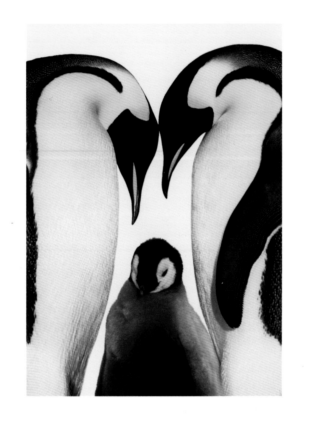

DEDICATION

To Gavriel Jecan,
my untiring travel companion
and fellow photographer,
without whose guidance,
patience, determined assistance,
and endless sacrifices
this book would simply
not be the book that it is.

—A.W.

CORPORATE SPONSORS:

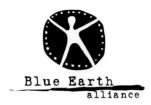

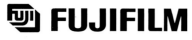

Canon

CANON USA

FUJIFILM

FUJI PHOTO FILM USA, INC.

gettyimages

SUPPORTERS:

Harriet S. Bullitt,

Katharyn Gerlich,

Dipti and Rakesh Mathur,

Jean Rhodes

IN MEMORIAM

Just as The Living Wild was nearing completion, I learned with great regret of the untimely death of John Sawhill. Under John's presidency, The Nature Conservancy grew into the world's largest conservation organization and protected more than 3 million hectares in the U.S. alone. All in just ten short years. What a legacy he has left us, what an inspiration he will always be.

—A.W.

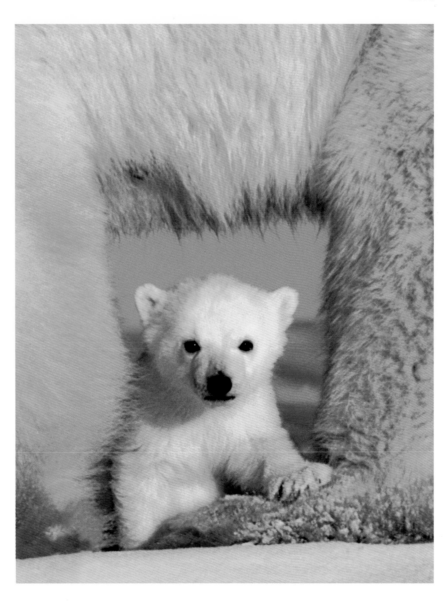

THE LIVING WILD

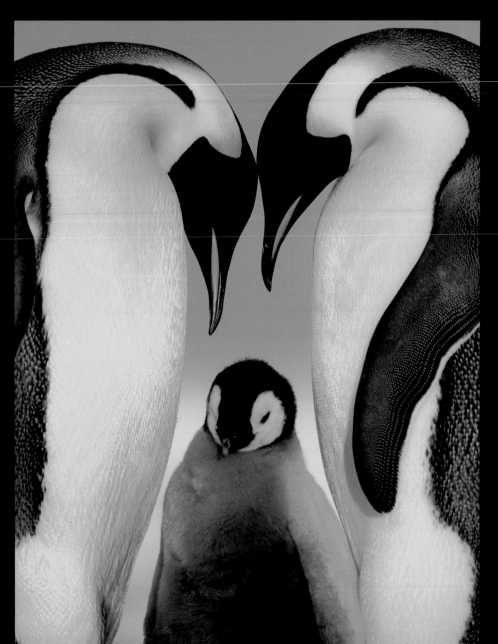

ACKNOWLEDGMENTS

The Living Wild has absorbed most of my attention for the last four years. It has taken me from the usual course of my business for nearly the entire time. My business survived because of my staff. They have not only played the largest role in the production of this book, but they have also had to keep the business moving forward. They have read, reviewed, listened, researched, conferred, argued, and consoled for too many hours, but have never lost their way in assisting with what I was trying to accomplish. I have listed them first among those to thank for their sacrifices and extraordinary talents: Ryan Bowe, Colin Bryn, Mel Calvan, Kate Campbell, Riko Chock, Christine Eckhoff, Bryan Ilyankoff, Gavriel Jecan, Erin Johnson, Christine Marie Larsen, Gilbert Neri, Ray Pfortner, Craig Scheak, Deirdre Skillman, Julie Sotomura, and Lisa Woods.

I wish to thank those who have graciously given their time and direct support to The Living Wild: Bob and Sue Barry, Deb Beaubein, Paul Brainerd, Ann Brown, Carol and John Burns, Lisa Chin and Nigel Green, Deb Crespin, Lisa Diekmann, Lance Douglas, Michael and Nancy Farrell, Matthew Felton, Betty and Murray Ferguson, Linda and Wayne Fricke, Mark Gardner, Katharyn Gerlich, Gerry Gerron, A. Tracy Harding, David D. and Susan W. Lewis, Gloria Lobb, James Martin, Meaghan McKenzie, Janet Van Kleeck McNae, Charles W. and Nancy Mertel, Bruce and Vicki Moore, Furman and Susan R. Moseley, George and Joyce Moss, Peggy and Tom Phillips, Bill Pope, Peter Potterfield, Fred and Mariana Quarnstrom, Carrie Rhodes, Jean Rhodes, Elizabeth and Jonathan Roberts, Mike Rich and Emily Wilson, Kathryn and Stephen Schipper, Amy Solomon, Richard Wohns, Ann Wyckoff (the Norcliffe Foundation), Martha Wyckhoff, Ann Wyman; Phil Borges, Malcolm Edwards, Natalie Fobes, Julee Geier, Marita Holdaway, David Johnson (Blue Earth Alliance); Tim Andree, Dave Metz, Michael Newler, Keith Paglin, Mike Zorich (Canon USA); Patrick Donehue (Corbis); Tom Curley, Jerry Nakao, Burt Park (Fuji Photo Film USA); Lewis Blackwell, Mark Getty, Jonathan Klein (Getty Images); and the Kongsgaard-Goldman Foundation. As our campaign continues, I wish to thank in advance all of those who join us to help bring this book and its message to the broadest audience possible.

Individuals, some of whom I have never met, many who have helped in the past, lent me their intelligence and resourceful assistance. I was especially pleased to have my high school alma mater approach us and select The Living Wild as a school project. They would ultimately provide our editor with valuable research. I wish to acknowledge Richard Shideler (Alaska Department of Fish and Game); Cathy Hedberg, Lucretia Robinson, Gary Thomsen (Chief Sealth High School staff); Chris Bhang, Elizabeth Boe, Justin Kuhn, Hannah Palmer, Joy Palmer, Jeff Pierson, Alec Sabin (Chief Sealth High School students); Fabia Barsic (Epson America); Mary Lewis (Jane Goodall Institute); Stephen R. Johnson (LGL, Ltd); Ed Marquand (Marquand Books); Dr. Janalee P. Caldwell (Oklahoma Museum of Natural History); Sir Ghillean Prance (Royal Botanic Gardens at Kew); Gary Luke (Sasquatch Books); Jeffrey Christiansen and Gaylen Goff (Seattle Aquarium); Don Engberg (Shedd Aquarium); Ed Goldstein and Nigel Homer (The Nature Conservancy); Declan Troy (Troy Ecological Research Associates); Jaimie Clark and Jim Clark (U.S. Fish and Wildlife Service); Dr. Robert J. Hudson (University of Alberta); and Dr. Laurence Frank (Laikipia Predator Project, University of California, Berkeley).

The travel and logistics required in completing this body of work necessitated help all along the way: friends and family meeting me (and sometimes, just my gear) at airports at all hours of the night and day; friends hand carrying bags of film through customs; organizations making special arrangements to accommodate me; nature guides, researchers, and biologists going out of their way to share special opportunities; generous friends hosting me; old and new friends providing much appreciated camaraderie for this sometimes isolated and weary traveler. The list includes, but is not limited to: Joan Alexander, Peter S. Bartlett, Andreas Bechstolsheim, Lee Berger, Desmond Berkowitz, Alan Bernstein, Justiniano F. Campa, Ramon Castellanos, Jagat Narayan Chaturvedi, H.S. Claire, Gansukh Dashvandan, Mike Fender, Joy Handyside, Khristina Horn, Mark Johnstad, Juan Carlos Lopez, Ian Mackenzie, Alfredo Maiquez, Jim and Teri Martin, Nico Martin, Robert Maughn; Nathan Myrhvold, Ellen Newman, Stefano Nicolini, Dan Parret, Alex Peltier, Pat Quillen, Anne and Mark Sturzenegger, Keren Su, Masao Uemura, Dick Wolfe, Christian Ziegler; Pablo Cervantes, Patricio Robles Gil, Patricia Rojo (Agrupación Sierra Madre); Eleanor Nicoles and Ellen Riechsteiner (All Around Travel); Mark Jorgensen (Anza-Borrego Desert State Park); Cynthia Carlisle and Daniel Tabon (Ara Fundación); Lorenzo Gasperini (Bogen Photo Corporation); Sheryl Carnegie, Debbie Davis, Phil Norton (Bosque del Apache National Wildlife Refuge); Tetsuo Hirasawa and Taro Maruyama (Canon Japan); Madan Rana and Sriyantra Rana (Chitwan Jungle Lodge); Gail Boucher (Churchill Chamber of Commerce); Lorenzo Sympson (Condor Project/Chile); Anne Lee and Dave Varty (Conservation Corporation Africa); Ken Kehrer (Denali National Park and Preserve); Tony Rivera (Ecosafaris); Russ Jarvis and Gordon Liddle (Falkland Island Government House); Guillermo Harris (Fundación Patagonia Natural/ Wildlife Conservation Society); Luis Orellana (Getty Images/Brazil); Stacey Green (Gettyone/ Seattle); Terry Elliott, "Tundra Tom" Faess, Dave Radcliffe, Bill Sirota (Great Canadian Ecoventures); Bärbel Krämer (Hapag Lloyd Cruises); Eduardo Alvarez (Harpy Eagle Recovery Project); Peter Luscomb and James Mejeur (Honolulu Zoo); Patricio Sarmiento, (Hotel Santa Clara); John Madunich, Dr. Richard Polatty, Eliza Tenza (Inca Floats, Inc.); Albert Chiang (Islands Magazine); Pete Jess (Jessco Operations, Inc.); HRH Princess Royal Salote Mafile'o Pilolevu Tuita of Tonga, Hon. Dr. Masasso Paunga, Minister Responsible for Tourism, Kingdom of Tonga; Norman and Cathy Galli, Mike Kirkinis, Howard Wolf (Kwando Lebala Camp); Monica Chavez and Roberto Lara (Manu Nature Tours); Ken Peterson (Monterey Bay Aquarium); Larry White (Monterey Bay Youth, Inc.); Scott Weir (Moss Tents); Dr. Bill Franklin, Dr. Isaac Ortega, Julie Young (Puma Project/ Chile); Floret Lyew (Quark Expeditions); Eduardo Nycander (Rainforest Expeditions); Diane Clark and Peter Clark (Rainforest Habitat); Adriana Bacheschi, Paulo Flieg, Juliana Gontijo, Fabio Luiz de Carvalho, Anne Thomsen (Refúgio Ecológico Caiman); Jacinto Jaramillo (Reina Silva); Anna Maria Alvarado, Lisa Barnet, Lucy Byrd Dorick, Irma Echevarria (Smithsonian Tropical Research Institute); Dr. William Burnham, Shawn Farry, Adam Green, William Heinrich, Angel Muela, Brian Mutch (The Peregrine Fund); Aaron Archibeque, Donna Stovall (Togiak National Wildlife Refuge); Semisi Taumoepeau and Peter Davidson (Tonga Visitors Bureau); Cuauhtémoc Chávez (UNAM, Instituto de Ecologia); Carlos Manterola (Unidos para la Conservación); Larry Richardson (U.S. Fish and Wildlife Service); Mike Hudson (Wau Ecology Institute); Marion Merlino (Wildlife Conservation Society); Lisa Diekmann, Kezha Hatier-Reiss, Rick McIntyre, Doug Smith (Yellowstone Park Foundation); and Peter Harrison, Shirley Metz, Werner Zender (Zegrahm Expeditions).

I owe an enormous debt to the immeasurable skills of the book's production team. They have persevered, facing so many unforeseen challenges: Alice B. Acheson, Richelle Barnes, Marlene Blessing, Kate Campbell, Quenton Cheung, Charlie Clark, Cathy Cohen, Peter Constable, Kai Davis, Nancy Duncan-Cashman, Christine Eckhoff, Joseph Eckhoff, Matthew Flor, Kris Fulsaas, Michelle A. Gilders, Louise Helmick, Rebecca Hom, Johnny Hubbard, Lou Kings, Stacey Lester, Marge Mueller, Gilbert Neri, Randl Ockey, Tim Perciful, Ray Pfortner, Jay Sakamoto, Craig Scheak, Deirdre Skillman, Gary M. Stolz, Brian Tyhuis, Curt Waller, Elizabeth Watson, Jason Wiley, Lisa Woods, Annie Woodward, and Gordon Yuen.

At the end of 1998, I lost my best mentor, Dr. Alan Lobb. He was my finest critic. Alan and his devotion to nature have always inspired me to stay on the path I have chosen and never to question its course.

—A.W.

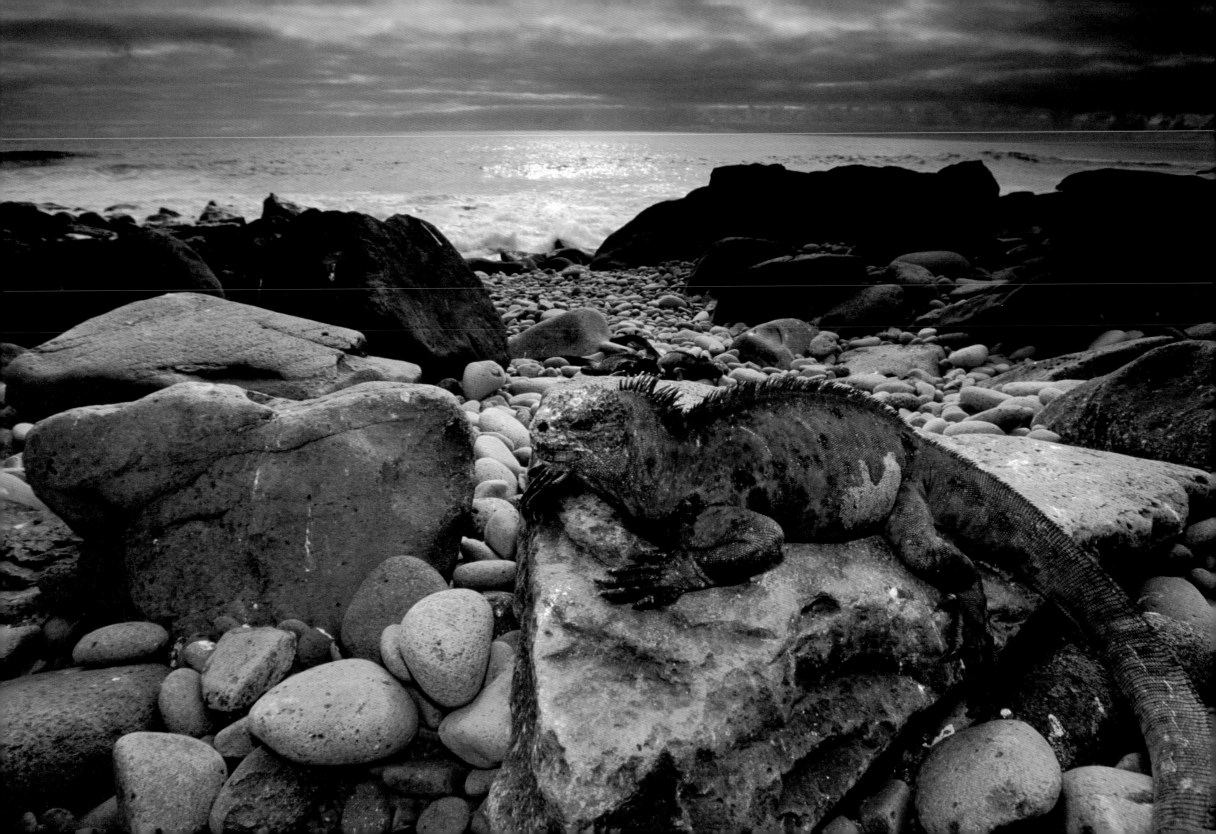

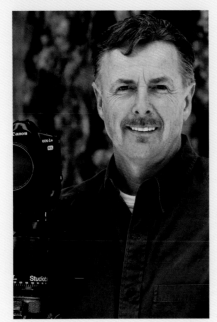

© GAVRIEL JECAN

A MESSAGE FROM
ART WOLFE

◄ MARINE IGUANA ⌒
(*Amblyrhynchus cristatus*), ISLA ESPAÑOLA,
GALÁPAGOS ISLANDS, ECUADOR
► ADÉLIE PENGUIN ⌒
(*Pygoscelis adeliae*), PETERMANN ISLAND,
ANTARCTICA

THE LIVING WILD

6

With every major book project that I've undertaken over the last twenty-five years, there have been experiences that have colored my life and my attitudes. *Tribes* provided memorable encounters with indigenous cultures from some of the world's most remote locations. While working on *Light on the Land*, I witnessed extraordinary moments when light and form miraculously came together. With *Migrations*, my senses were assailed with the sight, sound, and smell of two million wildebeest crossing the African plains. *Migrations* was my first book in which form, style, and pattern took precedence over biology. It was a book that reflected the essence of what I was photographing, not simply the reality of a species' existence.

As I began working on *The Living Wild*, I knew that this book would be unique in many respects. Looking forward to the new millennium, we are faced with incredible challenges. We are in danger of losing that which defines our planet's wonderful diversity of life. While the human population grows, other species are increasingly marginalized. Habitats are protected within national parks and reserves, but all too often such areas are protected only on paper. In many cases, these parks are able to do little more than preserve a stunning vista. To protect viable wildlife populations, parks and reserves must be able to weather natural changes like fire and flood, and permit the exchange of animals between populations. At the moment, few of the world's protected regions are large enough to sustain viable populations of the largest animals.

With this in mind, I decided to photograph *The Living Wild* from a perspective that placed as much emphasis on the environment as on the animal within it. After all, an animal without habitat is simply a curiosity biding time to its extinction. But an animal within its habitat is a vibrant representation of natural selection. To accomplish this broader photographic vision, I used wide-angle lenses whenever possible. Doing so allows the subject to hold center stage in the image, while still offering a satisfying proportion of the surrounding environment. Examples of this approach can be seen in my images of the elephant seals on South Georgia Island (*on the cover*) and the scarlet macaws in the Peruvian Amazon (*on the back cover*). Using a wide-angle lens also requires the photographer to get close. Many of these photographs were taken within 1 to 2 meters of the subject. Often I could not get so close to an animal, however, and I relied heavily on my telephoto lenses. Common sense and respect for wildlife govern my own photographic practices. And increasingly, parks and reserves wisely regulate how close visitors can approach an animal, ensuring the safety and well-being of both the wildlife and the viewer.

There are more than 140 different species included in this book. Each was selected because it is either a key representative of its habitat, or because it has a commanding presence in the minds of people around the world. Many could be categorized as "charismatic." They include the giant panda, tiger, polar bear, mountain gorilla, and African elephant. I do not mean to imply that other species, most notably the insects, are not important; from an ecological perspective they certainly are. However, conservation efforts around the world have often focused on large mammals to act as vanguards for greater preservation goals. Ensuring the preservation of viable wild populations of jaguars, African forest elephants, or lowland gorillas requires protecting vast areas. Within those areas countless other organisms can thrive, riding the conservation coattails of the animals that can galvanize public concern.

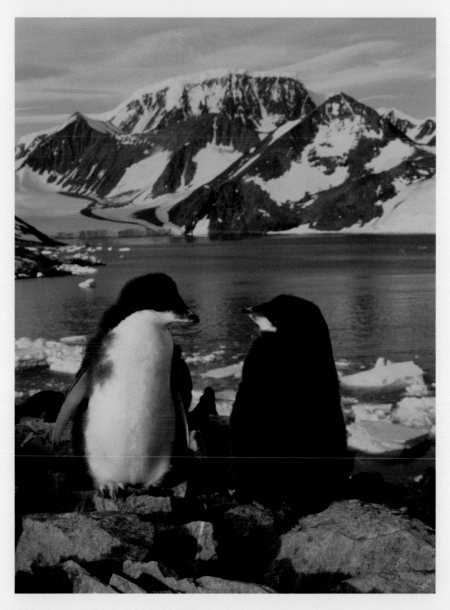

In addition to including animals that are now considered extremely rare (such as the California condor, Przewalski's horse, Florida panther, and golden frog), I have included some of the success stories of conservation: animals that were once driven to the brink of extinction, but that have been brought back to healthier population levels through adherence to environmentally sound policies (for example, the gray whale and bald eagle). Other species, although not generally considered rare, such as the polar bear, elk, walrus, and brown bear, have seen their populations decline in some areas as a result of environmental pressures that include pollution, habitat destruction, and overhunting.

The images I include on these two pages are two in this book that I find particularly poignant: the Bornean bay cat and Adélie penguins. The Bornean bay cat is one of the most mysterious carnivores on the planet. Until the 1990s, this small cat was known from just seven specimens. Little is known of its ecology, or its population; surveys conducted in the 1980s failed to find even one wild cat. The animal had never been photographed until I managed to get a picture of one in 1998. Why did this opportunity arise? Because in the late 1990s, much of Borneo was in flame—fires set by loggers had been made worse by drought, and the rare cat was driven from its home and into the hands of humans. My reaction at seeing this rare and elusive animal was tempered by the knowledge that the only reason it was within reach was because of environmental destruction. What a tragedy it would be if the image you see here—one of only two captive animals (the other being the bactrian camel on page 8) included in this book—becomes an epitaph for an entire species. Now you see it, now you don't.

While the fires burned in Borneo, researchers at the ends of the Earth—in Antarctica—were finding that another species was facing an increasingly uncertain future, and that its future and ours are more closely linked than many would imagine. Adélie penguins once crowded rookeries along the Antarctic Peninsula. Islands I remember as teeming with life are now quiet, many colonies all but deserted. Since 1950, the mean temperature of the Peninsula has risen by 3°C, while winter months are, on average, 6°C warmer. Rising temperatures result in more precipitation, and in Antarctica that means more snow. For the Adélie, more snow during the breeding season translates to failed nests and starving, freezing chicks. Warmer temperatures also mean that the winter ice pack is diminishing in size and floating ice sheets are breaking apart. If the Western Antarctic Ice Sheet were to melt, global sea levels would rise by more than 4 meters—and that would affect us all. The Adélie penguin may well be our "canary in the coal mine." Its decline should serve as a warning that global warming is no longer an abstract, far-in-the-future problem. It is here and we must solve it.

I have taken more than one million images in my photographic career,

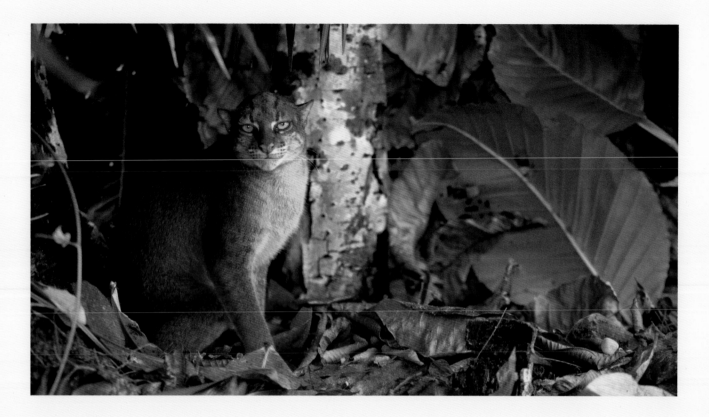

and within those million slides are pictures of over one thousand species. I have photographed in more than fifty countries, covering every type of habitat from polar to tropical, and from oceanic islands to high mountains. While there are many species that I still want to photograph, there are some that no one will ever have the opportunity to see or photograph again: the thylacine, least hare-wallaby, Okinawa flying fox, Falkland Island wolf, Mexican grizzly bear, Syrian wild ass, bluebuck, black-backed bittern, Labrador duck, Cuban red macaw, and Seychelles parrot. They, and too many others, are extinct.

But this book is not about the species we are too late to save. It is about the species that we still have time to save. *The Living Wild* provides a look at a world of animals that few get the chance to see in their natural habitat. It also presents an honest look at how these animals are doing at this point in time. The beginning of the new millennium may be a somewhat arbitrary date (after all, it is the year 5760 for Jews, and the year 1420 for Muslims), but it gives us all an opportunity to take stock of where we are and where we want to go. Each of the writers contributing to this book provides compelling a statement about the role of conservation today and in the future. The Harvard biologist E. O. Wilson once said, "There's one good thing about our species: We like a challenge." We can only hope that he is right, and that it is a challenge we can rise to meet.

BORNEAN BAY CAT

(*Felis badia*), BORNEO, MALAYSIA

ART WOLFE

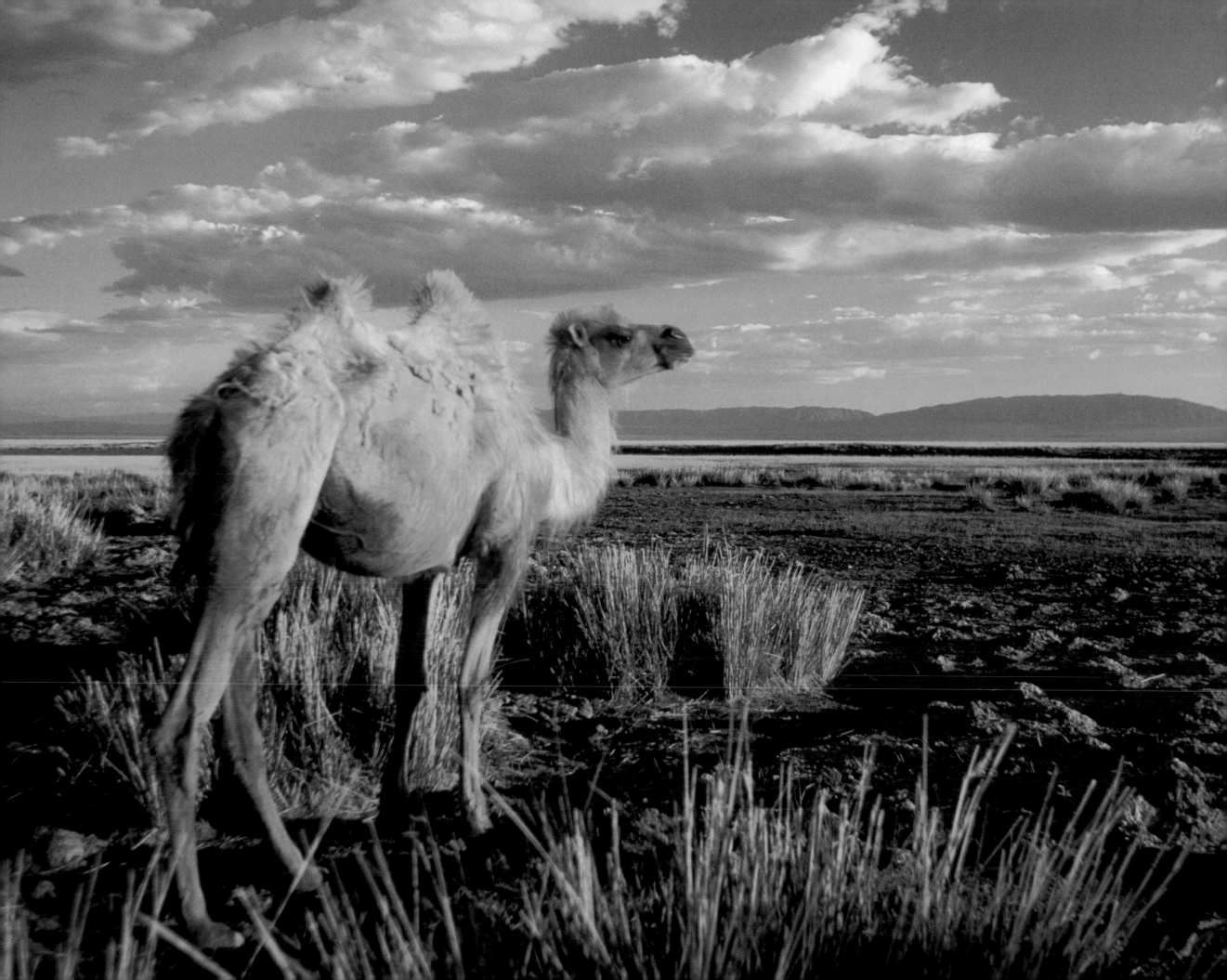

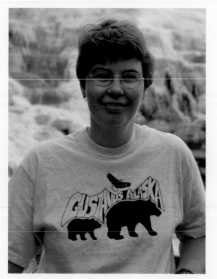

© VALERIE GILDERS

No one knows how many species there are on planet Earth. Nearly two million have been identified and named, but biologists put the actual total at between three and thirty million (some go as high as eighty million in the belief that the tropical rainforests have yet to reveal their full complexity). Such a difference between the known and the potentially unknown presents us with a paradox: we have countless new species to discover and learn from in the coming years, but we are also losing species through our direct actions (or our negligence) at such a rate that species are vanishing before we have had a chance to register their existence, much less name them.

There is a well-known adage that asks: "If a tree falls in the forest and there is no one there to hear it, does it still make a sound?" Perhaps in light of our current predicament, we can also ask: "If an unknown species vanishes before it has been discovered, have we lost anything?"

Our planet's biodiversity is the result of more than four billion years of evolution. Species have evolved to exploit a range of habitats from thermal pools to the surfaces of glaciers, from ocean depths to mountaintops, and from humid tropics to dry deserts. However, during the course of evolution more than 99.99 percent of all the species that ever existed have become extinct.

Scientists recognize five great extinctions: the Ordovician, 440 million years ago (MYA); the Devonian, 370 MYA; the Permian, 250 MYA; the Triassic, 210 MYA; and the Cretaceous, 65 MYA. Each of these events was precipitated by a natural event such as a gradually changing climate, volcanic or tectonic activity, or a major meteor strike. But we are now in the midst of a sixth great extinction, and we are the cause. We threaten other species by destroying their habitat, by introducing exotic species, and by overhunting. Unless human expansion is curtailed, we risk losing half of all species (mainly from the tropical rainforests) in the next 100 years. Why is this great extinction so different from earlier ones? For one thing it is occurring at an unprecedented rate (even the dinosaurs disappeared over millennia, and their descendants are the birds we cherish today). The sixth great extinction is also an arbitrary one. It has nothing to do with natural selection or the "survival of the fittest." Animals are not being outcompeted by a better-adapted species; they are being eliminated as their habitats are razed. If current trends continue, we will be left with homogeneous environments where the only wildlife is in the form of the opportunistic generalist that can make a home alongside us (like the brown rat, house mouse, and urban coyote or red fox).

We may not know how many species there are in the world, but we understand enough to fear what will happen if insects continue their decline, if birds vanish from our forests and grasslands, or if elephants and primates vanish from the tropics. A forest

without animal life is doomed to die, just as an animal without habitat cannot hope to survive. We too are animals, and as such we require a healthy and functioning habitat. Without insects, many of our crops would not be pollinated; without birds and mammals, many plants would fail to distribute their seeds; and without the full diversity of life, we would lack the vast majority of medicines and foods upon which we have come to depend. The argument for conservation can be one that recognizes the intrinsic value of all life on earth, or it can be one that builds on a utilitarian need. Whichever argument is used, the argument must still be made. And lest we fear that the task ahead is too vast, more than a third of the Earth's species are now known to inhabit just 1.4 percent of its land surface, some 2.1 million square kilometers, mainly in the tropical rainforests. The conservation of our planet's biodiversity is not only necessary, it is also achievable.

The species included in this book are those that draw people to zoological collections, that make people plan a trip-of-a-lifetime to Africa, or Alaska, or Antarctica. They are the species that people dream of seeing when they visit a national park or refuge. If you travel to any of these destinations, you hear about the "Big Five" or "Big Three" as people list the animals that they most want to see. Those names may differ with the location, but they have underlying similarities: They are the wolf, bear, bison, lion, leopard, elephant, and rhino. Each of these species is charismatic in its own way. They are also increasingly marginalized, pushed out of their former range as people move in. These are species that do not adapt well to competition with people, and many people do not wish to share their backyards with animals that can (however rarely) be a threat. The result is smaller and smaller populations of large mammals (particularly predators), fragmented habitats that are incapable of supporting their former diversity, and the steady loss of genetic diversity that comes from lack of exchange between populations and increased inbreeding.

The essays herein, surrounded by Art Wolfe's dramatic photographs, allow a glimpse of past successes and failures and a future still filled with possibilities. The writers drawn together for this book come from a variety of backgrounds. Jane Goodall and George B. Schaller are both veterans of prolonged fieldwork in remote corners of the world, and they have a unique perspective on the rigors of conservation. Richard Dawkins is the evolutionary biologist who gave us *The Selfish Gene* and who is always ready to challenge those who would relegate evolution to being simply another theory. William Conway, former general director of the Wildlife Conservation Society, has overseen hundreds of research and education programs, and John C. Sawhill, as president of The Nature Conservancy, headed an organization that runs the world's largest system of privately owned wildlife refuges.

The Living Wild, in both words and pictures, is more than a call for action. It is a stunning illustration of just what is at stake.

Michelle Gilders   MICHELLE A. GILDERS

◀ BACTRIAN CAMEL

(*Camelus bactrianus*), GREAT GOBI PROTECTED AREA, MONGOLIA

▶ CHIMPANZEE

(*Pan troglodytes*), MAHALE MOUNTAINS NATIONAL PARK, TANZANIA

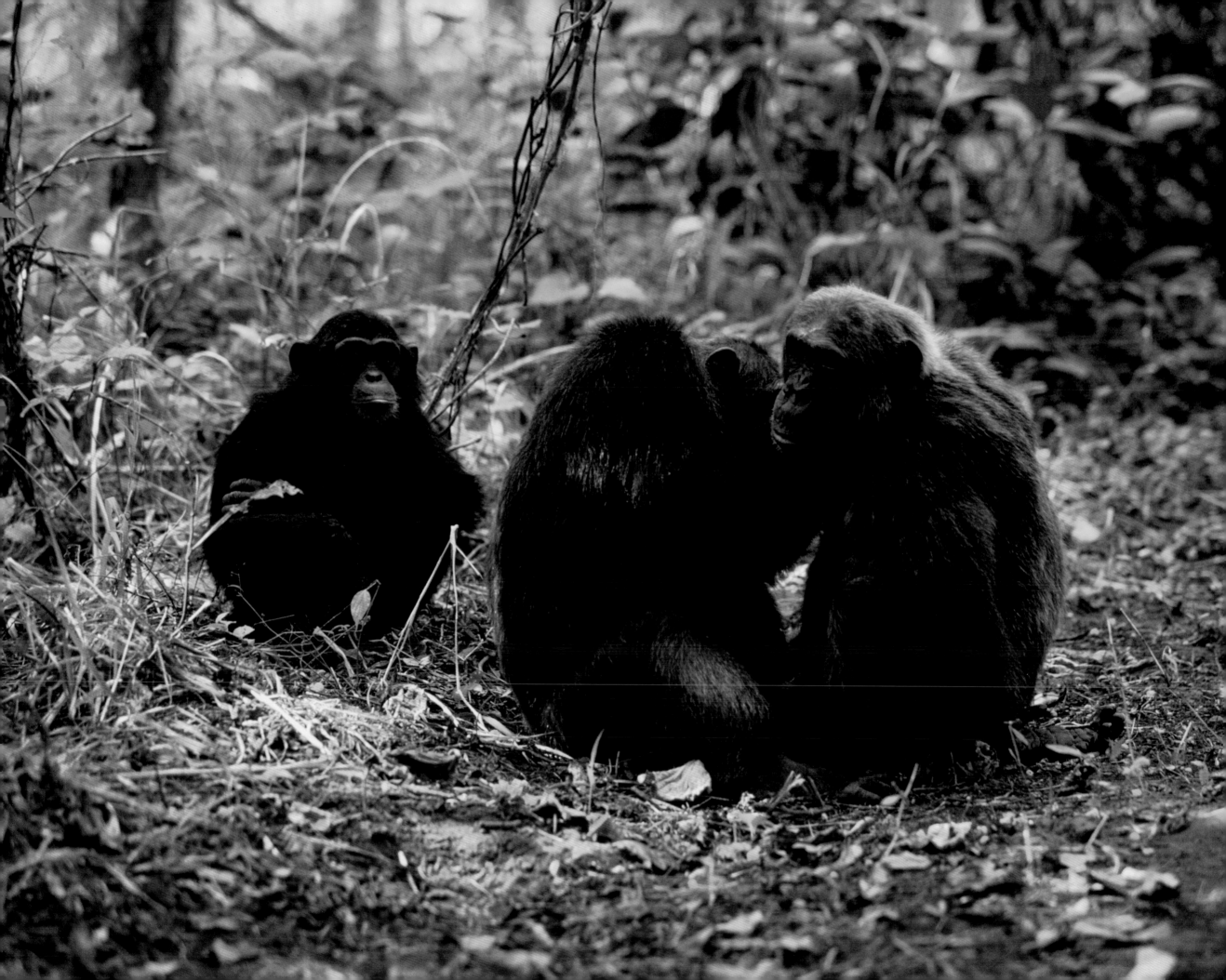

CONTENTS

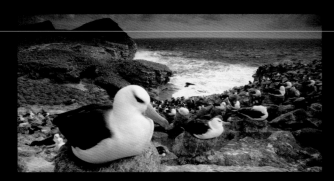

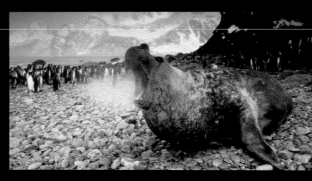

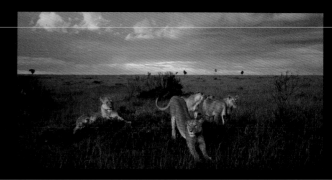

ISLAND & OCEAN 18   POLAR & SUBPOLAR 58   SAVANNAH, DESERT & STEPPE 92

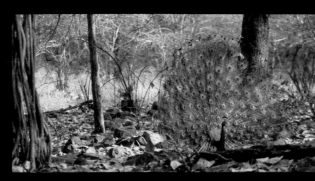

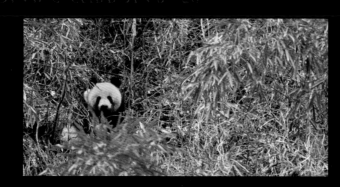

MOUNTAIN 132   TEMPERATE 158

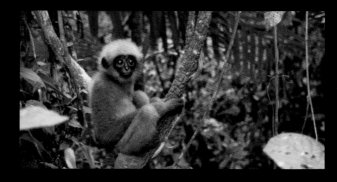

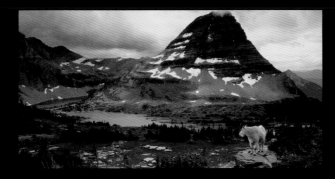

SUBTROPICAL 186   TROPICAL 212

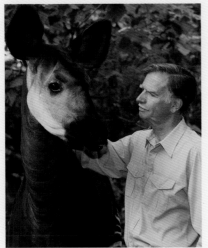

© DENNIS DEMELLO/WILDLIFE CONSERVATION SOCIETY

S aving nature has always been exhilarating, frustrating, poignant, and controversial. It is becoming more so. Wildlife conservation is increasingly in conflict with ideas of human rights and social justice, as well as with economic aspirations, and it is increasingly complex. Consider these comments from several frontline conservationists:

"The damned house cats are the main problem, not the monkeys as I first thought," Carl Jones confided, describing the loss of sixty of the gentle, nearly extinct pink pigeons he is breeding and reintroducing on the Indian Ocean island of Mauritius. "If we can keep the cats down, the birds will live."

"It is the situation of the panhandling elephants, most of all—so sad," lamented Pisit na Patalung, director general of Thailand's National Zoological Park Organization and secretary of the Committee on Environment, as he described Bangkok city wildlife problems. "But it's pythons, too. . . . "

"For God's sake we're killing almost as many dogs and cats in this country each year as some of the food animals we eat, over twenty-five million!" exclaimed my old friend, Roger Caras, president of the American Society for the Prevention of Cruelty to Animals.

"For the most part, there just isn't anything for a big carnivore to eat, no habitat left," Ullas Karanth explained, as we discussed tigers in his region of southwestern India. "But the tiger is not going to disappear overnight; the people care."

Improbably, millions of people do care, but wildlife populations are in crisis. Although there is still time to save a sampling of Earth's living wild, there is no longer any doubt that many, probably most, of the larger species will be lost, as well as thousands upon thousands of smaller ones of which we are not even aware.

The four main threats to wildlife are the same everywhere: habitat destruction, overhunting, introduction of alien species (especially domestic animals and farm crops), and disease. All the threats are fundamentally alike, but almost every solution is different. Saving wildlife has come to be as dependent upon understanding as upon caring. Patalung's elephants, Jones's pink pigeons, Caras's domestic animals, and Karanth's tigers all provide portholes to understanding. But what is the big picture?

THE BIG PICTURE. In few places is the wildlife situation as dire as that in crowded India, but many nations are headed that way. Consider the words of my colleague, Ullas Karanth. For thirty years, Ullas has been student, farmer, and then scientist near the Nagarahole National Park in southwestern India:

India is one-third the size of the continental United States but supports about a billion people. Most (60 to 75 percent) are poor, live off the land, use wood for fuel, and are unlettered. One-fifth of the world's cattle are raised in India. Set within this matrix of shrinking natural landscapes and poverty is an urbanized middle class approximately the size of the population of France.

Nagarahole has three major large carnivores. Asiatic wild dogs live in packs, and a pack has to kill roughly a small, cow-sized animal every day. A single leopard has to make such a kill every ten days or so, and a tiger once a week. There are twenty to twenty-five breeding female tigers in the national park.

I found that the densities and biomass of herbivorous mammals in Nagarahole were over ninety hoofed animals per square kilometer and, including elephants, a biomass of 15,000 kilograms for every square kilometer of land. The fauna was incredibly rich—but fragile. But the three predators were taking most of what was available. There was no room for another major predator, particularly if that predator sold the meat to nearby markets.

Nagarahole was long used as an extractive reserve by a variety of interests. It was logged, burned, and intensively hunted, and in the 1960s, there was little wildlife left. In the 1970s a new social chemistry arose in India and the influence of Indira Gandhi, a strong wildlife conservationist, was felt. A growing middle class liked to watch animals and pushed for reserves. This depended upon a forestry department with a militarylike structure capable of enforcement of wildlife laws.

With the enforcement of no-hunting laws and curbing of the inappropriate cutting practices of the forestry department itself, wildlife resurged, and by the 1980s Nagarahole was again a magnificent wildlife area.

Popular suggestions that biodiversity conservation could be effected through "sustainable use" and that there should be a linking of exploitation of biodiversity to global markets to create economic incentives for local stakeholders could not work in Nagarahole; the numbers were against it [as they are in most of the world].

In 1998, as president of the Wildlife Conservation Society (WCS), I rejoiced in the achievement of my Brazilian colleague, Marcio Ayres, whose many years of hard work with local communities and national officials were rewarded with the establishment of the huge Amana Sustainable Reserve. This is the largest contiguous rainforest reserve in the world, an area bigger than Costa Rica! It is home to tapirs, jaguars, anacondas, hyacinth macaws, ivory-colored uakari monkeys, and hundreds of thousands of other species—a marvelous example of both community-based conservation and national support.

The area's locals, Brazil's president, park officials, and WCS exchanged congratulations and expressions of hope. The euphoria was special, for the world is running out of areas that can be made into reserves. Later in the same year, however, we found that even more Amazon land had been newly lost than newly saved—burned and deforested for agriculture. But the problem is not confined to the Amazon. In one of thousands of close-to-home examples, the Maryland Office of Planning recently predicted that this tiny state would lose 330,000 acres of forest between 1988 and 2020.

We have all heard that human populations are increasing and wildlife is disappearing; We also hear that things are getting better. Outside Africa and India, human life expectancies have dramatically increased and large numbers of people are better fed and cared for today than fifty years ago. To many of us, most environmental problems appear solvable. But what about saving wildlife?

Eleven percent of the remaining birds, 18 percent of the mammals, 5 percent of the fish, and 8 percent of terrestrial plants are now seriously threatened with extinction. Almost all big animals are in trouble, as are storks and cranes, pythons and crocodiles, great apes (in fact, most of the primates), elephants, and rhinos.

Over half of all terrestrial species of plants and animals are found in tropical evergreen forests. According to tropical ecologist John Terborgh, only about 7.5 million square kilometers of tropical evergreen forest remain. If deforestation continues at the same rate as it did between 1979 and 1989, the last tropical evergreen forest tree will fall in 2045. But the deforestation rate is increasing. And that is only part of the story.

Sarah Elkan brushes buzzing flies from an ugly fragment of raw meat and skin to better see its hair and identify its species. Surrounded by doubtful timbermen and tribespeople, she is monitoring a bushmeat market for WCS, deep in the hot Congo forest; trying to determine what is being killed, where, who is eating it, and what the alternatives are. At the other end of the village, her husband, Paul, talks with two hunters. Responding to countless visits, they have come to turn in their wire "game" snares and take employment as wildlife rangers. The great forest for miles around is quiet.

The bushmeat harvest in the tropical forests of Africa is now about one million metric tons each year; that in the Brazilian Amazon is estimated at 67,000 to 164,000 metric tons per year. Wildlife kill figures from rural towns and villages can be so large as to be almost incomprehensible. A 1982 study revealed that the 574,000 people of the rural population of the Brazilian state of Amazonas were *annually* killing an estimated 2,824,662 mammals and 530,884 birds. In 1998, bushmeat hunters in Cameroon are said to have killed over 800 gorillas, selling their bodies for about forty dollars each.

But tropical hunting "takes" are not just a local problem; U.S. wildlife imports from 1980 through 1985 averaged 12,000 to 14,000 primates, 6 million raw fur skins,

800,000 live birds, 300,000 to 500,000 live reptiles, 2 million to 4 million reptile skins, and 125 million live "ornamental" fishes. When I studied the hide and skin trade during 1968 and 1969, the importation of big-cat skins into the United States. was 3,165 cheetahs, 17,490 leopards, 23,347 jaguars, and 262,030 ocelot skins. That, at least, has been stopped.

The U.S. dog and cat "kill" number is only the tip of a worldwide domestic animal iceberg. There are now about 17 billion domestic animals utilizing former wildlife habitat. More than a billion of these are ruminants—cows, goats, sheep—and they dominate at least 3 billion hectares of land. While humane organizations worry about cruelty to domestic animals, no one mentions the suffering imposed upon wild animals whose habitats they overrun. Another 1.7 billion hectares are even more compromised for crops. Vegetarianism is not a solution. At the same time, we are besieged by reports of acid rain, decreases in tropical forest rainfall, ozone depletion, global warming, coral bleaching, phytoplankton blooms, cancer epizootics in fishes, and such declines as the worldwide loss of amphibians.

The magnitude of the survival problem for wildlife, and ultimately for ourselves, is contained in five percentages: Over 40 percent of Earth's total terrestrial photosynthetic productivity (green plant and crop productivity) is now appropriated by people. So is 25 to 35 percent of the primary productivity of the ecosystems of the oceans' continental shelves (their fishes, mollusks, and crustaceans) and 54 percent of all runoff in rivers, lakes, and other accessible sources of freshwater. Protected areas amount to only 4 to 6 percent of Earth's land and 0.5 percent of its seas.

WHAT KIND OF WORLD FOR WILDLIFE? Too many people are the root of wildlife's problems, yet in 1998 the United Nations revised its World Population Projections sharply downward. The new estimate for 2050 is 8.8 billion, rather than 10 billion or 12 billion. Average global fertility has dropped to 2.7 births per woman as opposed to 5 in the early 1950s. Do we dare hope for a future wherein human effects upon the environment have diminished and considerable wildlife remains? Millions would have to work to make such a vision become reality and it could only be accomplished on a foundation of scientifically sound information. Here is a poignant report from Bangkok's Pisit na Patalung:

There are over 200 elephants panhandling on the streets of Bangkok. They were saved from abandoned timber camps. Now they are living on "treats" of sugarcane and bananas, purchased from their mahouts and fed to them by tourists. Of course, they can't survive on bananas and sugarcane. They have skin problems and eye problems, and are being hit by cars. The situation is terrible! They have no future.

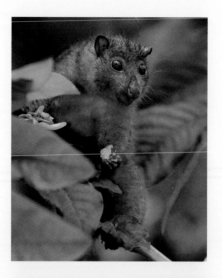

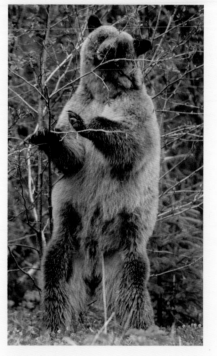

▲▲ NORTHERN COMMON CUSCUS
(*Phalanger orientalis*), NEW BRITAIN ISLAND, PAPUA NEW GUINEA
▲ GLACIER BEAR
(*Ursus americanus*), GLACIER BAY NATIONAL PARK, SOUTHEAST ALASKA, USA

WILLIAM CONWAY

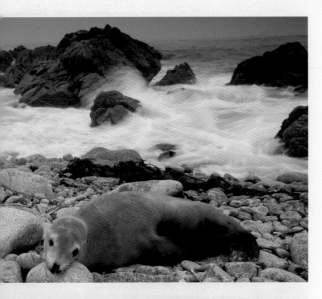

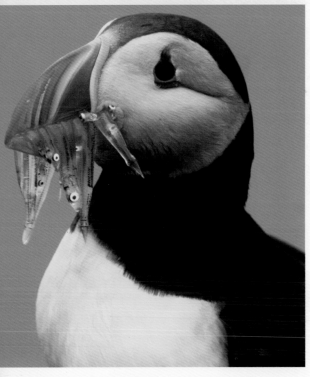

THE LIVING WILD

Bangkok is sprawling into former forest and Pisit's staff is constantly removing monkeys and pythons from around people's houses; about fifty pythons a month! "We take them someplace and release them," he says. But, of course, there really isn't any place he can release them where they can survive.

GETTING INFORMATION FROM THE FIELD. *Shahtoosh.* Squinting through a powerful telescope, a tall, weathered man braces himself against the cold Tibetan wind. The altitude is 16,000 feet. He is assessing the numbers, sex, and age distribution of a distant herd of Tibetan antelopes trekking through the snow of the vast plain below him. His keen gray eyes have observed jaguars in the Mato Grosso, lions on the Serengeti, tigers in India's Kanha, snow leopards in Pakistan, and giant pandas in China's Wolong Mountains. For each species, each wild place, George Schaller's scientific reports, popular writings, and personal persuasion have inspired concern, created understanding, and helped protection.

Tibetan antelopes or chiru are at the center of a struggle about "shahtoosh," and one of WCS's 350 field projects. For thousands of years, the warmest, finest fur on Earth has enabled great herds of the handsome little antelope to survive in its harsh environment in populations exceeding half a million, migrating back and forth across Tibet's highest grasslands. In recent years, however, it has become the victim of unchecked slaughter stimulated by the kind of people, mostly Americans, who take a perverse pride in paying upward of $2,000 for a "shahtoosh" shawl.

Schaller has discovered that the antelope population is now less than 75,000 and rapidly declining. Chinese officials reacted swiftly with strong punishments for poachers, but guards are few and the rewards of poaching very high.

Jaguars. At the National Autonomous University of Mexico, field scientists, representing almost every country in Latin America, are conducting a final review of a heavily marked map prepared by WCS's GIS (Global Information System) expert, Eric Sanderson. It extends from Mexico to Argentina and is the final iteration of four days of data sharing and comparison. This is the first collation of all that is known by the world's top jaguar experts about where jaguars still live, where they have been killed out, where their status is unknown, and, most important, the areas of highest priority for conservation action. It is a scientific blueprint for jaguar survival.

Penguins. Kneeling over a garbage pit on the Patagonian coast, their faces reflecting distaste for their task, three biologists cut open the bellies of one dead penguin chick after another. "A single squid beak," notes Dee Boersma to her Argentine students, as they record yet another casualty in a starvation die-off in the ongoing saga of Punta Tombo's penguin population.

The seventeen-year-old study at Tombo, which is following more than 40,000 marked Magellanic penguins, is a powerful diagnostic tool for judging the well-being of Patagonia's coastal wildlife. Here penguins, cormorants and other seabirds, elephant seals, and Patagonian sea lions compete with the Southern Hemisphere's fastest-growing fishery near Patagonia's top ecotourism site. One discovery of the coastal studies showed that 41,000 penguins were dying each year from oil pollution—primarily from illegal oil tanker ballast washings offshore. This has now been stopped—we hope.

Physics Nobelist Richard Feynman has said, "Science is a method of finding things out . . . a method based on the principle that observation is the judge of whether something is so or not." What WCS scientists and conservation biologists from other organizations are trying to do is to find facts, discover patterns, and set forth principles that can lead to predictions of what might happen in similar situations, and thus lead to conservation. Their litany is: "discover, involve, protect." It results in such things as parks and reserves; wildlife movement corridors; the training of local conservationists; community-based conservation; fishing, hunting, and timber regulations; disease control; and estimates of wildlife carrying capacity. The science-based approach to conservation, led by the WCS, is fundamental, but there are as many approaches as there are conservation organizations.

WHICH WILDLIFE SHOULD BE SAVED FIRST? Conservationists have devoted much effort to developing priority systems. These vary from long lists of unique or charismatic animals to wide-ranging representational approaches, with global maps of important "ecoregions" or "hot spots," rich in biodiversity. After all, saving wildlife usually comes down to saving habitat—but not always.

Priority setting helps us focus limited resources, but it tells us little about *how* to achieve conservation. Joshua Ginsberg observes, "We must find ways to protect ecosystem function and ensure long-term stability, or priority-setting exercises will simply be historical notes." There probably is no sure way "to protect ecosystem function," especially when ecosystems are big. But when they are small, they are very vulnerable.

The survival of the most biodiverse habitats is usually dependent upon pollination or "planting" by key species of animals, so the future of their vegetation can be lost overnight with the decline of those animals. Alluding to the role of birds and mammals in replanting forests with seeds passed through their digestive tracts, Andrew Mack characterized Papua New Guinea forests, which can have 228 species of tree per hectare, as "500 years of animal droppings." Biodiversity, which refers to the number of species, is such an overwhelming conservation focus that other fundamentals often get lost;

for example the number of species' populations, their biomass, intrinsic needs for migration, as well as ecological obligations, such as avoidance of habitat fragmentation.

Whatever approach we choose, numbers of species cannot be the only criterion. Medium-sized and large species are the most threatened component of biodiversity, but there are many times more threatened invertebrates. Indeed, there are thousands more species of beetles than of all the species of mammals, birds, reptiles, amphibians, and fishes combined. Thus we cannot deal with wild species as if all were of equal value.

The continued survival of two species of endangered elephants is of greater importance to society and to the ecology of very large areas of nature than two species of tiger beetles or guppies or warblers. Four species of endangered great apes are of far higher priority than four of marmosets. Conservation cannot be value-free, and is not ecologically. (My view seemed so politically incorrect to fellow conservationist Lee Durrell that she asked me if I really meant it—but then admitted that her own excellent organization, the Durrell Wildlife Trust, had chosen to save only certain species.)

STRATEGIES. WCS focuses upon "landscapes and landscape species" in its priorities, a different but compatible approach with the important work of The Nature Conservancy and the World Wildlife Fund, for example. Emphasizing ecosystem function *and* species as the keys to achieving conservation, WCS works to save the creatures that require the largest, most diverse areas in a landscape. The idea is not only to ensure their survival, but also to have the greatest positive impact on biodiversity as a whole by saving habitats overlapping the needs of many other species. While parks play a critical role, they are rarely large enough to ensure the success of ecologically functional populations.

In 1987, William Newmark published a sobering study of some of the largest protected national parks in North America. He found that twenty-seven species of mammals had already become extinct in one or more of these great parks. Not surprisingly, the number of extinctions was, in general, inversely proportional to the size of the park. But big predators are a special problem. A female jaguar in Peru requires a minimum of 20 square kilometers for herself and her cubs, while a pair of harpy eagles needs about 50. The 2-million-hectare Manú Reserve system supports only ten families (sixty individuals) of giant otters. Colonial animals such as seals and sea lions, penguins, and auks can exist only where there is access to very large and reasonably concentrated food supplies, which is why their breeding sites are so uncommon and vulnerable.

Even without global climate change, refuge resources alter over time, becoming less suitable for many original denizens. Habitat preservation alone does not assure species preservation through simple protection and benign neglect. There is no substitute for active ecosystem and species-care, especially from now on, since we have limited wildlife to smaller and smaller areas. Most nature reserves will ultimately become more or less artificial. Thus to preserve a significant proportion of the creatures we hold dear, we must be prepared to back up some of their wild populations with captive reservoirs, to translocate them, treat their illnesses, and control their numbers, as needed.

HUMANE WILDLIFE CONSERVATION. The saving of wildlife is a social process subject to widely disjunct cultural values. Only culture sustains much of India's wildlife, especially elephants, which kill as many as 300 people every year. Where a sympathetic culture does not exist in India, virtually all wildlife is killed. Yet people with sympathetic attitudes can lose their way.

In Massachusetts, animal rights advocates attacked wildlife officials trying to control abnormally large populations of gulls. The gulls are destroying colonies of threatened roseate terns. Others have lobbied to prevent conservationists from clearing introduced rabbits and goats from islands in many parts of the world, where they have eventually caused the extinction of several native species of plants as well as animals. While such actions are stimulated by good intentions, they reveal a mental separation of intentions from results, plus a failure to assume responsibility for consequences.

Domestic goats, rabbits, pigs, dogs, and cats are a particular scourge to wild animal populations, especially in confined areas. The only hope many island creatures have, whether they be Galápagos giant tortoises and land iguanas, Round Island boas or Howe Island rails, is the extermination of introduced domestics. Yet action has repeatedly been shelved by emotional charges of potential cruelty. We find it hard to kill individual animals to save whole species. But we need to temper our feelings with information and understanding. Cats are a terrible problem.

In 1894, the strange and charming little Stephen Island wren of New Zealand was discovered and extirpated, all in the same year, by a lighthouse keeper's cat—a whole species! Surely this is a one-of-a-kind event, occasioned by the coincidence that this was a rare species in a confined area . . . with a fast cat. Or is it? A study of seventy-seven town cats in Great Britain showed that "The delightful well-fed domestic cat may be the major killer of small birds and mammals in urban and suburban communities." Some cats killed as many as 400 birds and mammals in a single year!

My friend Stanley Temple, a University of Wisconsin professor, calculates that there are now about 2 million feral cats in Wisconsin, and as many as 100 million in the United States as a whole. The effect of these legions of unnatural predators upon small birds

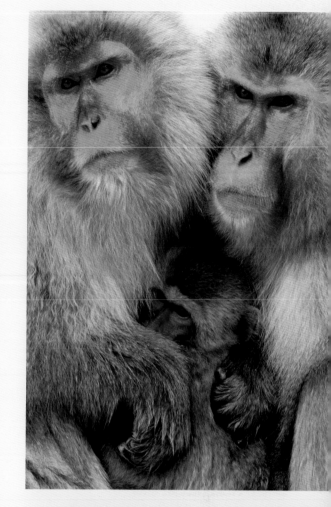

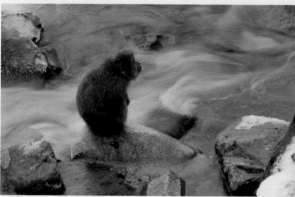

JAPANESE MACAQUE
(*Macaca fuscata*), JAPANESE ALPS. HONSHU
ISLAND. JAPAN

WILLIAM CONWAY

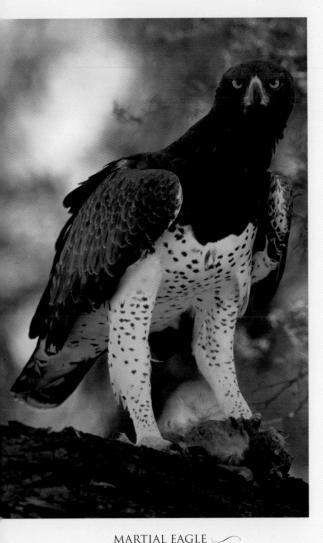

MARTIAL EAGLE ⌣
(*Polemaetus bellicosus*), SAMBURU NATIONAL
PARK, KENYA

boggles the mind. But sometimes shortsightedness is even more troublesome than cats.

In 1988, at a time when African elephants were being killed by ivory poachers for souvenir carvings and piano keys at the rate of one every eight minutes, and the elephant population had dropped 50 percent in ten years, *TIME* magazine published a detailed description of the situation and of the elephant's impending extinction. Mr. Paul Sarnoff of Baldwin, New York, responded indignantly. He wrote: "You emphasized the ivory trade of Asia but failed to note the economic impact an ivory ban would have on craftsmen of artistic ivory creations in other parts of the world. Which is more important, an elephant or a human being?" Mr. Sarnoff saw the protection of elephants as an infringement upon the well-being of the ivory carver—but what of the tour guide and tourist; of every human being, whether scientist, dreamer, tribesman, or poet? Such views are not uncommon, but how can we justify trades that destroy themselves as well as elephants?

MEGAZOOS. In 1987, Kenya's Nakuru National Park was completely fenced as a conservation measure, and I flew down from Nairobi to see the result with WCS ecologist David Western. The park is small, about 184 square kilometers, much of which is shallow salty Lake Nakuru, renowned as a feeding place for hundreds of thousands of lesser and greater flamingos. From the Cessna, the park fence was easily seen: 3 meters high, electrified and solar powered, surrounded by farms. Also visible were bomas for the rhino reintroduction program and a growing herd of Rothschild's giraffes, introduced some years ago. Overwhelming the view was a vast blanket of pink that covered much of the lake, more than half a million flamingos. On the ground, by truck, I was delighted by extraordinary numbers of warthogs, waterbuck, and impala.

Nakuru National Park has become a megazoo, a living museum rather than part of a larger more or less wild functioning ecosystem. From now on, Nakuru's animals will have to be cared for; managed ecologically, behaviorally, genetically, and demographically. Eventually, some will have to be selectively mated, culled, and treated for disease. Their habitat will have to be monitored and supervised; the health, regeneration, and distribution of its plants watched over with as much care as that of its animals.

The cost to Kenya of such sophisticated park management will be much higher than the simple protection services of the past. What is happening at Nakuru is typical of what is happening over most of the world: the increasing loss of wild land; the insularization of parks and refuges and their alteration. The nature of the challenge in saving wildlife becomes more vivid when visualized in terms of elephants and wildebeest.

If elephants and wildebeest are to survive, they must be distributed broadly and abundantly enough to survive chance events, such as natural disasters and disease, and within sufficient habitat to obtain food, space, and water in suitable climatic zones on a sustainable basis. Those are the essentials: Then it gets complicated.

Where will these elephant and wildebeest zones be? Is the fact that there are "enough" elephants in Gabon and wildebeest in Tanzania sufficient for Kenya? Is a minimal, biologically calculated population number adequate replacement for the elevating spectacle of great herds? Which nations and communities will seek the honor and profits of caring for them; the expense of overseeing their protection, monitoring their health and habitat, resolving their bound-to-increase conflicts with human beings; and also the heartbreak of culling them to control populations for sustainable management? And if it is decided to "give up" elephants and wildebeest, are we also prepared to give up the remarkable panoply of other mammals and birds and plants that are dependent upon their ongoing ecological services as "architects of the savannah"?

Alas, there are many "Nakurus." Cotton fields border one side of Tanzania's great Serengeti, and wheat lands confine Kenya's Mara. Africa's last 650 mountain gorillas dwell in a tiny area encircled by some of the most intensely cultivated farms in the world. Elephants, gaur, three species of deer, and two of gibbons are similarly surrounded in Thailand's poorly protected Khao Yai National Park.

FUTURE HABITAT? What will Africa be like in the future? What of the few remaining Asian forests? The great Amazon jungles? Imagine them crisscrossed with roads, huge agribusinesses, parking lots, cities, suburbs, reshaped rivers and streams, orderly tree plantations rather than great diverse forests, vast artificial ecosystems.

Most larger species will become dependent upon us. We will have to determine which of their populations will persist and which will not; which predators and how many can be sustained; where and how much of which creatures' populations they will be allowed to kill. And we will have to determine, in many instances, which animals will live and which will die . . . a morass of complexity, scientific and ethical, of our own making.

When it comes to large predators, WCS's Alan Rabinowitz says, "Big cats, bears, and the like simply won't stay in parks [unless they are fenced]. They will roam beyond the borders and come into conflict with humans." Maurice Hornocker, of the Hornocker Institute, is more hopeful, "Pumas, bears, and wolves can be taught to avoid people and livestock, but this requires people, including ranchers, to be knowledgeable and careful in big-cat country."

Very big, bold projects are believed by many to offer wildlife its best long-term chances. The "Wildlands Project" in the United States, designing a continental wilderness recovery strategy, plans an interconnected, continental-scale system of protected wildlands linked by corridors. It is nothing less than inspiring. WCS's Archie Carr, son of the famous sea turtle biologist, has conceived a grand plan for Central America. Called *Paseo Pantera* (Path of the Panther), it is trying to link the individually small parks and wild spaces of seven Central American nations to create a connected ecosystem large enough to save panthers, jaguars, tapirs, and the other big wild denizens of Mesoamerica. Moreover, the presidents of all these countries have met and are working on the concept; but it is a difficult one that cuts across political and social aspirations, not to mention economic ones. More often, I fear, the future will bring desperate rescue attempts for vanishing species on a one-by-one basis, with captive breeding and reintroduction—where habitat survives. The successful California condor and peregrine falcon programs are examples. But such efforts find few places where introduction is possible, and they are not easy.

The last wild herds of Arabian oryx were exterminated by hunters in Oman in 1972. A few captive animals were gathered together and bred in collaborating collections and reintroductions began in the early 1980s. Happily, the strange and beautiful lance-horned antelope's numbers soon exceeded 300. Success! Then in 1998–99, a local tribal dispute erupted and most oryx were slaughtered once again. The remaining 100 were captured and returned to captivity. Their future is unclear.

Chinese conservationists and their foreign collaborators report that giant panda monitoring is poor, poaching still takes place, and there are major conflicts between panda reserves and local communities. Panda numbers in nature are thought to be between 500 and 1,000 (a new census is underway), but the population appears to be fragmented into thirty-two isolated groups—a prescription for extinction. Unless there are major changes in its management, the panda's future is grim. There are 104 in captivity in China, but their pedigrees are problematic and there are many biomedical concerns. It may be that the only way the panda can survive into the twenty-second century is as a "metapopulation," involving interchanges between captive and wild animals.

In 1974, there were only four Mauritius kestrels left on this Indian Ocean island. By 1984 nearly 400 had been reared in captivity and 331 released. There are now 600 in the wild. On the same island, there were but 6 male and 2 female echo parakeets left by 1987. The extraordinary aviculturist Carl Jones did it again. As a result of his efforts, 22 have been released in the last three years and there are now 100 in the "wild."

By far the most impressive and successful of such efforts with birds has been the extraordinary campaign of The Peregrine Fund. Initiated by Professor Tom Cade at Cornell University, in New York, following the peregrine's near demise as a result of pesticide poisoning, the Fund has bred well over 3,000 peregrines and restored them to their old aeries across the country. Its techniques have been so successful that they have been utilized with many other birds of prey, including the bald eagle.

For some key species, the almost-dodos, the only viable "habitats" with sufficient security and carrying capacity for the foreseeable future may be in zoos. For example, the WCS's Bronx Zoo had success in reintroducing the "buffalo," the American bison, to the empty ranges where it once lived in the West until early in the 1900s. Such care will be a contribution to the preservation of biodiversity—and a valuable gift to the maintenance of future options. Captive populations like these can become linchpins for habitat restoration.

UNINTENDED CONSEQUENCES. When I am asked, "What worries you most when planning a conservation project?" I usually answer, "Unintended consequences." At the beginning of the twentieth century, sea otters and elephant seals were nearly extinct. There seem to have been only about 1,000 to 2,000 otters and fewer than 100 elephant seals. Now there are 125,000 seals, but the sea otters are again in jeopardy. After years of population growth, their population in the Aleutian Islands has dropped more than 90 percent since 1990. With their decline, sea urchin numbers have exploded, destroying the kelp forests, which are important to fish. The decline appears to be the result of greater predation by killer whales, which are eating the otters because their preferred prey, Alaskan seals and sea lions, have declined. In turn, the seals and sea lions have probably declined because their prey (fish) has decreased because of the burgeoning fisheries in the area. Unintended consequences!

Why *do* we need a blackburnian warbler or a black rhino, an egret, an eagle, an eland, a tiger, a turtle, a gorilla, or a gazelle? There is little reason to hope that any of these creatures possesses panaceas for the problems of cancer, AIDS, or poverty. They are not pollinating our crops or purifying our water. Their loss, even altogether, would hardly result in some vast ecological dilapidation that would endanger civilization. They are simply and wonderfully fascinating or frightening, beautiful, inspiring, instructive, or just plain agreeable. Who among us can make this enough for civilization?

If good-to-eat or competitive species are to persist, their conservation will have to be supported, at some level, by the few wealthy human societies that care enough to do so, and for a very long time. And these societies will have to work closely and supportively with local communities and economies to succeed. They will have to buy time.

Wildlife conservation is destined to be among the greatest challenges of the twenty-first century. Perhaps the world's new heroes will be recognized not for landing on a barren Moon, but for helping to prevent Earth from becoming one; for preserving wild creatures and wild places against the odds.

William Conway

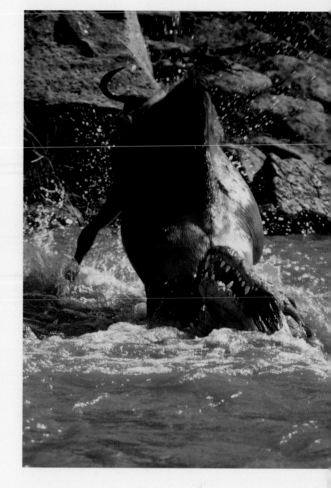

COMMON WILDEBEEST
(*Connochaetes taurinus*) AND
NILE CROCODILE
(*Crocodylus niloticus*),
MASAI MARA NATIONAL RESERVE, KENYA

WILLIAM CONWAY

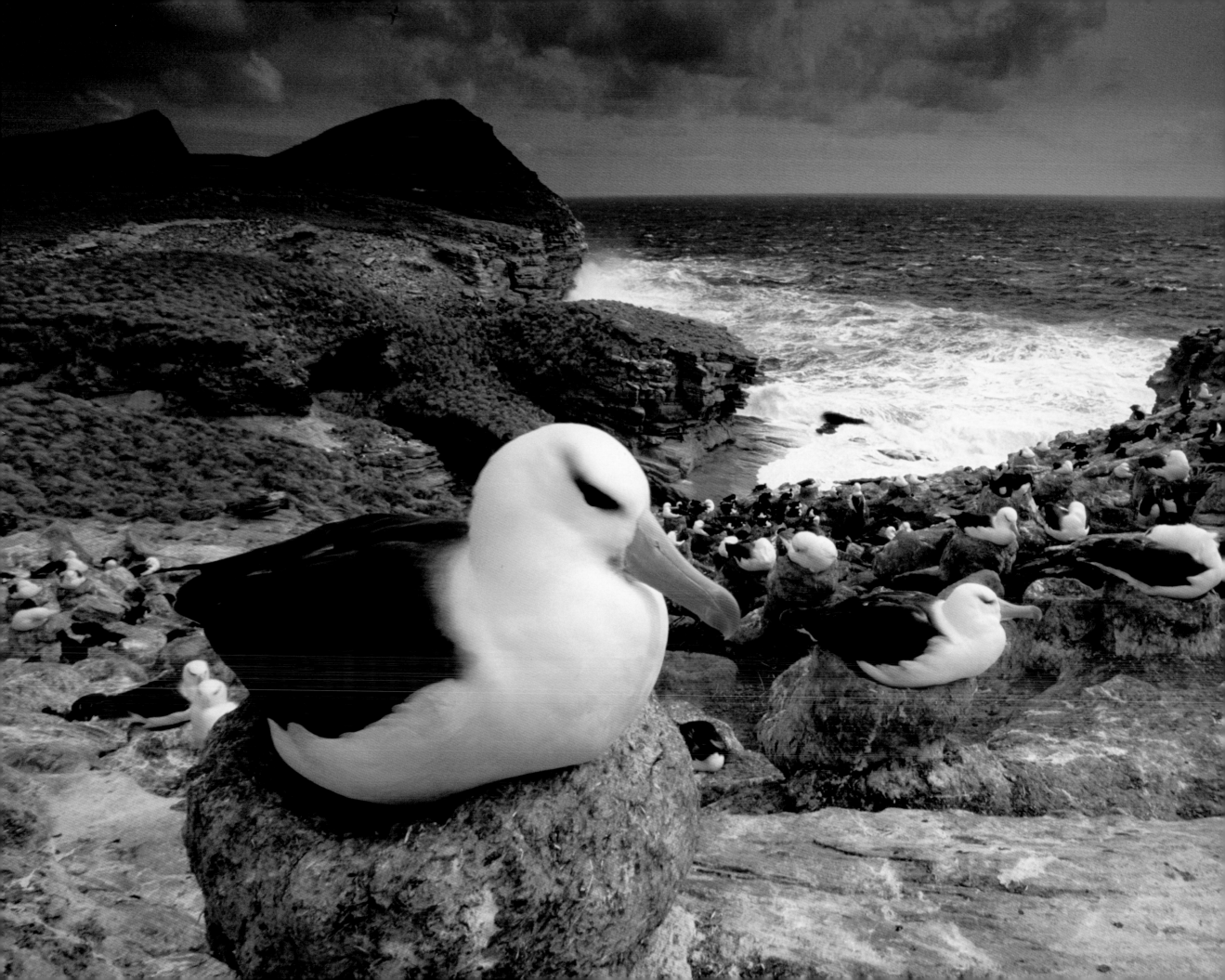

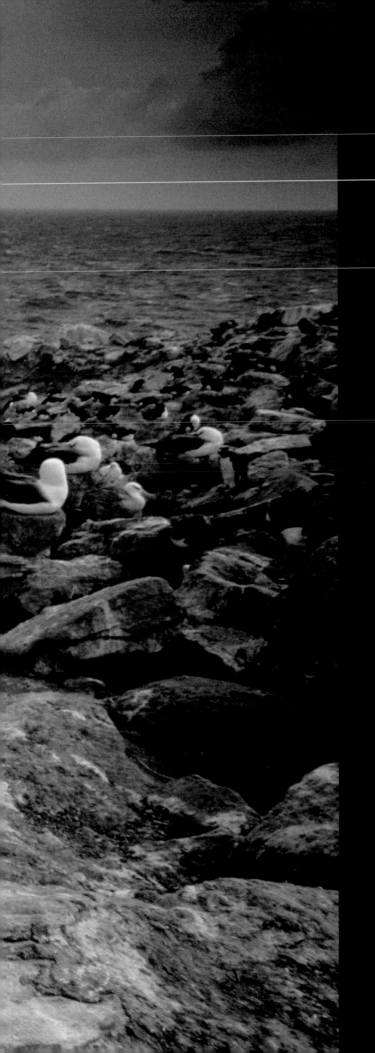

ISLAND & OCEAN

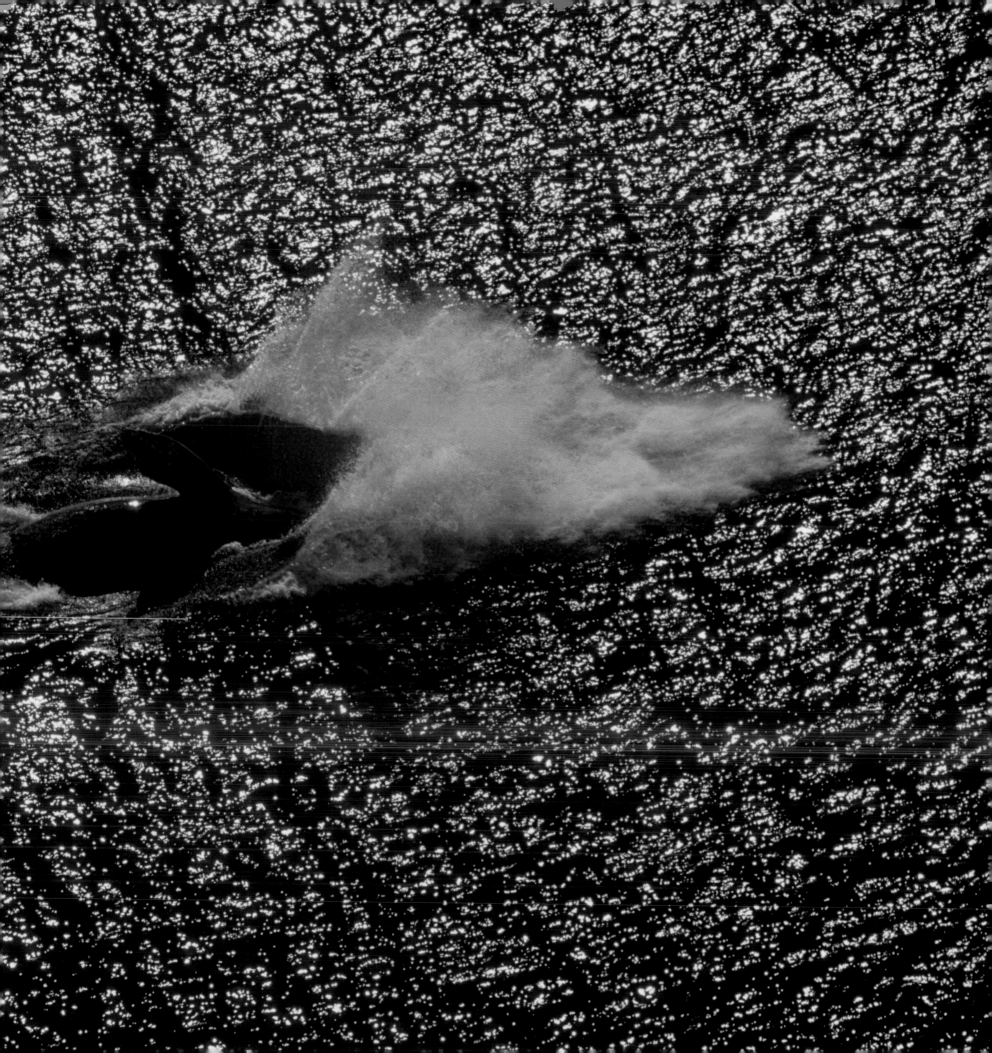

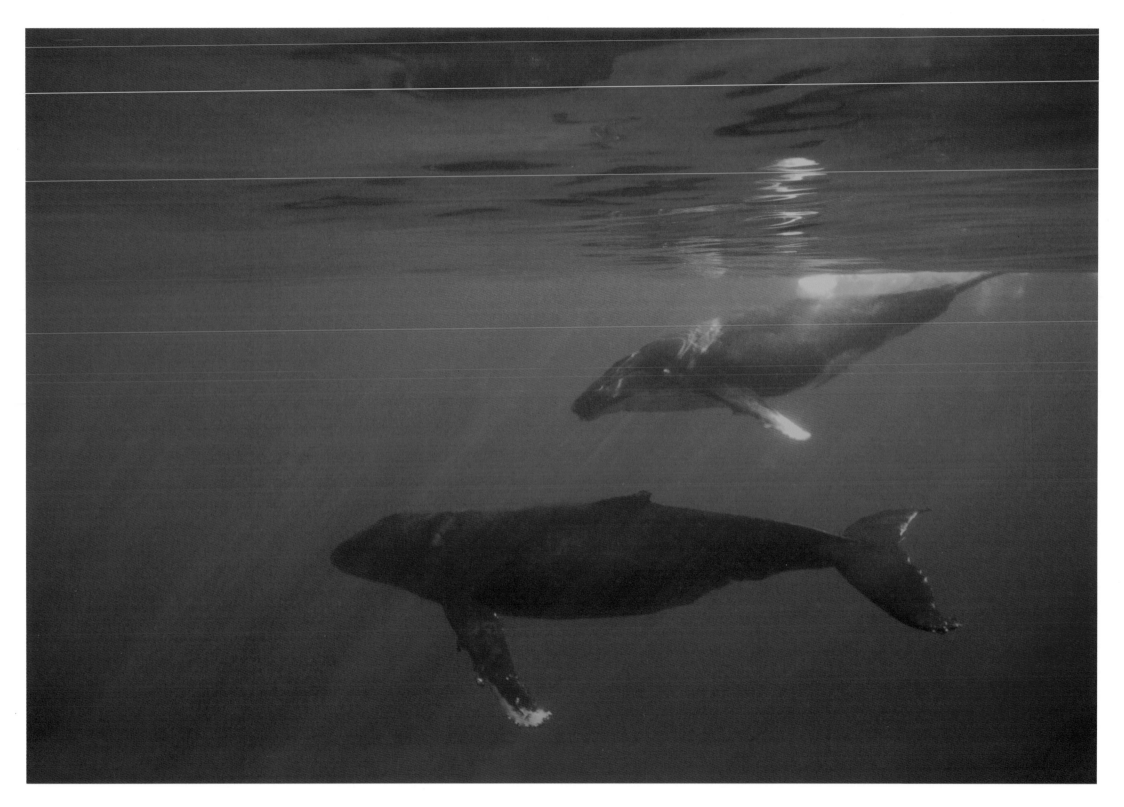

◀◀ BLACK-BROWED ALBATROSS ～

West Point Island, Falkland Islands, United Kingdom

◀ GRAY WHALE ～

Laguna San Ignacio, Baja California, Mexico

HUMPBACK WHALE ～

Tonga, South Pacific

ISLAND & OCEAN

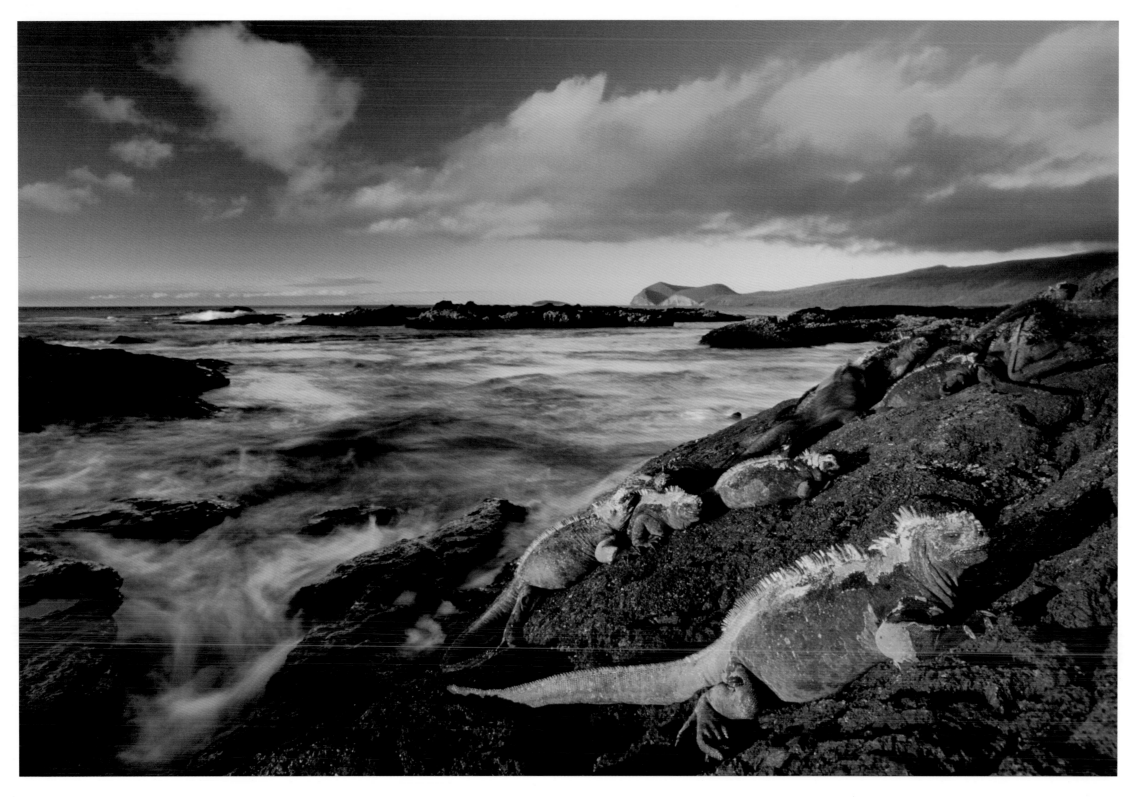

MARINE IGUANA

Isla Fernandina, Galápagos Islands, Ecuador

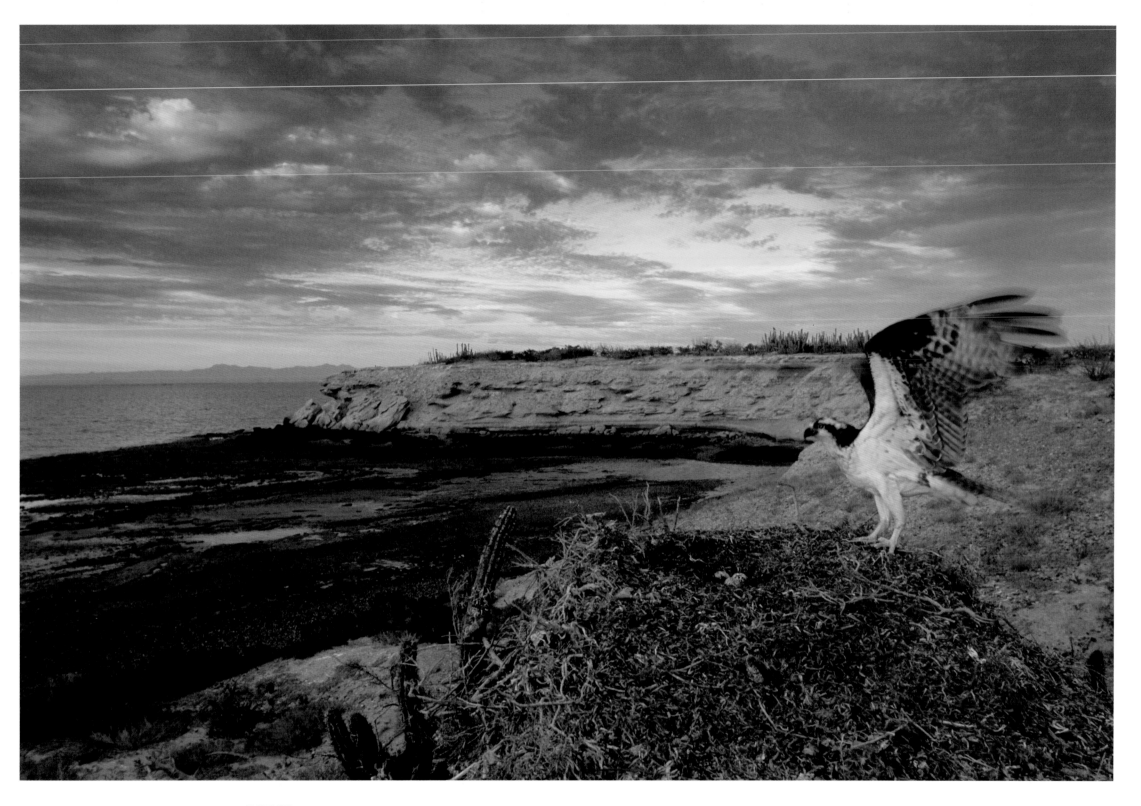

OSPREY

Laguna San Ignacio, Baja California, Mexico

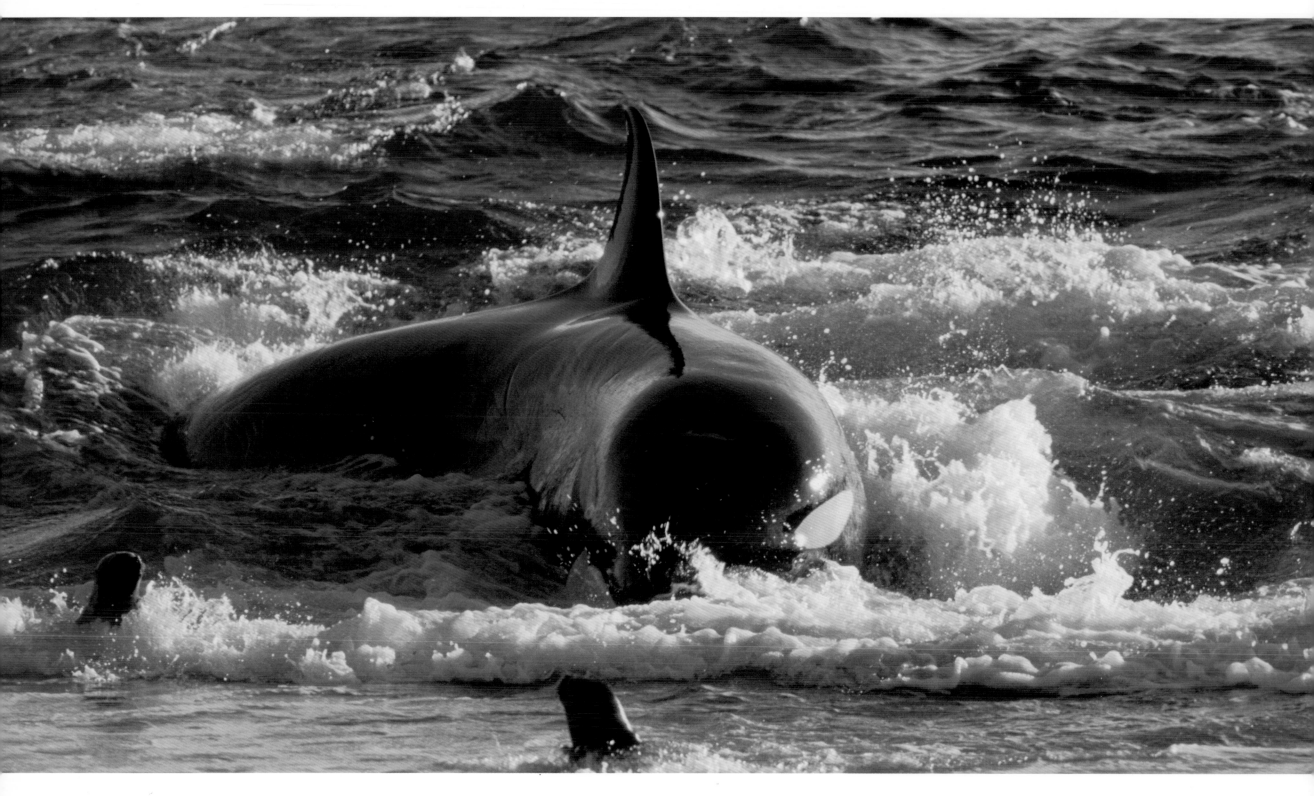

ORCA AND SOUTHERN SEA LION
PENÍNSULA VALDÉS, ARGENTINA

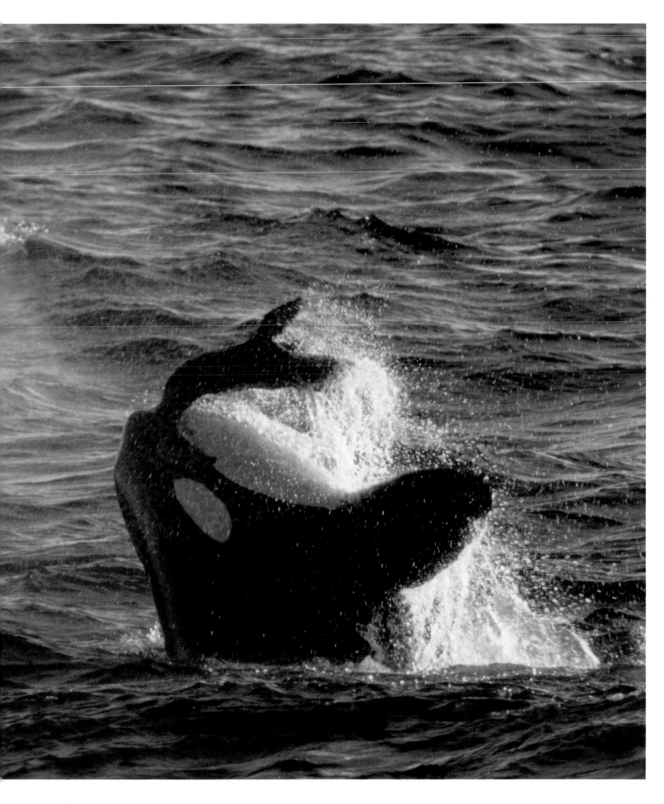
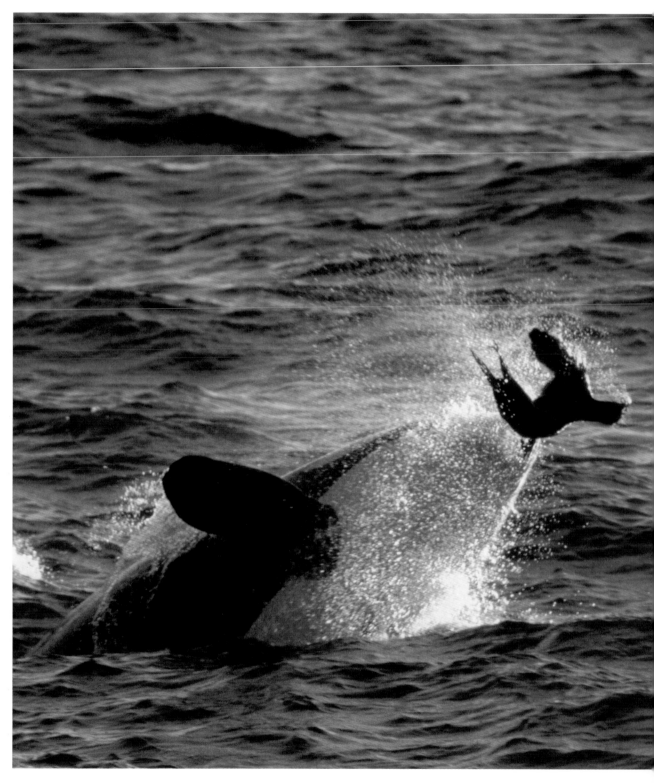

▲ AND ▶ ORCA AND SOUTHERN SEA LION
Península Valdés, Argentina

ISLAND & OCEAN

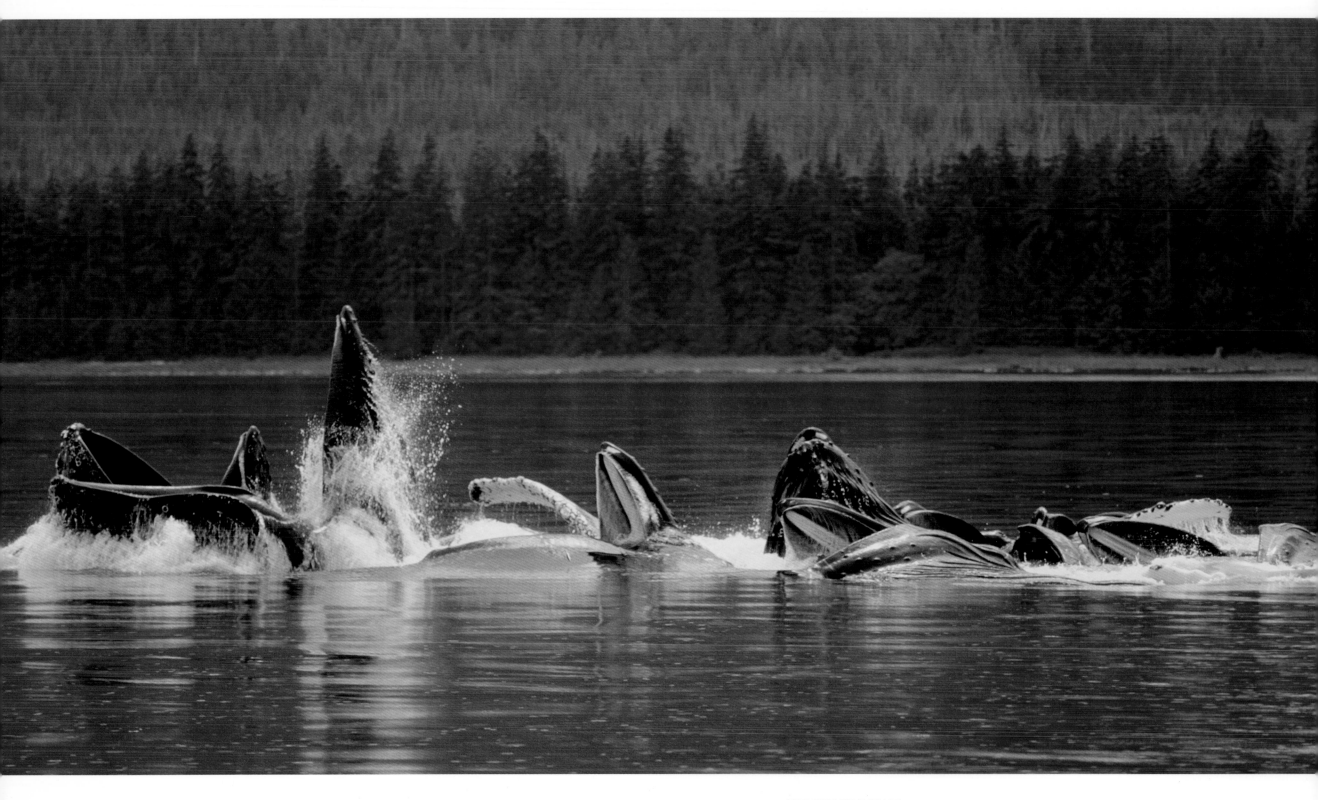

HUMPBACK WHALE

FREDERICK SOUND, SOUTHEAST ALASKA, USA

THE LIVING WILD

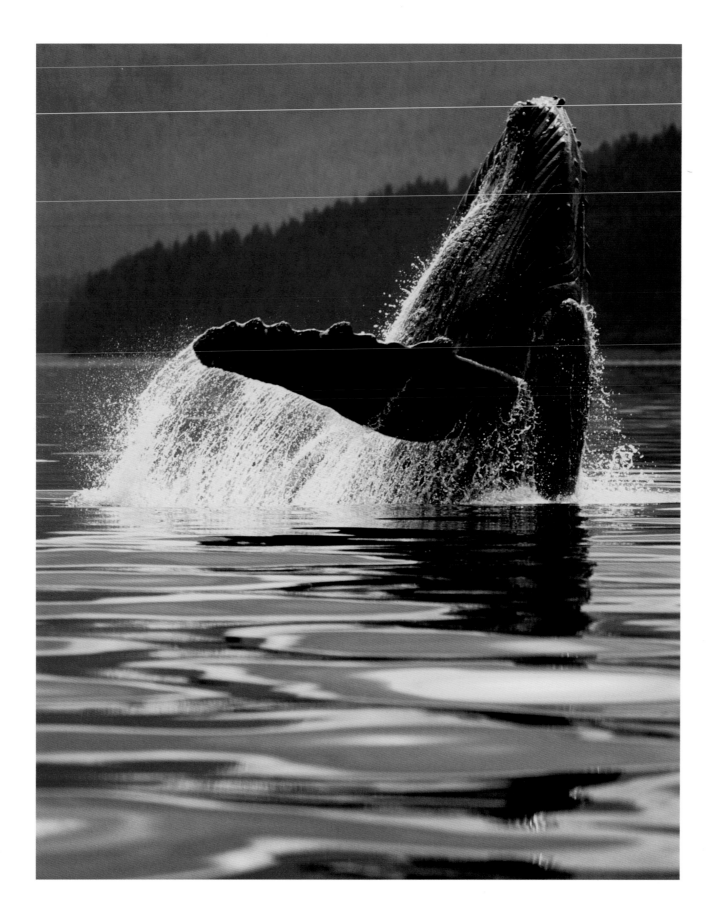

HUMPBACK WHALE

ISLAND & OCEAN

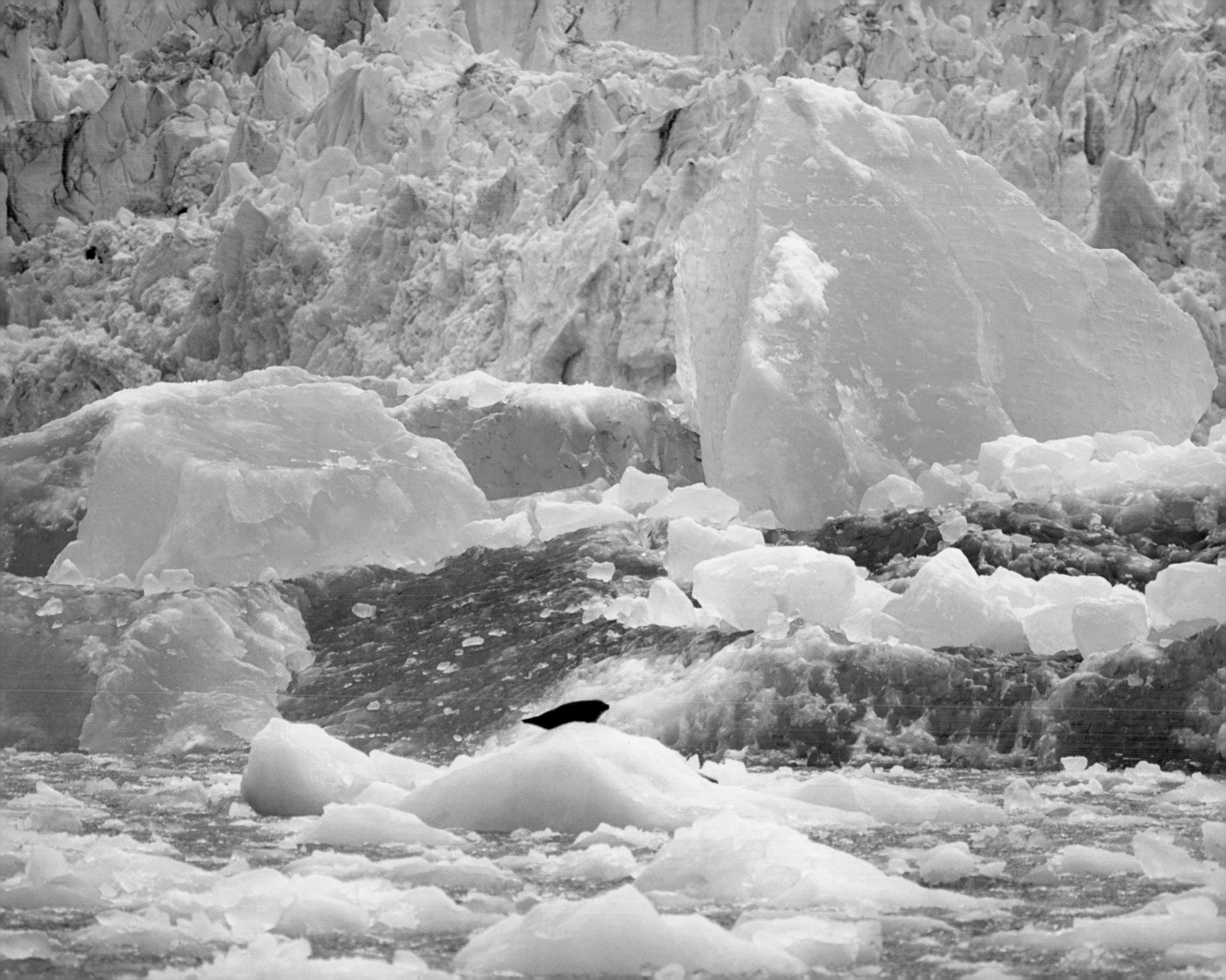

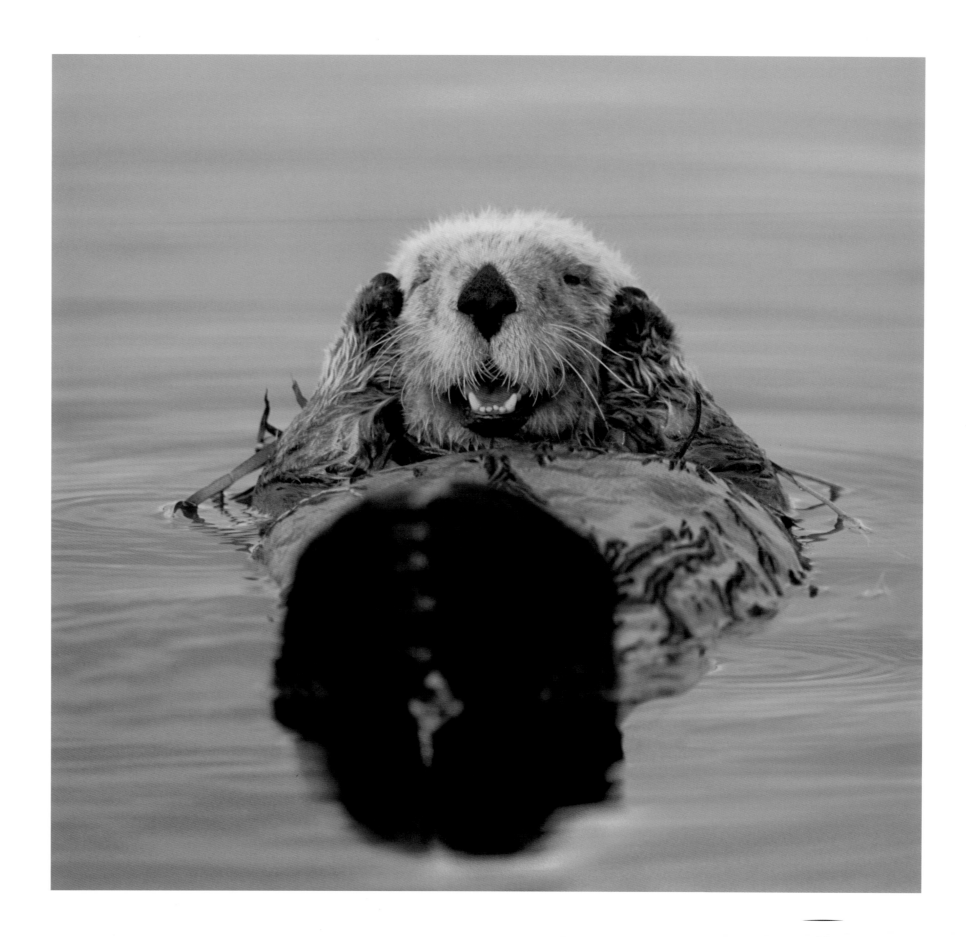

◄ HARBOR SEAL ～

TRACY ARM, SOUTHEAST ALASKA, USA

SEA OTTER ～

MONTEREY BAY, CALIFORNIA, USA

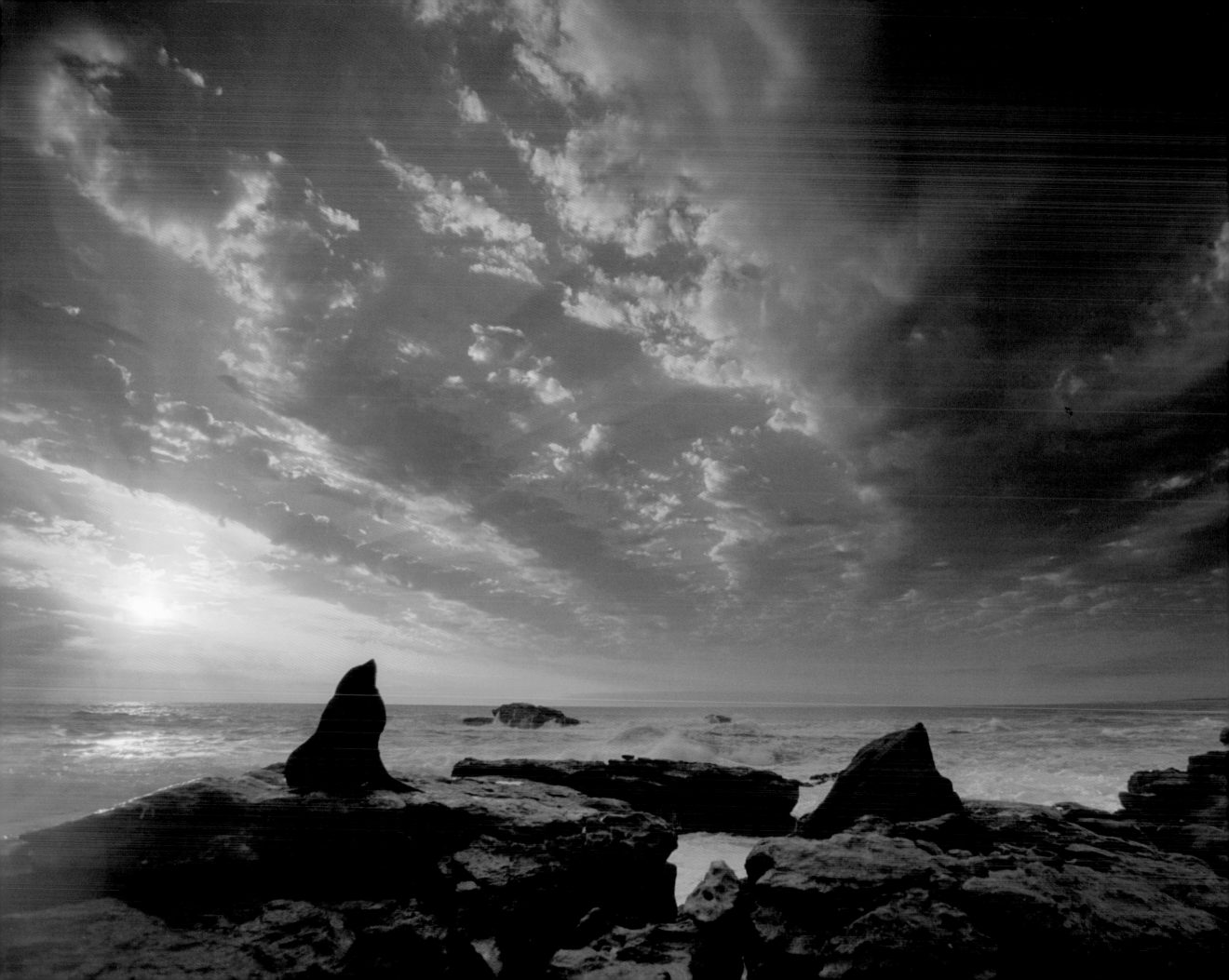

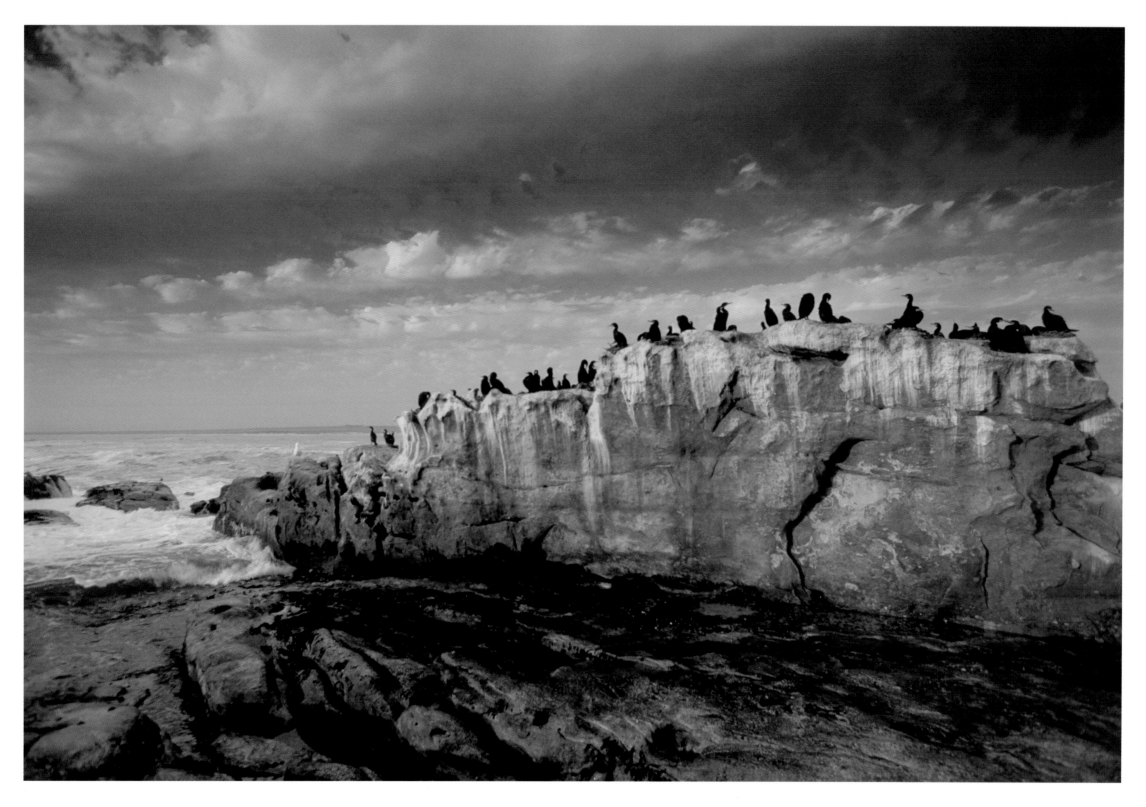

◀ CAPE FUR SEAL

ATLANTIC COAST, SOUTH AFRICA

CAPE CORMORANT

ATLANTIC COAST, SOUTH AFRICA

ISLAND & OCEAN

31

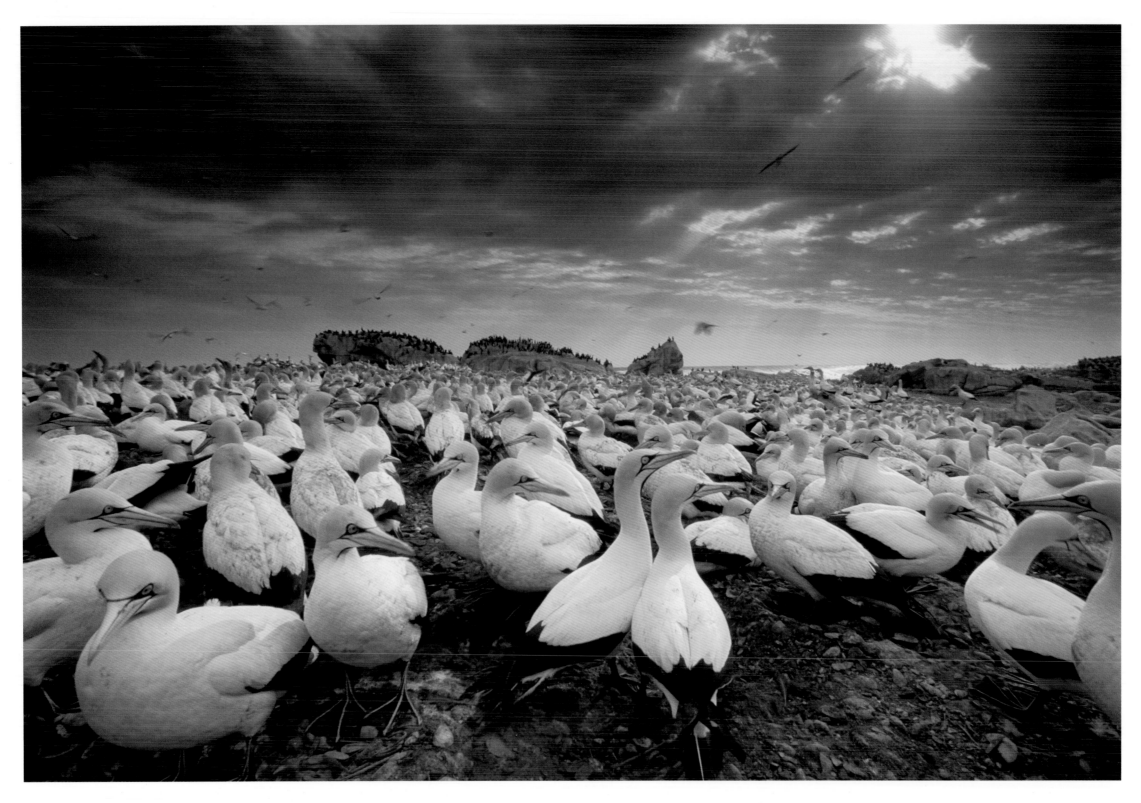

CAPE GANNET

Atlantic Coast, South Africa

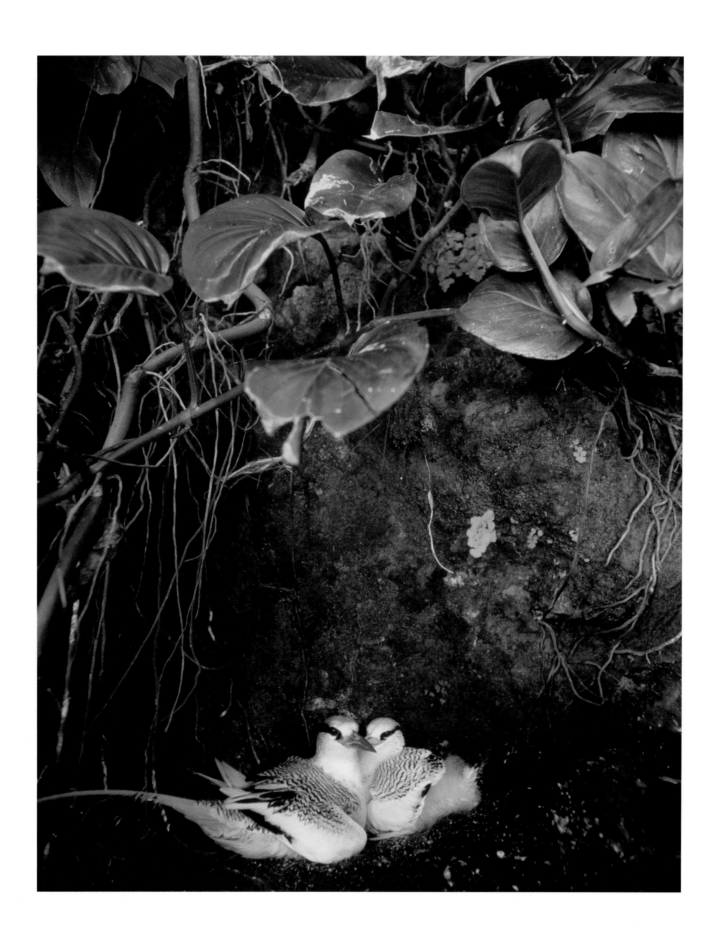

RED-BILLED TROPICBIRD

Islas Bocas del Toro, Panama

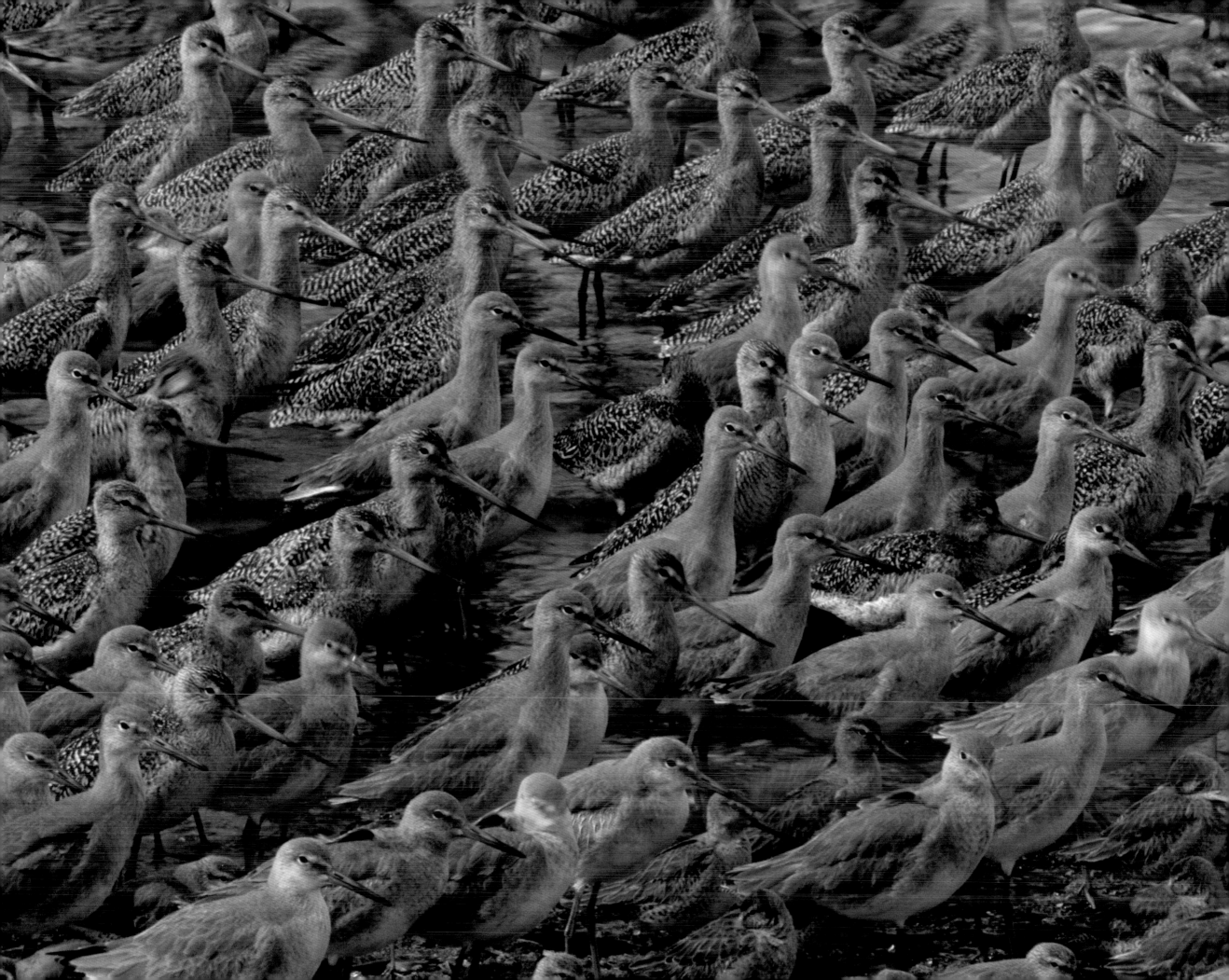

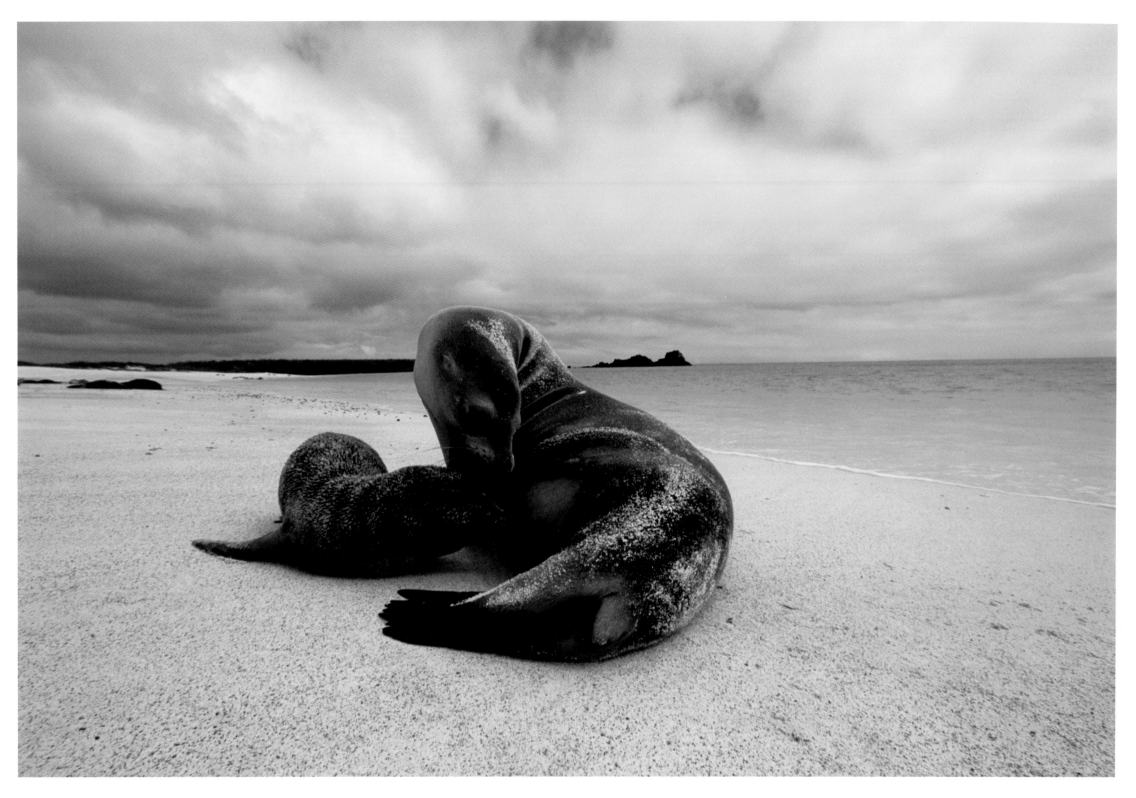

◄ MARBLED GODWIT, WILLET, AND SHORT-BILLED DOWITCHER ～   GALÁPAGOS SEA LION ～

Laguna San Ignacio, Baja California, Mexico   Isla Santa Fé, Galápagos Islands, Ecuador

ISLAND & OCEAN

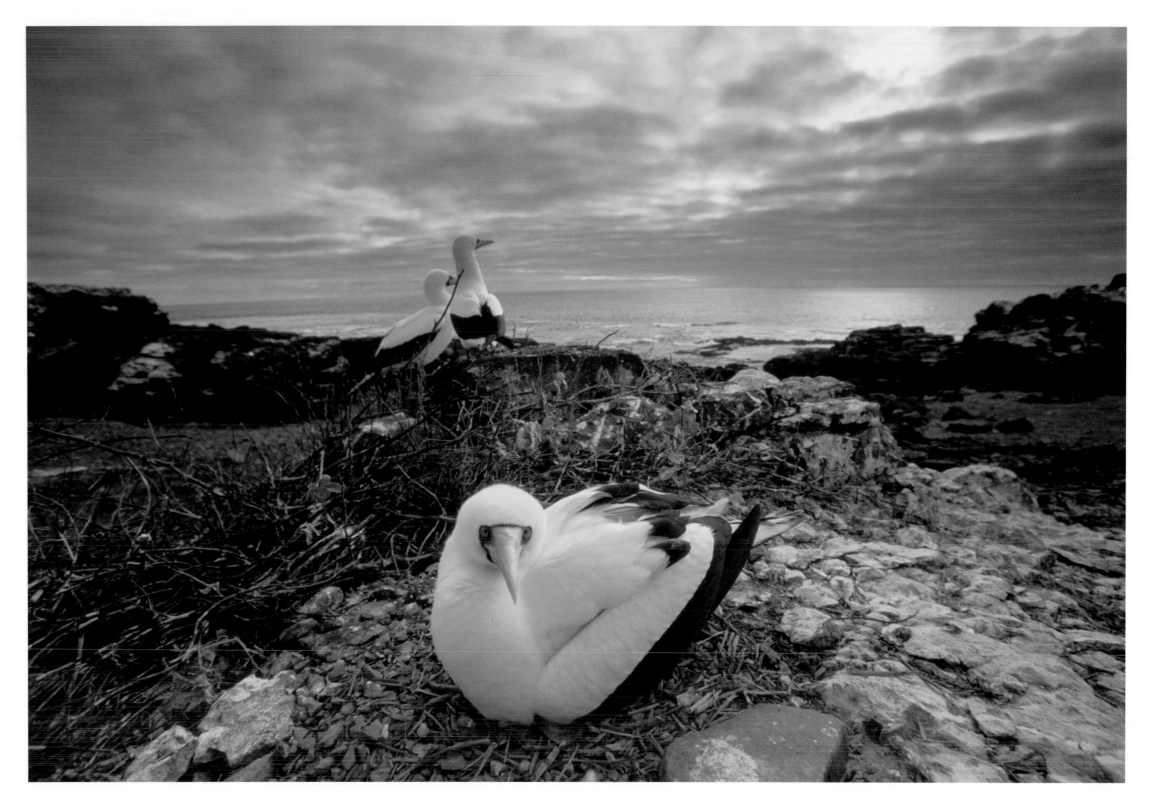

MASKED BOOBY

Isla Española, Galápagos Islands, Ecuador

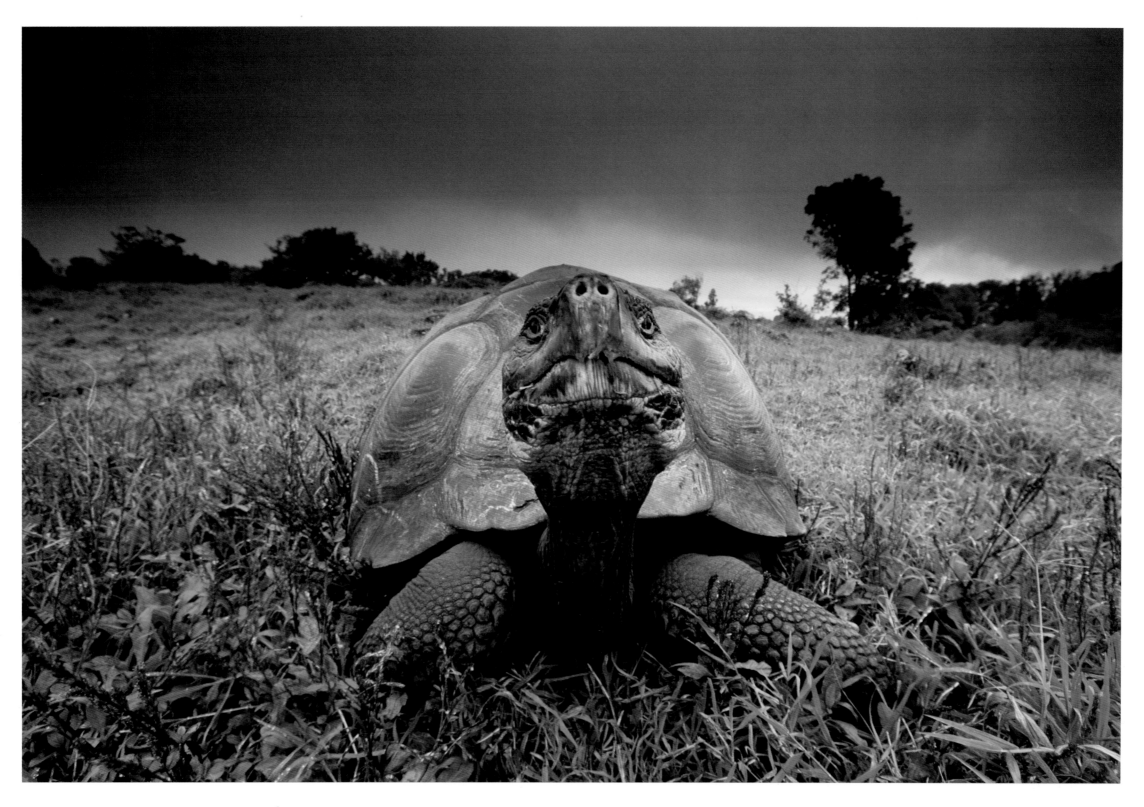

GALÁPAGOS GIANT TORTOISE

Isla Santa Cruz, Galápagos Islands, Ecuador

▶ COW-NOSED EAGLE RAY

Islas Bocas del Toro, Panama

ISLAND & OCEAN

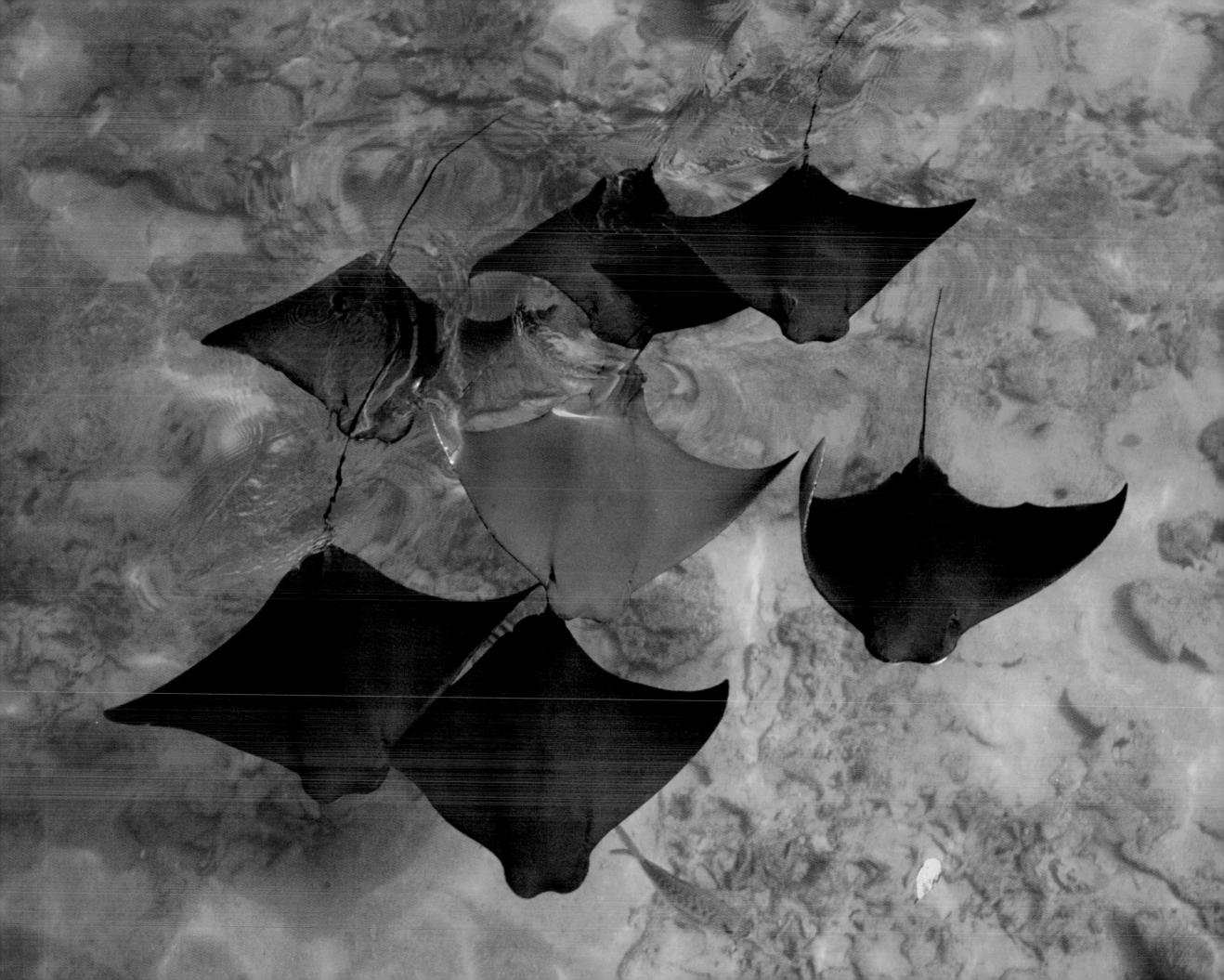

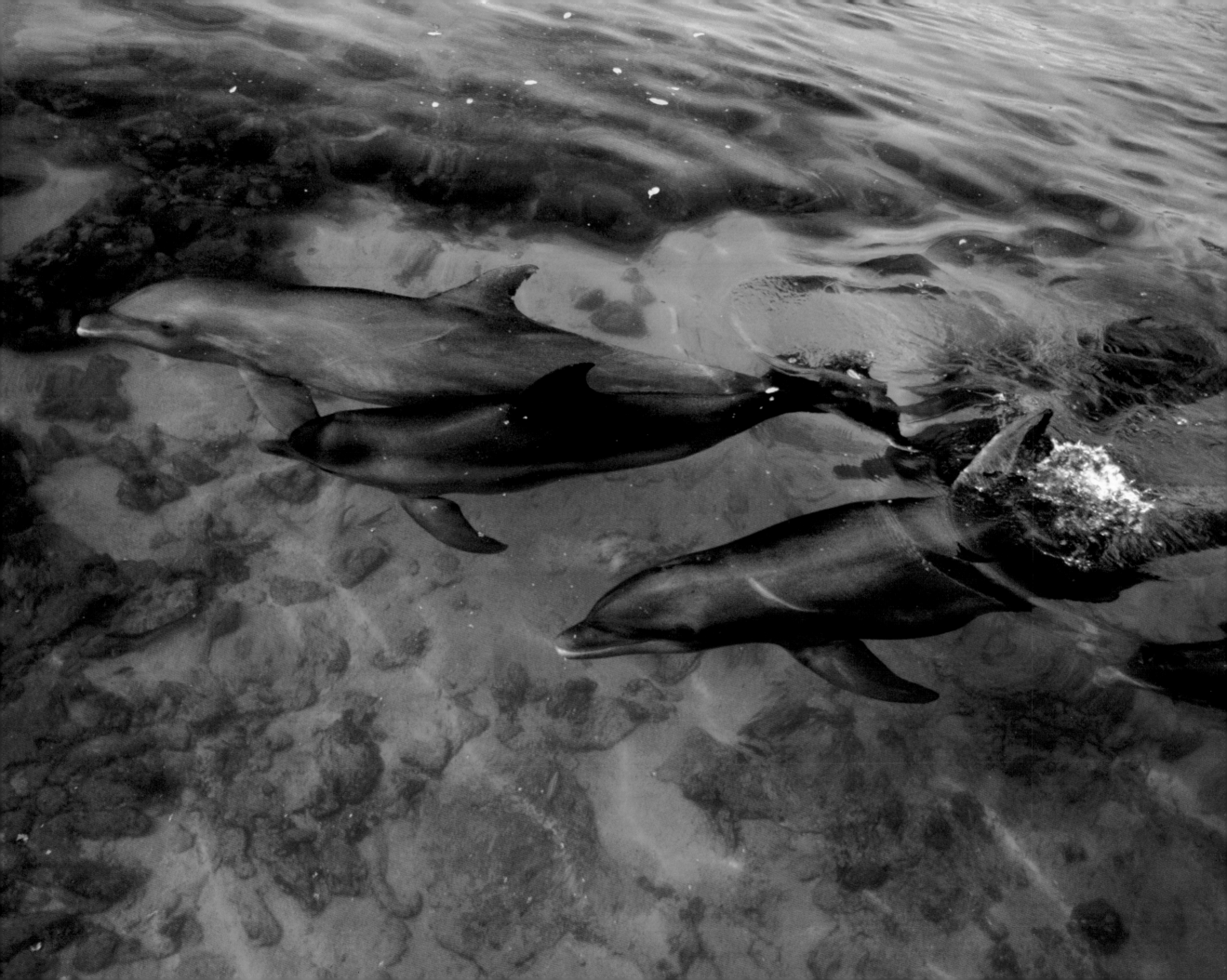

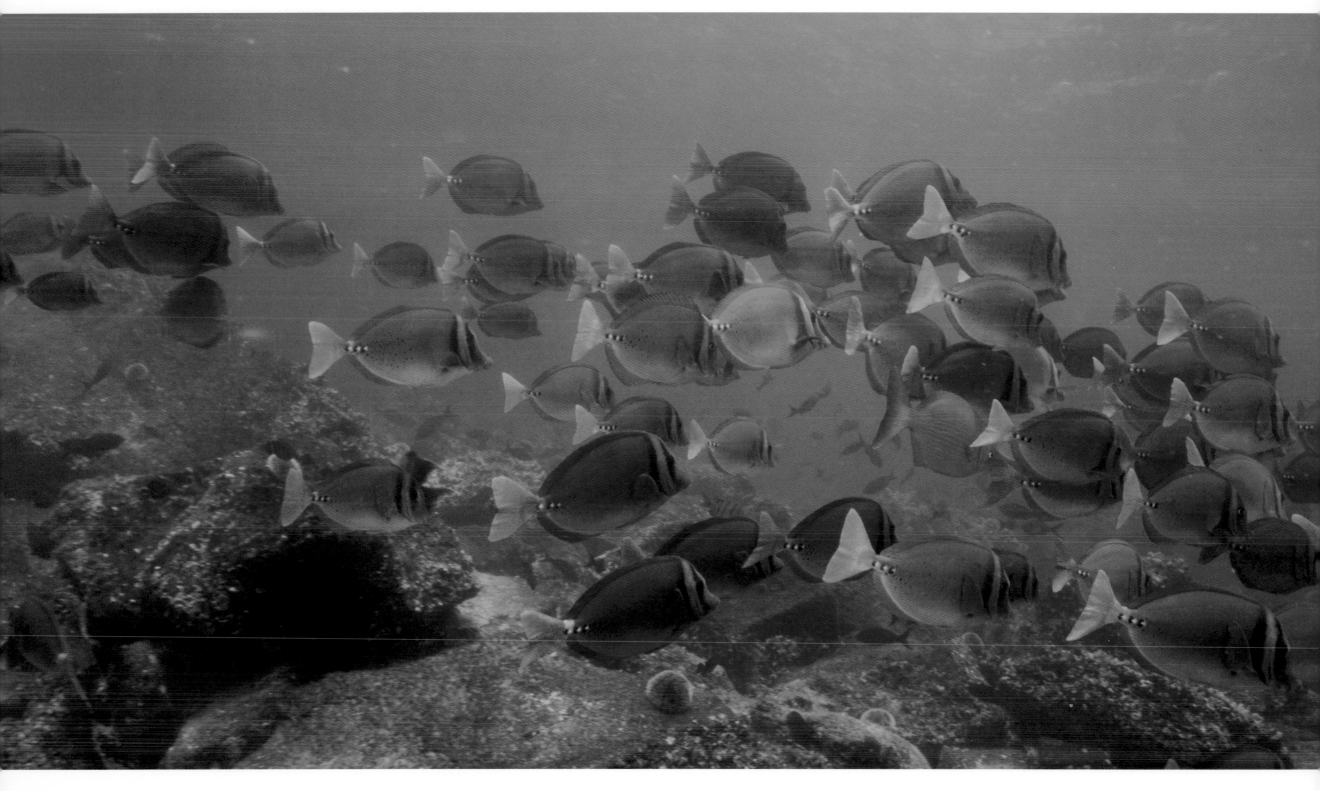

◄ BOTTLENOSE DOLPHIN

Islas Bocas del Toro, Panama

GALÁPAGOS SURGEONFISH

Isla Fernandina, Galápagos Islands, Ecuador

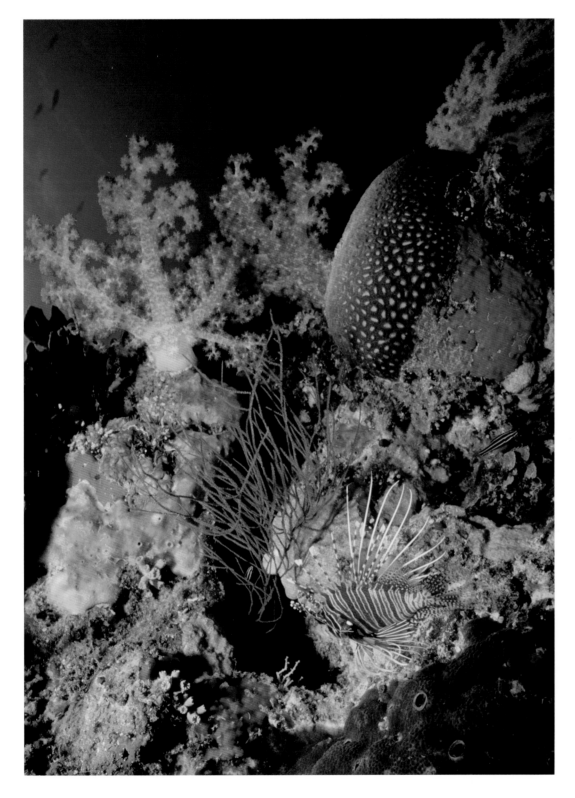

LIONFISH
Pulau Sipadan, Malaysia

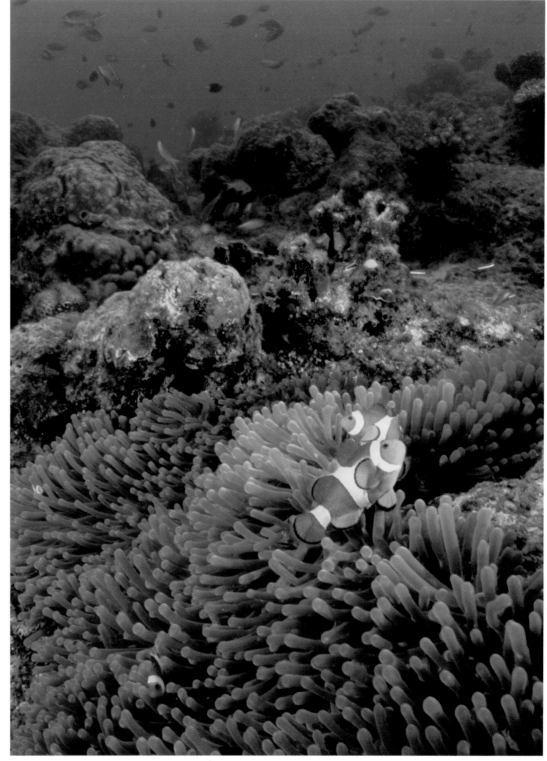

CLOWNFISH
Pulau Sipadan, Malaysia

ISLAND & OCEAN

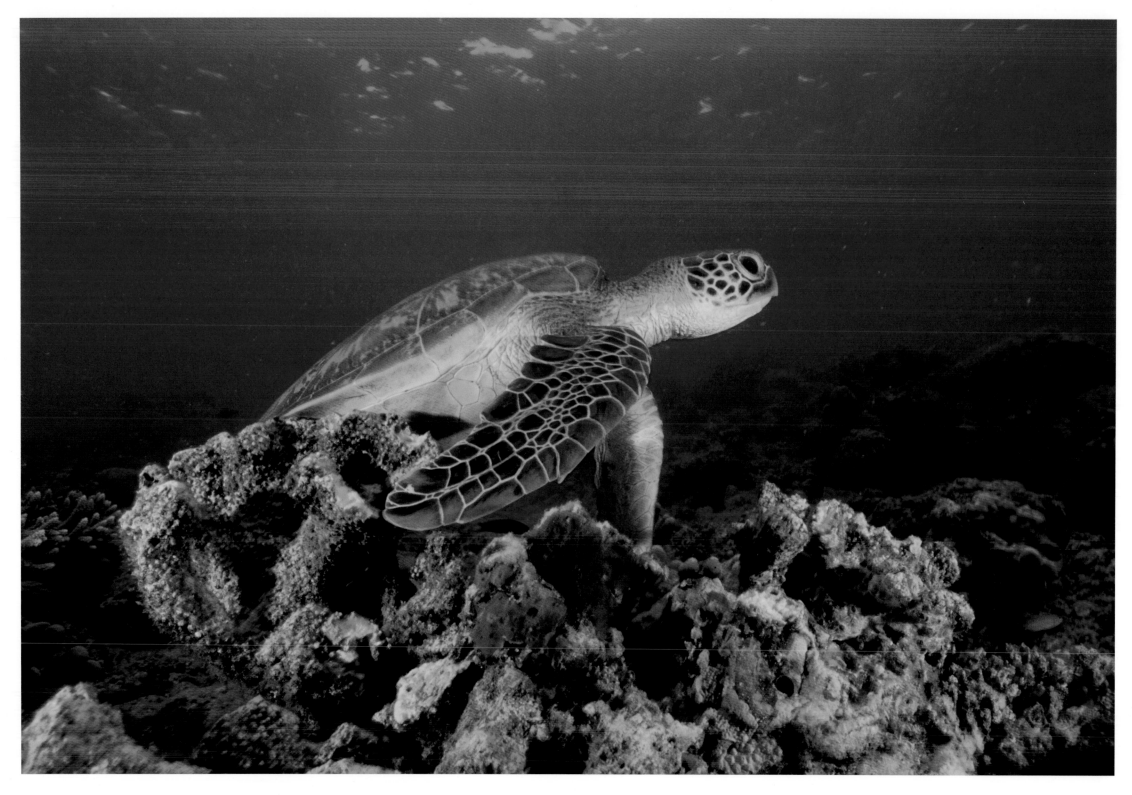

GREEN SEA TURTLE

Pulau Sipadan, Malaysia

► CORAL REEF

Pulau Sipadan, Malaysia

THE LIVING WILD

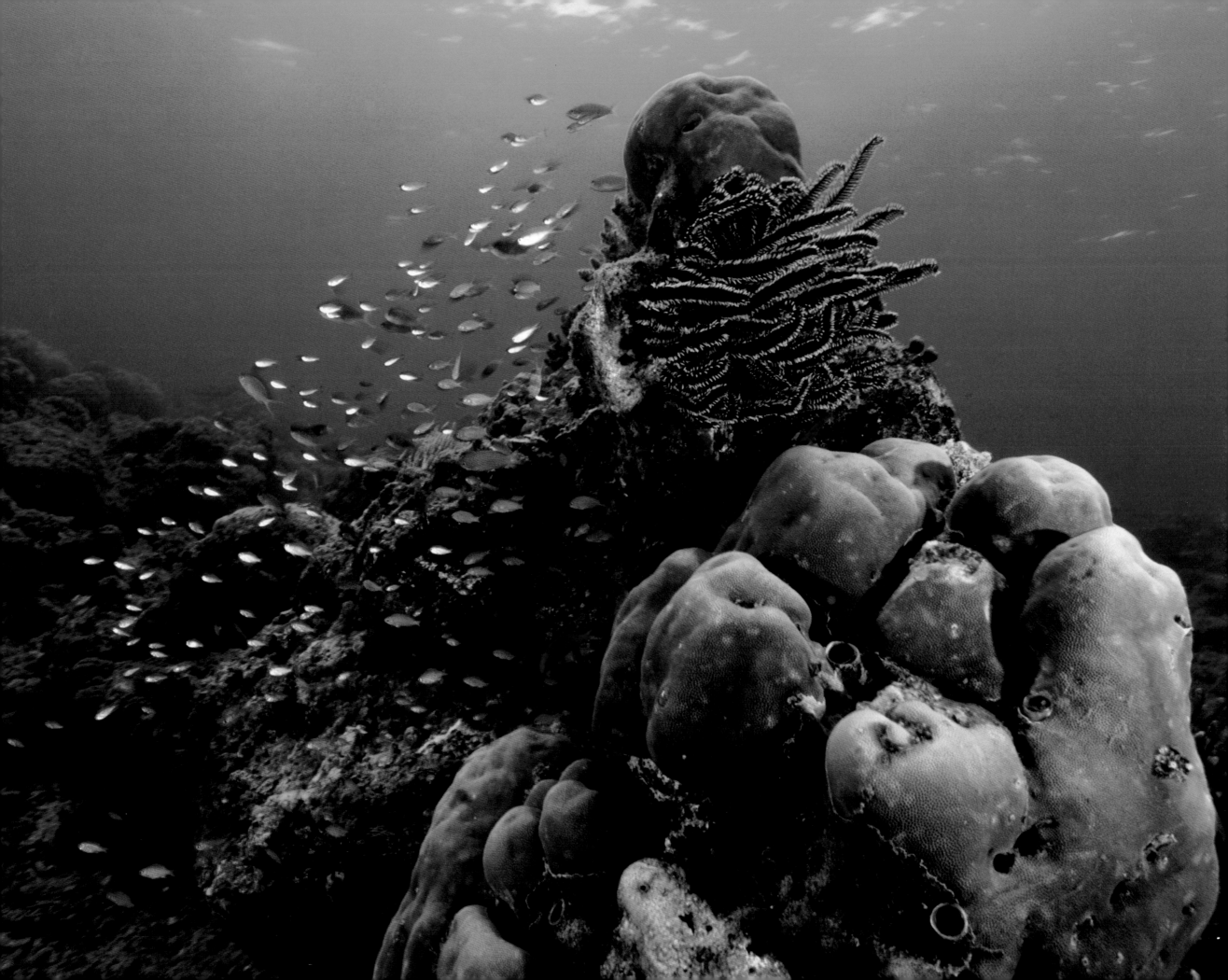

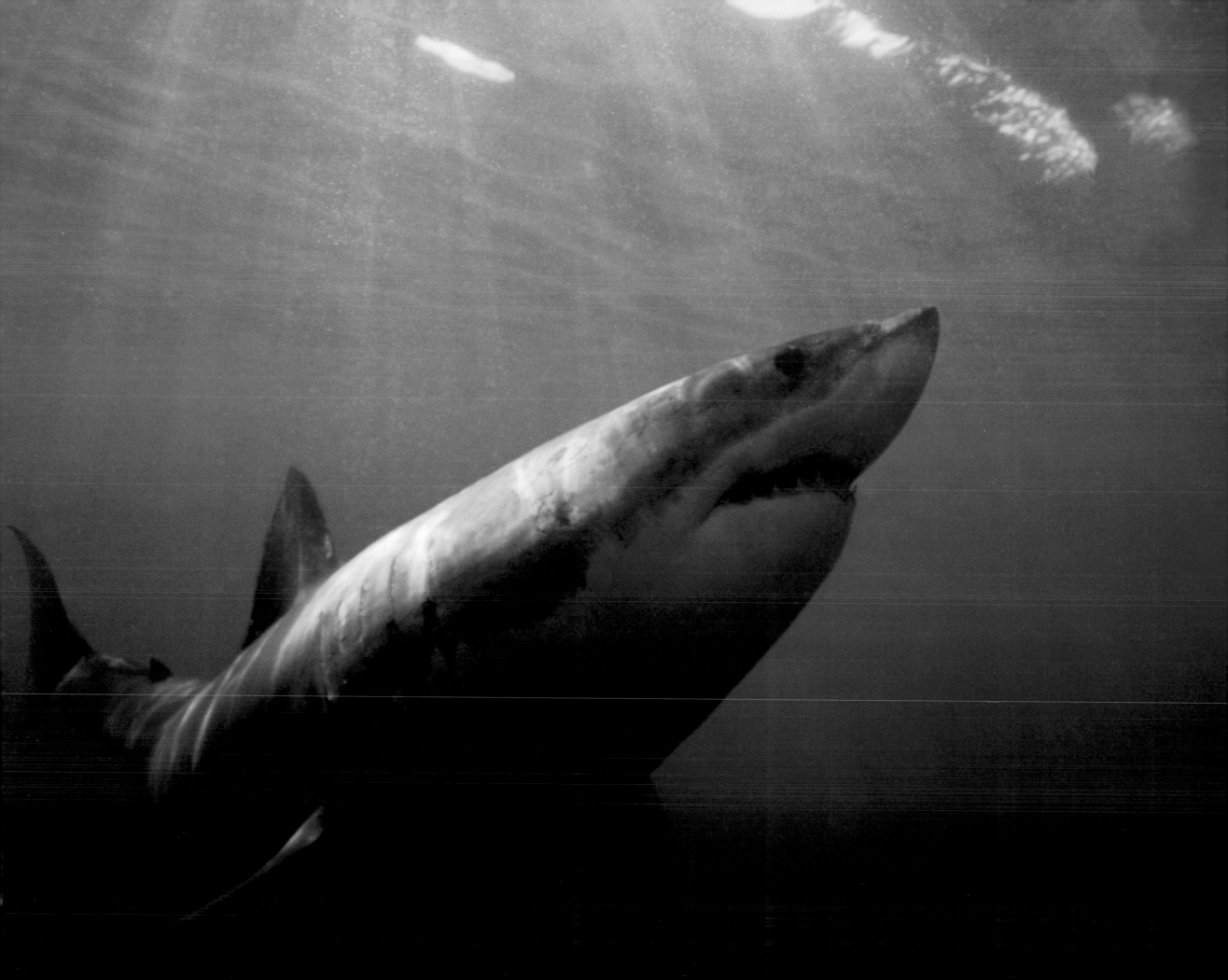

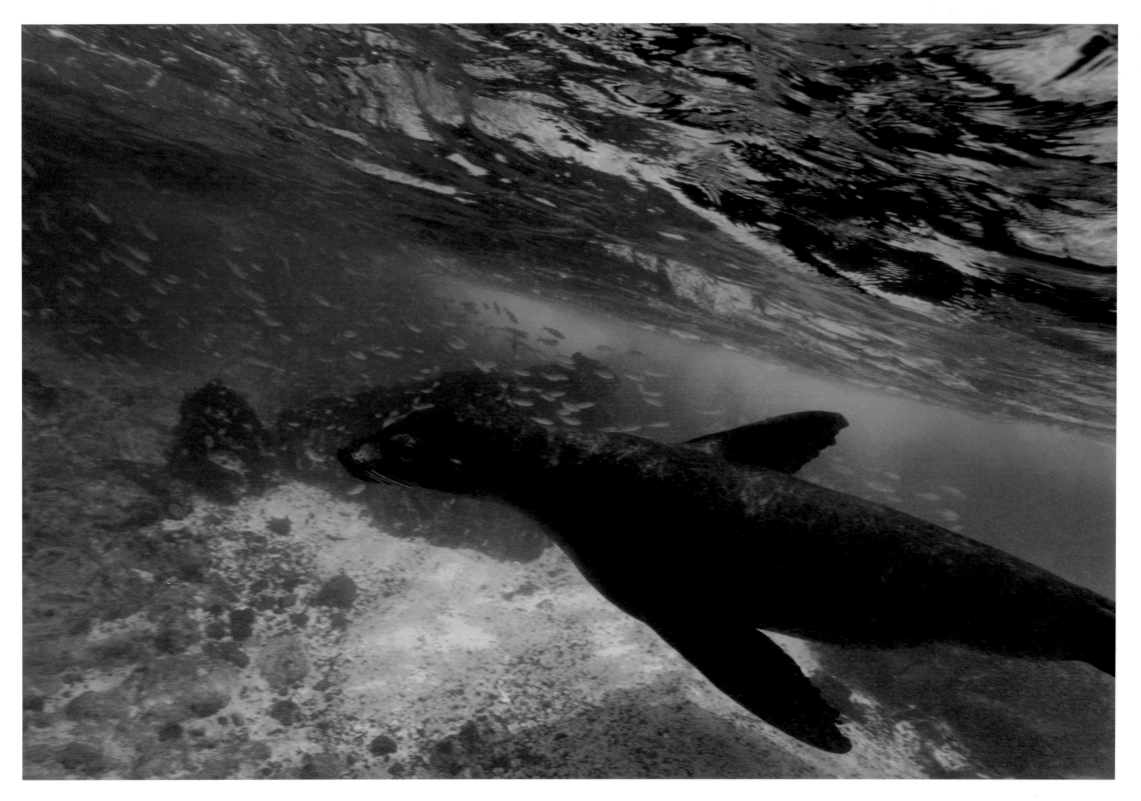

◄ GREAT WHITE SHARK
SOUTH COAST, SOUTH AFRICA

GALÁPAGOS SEA LION
ISLA SEYMOUR, GALÁPAGOS ISLANDS, ECUADOR

ISLAND & OCEAN

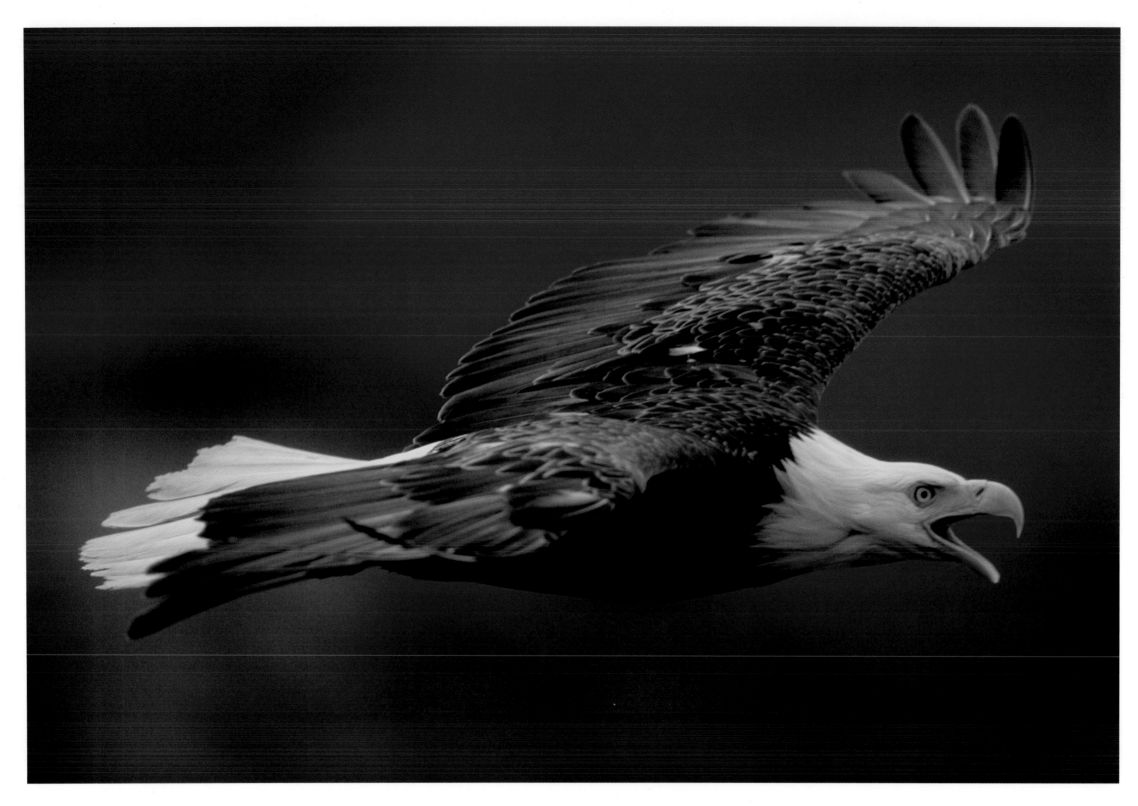

BALD EAGLE
Unalaska Island, Alaska, USA

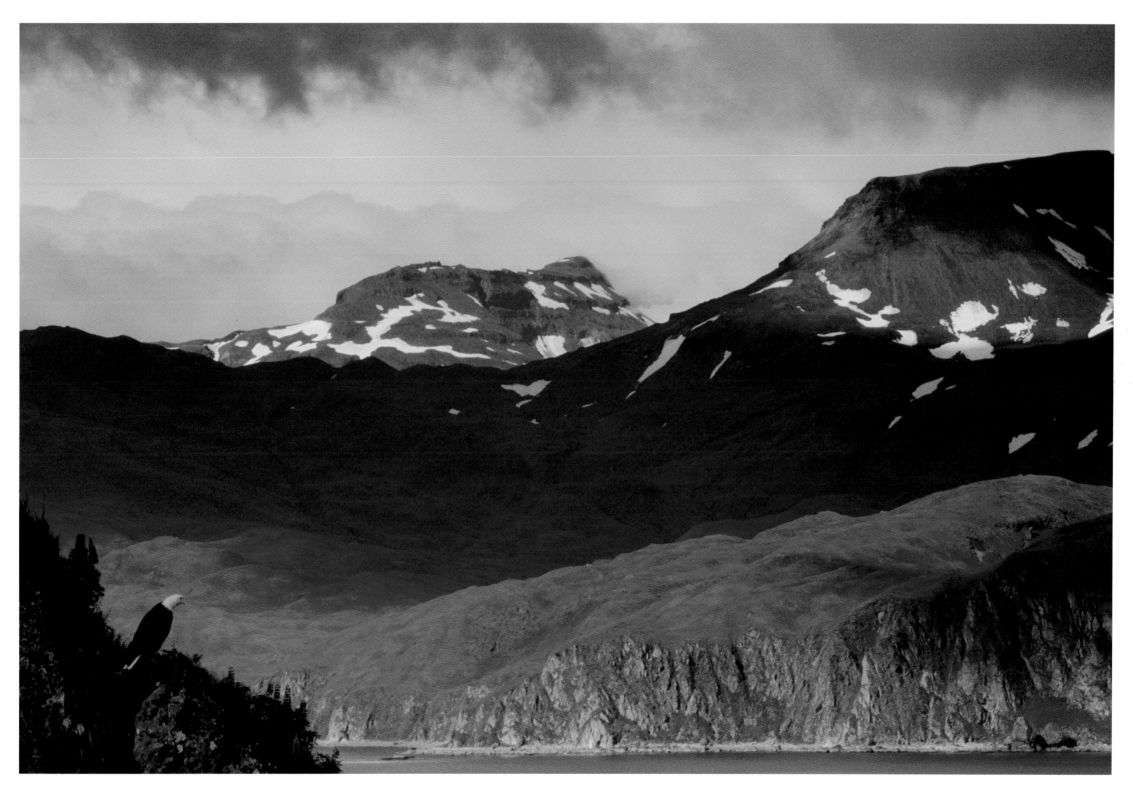

BALD EAGLE
Unalaska Island, Alaska, USA

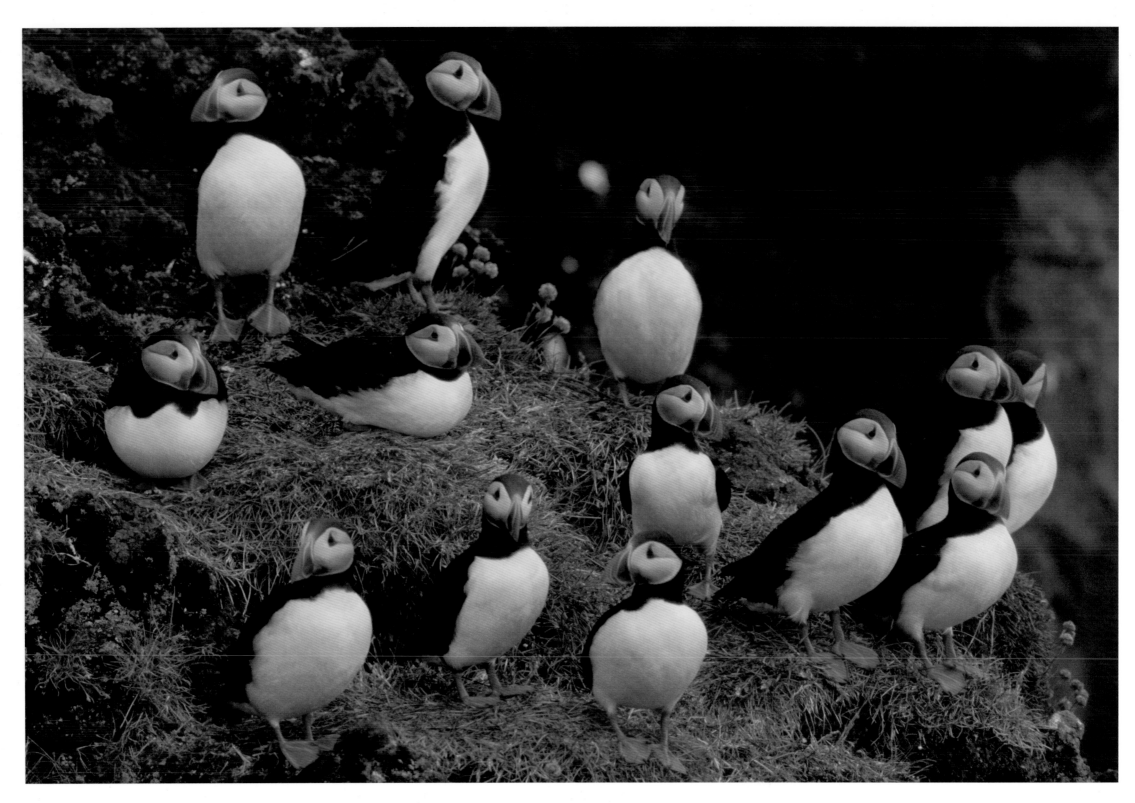

ATLANTIC PUFFIN
VESTMANNAEYJAR, ICELAND

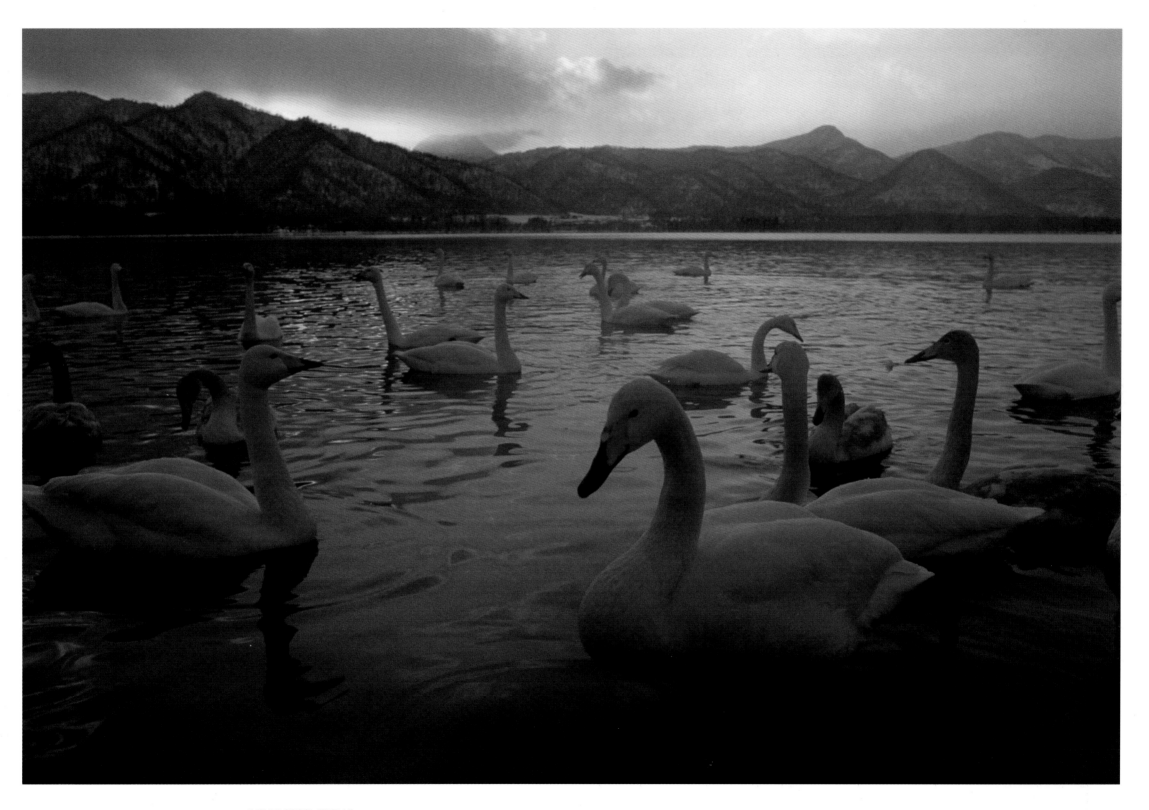

WHOOPER SWAN

HOKKAIDO ISLAND, JAPAN

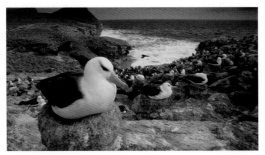

BLACK-BROWED ALBATROSS
(*Diomedea melanophris*)

West Point Island is one of 420 islands that form the Falklands in the South Atlantic. It is here that a colony of black-browed albatross sits. Several hundred thousand birds nest in the Falklands from October until April, each pair incubating a single egg on a conical mud nest. The Falklands contain the largest black-browed albatross colony in the world on Steeple Jason Island. On West Point, the albatross share their island home with gentoo penguins (*Pygoscelis papua*), upland geese (*Chloephaga picta leucoptera*), and the Falkland Island flightless steamer duck (*Tachyeres brachypterus*). The lack of terrestrial predators has resulted in almost fearless wildlife. Here the only natural predators come from the sky, in the form of skuas and caracaras. However, when people settle such places they often bring cats, dogs, and (unintentionally) rats with them, upsetting the balance between predator and prey and devastating vulnerable bird colonies.

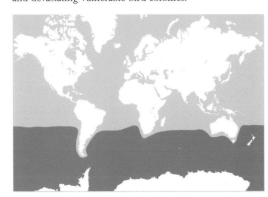

AW: Whenever I encounter extraordinarily relaxed animals, I try to capitalize on the situation. In this example, I have not only been able to photograph these albatrosses at close range with a wide-angle lens, but, since they remained so still, I was able to stop down to f/22, bringing all into focus. I used a polarizing filter to bring out the deeper blue of the ocean's surface. I also used a 2-stop graduated neutral density filter to darken the sky and bring the entire composition into an even exposure.

Canon EOS-3, Canon EF 17–35mm lens, f/22 at 1/8 second, polarizing filter, 2-stop graduated neutral density filter, Fujichrome Velvia film

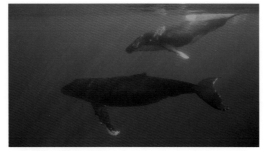

GRAY WHALE
(*Eschrichtius robustus*)

At one time, gray whales could be found in both the North Pacific and North Atlantic Oceans. North Atlantic grays became extinct by 1700 after several centuries of intense whaling. In the Pacific, the two populations of gray whales have come close to sharing a similar fate. The western population once inhabited the waters off China, Japan, and Korea. Those that bred in the Inland Sea of Japan were eliminated by 1900, while those off southern Korea had largely vanished by 1933. Sporadic sightings suggest that a remnant population of tens or a few hundred survive. Eastern Pacific gray whales have also been pushed to the brink by whalers. By the early twentieth century, only a few thousand animals remained. Full protection (with the exception of some native whaling) came in 1946 and an estimated 23,000 gray whales now ply the west coast of North America. Today coastal development and disturbance present new and unknown risks.

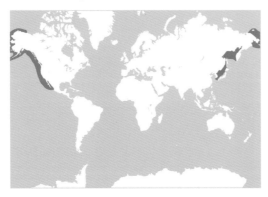

AW: Each fall, gray whales leave their summer home in the Bering and Chukchi Seas and travel down the west coast of North America. They head to the protective waters along Baja's Pacific Coast, and spend the winter months feeding, resting, mating, and giving birth. From the aerial perspective of an ultralight, I photographed a breaching gray whale with my favorite aerial lens, the 70–200mm zoom.

Canon EOS-3, Canon EF 70–200mm lens, f/2.8 at 1/1000 second, Fujichrome Astia film

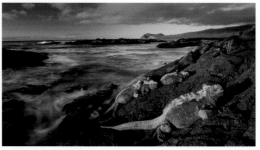

HUMPBACK WHALE
(*Megaptera novaeangliae*)

The humpback whale's scientific name—*Megaptera novaeangliae*—translates to "big-winged New Englander." The humpback is unique. No other member of the Balaenopteridae family has the long, tapering pectoral flippers of this species. The pectorals usually measure about a third of the animals' head and body length—thus, a 12.5-meter-long animal sports pectorals more than 4 meters in length. Adults attain an average weight of about 30,000 kilograms (the equivalent of six average male African elephants [*Loxodonta africana*]). Female humpbacks give birth to a single offspring after an 11- to 11.5-month gestation. The infant whale is 4 to 5 meters long at birth and weighs about 1,350 kilograms. The youngster is suckled for nearly a year and stays close to its mother for some time after it is weaned. In most populations, females give birth every two years, although they have been known to birth annually.

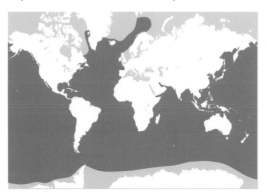

AW: Few personal experiences compare with the "adrenaline rush" I felt as I watched a humpback whale with her second-year calf ascend from the blue depths below me. For a few seconds it appeared as if they were headed directly toward me, but at the last moment, they veered away and broke the surface approximately 10 meters from me. After taking in a few breaths of air on the surface, they descended, leaving me floundering, in total awe, on the water's surface.

Canon EOS-1N, underwater housing, Canon EF 15mm lens, f/8 at 1/60 second, Fujichrome Astia film (pushed 1 stop)

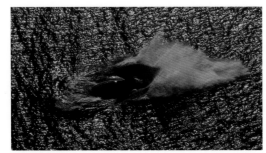

MARINE IGUANA
(*Amblyrhynchus cristatus*)

The marine iguanas of the Galápagos Islands are the only marine lizards in the world. It is likely that these unique creatures were among the first animals to reach the Galápagos—via natural rafts—following the islands' formation approximately four to five million years ago. Originally land dwellers, they gradually evolved to take advantage of the productive marine environment. Averaging 0.6 to 1 meter in length, they are typically black or dark gray in color, although some local populations can be more colorful. On Isla Fernandina, there are red phase marine iguanas, while in other areas iguanas sport a greenish tint. Although only a single species is recognized, isolation on the Galápagos' myriad islands has enhanced diversity and spawned numerous subspecies. Population estimates range from 200,000 to 300,000 animals, with as many as 8,000 individuals found in a single kilometer of coastline.

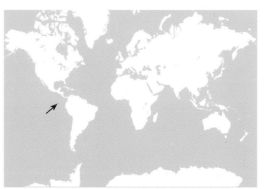

AW: In this image, marine iguanas absorb the last warming rays of the setting sun. These aquatic reptiles had just emerged from the sea after feeding on marine algae. I slowly approached the iguanas with a tripod and camera with a 17–35mm wide-angle lens. I had already spread the legs of the tripod so that I could minimize my movements once I got close. I used a polarizing filter to bring out the color in the clouds and heighten the contrast between the waves and the blue water. I also used a 2-stop graduated neutral density filter to darken the sky.

Canon EOS-3, Canon EF 17–35mm lens, f/22 at 1 second, polarizing filter, 2-stop graduated neutral density filter, Fujichrome Velvia film

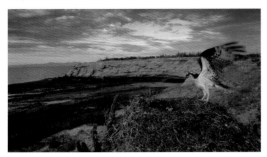

OSPREY
(*Pandion haliaetus*)

As has been the case with many birds of prey, ospreys experienced dramatic population declines during the 1950s and 1960s as their prey—fish—became contaminated with DDT. As the pesticide was concentrated up the food chain, it adversely affected breeding by thinning the birds' eggshells and thus reducing nesting success. With careful protection and pollution controls, their numbers have rebounded. Ospreys are mainly found along coasts and near other bodies of water. The 1.4-kilogram birds have a wingspan of about 1.6 meters, and they use their long talons to snag fish swimming within a meter of the water's surface. In addition to fish, they may also take birds, small mammals, and amphibians. Ospreys mate for life and often use the same nest year after year, adding to it when they return. Two to four eggs are laid, and both parents incubate; when they hatch, the female usually guards the nest while the male fishes.

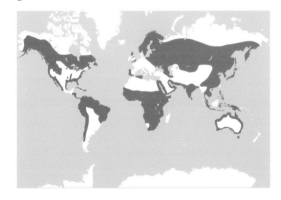

AW: On a tiny island located inside Laguna San Ignacio there is a large population of nesting ospreys. Nests can be found at about 100-meter intervals. I took this image using a 17–35mm wide-angle lens. I placed my tripod near the nest and used a 2-stop graduated neutral density filter to darken the clouds, plus fill flash to highlight the bird. I tripped the shutter using remote control.

Canon EOS-3, Canon EF 17–35mm lens, f/16 at 1/8 second, 2-stop graduated neutral density filter, fill flash, Fujichrome Velvia film

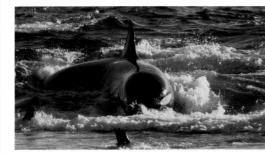

ORCA
(*Orcinus orca*)

At maximum lengths of 8.5 meters (females) and 9.8 meters (males), and weighing up to 5,500 kilograms (females) and 9,000 kilograms (males), orca are the largest members of the dolphin family (Delphinidae). These instantly recognizable cetaceans can be found in most of the world's oceans and seas. Feeding on fish, seals and sea lions, and other cetaceans, orca concentrate in coastal waters where prey is plentiful. They are efficient hunters, often employing innovative techniques to catch their prey—for example rushing a beach in Argentina, or breaking through ice to force prey into the water. Orca are highly social animals, and pods may comprise two to forty members. Such pods usually consist of related animals, with one large mature male leading the group. Within the pod, numerous "intrapod groups" form, each made up of a female and her generational offspring.

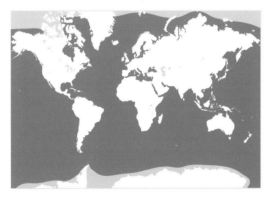

AW: One of the most incredible events I have ever witnessed is orca hunting sea lions on the beaches of Argentina's Península Valdés. The main challenge in taking this photograph and the two on page 25 was determining the proper exposure: a black-and-white animal and backlit water are both difficult subjects. First, I determined how fast a shutter speed was required to freeze the action. Then I put my camera on manual exposure and spot read off the neutral gray rocks on the beach.

Canon EOS-1N/RS, Canon EF 600mm lens, Canon Extender EF 1.4x, f/8 at 1/500 second, Fujichrome Velvia film

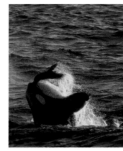 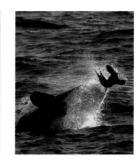

ORCA
(*Orcinus orca*)

Orca calves weigh about 180 kilograms at birth, and may be 2.4 meters long. Females are 12 to 16 years old when they have their first surviving calf and are likely to have about five calves during the course of their lives. Although often considered "wolves of the sea," orca have never been a demonstrable threat to humans. Still, they have come into conflict with humans over perceived safety risks and in competition over fish resources. During the 1950s, orca were routinely machine-gunned, while in more recent years animals have been shot and killed by commercial fishermen for stripping longlines. Orca have never been a focus of the whaling industry, but hundreds have been taken in some years (in the former Soviet Union, Norway, Greenland, and Japan) for their oil. Certain regional populations have also faced regular captures to supply animals to aquariums. There are an estimated 100,000 orca worldwide.

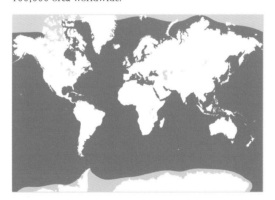

AW: In these two images, an orca is teaching its calf how to hunt. The adult has already caught a sea lion and shows its youngster how to incapacitate the prey by tossing the sea lion with its mouth and then flipping the unfortunate animal into the air with its powerful flukes. Here, as for the photograph on page 24, my starting point was to set a shutter speed fast enough to capture the action clearly.

Canon EOS-1N/RS, Canon EF 600mm lens, Canon Extender EF 1.4x, f/8 at 1/500 second, Fujichrome Velvia film

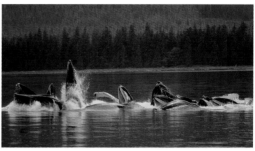

HUMPBACK WHALE
(*Megaptera novaeangliae*)

Every spring, humpback whales migrate across the North Pacific from Hawaii to Southeast Alaska. In Alaska, the cold waters support a vast array of animal life, including millions of fish and shrimplike crustaceans. When baleen whales, such as humpbacks, feed on these organisms they do so by taking a huge amount of water into their mouths—along with the fish. They then force the water out through their baleen plates, but keep the food safely inside. By feeding cooperatively, humpback whales are able to increase their chances of success even more. Groups of two or more whales—sometimes more than a dozen—dive beneath a school of fish or krill and blow a spiral of bubbles that corrals the prey within a "bubble net." The fish are disoriented by the bubbles, and when the bubbles reach the surface of the water, the whales swim up through the ball of fish, scooping up a concentrated mass of food.

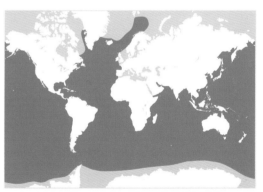

AW: To get this shot, I scanned the water until I located the telltale circle of tiny bubbles breaking the placid surface. Fixing my focus on the bubbles, I waited a few moments before the calm erupted into a few seconds of frantic feeding as the humpbacks rose up to 3 meters above the water's surface in pursuit of krill. I had already calculated my fastest exposure time by setting my aperture to f/5.6 and taking the corresponding shutter speed off the distant neutral-toned ridges.

Canon EOS-1N, Canon EF 70–200mm lens, f/5.6 at 1/125 second, Fujichrome Provia film

NOTES FROM THE FIELD

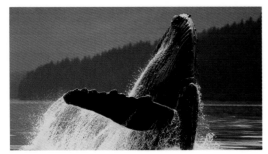

HUMPBACK WHALE
(Megaptera novaeangliae)

The behavior of humpback whales includes breaches, tail and flipper slaps, and tail-lobs. This behavior, plus their proximity to the coast, makes humpbacks a focus for whale-watchers. What made them attractive to whalers was their slow swimming speed. Between 1904 and 1939, 102,298 whales were killed in the Southern Hemisphere. Protection came in 1966, and their numbers are recovering slowly; today there are 15,000 to 20,000 humpbacks, approximately 15 to 20 percent of the pre-whaling population. While the whales no longer have to fear whalers, they increasingly have to share their coastal habitat with people. The oceans are filled with ships, fishing boats, and pleasure craft, all of which generate noise and disturbance. Whales are highly acoustic animals, and it is not clear if such noise pollution may affect their chances for a full recovery.

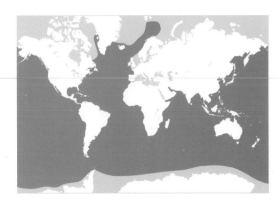

AW: One of my most exhilarating photographic experiences occurred off Point Adolphus in Southeast Alaska. An adolescent humpback whale breached nine times in a row directly in front of my small fishing boat, just 15 meters away. When the whale breached, it stayed above the water's surface for only a few seconds, intensifying the drama of framing, focusing, and triggering the shutter. Here I relied on autofocus, while I had already determined the correct exposure by manually taking an exposure reading off the distant gray cliffs.

Canon EOS-1N, Canon EF 70–200mm lens, f/4.5 at 1/500 second, Fujichrome 100 film

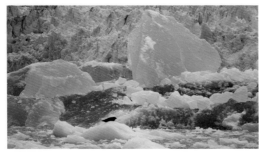

HARBOR SEAL
(Phoca vitulina)

While not as closely associated with ice as are other northern seals, harbor seals in Alaska are frequently seen in glacially calved fjords. Harbor seals are widely distributed, but conflicts with commercial fishermen (arising from their propensity for stealing fish from gillnets) have led to local declines. Elsewhere the disturbance of pupping areas, hunting, pollution, and disease each have varying levels of influence. In Europe, canine distemper has wiped out over half the animals in some areas. Accurate population estimates are difficult because the seals can only be counted when hauled out, but the best estimates suggest populations of 50,000 in Europe, 10,000 to 15,000 in eastern Asia, 40,000 along North America's west coast, 30,000 to 45,000 in the western Atlantic, and the largest concentration, 260,000, in Alaska.

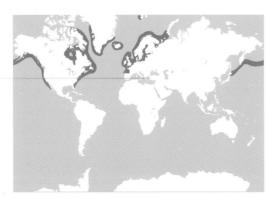

AW: Where glaciers meet the sea, enormous walls of ice, often more than 100 meters high, calve into the ocean, creating thousands of floating icebergs and "bergy-bits." Harbor seals often climb onto the icebergs seeking a safe place to rest. In this photograph, the beautiful color of the ice serves as the main compositional element, while the lone seal is discovered only upon closer examination.

Canon EOS-1N, Canon EF 70–200mm lens, f/11 at 1/60 second, Fujichrome Velvia film

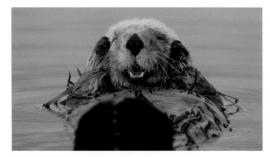

SEA OTTER
(Enhydra lutris)

Long sought by hunters for their thick pelts (at times pelts sold for more than US$1,000), sea otters may once have numbered 300,000 animals. Three subspecies range from Baja California to Oregon (*E. l. nereis*), Oregon to the Aleutians (*E. l. kenyoni*), and the Russian Far East to Japan (*E. l. lutris*). By 1911, under intense hunting pressure, the worldwide population was reduced to just 1,000 to 2,000 animals. Protection has seen the population rebound, and today between 100,000 and 150,000 otters survive, the vast majority in Alaska. The sea otters found along the California coast are southern sea otters (*E. l. nereis*). Thought extinct in the 1920s, a small group of 50 to 100 animals survived near Monterey. By the 1970s, this population had grown to about 1,800 individuals, and otters have since reclaimed portions of their former range, although attempts to reintroduce animals into British Columbia, Washington, and Oregon have largely failed.

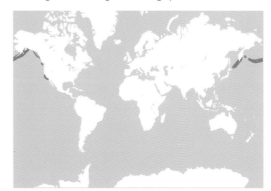

AW: Sea otters are extremely difficult to photograph. Their open water habitat gives them an unrestricted line-of-sight. To get this photograph, I traveled to a calm, protected saltwater slough in Monterey Bay. Working from a Zodiac raft with a wood platform gave me a perfect base. My lens had a built-in image stabilizer, so I was able to add a 1.4 extender and still get smooth, fairly slow exposures. By drifting toward the otter, I was able to run several rolls of film through my camera without disturbing my subject.

Canon EOS-3, Canon 500mm IS lens, Canon Extender EF 1.4x, f/16 at 1/60 second, Fujichrome Velvia film

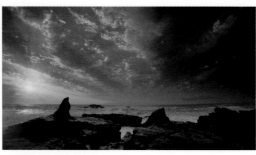

CAPE FUR SEAL
(Arctocephalus pusillius pusillius)

A. p. pusillius is one of eight species of southern fur seals. The species is divided into two subspecies: the Cape fur seal of southern Africa and *A. p. doriferus* of Australia. The African subspecies ranges along the coasts of Angola, Namibia, and South Africa, within 220 kilometers of shore. They feed primarily on fish, cephalopods, and crustaceans, and are capable of diving to depths of more than 200 meters. Bulls may weigh in excess of 350 kilograms and begin to compete for territories of 10 to 20 square meters in October; the males then guard groups of females that congregate within that area. Fur seals were heavily hunted in South Africa, beginning in 1610. Populations were much reduced by the late nineteenth century, but have now recovered. The South African population may now number two million animals, with some 34,000 still harvested each year.

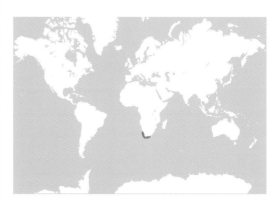

AW: While photographing along South Africa's west coast, I spotted a lone fur seal bull sitting on a rock. As the sun was setting and the dramatic clouds began to change color, I decided to approach the drowsy animal. I crossed the slick rocks, getting as close to the fur seal as I dared, about 2 meters away. I used a polarizing filter and a 2-stop graduated neutral density filter. This allowed me to retain detail in both the clouds and the pounding surf. The most difficult task in executing this photograph was keeping the salt spray from coating my filters.

Canon EOS-3, Canon EF 17–35mm lens, f/16 at 1/15 second, polarizing filter, 2-stop graduated neutral density filter, Fujichrome Velvia film

THE LIVING WILD

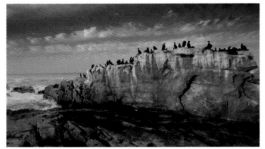

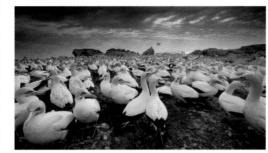

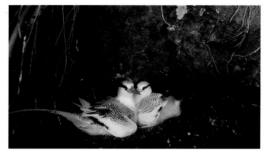

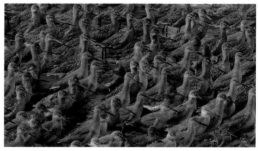

CAPE CORMORANT
(*Phalacrocorax capensis*)

CAPE GANNET
(*Morus capensis*)

RED-BILLED TROPICBIRD
(*Phaethon aethereus*)

MARBLED GODWIT
(*Limosa fedoa*)

Cape cormorants are large birds, measuring about 64 centimeters in length. They are the most abundant cormorant on South Africa's shores and breed in large numbers on offshore islands. Cormorants are easily identifiable by their long sinuous necks, long wings (Cape cormorants have a greater-than-1-meter wingspan), wedge-shaped bills, and hooked bills. Adult Cape cormorants are black, with a dark brown breast and foreneck; their throats are distinctively yellow. At sea, cormorants sit low in the water; their feathers are not waterproof as is the case in most other bird species. They chase fish underwater, diving down by "jackknifing" from the surface, and using both their wings and legs for propulsion. Once a fish is caught, the bird returns to the surface and swallows its catch whole. Back on shore, cormorants typically sit with their wings extended, drying their feathers in the sun.

Cape gannets are large birds, measuring 84 to 89 centimeters in length. They are mainly white, with a yellowish crown and nape, while their primaries, secondaries, and all twelve of their tail feathers are a blackish-brown (in the northern gannet [*Morus bassana*] only the primaries are blackish-brown). Their long, sharp bills are blue-gray in color, marked with distinctive black lines, and adults also have a black gular stripe on their throats. Their eyes are marked by a cobalt blue eye-ring. Gannets are gregarious birds, and are considered common along South Africa's coasts. They feed on fish, such as pilchards, mackerel, and anchovies, diving into the water at high speed to catch their prey. They nest in colonies from August to December, often congregating in large numbers along rocky shorelines and offshore islands. A single egg is laid on a mound nest made of guano, mud, and sticks. Both sexes tend the chick.

Tropicbirds are found throughout the tropical and subtropical regions of the Atlantic, Indian, and Pacific Oceans. As adults, these tern-sized birds carry two extremely elongated tail feathers; these streaming plumes may be almost a meter in length. Tropicbirds feed on squid and small fish, often hunting at night when the squid rise to the water's surface. The birds are highly acrobatic, and will turn sharply in midair, plunging into the water after their prey. Like many highly aerial species, tropicbirds are clumsy on land. They return to shore only to breed and favor those nesting sites that allow them to become airborne again with ease—such as a cavity in a rock face. The nest is a simple depression, perhaps lined with a few feathers, and a single egg is incubated for 42 to 46 days.

During their spring mating season, male marbled godwits perform stunning aerial displays known as ceremonial flights. The males climb to about 50 meters above the prairie meadows and slowly execute a series of large circles. They call with a loud "karrack," which makes them very conspicuous to observers. Once the high-flying circles have been completed, the male folds its wings and plummets downward, pulling up at the last moment to land. If the male has successfully caught the eye of a female, they will share the three-week incubation of their four eggs, laid in a simple ground scrape; they also share in the responsibilities of raising the chicks to fledging—which takes about a month. As many as three pairs of nesting godwits may be found in every square kilometer of prime, undisturbed, wetland habitat. Sadly, such prime wetland habitat is becoming increasingly rare.

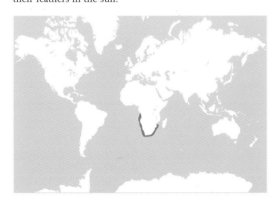

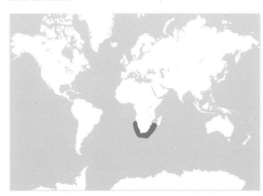

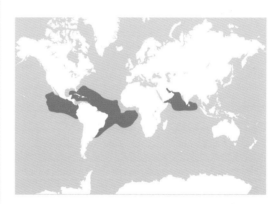

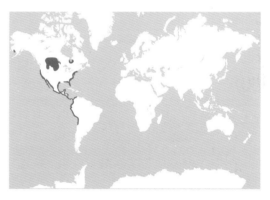

AW: Moments before the sun set over the Southern Atlantic, I photographed this group of cormorants perched on granite rocks lining the ocean's edge. One of the most exciting yet frustrating aspects of photography is how short a time the truly great light lasts. Fortunately in this case, gannets, fur seals, and cormorants were all in very close proximity, allowing me to get exposures of all three subjects during the last twenty minutes of daylight. Earlier in the afternoon, I had already decided on my sunset shooting location.

Canon EOS-3, Canon EF 17–35mm lens, f/11 at 1/30 second, 2-stop graduated neutral density filter, Fujichrome Velvia film

AW: Thousands of gannets colonize an isolated point along South Africa's Atlantic coast. With no terrestrial predators, they have virtually no fear of people. In photographs such as this, it is necessary to get the camera low to the ground and yet still have it mounted to a sturdy tripod to allow for smaller f-stops and long shutter speeds. I use versatile tripods, such as the Gitzo brand, that permit a full range of angles.

Canon EOS-3, Canon EF 17–35mm lens, f/16 at 1/15 second, polarizing filter, 2-stop graduated neutral density filter, Fujichrome Velvia film

AW: The beautiful light plumage of tropicbirds in flight creates a striking contrast to the deep blue skies. On land, the tropicbird presents a different image; it is ill equipped to walk far. In many nesting locations, it simply nests where it lands. But on the tiny wooded island where I photographed this mother and chick, the birds had to negotiate a steep slope to find a suitable nest site. I photographed these birds using a 17–35mm wide-angle lens so that I could incorporate more of the habitat surrounding the nest.

Canon EOS-1N, Canon EF 17–35mm lens, f/11 at 1/4 second, Fujichrome Velvia film

AW: This large flock of shorebirds was concentrated on the only beach left exposed by the high tide. Fortunately, there was a hill above the birds, providing a perspective that allowed each and every bird to be separated visually from all the others. This perspective also enabled me to get all of the birds into focus without having to use my smallest aperture settings. This was important because small aperture settings require the longer exposures that I wanted to avoid, given the potential for movement among so many birds.

Canon EOS-3, Canon EF 400mm lens, f/11 at 1/30 second, Fujichrome Astia film

NOTES FROM THE FIELD

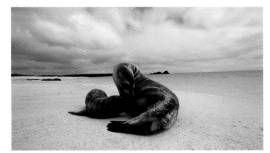

GALÁPAGOS SEA LION ∾
(Zalophus californianus wollebaeki)

The Galápagos sea lion, a subspecies of the California sea lion, is restricted to the remote archipelago located 1,000 kilometers off the Ecuadorian coast. They are highly coastal and are rarely seen more than 16 kilometers offshore. It is this coastal distribution that has successfully isolated the Galápagos subspecies from other populations, undoubtedly setting them on the path to full specific status sometime in the future. Galápagos sea lions will breed on sandy or rocky beaches, but favor those areas near protected or calm waters. Pups may be born throughout the year, although a peak does occur from August to October. The young pups weigh about 6 kilograms at birth, and their mothers remain with them for several days before heading out to sea to hunt for fish and cephalopods. Once the pups are about a week old, they are usually left alone during the day, with the females returning to suckle them at night.

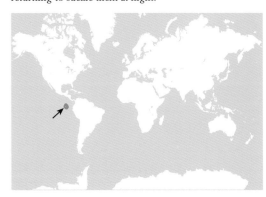

AW: A sea lion suckles its young pup on Isla Santa Fé's sandy shore. Protected from hunting, these sea lions have lost their fear of humans. To get this shot, I crawled up to the relaxed animals and began photographing them with a 14mm wide-angle lens. I handheld the camera to increase my mobility and attain a perspective from as close to the sand's surface as possible.

Canon EOS-3, Canon EF 14mm lens, f/11 at 1/250 second, Fujichrome Velvia film

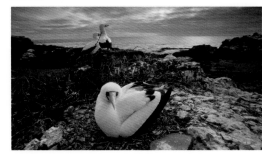

MASKED BOOBY ∾
(Sula dactylatra)

Also known as the blue-faced booby, the masked booby is a large seabird with a 1.5-meter wingspan. The species shows some color variation—for example legs may be grayish-blue or orange, and the stout bills may be yellow or orange—and these differences may indicate subspecies. Boobies are ungainly on land; they often nest on high cliffs so that they become airborne by simply stepping off the rocks. They generally nest from November to February, laying two eggs about five days apart; they do not make a nest, but lay their eggs on bare ground. Although no nest is constructed, pairs often engage in ritualistic exchanges of twigs and stones as they cement their bond prior to egg-laying. The first chick to hatch has a distinct advantage over the second, and will often kill its sibling. As fish-eaters, boobies are vulnerable to marine pollution, entrapment in nets, and fluctuating marine productivity associated with El Niño events.

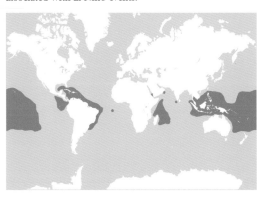

AW: Dozens of people each day will pass within 0.5 meter of this masked booby, incubating its eggs along the only footpath on Isla Española. This bird, like so much of the wildlife of the Galápagos Islands, exhibits amazing tolerance of humans. I selected my 17–35mm wide-angle lens to depict both the subject and its dramatic environment. I used a polarizing filter to reduce the glare off the distant ocean, a 2-stop graduated neutral density filter to bring the overall exposure into balance, and a fill flash to add a little light to the backlit booby.

Canon EOS-3, Canon EF 17–35mm lens, f/22 at 1/8 second, polarizing filter, 2-stop graduated neutral density filter, fill flash, Fujichrome Velvia film

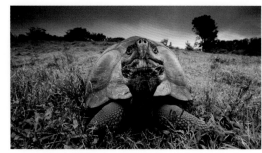

GALÁPAGOS GIANT TORTOISE ∾
(Geochelone elephantopus)

The Galápagos Islands were named after the large tortoises that inhabit the archipelago; "galápagos" is Spanish for turtle. Once, 250,000 tortoises lived here. Weighing 50 to 270 kilograms (males are larger than females) and measuring 1.5 meters over their carapaces, giant tortoises may live for more than 200 years. Of fourteen subspecies, three are extinct and one is now represented by just one animal. Isolated on different islands, subspecies can be identified by the shape of their shells. During the nineteenth century, tens of thousands of tortoises were killed by sailors; since the animals can survive for long periods with no food or water, they were often transported alive to provide meat during long voyages. Today, approximately 15,000 giant tortoises remain, threatened by feral animals (dogs, cats, and donkeys) introduced by humans, both natural and human-related fires, and environmental perturbations such as El Niño.

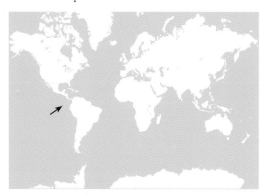

AW: A giant tortoise peers inquisitively into my wide-angle lens. Perhaps attracted to their own reflections, these large reptiles are easy to photograph once you locate one. If disturbed, their heads recoil back into their carapace, but if you remain still for just a brief moment, their heads will pop out again and you can resume photographing. It is that simple!

Canon EOS-3, Canon EF 17–35mm lens, f/22 at 1/8 second, Fujichrome Velvia film

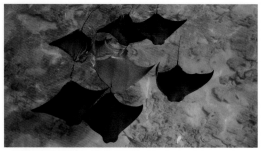

COW-NOSED EAGLE RAY ∾
(Rhinoptera bonasus)

Members of the family Myliobatidae (which consists of about twenty species), cow-nosed eagle rays have a broad, flat body with winglike pectoral fins. They measure about a meter across. Their whiplike tail has a single barbed spine at its base, and their heads are rounded with an indentation in the middle—which gives them their name. They average 10 to 20 kilograms, but can weigh up to 32 kilograms. They are found in temperate and subtropical waters and are often seen in large schools—some groups exceed 10,000 individuals. The rays seem to prefer the sandy or muddy bottoms of shallow waters where they forage for mollusks and large crustaceans. They find their prey by squirting water from their mouths to clear away the sand or silt, and are capable of unearthing a shellfish covered by up to 30 centimeters of material; they ingest only the soft flesh, spitting out the crushed shells.

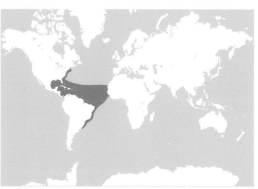

AW: While I was exploring the shallow mangrove islets of Islas Bocas del Toro, a school of cow-nosed eagle rays passed within a few meters of my boat. I asked the skipper to circle back as I grabbed my camera and 28–70mm lens. From the bow of the boat, I managed to take several exposures as the rays glided past. I calculated the exposure by spot reading off the lightest-colored ray in the center.

Canon EOS-3, Canon EF 28–70mm lens, f/5.6 at 1/250 second, Fujichrome Provia film

THE LIVING WILD

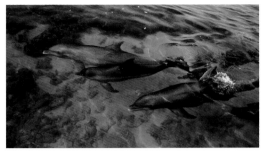

BOTTLENOSE DOLPHIN
(Tursiops truncatus)

Bottlenose dolphins are well known to the public through their acrobatic displays in aquariums. These large dolphins (up to 4 meters in length) are found throughout the Atlantic Ocean and its adjoining seas (a similar species, *T. aduncus*, inhabits the Pacific Ocean). Endowed with a brain that is larger than that of humans, bottlenose dolphins live in social groups that involve male coalitions and territorial defense, at least in some areas. Still considered common throughout most of its range, bottlenose dolphins are vulnerable to coastal development, harmful interactions with fisheries, and pollution. In 1987–88 an estimated half (800 to 1,000) of the U.S. mid-Atlantic coastal population died during an 11-month epidemic believed to have been caused by a morbillivirus. Dolphins that died were also found to have elevated levels of PCBs in their bodies, suggesting that their immune system may have been compromised.

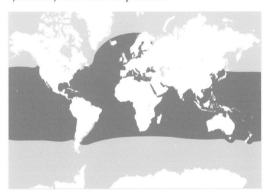

AW: In the rich waters along Panama's Caribbean coast, a pod of dolphins keeps pace with our small boat. Using a polarizing filter and a 70–200mm lens enabled me to reduce the surface reflection and capture the playful animals as they swam past.

Canon EOS-1N, Canon EF 70–200mm lens, f/4 at 1/250 second, polarizing filter, Fujichrome Velvia film (pushed 1 stop)

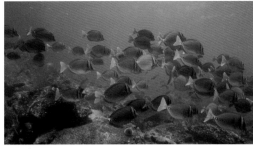

GALÁPAGOS SURGEONFISH
(Prionurus laticlavius)

There are almost 1,000 different species of surgeonfish found in the world's tropical seas. These oval-bodied fish are reef-dwellers named for the scalpel-like spines that lie just in front of their tails; they are sometimes referred to as doctorfish. The surgeonfishes' spines are used in territorial disputes with other fish and can inflict serious injury on an intruder if the surgeonfish lashes its tail from side to side. They do not school like other fish, but do travel in small groups. They feed on the small plants and animals that inhabit the reef, scraping them off the rocks and corals with their small incisorlike teeth. Juvenile surgeonfish look very different from the adults, and can easily be mistaken for a completely different species; the juveniles of the Galápagos surgeonfish are solid yellow.

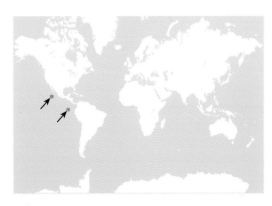

AW: Surgeonfish rise from a Galápagos reef. When being photographed underwater, brightly colored fish quickly take on a bluish cast as they descend in the water column. To counter this effect, most underwater photographers use a flash. Unfortunately, even though I used a high-powered flash, with a group of fish this large, and this far from my camera, the flash was not strong enough to bring out the brilliant yellow of the fishes' tails.

Canon-EOS 1N, underwater housing, Canon EF 20mm lens, f/8 at 1/125 second, single flash unit, Fujichrome MS100/1000 film (exposed at ISO 400)

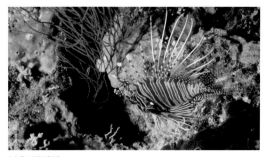

LIONFISH
(Pterois volitans)

At about 38 centimeters in length, the elaborately attired lionfish is an eye-catching marine reef species found throughout much of the Indian and Pacific Oceans. Its fanlike pectorals, branched dorsal fin, and brightly striped body serve as warning to would-be predators that its spines are charged with a powerful venom that can be fatal even to humans. Lionfish favor shallow reefs, and are often found concealed in caves and crevices during the day. At night, they emerge from their hiding places to hunt on the reef; they feed on crabs, shrimp, and small fish. Despite their venom, lionfish have become popular aquarium fish, and as such they have become a favored target of collectors. Many fish collected from reefs die in transit, and some reefs have become depleted of these and other sought-after species.

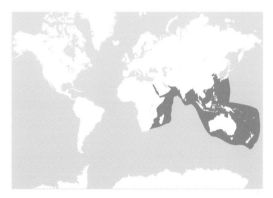

AW: A single lionfish hangs in the water among a variety of corals. I am always surprised when I see the results of using flash underwater. Without flash, every element in this composition appeared as a shade of blue to the naked eye. The shorter wavelengths of light, especially red, are quickly absorbed in the water column, leaving only the longer wavelengths, especially blue, even in this relatively shallow depth.

Canon EOS-1N, underwater housing, Canon EF 20mm lens, f/11 at 1/30 second, Fujichrome Velvia film

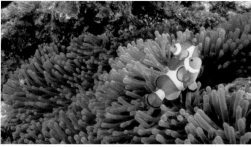

CLOWNFISH
(Amphiprion ocellaris)

Measuring about 8 centimeters in length, the distinctively colored clownfish inhabits the coral reefs of the tropical Pacific. Typically found at depths of 2 to 15 meters, clownfish are closely associated with several sea anemones (*Stoichactis kenti, Stichodactyla gigantea, S. mertensii,* and *Heteractis magnifica*). These species form a symbiotic relationship in which both benefit from their affiliation. Clownfish are highly territorial, and their displays and threatening behavior drive other fish away from the anemones, possibly protecting the cnidarians from predators. The clownfish also serve as "cleaners," keeping the anemones clean and free of detritus by eating any material that drifts into them. In return for their services, the small fish are protected by the anemone's stinging tentacles. To protect themselves from the anemone's neurotoxins, the clownfish develop a thick mucous coat that prevents the stinging cells from firing.

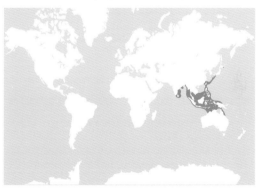

AW: A pair of clownfish hover cautiously above their security blanket, a large sea anemone amid the coral reefs that skirt Sipadan Island's shallows. The slightest movement sends the fish scurrying into the anemone's maze of tendrils. To photograph these tiny fish, I selected a 20mm lens to convey their dramatic environment.

Canon EOS-1N, underwater housing, Canon EF 20mm lens, f/16 at 1/30 second, two flash units, Fujichrome Velvia film

NOTES FROM THE FIELD

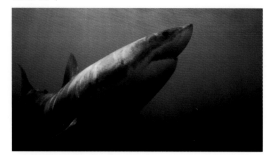

GREEN SEA TURTLE
(*Chelonia mydas*)

The green sea turtle is one of seven species of marine turtles. These large turtles have shell lengths of 0.9 to 1.1 meters and weigh 90 to 137 kilograms; exceptionally large animals reach 150 kilograms. Adults are mainly herbivorous, feeding on seaweeds and sea grasses, while immatures are carnivorous. Green sea turtles were once common in most of the warm oceans of the world, but they have become scarce due to overharvesting. Turtles are killed by people for food (both adults and eggs), leather, and jewelry. Other threats to their survival include coastal development and the disturbance of nesting sites, pollution (including ingestion of plastics), collisions with boats, and entanglements in fishing nets and bottom longlines. Green sea turtles can live for more than 50 years, and while females may reproduce every 2 or 3 years, laying 100 or more eggs at a time, only a handful of young survive to maturity.

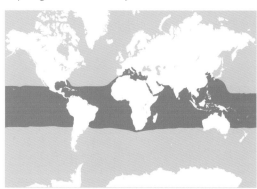

AW: A green sea turtle settles on the coral-covered sea shelf surrounding Malaysia's Sipadan Island. Renowned for its spectacular sea life, Sipadan is an important breeding ground for both hawksbill (*Eretmochelys imbricata*) and green sea turtles. To get this photograph, I positioned two electronic flash units each just over 0.5 meter out on either side of my underwater housing. By doing so, I was able to avoid illuminating the myriad of tiny particles suspended in the water between the camera and the turtle.

Canon EOS-1N, underwater housing, Canon EF 20mm lens, f/16 at 1/30 second, two flash units, Fujichrome Velvia film (pushed 1 stop)

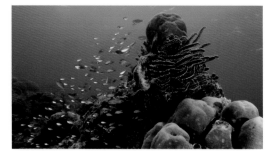

CORAL REEF

Reef-building corals grow in the tropics where the water temperature is above 21°C, and where sunlight can penetrate the clear water. The physical reef is built on the calcium carbonate skeletons of dead corals, with living coral on top. While many corals are carnivorous, feeding on zooplankton, others live in symbiotic relationships with algae, and it is this association that prevents them from growing in water deeper than about 70 meters. Reef growth is largely controlled by changes in sea level. As sea level rises, corals grow upward at a rate of 0.3 to 1.5 centimeters a year. Natural, slow rises in sea level have sustained such growth rates for the last 100,000 years. Accelerated sea level changes, caused by global warming, may result in such rapid increases in water depth that the corals will be unable to keep up; other threats to reef ecosystems include pollution, dredging, collecting, and boat collisions.

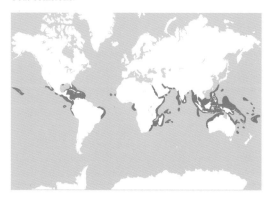

AW: The tropical waters surrounding Sipadan Island provide some of the best diving opportunities in the world, a fact that a novice diver like myself found irresistible. In this photograph, a cluster of living corals rises above the surrounding sea shelf, providing a safe haven for countless fish that disappear into the numerous crevices when threatened.

Canon EOS-1N, underwater housing, Canon EF 20mm lens, f/11 at 1/60 second, two flash units, Fujichrome Velvia film (pushed 1 stop)

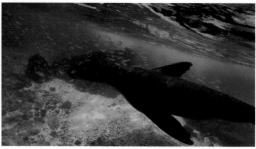

GREAT WHITE SHARK
(*Carcharodon carcharias*)

The great white shark is the largest member of the Lamnidae family (that includes mako [*Isurus oxyrinchus*] and porbeagle [*Lamna nasus*] sharks). Great whites can reach more than 6 meters in length. Coastal in distribution, they are generally found in temperate waters. Favoring large mammalian prey such as sea lions and elephant seals, great whites concentrate in areas with large prey populations. With their hydrodynamic shape; blunt, pointed snout; and large, powerful tail, they cruise the waters looking for a telltale silhouette above them. When potential prey is spotted, the shark hits from below, incapacitating its target with a bite and then returning to feed on the dying animal. Often considered "cold-blooded fish," great whites are able to maintain a body temperature 5°C to 11°C above that of the surrounding water—something that makes their muscles function with high efficiency. They are second only to orca (*Orcinus orca*) as the oceans' top predators.

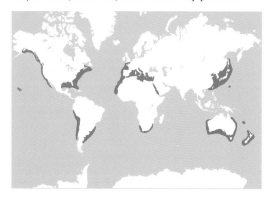

AW: Ever since *Jaws* terrified its first audience, the population of the much-maligned great white shark has declined steadily from being fished and netted. Most attacks on humans are a case of mistaken identity: sharks mistaking humans for sea lions, their natural prey. For this shot, the fishing boat I was on anchored between two islands off the coast of South Africa. The channel between these islands is referred to locally as "Shark Alley." From a shark cage, I photographed this 3.6-meter shark as it passed within a meter of me.

Canon EOS-1N, underwater housing, Canon EF 15mm lens, f/8 at 1/60 second, Fujichrome Provia film

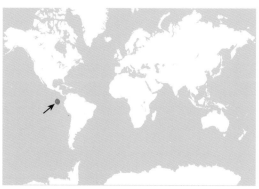

GALÁPAGOS SEA LION
(*Zalophus californianus wollebaeki*)

Galápagos sea lions are capable of diving more than 180 meters, although most of their dives average 37 meters. Foraging trips last about 15 hours, and a sea lion may make nearly 200 dives during that time. A dive typically lasts less than three minutes. In recent decades, disruptions in the marine food chain have had significant impacts on sea lion numbers. Island inhabitants are often, by virtue of their limited distribution, particularly vulnerable to both natural and human-induced disturbances. Sea lions were intensively hunted by humans during the nineteenth century, but recovered when demand for seal products declined. Additional population declines occurred in the 1970s when an epidemic swept through the islands, then in 1982–83 a strong El Niño caused a precipitous decline in marine productivity and thousands of sea lions starved or succumbed to disease. Their 50,000-strong population was more than halved, and recovery has been slow.

AW: A sea lion passes close by as I turn and pan the camera toward it. Playfully curious, sea lions repeatedly swam circles around me as I floundered in the strong currents and ocean swells that regularly flushed this submerged volcanic cone off Isla Seymour.

Canon EOS-1N, underwater housing, Canon EF 20mm lens, f/8 at 1/125 second, single flash unit, Fujichrome MS100/1000 film (exposed at ISO 400)

THE LIVING WILD

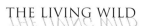

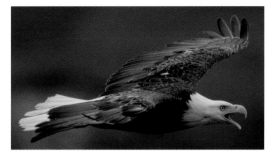

BALD EAGLE
(*Haliaeetus leucocephalus*)

The bald eagle is the only eagle unique to North America. It is also a conservation success story. Twenty-five years ago, bald eagles were highly endangered outside of Alaska. In the eighteenth century an estimated 25,000 to 75,000 eagles nested in the contiguous United States. By the 1960s there were fewer than 450. The birds were victims of habitat destruction, hunting (before 1953 a legal bounty system claimed the lives of more than 100,000 eagles), and pollution. DDT contaminated their food and led to the birds laying thin-shelled eggs that failed to hatch. The U.S. Fish and Wildlife Service began a captive breeding program and gradually reintroduced birds into the wild. This program, combined with habitat protection and the banning of DDT, all contributed to recovery. While today's population does not approach the former abundance, there are an estimated 4,500 breeding adults in the contiguous United States; an additional 30,000 thrive in Alaska.

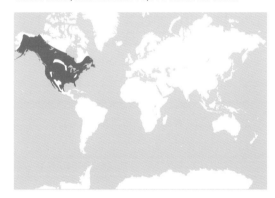

AW: A bald eagle glides past my location. I am 100 meters above this eagle's nest, which is located on a grassy promontory overlooking the Bering Sea. More curious than upset, the eagle lifted off its nest to scrutinize me before descending to its aerie again. As the eagle flew past, I panned with my camera on autofocus and got six sharp images.

Canon EOS–1N/RS, Canon EF 600mm lens, f/4 at 1/125 second, Fujichrome Velvia film

---

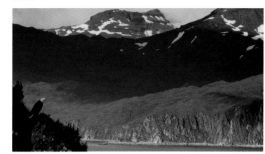

BALD EAGLE
(*Haliaeetus leucocephalus*)

Named for their conspicuous white heads, bald eagles do not actually achieve their distinctive plumage until at least four years of age. As immatures, they resemble golden eagles (*Aquila chrysaetos*). The sexes are identical and, as with most raptors, females are larger than males. Their sweeping wingspan may be up to 2.3 meters across, and the large eagles weigh 3.6 to 6.4 kilograms. Bald eagles are found throughout Alaska (except the far north and west), including the Aleutians. They are closely associated with water, and the highest densities occur along the coast and near rivers and lakes. They feed on fish, particularly spawning salmon, and will take waterfowl and small mammals. In general, however, they tend to be more scavengers than active hunters. During the winter, thousands of eagles migrate to southern Alaska and coastal British Columbia, congregating along rivers to feed on the last salmon runs of the year.

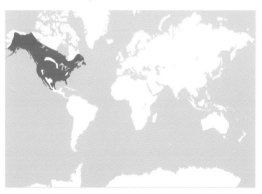

AW: Few environments characterize Alaska's stunning grandeur more effectively than the chain of remote mountainous islands that make up the Aleutians. The bald eagle thrives in this rich marine environment. With no ground predators, the eagles nest in the dense grass that carpets these treeless islands. I wanted to make the environment the main element of this image, with the bald eagle waiting to be discovered. I used a 2-stop graduated neutral density filter to darken the bright sky.

Canon EOS–1N/RS, Canon EF 70–200mm lens, f/16 at 1/15 second, 2-stop graduated neutral density filter, Fujichrome Velvia film

---

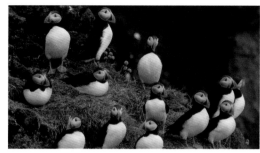

ATLANTIC PUFFIN
(*Fratercula arctica*)

The Atlantic or common puffin is one of just three puffin species. The other two species (horned [*F. corniculata*] and tufted [*F. cirrhata*]) are found in the North Pacific, while the Atlantic puffin is restricted to the Atlantic coasts of Western Europe, Iceland, Greenland, Atlantic Canada, and New England. The dramatic colors of the birds' bills are probably an indication of health and fitness—two factors that help in mate selection. Puffins feed by diving into the water. They are good swimmers, and these members of the auk family (Alcidae) fill a similar ecological niche in northern waters that penguins fill to the south. Puffins have experienced localized declines in numbers in recent years, particularly in areas of coastal development. Once common in many areas, nesting colonies are disappearing in more accessible regions. They remain reasonably abundant in more isolated locations.

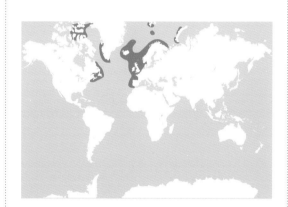

AW: There were two challenges to getting this image. First, to get close enough to fill the frame with the puffins, I had to crawl along the steep, wet, grassy slope until I came to a concealed vantage point. Second, to get all the puffins in focus, I had to stop down to an f/16 aperture opening and use a very slow shutter speed. I took several rolls of film, until I was confident of getting at least a few images in which all the birds were sharp.

Canon EOS–1N/RS, Canon EF 600mm lens, f/16 at 2 seconds, Fujichrome Astia film

---

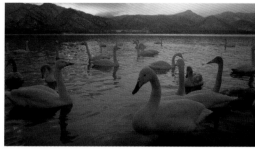

WHOOPER SWAN
(*Cygnus cygnus*)

At up to 1.6 meters in length, the whooper swan is an impressively large, regal bird. It has a broad, high bill with significantly more yellow on it than found on the tundra or Bewick's swan (*Cygnus columbianus*); both sexes look alike. Whoopers range across Eurasia, breeding in the north and wintering in the south. They favor wetland habitats, including coasts, lakes, rivers, and tundra. During their migration, they may fly at altitudes of up to 8,230 meters, often in flocks that form a V. Swans have faced severe hunting pressure in the past, and many populations were devastated in the early years of the twentieth century. Protection from hunting has allowed numbers to rebound, but habitat loss, the disturbance of nesting sites, lead poisoning, and other forms of pollution continue to take their toll.

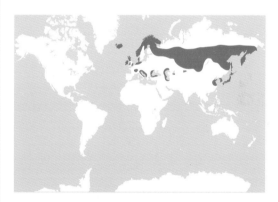

AW: These whooper swans spend the winter on a large lake located on Hokkaido, Japan's northernmost island. The normally shy swans overcome their fear of humans when biologists distribute grain to get them through the winter. I used a 17–35mm wide-angle lens placed low and close to the nearest swan to capture both the birds and their setting. I stopped down to f/16 for sharpness throughout the composition and then used a 2-stop graduated neutral density filter to darken the sky and provide a more even exposure.

Canon F3, 17–35mm lens, f/16 at 1/15 second, 2-stop graduated neutral density filter, Fujichrome Provia film (pushed 1 stop)

NOTES FROM THE FIELD

POLAR & SUBPOLAR

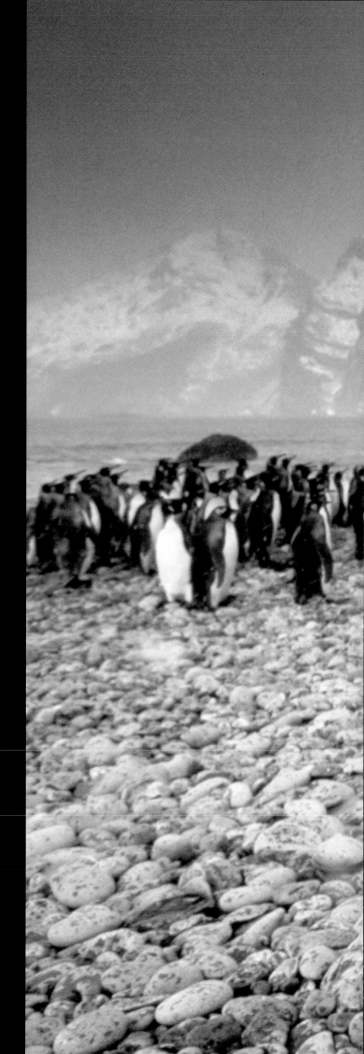

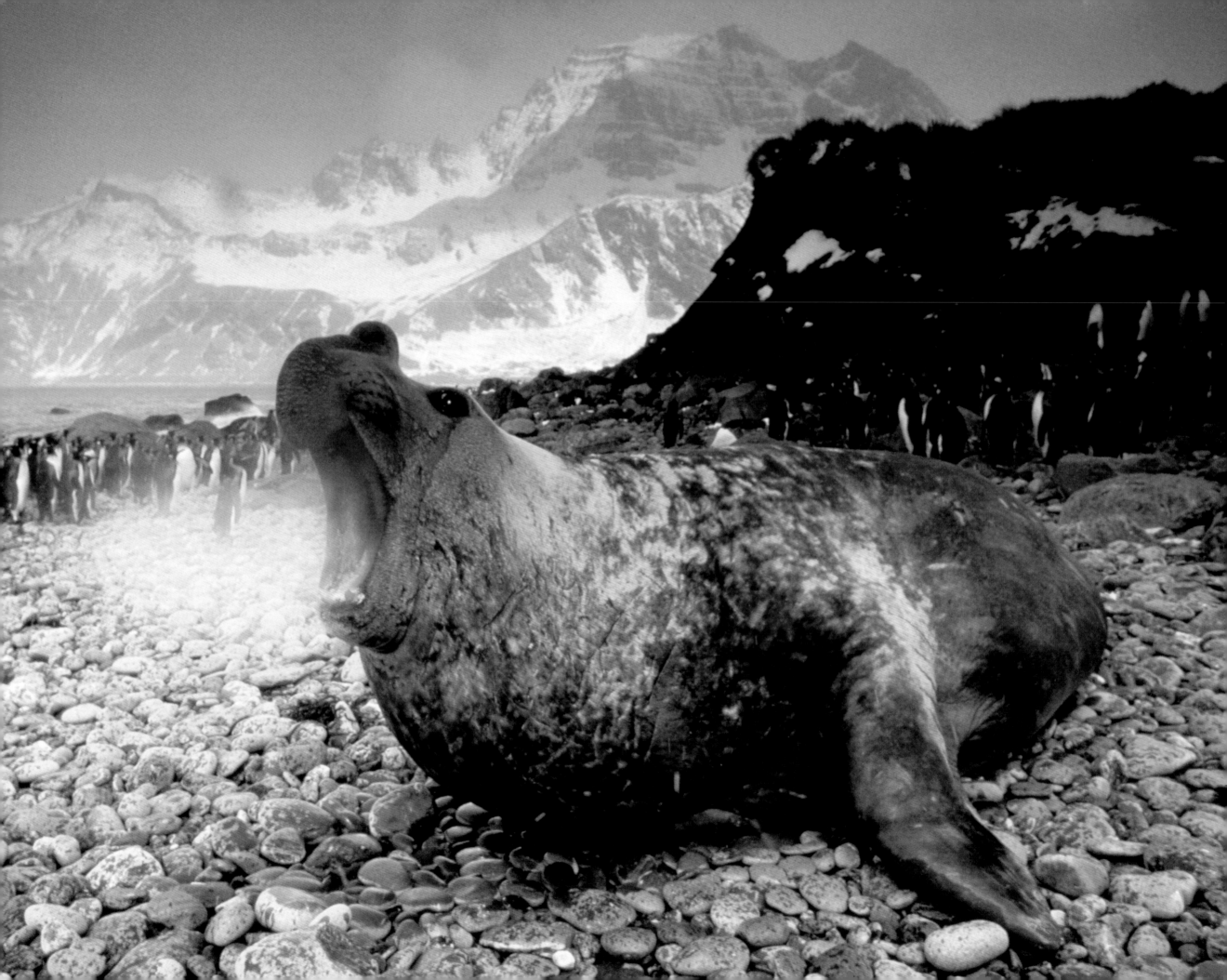

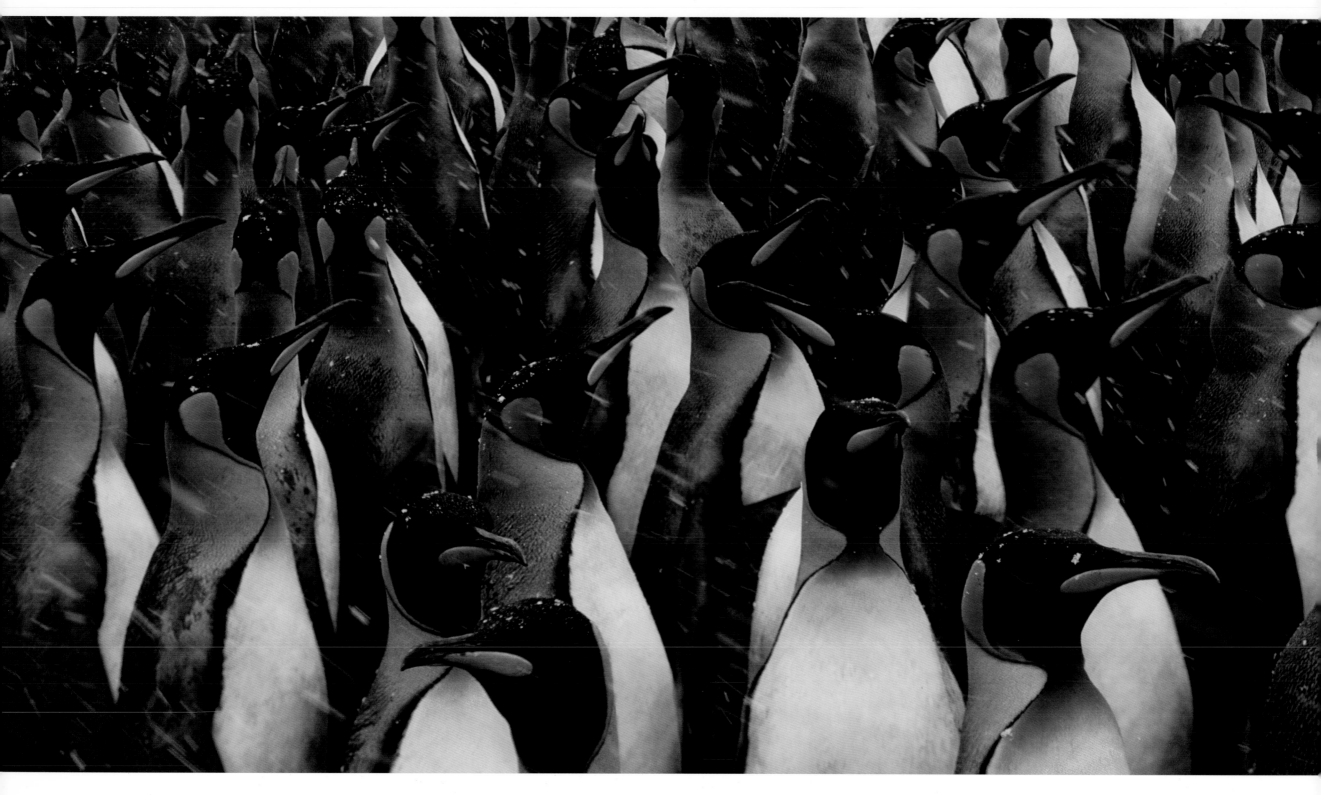

◄ SOUTHERN ELEPHANT SEAL ‿

South Georgia Island, United Kingdom

KING PENGUIN ‿

South Georgia Island, United Kingdom

THE LIVING WILD

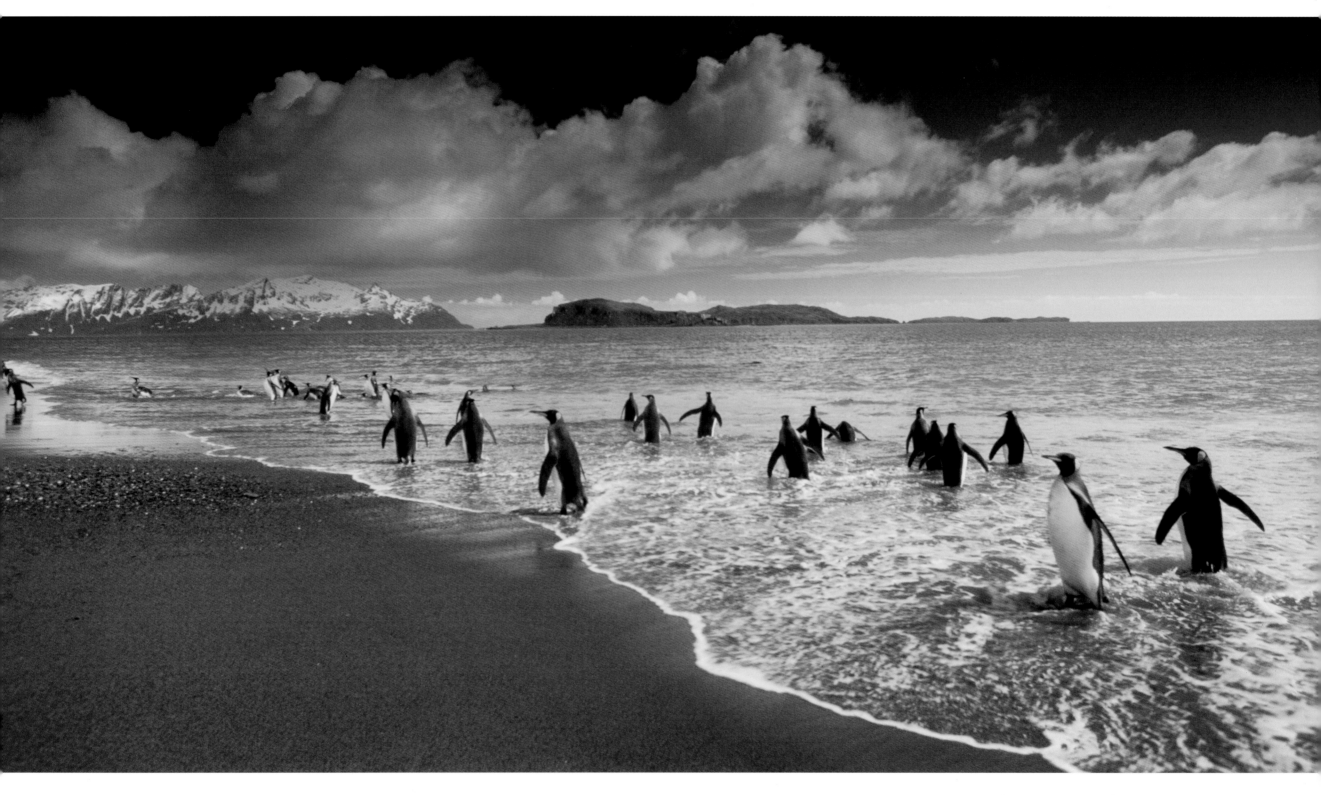

KING PENGUIN

Bay of Isles, South Georgia Island, United Kingdom

POLAR & SUBPOLAR

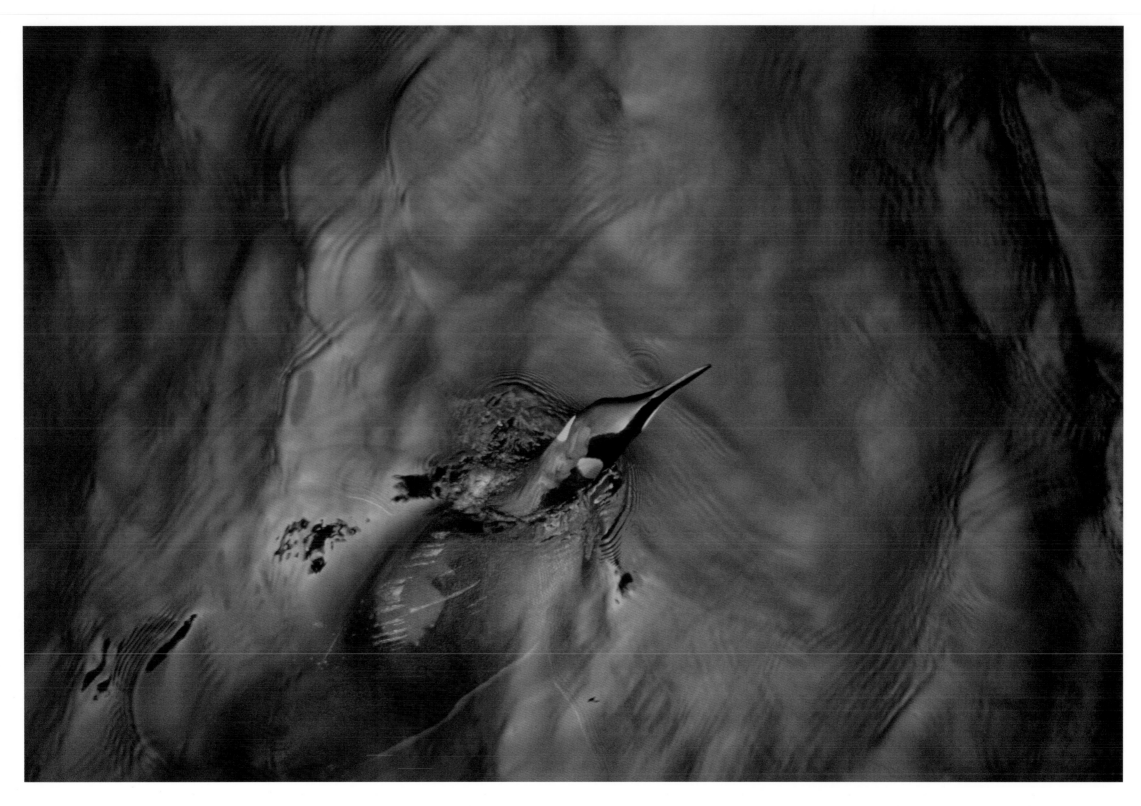

KING PENGUIN
South Georgia Island, United Kingdom

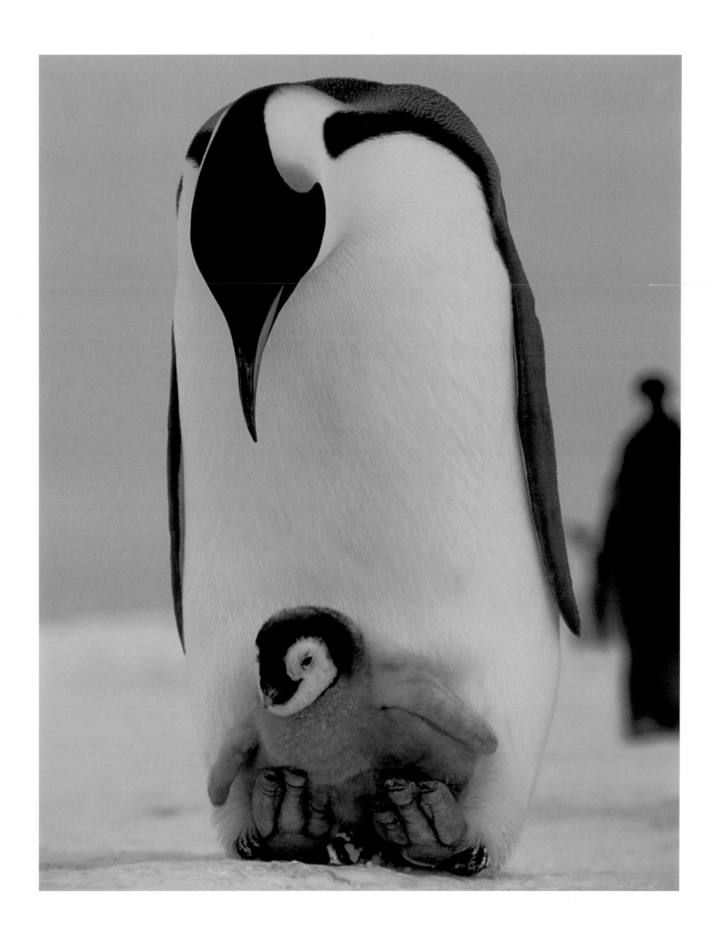

EMPEROR PENGUIN

WEDDELL SEA, ANTARCTICA

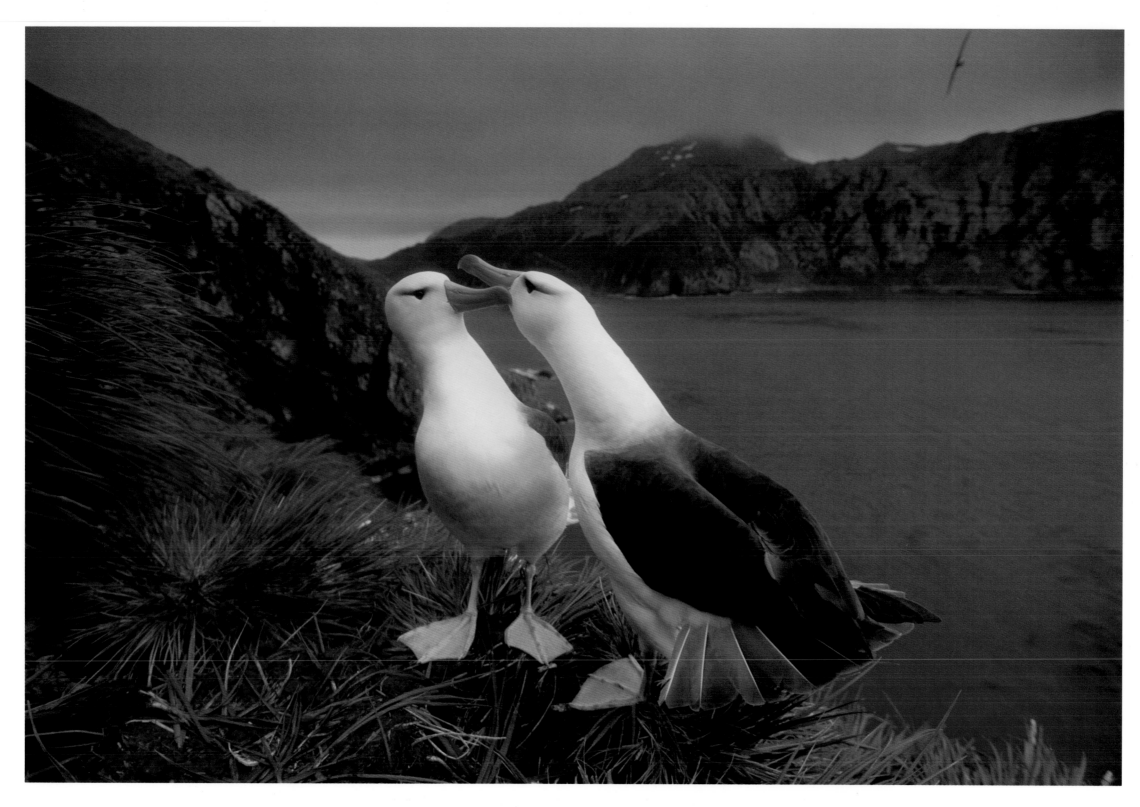

BLACK-BROWED ALBATROSS
SOUTH GEORGIA ISLAND, UNITED KINGDOM

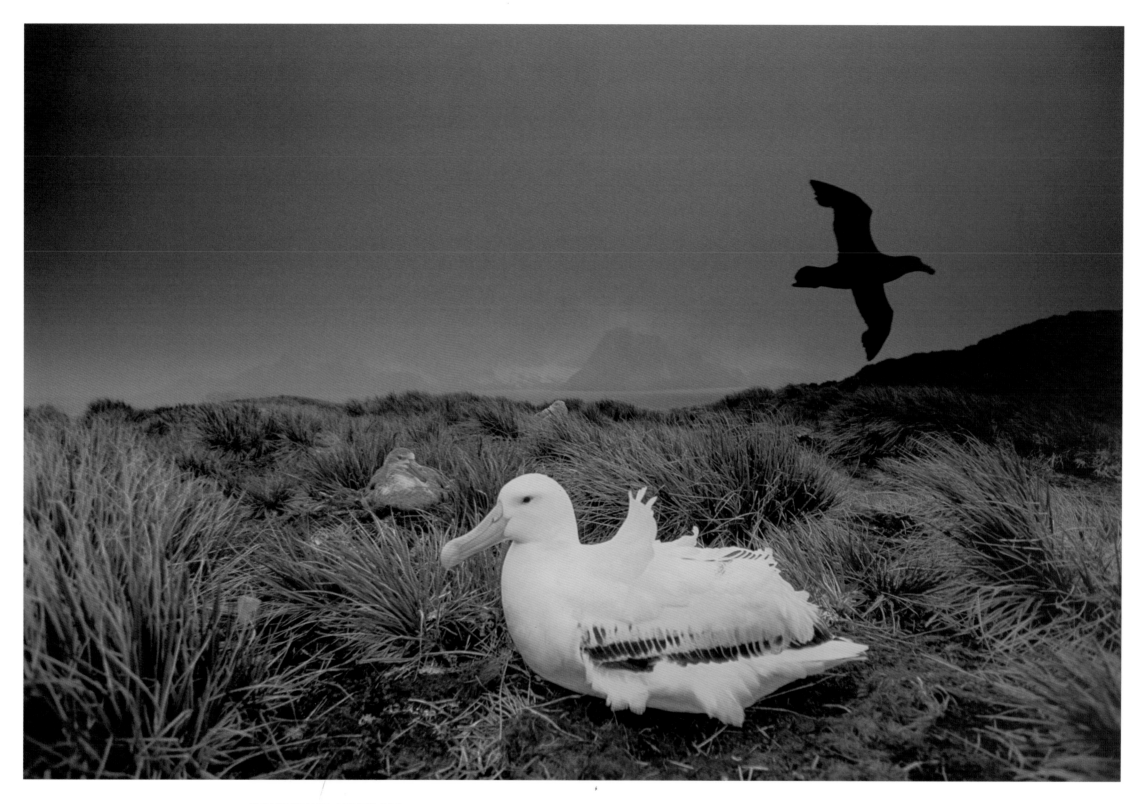

WANDERING ALBATROSS

King Haakon Bay, South Georgia Island, United Kingdom

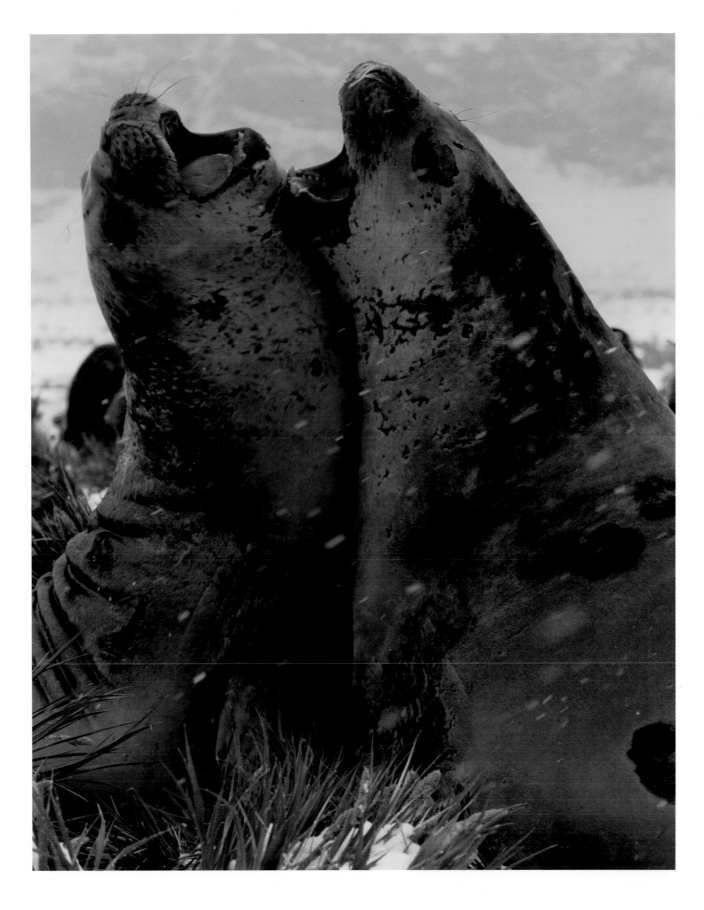

SOUTHERN ELEPHANT SEAL

SOUTH GEORGIA ISLAND, UNITED KINGDOM

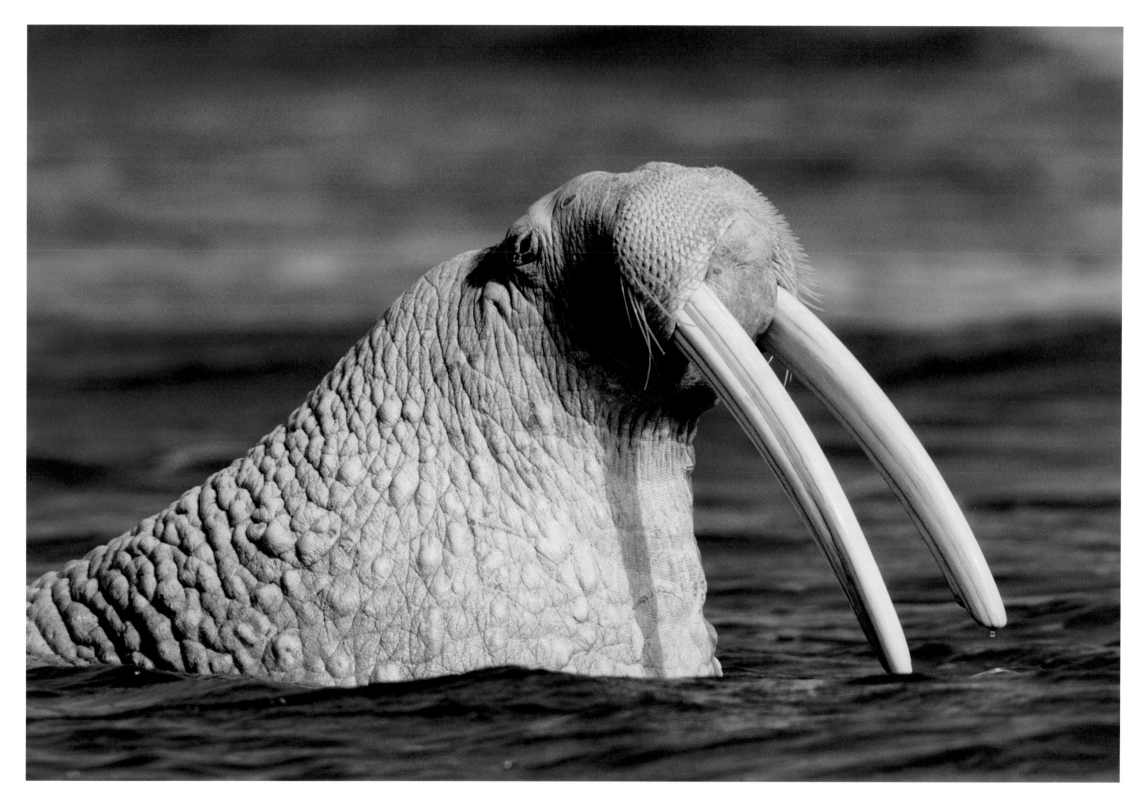

WALRUS

Togiak National Wildlife Refuge, Alaska, USA

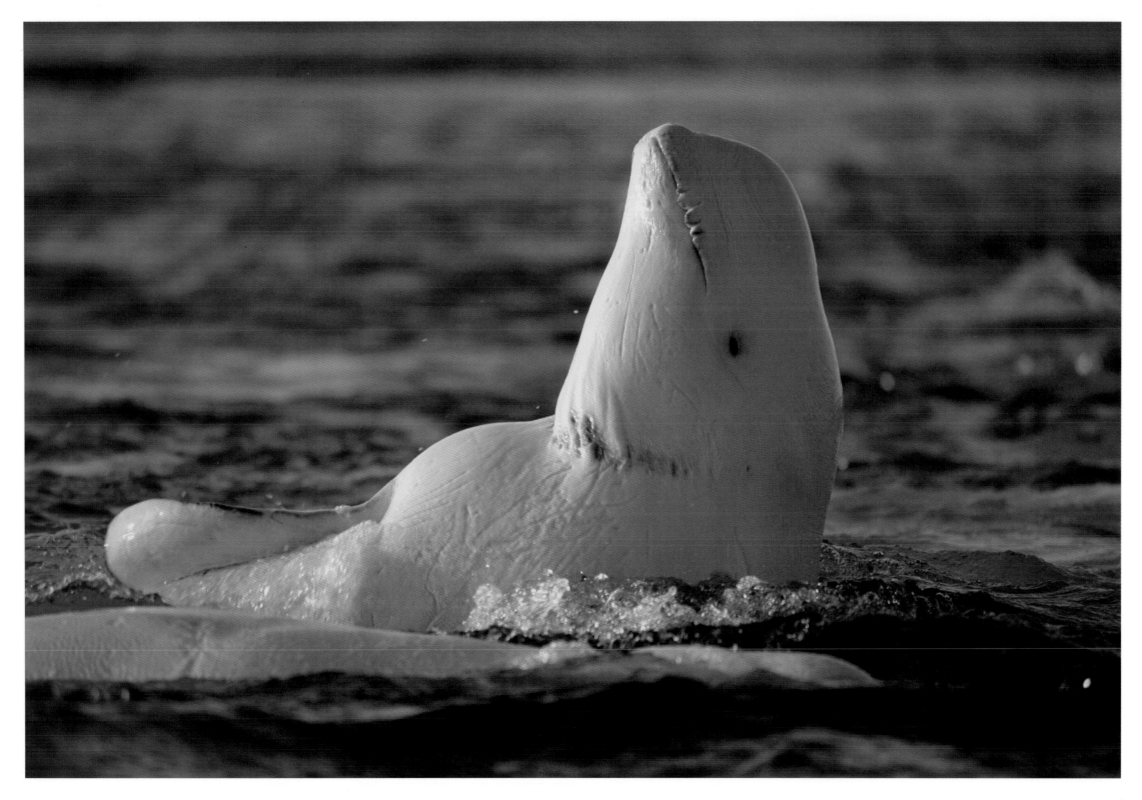

▲ AND ▶ BELUGA WHALE
SOMERSET ISLAND, NŪNAVUT, CANADA

THE LIVING WILD

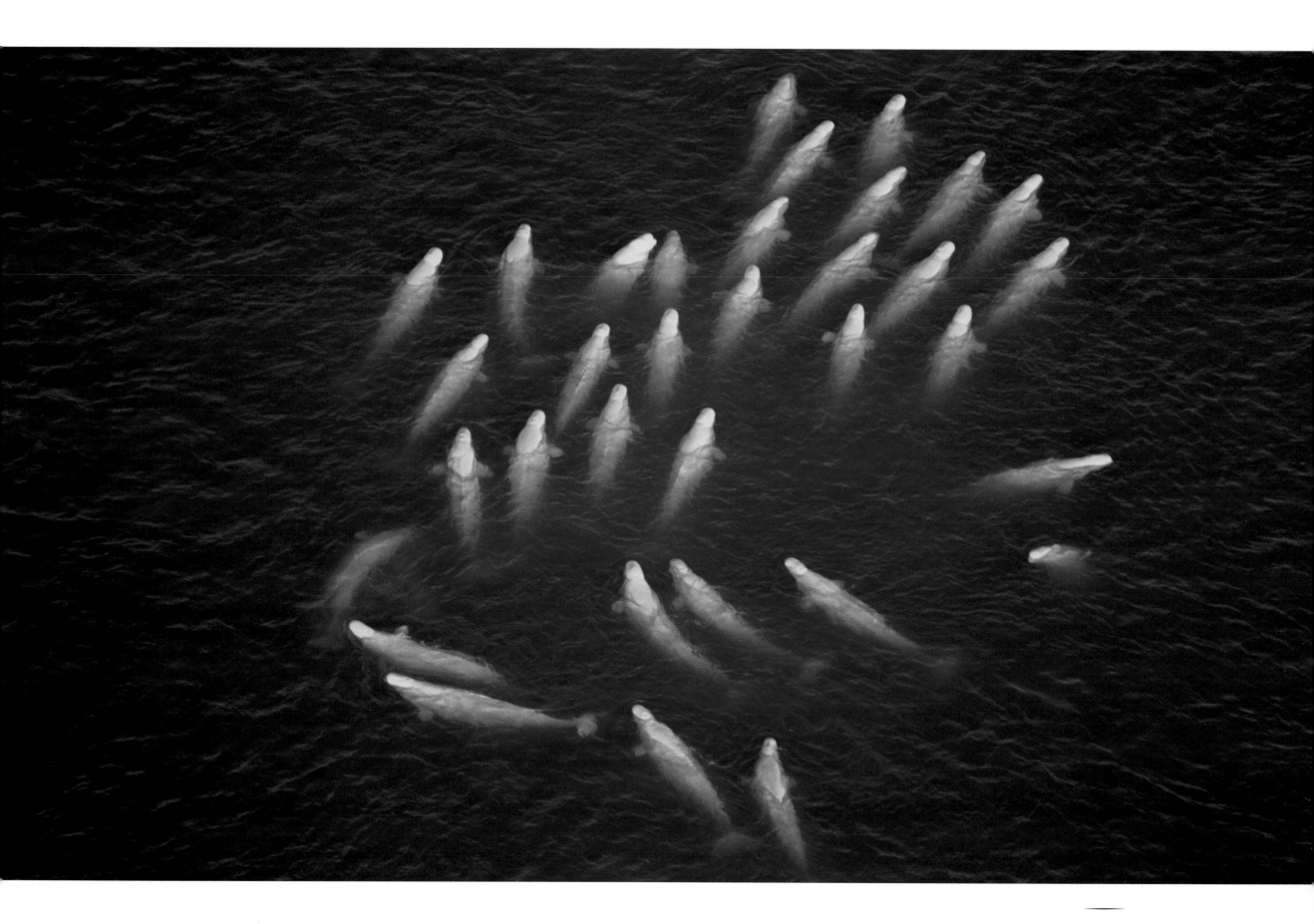

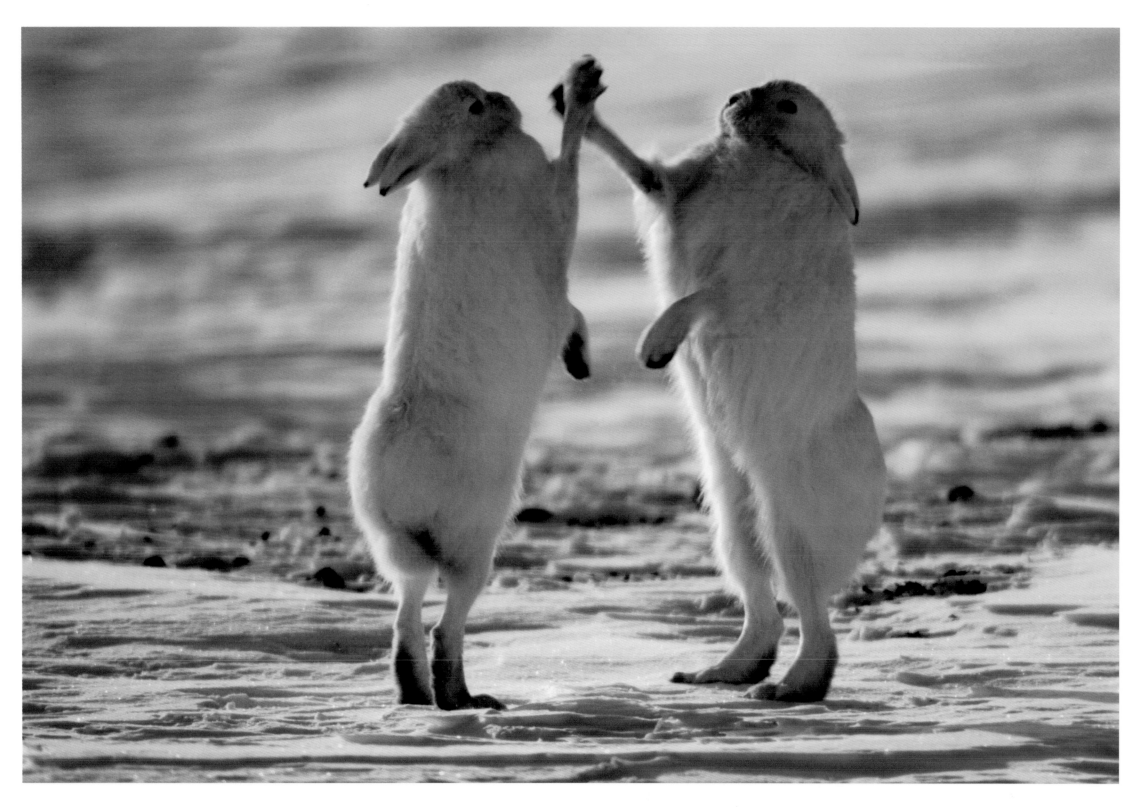

ARCTIC HARE
Ellesmere Island, Nunavut, Canada

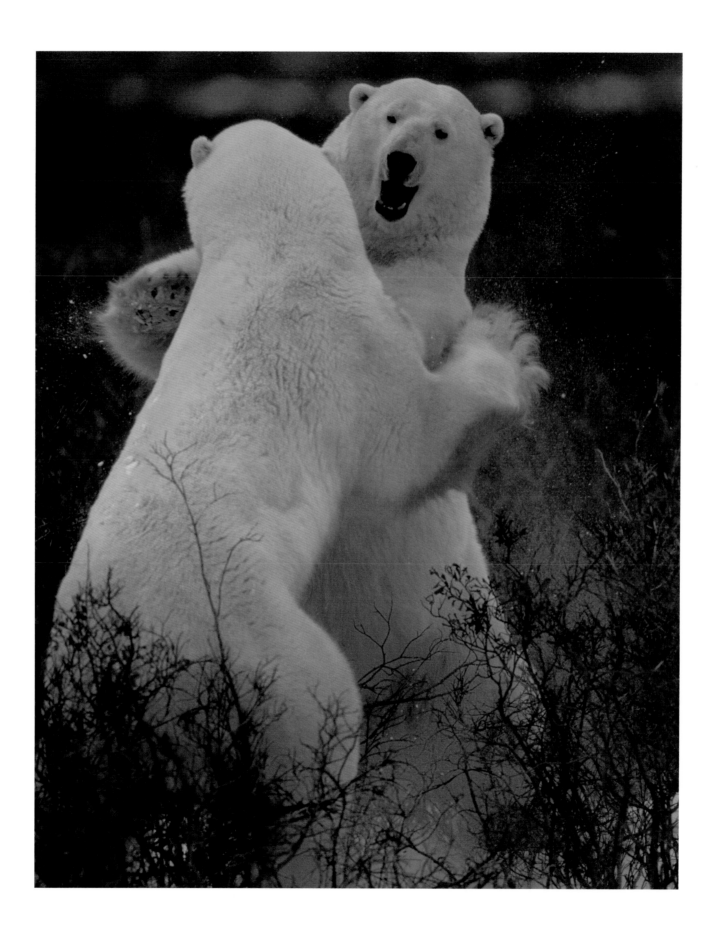

POLAR BEAR
CHURCHILL, MANITOBA, CANADA

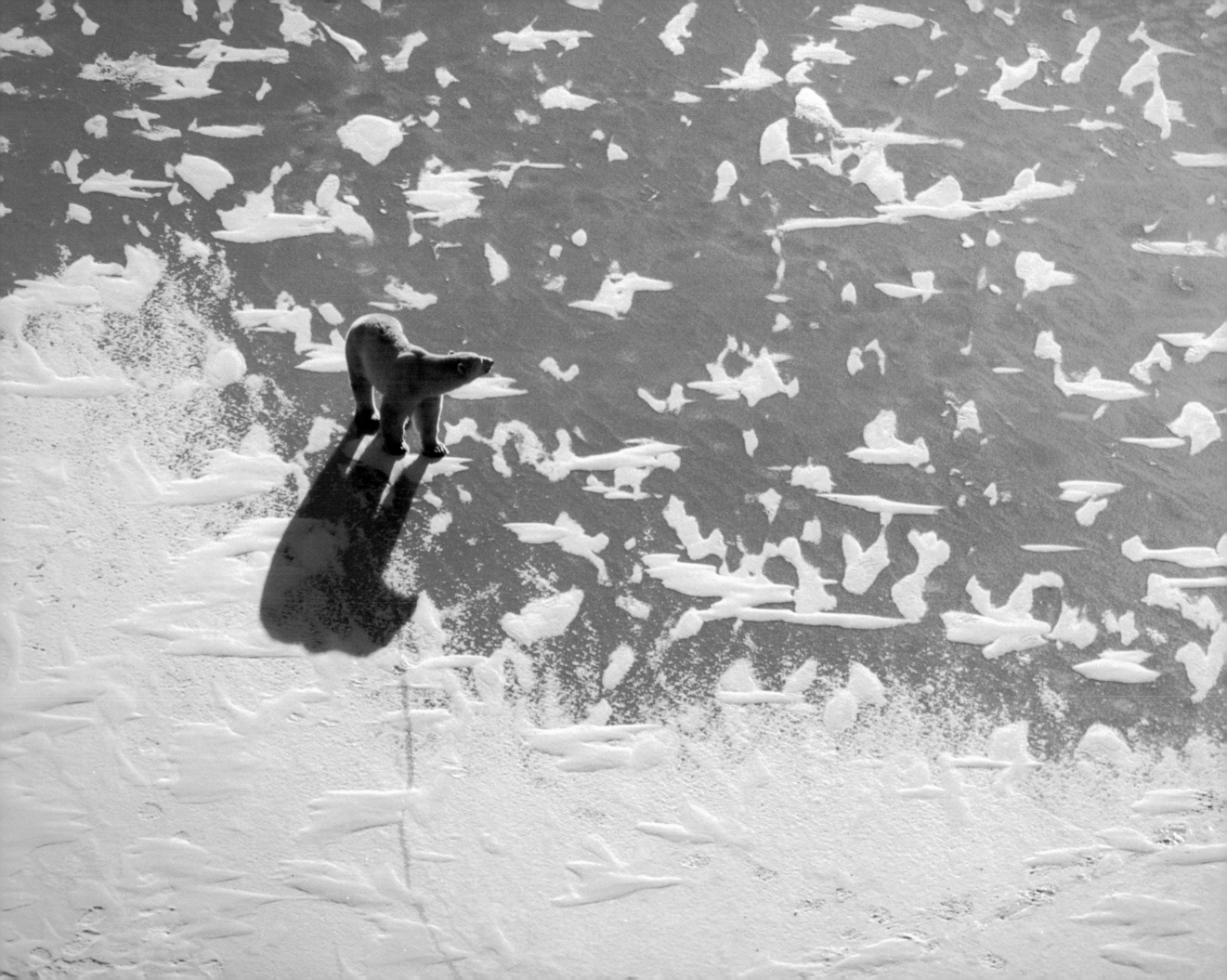

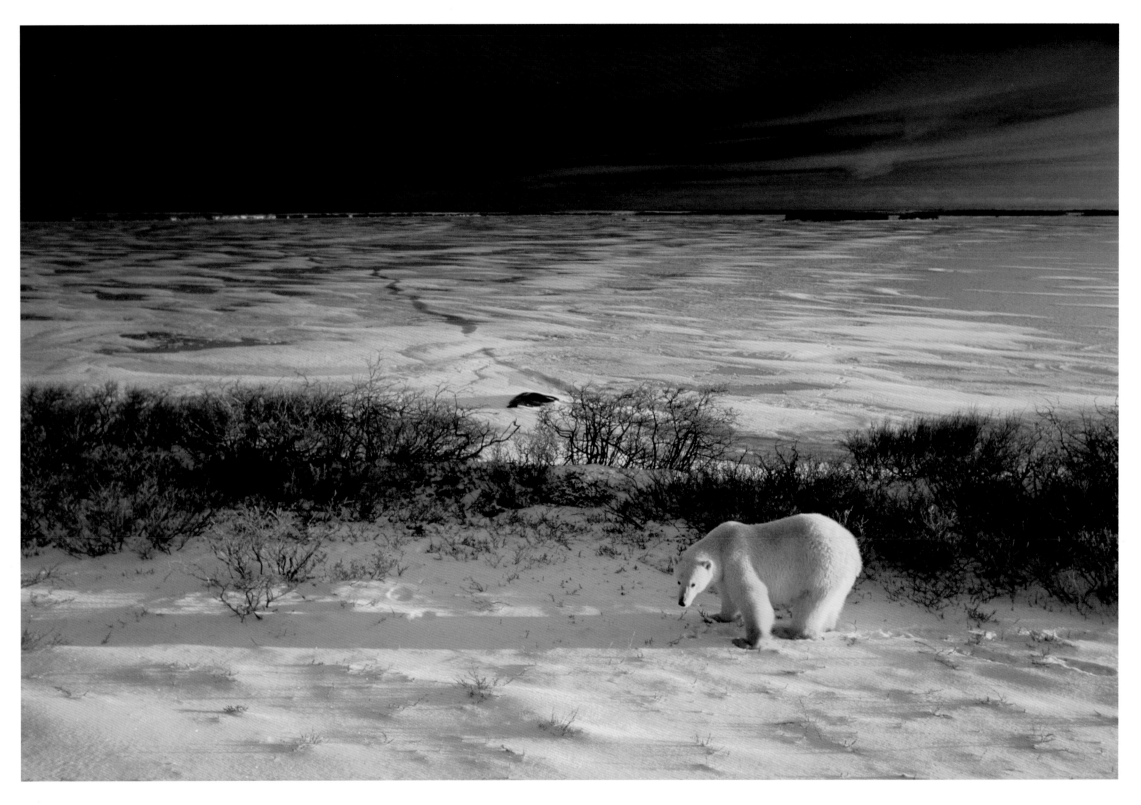

◀ AND ▲ POLAR BEAR
CHURCHILL, MANITOBA, CANADA

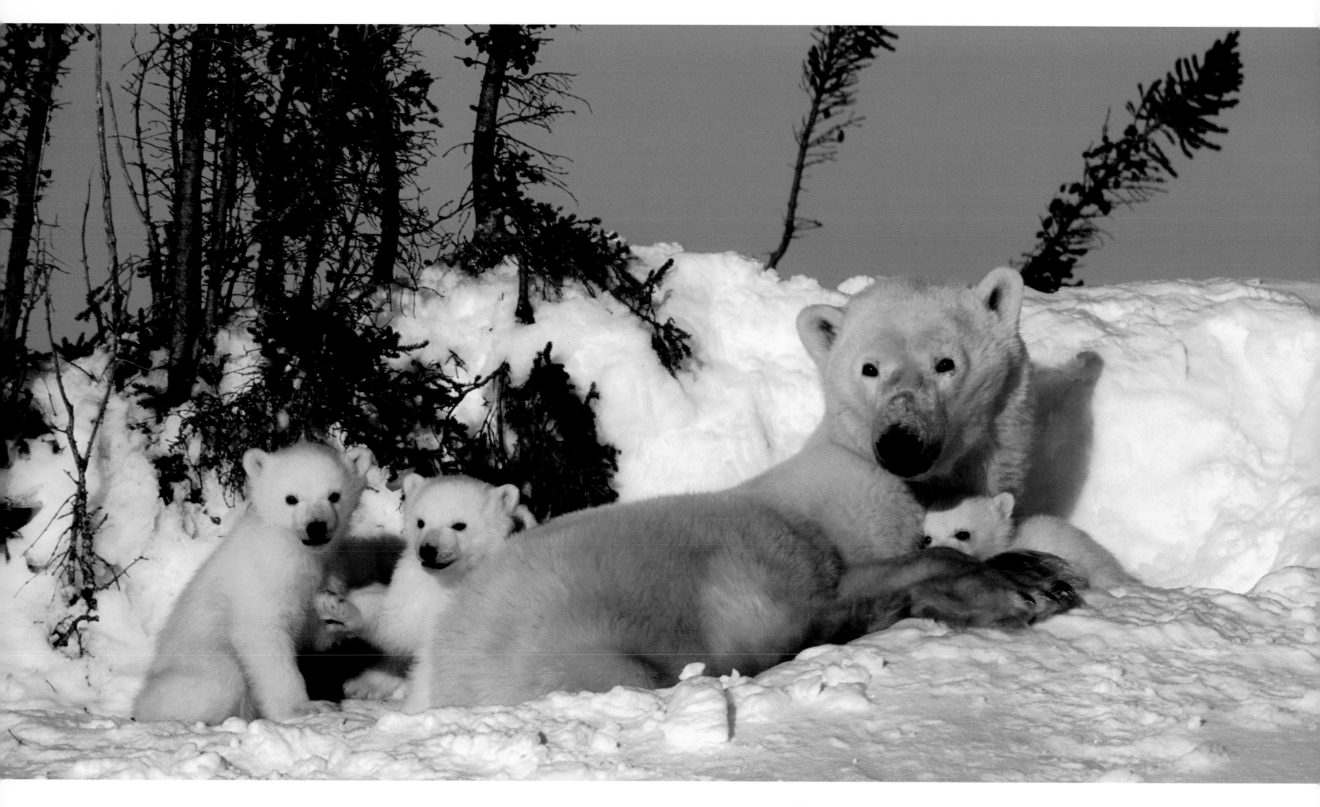

POLAR BEAR

THE LIVING WILD

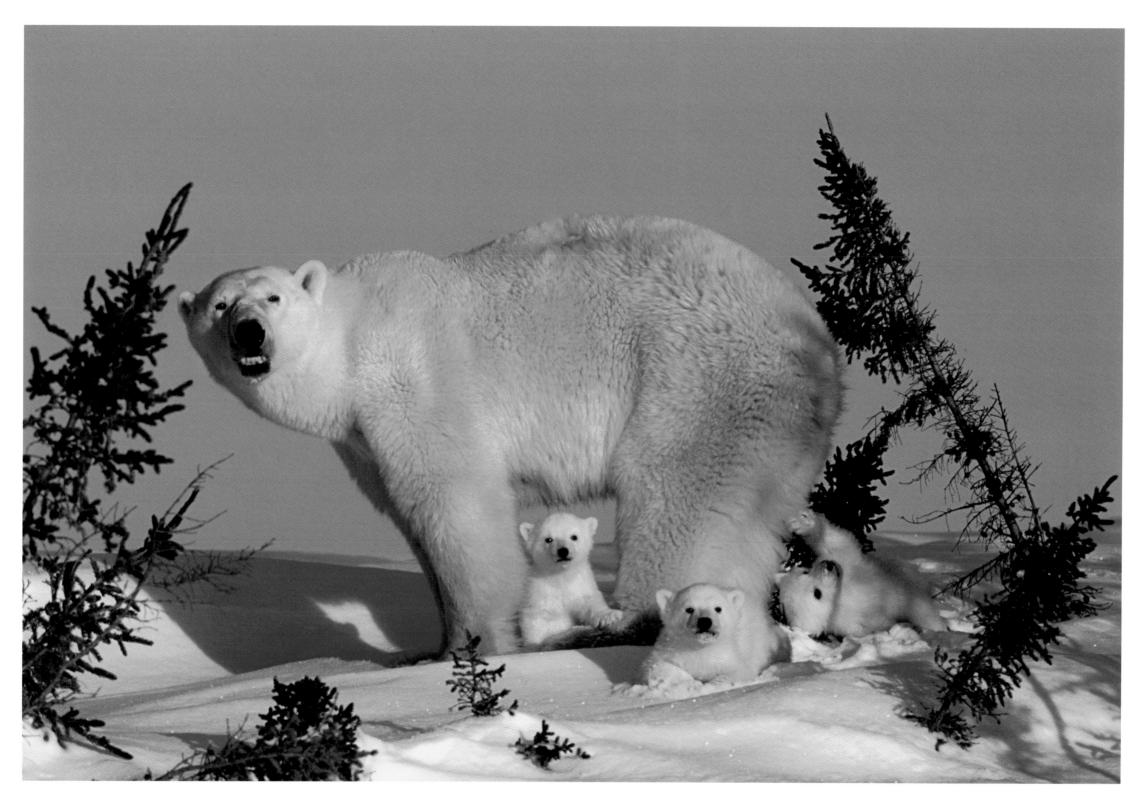

POLAR BEAR

CHURCHILL, MANITOBA, CANADA

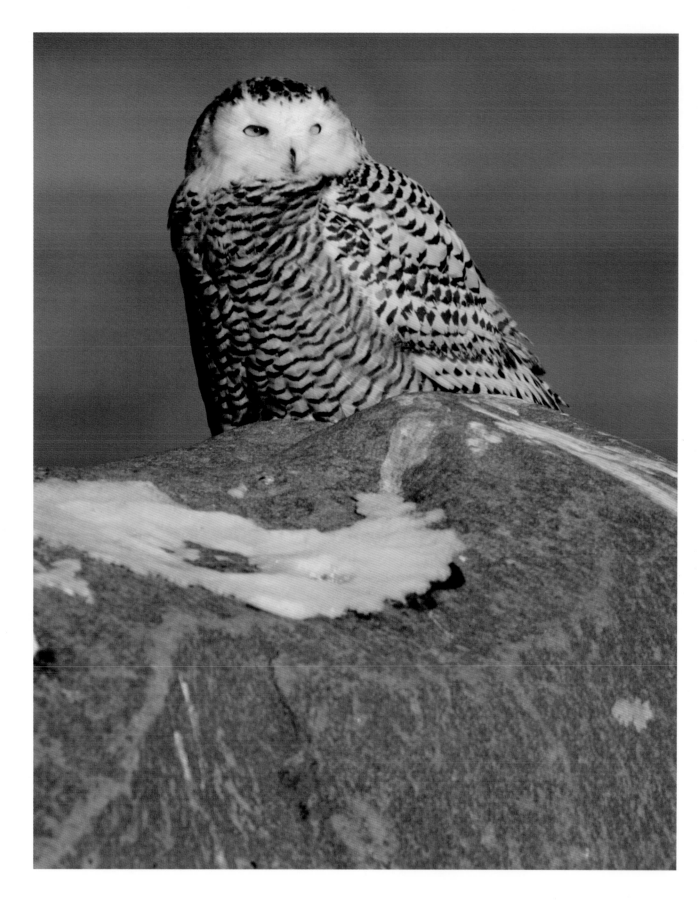

SNOWY OWL
CHURCHILL, MANITOBA, CANADA

► MUSKOX
NUNIVAK ISLAND, ALASKA, USA

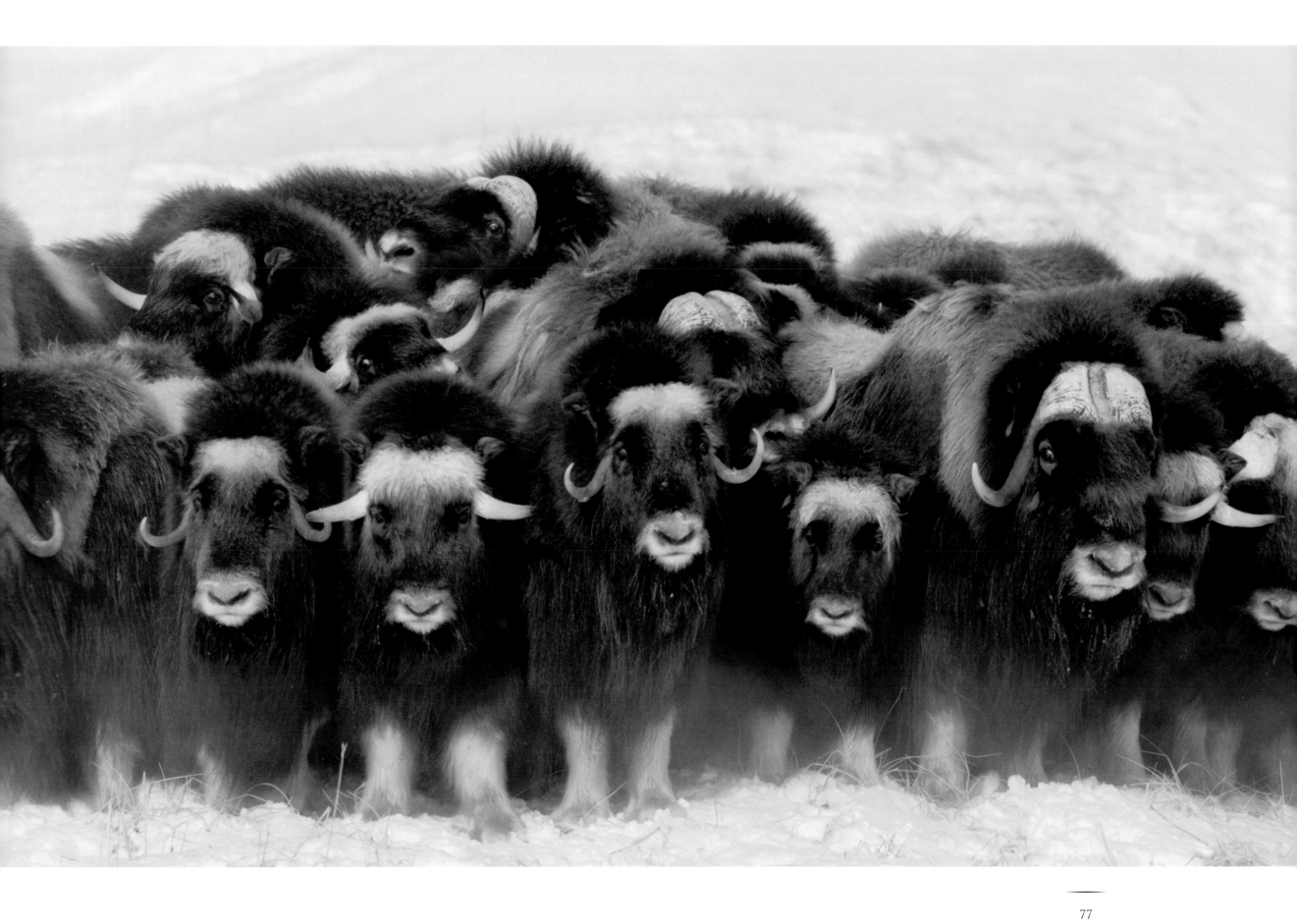

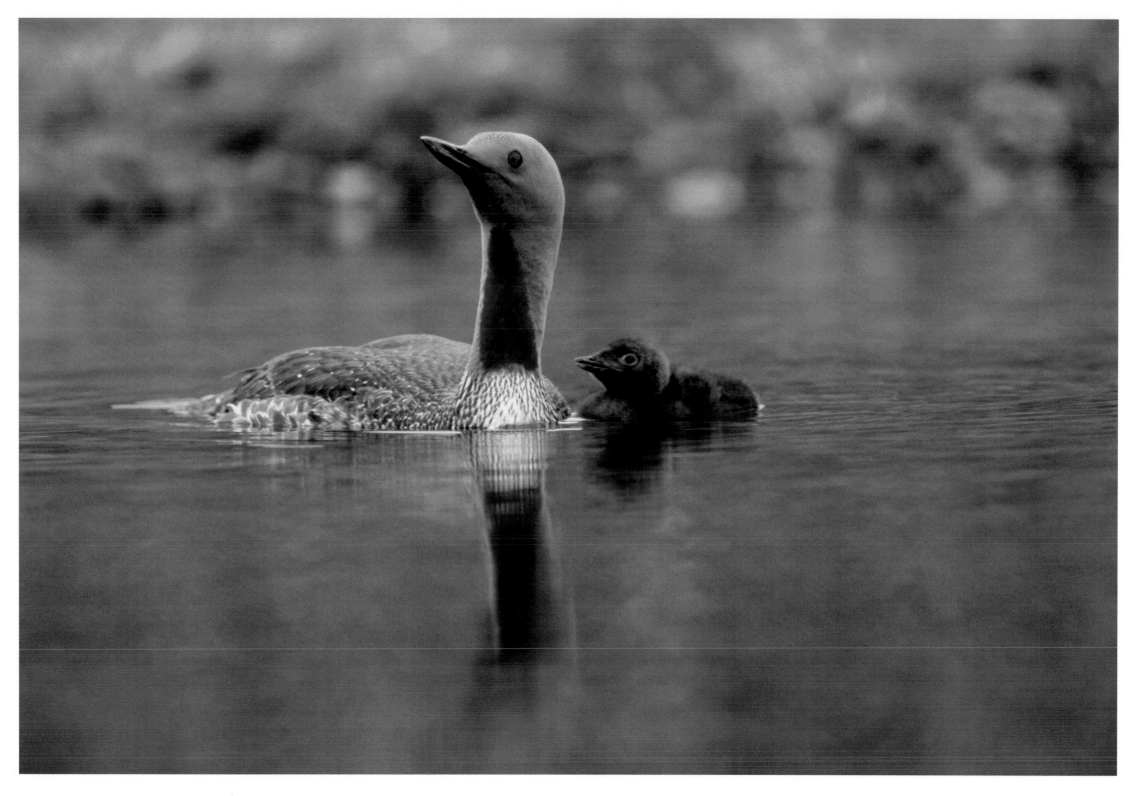

RED-THROATED LOON ⌒

JÖKULSÁRLÓN LAGOON, ICELAND

▶ PEREGRINE FALCON ⌒

ARTILLERY LAKE, NORTHWEST TERRITORIES, CANADA

THE LIVING WILD

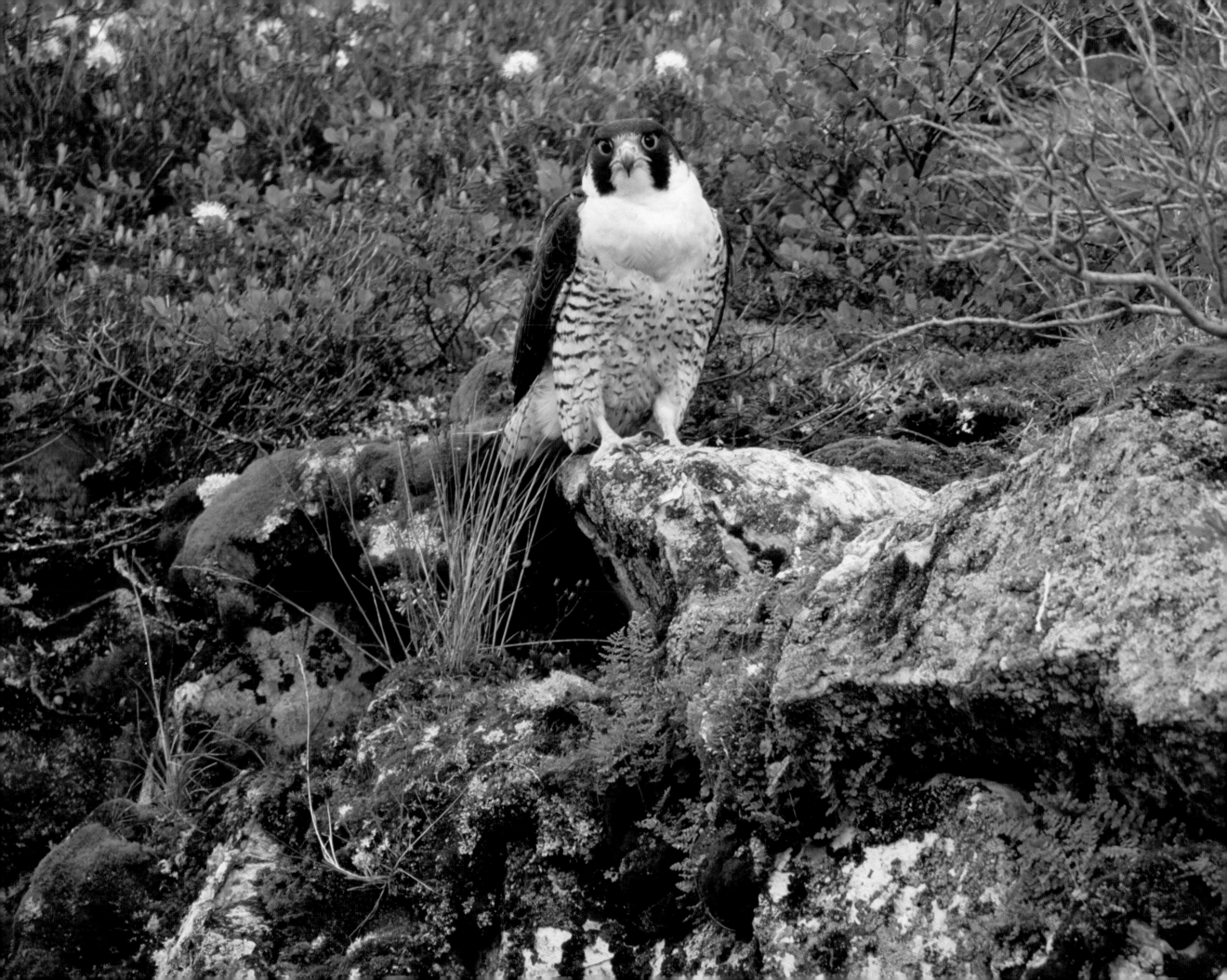

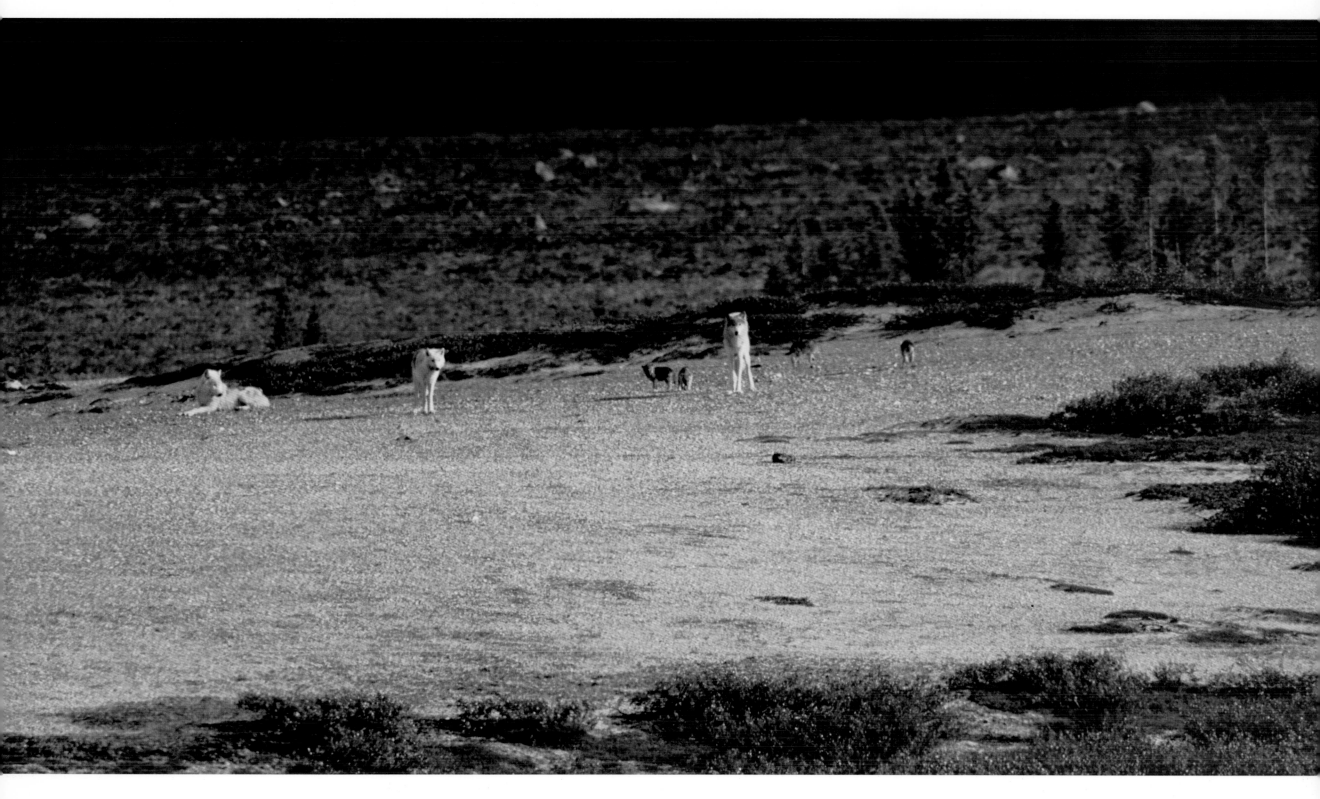

ARCTIC WOLF

ARTILLERY LAKE, NORTHWEST TERRITORIES, CANADA

THE LIVING WILD

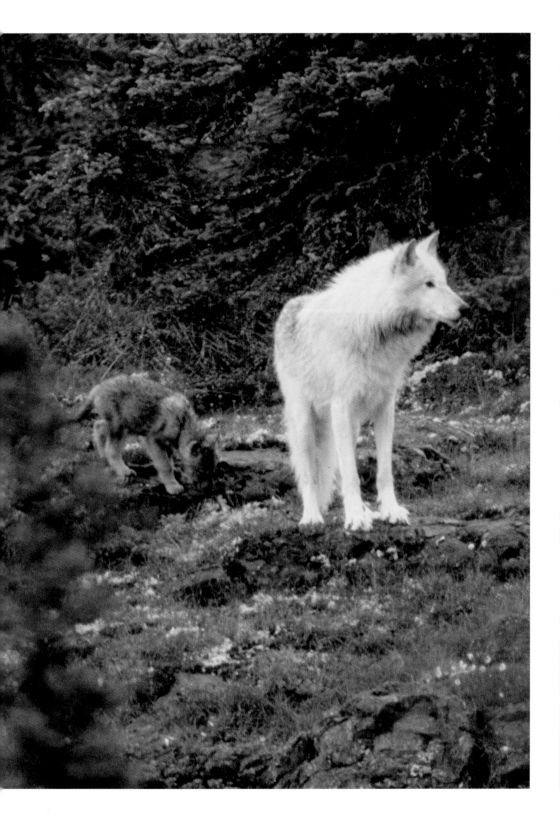

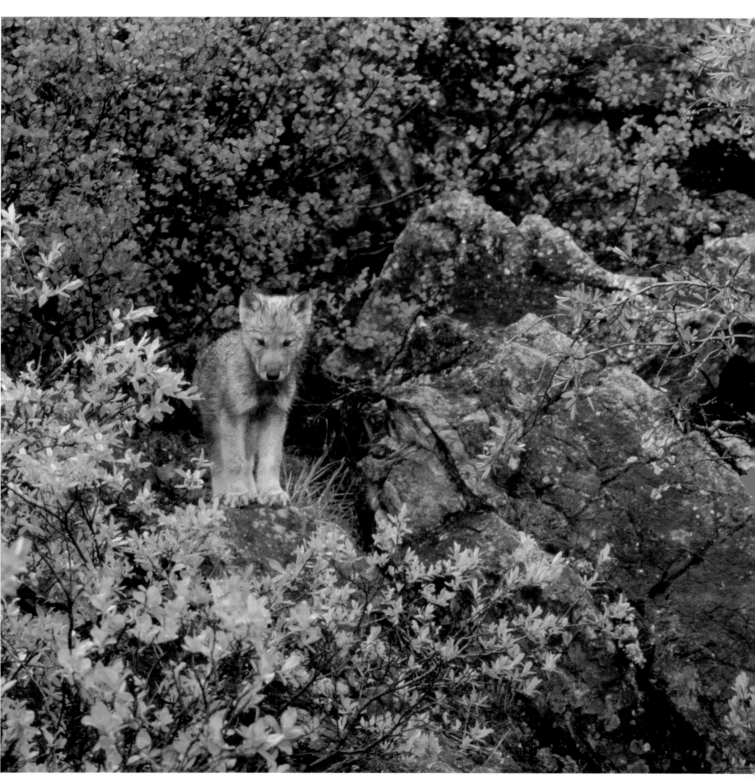

◄ AND ▲ ARCTIC WOLF 〜
ARTILLERY LAKE, NORTHWEST TERRITORIES, CANADA

POLAR & SUBPOLAR

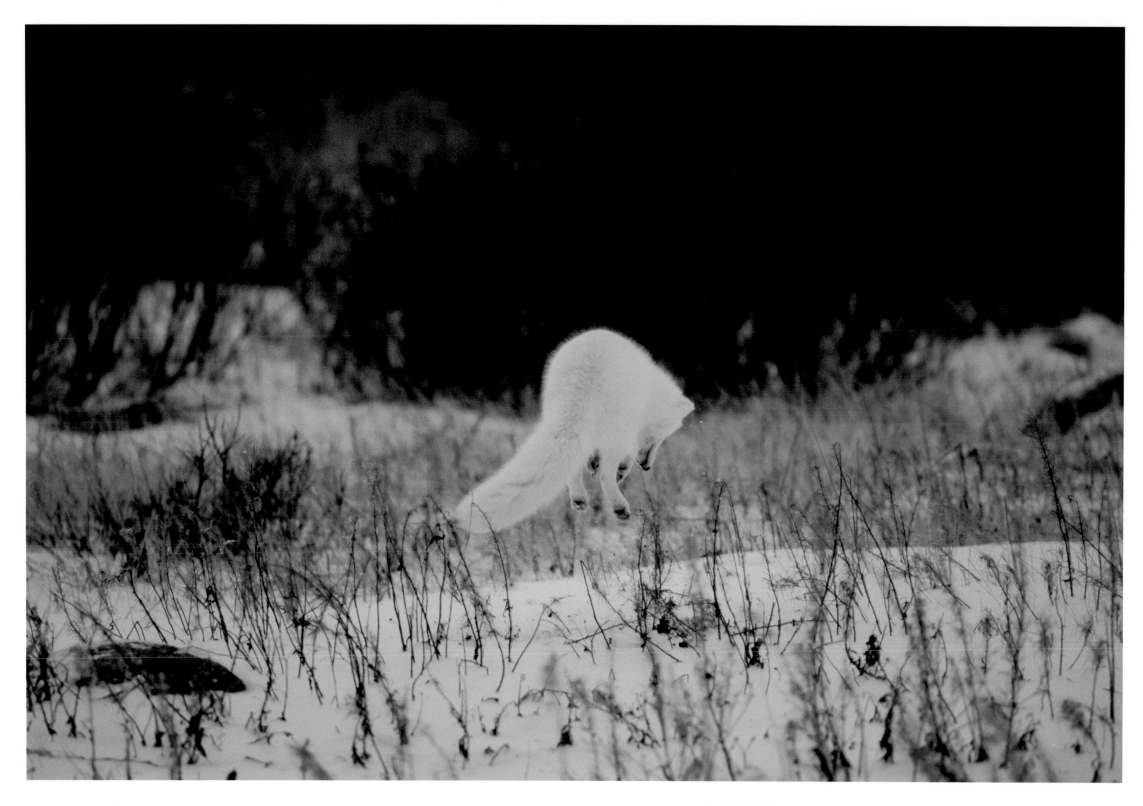

ARCTIC FOX
CHURCHILL, MANITOBA, CANADA

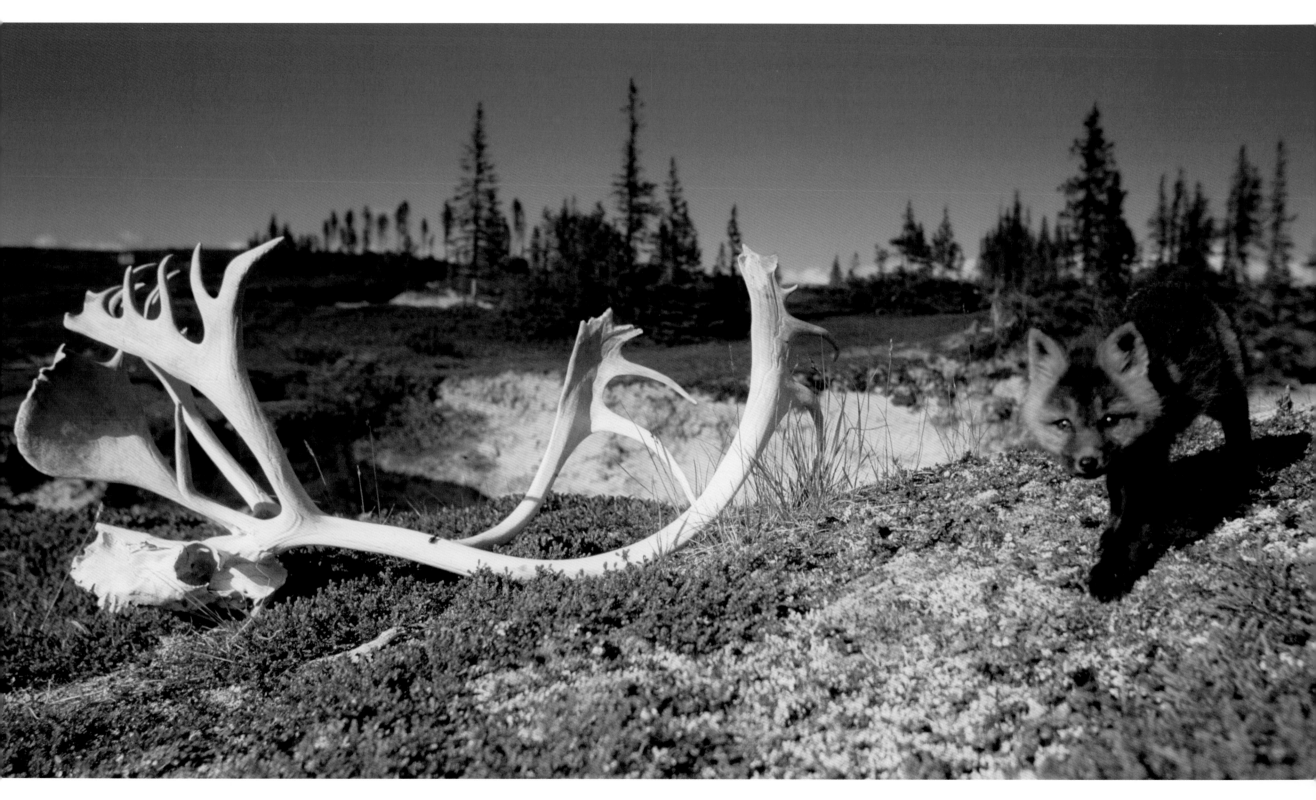

RED FOX

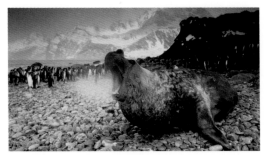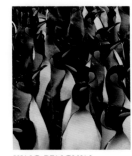

SOUTHERN ELEPHANT SEAL
(*Mirounga leonina*)

Southern elephant seals are the largest of the pinnipeds. Males are 4.5 to 6 meters long and can weigh up to 3.7 metric tons, while females are 2 to 3 meters long and weigh between 400 and 600 kilograms. Males reach sexual maturity at about 6 years of age, but do not compete for mates until they are at least 10. They do not defend territories, but establish a hierarchy in which the highest-ranking "alpha" male is able to dominate a beach (the "beachmaster") and thus mate with the most females. A beachmaster is usually at least 12 years old, although in heavily hunted populations, males begin mating 2 to 3 years earlier than males in nonexploited populations. Even though the alpha male is able to monopolize most of the females on his beach, other males will take any opportunity they can (for example when the alpha male is distracted by another interloper) to mate with a member of the alpha's harem.

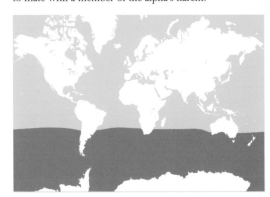

AW: Elephant seal bulls are so grotesque that they are almost endearing, or perhaps I have spent too much time in the field. To record this scene, I chose a 17–35mm wide-angle lens so that I could not only photograph the bull, but also the spectacular backdrop of rugged mountains, shoreline, and king penguins (*Aptenodytes patagonica*). As I cautiously approached this 3-metric-ton seal, the bull bellowed out a warning. In the cold temperature, his moist, warm breath was recorded on film. Fortunately, the smell of his breath was not.

Canon EOS-1N/RS, Canon EF 17–35mm lens, f/11 at 1/30 second, Fujichrome Velvia film

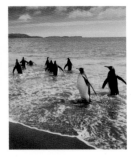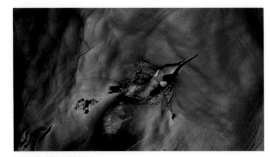

KING PENGUIN
(*Aptenodytes patagonica*)

King penguins are the second-largest penguins in the world (only the emperor penguin [*Aptenodytes forsteri*] is larger). Weighing up to 15 kilograms and standing about 95 centimeters tall, king penguins are most often seen concentrated in groups at their sub-Antarctic breeding colonies. Worldwide there are about two million adult king penguins, with over half a million on South Georgia alone. King penguins lay a single egg, which is incubated on the adults' feet under a brood patch. Pairs generally raise just a single chick every two years. The eggs are usually laid in November (although some late-breeders delay laying until January), with both parents taking turns at incubating the egg until it hatches after 54 or 55 days. The young chicks are completely dependent on their parents for food, and both sexes catch squid and fish to feed to their offspring.

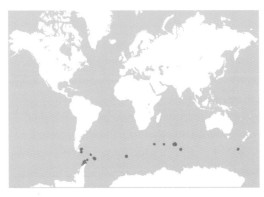

AW: Page 60 – I selected a 90mm tilt-shift lens, to allow maximum depth of field without the necessity of small aperture settings. This in turn permits the use of the faster shutter speed needed to freeze the motion of the birds. The added element of blowing snow heightens the drama.

Canon EOS-1N/RS, Canon TS-E 90mm lens, f/4 at 1/125 second, Fujichrome Astia film

AW: Page 61 – The unusually placid day, combined with a wide-angle lens and polarizing filter, creates an almost tropical impression.

Canon EOS-1N, Canon EF 17–35mm lens, f/16 at 1/125 second, polarizing filter, Fujichrome Velvia film

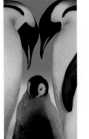

KING PENGUIN
(*Aptenodytes patagonica*)

Penguins evolved during the Eocene era, forty to fifty million years ago, from gull-like birds capable of flight. It is likely that at some point during their evolution, penguins could both fly and swim. Today, however, penguins are aquatic rather than aerial. They possess very dense plumage that traps air next to their skin, keeping them warm in the frigid polar and subpolar cold, and they have warm a "underfelt" of down beneath their outer layer of feathers. Penguins also have a thick layer of fat under their skin, which further insulates them from the cold. In fact, they are so well insulated that they can easily overheat. Excess heat is radiated away through the bare skin on their faces, flippers, and feet. Rather ungainly on land, in the water penguins literally fly through the fluid medium. King penguins routinely dive to depths greater than 50 meters, with their deepest dive recorded at 250 meters.

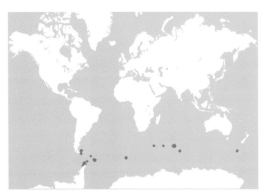

AW: Like many of my colleagues, I delight in capturing subjects in unusual ways. From the vantage point of a ship's deck, I photographed a group of king penguins as they swam by. The unusual angle combined with the pleasing texture of the water's surface makes for a memorable image. I used a polarizing filter to make the penguin more obvious.

Canon EOS-1N, Canon EF 70–200mm lens, f/5.6 at 1/60 second, polarizing filter, Fujichrome Astia film

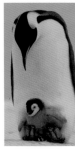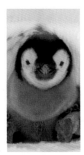

EMPEROR PENGUIN
(*Aptenodytes forsteri*)

Emperors are the largest of the eighteen species of penguins. They average about thirty kilograms in weight, but can reach 40 kilograms. Of the approximately thirty known breeding colonies of emperors, all but two are located on the sea ice that borders the Antarctic continent. Emperors have a unique breeding cycle, for theirs encompasses the harsh Antarctic winter. Colonies assemble in April and May—at the end of the Antarctic summer and as soon as the sea ice has thickened. Pairs conduct an elaborate three- to five-week courtship and the single egg is laid in May and early June. The male takes charge of the egg within hours of its appearance, placing it carefully on top of his feet, and the female heads off to sea. The male then incubates the egg for 65 days, weathering temperatures of -20°C and winds of 200 kilometers per hour. Males will lose up to 40 percent of their body weight before their mate returns.

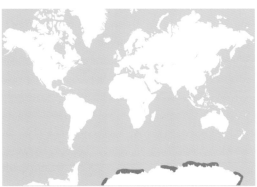

AW: All pages – There are two challenges in photographing intimate portraits of emperor penguins: First, to simplify the image by singling out a few individuals in the midst of these enormous rookeries; and second, to maintain an unobstructed view of the subject. Often I would be lying on the ice, looking through my viewfinder, when everything would suddenly go white. I would look up to see a curious penguin standing directly in front of my lens, bending over to examine it.

All pages – Canon F3, Canon EF 70–200mm lens, f/8 at 1/60 second, Fujichrome Velvia film

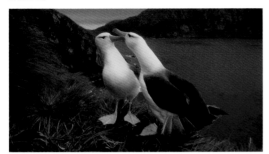

BLACK-BROWED ALBATROSS
(*Diomedea melanophris*)

With a worldwide annual breeding population of about 682,000 pairs, the black-browed albatross is the most abundant of the world's fourteen albatross species. They are circumpolar in distribution, with most breeding in the Falkland Islands. They return to land in mid-September, and begin laying their eggs in October. The single chick hatches after a 68- to 72-day incubation, and fledges at 16 or 17 weeks of age, leaving the nest in April. Colonies are usually found on cliffs or other elevated locations where the large birds (they have a 2.4-meter wingspan) can make use of updrafts to get airborne. Perfect gliders in the air, on land they are ungainly and clumsy. At sea, they are scavengers, picking krill and squid from the water's surface. It is likely that they feed extensively at night, when the creatures rise to the surface, and there are indications that they use their sense of smell to locate food.

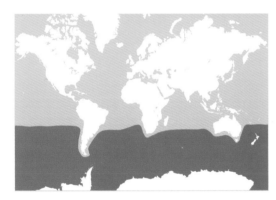

AW: On a cloudy, windy afternoon on South Georgia Island, I sat quietly eating my lunch amid tussock grass, when a pair of black-browed albatrosses landed at my feet. As there were no nests nearby, I think the birds were just curious. Never wanting to miss a photo opportunity, I put down my sandwich and picked up my camera and a 17–35mm wide-angle lens. When one of these birds saw its reflection in my lens, it leaned forward and gently nibbled at the camera.

Canon EOS-1N, Canon EF17-35mm lens, f/11 at 1/60 second, Fujichrome Astia film

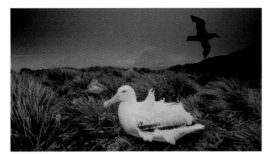

WANDERING ALBATROSS
(*Diomedea exulans*)

The wandering albatross roams the southern oceans, returning to land only to nest. Breeding colonies are found on several sub-Antarctic islands, including South Georgia. They are spectacular gliders and have the largest wingspan (3.4 meters) of any living bird. Predominantly squid feeders, albatross have been significantly impacted by baited longline fisheries. Longline fishing boats set lines more than 125 kilometers in length and containing thousands of hooks, all in search of tuna. An estimated 9,500 wandering albatross are hooked and killed each year as part of the unintentional fishery bycatch. In addition, there are only an estimated 20,000 breeding pairs of wandering albatross, and where colonies have been monitored they have declined by as much as 50 percent in the last 30 years. Unless these declines are arrested, it is likely that the wandering albatross will disappear from much of its range.

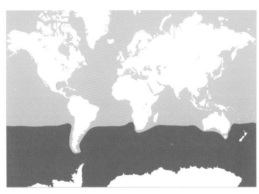

AW: Wandering albatrosses on islands without predators show little fear of people. I slowly crawled to within 1.5 meters of this nesting albatross and used a 17–35 mm wide-angle lens. Every few minutes a southern giant petrel (*Macronectes giganteus*) glided past. I calculated the depth of field I would need to get both the albatross and petrel in focus and what shutter speed would be necessary to freeze the petrel's motion. I pushed my 100-speed film to 200 ISO and triggered the shutter every time the petrel flew over. The best composition I got is the one you see here.

Canon EOS-1N/RS, Canon EF 17–35mm lens, f/11 at 1/250 second, Fujichrome Astia film (pushed 1 stop)

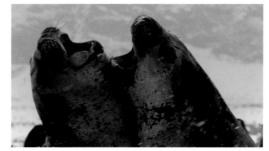

SOUTHERN ELEPHANT SEAL
(*Mirounga leonina*)

Young seals often spar with each other on the beach, but such activity has less to do with mating and establishing dominance than it does with the animals jostling for position or reacting to an inappropriately placed flipper or sand flicked into an eye. When the animals finally venture into the water, these ungainly "landlubbers" become highly efficient aquatic predators. They spend as much as eight months of the year in the open ocean, making deep dives that can exceed 1,400 meters (the depth record for all air-breathing vertebrates—1,581 meters—was set by a male northern elephant seal [*M. angustirostris*] off Alaska). The seals spend 90 percent of their time below the surface and often spend just a couple of minutes at the surface between dives. They forage along the ocean floor, searching for cephalopods and fish, and while most dives have an average duration of 10 to 20 minutes, they may last two hours.

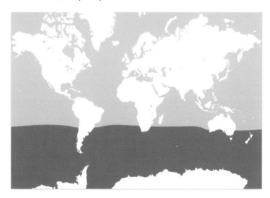

AW: Adolescent elephant seals are exceptionally engaging subjects as they jostle and spar with each other. When the seals are in the middle of such battles, they ignore virtually everything else, making it possible for me to reposition myself frequently without disturbing them. This also means that it is possible to create many different compositions of the same subject.

Canon EOS-3, Canon EF 70–200mm lens, f/8 at 1/125 second, Fujichrome Provia film

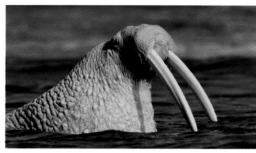

WALRUS
(*Odobenus rosmarus*)

The walrus, found only in Arctic and sub-Arctic regions, is well-adapted to the cold—its skin is 2 to 4 centimeters thick and the underlying blubber up to 10 centimeters thick. The long tusks (actually upper canines) occur in both sexes. Commercial hunting—mainly for ivory—began in earnest in the eighteenth and nineteenth centuries. By the early twentieth century Pacific walrus (*O. r. divergens*) were reduced from an estimated 250,000 to no more than 50,000; the Atlantic walrus (*O. r. rosmarus*) population also declined dramatically. Protection from hunting allowed a complete recovery of the Pacific subspecies by the early 1980s, but by 1990 their numbers were once again in decline, amid concerns about excessive subsistence harvests, ivory poaching, and an increase in clam-dredging. Today, there are an estimated 200,000 Pacific walrus, and 30,000 Atlantic walrus.

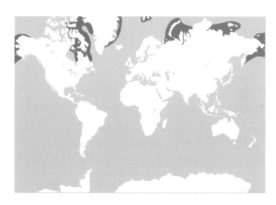

AW: Walrus are unlikely looking animals with huge, largely hairless bodies, and sporting long ivory tusks. As I photographed a walrus colony near Cape Peirce in Western Alaska, I saw an occasional walrus leave the beached colony and swim parallel to the shore. Recognizing the potential for a unique perspective, I positioned myself among some boulders near the water and waited for a walrus to swim by. I also kept the camera and lens low and as close to the water's surface as possible to create the perspective of being in the water with the animal.

Canon EOS-1N/RS, Canon EF 600mm lens, Canon Extender EF 1.4x, f/8 at 1/125 second, Fujichrome Velvia film

NOTES FROM THE FIELD

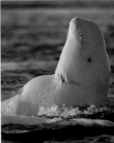 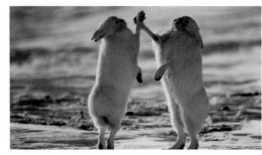

BELUGA WHALE
(*Delphinapterus leucas*)

Beluga whales (also known as white whales or belukha) are found in the Arctic Ocean and its adjacent seas. They have been known to swim up rivers for thousands of kilometers, but are more usually found in coastal regions and in deep water far from shore. While some populations are sedentary, others undertake long annual migrations—those in the High Arctic are more likely to undertake long migrations to avoid the winter ice. The global population is estimated at 100,000, with half of those in U.S. and Canadian waters—native people kill approximately 2,200 each year and a commercial harvest in Russia may take upward of 1,000 animals. Several subpopulations—including those in Baffin Bay, Hudson Bay, James Bay, and the St. Lawrence Estuary—have been greatly reduced by hunting, and in the case of the St. Lawrence, recovery is hampered by pollution, including polychlorinated biphenyls (PCBs) that inhibit successful reproduction.

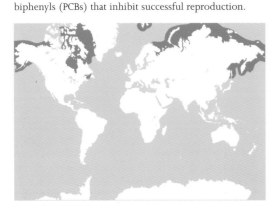

AW: Page 68 – Beluga whales enter warm, shallow river estuaries to shed their skins. To get this photograph, I simply waited next to the river channel. Naturally curious, several whales swam close and a few even poked their heads out of the water to get a better view of me.

Canon EOS-1N, Canon EF 600mm lens, f/8 at 1/125 second, Fujichrome 50 film

AW: Page 69 – To get a different perspective, I flew above the Somerset Island coastline. My favorite shot was this one, where thirty-four whales form a beautiful pattern.

Canon EOS-1N, Canon EF 70–200mm lens, f/3.5 at 1/125 second, Fujichrome 50 film

---

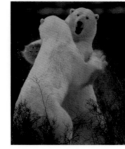 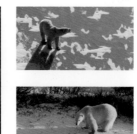

ARCTIC HARE
(*Lepus arcticus*)

Found on the tundra of Canada and Greenland, arctic hares are the northernmost of the lagomorphs (rabbits, hares, and pikas). Unlike rabbits, hares do not usually dig burrows. Instead their young lie hidden in nests or depressions in the ground (called "forms"). They are typically herbivorous, feeding on grasses, twigs, and bark, although they are also known to catch and eat voles. During the winter months arctic hares must endure temperatures below -40°C and snow cover that may last for more than nine months. The breeding season typically begins in May, with males boxing with each other, and even with females to secure mating rights. Such matches can sometimes result in serious injuries. Northern hares usually have only a single litter each year, and usually give birth in June after a 50-day gestation period; an average of five "leverets" make up each litter.

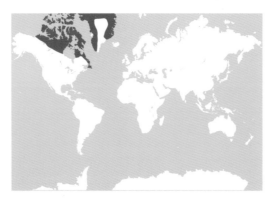

AW: Arctic hares are remarkably large, weighing up to 5.4 kilograms. While visiting Ellesmere Island, the last body of land before the North Pole, I encountered large groups of these tame hares. On several occasions, the hares would stand and begin punching each other. The most difficult task in taking this photograph was keeping both myself and my camera equipment operating in the -33°C April weather.

Canon F3, Canon EF 400mm lens, f/5.6 at 1/125 second, Fujichrome 100 film

---

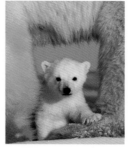 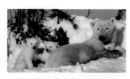 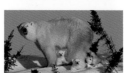

POLAR BEAR
(*Ursus maritimus*)

An estimated 28,000 to 40,000 polar bears roam the frozen Arctic Ocean and its coastlines. They feed mainly on ringed seals (*Phoca hispida*), but will also eat stranded marine mammals, small land mammals, seabirds, and occasionally young walrus (*Odobenus rosmarus*). At Churchill, Manitoba, bears spend the summer and fall stranded on land after the ice retreats from Hudson Bay. With little to eat, the bears spend most of their time resting. Researchers have taken advantage of this annual concentration, and their studies reveal a disturbing trend. In the last two decades the weight of adult females has declined, and cub mortality has increased. Since the average female bear is capable of producing, at most, five litters in her lifetime, any decline in reproductive fitness is of concern. The reason for the decline is unknown, but some researchers believe climate change could be a contributing factor.

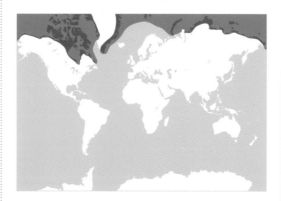

AW: Page 71 – I pushed my film one stop to gain the speed needed to freeze the action.

Canon EOS-3, Canon EF 600mm lens, f/5.6 at 1/250 second

AW: Page 72 – This helicopter image is all about pattern and shadow.

Canon EOS-3, Canon EF 70–200mm lens, f/5.6 at 1/500 second

AW: Page 73 – A wide-angle lens emphasizes the habitat.

Canon EOS-3, Canon EF 17–35mm lens, f/16 at 1/15 second

All pages – Fujichrome Velvia film (page 71 only: pushed 1 stop)

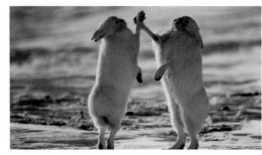

POLAR BEAR
(*Ursus maritimus*)

The polar bear is believed to have diverged from an ancestral stock of brown bears over 125,000 years ago. Today it ranges across the circumpolar Arctic. Radio-collared females in Alaska are known to travel between 2,100 and 5,200 kilometers annually, often within home ranges 150 to 300 kilometers across. Male movements are unknown because males cannot be collared; their necks are wider than their heads and the collars slide off. Polar bears seem to exist far from human influence, but that is not the case. In Norway's Svalbard archipelago, researchers found that 7 of 450 female bears showed signs of hermaphroditism (bearing partial penises). Norway's bears are exposed to significantly more polychlorinated biphenyls (PCBs) than bears in Alaska or Canada, and although a direct causal link has not yet been established, pollution from Europe, North America, and Asia is the likely culprit.

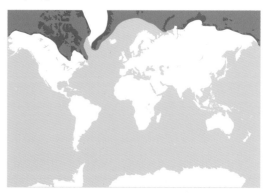

AW: All pages – For the final shoot for *The Living Wild*, I was extremely lucky. I went to Churchill to photograph cubs newly emerged from their winter dens. Not only did I find several sows with new cubs, but I found them in near-perfect late-afternoon light. I set my camera on manual exposure, taking a reading on the snow. I then set my aperture to overexpose by two stops from what my camera showed to be the correct exposure. This gives me the most accurate exposures for white animals in the snow.

All pages – Canon EOS-3, Canon EF 500mm lens, Canon Extender EF 1.4x, f/11 at 1/250 second, Fujichrome Provia film

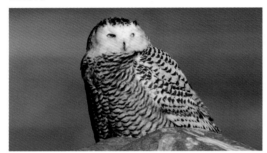

SNOWY OWL
(*Nyctea scandiaca*)

Snowy owls are found across the circumpolar Arctic and are found farther north than any other bird. They can survive ambient temperatures below -62.5°C—in part because of their extremely low thermal conductance; they lose minimal heat through their skin. Snowy owl populations fluctuate wildly in response to prey availability, and in many areas their numbers track fluctuations in lemming populations. When lemmings are abundant, snowy owl numbers may increase by a factor of ten. Although the owls may forego breeding if prey is scarce, when they do nest, they do so in a simple ground scrape that is slightly elevated above the surrounding tundra. Females lay five to seven eggs, and it is the female who incubates the clutch for 30 to 38 days. Female owls can be identified by the dark bars and spots on their plumage; males are usually pure white.

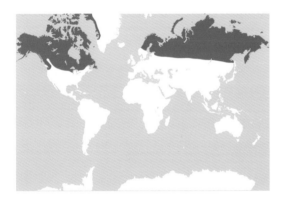

AW: Over the years, I have found snowy owls to be very elusive and frustrating subjects. Constantly alert, and favoring wide-open spaces, the owls usually take flight long before I can get close enough for a satisfying image. While photographing polar bears near Churchill, I discovered this owl perched on a snow-swept rock and, unlike so many times before, this bird allowed me to approach to within 20 meters.

Canon EOS-1N/RS, Canon EF 600mm lens, f/11 at 1/125 second, Fujichrome Velvia film (pushed 1 stop)

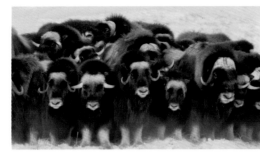

MUSKOX
(*Ovibos moschatus*)

Muskox represent some of the last of the "Pleistocene megafauna." Their standard defensive response to attack—to form a closed circle or semicircle—may be efficient when facing wolves (*Canis lupus*), but it made them easy targets when facing humans. By the early twentieth century, these 1.5-meter-tall, 200- to 410-kilogram bovids had been eradicated from Alaska and much of Canada—most killed for food by whalers, natives, and hide-hunters. Once found across the Arctic, from North America to Greenland and Eurasia, today the sole species of the genus *Ovibos* survives in small reintroduced populations in Alaska, numbering approximately 2,220 animals, including about 500 individuals on Alaska's Nunivak Island; on Greenland, where both indigenous groups and reintroduced animals collectively number 12,100 to 15,100; and in Arctic Canada, which has the largest population—109,000—mainly on Banks and Victoria Islands.

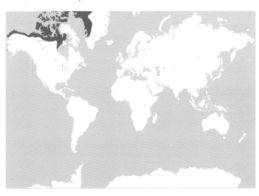

AW: A large herd of muskox demonstrates their primary means of defense by forming a tight circle with heads and horns facing outward. This enables them to gore their primary predator, the wolf. This classic defense posture also allowed me to approach fairly closely. To determine the proper exposure, I spot read off their massive horns—a medium gray in a bright snow setting with very dark animals.

Canon F3, Canon EF 300mm lens, f/11 at 1/125 second, Fujichrome 100 film

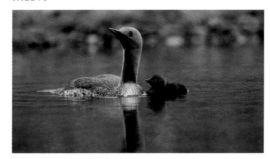

RED-THROATED LOON
(*Gavia stellata*)

Red-throated loons occur widely across much of the Holarctic. They breed in northern latitudes, particularly in coastal Alaska, Arctic Canada, Greenland, Iceland, northern Europe, and northern Russia, where they favor small ponds and lakes about 0.5 hectare in size. The loons (known as divers outside of North America) build nests of mud and vegetation, often on small islands in their chosen water body. Clutches typically consist of two eggs that are laid two days apart. The first chick to hatch has a much better chance of survival than the second. The young chicks are able to swim within 24 hours of hatching and are fed—small fish and invertebrates—by their parents until fledging at five or six weeks of age. Wintering birds head south to winter along the eastern and western seaboards of North America, northwestern Europe, Japan, eastern China, and Korea.

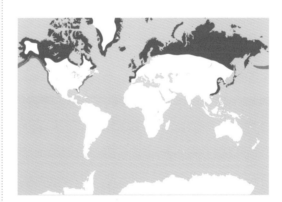

AW: While touring Iceland, I came across this adult and chick in a narrow pond along the highway. Since the loon had chosen to nest along a fairly busy highway, the birds were well habituated. To photograph them, I used a 600mm lens and activated the automatic focus on my camera. This allowed me to follow focus, since the birds were in continuous motion. I also lowered the camera on my tripod as close to the ground as possible. By doing so, I gained a better view of the birds, and this position also appeared to be less intimidating.

Canon EOS-1N, Canon EF 600mm, Canon Extender EF 1.4x, f/8 at 1/125 second, Fujichrome Astia film

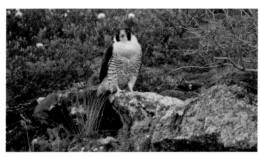

PEREGRINE FALCON
(*Falco peregrinus*)

The peregrine falcon was once widespread throughout the world. Nineteen subspecies are recognized, including three in North America (*tundrius*, *pealei*, and *anatum*). Breeding populations were decimated, especially during the 1950s and 1960s, largely due to contamination from pesticides such as DDT that interfered with successful reproduction. In western Europe and North America many populations were designated as endangered. Protection, the banning of DDT and related pesticides, and reintroduction programs have seen the peregrine make at least a partial recovery in some areas. They can be found in a variety of wetland habitats where they hunt ducks and shorebirds; they have even settled in some cities where they prey on pigeons. When diving on their prey, peregrines may reach speeds of 300 kilometers per hour, literally knocking their target out of the sky. They are capable of recovering from a G force that would cause a human to lose consciousness.

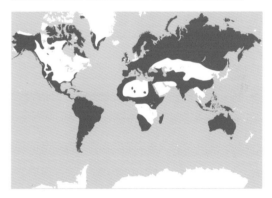

AW: In selecting images for inclusion in *The Living Wild*, a sense of habitat was my primary criteria. I preferred this image over several tighter portraits, because it includes the plants that also struggle for existence in this harsh Arctic environment. The falcon was perched on a basalt cliff with its nest tucked away in a protective crack along the cliff. The bird routinely perched in this same spot before entering its nest. To get this shot, I approached the cliff from below and waited for the falcon to return from a hunting foray.

Canon EOS-3, Canon EF 600mm lens, f/16 at 1/30 second, Fujichrome Velvia film

NOTES FROM THE FIELD

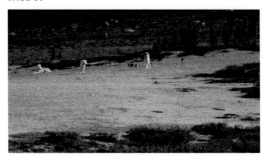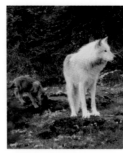

ARCTIC WOLF
(*Canis lupus arctos*)

Arctic wolves inhabit Arctic Canada and parts of coastal Greenland. A subspecies of the gray wolf, arctic wolves are often white, although they can be black or gray. They have thick coats with a dense undercoat of hairs and an overcoat of coarse, hollow guard hairs. These layers trap air and provide effective insulation against the cold. Other adaptations include small ears, short muzzles, and relatively short legs, compared to their southern relatives. Arctic wolves are stocky canids, weighing up to 55 kilograms, making them among the largest of wolves. They may range over more than 2,000 square kilometers of tundra, feeding on a variety of prey from voles and lemmings to caribou (*Rangifer tarandus*) and muskox (*Ovibos moschatus*). Packs range in size from seven to twenty-five animals, and pack cohesion is greater than that found in wolves to the south; lone wolves would have a difficult time surviving in such a harsh environment.

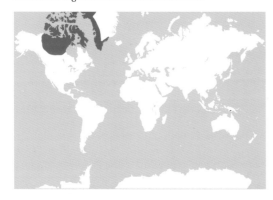

AW: In northern Canada, wolves have been hunted and trapped for over 150 years and they are extremely difficult to photograph. To take this photograph, I remained hidden behind a small willow 0.5 kilometer away. I attached a 2x extender to my 600mm lens, creating the equivalent of a 1200mm lens. I used two tripods, one under the lens and the other under the camera body to maximize stability. Often, when using this combination, I have to contend with heat waves rising from the surface of the land that can disrupt the clarity of the image.

Canon EOS-3, Canon EF 600mm lens, Canon Extender EF 2x, f/8 at 1/125 second, Fujichrome Velvia film

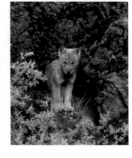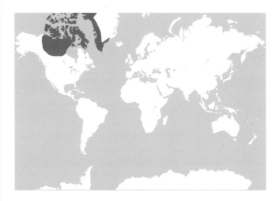

ARCTIC WOLF
(*Canis lupus arctos*)

The remote environment inhabited by arctic wolves (and the corresponding low human population density) has protected the wolves from widespread harassment by people. In many areas of northern Canada, wolf population densities average just one wolf for every 520 square kilometers. Censuses, and other figures based on prey availability, suggest that there are about 200 wolves in the Queen Elizabeth Islands (including Ellesmere Island), 1,100 on Banks and Victoria Islands, 2,100 on Baffin Island (subspecies *manningi*), fewer than 100 in Greenland (these animals are believed to have migrated across the ice from Canada), and 5,000 to 15,000 in the Northwest Territories, although these figures include a number of subspecies in addition to *arctos*, including *columbianus*, *griseoalbus*, *hudsonicus*, *mackenzii*, *nubilus*, *occidentalis*, and *pambasileus*.

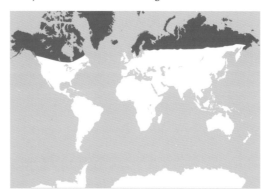

AW: Page 81 (left) – As I sat eating my lunch, I caught a glimpse of white across a small clearing. I managed to take several exposures as an adult arctic wolf and small pup emerged from the trees—before they reentered the forest, apparently without ever detecting my presence.

AW: Page 81 (right) – A four-month-old wolf pup watches me watching him from across a small stream. Pups are often left on their own when the adults leave on hunting forays.

Both: Canon EOS-3, Canon EF 600mm lens, f/5.6 at 1/60 second, Fujichrome Velvia film (page 81, right, only: pushed 1 stop)

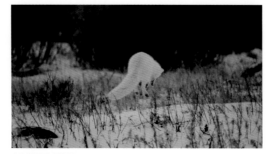

ARCTIC FOX
(*Alopex lagopus*)

Arctic foxes are the ubiquitous small predator of the circumpolar Arctic. Denning onshore during the summer, they often travel extensively across the sea ice in winter and have been sighted more than 800 kilometers offshore. Arctic foxes are opportunistic hunters and scavengers, feeding on carrion, lemmings, ground squirrels, fish, and even digging out seal pups from their lairs. They are often seen in association with polar bears (*Ursus maritimus*), scavenging from their kills. Foxes are highly adaptable and soon lose their fear of people, frequenting Arctic towns and villages. The high incidence of rabies in some fox populations can make this a tense association. Arctic foxes have long been harvested for their fur, and there is an annual worldwide harvest of 100,000–150,000 animals. Overhunting in Iceland and throughout Scandinavia has drastically reduced fox populations in those countries— with just a few hundred remaining in some cases.

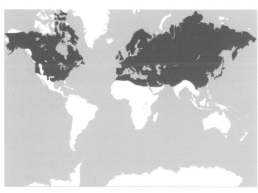

AW: During winter, the arctic fox uses its hearing as much as its sight when hunting. This is especially true when it is searching for small animals, such as lemmings, that live in a network of tunnels beneath the snow. By placing its head close to the snow's surface, the fox pinpoints the animal's location. Then with a vertical meter-high leap the fox lands, breaking through the snow's crust and capturing its prey. In this photograph, I have caught a fox as it springs upward. With a shutter speed of 1/250th of a second, I succeeded in freezing the fox in midair.

Canon EOS-3, Canon EF 600mm lens, f/4 at 1/250 second, Fujichrome Astia film

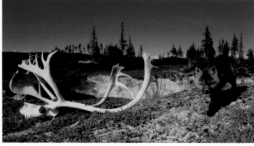

RED FOX
(*Vulpes vulpes*)

The ubiquitous red fox has one of the greatest natural distributions of any terrestrial mammal—perhaps exceeded only by humans (and formerly the gray wolf [*Canis lupus*]). They are equally at home in dense forests and open tundra, in towns and cities, and in alpine habitats up to about 4,500 meters elevation. Red foxes are typically reddish brown in color, with whitish underparts. However, several color variations are known, including the "cross fox" (shown here) and the "silver fox." About 25 percent of red foxes are of the cross fox variety. Cross foxes are somewhat darker than the typical red fox and have a single black line that runs down the middle of their back, with another that runs across the shoulders, forming the "cross" of its name. Red foxes have been heavily hunted throughout their range, for both sport and pelts. During the 1980s more than 500,000 pelts were being sold annually.

AW: To take this photograph, I placed a camera and 17–35mm wide-angle lens on a short tripod near a set of caribou (*Rangifer tarandus*) antlers located close to a fox den. Using a remote-control triggering device, I simply tripped the shutter as the pups played around the antlers. I remained motionless about 30 meters away.

Canon EOS-IN, Canon EF 17-35mm lens, f/16 at 1/30 second, Fujichrome Velvia film

THE LIVING WILD

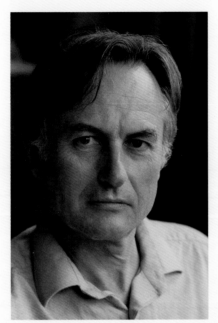

© CAROLYN DJANOGLY

The third planet is unique. Luxuriating over our sphere's surface, thinning up into the air, and etching its way down into the rocks is a layer in which something rich and new is added to the physics that unremarkably pervades the rest of the solar system. That special layer is, of course, the layer of life. It is not that the laws of physics are disobeyed at the planet's rim: Vanish the thought. But living matter deploys physics in unusual ways. So unusual—"emergent"—that the error of believing the laws of physics to be defied is forgivable. Which is just as well, because everyone has been tempted by that error, most people through history have succumbed to it, and many still do.

Darwin may not have been quite the first to resist the temptation, but the comprehensiveness with which he repudiated it entitles him to most of the honor. In spite of its title, his great book is less on the origin of species than on the origin of adaptation. That is to say, it is on the origin of the design illusion, that powerful simulacrum that led people to suspect, wrongly, that material causes are not enough to explain biology.

The illusion of design is at its strongest in the tissues and organs, the cells and molecules, of individual creatures. The individuals of every species, without exception, show it powerfully, and it springs forth from every picture in this book. But there is another illusion of design that we notice at a higher level—also so splendidly displayed in these pages: the level of species diversity. Design seems to reappear in the disposition of species themselves, in their arrangement into communities and ecosystems, in the dovetailing of species with species in the habitats that they share. There is a pattern in the intricate jigsaw of rainforest, say, or coral reef, which leads rhetoricians to preach disaster if but one component should be untimely ripp'd from the whole. In extreme cases, such rhetoric takes on mystical tones. The womb is of an earth goddess, all life her body, the species her parts. Yet, without giving in to such extravagance, there is a strong illusion of design at the community level, less compelling than within the individual organism but worth attention.

The animals and plants that live together in an area seem to fit one another with something like the glovelike intimacy with which the parts of an animal mesh with other parts of the same organism. A Florida panther has the teeth of a carnivore; the claws of a carnivore; the eyes, ears, nose, and brain of a carnivore; leg muscles that are suitable for chasing meat, and guts that are primed to digest it. Its parts are choreographed in a dance of carnivorous unity. Every sinew and cell of the big cat has meat eater inscribed through its very texture, and we can be sure that this extends deep into the details of biochemistry. The corresponding parts of, say, a bighorn sheep are equally unified with each other, but to different ends. Guts designed to digest plant roughage would be ill served by claws and instincts designed to catch prey. And vice versa. A

hybrid between a panther and a sheep would fall flat on its evolutionary face. Tricks of the trade cannot be cut from one and pasted into the other. Their compatibility is with other tricks of the same trade.

Something similar can be said of communities of species. The language of the ecologist reflects this. Plants are primary producers. They trap energy from the sun, and make it available to the rest of the community, via a chain of primary, secondary, and even tertiary consumers, culminating in scavengers. Scavengers play a recycling "role" in the community, and I use quotation marks advisedly. Every species, in this view of life, has a role to play. In some cases, if the performers of some role, such as scavengers, were removed, the whole community would collapse. Or its "balance" would be upset and it might fluctuate wildly, out of "control" until a new balance is set up, perhaps with different species playing the same roles. Desert communities are different from rainforest communities, and their component parts are mutually ill suited, just as— or so it seems—herbivorous colons are ill suited to carnivorous habits. Coral-reef communities are different from sea-bottom communities, and their parts cannot be exchanged. Species become adapted to their community, not just to a particular physical region and climate. They become adapted to each other. The other species of the community are an important—perhaps the most important—feature of the environment to which each species becomes adapted.

The harmonious role-playing of species in a community, then, resembles the harmony of the parts of a single individual organism. The resemblance is deceptive and must be treated with caution. Yet it is not completely without foundation. There is an ecology within the individual organism, a community of genes in the gene pool of a species. The forces that produce harmony among the parts of an organism's body are not wholly unlike the forces that produce the illusion of harmony among the species of a community. There is balance in a rainforest, structure in a reef community, an elegant meshing of parts that recalls coadaptation within an animal body. In neither case is the balanced unit favored *as a unit* by Darwinian selection. In both cases the balance comes about through selection at a lower level. Selection doesn't favor a harmonious whole. Instead, harmonious parts flourish in the presence of each other, and the illusion of a harmonious whole emerges.

At the individual level, to rehearse an earlier example in genetic language, genes that make carnivorous teeth flourish in a gene pool containing genes that make carnivorous guts and carnivorous brains, but not in a gene pool containing genes for herbivorous guts and brains. At the community level, an area that lacks carnivorous species might experience something similar to a human economy's "gap in the market." Carnivorous

RICHARD DAWKINS

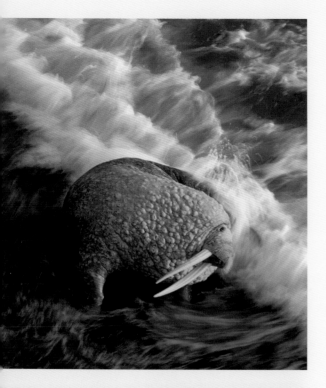

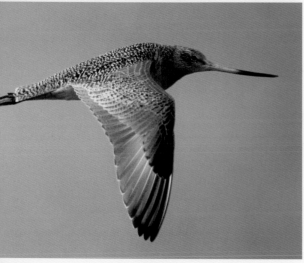

▲▲ WALRUS

(*Odobenus rosmarus*), TOGIAK NATIONAL
WILDLIFE REFUGE, ALASKA, USA

▲ MARBLED GODWIT

(*Limosa fedoa*), LAGUNA SAN IGNACIO,
BAJA CALIFORNIA, MEXICO

THE LIVING WILD

species that enter the area find themselves flourishing. If the area is a remote island that no carnivorous species has reached, or if a recent mass extinction has devastated the land and created a similar gap in the market, natural selection will favor individuals within noncarnivorous species that change their habits and become carnivores. After a long enough period of evolution, specialist carnivore species will descend from omnivorous or herbivorous ancestors.

Carnivores flourish in the presence of herbivores, and herbivores flourish in the presence of plants. But what about the other way around? Do plants flourish in the presence of herbivores? Do herbivores flourish in the presence of carnivores? Do animals and plants need enemies to eat them in order to flourish? Not in the straightforward way that is suggested by the rhetoric of some ecological activists. No creature normally benefits from being eaten. But grasses that can withstand being cropped better than rival plants can really flourish in the presence of grazers—on the principle of "my enemy's enemy." And something like the same story might be told of some animal victims of parasites—and predators, although here the story is more complicated. It is still misleading to say that a community "needs" its parasites and predators like a polar bear needs its liver or its teeth. But the enemy's enemy principle does lead to something like the same result. It can be right to see a community of species as a kind of balanced entity, which is potentially threatened by removal of any of its parts.

This idea of community, as made up of lower-level units that flourish in the presence of each other, pervades life. Even within the single cell, the principle applies. Most animal cells are communities of hundreds or thousands of bacteria, which have become so comprehensively integrated into the smooth working of the cell that their bacterial origins have only recently become understood. Mitochondria, once free-living bacteria, are as essential to the workings of our cells as our cells are to them. Their genes have flourished in the presence of ours as ours have flourished in the presence of theirs. Plant cells by themselves are incapable of photosynthesis. That chemical wizardry is performed by guest workers within the cells, originally bacteria and now relabeled chloroplasts. Plant eaters, such as ruminants and termites, are themselves largely incapable of digesting cellulose. But they are good at finding and chewing plants. The gap in the market offered by their plant-filled guts is exploited by symbiotic microorganisms that possess the biochemical expertise necessary to digest plant material efficiently. Creatures with complementary skills flourish in each other's presence.

And the process is mirrored at the level of every species' "own" genes. The entire genome of a polar bear or a penguin, of a caiman or a guanaco, is a set of genes that flourish in each other's presence. The immediate arena of this flourishing is the interior of an individual's cells. But the long-term arena is the gene pool of the species. Given sexual reproduction, the gene pool is the habitat of every gene as it is recopied and recombined down the generations.

This gives the species its singular status in the taxonomic hierarchy. Nobody knows how many separate species there are in the world, but we at least know what it would mean to count them. Arguments about whether there are thirty million separate species, as some have estimated, or only five million, are real arguments. The answer matters. Arguments about how many genera there are, or how many orders, families, classes, or phyla have no more status than arguments about how many tall men there are. It's up to you how you define tall and how you define a genus or a family. But—as long as reproduction is sexual—the species has a definition that goes beyond individual taste and does so in a way that is really important. Fellow members of a species participate in the same shared gene pool. The species is defined as the community whose genes share that most intimate of cohabiting arenas, the cell nucleus—a succession of cell nuclei through generations.

When a species splits off a daughter species, usually after a period of accidental geographical isolation, the new gene pool constitutes a new arena for intergene cooperation to evolve. All the diversity on Earth has come about through such splittings. Every species is a unique entity, a unique set of coadapted genes, cooperating with each other in the enterprise of building individual organisms. The gene pool of a species is an edifice of harmonious cooperators, built up through a unique history. Any gene pool, as I have argued elsewhere, is a unique written record of ancestral history. Slightly fanciful perhaps, but it follows indirectly from Darwinian natural selection. A well-adapted animal reflects, in minute detail even down to the biochemical, the environments in which its ancestors survived. A gene pool is carved and whittled through generations of ancestral natural selection to fit that environment. In theory a knowledgeable zoologist, presented with the complete transcript of a genome, should be able to reconstruct the environmental circumstances that did the carving. In this sense the DNA is a coded description of ancestral environments, a "genetic book of the dead."

The extinction of a species therefore diminishes us in a sense that the death of an individual perhaps does not. To be sure, every individual is unique, and to that extent irreplaceable. But the set of genes in a species' gene pool represents a unique solution to the problem of survival. An individual organism, by contrast, is only a permutation of the units of that solution: unique, but not unique in an interesting way. If an individual dies, there are lots more where it came from. It is just another deal from the same pack of cards. When the last individual of a species dies, the whole pack has been destroyed.

No doubt other species will arise to take its place, but they will take time to build up an equivalently intricate collection of mutually compatible genes, and their new solution to the problem of DNA preservation will always be different from the old. When the last (probably) Tasmanian wolf died in Hobart Zoo in 1936, we lost tens of millions of years worth of carnivorous research and development.

It is possible to take a robust view of extinction, even mass extinction. We can tough-mindedly point out that extinction is the norm for species throughout geological history. Even our own swath of chain-saw and concrete devastation is only the latest in a long series of cleanouts from which life has always bounced back. What are we and our domination of the world but another natural process, no worse than many before? The catastrophe that ended the dinosaurs had a consequence that might lead us to take a positively cheerful attitude toward it: us. From a more dispassionate point of view, every mass extinction opens up yawning gaps in the market, and the headlong rush to fill them is what, time after time, has enriched the diversity of our planet.

Even the most devastating of mass extinctions can be defended as the necessary purging that makes rebirth possible. No doubt it is fascinating to wonder whether rats or starlings might provide the ancestral stock for a new radiation of giant predators, in the event that the whole order Carnivora was wiped out. But none of us would ever know, for we do not live on the evolutionary time scale. It is an aesthetic argument, an argument of feeling, not reason, and I confess that my own feelings recoil. I find my aesthetics incapable of quite such a long view.

The dinosaurs are gone. I mourn them and I mourn the giant ammonites, and before them the mammal-like reptiles and the club moss and tree fern forests of the coal measures, and before them the trilobites and eurypterids: But they are beyond recall. What we have now is a new set of communities, our own contemporary buildup of mutually compatible mammals and birds, flowering plants and pollinating insects. They are not better than the communities that preceded them. But they are here, we have the privilege of studying them, they took agonizing ages to build up, and if we destroy them we shall not see them replaced. Not in our lifetime, not in five million years. If we destroy the ecosystems of which we are a part, we condemn not just our own generation, but all the generations of descendants that we could realistically hope to succeed us, to a world of devastation and impoverishment.

The case for conserving wild nature is sometimes made in terms of the crudest self-interest. We need the diversity of the rainforests because who knows where our next set of medicines and crop plants will come from? Well, if that is what it takes to mobilize support, so be it, though it rings hollow to me, hollow and even ignoble. The

justification for conservation to which I return is an aesthetic one, and what is wrong with that? Who, having looked through the pages of this book, could contemplate with anything but sorrow the extinction of any one of the species here pictured?

But the best is the enemy of the good. We live in an economic world (interestingly, the Darwinian world of wild nature is an economic one too) where everything has its price. It seems all too easy to take the aesthetic high ground and look down on selfish, utilitarian motives for saving rainforests and rare species. But what proportion of our own wealth, or our own time, are we prepared to sacrifice to such an end? Not much. Even before we get selfish, there are other calls on our charitable generosity. What about the victims of the latest earthquake, famine, tornado, or other human catastrophe? Many of the habitats of endangered species are also the homelands of human poor, who can be forgiven for seeing wild animals as competitors rather than as enhancers of life's richness. "Life's richness" can ring hollow, as hollow perhaps as your own child's stomach. The aesthetic view of wild nature is, from such a low vantage point, a luxury that the hungry cannot afford.

Let us not be too ready, then, to condemn those attempts by southern African states to make game parks "pay their way," perhaps by turning the need to "cull" into an excuse to sell big-game shooting licenses. Of course it seems obscene to gratify human blood-lust, especially in those cases in which the animals themselves are tame and trusting, and the "hunters" safely ensconced in vehicles, with experienced rangers on hand to protect them if they miss. But this too is an aesthetic judgment, and the practice can be defended on grounds of economic practicality, a defense that is not available to, for example, the mincing, strutting, primping bullfighter. Disagreeable as it sounds, I sometimes find it hard to maintain my confidence that the southern African solution to the problem of saving the elephant and the black rhinoceros is not the most practical one. Nevertheless, on balance I still prefer the solution of a total ban on all trading in ivory and rhinoceros horn.

Such inconclusive meditation is a sure sign that I have no easy solution to offer. I return to aesthetics: But this book persuades me that here are more than ordinary aesthetics. It is not just the streamlined beauty of a swimming whale, the muscular tautness of a stalking big cat, the iridescent extravaganza of peacock or scarlet macaw. It is not just the pleasure of gazing at a spectacle, and of reflecting on the privilege of being able to do what future generations may be denied. Evolutionary thinking can give our aesthetic a new depth. We are not just looking at an animal as if it were an ordinary work of art. If it is a work of art, it is one that has been perhaps ten million years in the crafting. This seems to me to make a difference.

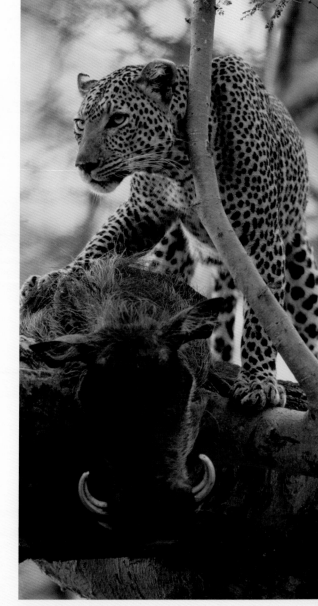

LEOPARD

(*Panthera pardus*) AND

WARTHOG

(*Phacochoerus africanus*),

Lake Nakuru National Park, Kenya

RICHARD DAWKINS

91

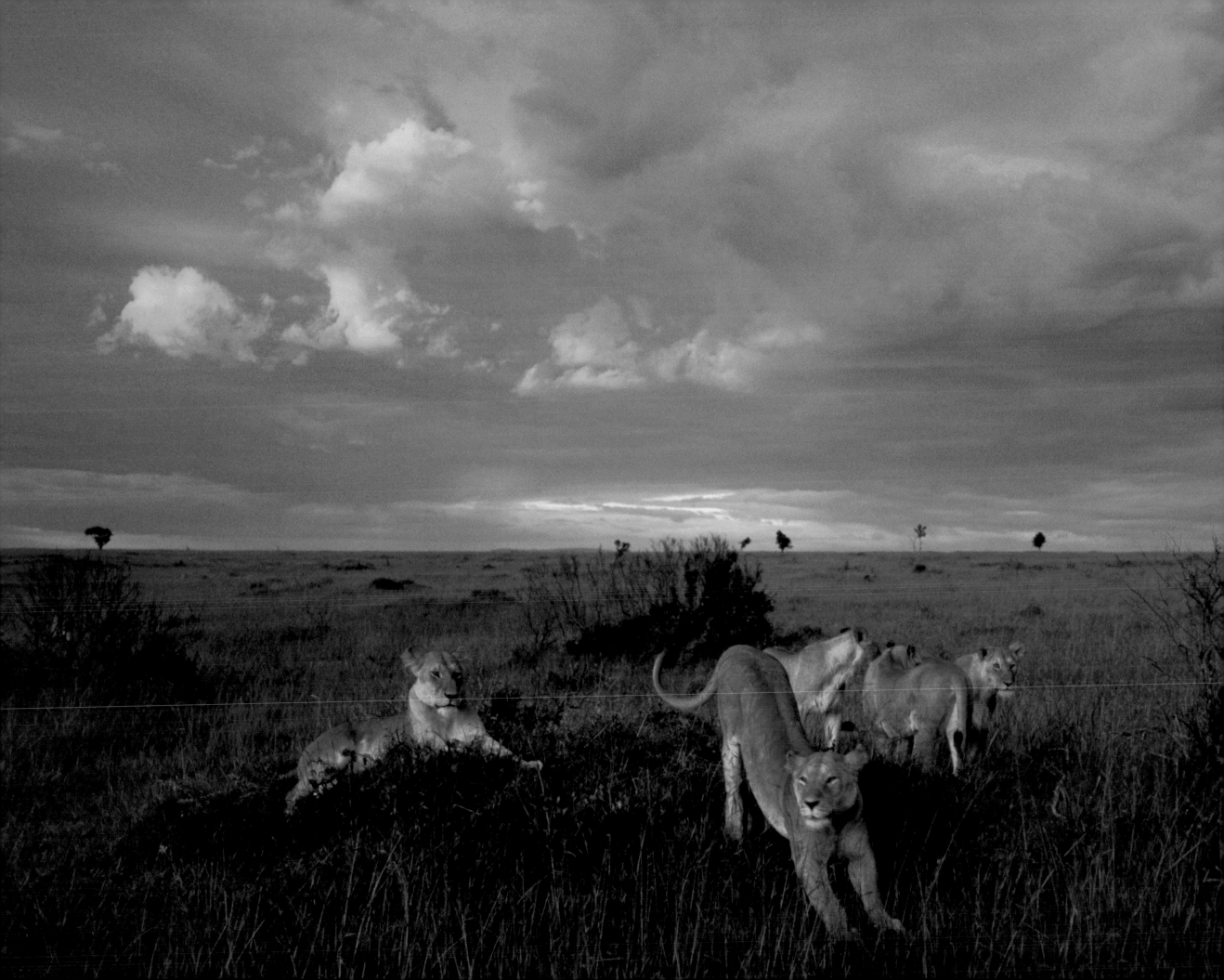

SAVANNAH, DESERT & STEPPE

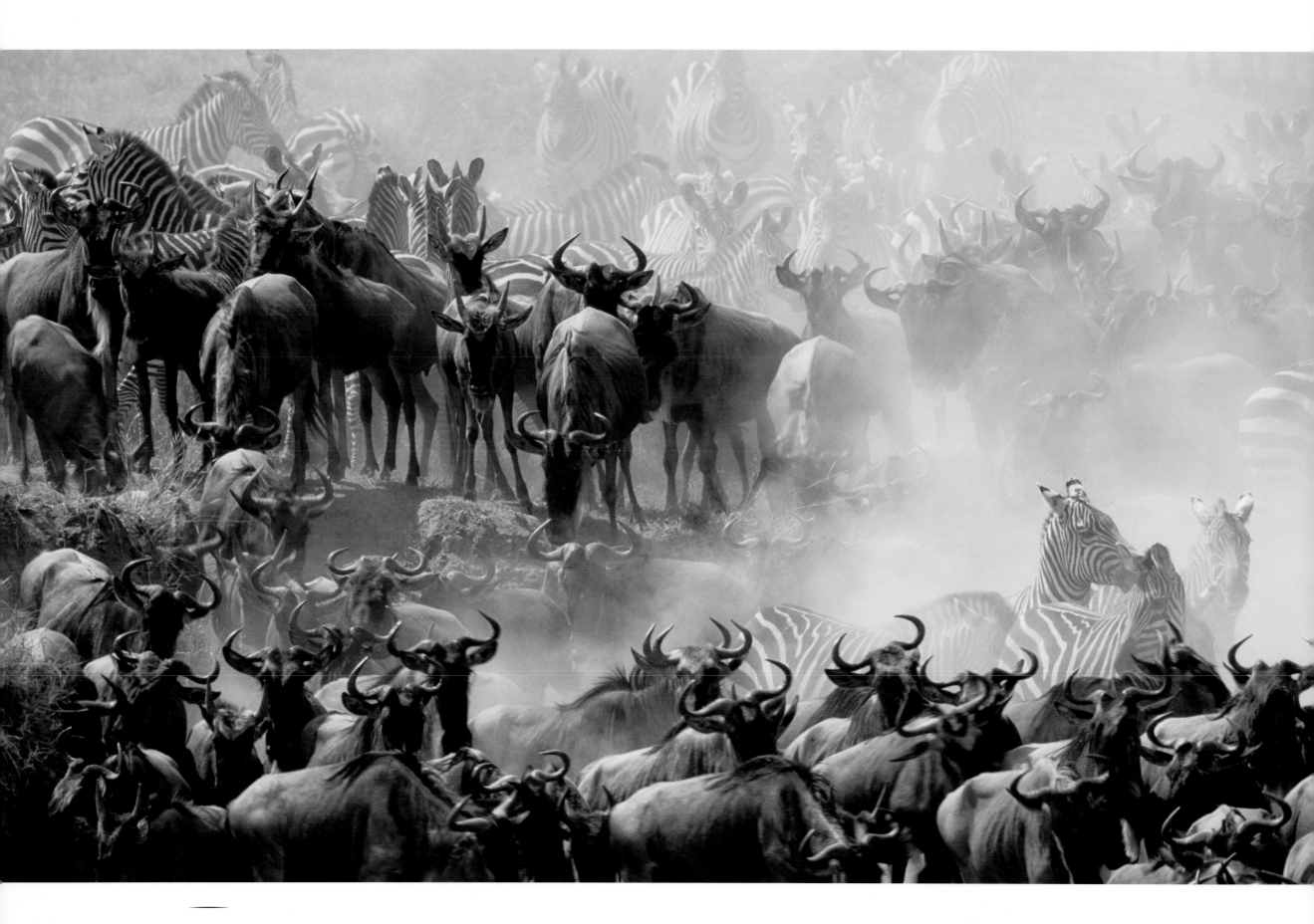

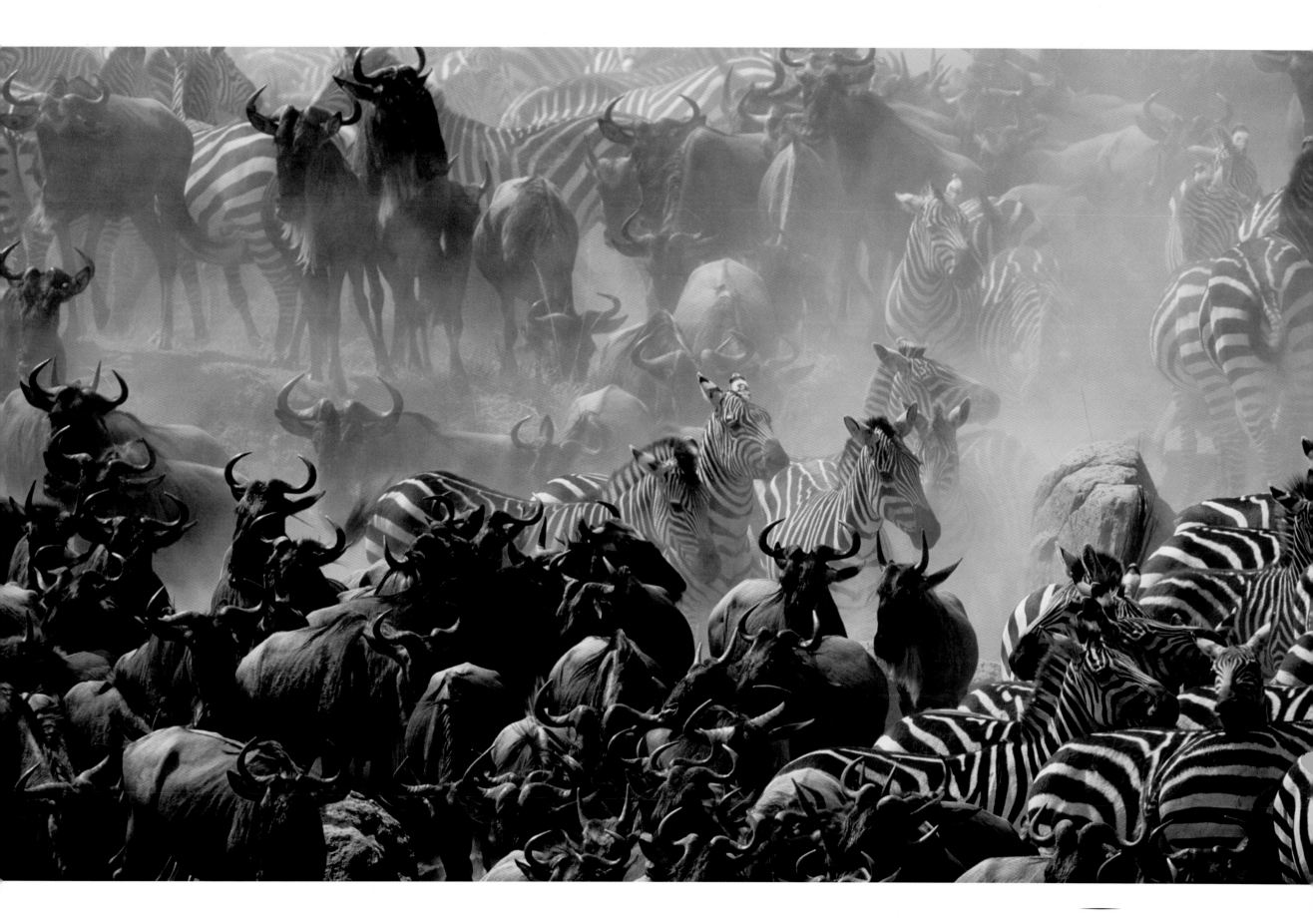

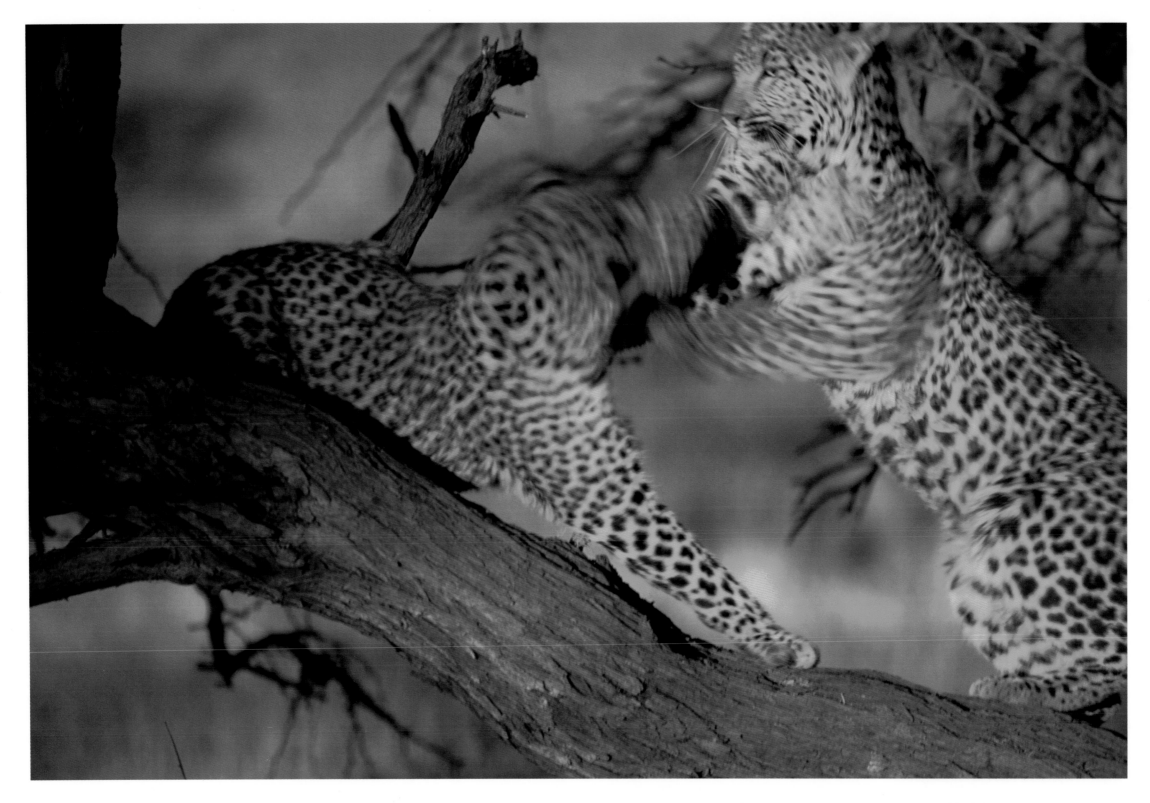

Masai Mara National Reserve, Kenya

◄ ◄ AND ◄ PLAINS ZEBRA AND COMMON WILDEBEEST ◠
Masai Mara National Reserve, Kenya

LEOPARD ◠
Londolozi Preserve, South Africa

THE LIVING WILD

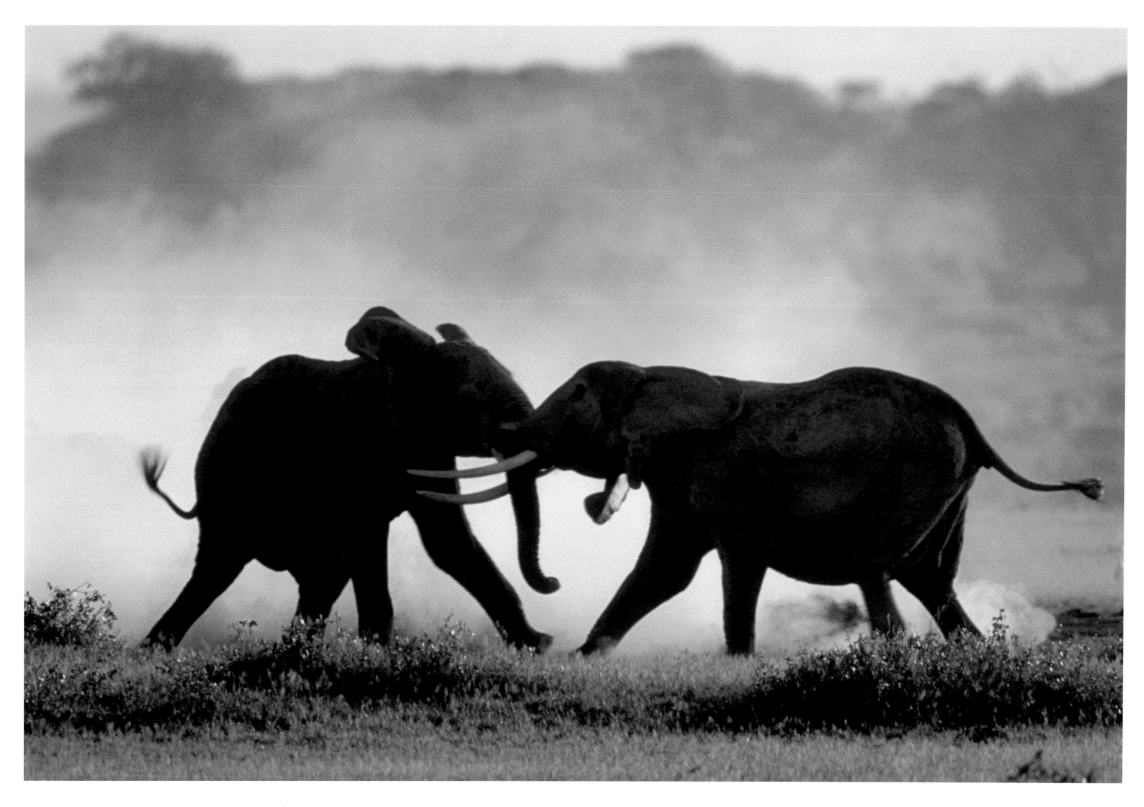

AFRICAN ELEPHANT
AMBOSELI NATIONAL PARK, KENYA

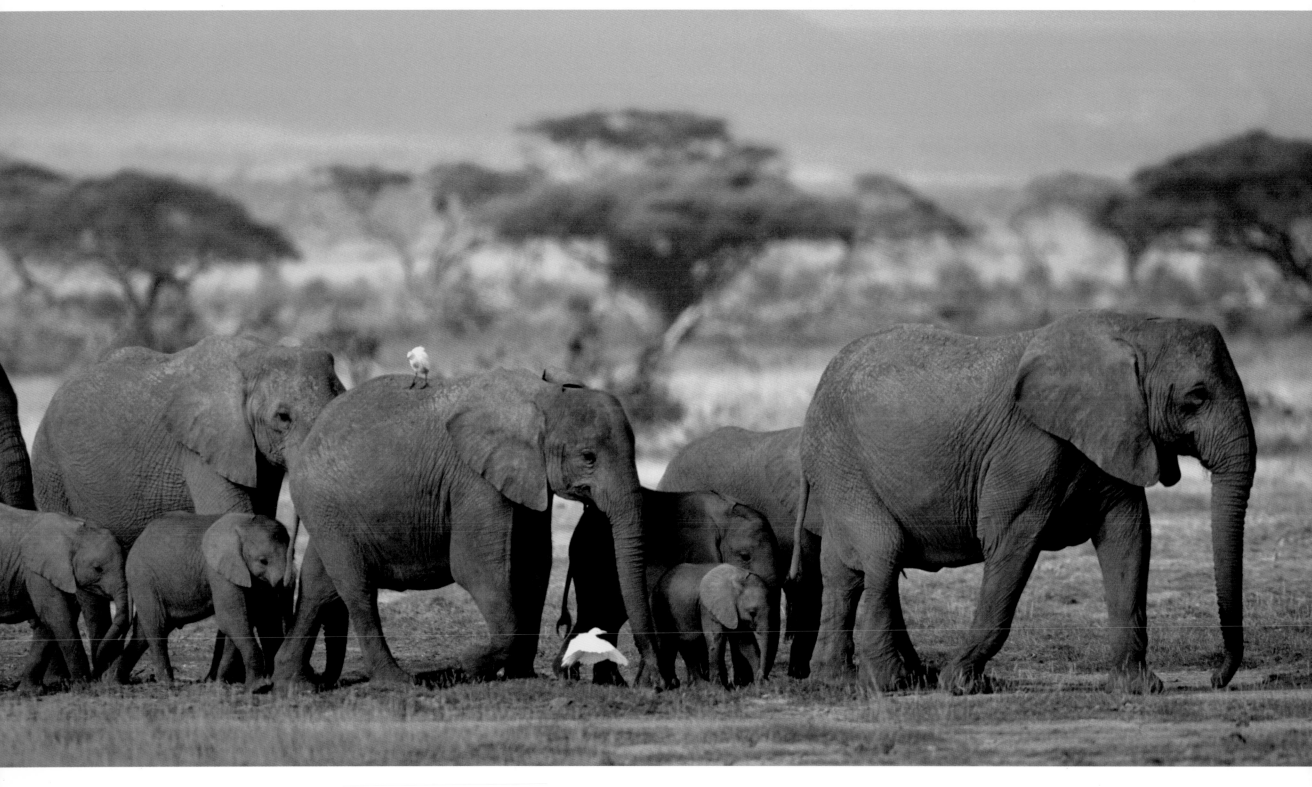

AFRICAN ELEPHANT
AMBOSELI NATIONAL PARK, KENYA

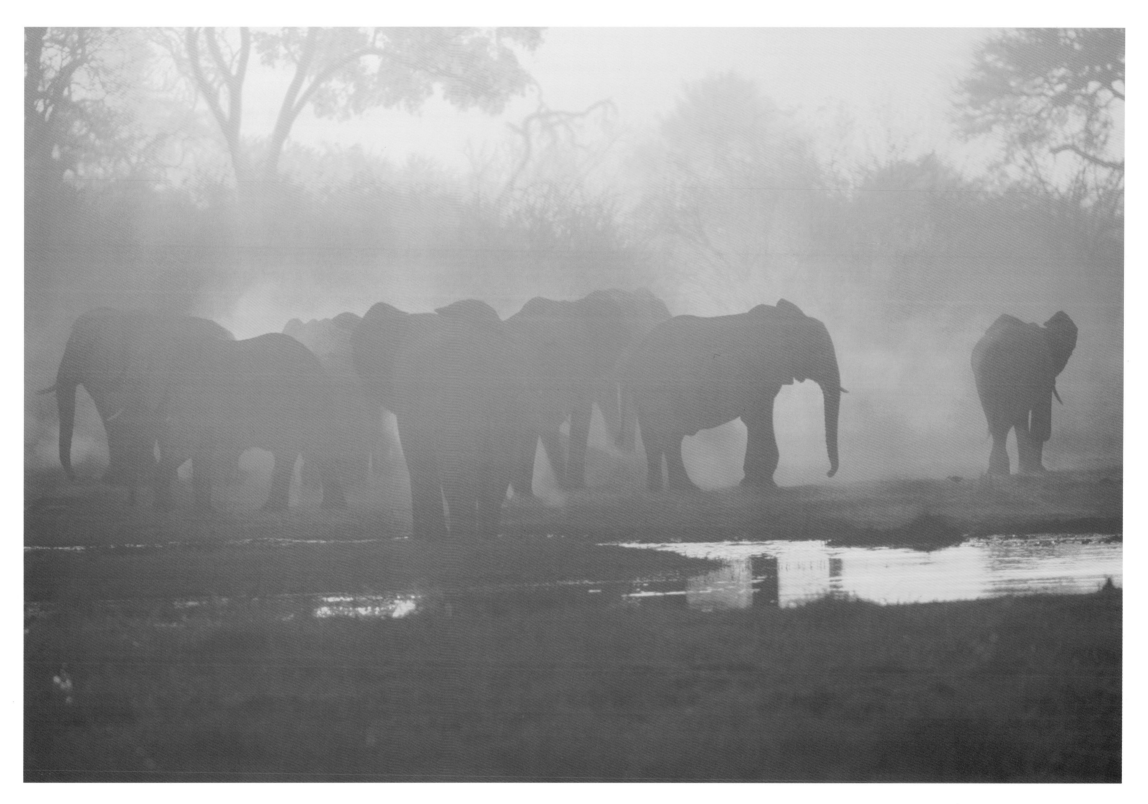

AFRICAN ELEPHANT

KWANDO, BOTSWANA

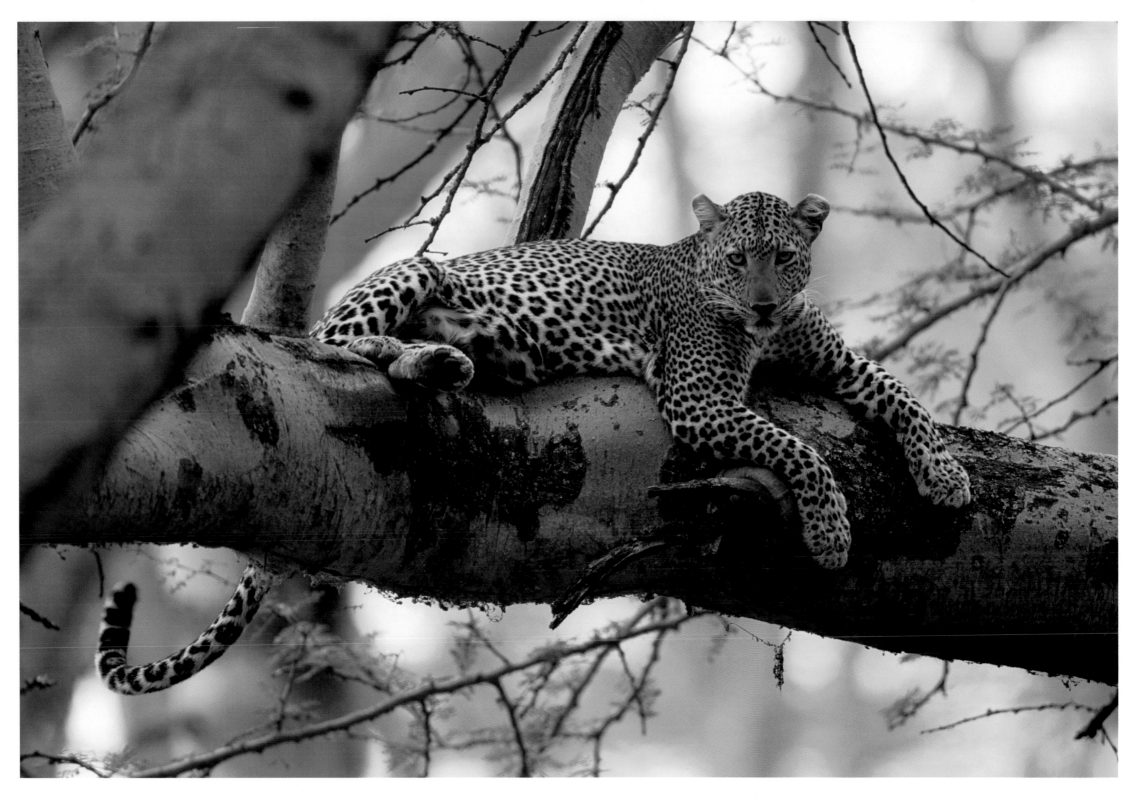

LEOPARD ~

Lake Nakuru National Park, Kenya

▶ CHEETAH ~

Phinda Reserve, South Africa

THE LIVING WILD

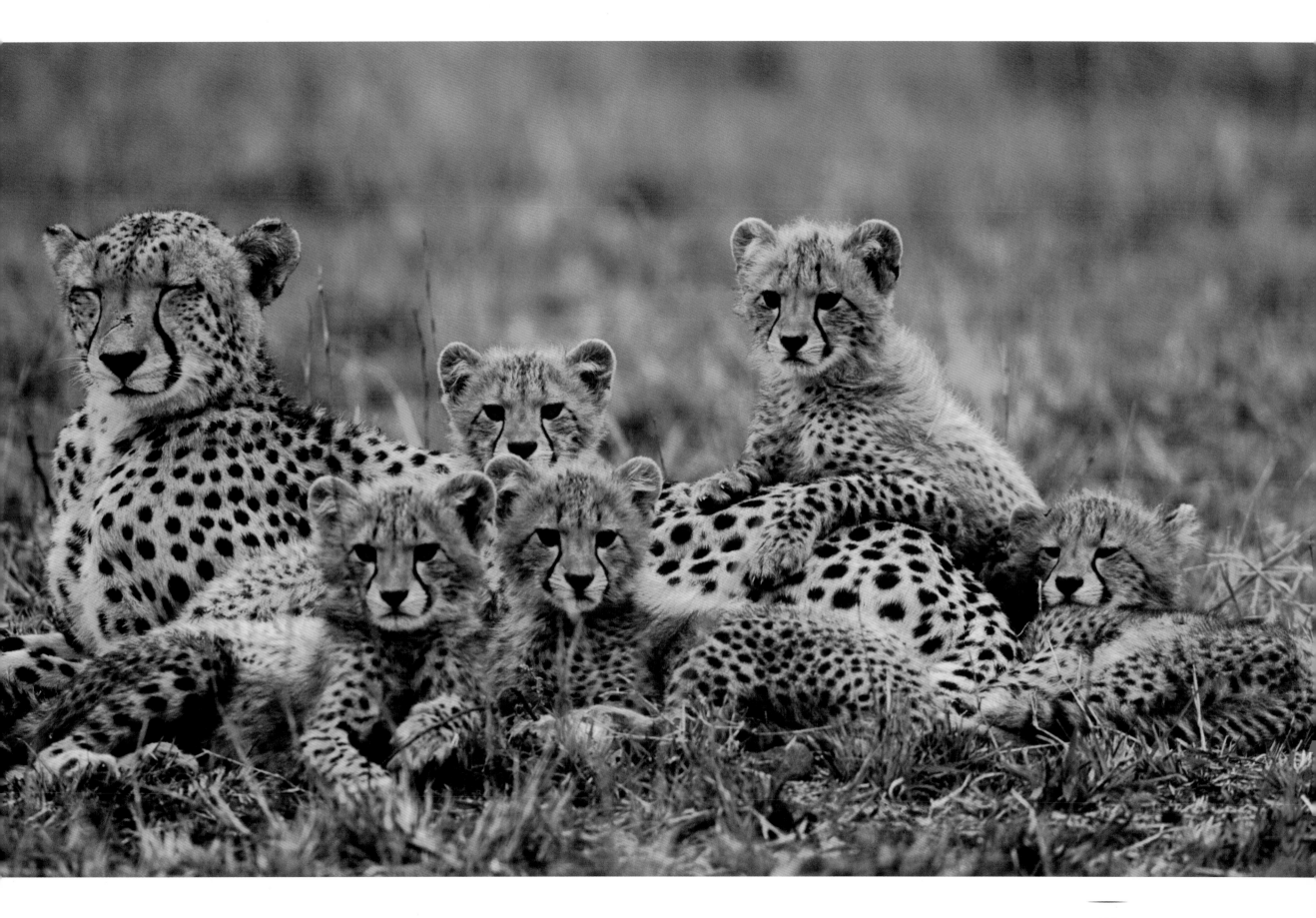

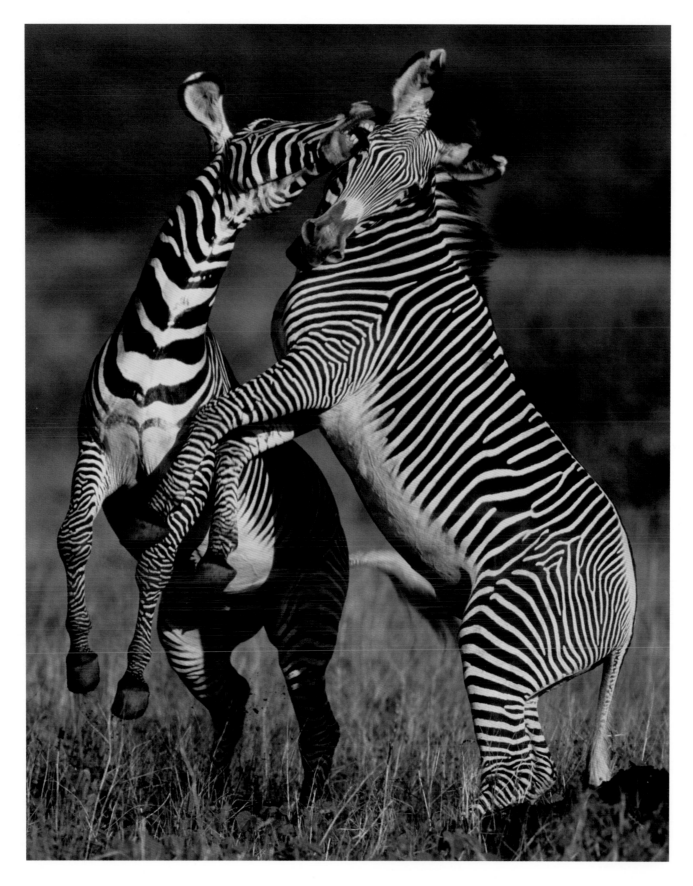

GREVY'S ZEBRA
SAMBURU NATIONAL PARK, KENYA

► IMPALA
MASAI MARA NATIONAL RESERVE, KENYA

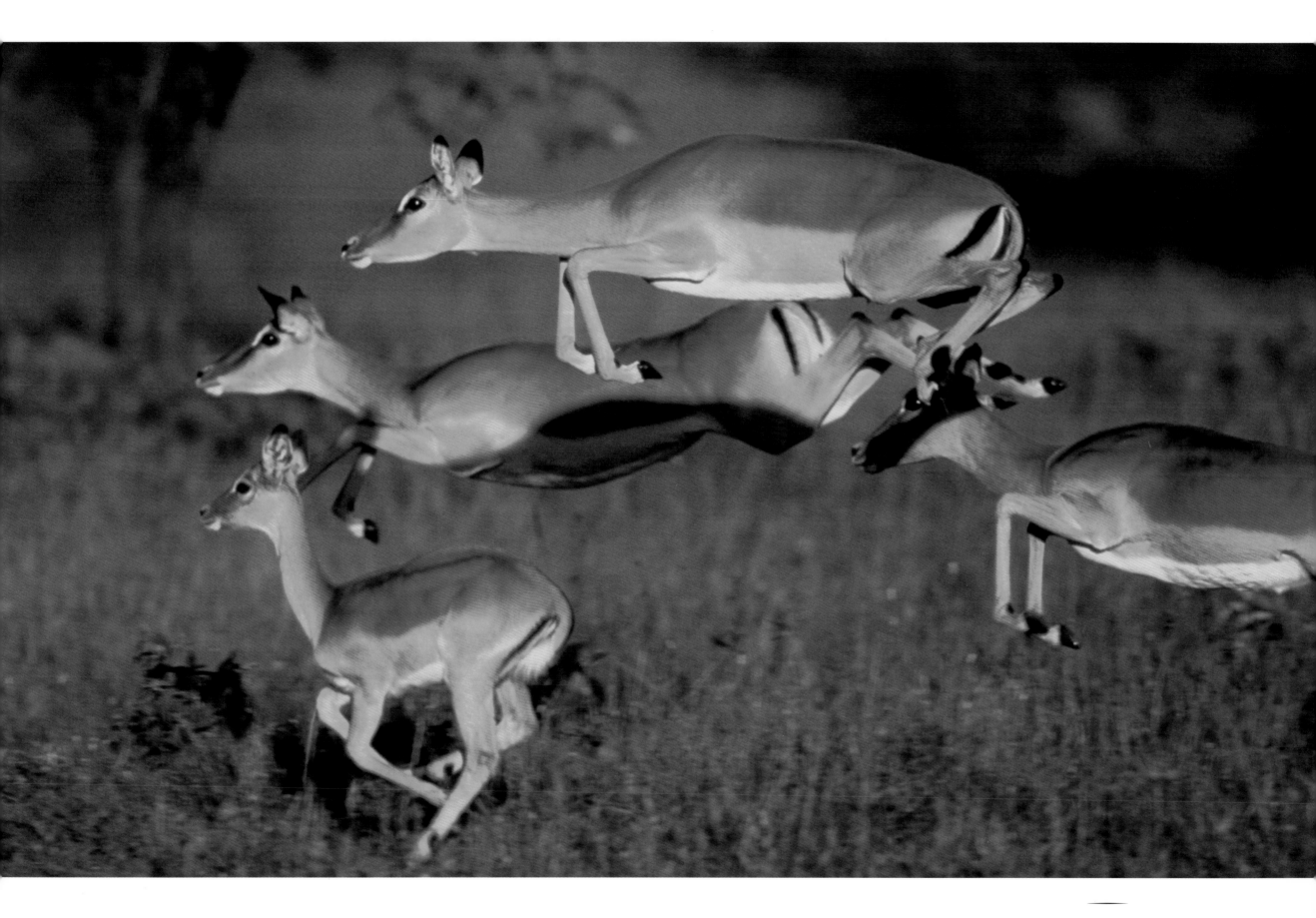

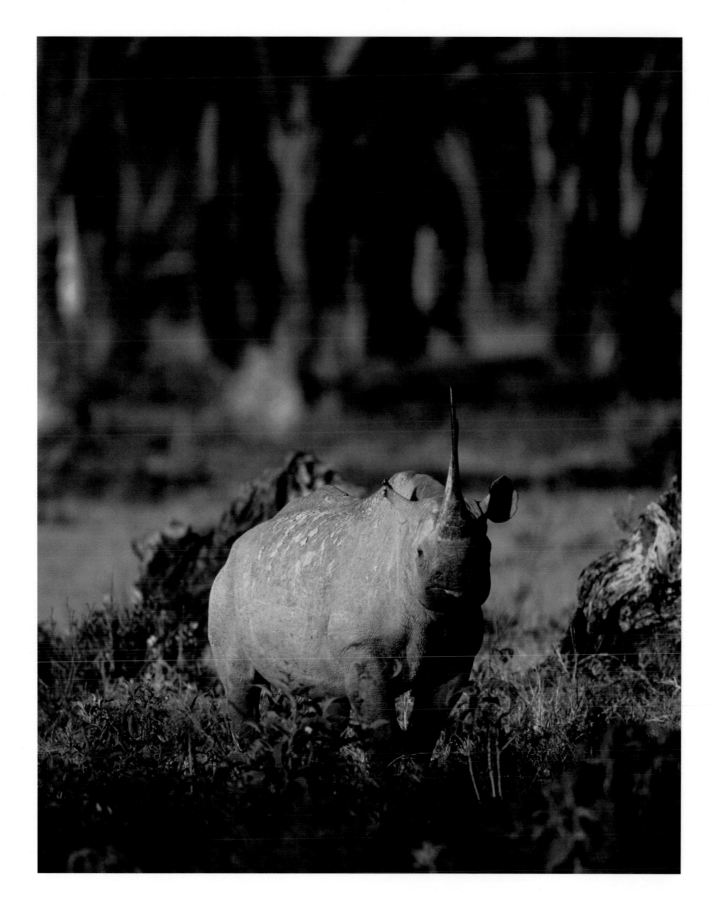

BLACK RHINOCEROS
NGORONGORO CONSERVATION AREA,
TANZANIA

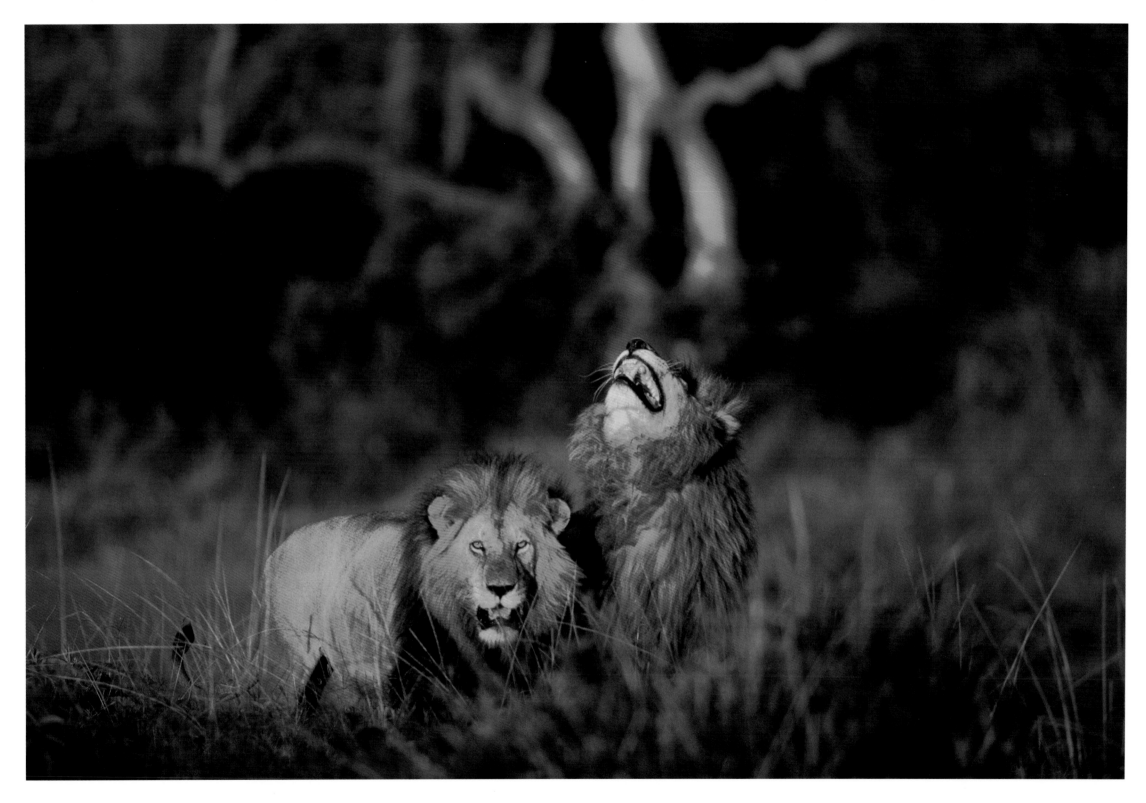

LION ⌒
MASAI MARA NATIONAL RESERVE, KENYA

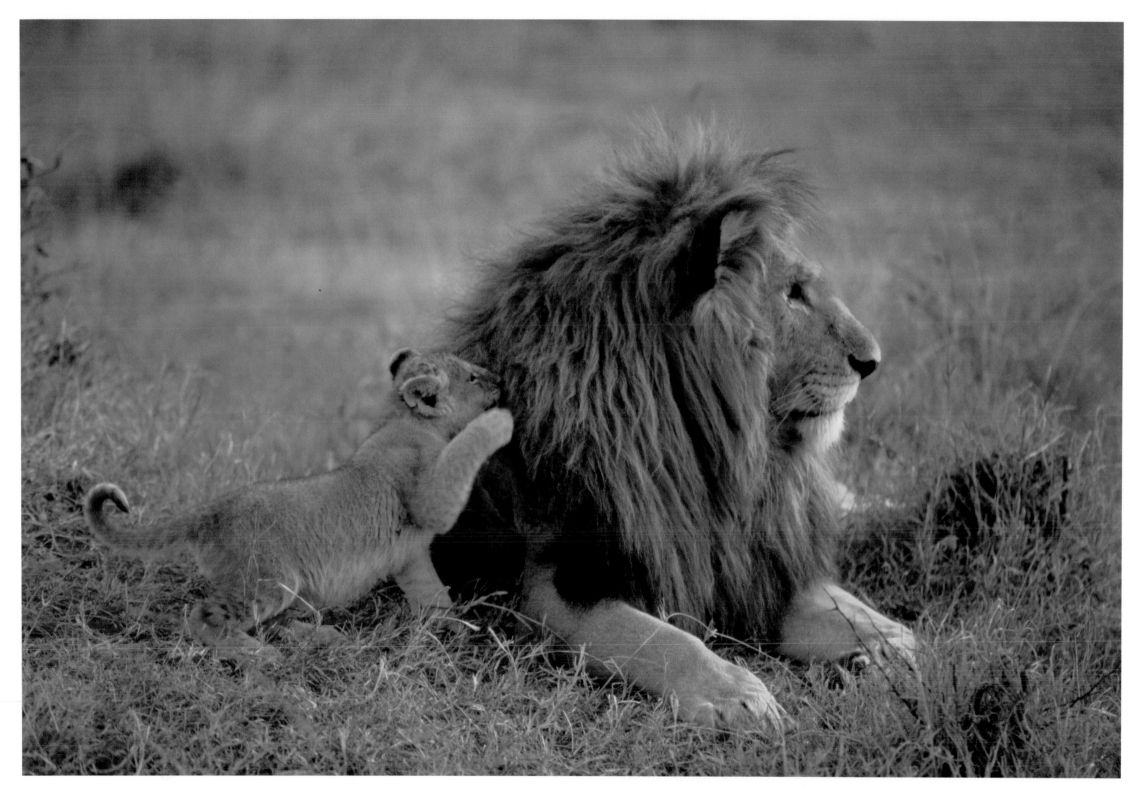

LION

MASAI MARA NATIONAL RESERVE, KENYA

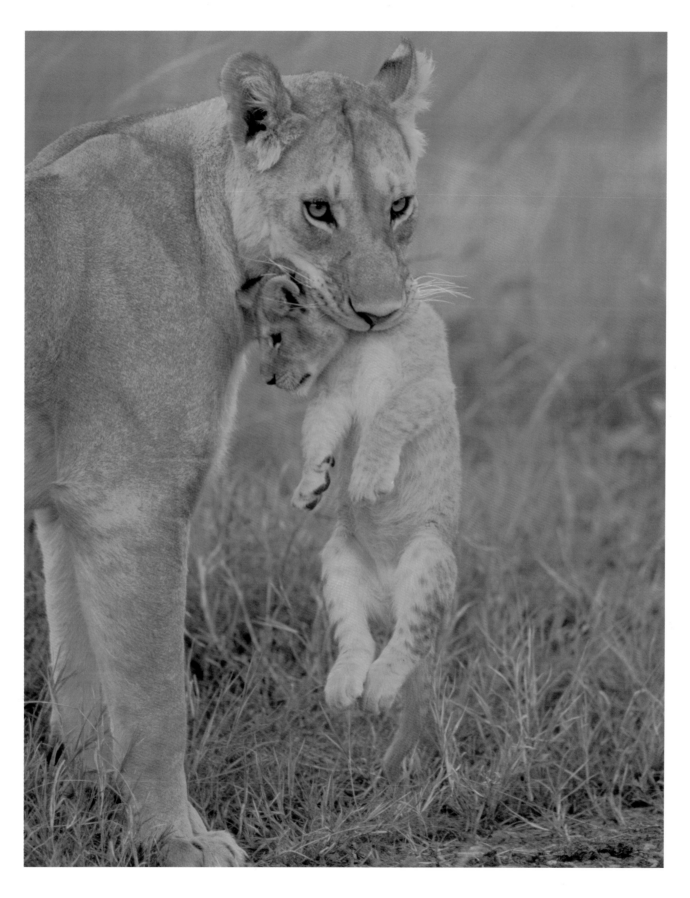

LION ～

SAVANNAH, DESERT & STEPPE

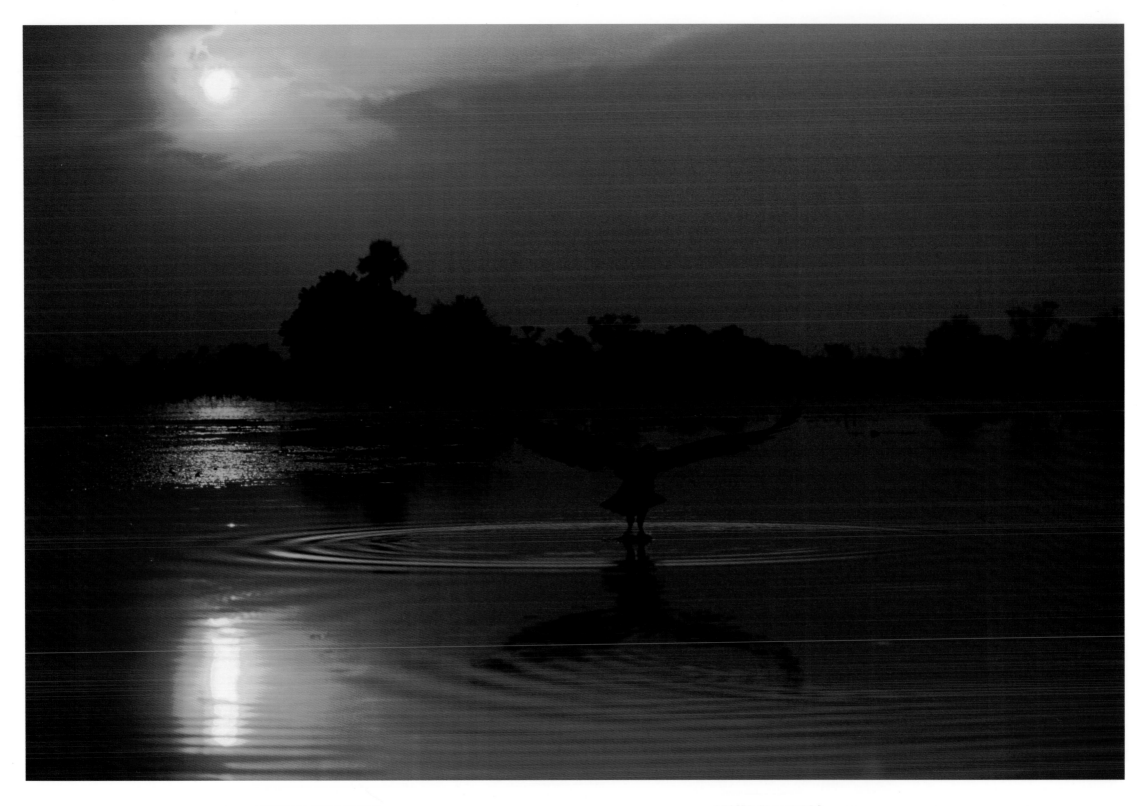

AFRICAN FISH EAGLE ⌣

Okavango Delta, Botswana

► LESSER FLAMINGO ⌣

Lake Magadi, Kenya

THE LIVING WILD

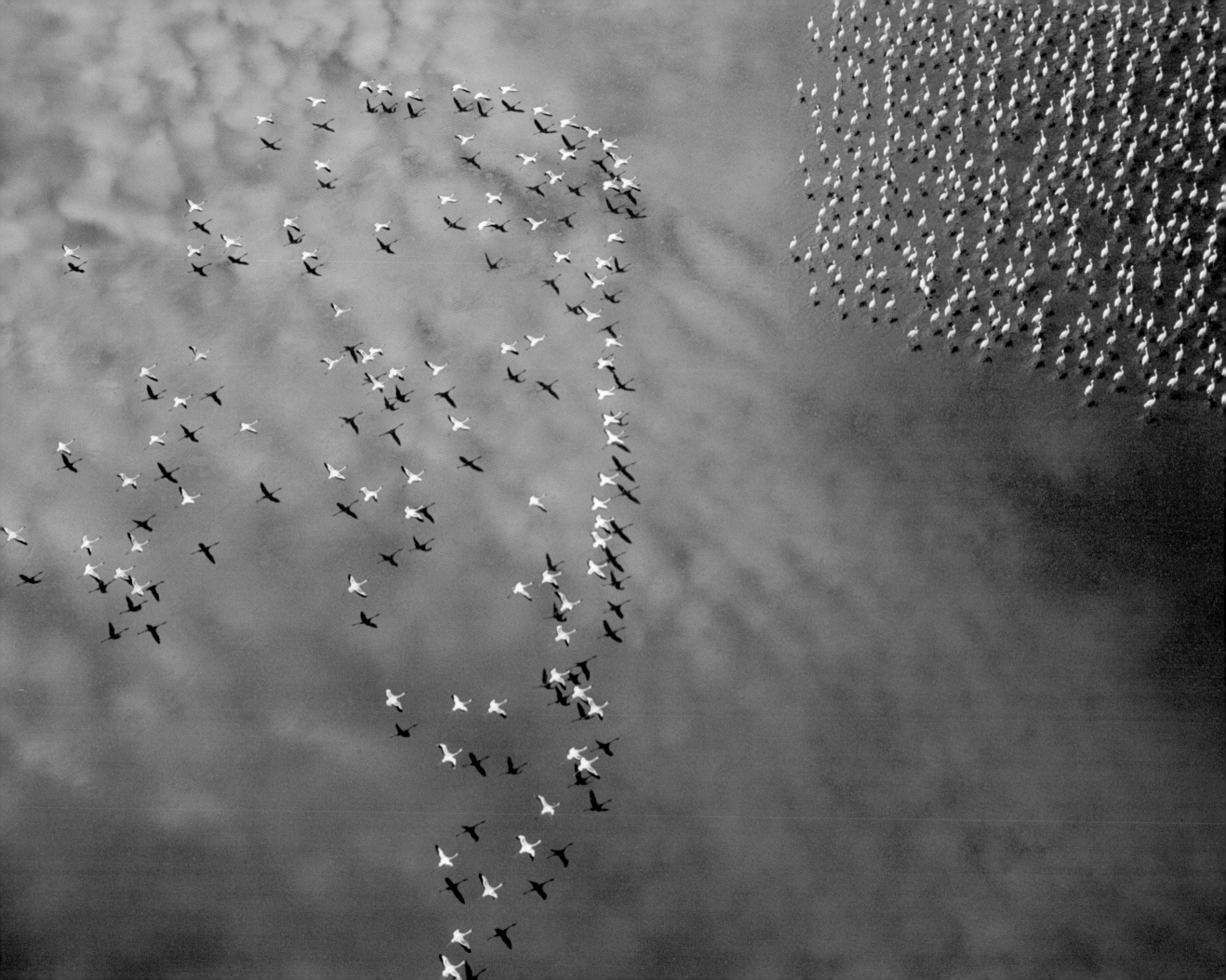

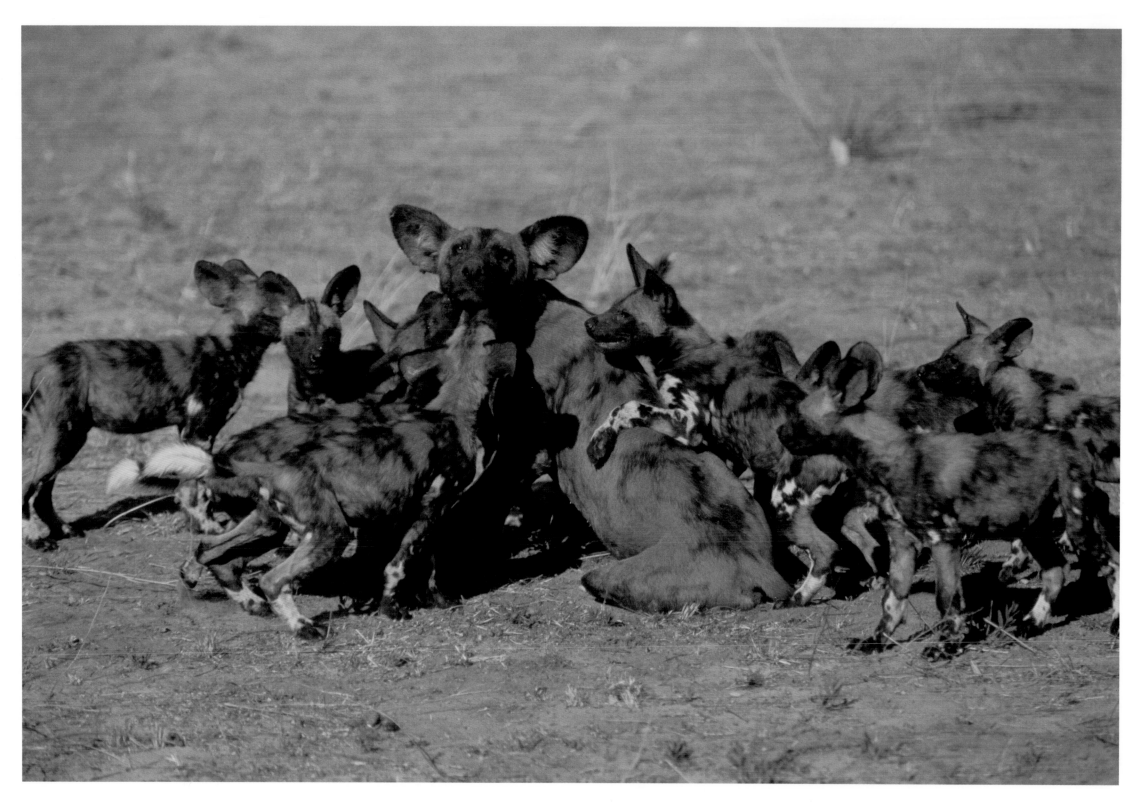

WILD DOG ﹏
KWANDO, BOTSWANA

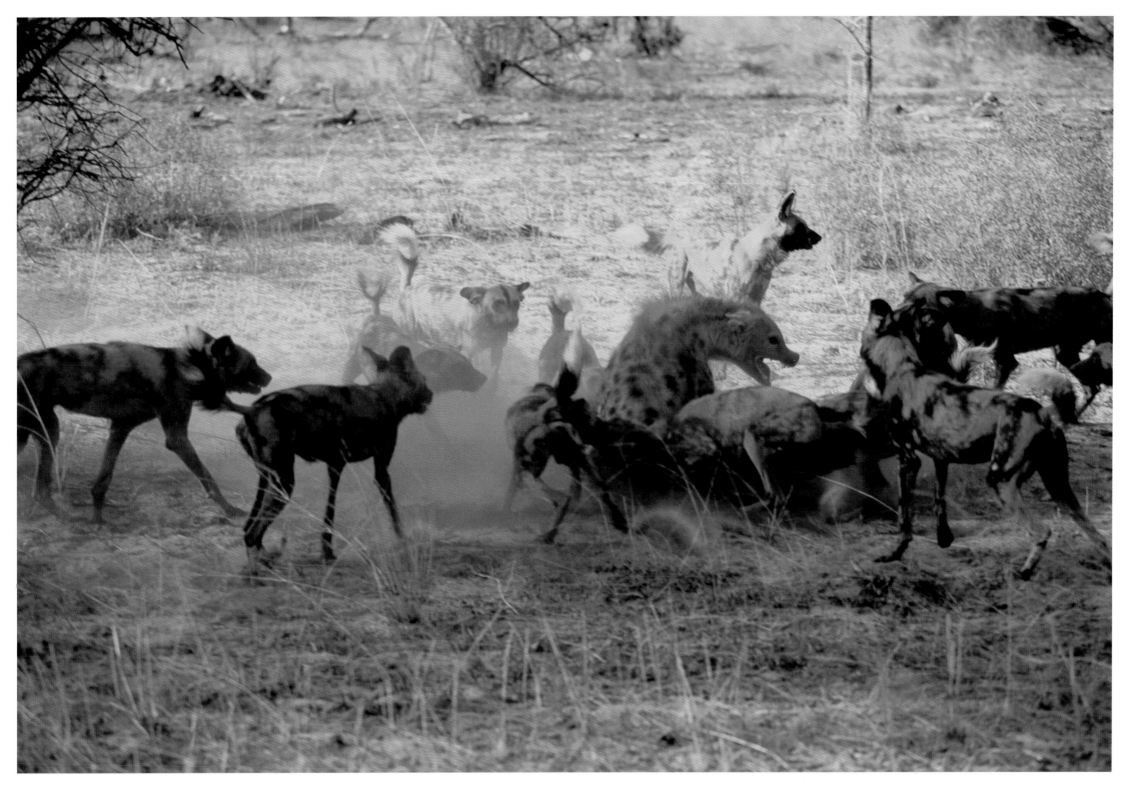

SPOTTED HYENA AND WILD DOG

Kwando, Botswana

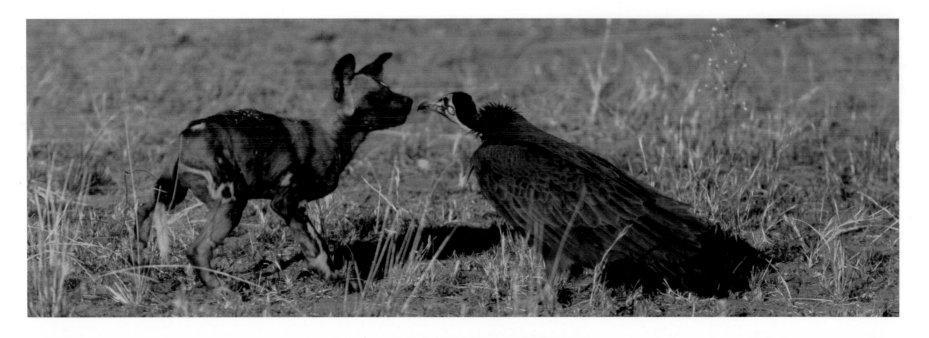

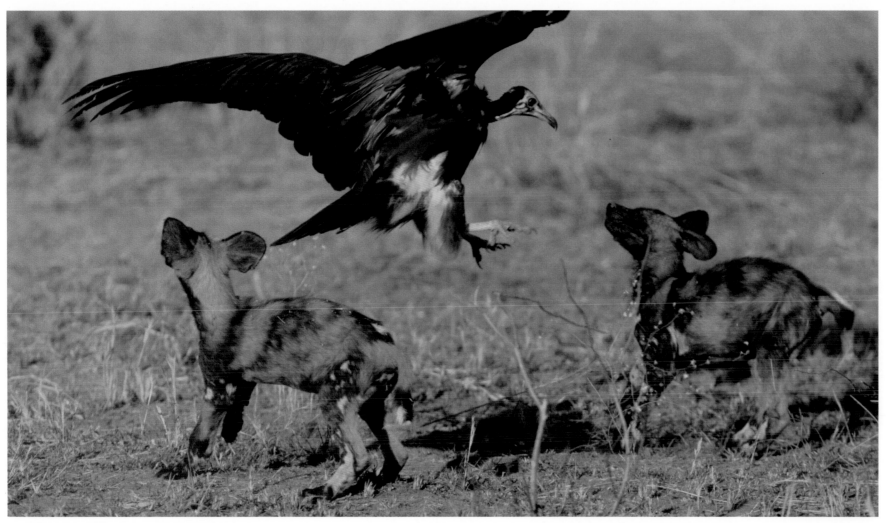

▲ AND ◄ HOODED VULTURE
AND WILD DOG ∼
KWANDO, BOTSWANA

► PRZEWALSKI'S HORSE ∼
HUSTAIN NURURU NATIONAL RESERVE,
MONGOLIA

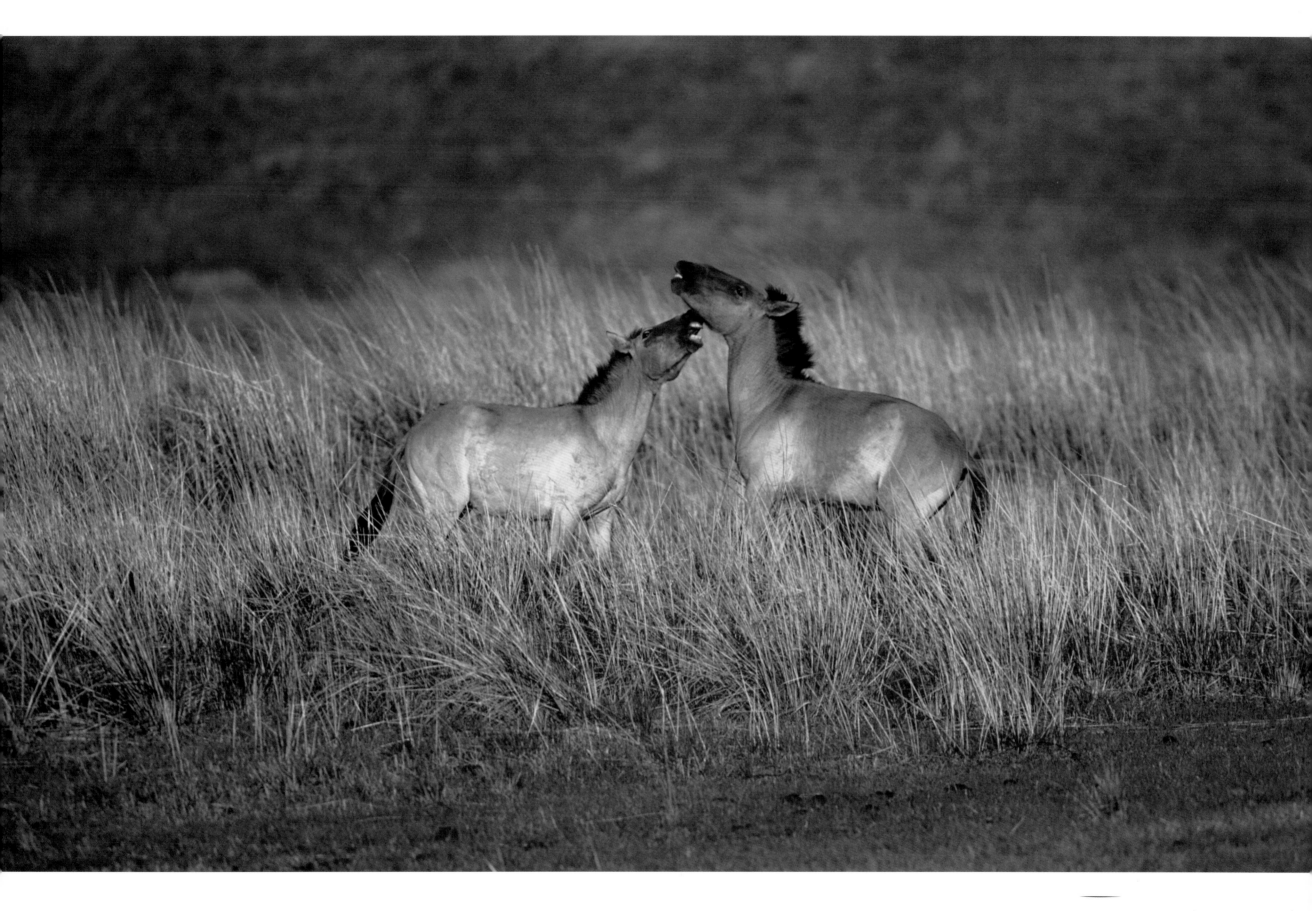

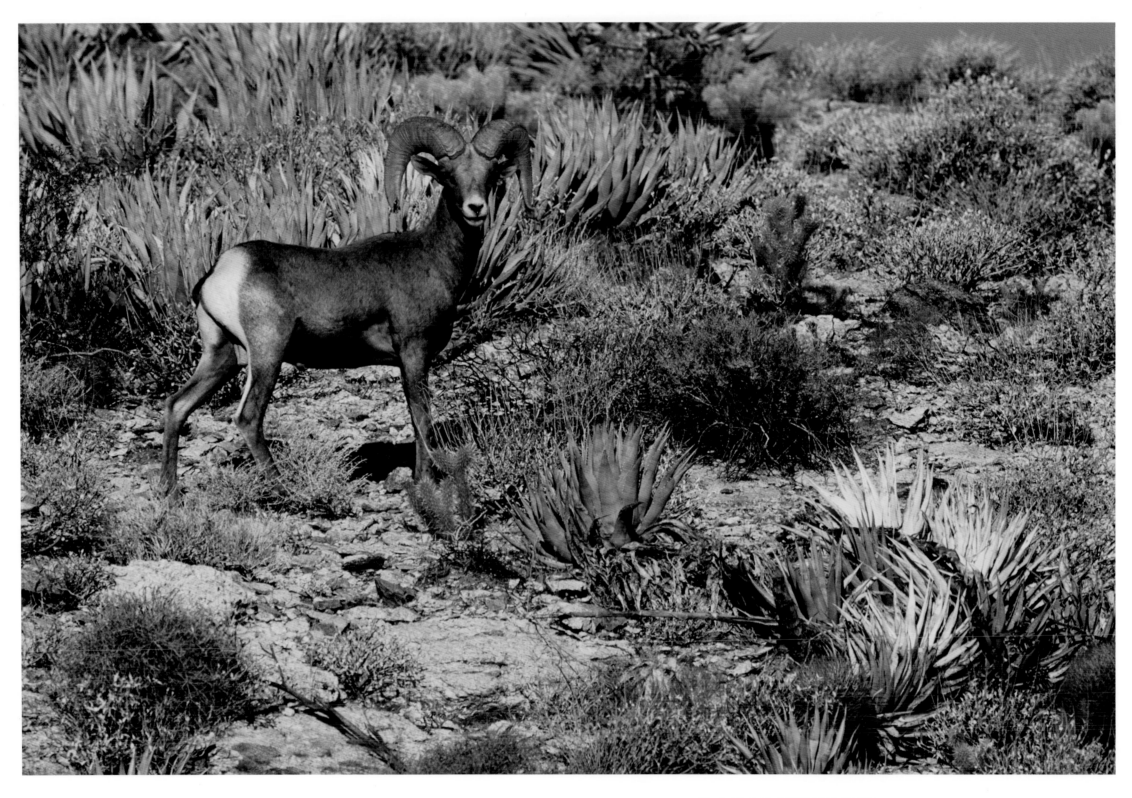

PENINSULAR BIGHORN SHEEP
Anza–Borrego Desert State Park, California, USA

THE LIVING WILD

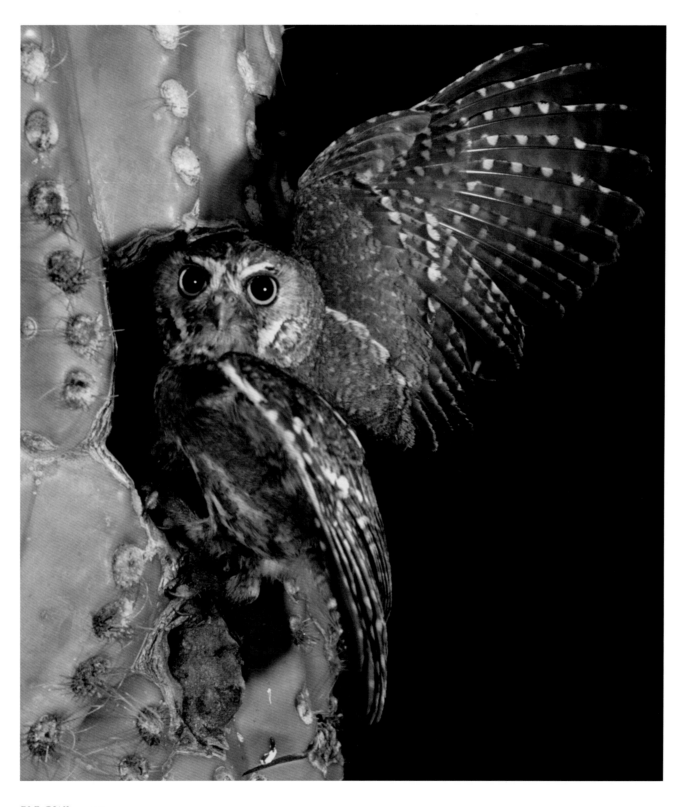

ELF OWL

Saguaro National Monument, Arizona, USA

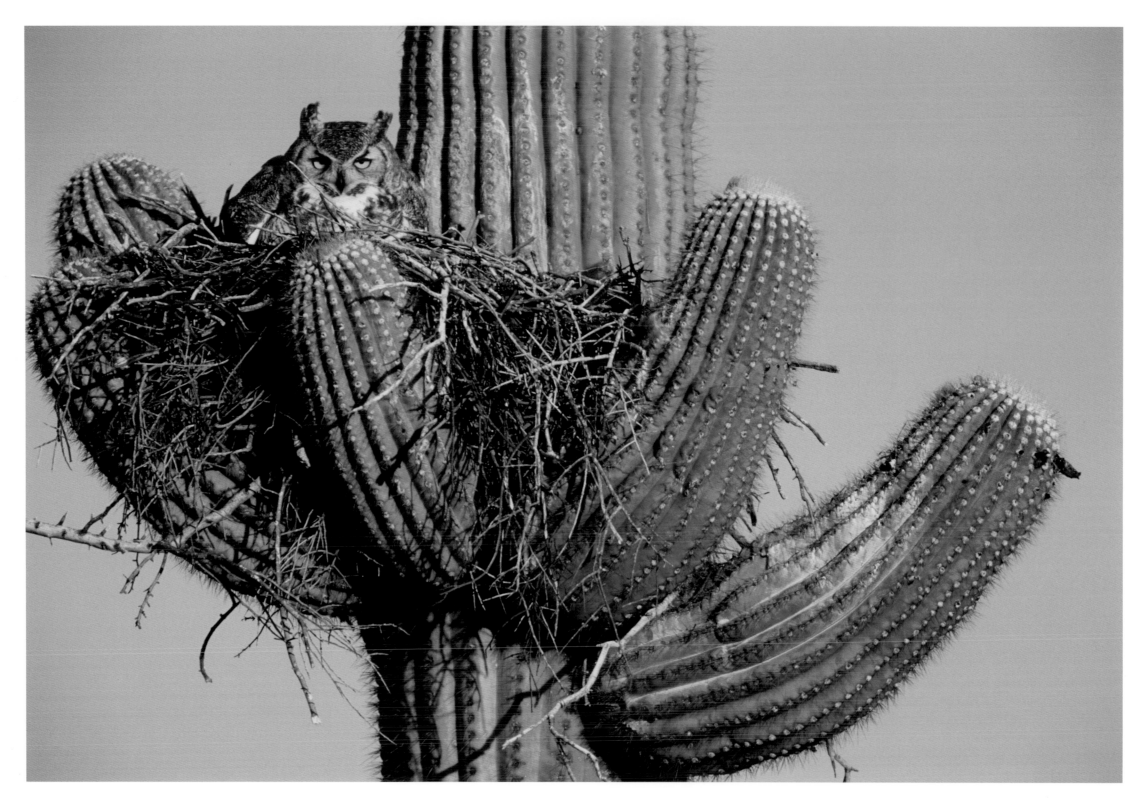

GREAT HORNED OWL

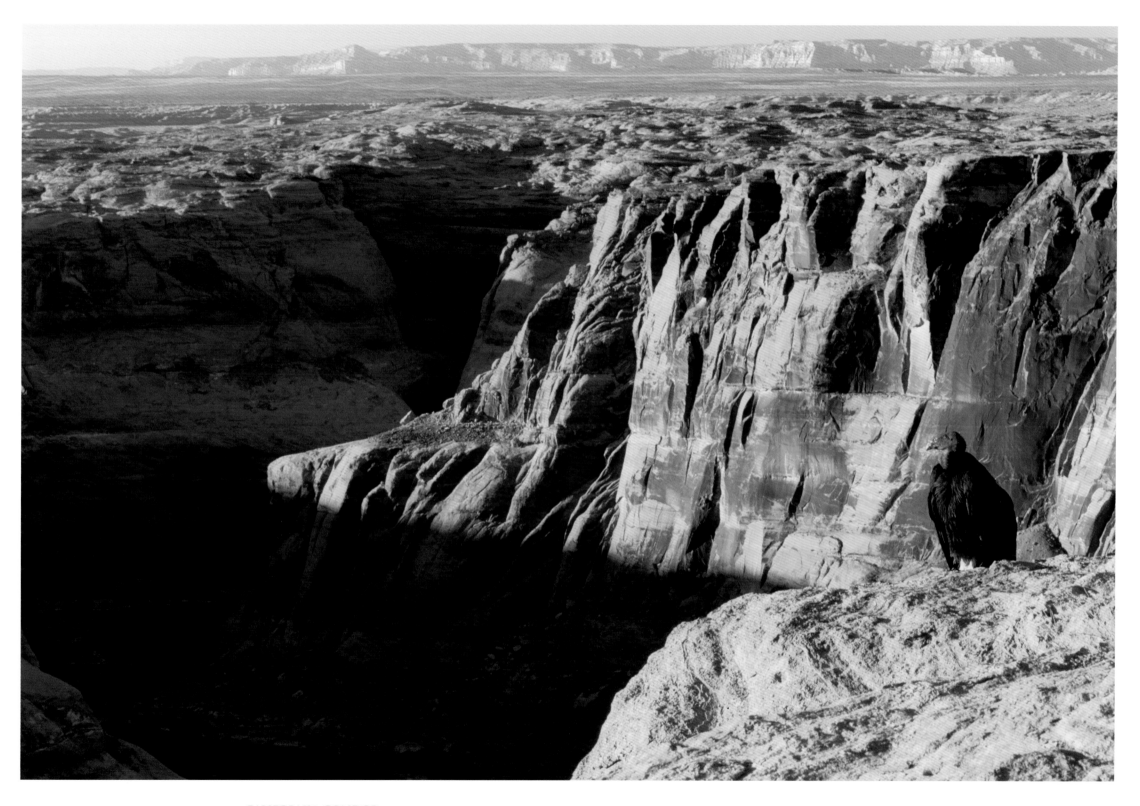

CALIFORNIA CONDOR
Colorado Plateau, Arizona, USA

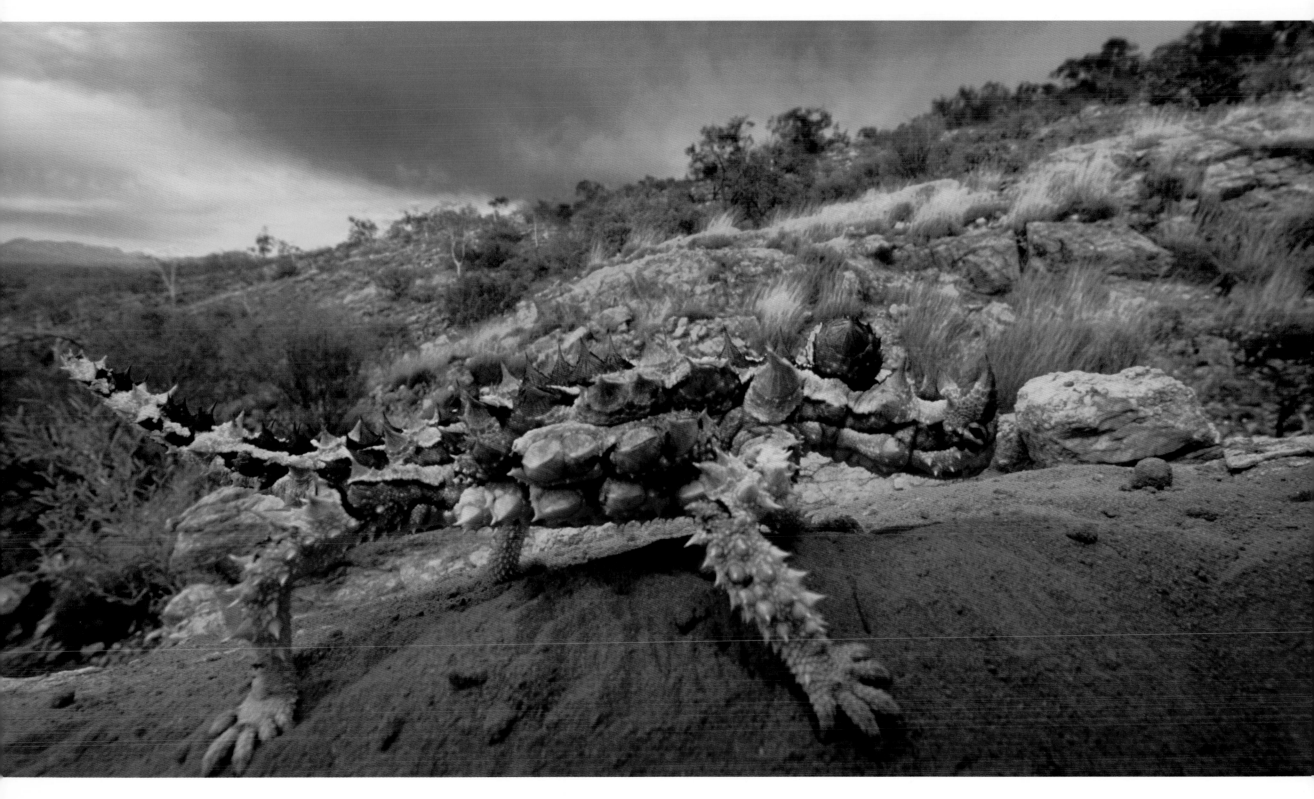

THORNY DEVIL

THE LIVING WILD

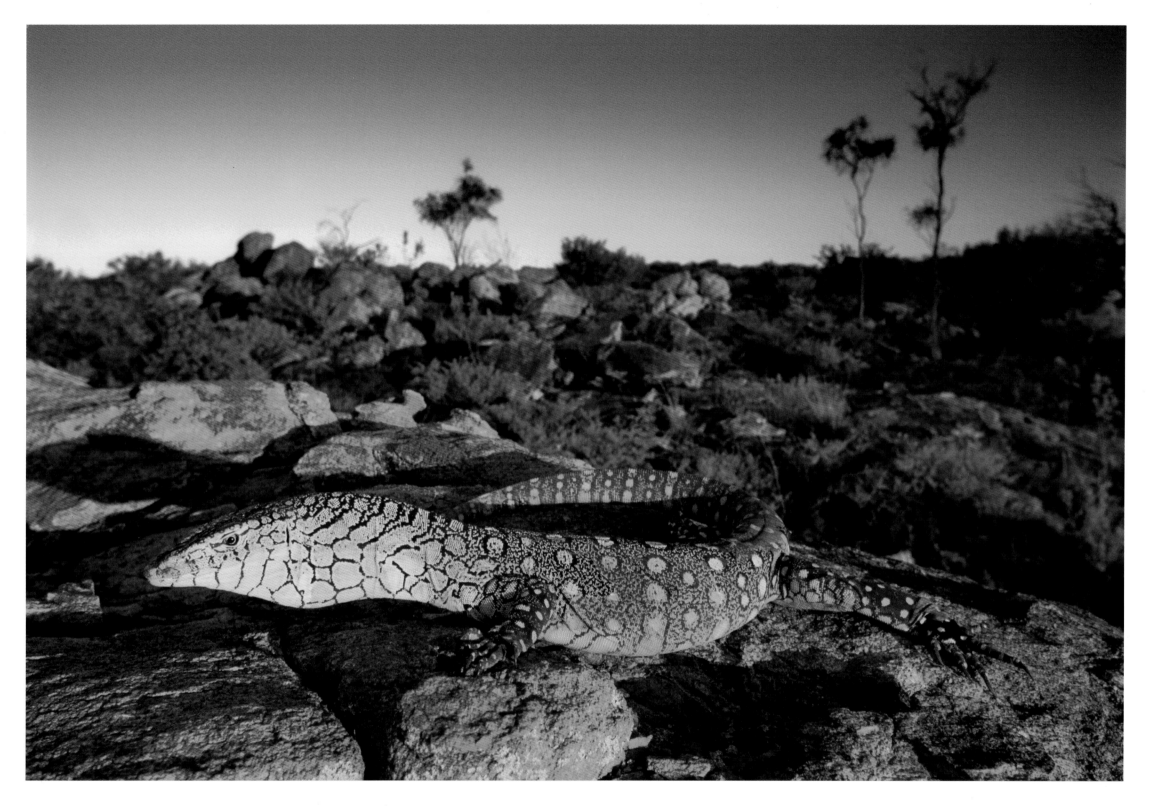

PERENTIE GOANNA

Macdonnell Ranges, Northern Territory, Australia

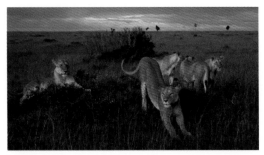

LION ⌒
(*Panthera leo*)

Lions are animals of the savannah, although they can sometimes be found in very arid environments such as the Namib or Kalahari Deserts. They typically occur from sea level up to about 5,000 meters elevation and their home ranges are 20 to 400 square kilometers. Lions may be active at any time of the day, and will even hunt during daylight hours—especially in those areas where they are protected. However, where lions are regularly persecuted by people, they may become exclusively nocturnal. Lions are well known for their inactivity; they rest for 20 to 21 hours each day. When they do hunt, it is the females who are typically the providers. Although lions may cooperate to bring down a wildebeest or zebra, much of that cooperation is perhaps inadvertent and opportunistic. Once on a kill, each lion looks out for its own interests. A particularly hungry lion may eat 50 kilograms at a single sitting.

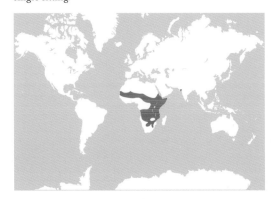

AW: A lion pride begins to stir as the last light of day illuminates them. This pride had been daytime hunters until the Masai population of the region increased dramatically. Now the lions hide during the day and hunt under the cover of darkness. For this photograph, I used a 20mm lens balanced on a beanbag on my vehicle's open window. I used a polarizing filter to bring out the clouds in the sky and a 2-stop graduated neutral density filter to provide a more even exposure.

Canon EOS-1N/RS, Canon EF 20mm lens, f/8 at 1/8 second, polarizing filter, 2-stop graduated neutral density filter, Fujichrome Velvia film

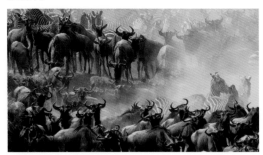

COMMON WILDEBEEST ⌒
(*Connochaetes taurinus*)

The common wildebeest or gnu is one of Africa's largest antelopes, standing almost 1.5 meters at the shoulder. Also known as the blue wildebeest, brindled gnu, or white-bearded wildebeest, *C. taurinus* is much lighter in color than the closely related black wildebeest (*C. gnou*) of South Africa. Common wildebeest are an integral part of the great migratory herds of ungulates still to be found in the Serengeti—Masai Mara of Kenya and Tanzania. Although some herds are sedentary, the vast majority of the more than 1.5 million wildebeest that throng the savannah move with the rains, seeking new pastures to graze as the seasons shift. Although wildebeest abound on these grasslands, their numbers have declined in other parts of Africa as farmers have encroached on previously undisturbed lands. The fences that farmers and ranchers build to protect their stock have, in many cases, impeded wildlife movements, with serious consequences during times of drought.

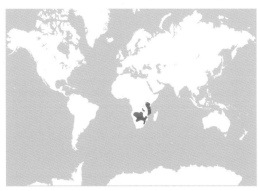

AW: The annual fall migration of wildebeest and zebra is a wildlife spectacular not to be missed. Here the migrating animals have become congested at the edge of the Mara River. It is a dangerous place for these ungulates, because Nile crocodiles (*Crocodylus niloticus*) await just below the water's surface. This scene was photographed from a high bank on the opposite side of the river. The elevated vantage point placed more animals in the same plane of focus, allowing me to use a faster shutter speed in order to freeze the motion of the restless animals.

Canon EOS-1N, Canon EF 600mm lens, f/11 at 1/250 second, Fujichrome Astia film

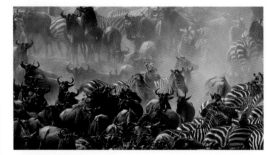

PLAINS ZEBRA ⌒
(*Equus burchelli*)

The four-million-year-old Serengeti–Masai Mara ecosystem straddles 25,000 square kilometers and is home to the greatest gathering of grazing mammals in the world today, including 200,000 plains (or Burchell's) zebra and 1.5 million common wildebeest. It has been recognized both as a biosphere reserve and as a World Heritage Site. Plains zebra live in habitats from savannah to open woodland; 90 percent of their diet is grass. While thousands may congregate during migration, zebra social organization is based on small family groups and bachelor herds. Although not considered threatened, plains zebra have declined in numbers and range due to hunting and competition with domestic livestock. The subspecies *E.b. burchelli*, formerly found in South Africa, is extinct, while Mozambique's *E.b. chapmani* is considered seriously endangered with fewer than 3,000 individuals remaining.

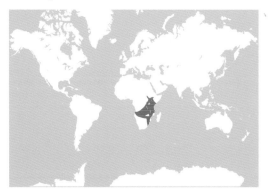

AW: Anxious migrating wildebeest waiting to cross the Mara River become more and more pressed between the crocodile-infested waters and the thousands of wildebeest arriving behind them. The compressed, agitated animals stir up a dust cloud that adds even more drama to this ageless scene.

Canon EOS-1N, Canon EF 600mm lens, f/11 at 1/250 second, Fujichrome Astia film

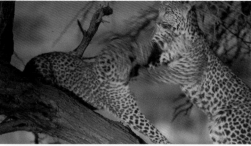

LEOPARD ⌒
(*Panthera pardus*)

Leopards are breathtakingly beautiful cats, standing up to 0.78 meter at the shoulder. Males weigh 37 to 90 kilograms, while females are somewhat smaller at 28 to 60 kilograms. Leopards are still considered common in parts of Africa, although their numbers have seen regional reductions in many areas due to human encroachment and poaching. In most of Asia, the species is now extremely rare. Subspecies throughout the Middle East and Asian subcontinent are considered to be critically endangered. Most of the Near and Middle Eastern populations number a few hundred animals; fewer than two dozen are found in Israel. The largest Asian population is in India, which has about 14,000 animals; 400 to 600 survive on Sri Lanka. In addition there are about 150 in Turkmenistan, barely 350 to 700 on the southeast Asian island of Java, and fewer than 50 in southeastern Siberia, Manchuria, and Korea.

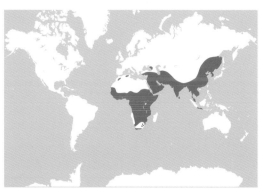

AW: Two adolescent leopard siblings engage in some lighthearted sparring. I was photographing sharp portraits of these two in the beautiful light of the setting sun when one suddenly pounced on the other. I instinctively clicked my camera at the unexpected movement. Although the light level was too low to get a sharp image, I liked the sense of motion that resulted.

Canon EOS-1N/RS, Canon EF 600mm lens, f/5.6 at 1/15 second, Fujichrome Velvia film

THE LIVING WILD
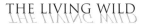

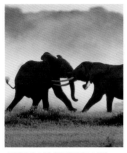
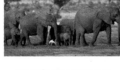
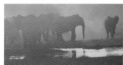
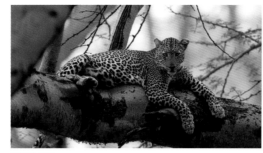

AFRICAN ELEPHANT
(*Loxodonta africana*)

Before the ivory trade decimated their numbers, 27 million elephants may have inhabited the African continent. Between 1860 and 1930, up to 100,000 elephants were killed each year—most to supply ivory for piano keys. During the first half of the twentieth century, there may still have been several million elephants, but in the 1970s the price of ivory jumped to more than US$100 per kilogram at times. By 1989 only 625,000 elephants remained, and an international ban on ivory was implemented to stem the downward spiral. With the ban in place, some populations began to increase. However, in 1997, the ivory ban was relaxed, allowing three countries to sell their stockpiles. Today, there are fewer than 600,000 elephants. Since both illegal and legal trade in ivory continues, and elephants are facing increasing competition with farmers and settlers for land, the elephant population can be expected to decline further.

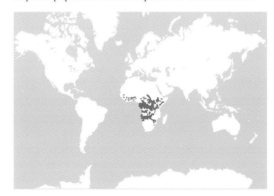

AW: Page 97 – I froze the action using a high shutter speed, underexposing to silhouette the two bulls for drama.

Canon EOS-1N, Canon EF 600mm lens, f/4 at 1/250 second, Fujichrome Astia Film

AW: Page 98 – I panned as the elephants passed by.

Canon EOS-1N, Canon EF 70–200mm lens, f/5.6 at 1/250 second, Fujichrome Velvia film

AW: Page 99 – The herd is backlit by the setting sun.

Canon EOS-3, Canon EF 600mm lens, f/16 at 1/60 second, Fujichrome Velvia film

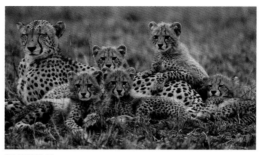

LEOPARD
(*Panthera pardus*)

Leopards are found in rainforests, riverine habitats, savannahs, woodlands, and even deserts. Although they often appear tolerant of encroachment by human settlements, their densities fall dramatically near areas of human activity, sometimes by a factor of 100. Before public opinion shifted against the fur trade, leopards were a popular target. In a single year (1968–69), an estimated 30,000 leopards were killed in East Africa, and during the 1970s leopard populations in Ethiopia, Kenya, Nambia, and Zimbabwe were reduced by 90 percent, largely due to poisoning by livestock ranchers. As people begin farming in what had been leopard habitat, conflicts often arise. Leopards patrol their territories regularly and are susceptible to poisoned baits. With less than 15 percent of leopard habitat within protected areas, conflicts between humans and leopards will only grow, and the species become increasingly marginalized.

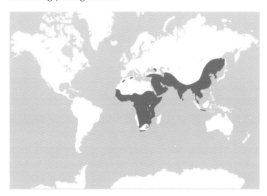

AW: I have shot thousands of leopard images over the years. Often I have had to contend with beautiful subjects in harsh light, rather than obscured subjects in great light. In this photograph, light, subject, and habitat come together to create one of my favorite images of a leopard. Had this been a sunny day, the entire composition would have been fractured by bright highlights and dark shadows, which would have made this otherwise simple composition busy and confusing.

Canon EOS-1N/RS, Canon EF 400mm lens, f/8 at 1/125 second, Fujichrome Velvia film

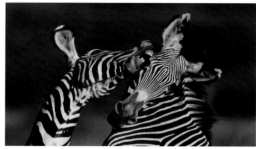

CHEETAH
(*Acinonyx jubatus*)

Cheetahs breed throughout the year, and females typically have three to five cubs, although they can have as many as eight. The cubs are reliant on their mother for 14 months, and despite her best efforts, only about 5 percent will survive to adulthood—that means that a female must have twenty cubs before she is able to raise even one to independence. This extremely low recruitment rate makes cheetahs very susceptible to population declines. Cheetahs also show little genetic variation within their population, which suggests that they went through a significant reduction, or "bottleneck," at some time in their history, potentially making them even more vulnerable to the effects of environmental disruption. Extirpated from India and much of Asia and North and East Africa, there are only an estimated 9,000 to 12,000 cheetahs in the wild. The largest population of about 2,500 is found in Namibia.

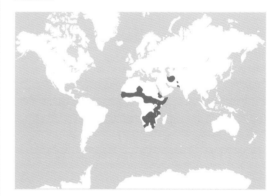

AW: A mother cheetah with five cubs has many responsibilities. The male does not participate in raising the offspring. It is the female that must provide enough food for her young and also protect them from other predators. Lions (*Panthera leo*) leopards (*Panthera pardus*), and brown hyenas (*Hyaena brunnea*) will kill the cubs if given the chance. I photographed this family on a late, cloudy afternoon. To gain a little more speed in the fading light, I pushed my Provia film 1 stop.

Canon EOS-1N, Canon EF 400mm lens, f/8 at 1/30 second, Fujichrome Provia film (pushed 1 stop)

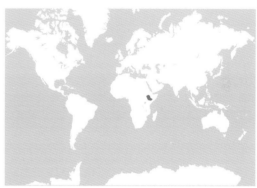

GREVY'S ZEBRA
(*Equus grevyi*)

Grevy's zebra have the narrowest stripes of any zebra; they look like walking optical illusions. They are the largest of the wild equids—only specially bred domestic horses are larger. Grevy's are found in "subdesert" habitats between the arid areas to the north favored by the African wild ass (*Equus asinus*) and wetter habitats to the south favored by plains zebra (*Equus burchelli*). They were once found in Egypt, Sudan, Somalia, Ethiopia, and Kenya; only northern Kenya still has significant numbers—probably fewer than 5,000. Loss of habitat, military activity, and poaching for their handsome skins have truncated their range and restricted most to national parks and preserves. Unlike other zebras, the key unit among Grevy's is that between female and offspring—all other groups are unstable and temporary. While females range widely in search of grazing and water, males may defend their territories year-round, vying with each other to mate with passing females.

AW: Zebras demonstrate interesting behavior when in tightly packed herds. These two were in a herd of about forty, when one bit the other's rump. The immediate response was a well-placed kick to the offender's chin. I ran several rolls of film through my camera as the encounter escalated. I first framed the fight horizontally, but switched to verticals as the zebras became more agitated. I had my driver keep moving in order to stay parallel to the zebras' ever-changing positions, while keeping the late-afternoon sun shining squarely in their faces.

Canon EOS-1N, Canon EF 600mm lens, f/8 at 1/250 second, Fujichrome Velvia film

NOTES FROM THE FIELD

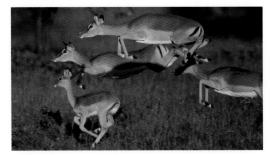

IMPALA
(Aepyceros melampus)

The impala is the only member of the genus *Aepyceros* (family Bovidae), although some have proposed classifying them with gazelles and kobs. Impala are found in open habitats, usually in woodlands and grasslands, and are highly gregarious. Females live in breeding herds of thirty to more than eighty animals, while males form herds on their own. Impalas are well known for their jumping ability—known as "pronking"—and can easily leap 3 meters vertically, covering 11 meters with each bound. Impalas are the staple diet for many of the savannah predators, including leopards (*Panthera pardus*) and lions (*Panthera leo*), and the impalas' leaping ability makes it harder for a predator to select and focus on a single animal. Impala also have a tendency to zigzag as they run, cutting in front of each other and creating a sudden, explosive mass of antelope able to confuse any would-be hunter.

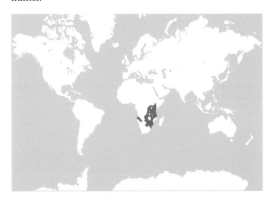

AW: This photograph represents a turning point for me. Up until this time, I had relied exclusively on manual focus when trying to film moving subjects. Just before departing for East Africa, I purchased a 600mm autofocus lens, suspecting that my reflexes were no match for the latest technology. When I spotted a herd of sprinting impala, I initiated the autofocus and panned with the movement of the animals. To my amazement, I was able to get several sharply focused frames.

Canon EOS-1N/RS, Canon EF 600mm lens, f/8 at 1/500 second, Fujichrome Velvia film (pushed 1 stop)

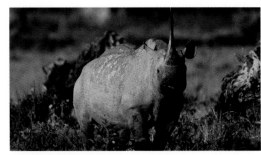

BLACK RHINOCEROS
(Diceros bicornis)

From an estimated 65,000 black rhino in Africa in 1970, only an estimated 2,400 survived in 1996. They are no longer found in the Central African Republic; Zimbabwe has only about 300 left; there are 1,000 in South Africa, 600 in Namibia, 400 in Kenya, and handfuls of individuals in a few other nations. Of seven subspecies, three are extinct, including *D. b. bicornis*, largest of the black rhinos that once lived throughout South Africa and Namibia. *D. b. brucii* of the Sudan, Ethiopia, and Somalia is also gone, as is *D. b. chobiensis* of southeastern Angola. Other subspecies number in the hundreds of individuals and may no longer be genetically viable. Several conservation plans have been implemented to protect the remaining rhinos, ranging from armed guards with a shoot-to-kill policy toward poachers, to the regular dehorning of animals—the latter may unwittingly save rhinos from poachers but make them vulnerable to predators.

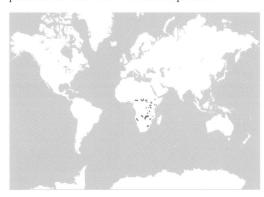

AW: A black rhino emerges from a sparse forest of acacia trees within Tanzania's Ngorongoro Crater. The crater has become a life-saving refuge for the rhinoceros, as it is easier to guard them there against poachers. After several days in the crater, the rhinoceroses' movements become fairly predictable. During the night, they sought the safety of the forest. Then, as the sun rose, they left for the plains to browse. Every morning we positioned our vehicle so that the rhinoceroses would pass close by on their way to the savannah.

Canon EOS-1N, Canon EF 600mm lens, f/5.6 at 1/60 second, Fujichrome Velvia film

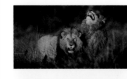
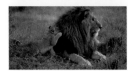
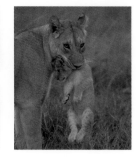

LION
(Panthera leo)

Lions are gregarious, social cats (a unique trait among felids). Related females live in permanent prides (of 4 to 37 animals), raising their cubs together, along with a number of attendant, unrelated males. Males tend to be tolerant of cubs in their pride, since they undoubtedly fathered them. When a new male takes over a pride, he invariably kills any young cubs, simultaneously eliminating future competitors and bringing females back into estrus. Since 1950, the lion population in Africa has been halved (estimates today range from 30,000 to 100,000). Lions are now rare in West Africa, and have been eliminated from much of South Africa and East Africa. When ranchers move their livestock into an area, lions are poisoned and shot out of existence. Soon they may be found only within protected parks where their low numbers raise concerns about inbreeding and the loss of genetic diversity.

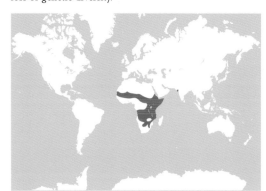

AW: All pages – Lions are excellent subjects for photography, illustrating so many different concepts—"regalness," "power," and even "tenderness."

Page 105 – Canon EOS-1N, Canon EF 70–200mm lens, f/5.6 at 1/60 second

Page 106 – Canon EOS-1N/RS, Canon EF 70–200mm lens, f/4 at 1/60 second

Page 107 – Canon EOS-1N, Canon EF 400mm lens, f/8 at 1/125 second

All pages – Fujichrome Velvia film

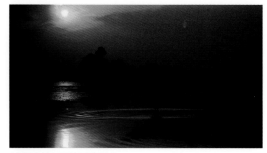

AFRICAN FISH EAGLE
(Haliaeetus vocifer)

With a wingspan of 2.1 meters, the African fish eagle is an imposing figure in the skies. Adult eagles have chestnut underparts, shoulders, and thighs, while their heads, necks, chests, backs, and tails are white. Their flight feathers are black. Although most African fish eagles are seen by lakes and rivers, immature birds may be forced from such prime wetlands to forage in far less suitable habitats, including dry-land regions where they must scavenge the remains of lion (*Panthera leo*) or leopard (*Panthera pardus*) kills. The fish eagle hunts like an osprey (*Pandion haliaetus*), gliding out over the water with its feet extended to snag fish, such as tilapia, cichlids, or nile perch (*Lates niloticus*). In addition to fish, the eagles also feed on ducks, young flamingos, shorebirds, lizards, and turtles. On occasion they will steal fish from herons, pelicans, and even kingfishers.

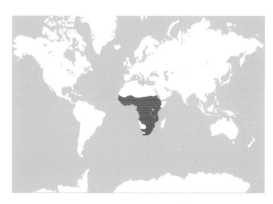

AW: While staying at a lodge in the Okavango Delta, I observed a rather tame African fish eagle perched in a tree overlooking a small dock. Late each afternoon, the eagle frequently dove for, and caught, fish that were attracted by the lights lining the dock. For this photograph, I simply calculated my exposure by manually spot reading the light in the sky to the left of the setting sun. In addition, I triggered a flash to partly illuminate the silhouetted bird.

Canon EOS-1N, Canon EF 70–200mm lens, f/16 at 1/250 second, Fujichrome Provia film

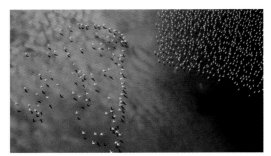

LESSER FLAMINGO
(*Phoenicopterus minor*)

Lesser flamingos flock to Kenya's Lake Magadi. Fed by hot springs that spew forth boiling water and calcium carbonate, this soda lake is an inhospitable environment. Daytime temperatures can exceed 65°C. However, the caustic waters do support algae and abundant crustaceans, and these in turn attract flamingos. Despite such spectacles of color, Africa's flamingos are facing dramatic population declines (both lesser and greater flamingos [*P. ruber roseus*] have declined by 40 percent in the last 15 years). The vast salt pans that support their breeding colonies have been drying up before the chicks are fledged. Some colonies have lost hundreds of thousands of chicks. In many areas the colonies are failing to reproduce at all. The reasons behind these failures are unknown but may be linked to global warming. In other areas, river diversion projects may be responsible for altering water discharge and evaporation rates, with devastating results.

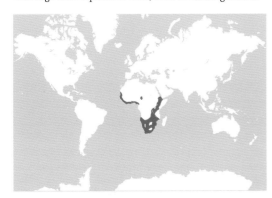

AW: Along Kenya's Rift Valley lie a series of ancient lakes that are home to hundreds of thousands of flamingos. The flamingos feed on tiny shrimplike organisms that thrive in the lake's caustic, alkaline waters. From an ultralight, I was able to get an incredible view as a flock of flamingos took to the air. I like this photograph, because it presents an interesting combination of texture, pattern, and perspective.

Canon EOS-1N, Canon EF 70–200mm lens, f/4 at 1/500 second, Fujichrome Velvia film

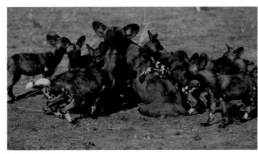

WILD DOG
(*Lycaon pictus*)

Wild dogs have long faced persecution from people. In the past, entire packs were routinely shot because ranchers believed they were indiscriminate killers of livestock and prized game animals. Wild dogs have also been marginalized by habitat losses and diseases spread by domestic animals. Their need for large home ranges makes them particularly hard to protect. The dogs no longer occur in North Africa, and they occur only sporadically in West and Central Africa, where the surviving populations are unlikely to be viable over the long term. They have also been eradicated from South Africa, except for small numbers in Kruger National Park. The largest continuous population, of about 1,000 animals, is found in Tanzania's Selous Game Reserve, with 300 to 600 occurring in Zimbabwe. There are about 300 in captivity. Once largely ignored by researchers and tourists alike, wild dogs are now attracting international attention.

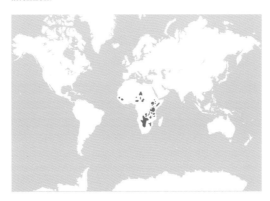

AW: Privilege has its drawbacks, as evidenced when an alpha female is besieged by her eleven demanding pups. When most pack members head out on hunting forays, one or two adults remain behind to protect the young. When the hunters return with the kill in their stomachs, the pups and their babysitters beg for food, initiating a regurgitation reflex and thereby ensuring food for all.

Canon EOS-3, Canon EF 70–200mm lens, f/8 at 1/125 second, Fujichrome Velvia film

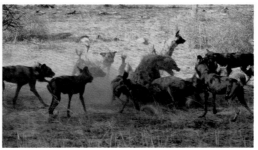

SPOTTED HYENA
(*Crocuta crocuta*)

Spotted hyenas and wild dogs (sometimes called Cape or African hunting dogs) share much of their range, although wild dogs are far rarer. While the spotted hyena population may be as high as one million (with estimates ranging from 100,000 to a million), only 2,000 to 5,000 wild dogs survive in Africa. On the undisturbed savannah, spotted hyenas are often the most plentiful of the large carnivores. Wild dogs are the smaller of the two species, weighing 17 to 36 kilograms, compared to 50 to 86 kilograms for the hyenas. Usually when hyenas and wild dogs come into conflict at a kill, it is the hyenas who easily win. Only when a lone hyena is outnumbered is the outcome likely to favor the smaller of the two predators. Although hyenas have earned a somewhat unfair reputation as scavengers, they are, in fact, efficient predators in their own right. Lions (*Panthera leo*) are more likely to scavenge hyena kills than vice versa.

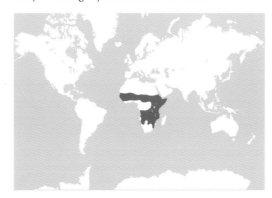

AW: An inexperienced spotted hyena suffers the consequences of having wandered too close to an active wild dog den. The ever-alert adult dogs immediately gave chase and easily caught the larger predator. After delivering several savage, chastising bites to the hyena's hindquarters, the dogs allowed the wounded animal to limp off into the surrounding forest.

Canon EOS-3, Canon EF 70–200mm lens, f/8 at 1/500 second, Fujichrome Velvia film

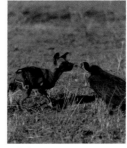

HOODED VULTURE
(*Necrosyrtes monachus*)

The hooded vulture is the smallest of Africa's vultures; its wingspan is still a large 1.7 meters. The dark brown bird has a pink face and foreneck that turn bright red when the vulture is excited. They are fairly common scavengers and will wait patiently to gain access to a kill. Their small size makes them ill equipped to compete with larger vultures at a kill, so they tend to finish off what the other birds leave behind. The presence of predators, such as wild dogs, often attracts the attention of hooded vultures. They will also follow cattle and goat herds. Vultures are not the only animals that wild dogs may have to share their kills with. The dogs are outweighed seven to one by lionesses (*Panthera leo*) and two to one by spotted hyenas (*Crocuta crocuta*). Where lions are abundant, wild dogs are usually scarce.

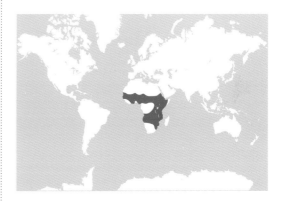

AW: Page 112 (top) – Hooded vultures scavenge scraps of meat around wild dog dens. For several days, we watched as wild dog pups chased, and then were chased by, the vultures. As the pups mature, the vultures become much more respectful.

AW: Page 112 (bottom) – Annoyed by constant harassment, a hooded vulture flies up, trying to land with open talons on one of its tormenters. The startled pups run, only to return for more mischief once the vulture has landed.

Both – Canon EOS-3, Canon EF 600mm lens, f/8 at 1/500 second, Fujichrome Velvia film

NOTES FROM THE FIELD

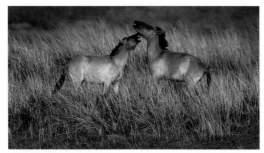

PRZEWALSKI'S HORSE
(*Equus caballus przewalskii*)

Przewalski's horse is the only wild horse to survive into modern times. Once common throughout Kazakhstan, Mongolia, and southern Siberia, they were all but eliminated by the mid-twentieth century by hunting and competition with domestic animals. The last reliable sighting in the wild was in 1968. To save them from extinction, biologists turned to captive wild horses. From an ancestral group of 13, the captive population grew to 1,200. In 1992, 16 were returned to Mongolia to be reintroduced into Hustain Nururu National Reserve, in what was to be the first of several reintroductions. In 1993 the first foal was born in the wild. The goal is to establish a self-sustaining wild population of 500 horses. Despite early successes, there are concerns that prolonged captive breeding may have reduced genetic diversity to the extent that long-term survival may be compromised; only time will tell.

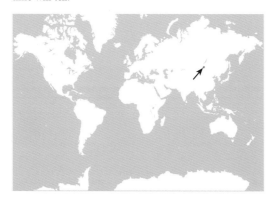

AW: Strong and spirited, wild Przewalski's horse (also known as Takhi) stallions challenge each other on the Mongolian steppe. Since their reintroduction into the wild, these horses are often confronted by packs of wolves trying to separate the young colts from the rest of the herd. I photographed these two animals from a hidden location atop a grassy knoll using a 600mm lens.

Canon EOS-1N, Canon EF 600mm lens, f/5.6 at 1/125 second, Fujichrome Velvia film

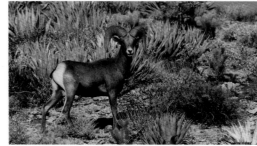

PENINSULAR BIGHORN SHEEP
(*Ovis canadensis cremnobates*)

Restricted to western North America, there may have been two million bighorn sheep before Europeans arrived. Six subspecies survive: Rocky Mountain (*O. c. canadensis*), California (*O. c. californiana*), Nelson (*O. c. nelsoni*), Mexican (*O. c. mexicani*), Weem's (*O. c. weemsi*), and Peninsular bighorn (*O. c. cremnobates*). The subspecies *O. c. auduboni*, formerly found in the Black Hills of South Dakota, was eradicated by hunting and competition with livestock. There are about 27,500 Rocky Mountain bighorns in the western mountain ranges, and 10,500 California bighorn. Of the four desert subspecies (collectively about 20,000), the rarest is the Peninsular bighorn, estimated at fewer than 300. Anza-Borrego Desert State Park was established in 1933, partly to protect this rare sheep. While Peninsular bighorn numbered more than 1,100 in 1979, their decline has been attributed to development, poaching, predation, and the introduction of diseases by domestic livestock.

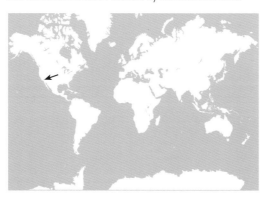

AW: The Peninsular subspecies of bighorn sheep (*O. c. cremnobates*) is rapidly decreasing in numbers throughout much of its traditional range. Developments such as golf courses are replacing wintering grounds. Researchers suspect an increased cougar (*Felis concolor*) population is also taking its toll. As I photographed these bighorn, I was amazed to see them eat cacti without being punctured by the razor-sharp spines. As long as I remained downslope from these majestic sheep, they remained relaxed, permitting me within 30 meters.

Canon EOS-3, Canon EF 400mm lens, f/11 at 1/60 second, Fujichrome Velvia film

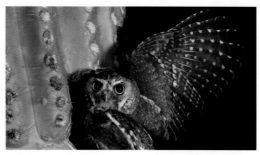

ELF OWL
(*Micrathene whitneyi*)

The petite elf owl—roughly the size of a large sparrow—has a limited distribution in desert lowlands, sycamore woodlands, and riparian habitats. They are completely nocturnal in habit and, as befits their small size, they hunt insects, centipedes, scorpions, and small lizards or birds. During the day they remain hidden in cavities within trees or cacti. Breeding takes place during early summer (May–June), and the females lay between two and five eggs. The owls are still fairly abundant in Arizona, but have been largely extirpated from California. The expansion of agriculture into shrubland and desert regions, river diversion projects, and dams have all taken their toll on the owls' habitats. Although resident in some areas, most owls leave the more northerly part of their range to spend the winter in Mexico.

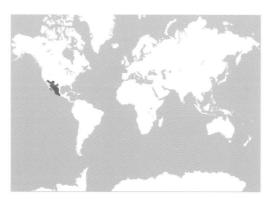

AW: Elf owls are tiny owls (15 centimeters high) that opportunistically move into the former nest cavities of gila woodpeckers (*Melanerpes uropygialis*), most often in saguaro cactus. While desert temperatures occasionally soar to 50°C, the owls are able to remain comfortably cool deep within the insulated trunk of the cactus. I photographed this owl from a stepladder placed 9 meters from its nest.

Canon F3, Canon EF 400mm lens, Canon Extender EF 1.4x, f/16 at 1/4 second, Fujichrome 50 film

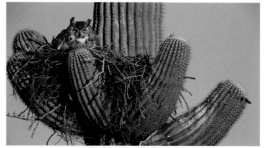

GREAT HORNED OWL
(*Bubo virginianus*)

Great horned owls are large reddish brown or gray birds, approximately 46 to 63 centimeters long with a wingspan of 0.9 to 1.5 meters. Female owls are 10 to 20 percent larger than their mates. They are named after their prominent "horns" or "ear tufts"—actually feathers unrelated to hearing. Owls are efficient hunters, diving to the ground from their perches to catch small mammals, birds, and even fairly large prey such as turkeys, herons, and young alligators. They have a broad distribution throughout the Americas, and range from dense forests to deserts, and from grasslands into urban areas. Of the twelve recognized subspecies of great horned owls, ten are found in North America. Territories of about 2 square kilometers are maintained by pairs, and although males and females only associate with each other during the breeding season, the same pairs may endure for many years.

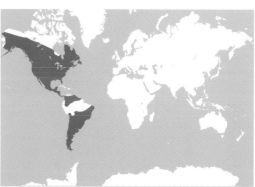

AW: Great horned owls have a widely dispersed range extending from the Arctic Circle to Patagonia. Like other owls, they do not build their own nests but move into the abandoned nests of other species. In this image, a great horned owl has nested in a former black hawk (*Buteogallus anthracinus*) nest located on a giant saguaro cactus. I photographed the owl with a 600mm lens. I deliberately avoided direct eye contact as I was mounting my lens on the tripod. Owls are easily intimidated, and if you stare at them, often they will take flight.

Canon EOS-1N, Canon EF 600mm lens, f/11 at 1/30 second, Fujichrome Velvia film

THE LIVING WILD

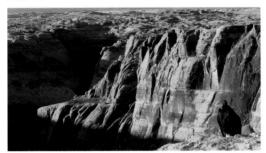

CALIFORNIA CONDOR
(*Gymnogyps californianus*)

California condors once ranged across much of western North America, from British Columbia to northern Baja California, and even east into Florida. They occurred in the Pacific Coast region until the 1800s and in Baja until the 1930s. They were declared extinct in the wild in 1987 following the capture of the last wild individuals for captive breeding programs. Their decline has been linked to shooting, capture, egg collecting, poisoning, impacts from pesticides and disturbance, and habitat loss. They lay a single egg every other year and their young do not become independent until at least a year old; they do not breed until six or eight years of age, which gives them an extremely low recruitment rate. The goal of the reintroduction program is to establish two geographically distinct, self-sustaining wild populations—one in Los Padres National Forest, the other along the Colorado River Plateau—each numbering at least 100 birds.

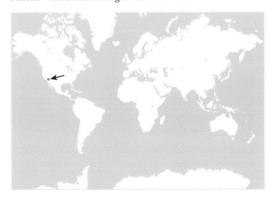

AW: The California condor, once extinct in the wild, is now being gradually reintroduced. More than 50 birds now survive in the wild, with a little over 100 still in captivity. One of the challenges of releasing captive-bred condors is that they show little fear of humans. In this photograph, a condor perches on a cliff overlooking Horseshoe Bend on the Colorado River. I was able to approach within 5 meters of this huge bird and used a 28–80mm wide-angle lens that allowed me to frame the condor within its spectacular backdrop.

Canon EOS-3, Canon EF 28–80mm lens, f/16 at 1/25 second, Fujichrome Velvia film

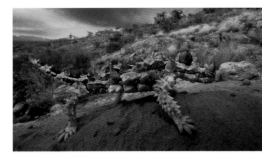

THORNY DEVIL
(*Moloch horridus*)

Australia's thorny devil or moloch is named after the god of the Old Testament who wrought human sacrifices from his followers. The startling lizard is only about 20 centimeters long, but its entire body is covered with thornlike spines. However, the spines are defensive rather than offensive in nature, and the small, orange-brown reptile is harmless, feeding only on black ants. The thorny devil inhabits Australia's sandy deserts, and its protective spines serve a dual purpose. In the desert, water is a rare commodity. In the early morning, dew settles on the devil and the animal channels the liquid to its mouth via a series of small furrows in its skin. Thus, not only do the spines deter would-be predators from making the lizard into a tasty meal, but they provide the desert dweller with the life-sustaining moisture it needs to survive.

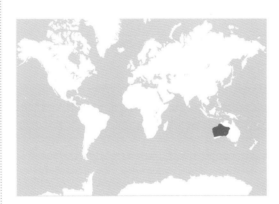

AW: Thorny devils are ideal photographic subjects: They often stand motionless, even as a photographer towers over them. To accentuate their threatening appearance, I placed a camera and 14mm wide-angle lens 2.5 centimeters from the lizard. At this range, the lizard appears enormous, while the extreme wide-angle lens includes the landscape. However, at 2.5 centimeters, the lizard was too close to focus clearly, so I stopped down to an aperture setting of f/22. Only then did the thorny devil become sharp, complete with the surrounding landscape.

Canon EOS-3, Canon EF 14mm lens, f/22 at 1 second, fill flash, Fujichrome Velvia film

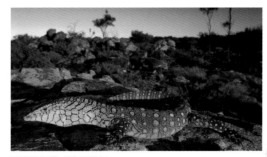

PERENTIE GOANNA
(*Varanus giganteus*)

The perentie is the second-largest lizard in the world—and the largest found in Australia—only Indonesia's Komodo dragon (*V. komodoensis*) is larger. Perenties inhabit the deserts and semiarid areas of most of the island continent. They can reach 2.5 meters in length (averaging 1.6 meters) and weigh up to 10 kilograms. They are efficient hunters, preying on snakes, other lizards, birds, and mammals, including small kangaroos, as well as feeding on carrion. In many ways they fill the predatory niche taken by mammals elsewhere in the world. Rabbits form a substantial part of their diet, since the perentie often enters burrows to hunt. Despite their size, perenties are not considered especially dangerous, and they often flee a perceived threat by climbing a tree and hiding among the branches; their coloration provides effective camouflage. If cornered, they are able to defend themselves—they possess large claws, strong jaws, and a heavy tail.

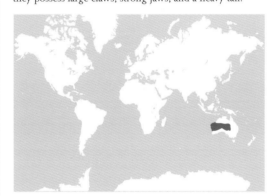

AW: Perenties are revered by the aboriginal peoples of Australia in art and legend as a source of inspiration, but also as a food source. These monitors are elusive, fast-moving predators, and can be difficult to approach. But in the early morning, when their bodies have been chilled by the cool desert night, they are rather sluggish. This meter-long perentie lies upon an east-facing rock to catch the first rays of the rising sun. I was able to move within 0.5 meter before taking my photographs.

Canon EOS-3, Canon EF 17–35mm lens, f/22 at 2 seconds, polarizing filter, 2-stop graduated neutral density filter, Fujichrome Velvia film

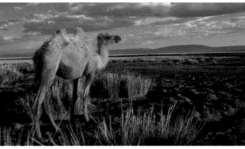

BACTRIAN CAMEL
(*Camelus bactrianus*)

Both species of camels—the Bactrian or two-humped camel and the dromedary or one-humped camel (*Camelus dromedarius*)—have been victims of successful domestication. Bactrian camels were probably first domesticated more than 4,500 years ago. They have been—and in many areas still are—used for transportation, meat, milk, wool, and hides. There are more than one million domesticated Bactrian camels in China and Mongolia, but wild—as opposed to feral—animals are far scarcer. Early in the twentieth century, wild camels were still relatively common and herds may have roamed from Kazakhstan all the way to Mongolia. Today there are only about 1,000 pure wild Bactrian camels left, their numbers concentrated in the Gobi Desert that straddles the border between northwestern China and southwestern Mongolia. Competition with pastoralists, hunting, and hybridization with domesticated animals are all contributing to their continued decline.

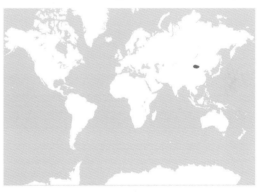

AW: Pure-blooded, wild bactrian camels are highly endangered animals. In this photograph, a camel gazes out over its desert landscape. This animal was caught as a youngster, then raised with other wild camels alongside domesticated camels in an effort to habituate them. Once habituated, they are bred to other pureblooded wild camels in an effort to increase their dangerously low numbers. One day it is hoped that an entire herd of purebred, wild camels will again roam the desert.

Canon EOS-1N, Canon EF 17–35 mm lens, f/11 at 1/15 second, Fujichrome Velvia film

NOTES FROM THE FIELD

AN ESSAY BY
JANE GOODALL

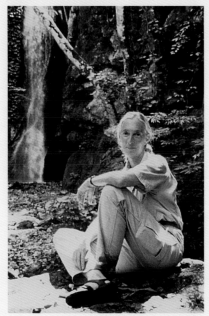

© KEN REGAN/CAMERA 5

*H*omo *sapiens*, the "intelligent" man, the ape that is somehow so different from all the other animals. Or is it? What makes our human species so special? Some would reply that it is because we are "made in God's image." Millions would assert that it is because we have a soul. Almost everyone, although many could not explain why, believes that our species, somehow, stands alone, apart from the rest of the animal kingdom. Certainly humans have big brains with a well-developed neocortex and the power to reason, solve problems, use and make tools, plan for the future, and to abstract, generalize, and conceptualize. We are self-aware and can manipulate the physical and social environment to our own advantage, individually or through cooperation. Our children have a long period of dependency, during which they acquire the skills they will need as adults. We enjoy long-term supportive and affectionate relationships. We experience emotions such as joy and sadness, fear and despair, and we feel pain. We have the capacity for love and compassion, forgiveness, loyalty, and altruism. We are also capable of hate and betrayal, brutality, sadism, and war. And, of major importance, we have a sophisticated spoken language that enables us to discuss the distant past, make plans for the far-ahead future, and discuss ideas so that they can grow free of the accumulated wisdom of the group.

Traditionally, western science has insisted that when any animals other than human animals exhibited any behavior similar to or the same as those listed above, this could be explained as purely instinctive, or innate. Animals might *appear* to be sad, depressed, or joyful; they might *seem* to use reason to solve a problem. But in fact, these behaviors were merely reflex responses to specific internal or external stimuli. To attribute individuality, reasoning power, or humanlike emotions to mere animals was to be guilty of anthropomorphism. Some scientists even said they believed that animals did not feel pain. To anyone who knows anything about animals, at least those with well-developed brains, this was absurd. But it made it easier to do cruel experiments or tests on animals and to subject them to the horrors of intensive farming, trapping, hunting, and so on.

It was fortunate that when I began the study of the chimpanzees in 1960 I had not been to a university. I did not know that chimpanzees were supposed to be without mind and emotions. I did not realize that I should have numbered rather than named the members of my study community, that their behavior was purely innate, that they were incapable of reason, that emotions that looked like ours were simply automatic responses triggered by different environmental situations. Nor did I know that only humans were supposed to have individuality. I went ahead and described the vivid and unique personalities whom I gradually came to know: David Greybeard and old Flo, Mike and Olly, Fifi and Gilka. Imagine my amazement when the erudite editor of *Nature* struck out my references to *he*, *she*, and *who* in an article I had submitted and substituted *it* and *which*.

With such obvious sexual differences, it was absurd to deprive them of gender simply because they were *merely* animals. (I put the *hes*, *shes*, and *whos* back—and they stayed!)

So how did this naïve young woman, with her abysmal lack of scientific sophistication, ever get to study chimpanzees? It was the famous anthropologist/paleontologist, the late Louis Leakey, who sent me to Gombe to study the behavior of the chimpanzee living there. He did not want to send a university student; he actually preferred to send someone whose mind was uncluttered with the reductionist theories of the time. It did make it hard for him to get a grant for me to start the study, but he succeeded in the end. He also had to overcome the prejudice against a *female* going into the bush on her own.

Louis believed that a knowledge of our closest living relatives, in their natural environment, would help him to better understand how our own earliest human ancestors may have behaved. He had spent his life searching for the fossilized remains of our earliest prehistoric ancestors in various parts of East Africa, where he and his wife, Mary, uncovered many of the skeletal remains that would help to establish Africa as the cradle of mankind. Darwin, back in 1872, had theorized that this was so, and his brilliant deduction had been confirmed by Raymond Dart in 1924 when he found the perfectly preserved skull of an immature *Australopithecus*, the Taung child, in the Sterkfontein cave of South Africa. In 1959, at Olduvai Gorge, the Leakeys uncovered *Zinjanthropus*, *Australopithicus boisei*—known as the Nutcracker Man—and then, some years later, the remains of *Homo habilis*. Anatomists, working with skillful artists, could reconstruct how these ancestors must have looked, and the artifacts found in association with their bones told something of their way of life. But behavior does not fossilize, and there were no clues as to their social life. So, Louis reasoned, we should learn what we could about the behavior of our closest living relatives, the modern great apes. Behavior common to modern humans and modern apes was probably present in a common ancestor, half-human, half-ape, millions of years ago—and, therefore, probably present in the first true humans. At least, Louis felt, he would then have a way of making reasoned guesses as to how Stone Age man behaved. John Emlen had already sent George Schaller to study a group of mountain gorillas for a year. And now Louis Leakey found three individuals prepared to go and study chimpanzees, gorillas, and orangutans. I set off for the Gombe Stream Game Reserve in 1960, Dian Fossey started observing mountain gorillas in 1967, and Birute Galdikas ventured into Indonesia to observe orangutans in 1971. If Louis had realized that the "bonobo" was, in fact, a fourth species of great ape, he would, without doubt, have dispatched a fourth eager young woman to study them!

I was twenty-six years old when I began my field study of wild chimpanzees in the Gombe Stream Game Reserve (now Gombe National Park). With me, for the first four months, was my remarkable mother, since the local British authorities of what was then the protectorate of Tanganyika refused to allow a young *girl* to go into the bush alone, especially one with no training. I wasn't even interested in becoming a scientist. But I had the qualities that Louis had deemed the most important: patience, the desire to learn about my subjects, and sheer determination to succeed. Of course, when I subsequently went to Cambridge University—for Louis insisted I would need a Ph.D.—I came in for much criticism from my scientific instructors and peers because of my anthropomorphic approach. Fortunately, because I was not interested in a career in science, I was able to withstand this disapproval. How wise of Louis to choose such a naïve observer!

Leakey's vision has been vindicated: Almost all textbooks that deal with human evolution talk about chimpanzee behavior as it relates to the probable behavior of our prehistoric ancestors. And the detailed, long-term observations of Dian Fossey and Birute Galdikas, along with information from all of the other ape studies that have followed, have further helped anthropologists piece together the steps from ape to man. At the time of this writing, the study of the Gombe chimps approaches its fortieth year—the longest unbroken field study of any group of wild animals. Fifi, who was a tiny infant when I began in 1960, is close to forty years old herself. When I gaze into her eyes today, I know that there are some memories from the early '60s that are unique to us. Fifi's mother, Flo, was one of the first chimpanzees, along with David Greybeard, William, and Olly, to lose her fear of the strange white ape who had invaded their territory. And as I recorded their behavior, they introduced me to the other members of the community. They were heady, those early days: making the first observations of tool using and tool making, seeing a group of supposedly vegetarian males cooperate in a hunt and kill a young colobus monkey, and subsequently watching the hunting of young bushpig, bushbuck, and baboons. Gradually learning the complex communication repertoire of these amazing chimpanzees—the embracing, kissing, patting on the back, crouching and bowing, holding out the hand, palm up, in a request for food. The swaggering, punching, and kicking. The tickling and laughing. Postures and gestures that looked like many that we make, and were used in the same context: They seemed to mean the same.

Eventually I came to realize the importance of early childhood experience in chimpanzee development, the big differences between individual females in their mothering techniques, and the importance of learning. Youngsters can learn by observing the behavior of others and imitating what they see. In this way, tool-using and tool-making skills are passed from one generation to the next. Affectionate, supportive bonds between family members can last throughout a life of more than sixty years. Orphaned infants are adopted, usually by older siblings, sometimes by nonrelated adults. Sadly, I eventually learned that

chimpanzees, like humans, have a dark side to their nature: They are aggressively territorial and have a hatred of strangers. This may lead to brutal attacks on individuals from neighboring communities. During one four-year period, a group of adult males systematically hunted down individuals of a smaller neighboring social group, brutally attacked them, and left them to die of their wounds. It was primitive warfare.

And we are still learning new things. We are finding out more about cultural variation between chimpanzee populations across Africa. Just recently we have been able to document cultural transmission from one community to another at Gombe—a pattern of tool use, never seen in the main study community in more than thirty years, is being utilized by a growing number of our group following the transfer of a young female from a neighboring community where the behavior is common. We have our third chance to study the development of the relationship between twins. We are still learning more about how different chimpanzee groups across Africa use the leaves of a variety of plants for medicinal purposes—leaves typically used as medicine by humans in the area.

Perhaps the most fascinating aspect of chimpanzee behavior is how like us they are—or how like them we are. In addition to these striking behavioral parallels, there are extraordinary genetic and biological similarities. We differ from chimpanzees in the structure of our DNA—our genetic building blocks—by only just over 1 percent. In fact, chimpanzees are closer to us than they are to gorillas in this respect, and closer than horses to zebras. Our blood is so similar to that of a chimpanzee that a human could be saved by a transfusion from a chimp, if the blood groups matched, and a chimp could be saved by blood donated by a human. Our immune system is remarkably like that of a chimp, which is why they are used as surrogate humans in certain kinds of medical experiments, particularly infectious disease research. Most importantly, our brain and central nervous system are uncannily similar to those of the chimpanzee. Which is why it makes sense to assume that many behaviors that look humanlike probably are humanlike in cause and function. "Bonobos" (once called pygmy chimpanzees) are just as close to us, if not closer, and gorillas also show many of these similarities.

All this has blurred the line once thought so sharp, drawn by us in our arrogance, between humans on the one side and all the rest of the animal kingdom on the other. And once we are prepared to accept that it is not only humans who have personalities and reasoned thought and, above all, who know emotions and are capable of mental as well as physical suffering, this leads to a new respect—a respect not only for chimpanzees and the other great apes and higher primates, but for so many of the other wonderful animals with whom we share this planet. Thanks to the work of many patient and dedicated wildlife researchers, we have learned something of the complex societies and communication

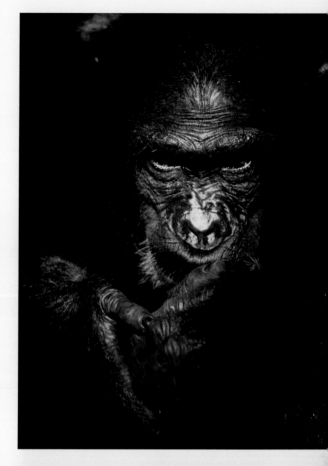

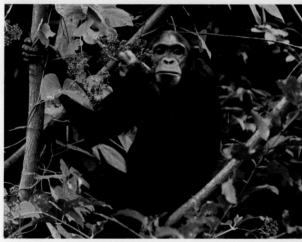

CHIMPANZEE

(*Pan troglodytes*), MAHALE MOUNTAINS NATIONAL PARK, TANZANIA

JANE GOODALL

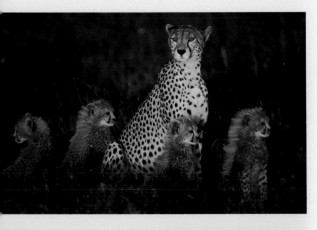

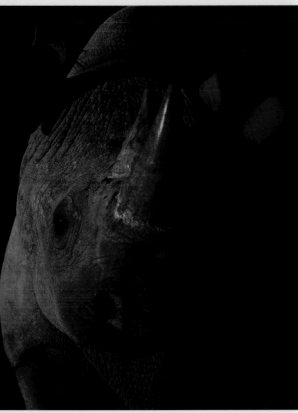

THE LIVING WILD

patterns of elephants and whales and dolphins, wild dogs and hyenas and jackals, hyraxes and mongooses, and a whole variety of other animals worldwide.

All these diverse creatures have adapted exquisitely during evolution to their own particular type of environment. We tend, however, to be most impressed by those who have brains similar to our own, whose outlook on life seems similar to ours. But this is just our egocentric bias. Equally fascinating are the incredibly complex societies of the social insects. And the extraordinary life-style of the little naked mole rats that is so like that of termites. The teeming life of the coral reefs, the myriad reptiles and amphibians. Truly the diversity of habitats and the variations in form and behavior of the flora and fauna associated with each provoke a sense of awe. And that feeling of awe, for me, is intensified when I gaze up at the brilliant star-studded African sky. The memory of the long moonlit nights that I spent in the Ngorongoro Crater with the utterly fascinating hyenas of the Scratching Rocks Clan will remain with me throughout my life. Bloody Mary, the matriarch; Lady Astor; poor, low-ranking Baggage, who was such a good mother to her twin cubs; and the henpecked males, smaller than the great females—Nelson, Southern Cross, Lord Dracula, and the rest. What vivid personalities.

How tragic that the growth of human population everywhere, coupled with the consumerism and greed of the affluent societies around the world, have already led to extinction for so many of our planet's forms of life. This is due largely to loss of habitat, but also to hunting for food, deliberate extermination, and, in some cases, competition from exotic species introduced accidentally or on purpose. The pollution of water, air, and land takes a terrible toll on some species of plants and animals; and global climate changes, accelerated by the activities of *Homo sapiens*, threaten thousands more. The largest study ever undertaken of the state of the world's wildlife, carried out recently by the World Conservation Union, found that one-quarter of all species of mammals—including nearly half of all monkeys and apes—are at risk of extinction.

Throughout the world there are many glorious wilderness areas that have been given protected status. In Tanzania alone there are eleven national parks—including the magnificent Serengeti, Ruaha, Kilimanjaro, and, of course, Gombe. But throughout the developing world, wildlife areas, even when protected, are often far from safe. Profits that can be made by poachers are, for the most part, well worth the risk of being caught, since—only too often—wildlife authorities are underfunded and corruption is rife. Civil war and movements of vast numbers of displaced and often desperate people make a mockery of the law—as in the famous Virunga National Park, where starving refugees, camped in the foothills, have set snares ever farther into the park simply to survive. Soldiers, armed militia, guerrillas show no respect for protected areas. In Congo-Zaire,

armed hunters are dispatched into the national parks to shoot bushmeat for state banquets; the animals are easier to approach. And the protected areas in the developed world are not safe either: Commercial interests often win out, for example, when there's an argument as to whether or not mining should be allowed in a conservation area, or a road built through it. Even tourism can be horribly damaging to fragile ecosystems.

The trouble is, there are too many *Homo sapiens* on planet Earth—some 6 billion of us as we move into the new millennium. The United Nations estimates that fifty years from now the total number of human beings will have risen to at least 8.8 billion. Ninety-five percent of this population growth will occur in developing countries—poor countries striving to attain the standard of living that is enjoyed by the affluent. And as they move toward this goal, the impact on the natural world will be devastating. The World Resources Institute estimates that although only some 5 percent of the world's people live there, nevertheless the United States uses one-third of the world's nonrenewable resources and one-fourth of the planet's commodities; the average U.S. citizen uses 300 times the energy used by a citizen of the developing world. As the percentage of people who can afford to join this materialistic, consumer-driven culture increases, as international corporations become ever more powerful, so will the squandering of our precious natural resources accelerate. Already between one-third and one-half of the Earth's land area has been significantly altered by human activities. Millions of hectares (about 200 million) of forest have been lost during the past twenty years. And so much of what is left has been fragmented by development: Only about one-fifth of the world's original forests remain in large, relatively natural ecosystems. As we continue to destroy the last of the great rainforests, so the planetary biodiversity diminishes, since more than 40 percent of all plant and animal species are found in these forests.

The plight of chimpanzees in the wild highlights the destruction of Africa's natural environment. At the turn of the century, there were somewhere between one and two million chimpanzees living throughout the equatorial forest belt that stretched from the coast of West Africa (Senegal in the north to Angola's Cabinda region in the south) eastward to western Tanzania and Uganda. Today, it is estimated that there are no more than 105,000. There is a similar decline in the populations of gorillas and "bonobos." Once chimpanzees were found in twenty-five nations. They are gone from four of those and are almost extinct in many others. Only in the heart of their range—in Congo-Brazzaville and Congo-Zaire, Gabon, and Cameroon—are there significant populations today, and they are decreasing, mainly as a result of the so-called bushmeat trade. For hundreds of years the forest-dwelling human groups of West and Central Africa have lived in harmony with their forest world, practicing subsistence hunting. Now things are different. Timber companies build roads that penetrate ever deeper into the last remaining tracts of virgin forest, and these roads provide access to commercial hunters from the towns. The hunters ride logging trucks to the end of the road, shoot everything they see—from elephants to bats, and including chimpanzees, gorillas, and "bonobos"—then load the meat onto the trucks for the return journey. The meat is sold in the big towns in West and Central Africa. This is not—and I repeat *not*—to feed starving people, but to cater to the cultural preference of many for the flesh of wild animals, for which they will pay more. Chimpanzee meat, along with monkey meat, has even been sold in restaurants in Belgium. This trade is rapidly pushing the remaining populations of chimpanzees, gorillas, "bonobos," elephants, and many other animals to extinction. In addition, the great apes run the risk of being caught in snares set by hunters for bushbucks and pigs. In some countries, the live animal trade accounts for more slaughter, since the mothers must be shot in order to capture their infants. Those that survive will be exported for entertainment, the pet industry, and (though less now than of yore) biomedical research. Remaining populations are becoming increasingly fragmented due to habitat destruction. Small remnant groups, with little or no opportunity for genetic exchange with other groups, will not survive over time due to lack of genetic diversity. The famous chimpanzees of Gombe are now isolated within their 78-square-kilometer national park, surrounded by farmland from which the forest has gone.

There are too few protected areas in Africa, and throughout the world, that are large enough to sustain natural populations of the large mammals such as the great apes, elephants, and rhinos. Less than 2 percent of the world's protected areas are larger than 1 million hectares, which is thought by some to be the minimum area necessary to ensure the survival of these large animals. Moreover, only about 6 percent of the natural world is strictly protected: Many so-called conservation areas actually allow activities such as mining, logging, hunting, and grazing.

It is not only the natural world that is suffering from human greed and exploitation. As human populations grow, and as more and more countries adopt the destructive technologies of the developed world, there is a massive increase in poverty, hunger, and illness. As the number of people in a given area increases, the point is reached when they can no longer live on the resources of the land. For the wealthy, this means importation from outside. For the economically poor, who have no money to buy food from elsewhere, and who can seldom move to new areas, it means growing poverty and hunger. Billions of people in the developing world have no adequate housing, no clean water, and no proper sanitation. Diseases spread fast in these conditions, particularly among children, and especially when family size increases, birth spacing is reduced, and infants

are weaned too early from the relative safety of breast milk. Millions of children die each year from malnourishment and diseases resulting from poor hygiene. The introduction of modern technology, without the resources or without the will to ensure environmental safety measures, has led to horrifying levels of pollution around the world. About four million children die from pollution-related illnesses each year, with a high percentage in the old Soviet Union and China. The devastating long-term effects of some synthetic chemicals on the environment, such as DDT and CFCs, have now been demonstrated. It was not possible to predict these effects; in fact, DDT and CFCs were once hailed as wonder chemicals. The tragedy is that petrochemical companies are still developing and releasing new synthetic chemicals, the long-term effects of which also cannot be predicted. There is growing evidence of increased disease, such as cancer, among people living in areas contaminated by a whole variety of chemicals—pesticides, fertilizers, industrial waste in landfills, and so on. Evidence that human fertility is being adversely affected is probably the one piece of good news, so far as the environment is concerned!

Throughout evolution there has been competition for the resources on which living organisms depend for their continued existence, and through the millennia countless species have lost out. But this time a different sort of extinction looms on planet Earth—an extinction caused by the constant manipulation of the natural world by just one species: ours. Humans have ruthlessly destroyed or persecuted other life forms that interfered with their plans for a good life. And humans, invariably, have won out because of our superior intellect. We make cruel traps and poisoned arrows and use modern bullets in our constant striving for domination. We destroy the habitat that was home to countless living beings and cover once-verdant land with concrete, dissecting the few places left for animals with kilometer upon kilometer of lethal roads.

Sadly, of course, humans of different ethnic and religious groups try to destroy and persecute each other. In some ways this is the most shocking of all. The intraspecific conflicts between different human groups in Africa today have resulted in terrible, long-drawn-out wars and massive suffering. And, again, the greed of the developed world has fueled these bitter wars, many of which have been financed almost entirely by the diamond trade. Wars have been waged since the earliest recorded history. With the advancement of technology, wars have caused increased suffering to humans and increased damage to the environment. The horrors of nuclear, chemical, and biological warfare are reminiscent of Dante's Inferno. Wars and the nightmare of ethnic cleansing as in Rwanda, Burundi, and many other parts of Africa, as well as Cambodia, China, the old Soviet Union, and the Balkans, have led to refugee problems of epic proportion.

Waves of refugees from Burundi and eastern Zaire have seriously impacted my own

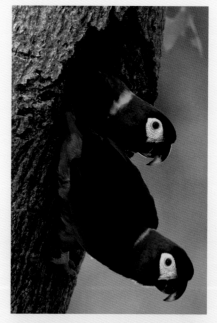

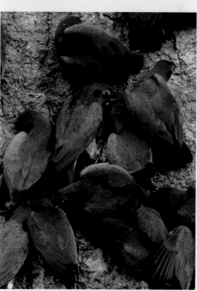

▲▲ YELLOW-COLLARED MACAW ⌒
(*Propyrrhura auricollis*), PANTANAL, BRAZIL
▲ BLUE-HEADED PARROT ⌒
(*Pionus menstruus*), RESERVA DEL MANÚ, PERU

JANE GOODALL

129

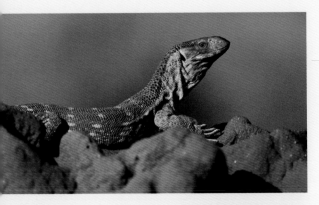

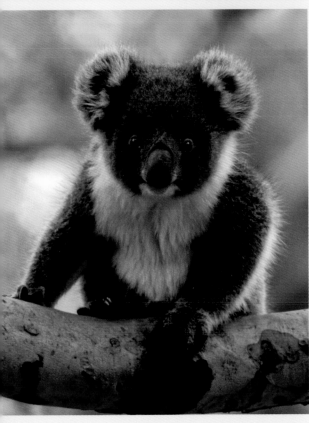

THE LIVING WILD

study site. Ethnic violence between Hutu and Tutsi in Burundi, just north of Gombe National Park, still simmers. A constant trickle of refugees spills over the border, and while most of them are gathered up by the U.N. High Commissioner for Refugees, many prefer to live illegally in the hills. The same is true for the Wabembe, who have been pouring over Lake Tanganyika in the thousands to escape the fighting on the western shore. This influx, in addition to the population growth of the local peasant farmers, explains why the forests outside the borders of the 78-square-kilometer national park are gone. When I arrived in 1960, the forested slopes that tumbled down to the clear water of the lake stretched for miles to the north, south, and east of the park. But as land was needed to grow more food, and as wood was needed to cook more meals, so chimp habitat, along with the chimps themselves, vanished. With tree cover gone, large amounts of the precious, thin layer of topsoil are washed down the steep slopes of the Rift escarpment into the lake, and the fish-breeding grounds are silting up. The local Waha population is poor, and people have traditionally lived by subsistence farming and fishing. How can we hope to save Gombe and its forests and chimpanzees when the people living around its borders increasingly struggle to survive?

The Jane Goodall Institute, along with a number of other like-minded groups, has long realized that all conservation efforts in the developing world are likely to fail unless the people living around the area to be conserved are themselves able to benefit. To try to find some solution to the problems facing both humans and wildlife in and around Gombe, we initiated a program to help the villagers. Lake Tanganyika Catchment Reforestation and Education Project has established tree nurseries in twenty-seven villages in the area. Villagers tend and then sell seedlings of fruit trees, fast-growing species for building poles, firewood, and so forth. Indigenous trees are reintroduced. Issues of soil erosion control and prevention are addressed. Conservation education programs have been implemented among the villagers, especially in the schools. A small program of micro-credit lending has been introduced, modeled on the Grameen Bank system. This enables groups of women to start sustainable development projects that will improve the quality of their lives, without destroying the environment. In cooperation with the regional medical authority, primary health care especially for women and children, AIDS education, and family planning consultation are delivered to the villages. In cooperation with UNICEF and the International Rescue Committee, hygienic latrines and freshwater will be installed in thirty-three villages. We work to improve women's education and provide some scholarships for girls to move on to secondary education. We expect that as women become better educated, family size will decrease as it has in other parts of the world.

In the four short years since it began, this program has improved the quality of life for many. And, in their turn, many of the villagers are now prepared to help us not only to preserve the national park, but to reintroduce indigenous forested areas elsewhere. In addition, the Gombe research program itself has boosted the surrounding economy, as we buy as many products as possible from villagers around the park and employ as many of them as possible as researchers and other staff. The field staff are proud of their work, talk about the chimpanzees to family and friends, care about them, and want to protect them as individuals. In all these ways we have shown that the conservation of the natural environment, particularly the forest, is important for people as well as animals. Trees and other vegetation matter not only because they are needed by chimpanzees for food and security, but because they protect and sometimes enhance the fertility of the soil, prevent erosion, and provide firewood, shade, and medicine.

The local and central governments support our research and help protect the national park, not only because we are clearly improving life for Tanzanians in the area, but also because Gombe attracts tourism and thus brings much-needed foreign exchange into the country. We are trying to set up a similar program around our large sanctuary for orphan chimpanzees in the western coastal region of Congo-Brazzaville. These programs, and others like them, provide hope for the future of Africa. And as people throughout the world become increasingly aware of the terrible damage we are inflicting on the environment, so technology and industry are coming to grips with many of the problems, finding new ways to live in better harmony with nature.

It is easy to become depressed about the global problems and just give up, sink into apathy. In a world where there are billions of other human beings and such vast problems, what difference can my behavior make? Imagine the power we have—the collective results of individual actions. Billions of people can use public transportation, walk, or cycle; turn off taps and lights; pick up litter in public places. We can choose not to buy products made by companies that have an environmentally bad reputation or those made by child slave labor in a far-off country. We can buy organically grown food.

Each one of us makes a difference. And this is true for animals, too. If we look back over the dogs or cats with whom we have shared part of our lives, we can quickly see how each one played a different role, affected us and those around us in different ways. And this we should consider in relation to wild animals, too. When a chimpanzee is killed, a distinctive personality and role is removed from his or her community. The adult female Gigi almost certainly caused an escalation in the intercommunity conflict that caused the deaths of so many individuals at Gombe in the mid-1970s. For she was sterile, constantly cycling, becoming sexually attractive, and so attracted the adult males around her. And these males, confident in a group, then went on boundary patrols that often ended in brutal attacks on individuals from neighboring social groups. Flo, the matriarch of her society in the 1960s, gave birth to Fifi, who has had the most successful reproductive career of all Gombe females. Trezia seems to have introduced a new tool-using culture into her community. And so on. It is the same with other big-brained animals. When an old elephant matriarch is "culled," her cultural wisdom, accumulated over many years, dies with her, and her unique personality will not be repeated. I am often criticized by conservationists for caring about individual animals rather than the species, but this cannot change my passionate conviction that each one of us, animal as well as human animal, has a role to play in this life. I think it is only through respect for individual lives that our world, already a place of great beauty, can eventually become also a place of peace that will enable future generations to enjoy the beauty.

Fortunately, more and more young people are becoming aware of the problems in their world. If only children can be empowered to act, their energy and enthusiasm and commitment can make a huge difference. As they find out about the environmental and social problems that are, sadly, part of their heritage, they have a vested interest in trying to put things right—for it will be their world tomorrow, they who will be the leaders, the workforce, the parents.

I am devoting more and more of my own time and effort into developing Roots & Shoots, our program for youth. This is a symbolic name: Roots creep under the ground and make a firm foundation; shoots seem small, but to reach the light they can break apart brick walls—symbolic walls of overpopulation, deforestation, soil erosion, desertification, poverty, hunger, disease, pollution, human greed, materialism, cruelty, crime, and warfare. The message of Roots & Shoots is one of hope: Hundreds of thousands of roots and shoots—young people—around the globe can break through and change the world. The program emphasizes the value of the individual in this process of change.

From kindergarten to university, the Roots & Shoots groups are involved in three kinds of hands-on projects that show care and concern for animals, for the local community, and for the environment around them. What they actually do depends on where they live and the nature of local problems, the age of the group, and the particular interests of the leaders or members. Groups are planting trees, cleaning rivers, rescuing animals, spending time with children in hospitals or with the elderly. They are learning and sharing the knowledge. And they are having fun, being enriched, even as they are making a difference. The program began in Tanzania, in the capital Dar es Salaam, and in the Kigoma region around Gombe and the chimps. Now it is rapidly spreading across the country. Today there are Roots & Shoots groups in thirty-eight states of the United States and in forty-seven countries around the world.

It is a program that seeks to break down barriers between ethnic, religious, and socioeconomic groups, between generations, between countries—and, as well, between humans and animals. And here the chimpanzees, with their humanlike qualities and their fascinating life histories, lead the way. Children identify so easily with little Flint, who died of grief at eight years of age, unable to cope with life after losing his mother. And the adolescent boys identify with Mike, who made use of empty tin cans to enhance his charging displays and, with an equal mixture of brains and courage, rose to the top-ranking position. Once these chimp histories have been shared, there is concern among the youth when they hear of the plight of the apes in the wild, their mistreatment in captivity. This paves the way for similar concern for elephants and cheetahs and wolves. And, finally, for the animals and environment of their own backyards. Once they see that their actions make a difference, nothing can stop them.

National and international conservation organizations, along with enlightened governments, are fighting to protect preserved areas and to create more. We can still visit countless areas of wilderness around the globe and know that, with increased local involvement, especially of the children, we can survive into the future. In Africa, despite its troubles, we can marvel at the continent's magnificent contrasts, from the extraordinary concentration of animals during the great migration on the Serengeti Plains to the stark beauty of the Namib Desert. There are the spectacular Victoria Falls, and the remote swamp forests of Endoke in the Congo Basin, where the animals, including elephants, gorillas, and chimpanzees, have not yet learned to fear humans. There are so many glorious wilderness areas throughout the rest of the world that it would take a lifetime to visit even a tenth with enough time to learn their secrets. An increasing number of species is becoming threatened and endangered, but this trend can sometimes be reversed, as with the peregrine falcon. And there is still much to discover: new species to be identified and described, new behaviors to be observed, medicinal plants (their benefits as yet unknown) waiting to be found in the forests. Somehow we must save what is left.

And so, as we begin the new millennium, let us pause and think back over our human record—not only the accomplishments and failures of our own species over the past hundreds of years, but our own, during our own lifetime. Knowledge and understanding, persistence and hard work, love and compassion are the most important tools we have. Let us rejoice in our humanity, our rationality, our power to effect change. Only if we understand will we care, only if we care will we help, and only if we help shall all be saved. That is our challenge: to save the natural world with all its glorious and diverse life forms, taking them with us into the next century to share with our children and theirs.

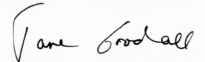

JANE GOODALL

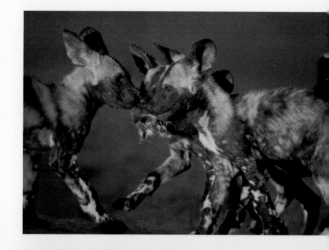

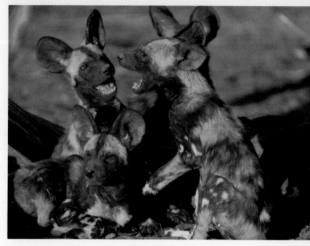

WILD DOG

(Lycaon pictus), KWANDO, BOTSWANA

MOUNTAIN

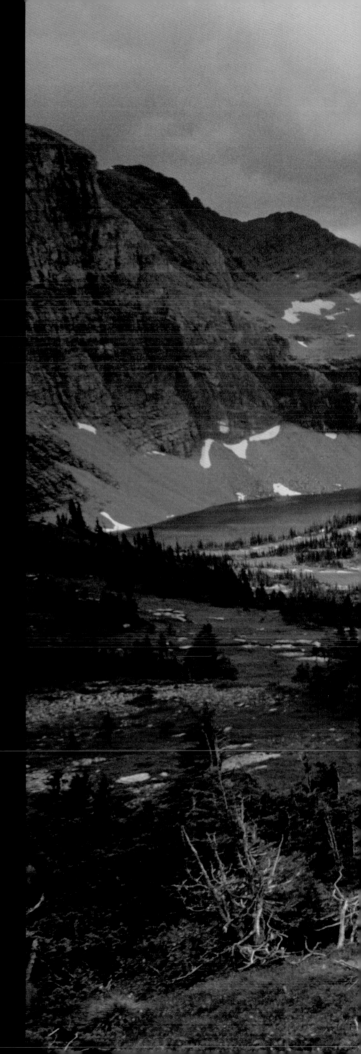

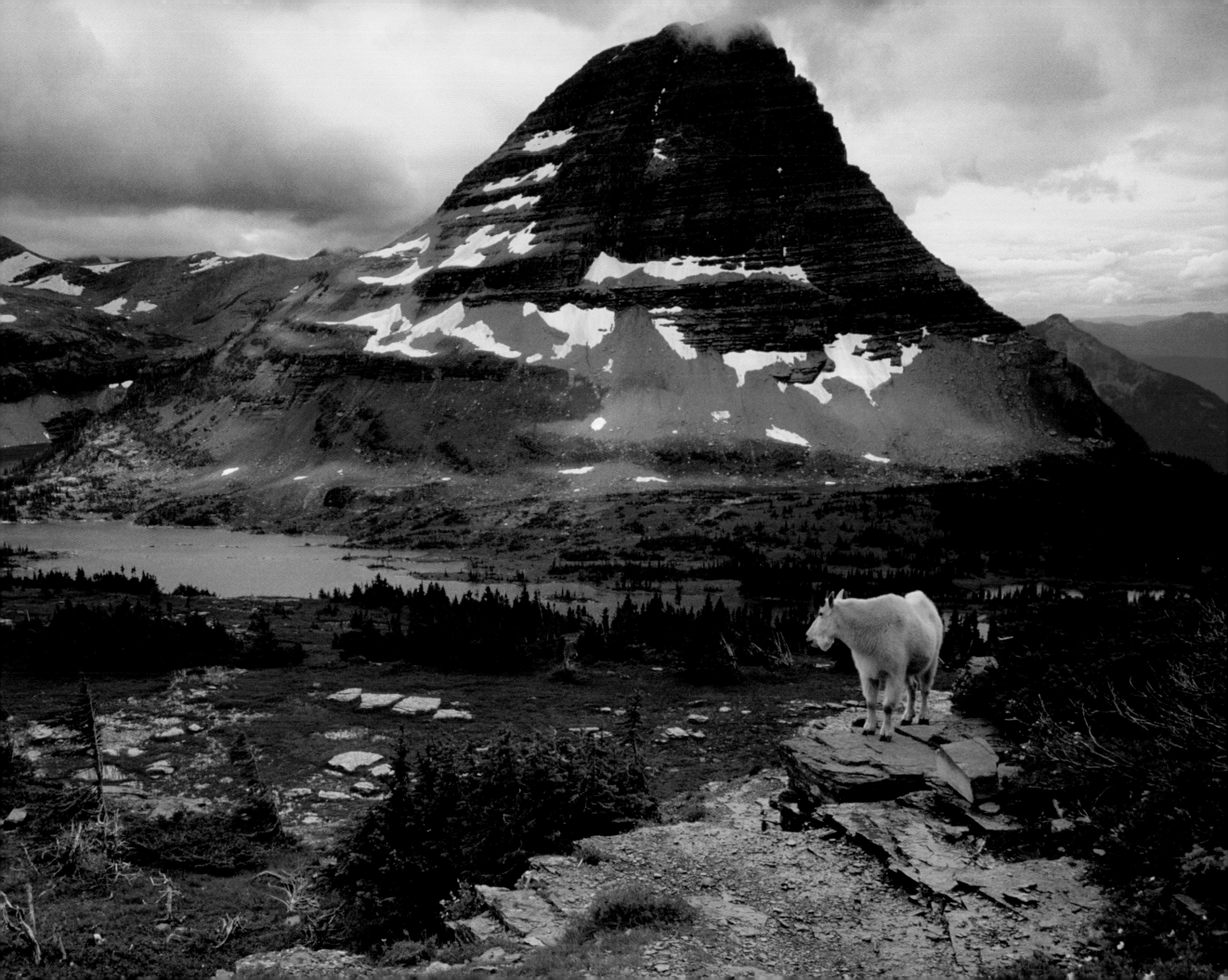

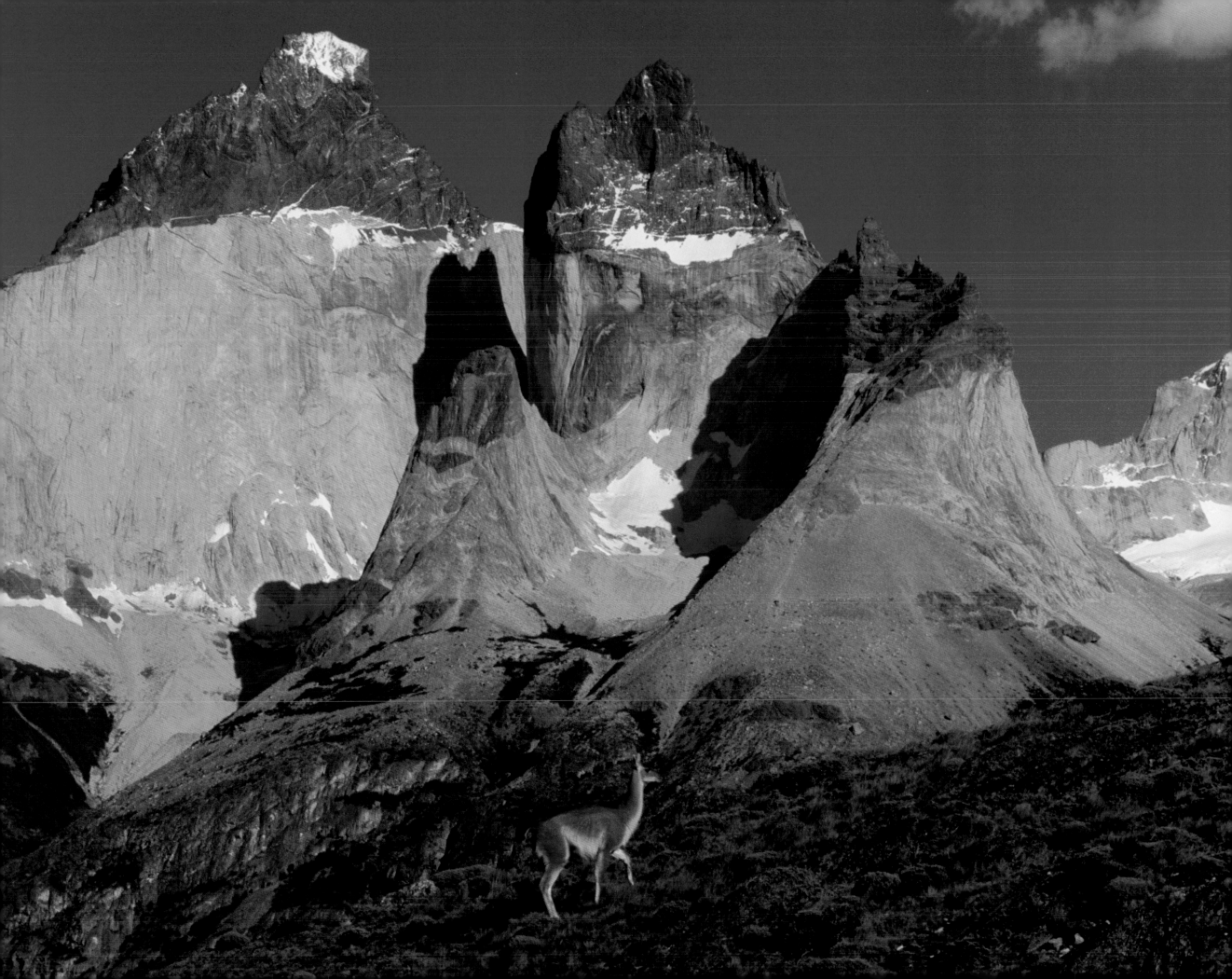

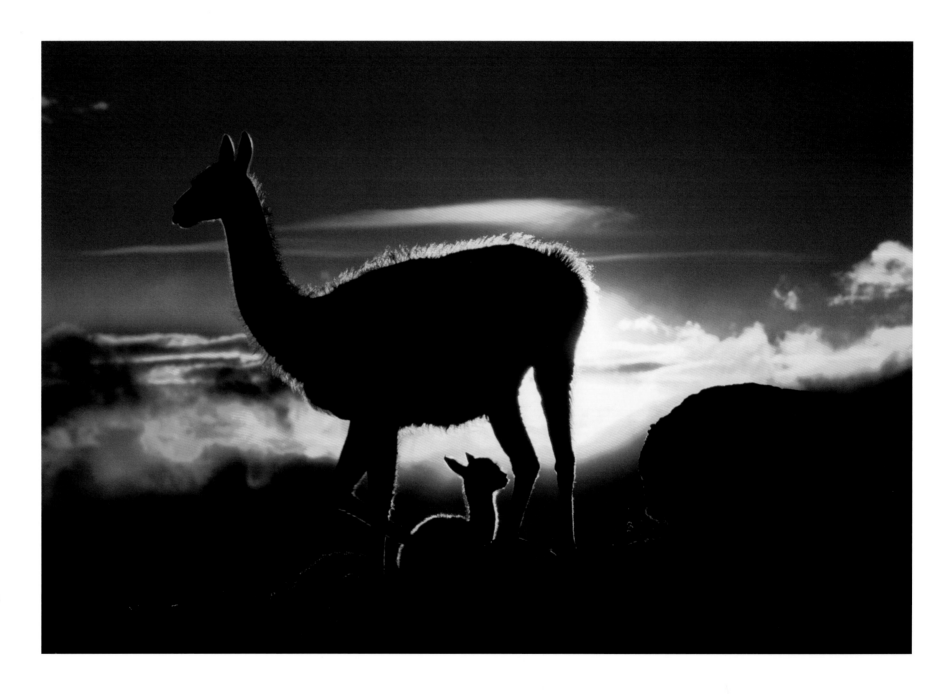

◄◄ MOUNTAIN GOAT

GLACIER NATIONAL PARK, MONTANA, USA

◄ AND ► GUANACO

TORRES DEL PAINE NATIONAL PARK, CHILE

MOUNTAIN

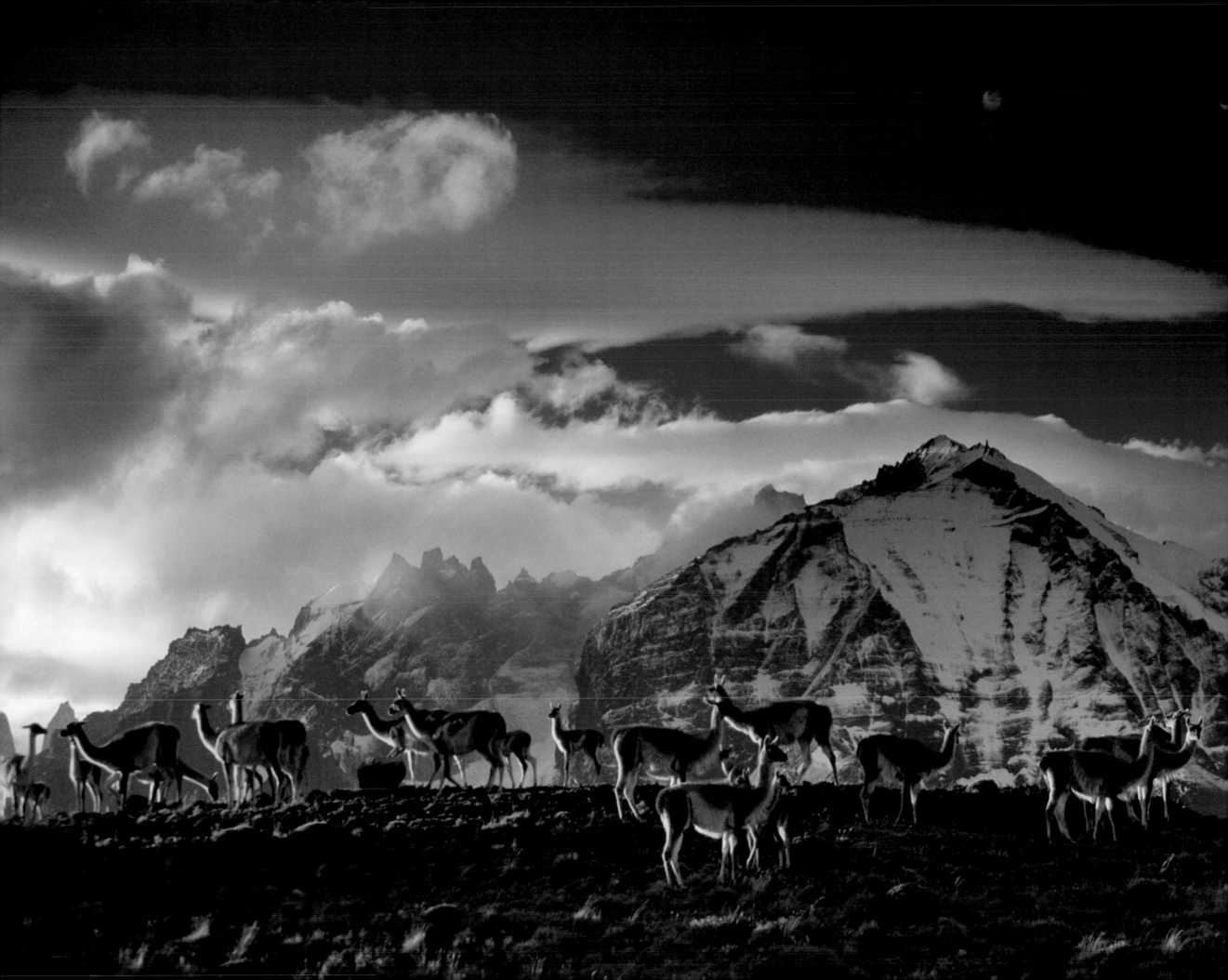

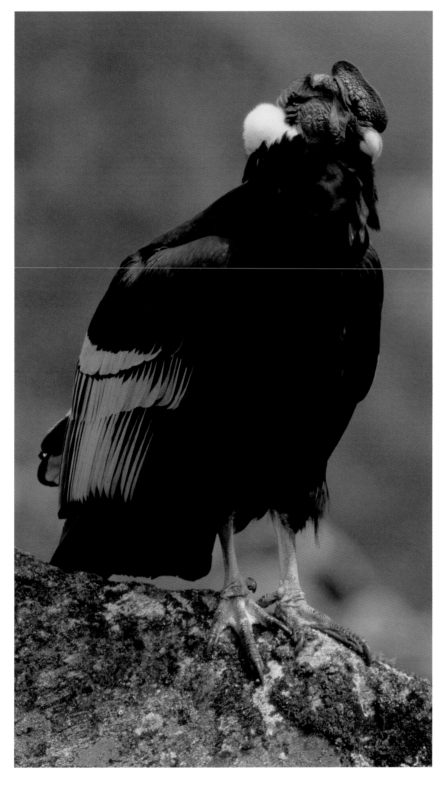

◄ GUANACO

TORRES DEL PAINE NATIONAL PARK, CHILE

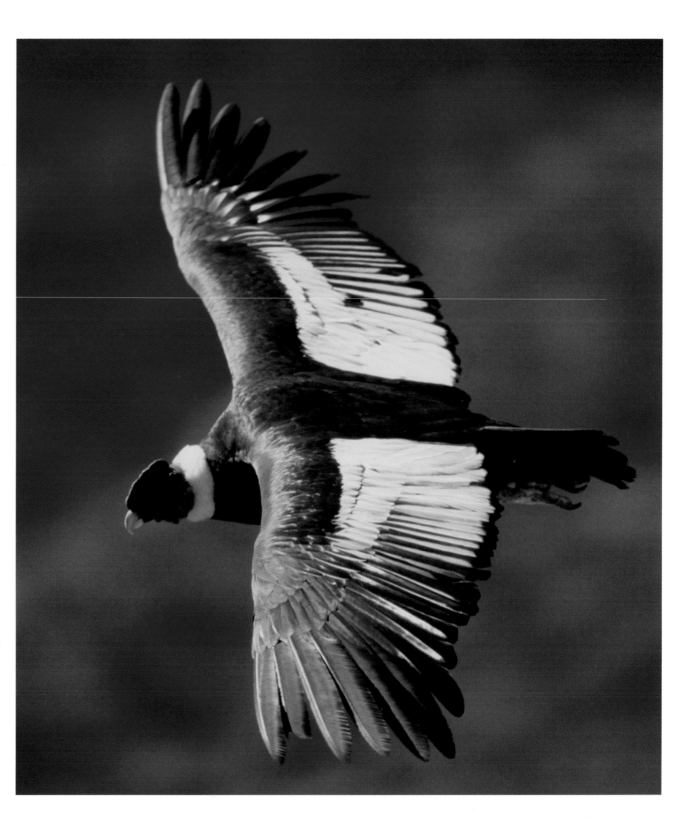

◄ AND ▲ ANDEAN CONDOR

PATAGONIA, ARGENTINA

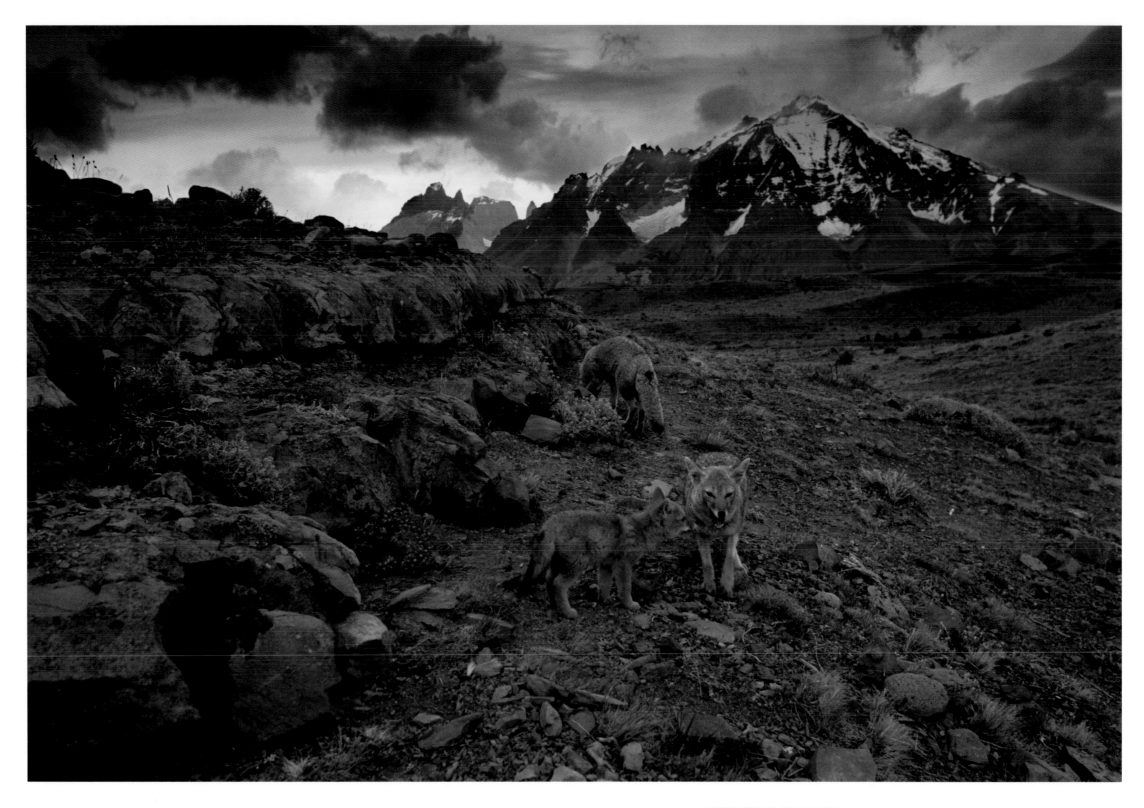

ARGENTINE GRAY FOX

Torres del Paine National Park, Chile

THE LIVING WILD

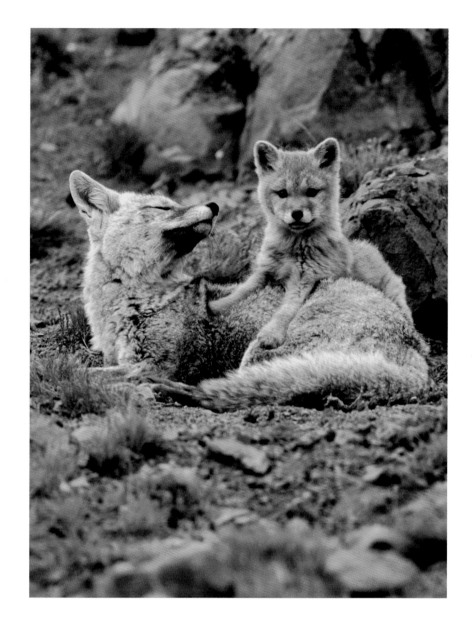

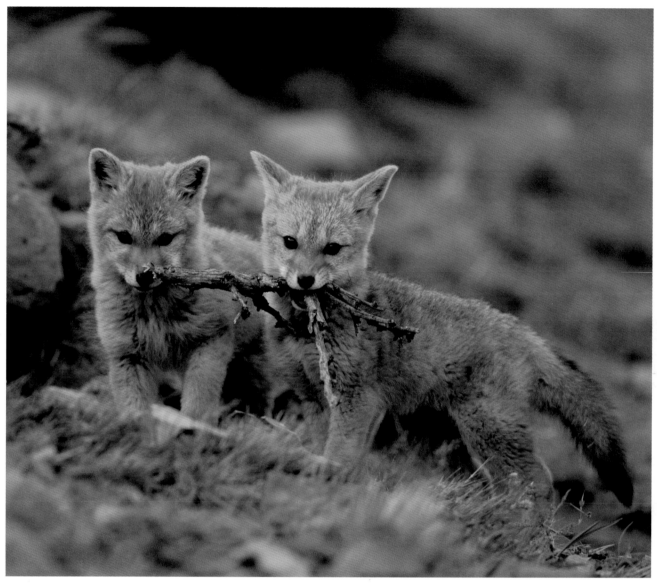

◄ AND ▲ ARGENTINE GRAY FOX ◦
Torres del Paine National Park, Chile

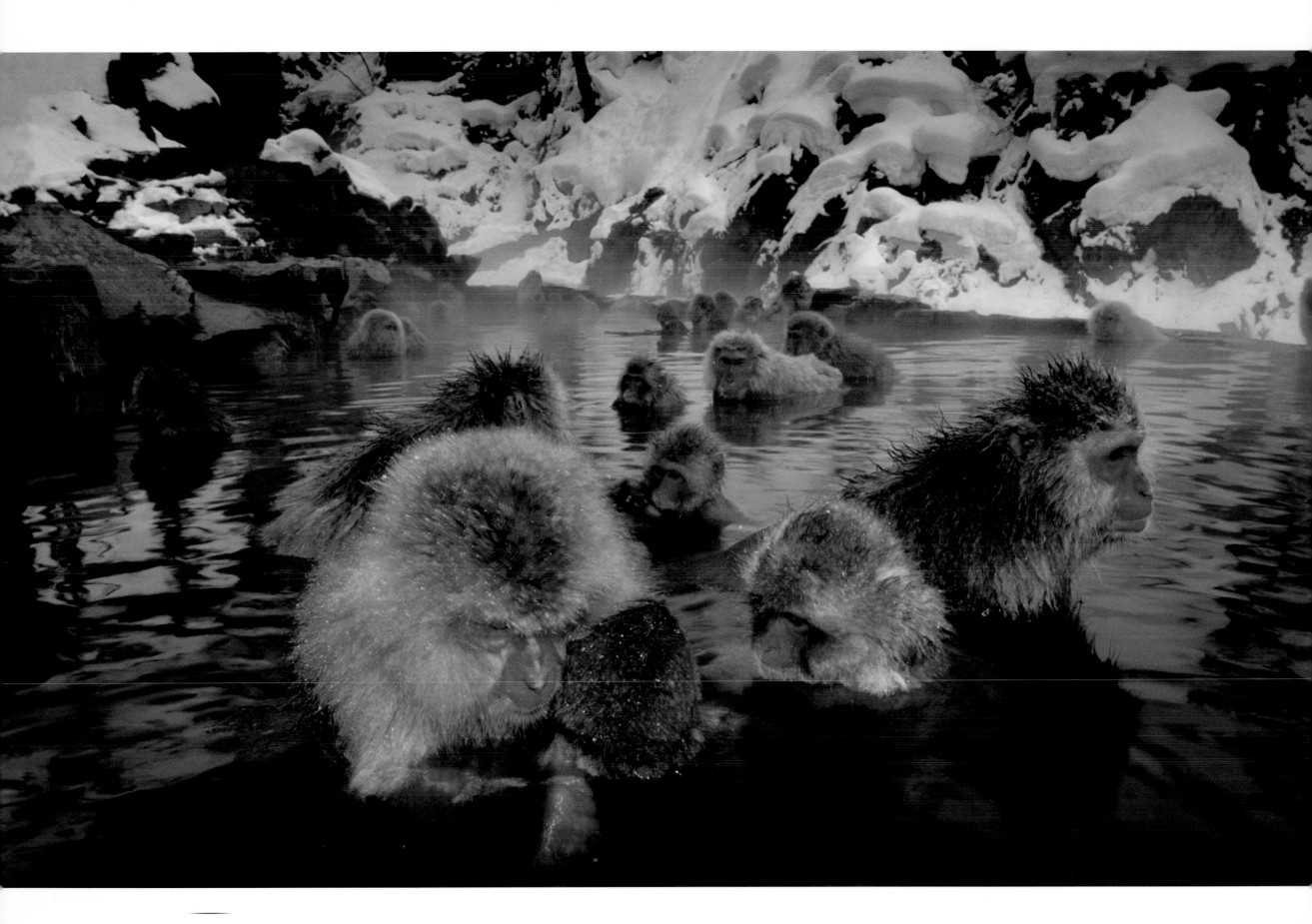

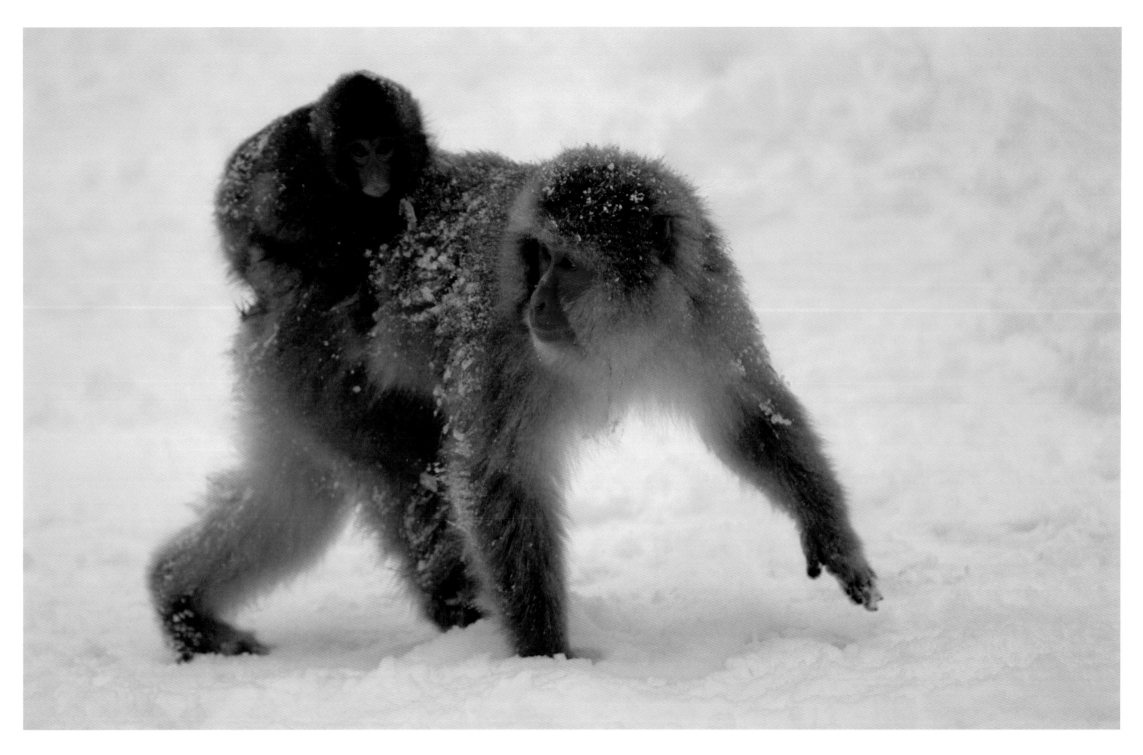

◂ AND ▴ JAPANESE MACAQUE

JAPANESE ALPS, HONSHU ISLAND, JAPAN

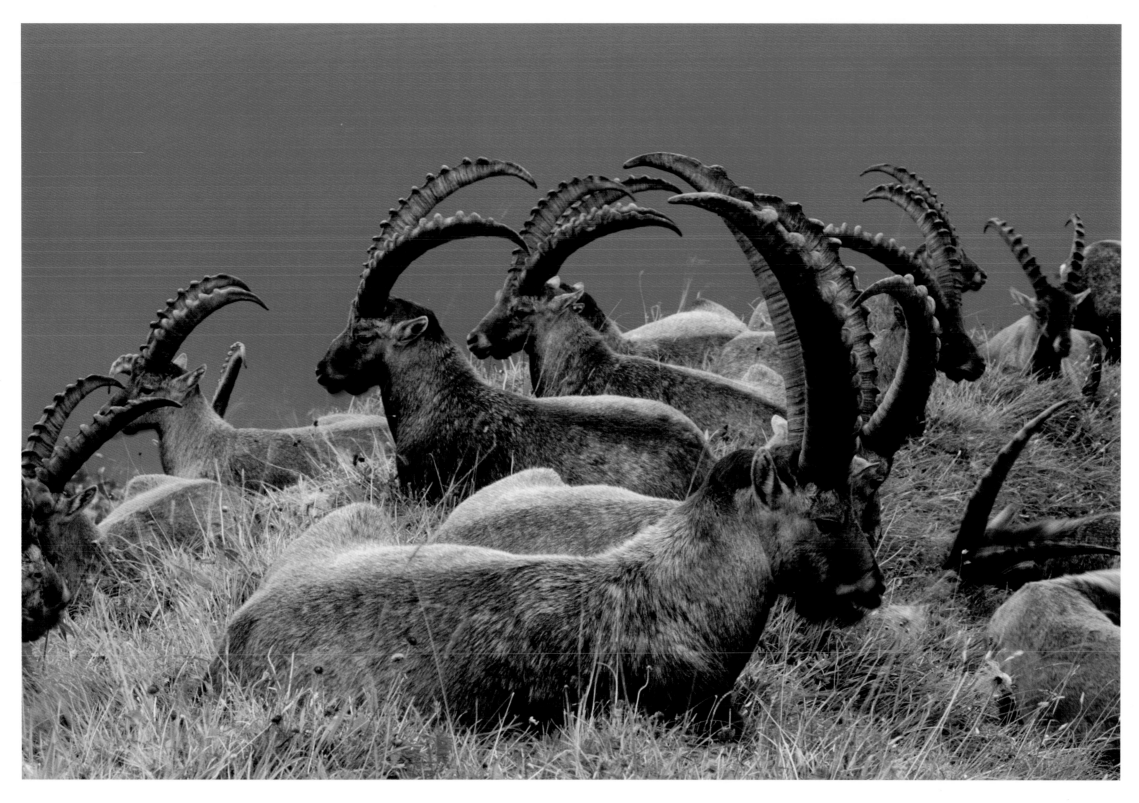

ALPINE IBEX

Interlaken, Alps, Switzerland

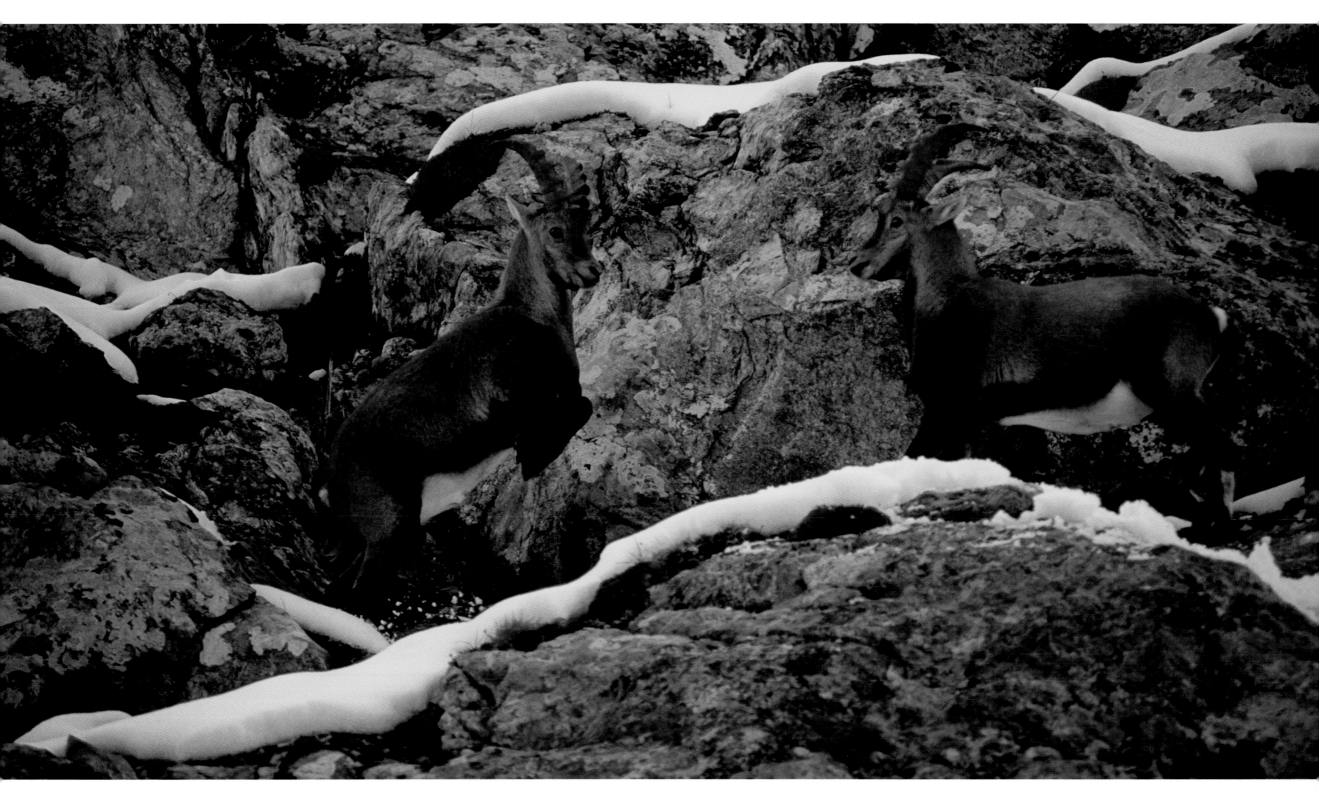

ALPINE IBEX
INTERLAKEN, ALPS, SWITZERLAND

MOUNTAIN

143

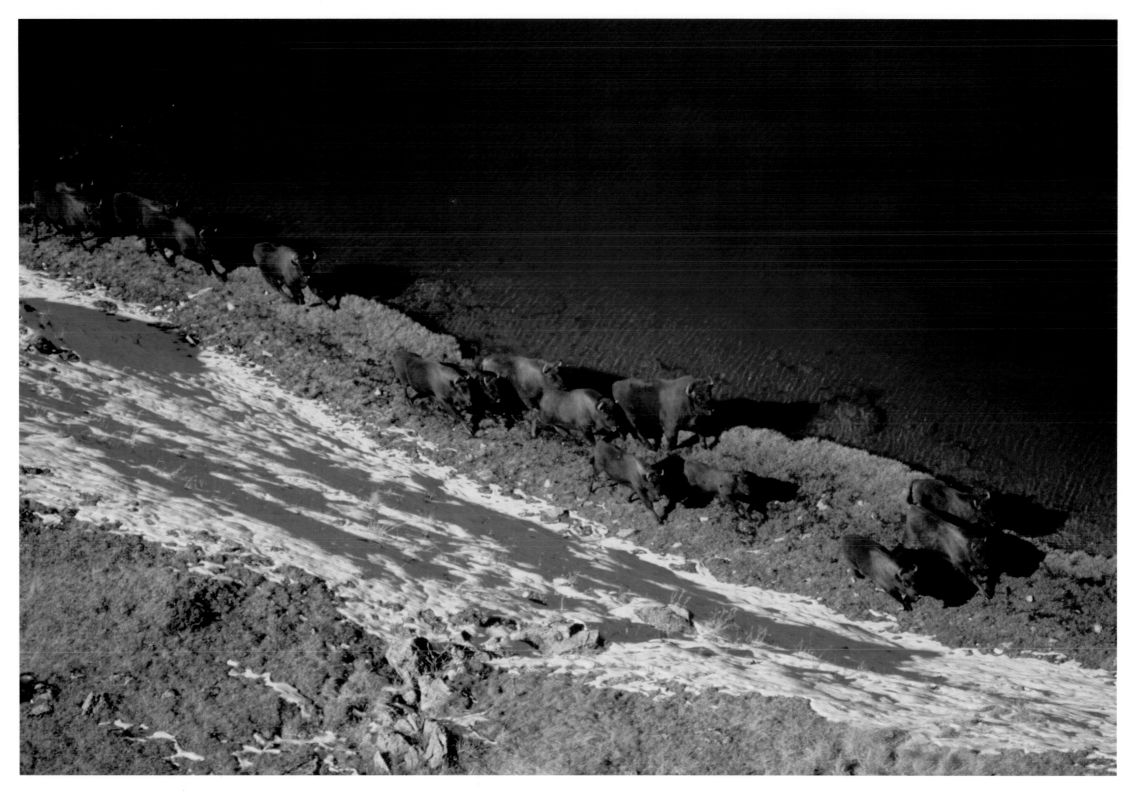

EUROPEAN BISON

Kavkazsky Zapovednik Biosphere Preserve, Russian Federation

► NORTH AMERICAN BISON

Yellowstone National Park, Wyoming, USA

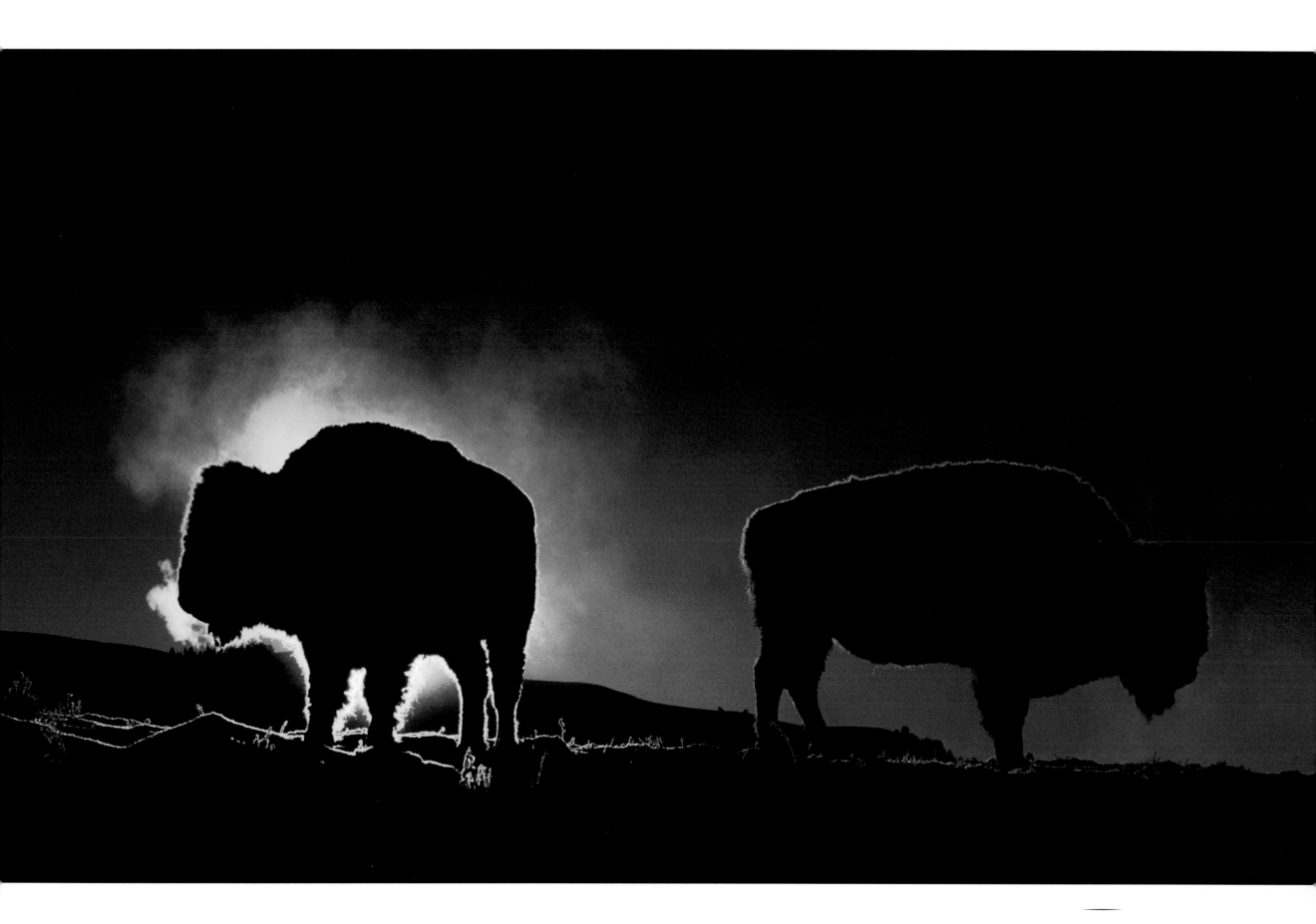

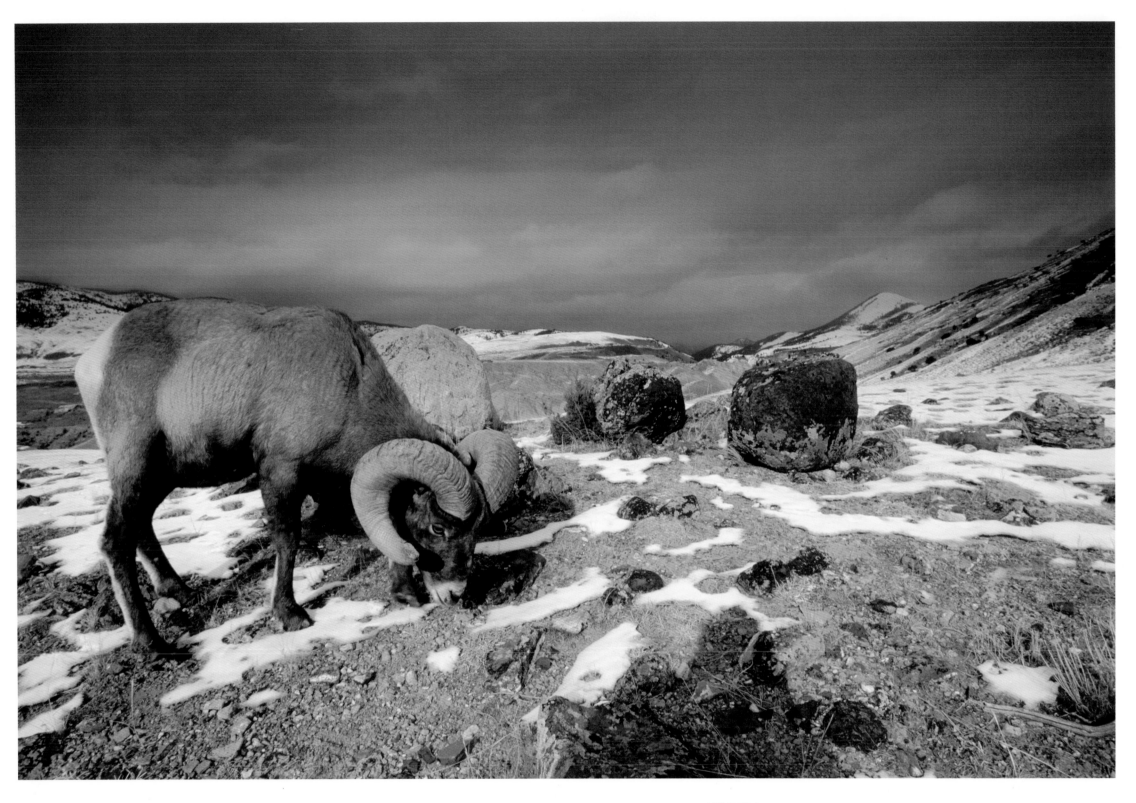

BIGHORN SHEEP ⌒

Yellowstone National Park, Wyoming, USA

► MOOSE ⌒

Denali National Park, Alaska, USA

THE LIVING WILD

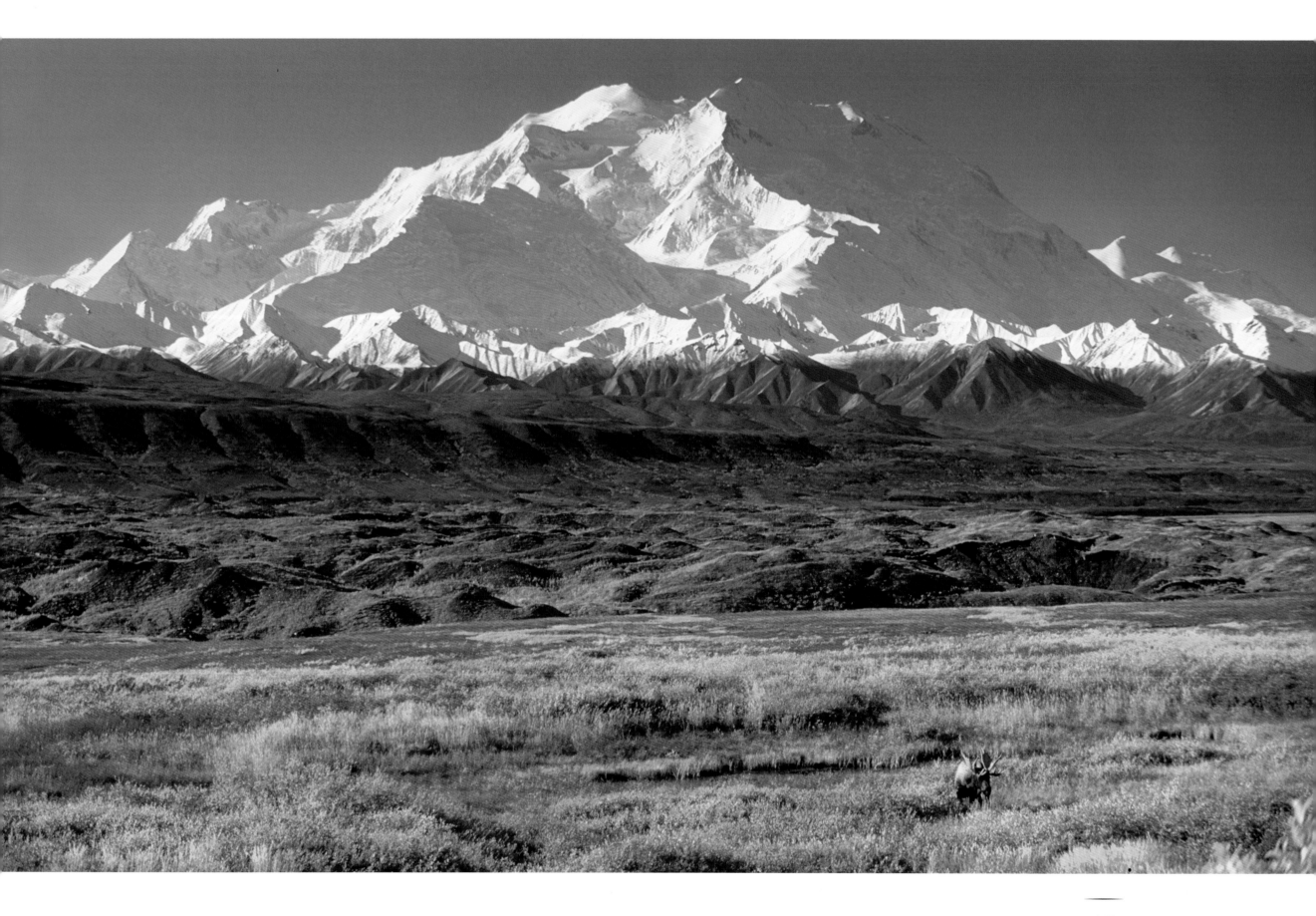

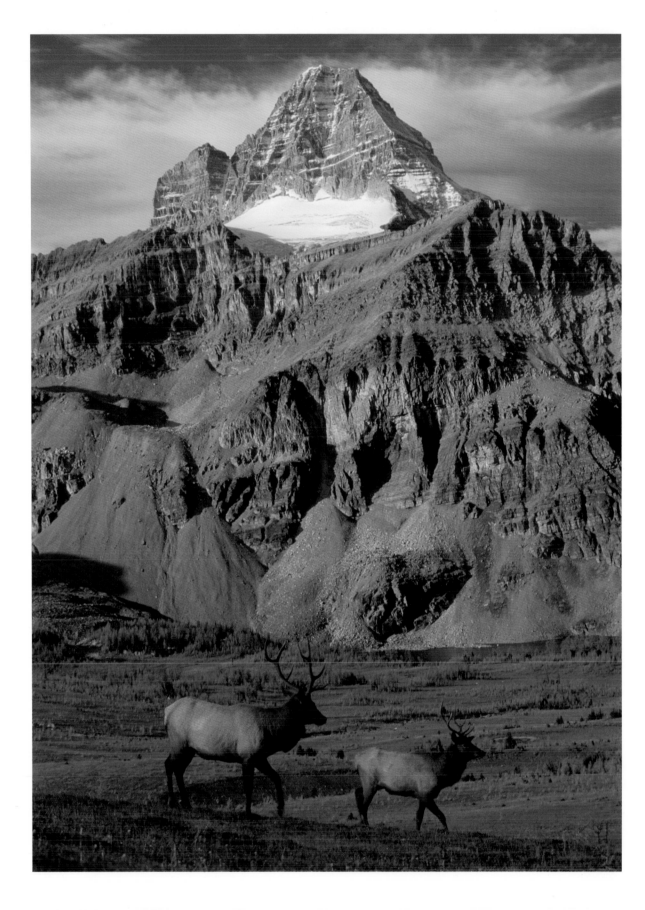

ELK
MOUNT ASSINIBOINE PROVINCIAL PARK,
BRITISH COLUMBIA, CANADA

▶ ELK
ROCKY MOUNTAIN NATIONAL PARK,
COLORADO, USA

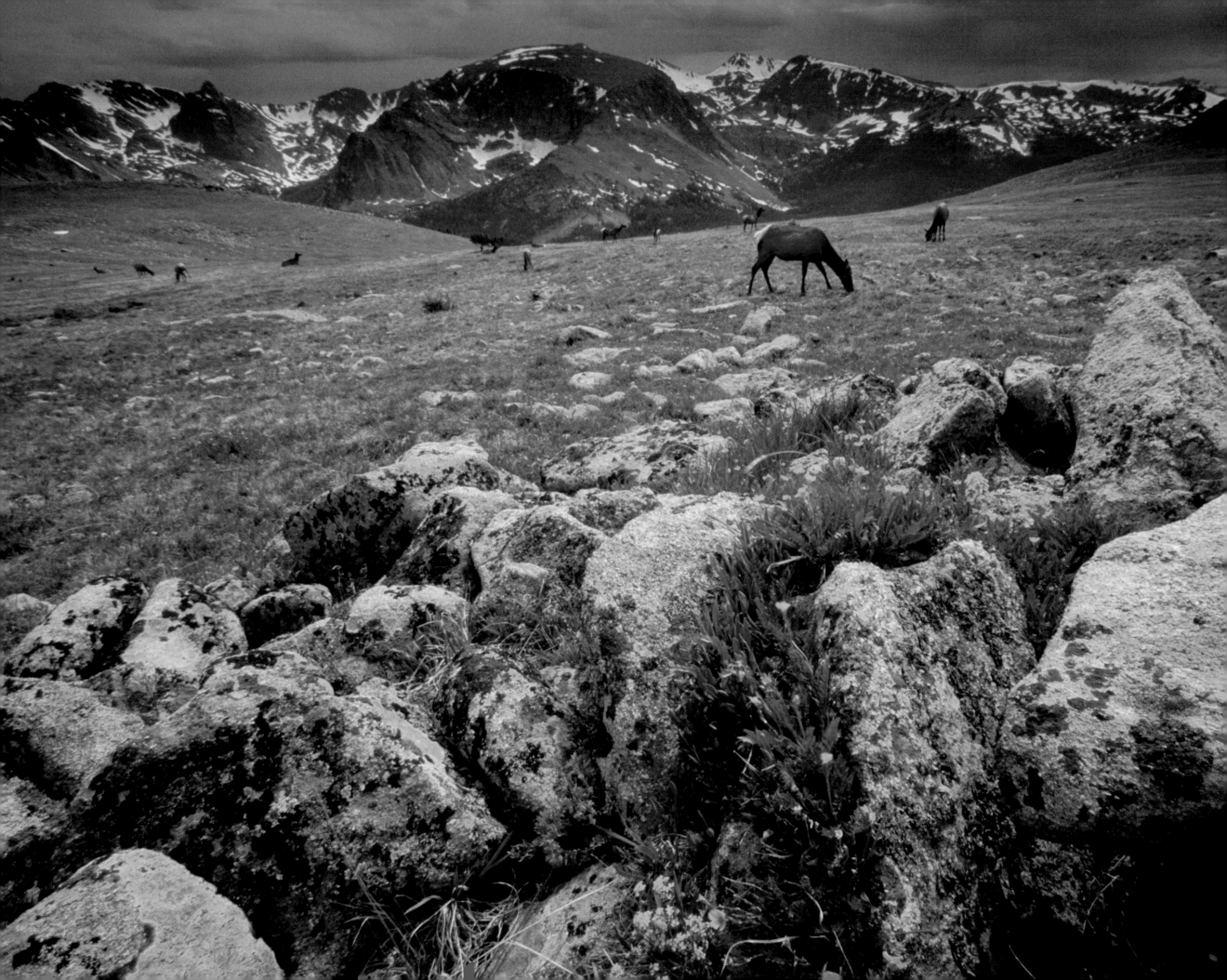

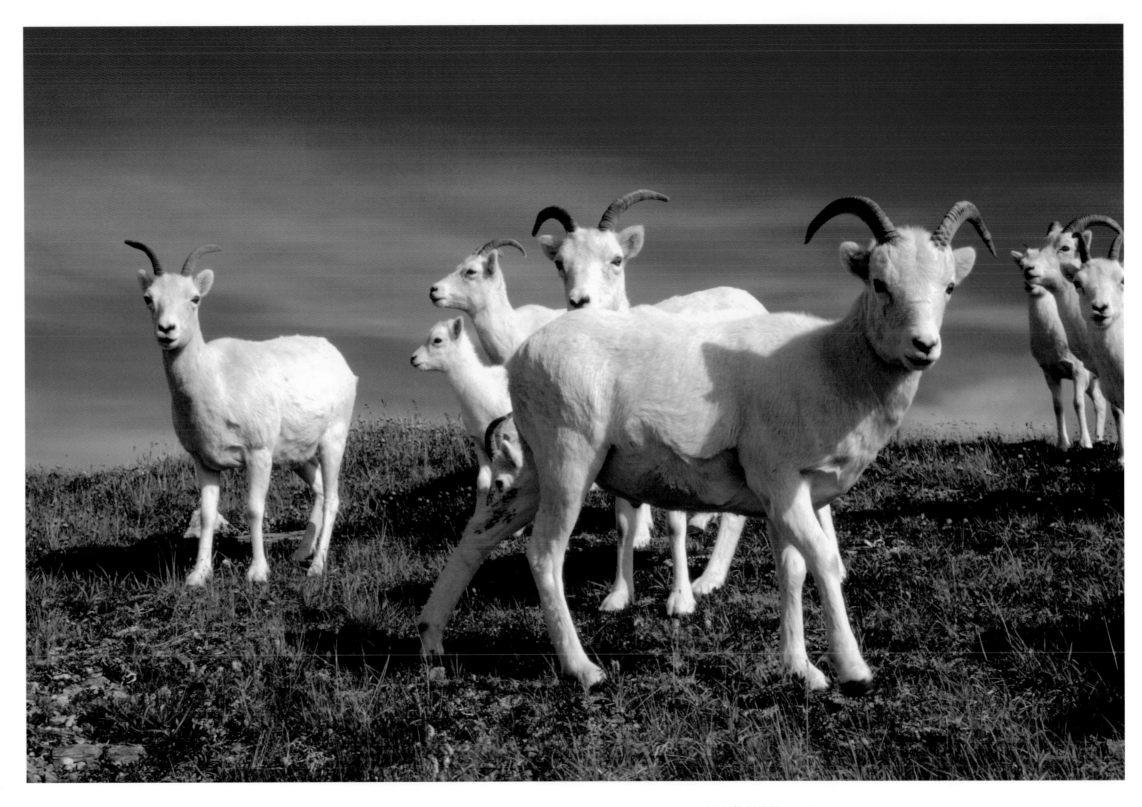

DALL'S SHEEP
Denali National Park, Alaska, USA

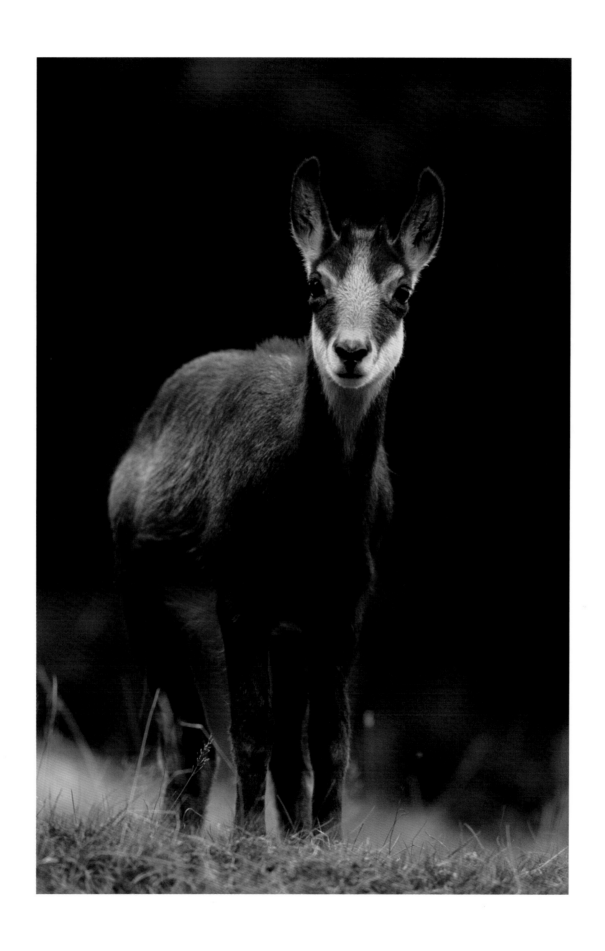

CHAMOIS
Chamonix, Alps du Valais, France

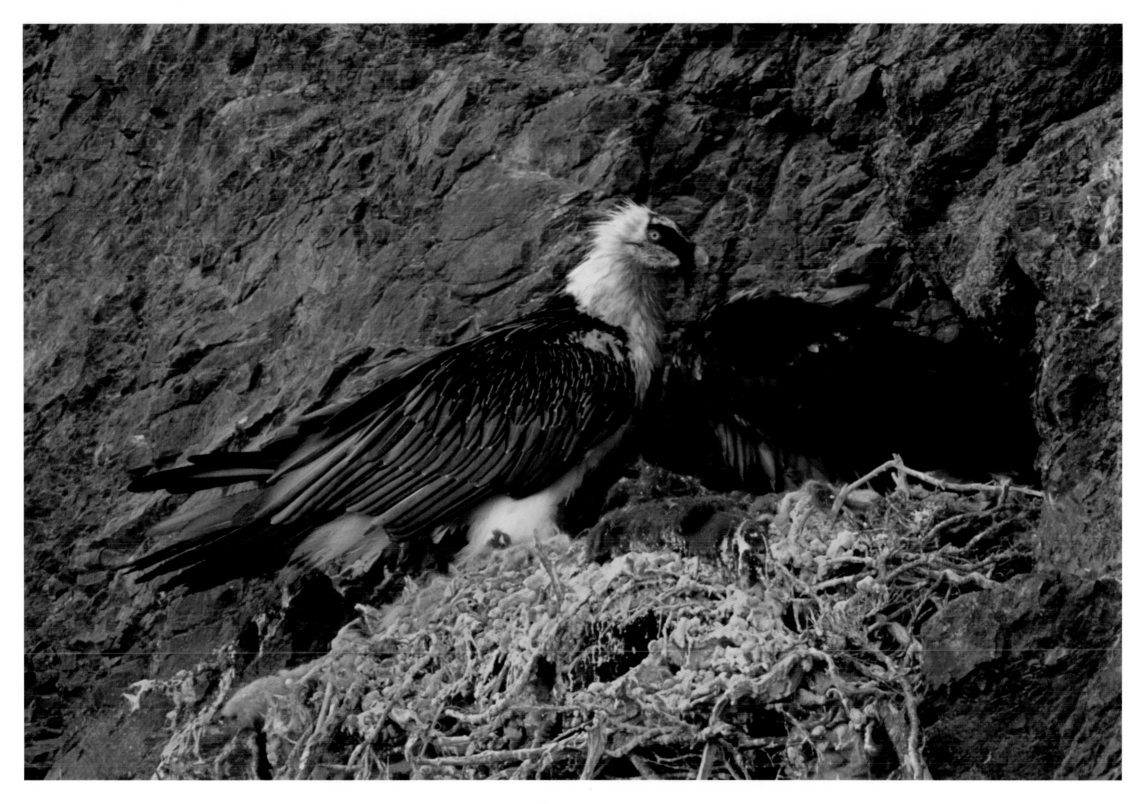

LAMMERGEIER

Gobi Gurvansaikhan National Park, Mongolia

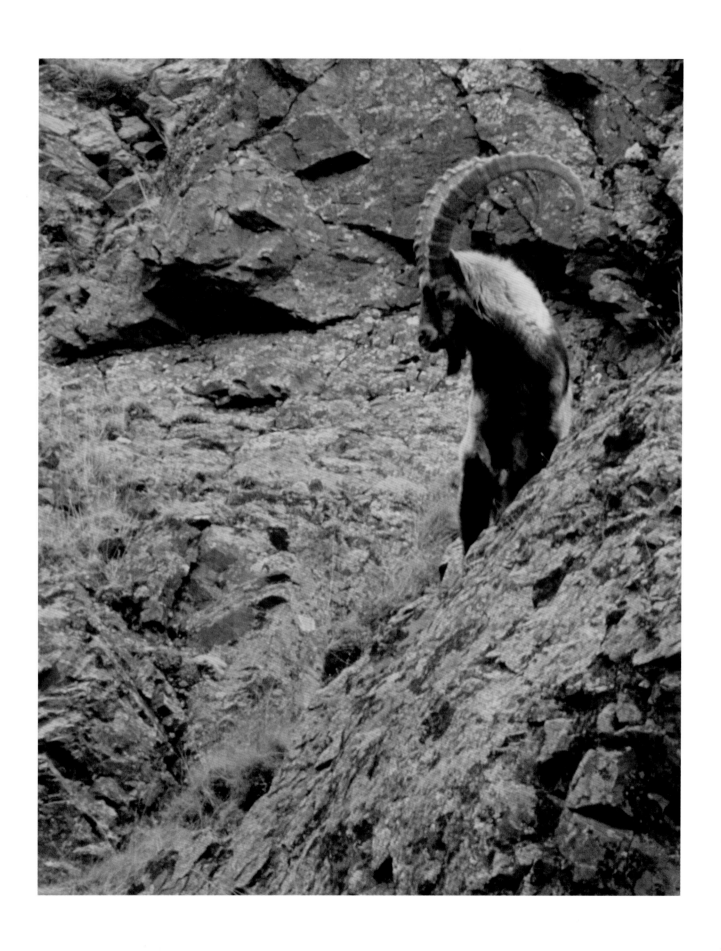

SIBERIAN IBEX

ALTAI MOUNTAINS, MONGOLIA

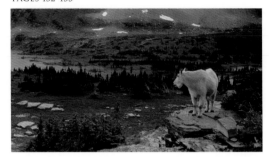

MOUNTAIN GOAT
(*Oreamnos americanus*)

Despite its name, the mountain goat is not a true goat, but a member of the goat-antelope tribe Rupicaprini in the subfamily Caprinae. There is only one species in this genus, and it is unique to North America. Mountain goats flourish in rugged terrain and are well adapted to steep slopes (although many show healed injuries, suggesting that they are not always surefooted). Goats can climb 460 meters in elevation in just 20 minutes in an astonishing display of agility and stamina. Their remote habitat has protected them against human encroachment, but as more people enter the backcountry, that may change. Mountain goats evolved to exploit a harsh physical environment that has significantly fewer predators than other habitats. Because they rely on their extreme habitat for protection, they show little fear of humans, making them a particularly easy target for hunters. There are 50,000 to 100,000 mountain goats in North America.

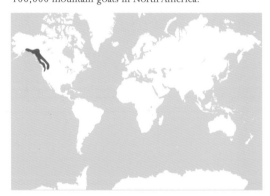

AW: A short hike from Logan Pass provides a spectacular view of Hidden Lake and the surrounding mountains. This is prime mountain goat habitat and the day I hiked this trail, a large billy goat miraculously appeared. Since the setting was so dramatic, I selected a 17–35mm wide-angle lens to encompass the entire vista, including the goat. Using f/22, every element of the composition came into sharp focus. I used a 2-stop graduated neutral density filter to darken the bright sky and bring the entire composition into an even exposure.

Canon EOS-1N, Canon EF 17–35mm lens, f/22 at 1/8 second, 2-stop graduated neutral density filter, Fujichrome Velvia film

---

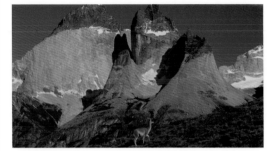

GUANACO
(*Lama guanicoe*)

Guanacos are the only wild members of the genus *Lama*. Their close relatives, llamas (*L. glama*) and alpacas (*L. pacos*), have been domesticated for at least 5,000 years. Guanacos survive in both mountain and plains habitats. Their hemoglobin has a much higher affinity for oxygen than that of other mammals, allowing them to function at high altitudes (up to 4,800 meters). Over the years guanacos have been eliminated from most of the lowland portions of their range. They have been alternately prized for their skin and despised as competitors with domestic sheep. There were as many as 50 million guanacos when Europeans first arrived in the New World. Today their population is less than 600,000. Ninety percent of those surviving live in southern Argentina and southern Chile.

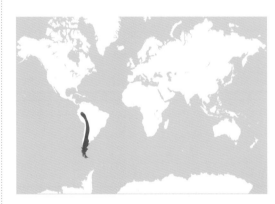

AW: Ancient glaciers carved the spectacular granite faces of Cuernos Towers in Torres del Paine National Park. For days I combed this region, looking for an animal to place in the foreground of this spectacular view. My perseverance finally paid off on the very last morning of my visit, as this lone guanaco strolled by.

Canon EOS-3, Canon EF 70–200mm lens, f/16 at 1/15 second, 2-stop graduated neutral density filter, Fujichrome Velvia film

---

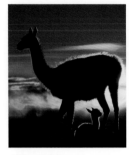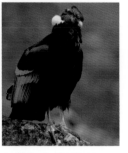

GUANACO
(*Lama guanicoe*)

Guanacos are small camelids with far more delicate features than their relatives in the Old World. Standing about a meter at the shoulder, guanacos weigh 100 to 120 kilograms. They have a slender build and long legs that can power them along at up to 56 kilometers per hour. Although often found in dry mountain habitats, guanacos, like many of the *Lama*, seem to delight in sitting or lying in water and will seek out streams and ponds. They live in family groups that average sixteen members and consist of a single adult male plus females and their dependent offspring. The guanaco infant or "cria" weighs 8 to 15 kilograms at birth and can run almost immediately. They suckle for 6 to 15 months, and youngsters of both sexes are driven from the herd by the adult male when they reach 13 to 15 months of age.

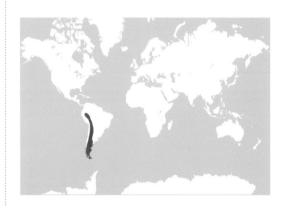

AW: Page 135 — I slowly approached this mother and calf, aligning the setting sun directly behind the mother's torso for a dramatic silhouette. For my exposure, I took a spot reading off the highlighted fur.

Canon EOS-3, Canon EF 70–200mm lens, f/11 at 1/125 second, Fujichrome Velvia film

AW: Page 136 — I chose an 80mm focal length to record this scene, allowing me to capture the landscape without losing the guanacos. I used a 2-stop graduated neutral density filter to keep the backdrop from washing out.

Canon EOS-3, Canon EF 70–200mm lens, f/16 at 1/30 second, Fujichrome Velvia film

---

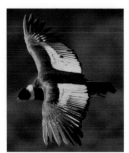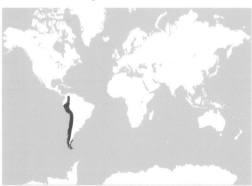

ANDEAN CONDOR
(*Vultur gryphus*)

The Andean condor is the largest raptor in the world. It measures approximately 1.3 meters in length and has a wingspan that can exceed 3 meters. With a range across the backbone of South America—the Andes—condors usually nest above 3,000 meters. Such high-altitude dwelling has protected them from large-scale human encroachment, but the population has suffered from mortality associated with ingesting pesticide-contaminated prey and being shot by farmers who blame the condor for livestock deaths (despite the fact that they feed largely on carrion). Condors do not reach sexual maturity until they are seven or eight years old, and the females only lay two eggs every other year (rarely are a pair able to successfully raise both chicks). With such a low recruitment rate, it can take many years for populations to recover from human-induced losses. No reliable population figures are available for the species as a whole.

AW: Page 137 (left) — To photograph this bird, I crawled over 100 meters to maintain a low and less intimidating profile. When I began photographing, the condor was so relaxed that it often closed its eyes.

Canon EOS-3, Canon EF 600mm lens, f/5.6 at 1/60 second, Fujichrome Velvia film

AW: Page 137 (right) — At times I watched as many as eighty condors soar below me. I panned my 400mm lens with the motion of this bird. The condors came so close I could have filled the frame using a 50mm lens.

Canon EOS-3, Canon EF 400mm lens, f/5.6 at 1/250 second, Fujichrome Astia film

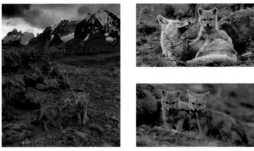
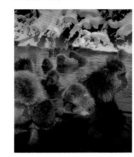
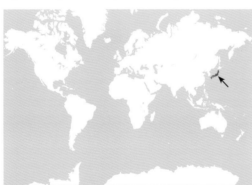

ARGENTINE GRAY FOX
(Pseudalopex griseus)

There are four species of South American fox. The Argentine gray fox is found in the low mountains and open plains of Chile, western Argentina, and Patagonia, where it favors open grasslands and forest edges. Hunting has resulted in population declines in all four species. Their skins are prized, and during the 1980s up to 100,000 Argentine fox skins were exported annually, the vast majority from Argentina. Although legally protected in much of its range (and benefiting from a global drop in the demand for fur), these foxes are still killed by farmers and ranchers who blame them for taking domestic fowl and sheep. Populations in Argentina are now believed to be stable; no reliable population figures are available for Chile. The subspecies, *P. g. fulvipes*, found only on Chiloé Island (in Chile's Los Lagos province about 960 kilometers south of Santiago), is considered the rarest South American canid.

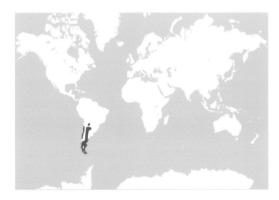

AW: All photos – I had to habituate these foxes by assembling three sticks and putting a bag on top to resemble my equipment. After three days, I replaced the decoy. I used an automatic, center-weighted setting for changing light levels and a remote so I could stay 75 meters away. Soon, by maintaining a very low profile, I was able to get very close to the den.

Page 138 – Canon EOS-3, Canon EF 17–35mm lens, f/16 at 1/30 second, 2-stop graduated neutral density filter

Pages 139 (left & right) – Canon EOS-3, Canon EF 70–200mm lens, f/5.6 at 1/125

All photos – Fujichrome Velvia film

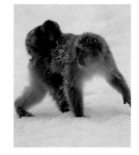
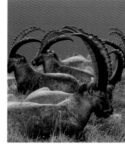
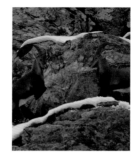

JAPANESE MACAQUE
(Macaca fuscata)

Japanese macaques are the most northern-ranging of primates—with the exception of humans. They live in the evergreen forests of Japan's highlands and mountains, where they feed on fruits, leaves, flowers, insects, and tree bark. Classified as endangered by the IUCN–World Conservation Union, Japanese macaques are threatened by a loss of habitat as their forests are logged. Although revered in much of Japan, the macaques also face opposition from farmers due to the damage they can inflict on crops. Macaques have declined dramatically since 1923, and in the early 1990s as many as 5,000 animals were culled from the population each year in response to complaints from farmers. One subspecies, *M. f. yakui*, found on Yakushima Island, is faring particularly poorly as habitat losses force animals to raid orange groves for food. The current population of the entire species is estimated at 35,000 to 50,000 animals, and declining.

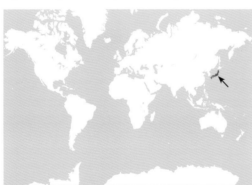

AW: Page 140 – I stopped down to f/16 to bring the entire scene into focus. I used a 2-stop graduated neutral density filter to darken the brighter snow-clad hillside selectively, and a fill flash to put a little light in the macaque faces.

Canon 3, Canon EF 17–35mm lens, f/16 at 1/4 second, 2-stop graduated neutral density filter, fill flash, Fujichrome Velvia film

AW: Page 141 – While taking portraits, I noticed some motion out of the corner of my eye. I had enough time to get this shot, thanks entirely to autofocus.

Canon EOS-3, Canon EF 70–200mm lens, f/4 at 1/125 second, Fujichrome Velvia film (pushed 1 stop)

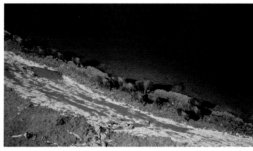

ALPINE IBEX
(Capra ibex ibex)

The alpine ibex could once be found throughout the European Alps, ranging in the mountains of France, Germany, Austria, Switzerland, and northern Italy. One of several ibex subspecies—although some authorities treat them as full species—the alpine ibex was almost hunted out of existence by the early nineteenth century. Its dramatic scimitar horns—present in both sexes and up to 1.4 meters long in males—were sought by sport hunters, and its body parts used for purported medicinal purposes. After decades of hunting pressure, a small population of just 60 animals was all that survived in Italy's Gran Paradiso National Park. A breeding program was established and gradually the herd grew and its animals were used to seed other herds. Today, more than 3,000 live in Gran Paradiso, and in excess of 12,000 can be found in Switzerland and other parts of Europe's highest mountain range.

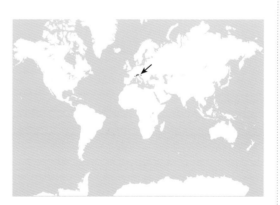

AW: Page 142 – I was able to get within 3.5 meters of this herd. I composed the photograph to create a cathedral-like opening through their horns. I stopped my lens down to f/16 to bring all of the herd into focus, and used a polarizing filter to bring out the color of the lake.

Canon EOS-1N/RS, Canon EF 70–200mm lens, f/16 at 1/8 second, polarizing filter, Fujichrome Velvia film

AW: Page 143 – In the Swiss Alps, I photographed ibex on the nearby cliffs. It was late afternoon on a cloudy day, so I pushed my film to get the sharpest image.

Canon EOS-1N, Canon EF 600mm lens, f/4 at 1/125 second, Fujichrome Astia film (pushed 1 stop)

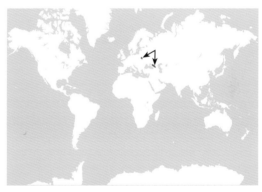

EUROPEAN BISON
(Bison bonasus)

In historical time, European bison could be found from England to southern Sweden, and from northern Spain east into Poland and western Russia. However, as the human population grew, the bison were eliminated. They survived in France until the sixth century, and in remote quarters of Germany until the eighteenth century. By 1900 they had been entirely extirpated, except for in the Caucasus Mountains and the Bialowieza Forest on the border between Poland and Belarus. These last remaining herds were gone by 1925. Fortunately 12 animals survived in captivity and their descendants have been reintroduced into the wild. The Bialowieza Forest now holds about 500 animals, and 2,900 occur in other areas, including the Caucasus Mountains. However, since all are descended from just a dozen animals, there has been a significant amount of inbreeding, with adverse impacts on life-span, juvenile mortality, and intercalf intervals.

AW: European bison inhabit a very different environment from that of their American cousins. From the perspective of a hovering helicopter, I photographed this herd as it ran along an alpine lake at an elevation of 3,300 meters in the Caucasus Mountains. I had been photographing these remote mountains, when I unexpectedly came across these animals. Normally these long-legged bison are found in only a few forest preserves in Russia and Poland.

Canon F1, Canon EF 70–200mm lens, f/4 at 1/500 second, Fujichrome 50 film

NOTES FROM THE FIELD

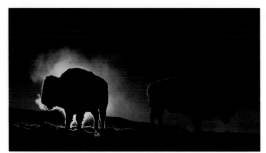

NORTH AMERICAN BISON
(Bison bison)

Before the arrival of Europeans, an estimated 50 million bison (B. b. bison) roamed North America's plains and more than 150,000 woodland bison (B. b. athabascae) could be found in western Canada. By 1890 fewer than 1,000 plains bison were left, victims of overhunting and a government plan to subjugate the Plains Indians. To the north, the woodland bison was reduced to 300. Today, there are 200,000 bison in North America, but most are in privately managed herds. The only free-ranging bison occur in Yellowstone National Park, Wyoming, and Wood Buffalo National Park, Northwest Territories. The woodland bison suffered further indignities in the 1920s when thousands of plains bison were released into the woodland bisons' range, where they promptly hybridized with the native subspecies. A selective breeding program has since isolated near-pure woodland animals, and today there are about 2,500 "pure" woodland bison.

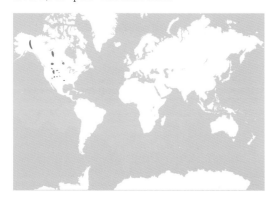

AW: A bison stands on a small rise to catch the first rays of the morning sun in Wyoming's Yellowstone National Park. The bitter cold of a long winter's night has left the animal encased in a mantle of thick frost. I photographed the bison with the intent of creating a silhouette by deliberately aligning the bison against the rising sun. I calculated the exposure by spot reading off the sky directly in front of the bison's head.

Canon EOS-3, Canon EF 70–200mm lens, f/16 at 1/250 second, Fujichrome Velvia film

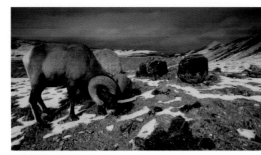

BIGHORN SHEEP
(Ovis canadensis)

Rocky Mountain bighorn (Ovis c. canadensis) are large sheep, with males weighing 73 to 143 kilograms and females somewhat smaller at 53 to 91 kilograms. While both sexes have horns, only the males sport the immense spiral horns that make them so popular with trophy hunters. Bighorn favor upland habitats, particularly alpine meadows that give them easy access to rocky cliffs. Such habitats provide a measure of protection from cougars (Felis concolor), grizzly bears (Ursus arctos), and humans. Sheep are remarkably surefooted when crossing treacherous rock faces, but even so, many slip and such injuries are frequently fatal—in the spring, bears often patrol the bases of cliffs to scavenge the carcasses of animals that fell during the winter. As is the case with many large mammals in North America, bighorn face increasing competition from livestock, habitat losses to residential and recreational developments, diseases spread by domestic sheep, and hunters.

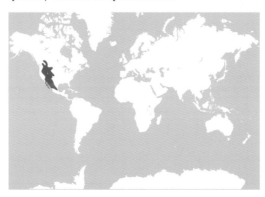

AW: I was watching a small band of bighorn rams grazing on the slope below me, waiting for a good opportunity to photograph them. One of the rams turned in my direction as he continued grazing. I reached for my 70–200mm zoom lens, but the ram surprised me by coming too close for this range of focal lengths. I switched to my 17–35mm wide-angle lens, sat very still, and got this image as the ram passed within 1 meter of me.

Canon EOS-3, Canon EF 17–35mm lens, f/11 at 1/30 second, Fujichrome Provia film

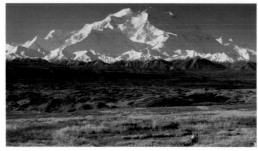

MOOSE
(Alces alces)

Denali (Mount McKinley) rises almost 6,100 meters, forming the centerpiece of the Alaska Range. Despite its imposing presence, the mountain can prove elusive due to frequent cloud cover. Moose are common in Denali National Park, where they browse willow, birch, and aspen. Known as elk in Europe, they once ranged across northern Europe and the Caucasus into Siberia, and from Alaska and Canada south along the Rockies and into parts of the American Northeast. However, excessive hunting resulted in substantial regional population declines. Moose disappeared from western Europe in the thirteenth century (surviving in Scandinavia), from the Caucasus in the early nineteenth century, and from much of the contiguous United States by the early twentieth century. Under careful management, they have returned to parts of their former range. An estimated 900,000 moose live in North America (mainly in Alaska and Canada), and one million in Eurasia.

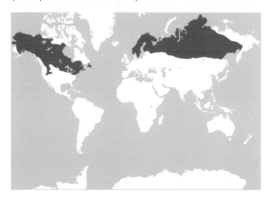

AW: Here I had to use a combination of filters and settings that greatly reduced my chance of success. I used my zoom lens at 80mm, so that Denali is slightly enlarged, as is the moose. A polarizing filter brought out the rich colors of the tundra, while darkening the sky. I used a 2-stop graduated neutral density filter to darken the sky and bring the entire scene into the same exposure. Stopping down to an f/16 setting brought every element into focus. All of this lengthened my exposure time, so the moving moose was blurred in most but not all of the exposures.

Canon EOS-1N, Canon EF 70–200mm lens, f/16 at 1/8 second, polarizing filter, 2-stop graduated neutral density filter, Fujichrome Velvia film

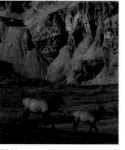 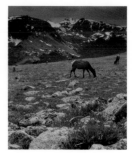

ELK
(Cervus elaphus)

Elk (also known as red deer or wapiti) are the largest of ten species in the "red deer" genus Cervus. They stand up to 1.5 meters at the shoulder and weigh 75 to 340 kilograms. North American elk are usually larger than their European relatives. The impressive antlers, found only in males, may measure more than 1.7 meters across. Elk are found in a wide variety of habitats, including lowlands, coniferous forests, open forests, grasslands, chaparral, and mountains. While elk are native to Europe (where they are known as red deer), North America, and Asia, they have been introduced to other countries (including Australia, New Zealand, and Argentina), where they can come into conflict with indigenous wildlife. Several subspecies of elk, found in Corsica and Sardinia, North Africa, and Asia Minor, as well as six subspecies found in China, the Tibetan Plateau, Central Russia, and Afghanistan, are considered to be highly endangered.

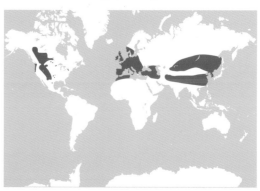

AW: Page 148 – Using a 70–200mm lens, I zoomed to arrive at the best composition, framing tightly around the elk and the summit of Mount Assiniboine. I used a 2-stop graduated neutral density filter to darken the sky and the snow, and stopped down to f/22 to attain sharp focus.

Canon EOS-1N/RS, Canon EF 70–200mm lens, f/22 at 1/15 second, 2-stop graduated neutral density filter, Fujichrome Velvia film

AW: Page 149 – I wanted to make the dramatic landscape the primary component here, so I selected a 17–35mm wide-angle lens to record this scene.

Canon EOS-3, Canon EF17–35mm lens, f/16 at 1/15 second, Fujichrome Velvia film

THE LIVING WILD

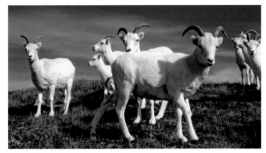

DALL'S SHEEP
(*Ovis dalli*)

Dall's sheep inhabit some of the tallest mountain ranges in Alaska, including the Alaska and St. Elias Ranges. During the summer they range high into alpine tundra habitats, moving downslope in winter to find areas with greater forage availability. Dall's sheep in the northern part of their range are creamy white in color, while those to the south tend to be brown with a white rump patch, muzzle, and white on the inside of their hind legs and forehead. Where the two races overlap, sheep can be found with more intermediate coloring; for example, the saddle-backed sheep of the eastern Yukon. Southern Dall's sheep are consistently larger than their northern relatives. A southern male weighs about 90 kilograms, while northern males weigh 75 to 90 kilograms. Their remote habitats have protected them from serious threats, but sport and subsistence hunting can result in local population declines. Most of the estimated 112,000 Dall's sheep reside in Alaska.

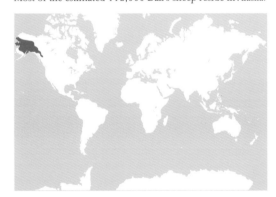

AW: I am always surprised at how relaxed animals become when they have lived their entire lives in zones where hunting is prohibited. This herd of lambs and ewes literally walked straight up to me on a ridge crest in Denali National Park. After a few moments of the herd and I studying one another practically face to face, the herd continued down the ridge.

Canon EOS-1N, Canon EF 17–35mm lens, f/16 at 1/60 second, Fujichrome 100 film

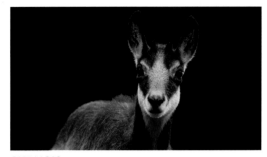

CHAMOIS
(*Rupicapra rupicapra*)

Two species of chamois inhabit the mountains of Europe: *R. pyrenaica* is confined to northwestern Spain, Pyrenees, and central Italy's Apennines, while *R. rupicapra* ranges through the Alps, Balkans, and Caucasus. Goatlike in appearance, the chamois stands 0.7 to 0.8 meter tall and has a stiff, coarse coat that forms a thick underfur in winter. Both sexes have slender, hooked black horns. In summer, chamois are found above 1,800 meters, where they stay close to cliff faces; in winter, they descend to below 1,100 meters. Hunting for meat and hides, combined with habitat loss and disturbance, has driven chamois from much of their former range. Several subspecies are highly endangered, including *R. r. cartusiana* of France's Massif de la Chartreuse (numbering about 150 animals) and *R. r. tatrica* of Poland and Slovakia's Tatra Mountains (numbering fewer than 1,000 individuals). The entire European population is estimated at 400,000.

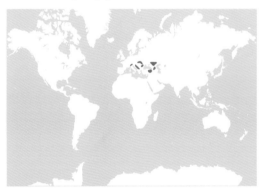

AW: While hiking along the trail to Le Buet in the Chamonix Region of the French Alps, I came upon this chamois grazing in an open clearing in an evergreen forest. I selected a 70–200mm lens to photograph the animal, because I wanted to isolate it against a solid, dark backdrop. In doing so, the lighter facial markings become more evident.

Canon EOS-1N, Canon EF 70–200mm lens, f/11 at 1/30 second, Fujichrome Velvia film

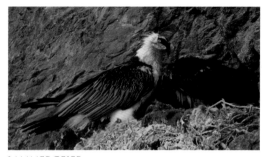

LAMMERGEIER
(*Gypaetus barbatus*)

The lammergeier or bearded vulture is a huge raptor, with a wingspan of over 2.5 meters. They have black wings and a black facial mask, while their bodies are a rich orange color, the result of mineral particles impregnated in their feathers. Inhabiting high mountain ranges up to 8,000 meters (but breeding only to 4,400 meters), lammergeiers feed on bones—they make up 85 percent of its diet. They favor the leg bones of animals like sheep and goats, and will also feed on rodents, birds, and reptiles. If they are not able to break the bones themselves, they will carry them up into the air and drop them from heights of 20 to 80 meters. Lammergeiers have declined throughout Europe, Asia, and Africa—mainly because of poisoning by ranchers who mistakenly blame them for killing livestock, and direct hunting. Most populations are now fragmented and the vulture is extinct in several parts of its former range.

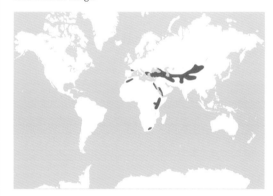

AW: I first saw these immense vultures while participating in a Mount Everest expedition in Tibet in 1984. To get this shot, I traveled to remote Mongolia. I assembled a blind across a steep mountain ravine from where the birds' nest was situated, and then spent two days watching them. During that time, I was fortunate to get nineteen exposures. Unfortunately, the light level was always so low in the deep recesses of the ravine that only four exposures turned out sharp enough to use.

Canon EOS-1N, Canon EF 600mm lens, Canon Extender EF 2x, f/8 at 1/8 second, Fujichrome Provia film (pushed 1 stop)

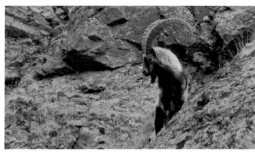

SIBERIAN IBEX
(*Capra ibex sibirica*)

The Siberian ibex is considered a species (*Capra sibirica*) by some, and a subspecies by others. Overhunting, poaching, habitat encroachment by people, and competition with domestic livestock have impacted the Siberian ibex like the alpine ibex in Europe. They are found in the mountains of eastern Kazakhstan, Tajikistan, Kirghizia, northern Afghanistan, Pakistan, and India; east into China's Sinkiang Province; and north into southern and western Mongolia and southern Siberia. Estimates from the late 1980s suggested that 100,000 animals could be found in the former Soviet Republics; approximately 10,000 to 15,000 animals were being hunted annually. Other estimates indicate there could be 60,000 Siberian Ibex in western China, 20,000 in Afghanistan and the western Himalayas, and 80,000 in Mongolia. Military activity and political instability may well have adversely impacted several of these populations.

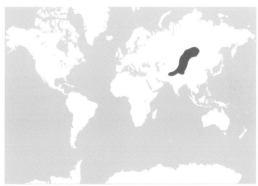

AW: A Siberian ibex traverses a steep slope high in Mongolia's Altai Mountains. These mountains are also home to a population of snow leopards (*Panthera uncia*) that primarily prey on argali sheep (*Ovis ammon*) as well as on the stately ibex. To get this photograph, I remained concealed in a blind for 12 hours near a mineral lick. In the late afternoon, this mature male appeared across a small ravine just above the lick.

Canon EOS-3, Canon EF 600mm lens, Canon Extender EF 1.4x, f/11 at 1/15 second, Fujichrome Velvia film

NOTES FROM THE FIELD

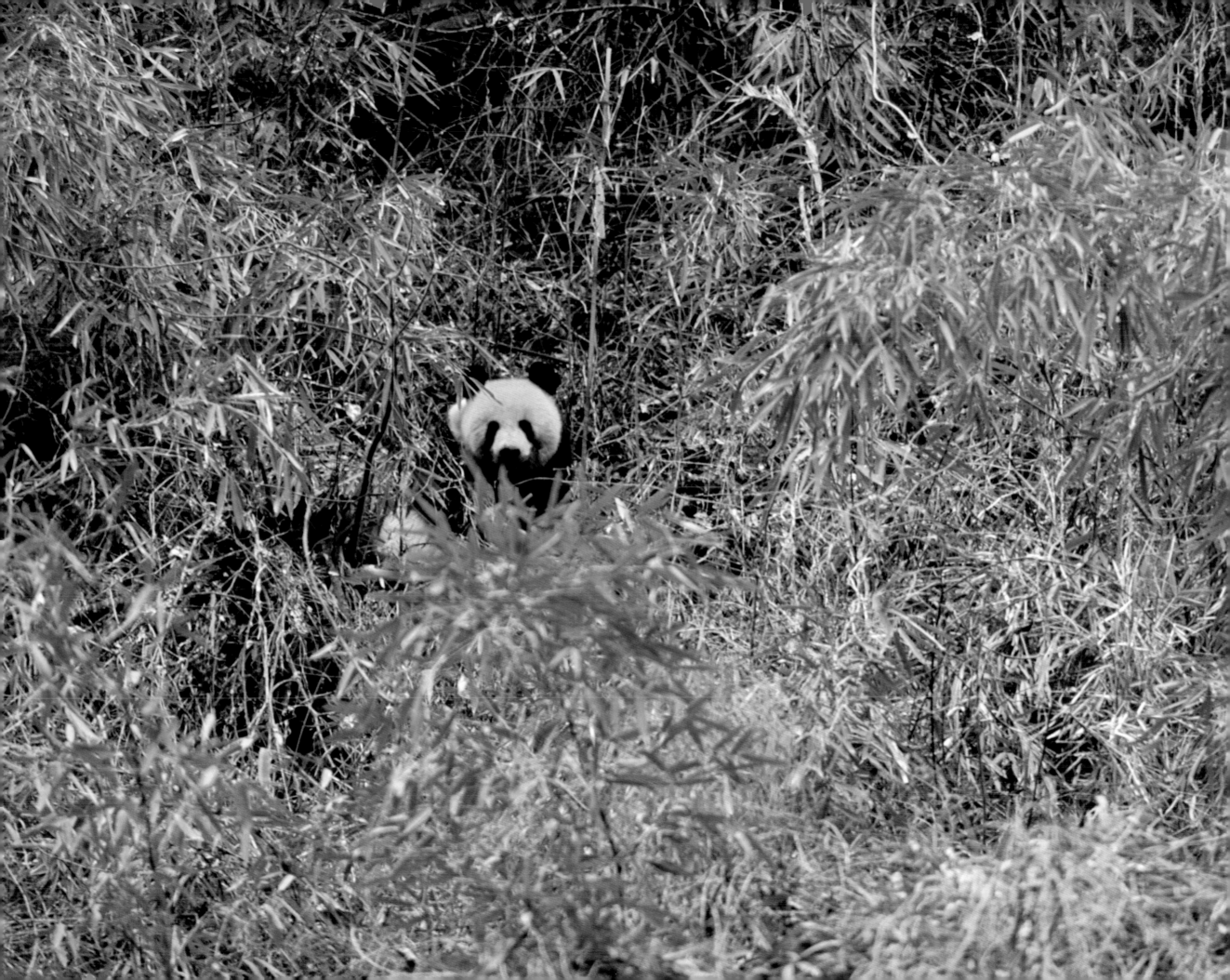

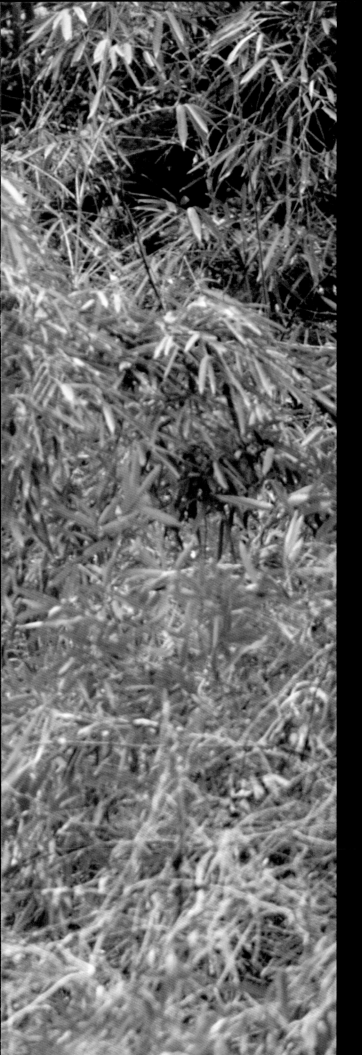

TEMPERATE

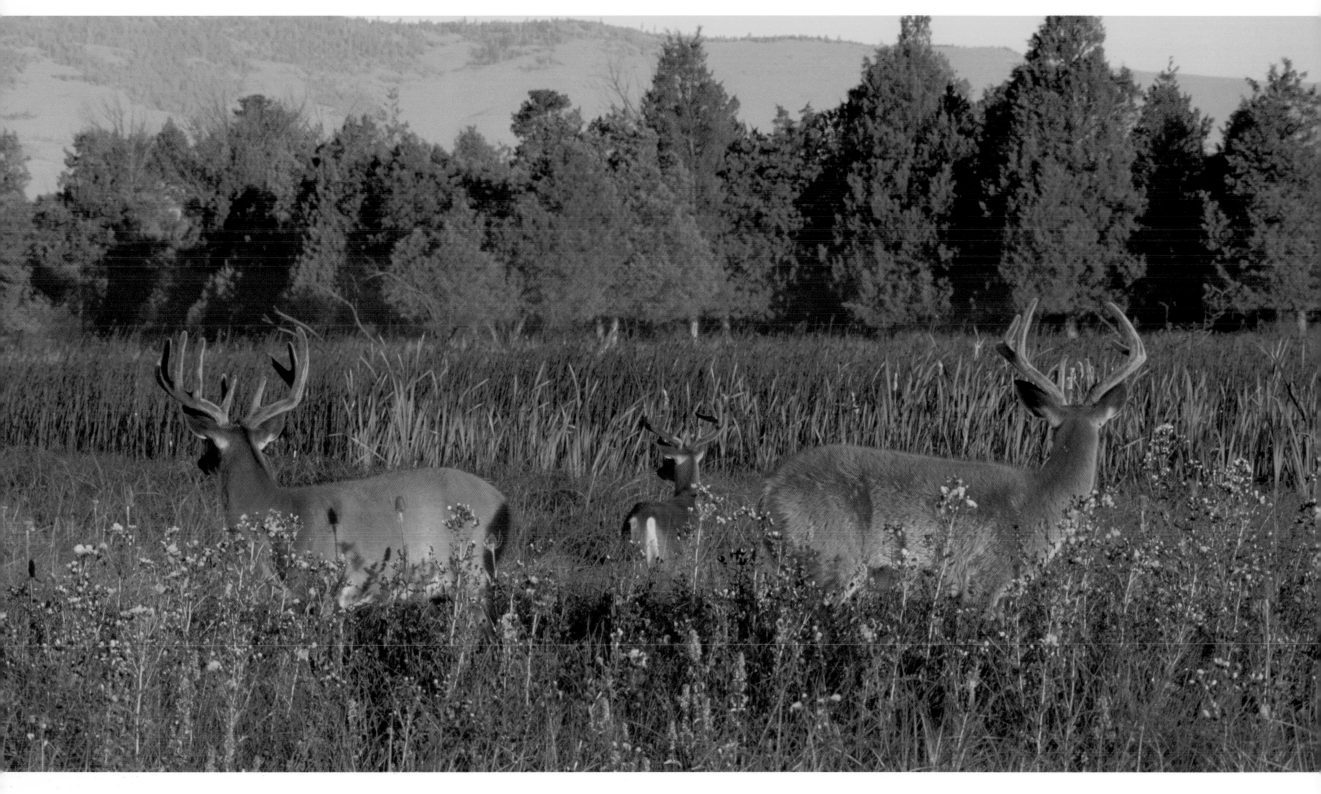

◄ GIANT PANDA

QINLING MOUNTAINS, CHINA

WHITE-TAILED DEER

NATIONAL BISON RANGE, MONTANA, USA

THE LIVING WILD

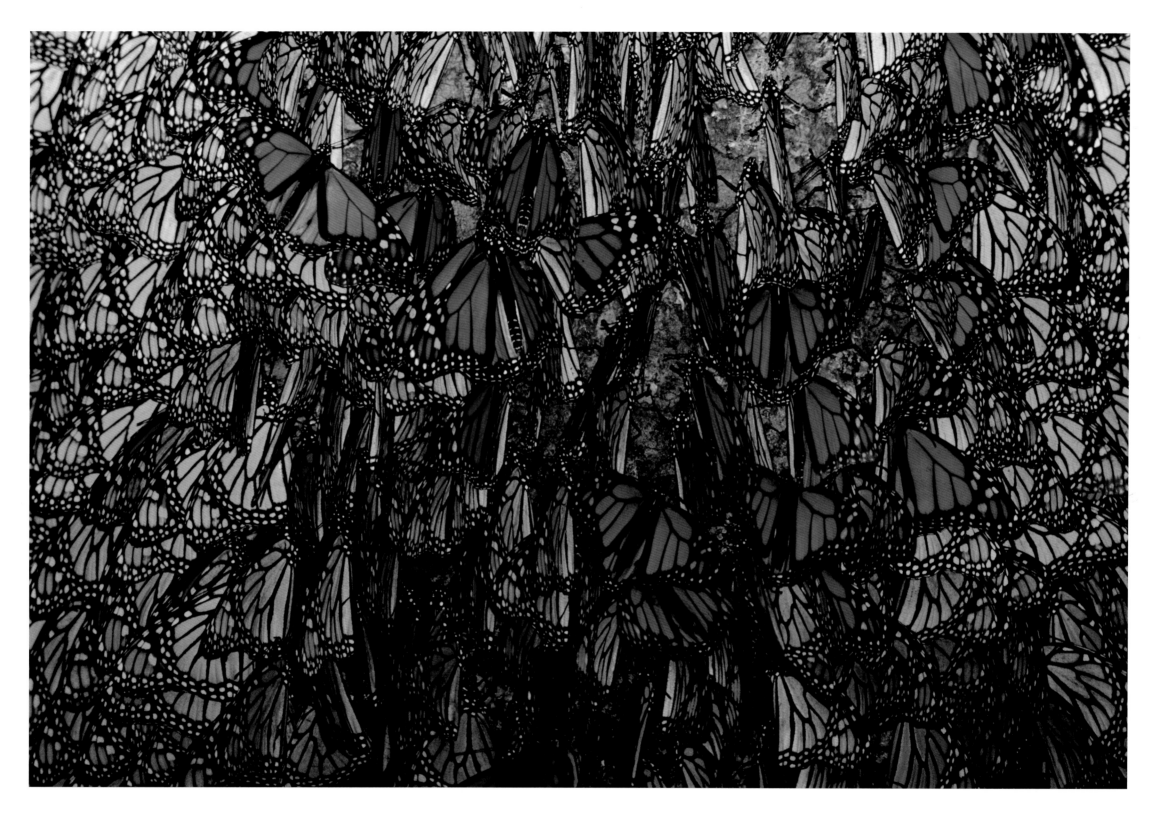

MONARCH BUTTERFLY

TRANSVOLCANIC RANGE, MICHOACAN, MEXICO

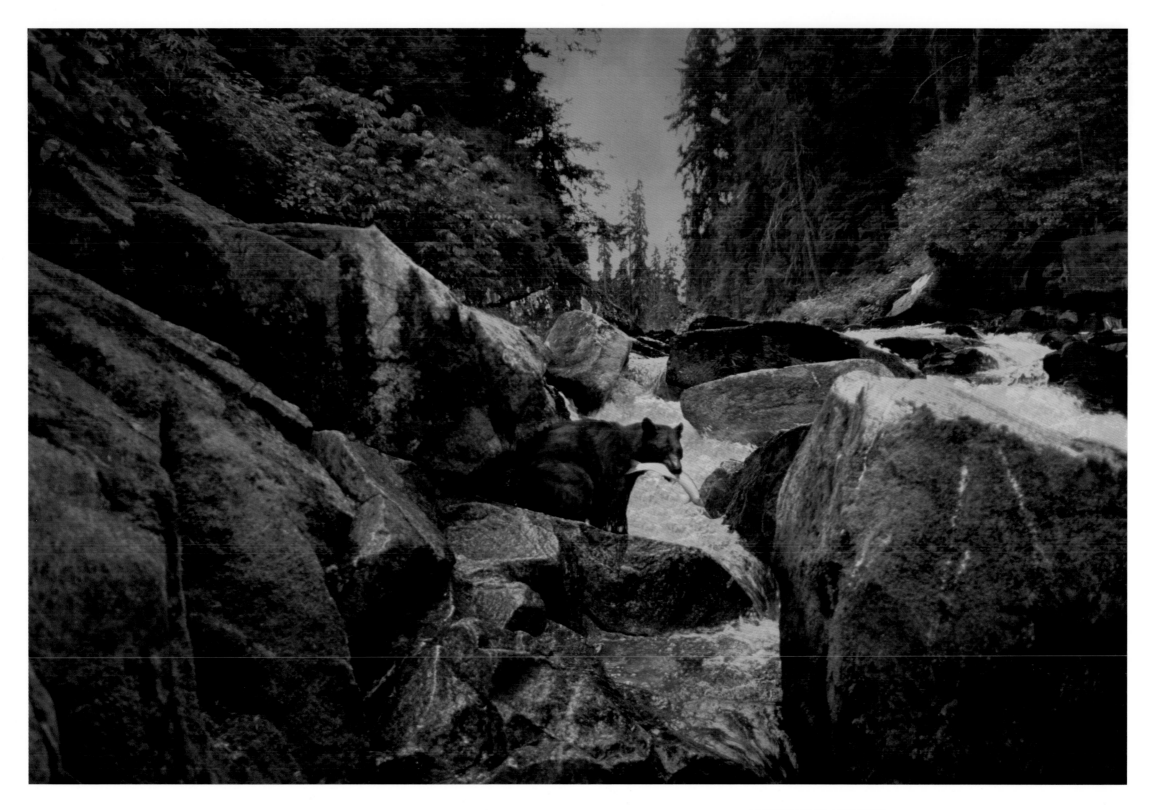

▲ AND ▶ AMERICAN BLACK BEAR

ANAN CREEK, TONGASS NATIONAL FOREST, ALASKA, USA

THE LIVING WILD

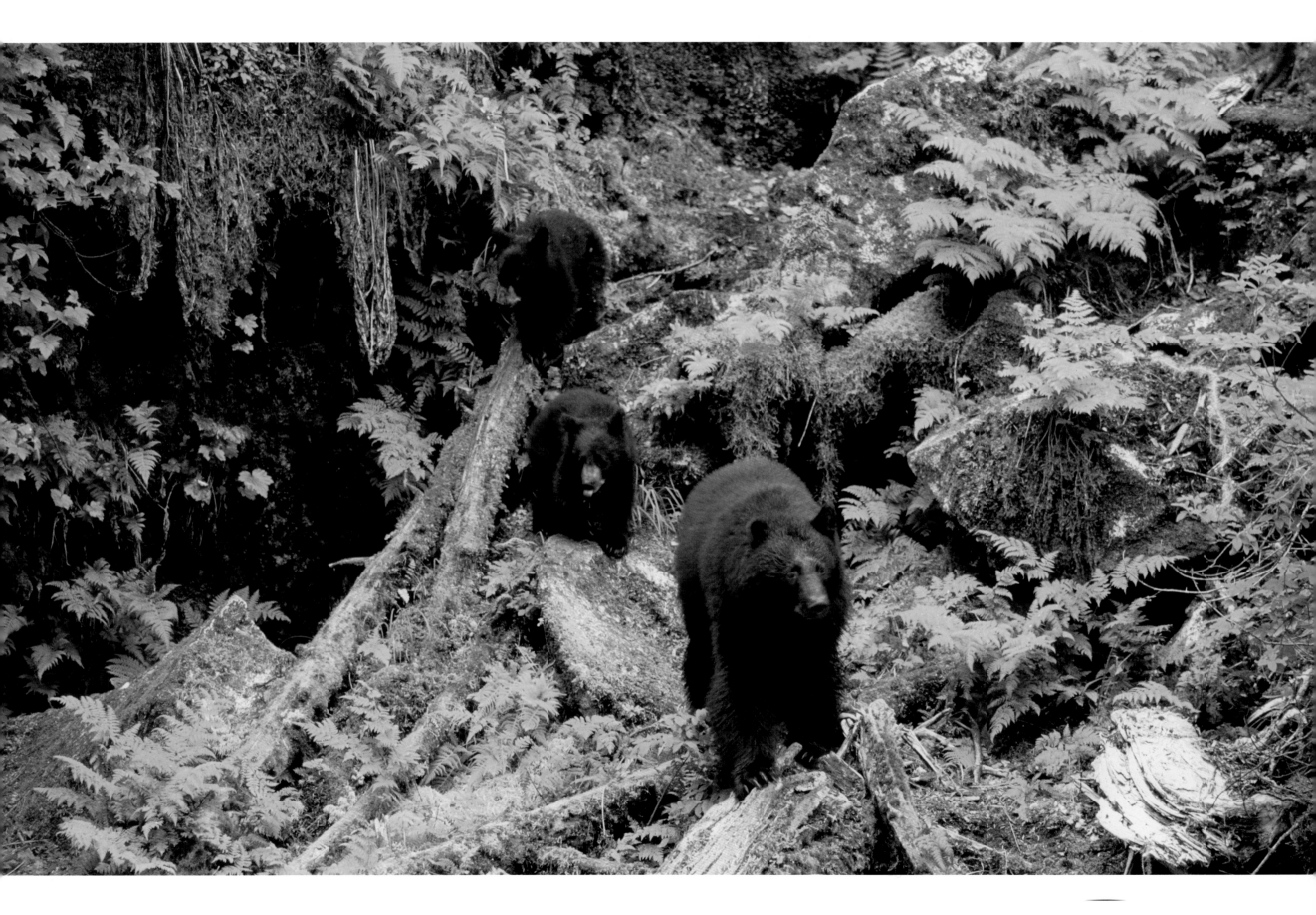

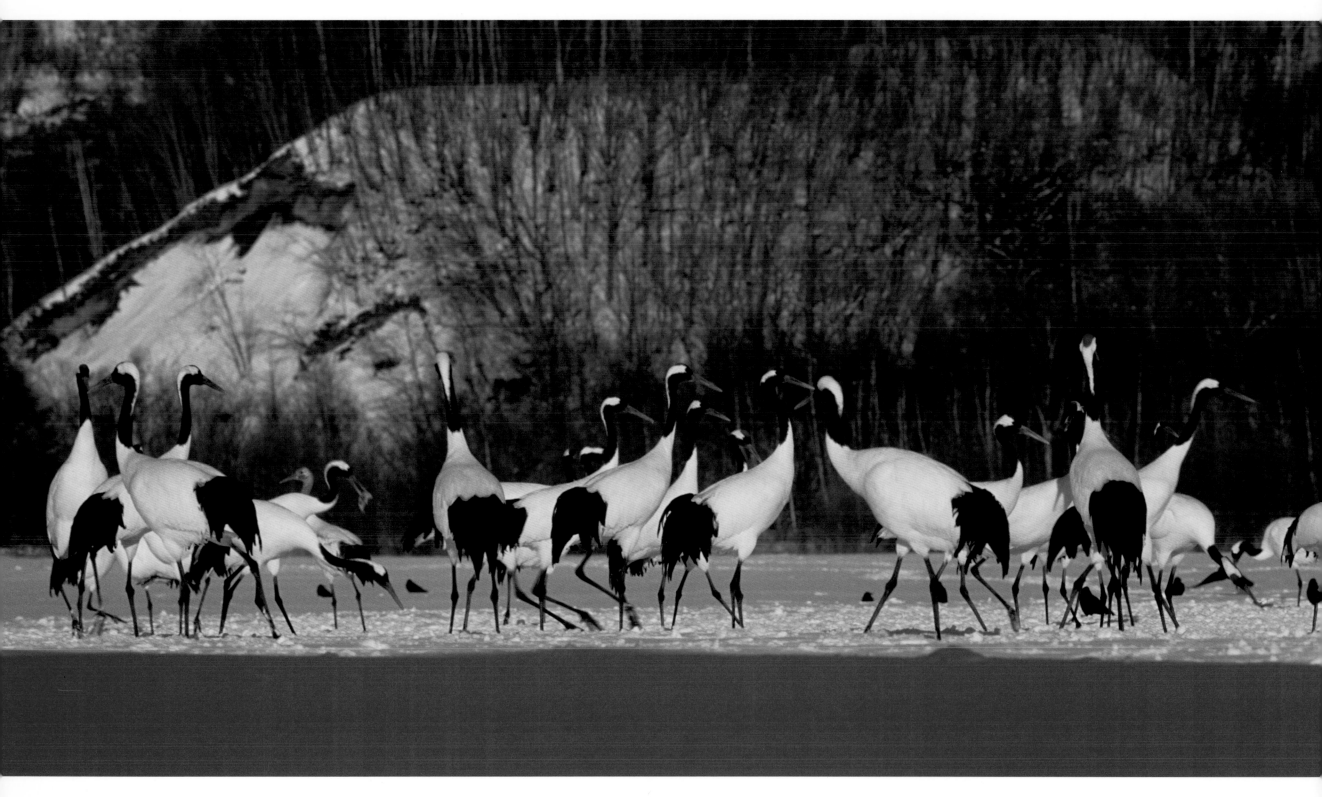

RED-CROWNED CRANE

Hokkaido Island, Japan

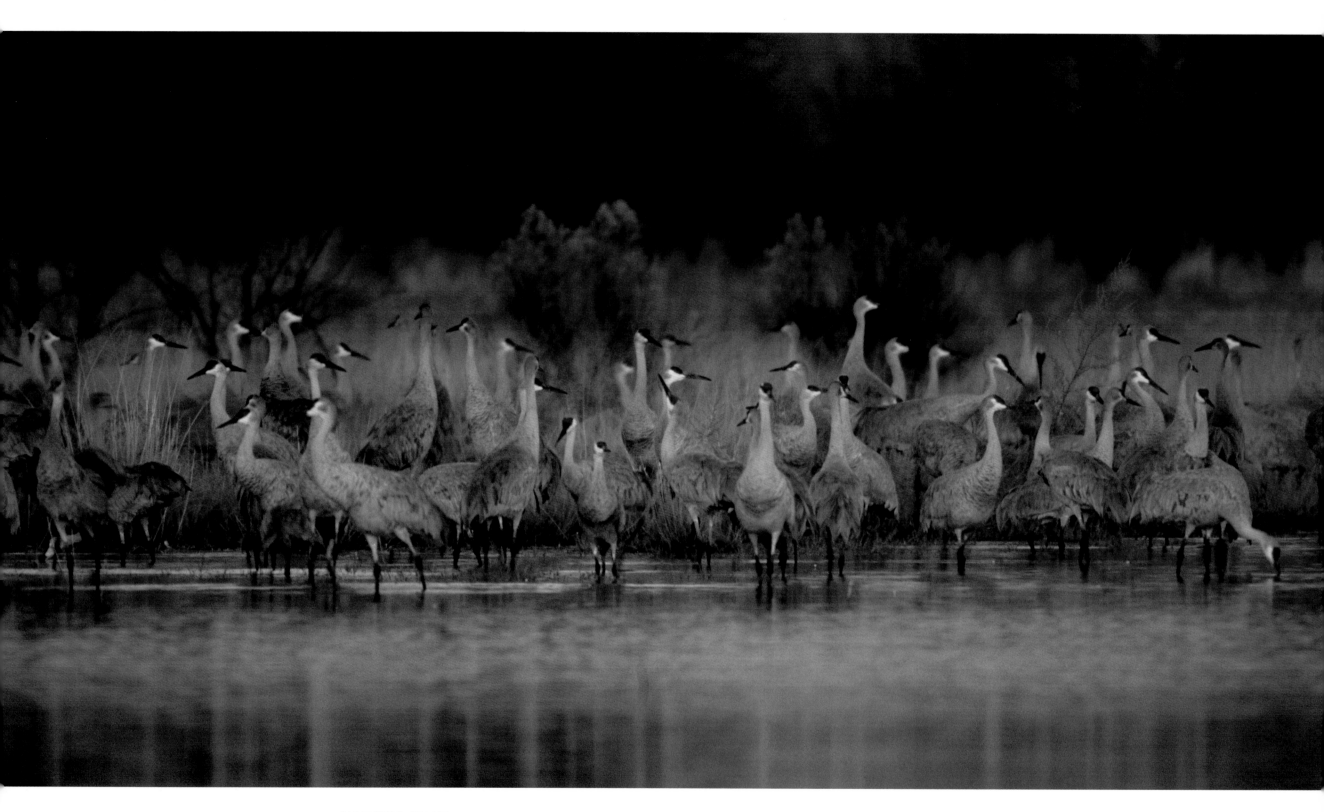

SANDHILL CRANE

Bosque del Apache National Wildlife Refuge, New Mexico, USA

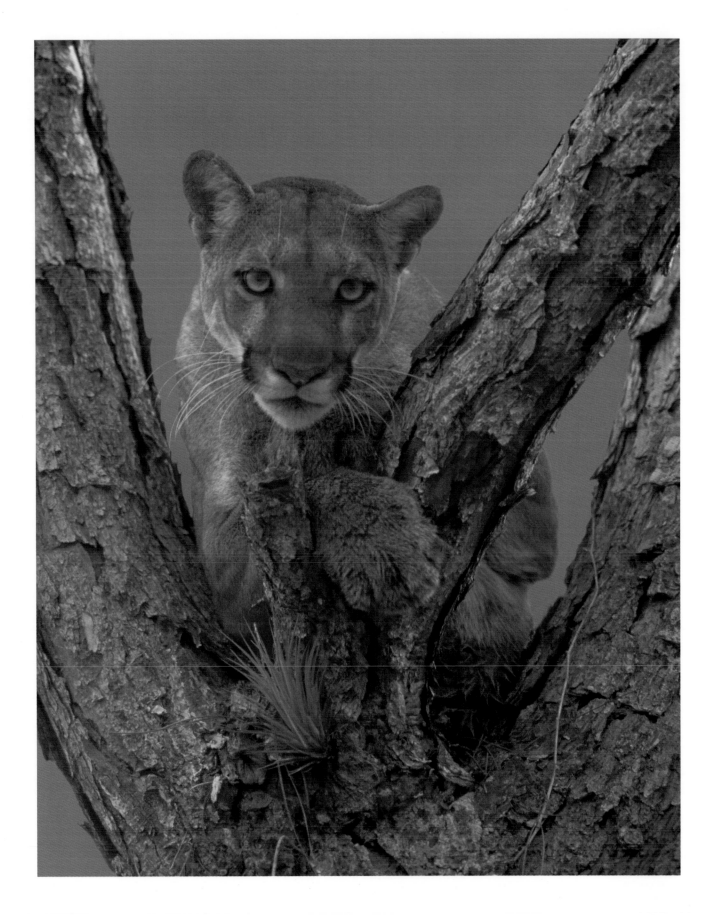

FLORIDA PANTHER

BIG CYPRESS SWAMP, FLORIDA, USA

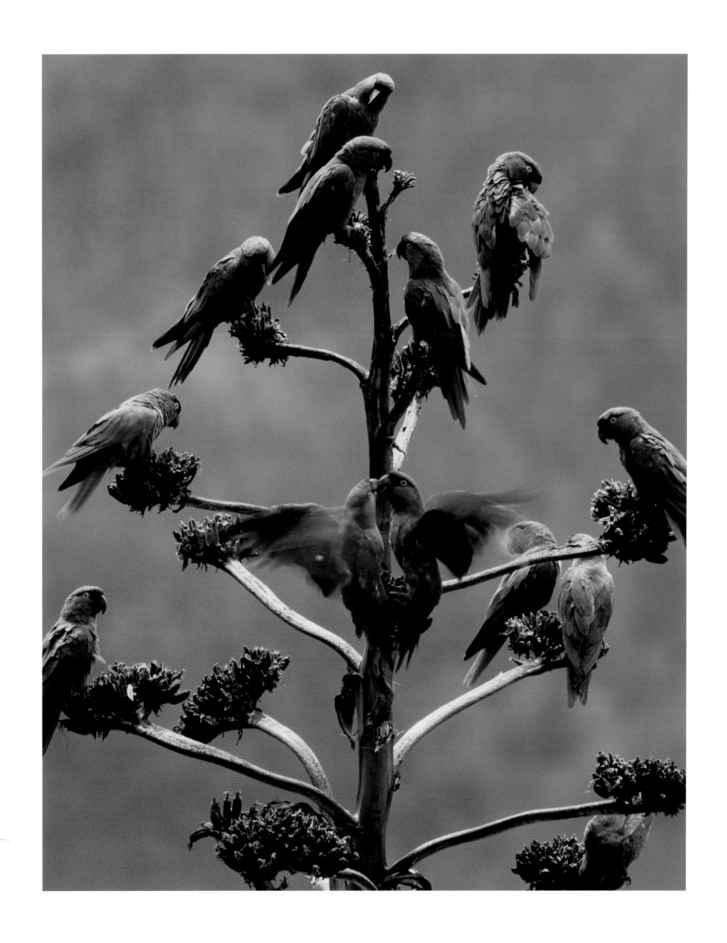

MAROON-FRONTED PARROT
SIERRA MADRE ORIENTAL, MEXICO

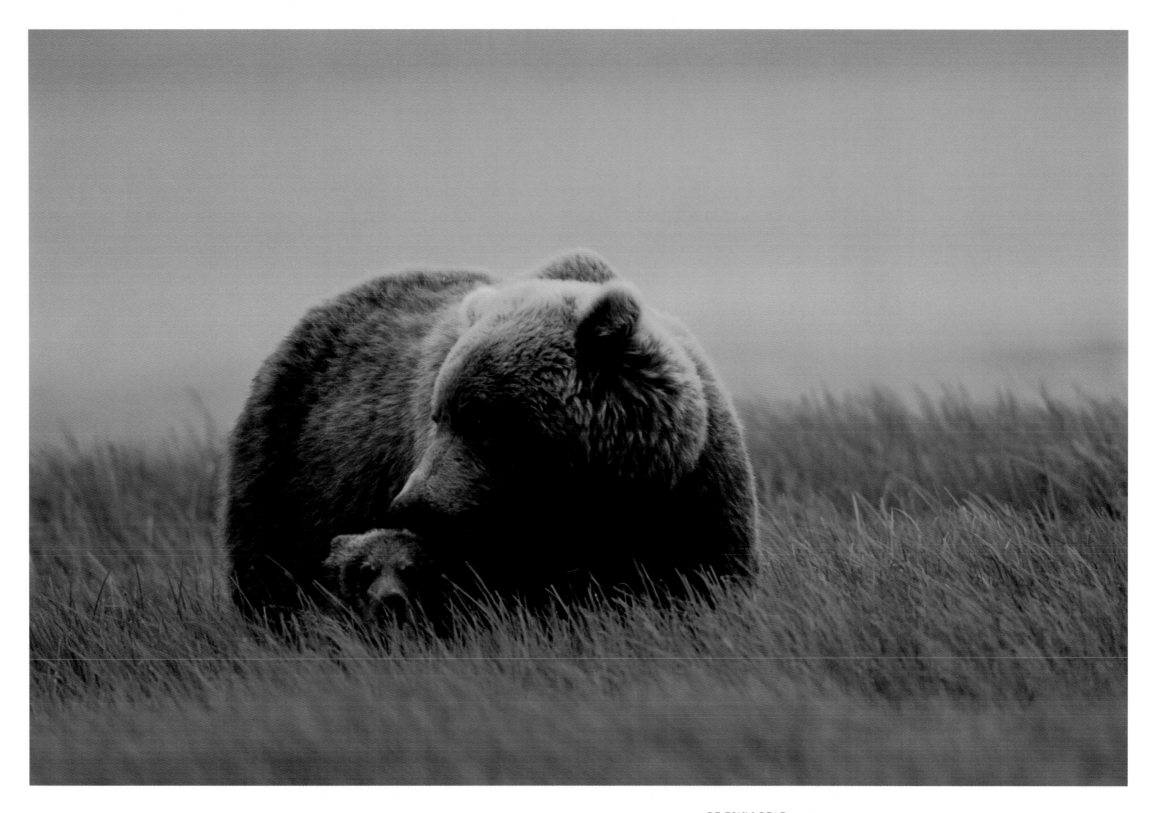

BROWN BEAR

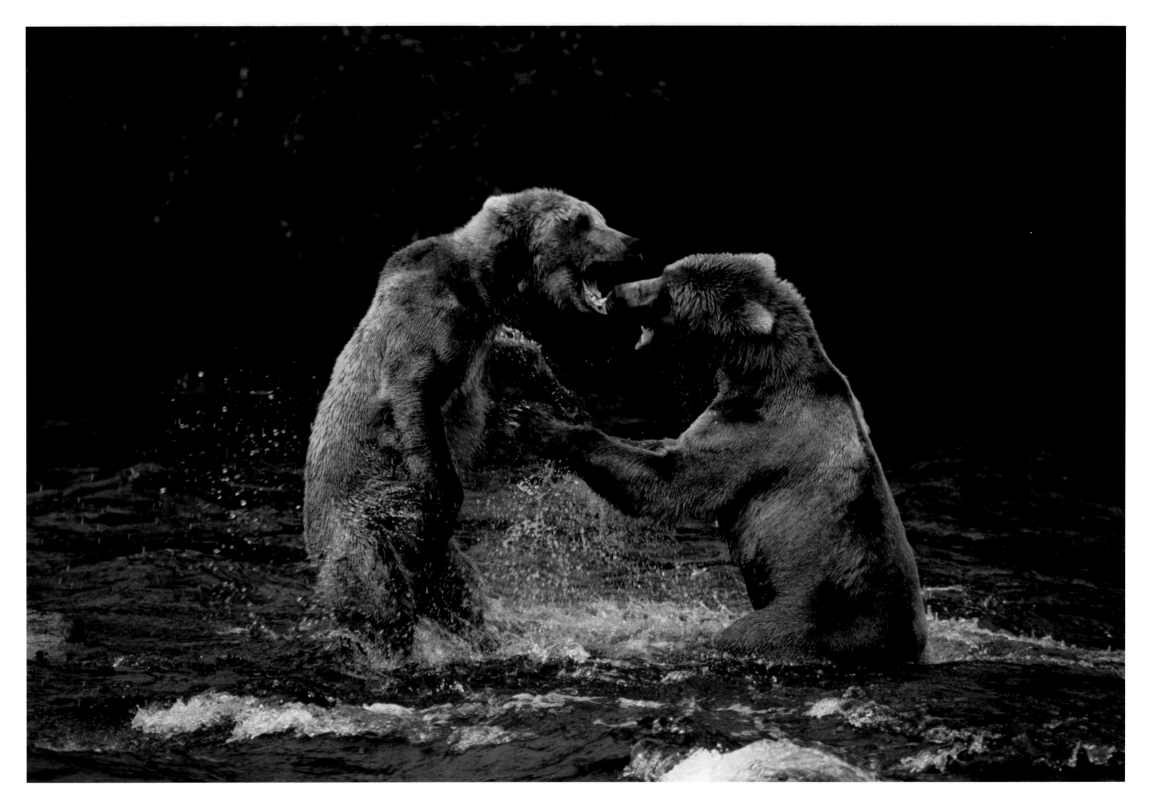

BROWN BEAR

McNeil River State Game Sanctuary, Alaska, USA

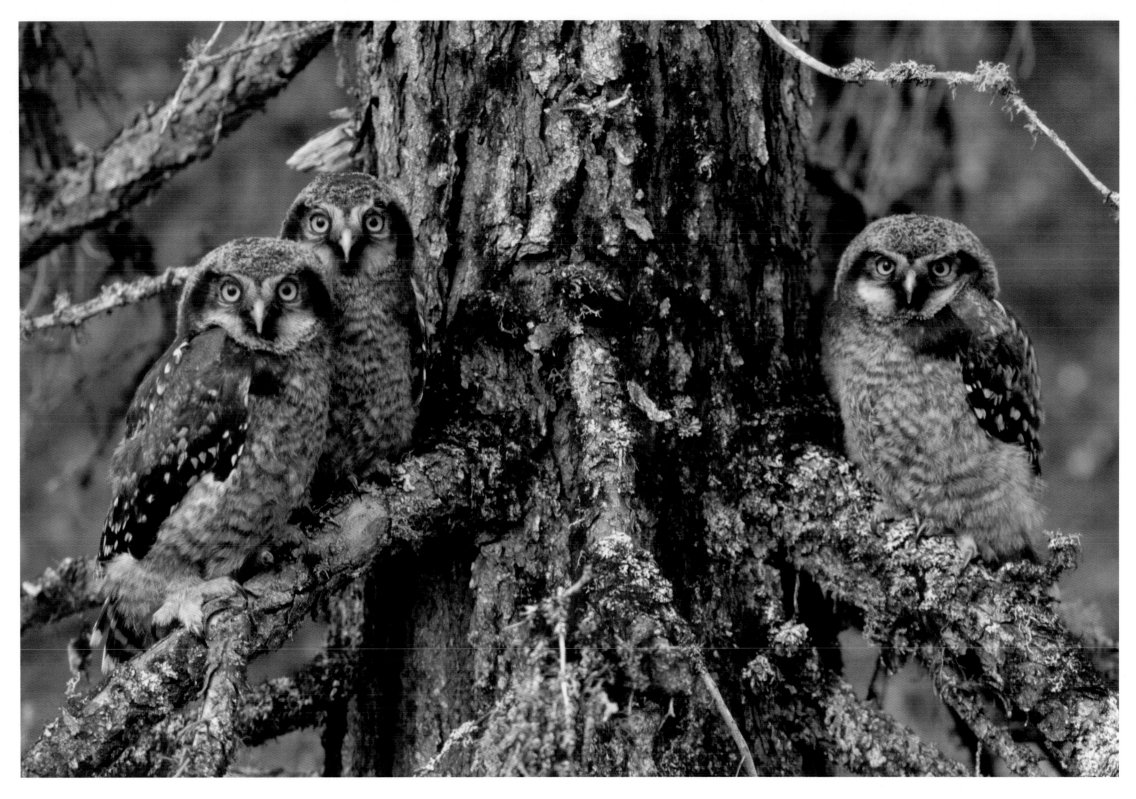

NORTHERN HAWK OWL

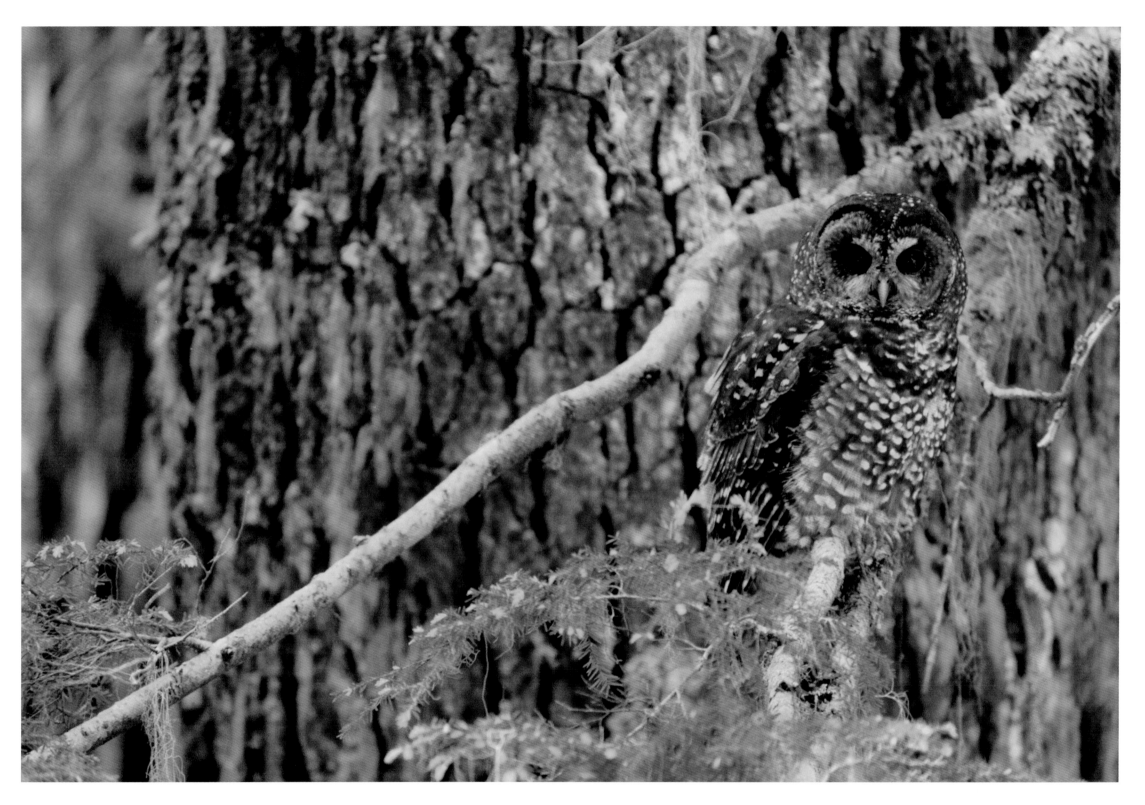

SPOTTED OWL

Cascade Mountain Range, Washington, USA

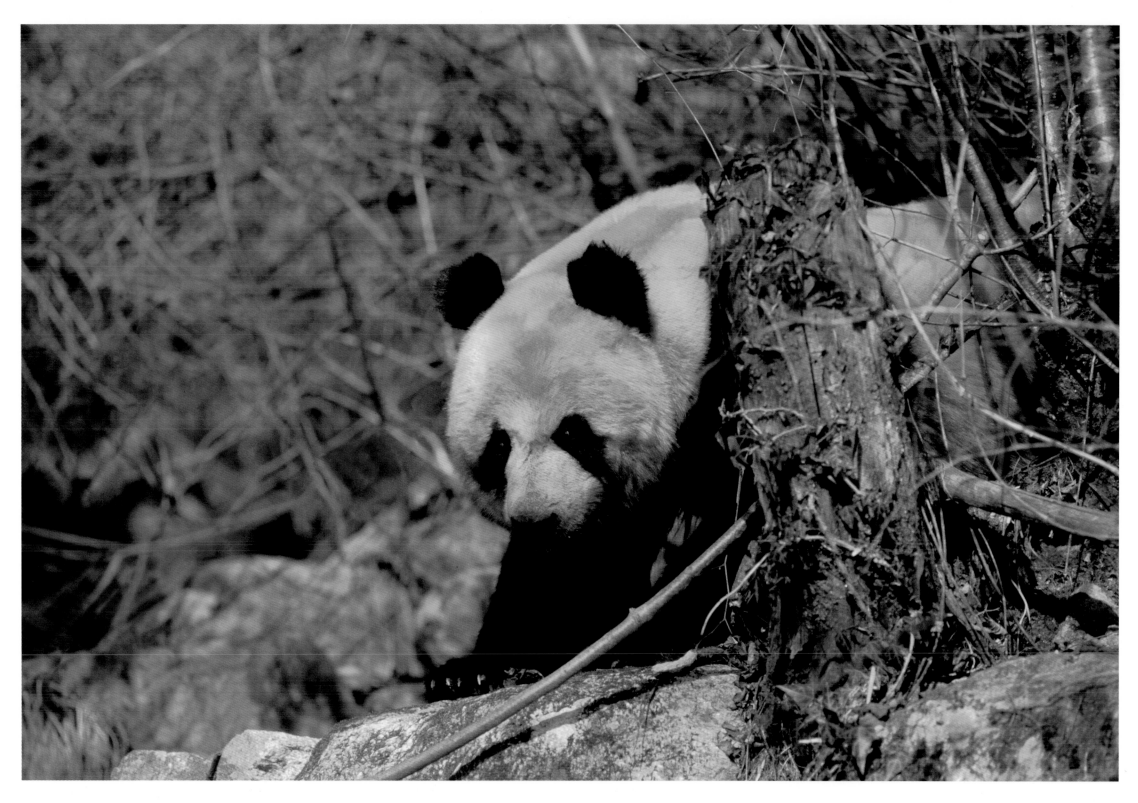

GIANT PANDA

QINLING MOUNTAINS, CHINA

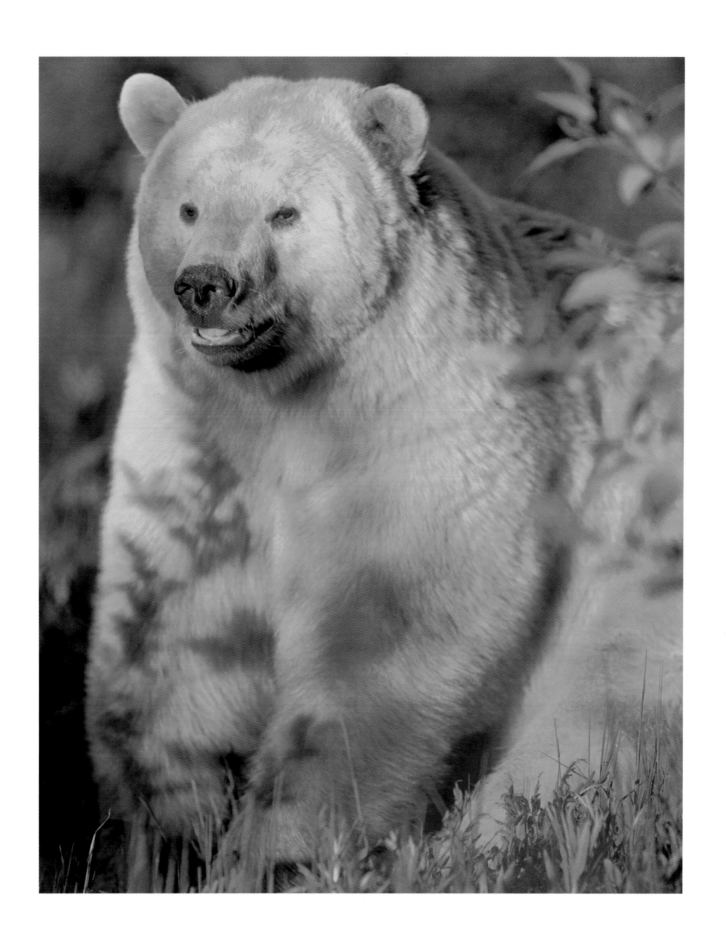

KERMODE BEAR

TERRACE, BRITISH COLUMBIA, CANADA

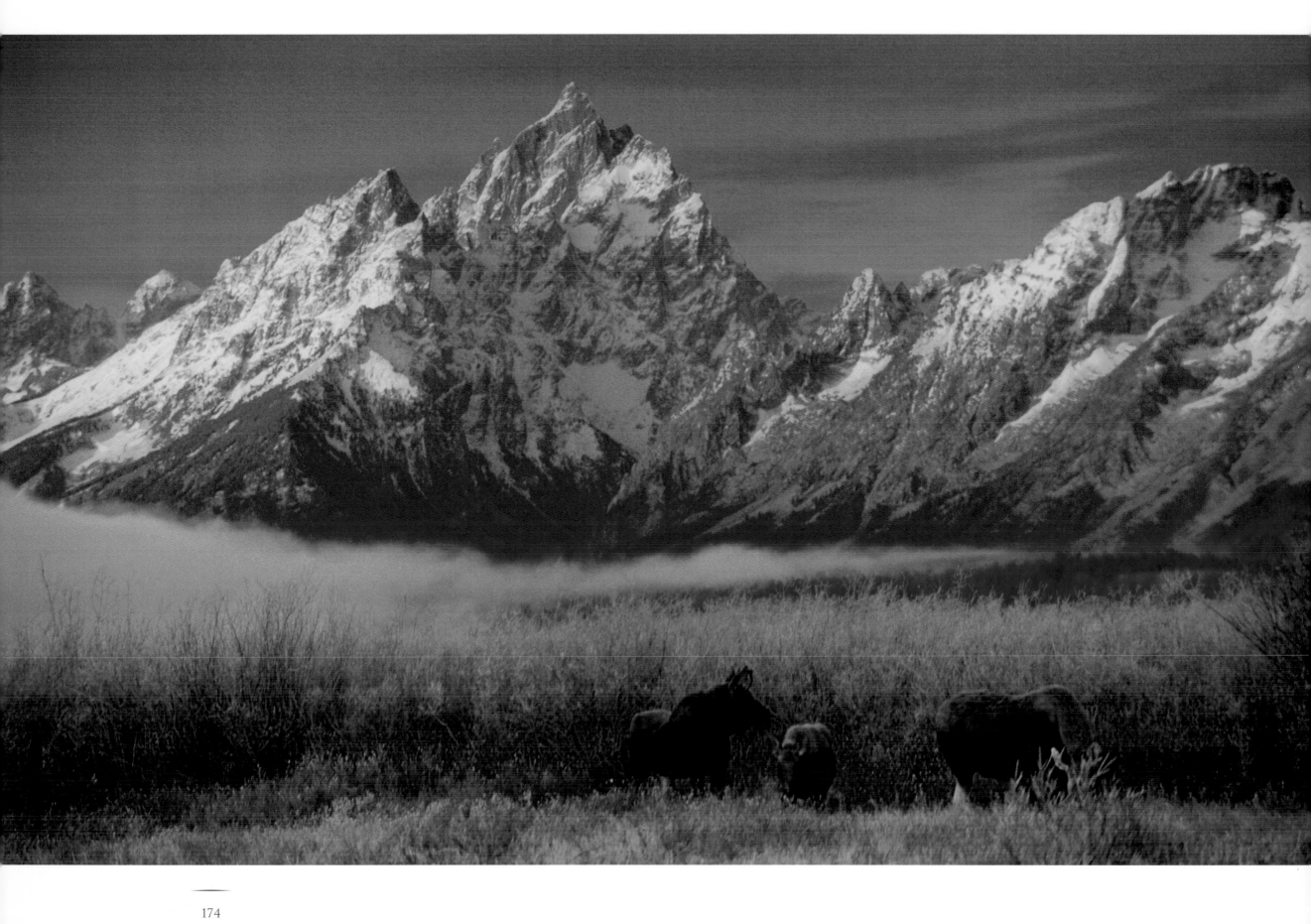

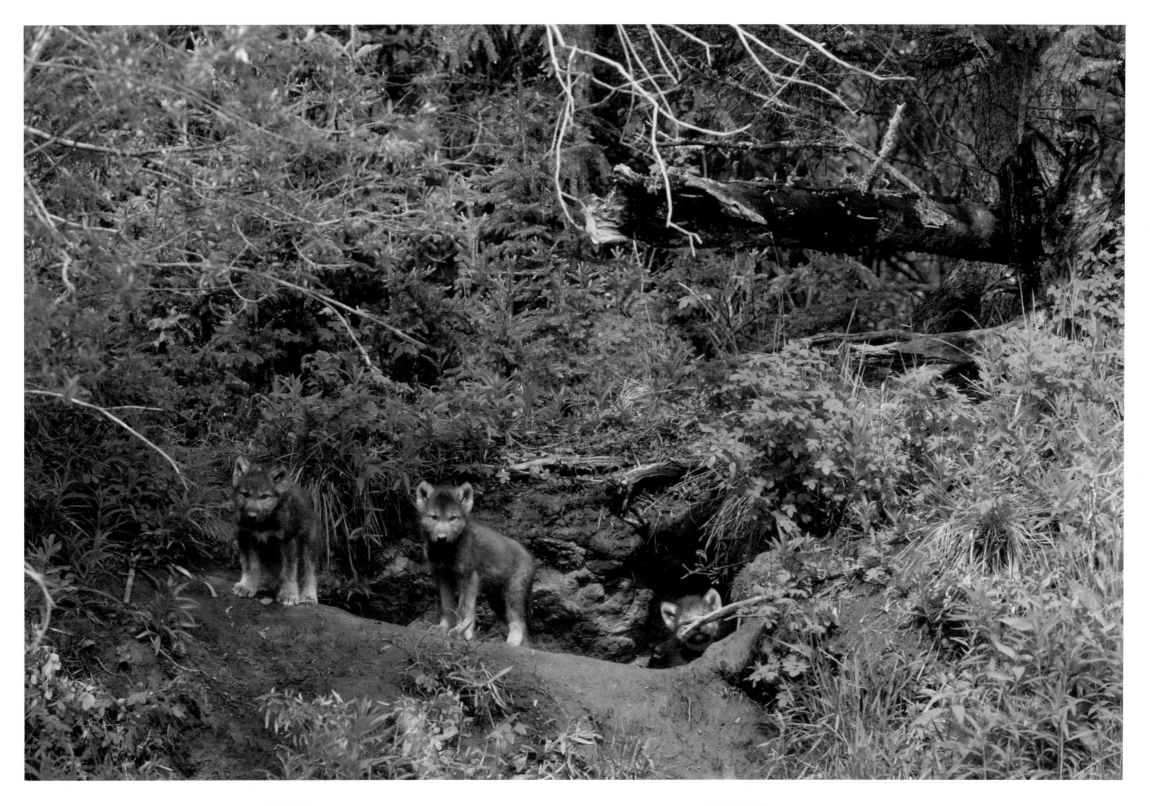

◄ MOOSE

Grand Teton National Park, Wyoming, USA

GRAY WOLF

Tok Junction, Alaska, USA

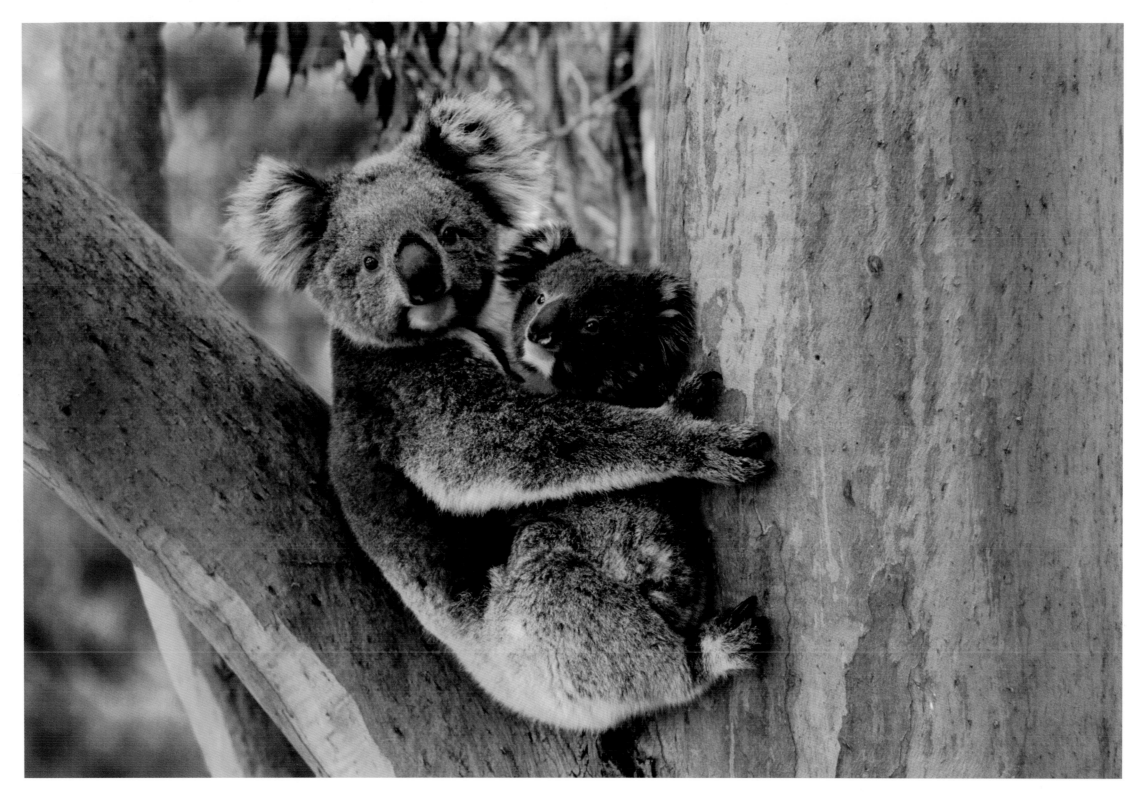

KOALA 〜

Kangaroo Island, South Australia, Australia

▶ WESTERN GRAY KANGAROO 〜

Flinders Chase National Park, Kangaroo Island, South Australia, Australia

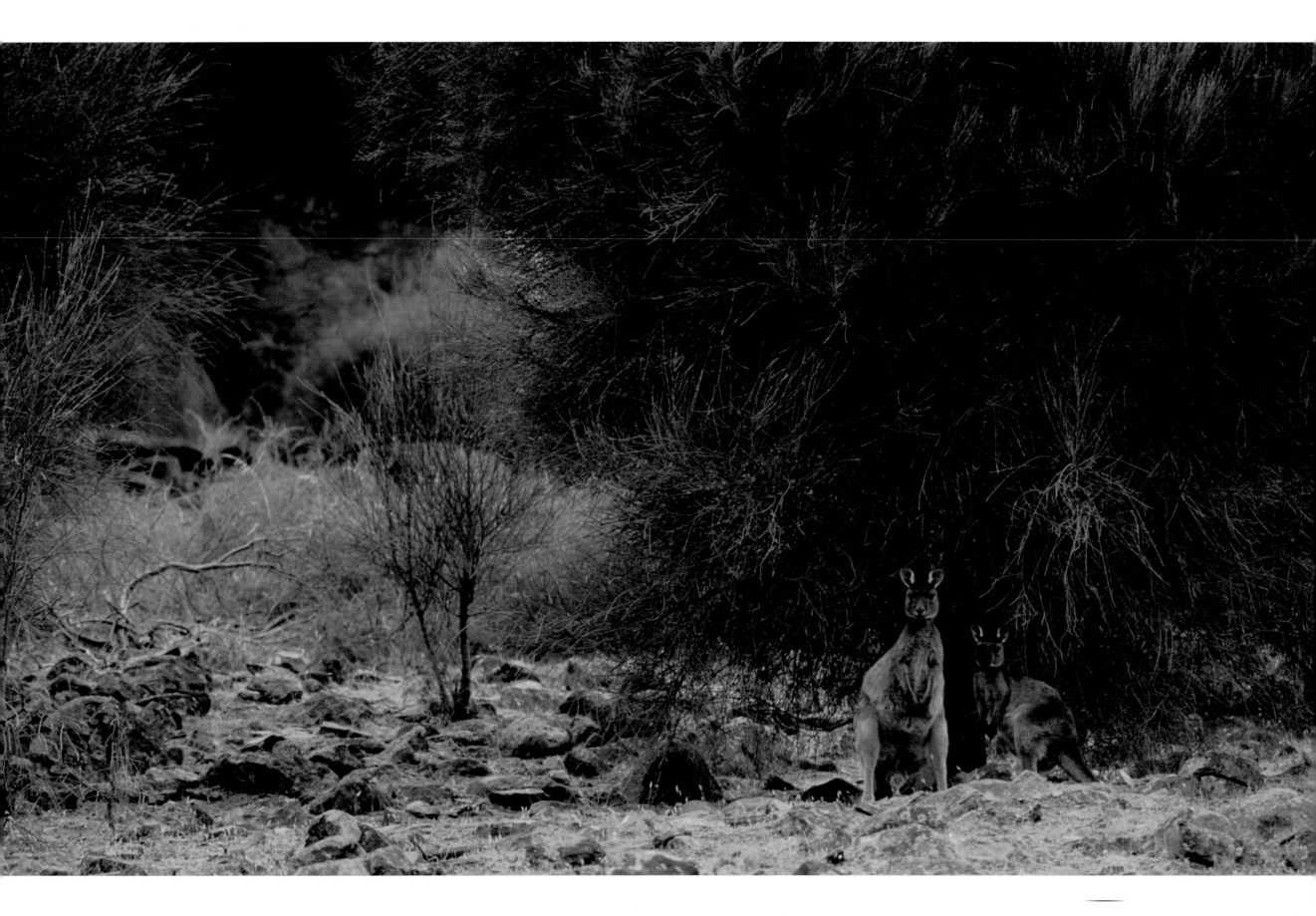

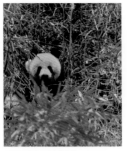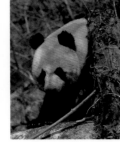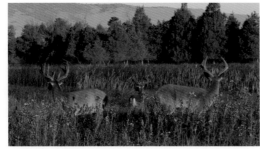

GIANT PANDA
(*Ailuropoda melanoleuca*)

The giant panda is the most unusual of the eight species of bears. There has been considerable debate about whether they should be considered bears, or members of the Procyonidae family along with raccoons (and lesser pandas [*Ailurus fulgens*]). It is now generally accepted that giant pandas are closely related to both bears and raccoons, with the former taking precedence. Pandas resemble other bears in their general body form; however, their striking coloration is unique. Their heads are also proportionately larger than those of other bears, in part because their jaw muscles are so large—all the better to chew bamboo with. The giant panda has become the icon of the global conservation movement, but changing climate and human encroachment have made it increasingly rare. Fewer than 1,000 are thought to survive in the wild, with about 113 in captivity. Despite harsh punishments for poachers—including death—animals are still killed for their skins.

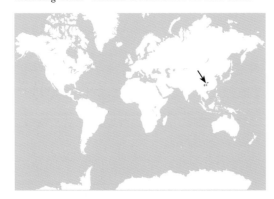

AW: Pages 158-159 –This panda paused in a small opening long enough that I was able to run two rolls of film through my camera to get this photograph.

Canon EOS-3, Canon EF 400mm lens, Canon Extender EF 1.4x, f/11 at 1/15 second, Fujichrome Velvia film

AW: Page 172 – I heard a panda approaching a stream for a drink. I waded in up to my thighs to a point where I thought the panda would emerge from the forest. Fortunately, I guessed right.

Canon EOS-3, Canon EF 70–200mm lens, f/8 at 1/250 second, Fujichrome Astia film (pushed 1 stop)

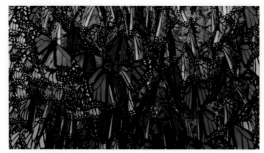

WHITE-TAILED DEER
(*Odocoileus virginianus*)

White-tailed deer in the northern part of their range stand more than a meter at the shoulder and weigh 100 to 150 kilograms; those in the southern United States are smaller, standing about 0.9 meter at the shoulder and weighing 50 to 100 kilograms, while those in South America are smaller still—standing 0.8 meter and weighing 30 to 55 kilograms. Whitetails are found in a variety of habitats, but avoid dense forests. They do not tend to aggregate in large groups; the key unit is mother and offspring. Before the arrival of Europeans in North America, there were an estimated 23 million to 40 million white-tailed deer. By 1900, only 300,000 to 500,000 remained. Conservation efforts, and the deer's highly adaptable nature, have since raised those numbers to around 14 million—about 2 million are killed annually by hunters. Two of the species' sixteen subspecies (*O. v. clavium* and *O. v. leucurus*) are considered endangered.

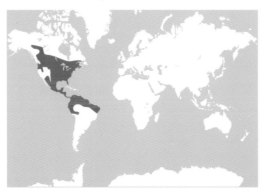

AW: I like this image for two main reasons. First, the early morning light and beautiful habitat combine to give the photograph a rich sense of place. Second, the deer seem to be bearing silent witness to an unseen drama. The three bucks simultaneously turned their heads away from me and intently followed the movement of a black bear (*Ursus americanus*) crossing the marsh behind them. The fact that the faces of the deer—and the bear—cannot be seen gives the composition an air of mystery.

Canon EOS-1N/RS, Canon EF 70–200mm lens, 2-stop graduated neutral density filter, f/16 at 1/15 second, Fujichrome Velvia film

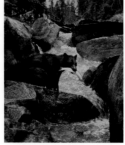

MONARCH BUTTERFLY
(*Danaus plexippus*)

Monarch butterflies are found in many parts of the world, but are concentrated in the Americas. The North American monarchs are well known for their incredible migrations—some travel more than 2,900 kilometers to their wintering grounds. Butterflies from the northwest United States spend the winters in California, while those from the East Coast migrate to the mountains of Mexico. The Mexican wintering locations were discovered only in 1975, and it is here that millions of the butterflies congregate in roosting trees. Not all monarch populations migrate. Those in tropical regions, for example Southeast Asia and much of Central America, are fairly sedentary, although they may make altitudinal migrations. The isolated locations of many butterfly roosts have protected them from harm, but since so few have been discovered, it is vital that all are protected.

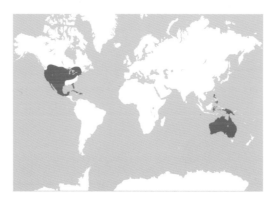

AW: Every year an astounding 100 million monarch butterflies overwinter in the mountains north of Mexico City. Preserves have been established to ensure minimal disturbance of these delicate insects. By carefully placing my camera and lens on two different tripods on a slope above the tree where the butterflies were roosting, I was able to have my film plane parallel to the tree trunk. This positioning ensured that all the butterflies were in focus at the same time. Finally, I used a fill flash to stop any motion among the mass of wings.

Canon EOS-3, Canon EF 600mm lens, f/11 at 1/4 second, fill flash, Fujichrome Velvia film

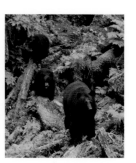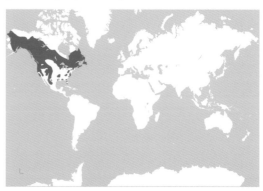

AMERICAN BLACK BEAR
(*Ursus americanus*)

The range of the American black bear has declined substantially as its habitat has been altered. However, black bears are remarkably opportunistic and are often attracted to towns and farms, where they scavenge. They are of little threat to people, except when wounded or protecting their young. But even so, they are frequently killed when they prey on livestock or roam into settled areas. While the North American population may be as high as half a million, they are facing increased hunting and poaching in many areas, partly to satisfy demands for body parts—such as gallbladders—that are used in eastern traditional folk medicines. The United States is the largest supplier of gallbladders to South Korea, with China, Japan, and Taiwan also significant markets. Among the black bear subspecies, only 500 to 1,000 Florida black bears (*U. a. floridanus*) are thought to survive, while the Louisiana black bear (*U. a. luteolus*) may number just a handful of individuals.

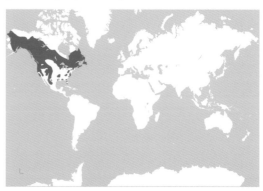

AW: Page 162 – I particularly like a single composition that conveys so much information: Here we see not only a bear, but what the bear has caught and where it has caught it.

Canon EOS-1N, Canon EF 20mm lens, f/11 at 1/15 second, Fujichrome Provia film

AW: Page 163 – When salmon are running, bears congregate in high densities in Alaska's Tongass National Forest. In this photograph, a sow cautiously approaches a salmon stream. The reason: The cubs accompanying her are vulnerable to attack.

Canon EOS-1N, Canon EF 400mm lens, f/4 at 1/125 second, Fujichrome Provia film

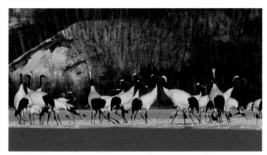

RED-CROWNED CRANE
(*Grus japonensis*)

Red-crowned cranes (also known as Japanese or Manchurian cranes) are the second-rarest crane species in the world, numbering 1,700 to 2,000 birds in the wild (only the whooping crane [*Grus americanus*] is rarer, numbering about 300 birds). The cranes breed in wetland habitats in the temperate parts of East Asia, and winter along rivers and in marshes in Japan, China, and along the Korean Peninsula. Two main populations exist—a migratory population in northeastern China and Russia, and a resident population on Japan's Hokkaido Island. The latter comprises about 600 birds. The species is threatened by habitat loss as its wetlands are converted to agricultural use, and by water control and diversion projects (including dams on the Amur and Yangtze Rivers) that disturb and significantly alter habitat. About 300 cranes winter in the Korean Demilitarized Zone, making them vulnerable to international conflict and other human activity.

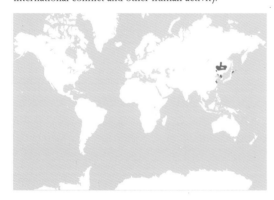

AW: Red-crowned cranes are among the most revered animals in Japan. Their commanding 1.5-meter height, striking black-and-white plumage, and delicate, graceful lines, make it easy to understand why. I traveled to Hokkaido in January for this image, visiting fields where local farmers leave behind some of their grain for the birds to feed on during the harsh winter months. On one farm, a viewing station has been established so the Japanese can see their favorite bird up close.

Canon EOS-1N, Canon EF 800mm lens, f/11 at 1/60 second, Fujichrome Velvia film

---

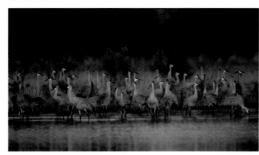

SANDHILL CRANE
(*Grus canadensis*)

Sandhill cranes are elegant birds standing 1.2 meters tall. They often congregate in wetland habitats where they consume plant tubers, corms, berries, and grains, as well as insects, earthworms, rodents, and frogs. Their courtship displays are elaborate "dances," and they emit loud calls that resemble a low-pitched rattle. With a global population of half a million, they are the most numerous of the fifteen crane species. There are six recognized subspecies of sandhill cranes. Three are migratory— the lesser, greater, and Canadian. However, the three nonmigratory subspecies are much rarer. Both the Cuban subspecies, with a population of about 300, and the Mississippi subspecies, estimated at 120, are critically endangered. The Florida subspecies has more robust numbers, with its population between 4,000 and 6,000 individuals. As habitats are increasingly lost to developers, isolated subspecies will become even more marginalized.

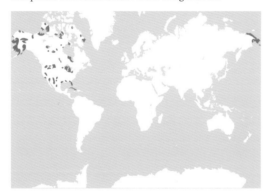

AW: Sandhill cranes winter along New Mexico's Rio Grande, where fields of grain are left unharvested to ensure ample feed for the hungry migrants. In this photograph, a small flock gathers along the shore of a lake adjacent to the river. The post-sunset glow provides enough light to bathe the birds in soft pastel hues.

Canon EOS-1N, Canon EF 600mm lens, Canon Extender EF 1.4x, f/5.6 at 1 second, Fujichrome Velvia film (pushed 1 stop)

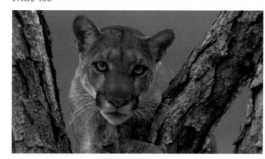

FLORIDA PANTHER
(*Felis concolor coryi*)

The Florida panther is a highly endangered subspecies of mountain lion. It once lived throughout much of the southern United States, but today only thirty to fifty exist in the Florida wilds. There is only one self-sustaining population. Even more worrisome is that more than 90 percent of male panthers have an extremely high proportion of abnormal sperm, and 65 percent are cryptorchid (a condition where one or both of the testicles fails to descend, which can lead to complete sterility). These discoveries all suggest that inbreeding is having a severe impact on genetic health. Since 1988 researchers have been freeze-storing sperm from male panthers, and a captive breeding program has been established. Some animals from an adjoining subspecies in Texas have been introduced into northern Florida in an attempt to prevent further genetic degradation. The Florida panther remains one of North America's most endangered animals.

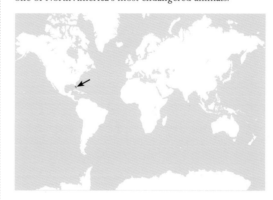

AW: Finding and photographing the North American cats in the wild is a major challenge for any photographer. When it comes to the Florida panther, chance encounters are almost impossible. To photograph this panther, I joined biologists whose field techniques and knowledge enable them to keep an accurate census of these highly endangered felines. It was while taking this particular image that I first had the idea for this book.

Canon EOS-3, Canon EF 400mm lens, f/8 at 1/125 second, Fujichrome Velvia film

---

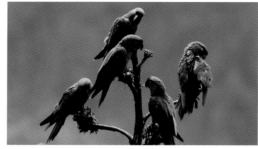

MAROON-FRONTED PARROT
(*Rhynchopsitta terrisi*)

Endemic to Mexico, maroon-fronted parrots are found within an 18,000-square-kilometer region of the Sierra Madre Oriental in northeastern Mexico—although less than half that area consists of suitable pine forest habitat. The birds are mainly found at between 2,000 and 3,000 meters, and they feed on pine seeds, acorns, and nectar. The birds make seasonal migrations in response to the availability of pine seeds, moving somewhat north during the summer and south in the winter. They nest on limestone cliffs, establishing their nests within holes in the rock; outside of the breeding season the parrots roost communally in trees. The highly localized population is considered very rare and declining. The parrots are threatened by habitat destruction from logging, agriculture, and grazing, and the total population is estimated at no more than 2,000 birds.

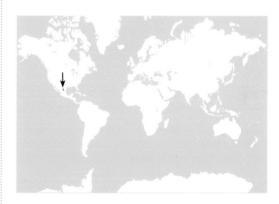

AW: Maroon-fronted parrots are gregarious, large parrots that nest on cliffs in the Sierra Madre Oriental of Mexico. To take this image, I had to climb up a steep hillside and place my camera just below their nests. In the morning, the parrots congregated on the agave plants below the cliffs. Using my 600mm lens and a 1.4 extender, I was able to get a pleasingly tight composition of a flock of birds. By photographing from slightly above the parrots, I filled the background with a distant hillside, allowing the green of the birds to stand out against a neutral color.

Canon EOS-3, Canon EF 600mm lens, Canon Extender EF 1.4x, f/11 at 1/30 second, Fujichrome Velvia film

NOTES FROM THE FIELD

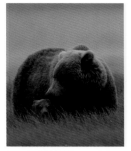
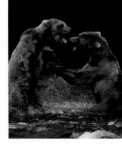

BROWN BEAR
(Ursus arctos)

The brown or grizzly bear has one of the largest natural distributions of any mammal, including mountains, tundra, forests, open plains, and coastlines. Grizzlies survive in less than 2 percent of their former range in the contiguous United States, and number just 1,000 (the California golden bear subspecies [U. a. californicus] became extinct in 1922 [it was made the state animal in 1953] and the Mexican grizzly [U. a. nelsoni] has also vanished). Since the population in the contiguous United States is fragmented, many of the isolated groups may not be reproductively viable. Similar concerns exist for relic populations in Europe. Grizzlies have substantial strongholds in Alaska and Canada (about 55,000 bears), and Eurasia (about 130,000 animals), but their need for large home ranges, the potential for dangerous encounters as people encroach on their habitat, and the growing problem of poaching all place increasing pressures on the species.

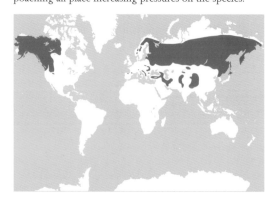

AW: Page 168 – When I photograph bears, I always make sure they are aware of my presence, and I do not approach too closely. This is even more imperative when cubs are present.

Canon EOS-1N, Canon EF 600mm lens, f/8 at 1/60 second, Fujichrome Provia film

AW: Page 169 – To stop the motion of these two energetic bears and get the sharpest image possible, I pushed my film 1 stop and used the widest possible aperture.

Canon F1, Canon EF 800mm lens, f/5.6 at 1/250 second, Fujichrome 100 film (pushed 1 stop)

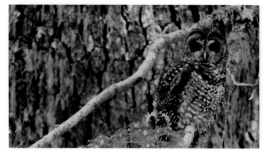

NORTHERN HAWK OWL
(Surnia ulula)

The northern hawk owl is a bird of the boreal forest. It favors both coniferous and deciduous forests that have regular clearings, and may also be found in more open tundra habitats. It tends to be a resident species, and its population is known to fluctuate greatly in response to changes in prey abundance. Unlike most owls, the northern hawk owl is a daylight hunter that relies more on sight than hearing to find its target; during the long winters it also hunts in the dark. Its preferred prey are voles and mice, but it will also take insects, hares, and birds such as grouse. The owl earned its name because of similarities in its behavior and appearance to hawks—including pointed wing tips, a long tail, and a swiftlike flight pattern. These owls do not build a nest, but normally lay their eggs in a cavity inside a tree.

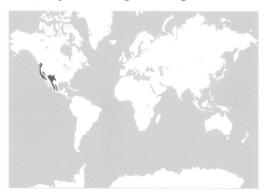

AW: Northern hawk owlets exhibit a behavior commonly known as "branching." This refers to their habit of exploring the limbs of surrounding trees once they have outgrown their nest cavity. At this age, the young owls are capable of flying short distances. To avoid disturbing these birds, I chose a 400mm f/2.8 lens so that I could shoot reasonably fast exposures in the dark spruce forest while also keeping my distance.

Canon EOS-3, Canon EF 400mm lens, f/11 at 1/15 second, Fujichrome Velvia film

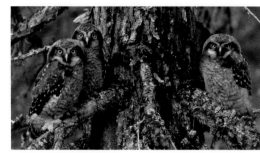

SPOTTED OWL
(Strix occidentalis)

Spotted owls are entirely restricted to British Columbia, the western United States, and parts of northern Mexico. They favor old-growth forests dominated by firs, but also make use of hardwood habitats. They seem to select forests that are at least 200 years old, although they may nest in old second-growth areas, where trees are 70 to 140 years old. There are three recognized subspecies: S. o. caurina (northern spotted owl), S. o. lucida (Mexican spotted owl), and S. o. occidentalis (California spotted owl). Spotted owls are nonmigratory, but may move to lower elevations during the winter months. Habitat destruction and fragmentation, particularly the logging of old-growth forests, represents the most serious threat to the owls. Less than 13 percent of the Pacific Northwest's ancient forests survive; there are fewer than 100 pairs of northern spotted owls in British Columbia, and probably fewer than 2,000 pairs in Washington and Oregon.

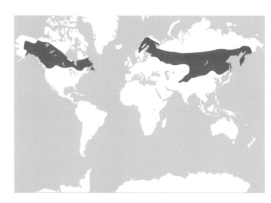

AW: I have always been drawn to owls, so much so that I spent nine years working on a book devoted solely to the owls of North America. It was during this time that the little-known spotted owl rose to national prominence. It became the rallying symbol in the battle to save the old-growth forests of the Pacific Northwest. In this photograph, a spotted owl perches on a western hemlock. Although the owl is extremely difficult to find in the dense, dark forest, once found, it is easy to approach because it shows little fear of people.

Canon EOS-1N, Canon EF 400mm lens, f/8 at 1/8 second, Fujichrome Astia film

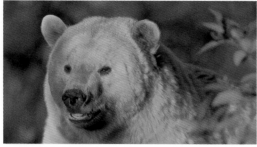

KERMODE BEAR
(Ursus americanus kermodei)

Kermode bears look like miniature polar bears lifted from the ice pack and deposited in the coastal rainforests of British Columbia. In fact, they are a rare color-form of the American black bear. Kermodes are named after a former director of the Royal British Columbia Museum; other names for the stunning creamy-white animals include the evocative "spirit bear" or "ghost bear." As with the other color-forms of black bears (such as the glacier bear of Alaska), Kermodes are the result of a double recessive gene. When an animal has two recessive "white" genes— one received from each parent—it has the distinctive white coat. Animals with only a single recessive gene look black, but if they mate with another "carrier," an average of 25 percent of their offspring will be Kermodes. Princess Royal Island on British Columbia's west coast has a particularly large number of Kermode bears, with 7 to 15 percent of the island's 130 black bears born white.

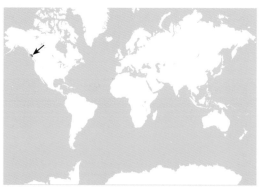

AW: For two days in a row, I found this large male Kermode bear feeding on a carpet of clover in a forest clearing. What surprised me most about these two encounters was how accepting the bear was of my presence. At times, I photographed from just 5 meters away. In the late afternoon, the bear left the clearing and went swimming in a nearby beaver pond to cool off.

Canon F3, Canon EF 300mm lens, f/5.6 at 1/60 second, Fujichrome Velvia film

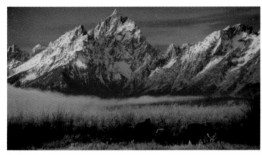

MOOSE
(Alces alces)

The moose is the largest member of the deer family (Cervidae), standing 1.4 to 2.3 meters at the shoulder and weighing 200 to 825 kilograms, with adult males being particularly large. They are unmistakable animals with broad muzzles, immense antlers, and a pendulous "bell" hanging under their throats. Moose can usually be found in wooded habitats that get some amount of snowfall each winter. They are browsers, feeding on shrubs and trees, as well as aquatic vegetation, sometimes immersing themselves completely to reach submerged plants; they consume nearly 20 kilograms of plant material daily. Often solitary, moose may congregate if the habitat is particularly favorable. Small groups may actually consist of an adult female, calf-of-the-year (twins are common), and older, independent offspring.

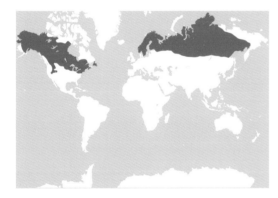

AW: To capture this scene on film required a little innovation. I used an 70–200mm lens to create a balanced composition. I stopped down to f/11 to bring all elements into focus. I used a polarizing filter to intensify the alpenglow. And since there was a 4-stop difference in light levels between the summits and the moose, I used two 2-stop graduated neutral density filters to bring the entire scene into an even exposure. All the filters and an f/11 aperture made my shutter speed very long. The only usable shots came when all of the moose were motionless.

Canon EOS-1N, Canon EF 70–200mm lens, f/11 at 1 second, polarizing filter, two 2-stop graduated neutral density filters, Fujichrome Velvia film (pushed 1 stop)

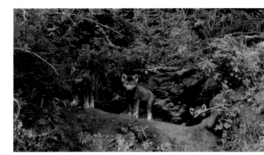

GRAY WOLF
(Canis lupus)

The gray wolf epitomizes the persecuted animal. The wolf as villain is a part of human culture. In the contiguous United States, wolves were virtually eliminated by the early twentieth century; federal extermination campaigns gave official sanction to bounty hunters. An estimated 2,700 wolves live in the contiguous United States today (many as part of carefully controlled reintroduction projects); an additional 5,900 to 7,200 are found in Alaska. Thirty thousand may survive in Canada, and perhaps 50,000 in the Russian Federation. Elsewhere wolves survive only in remnant populations. While it was once thought that wolves would exterminate their prey (and thus harm big-game populations sought by human hunters), it is now recognized that viable predator populations are vital to a healthy ecosystem. Still, when wolves move out of protected areas and onto ranchland, they enter a conflict they cannot win.

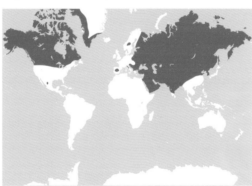

AW: Gray wolves are difficult to see, even in northern Canada and Alaska where relatively large populations still exist. They often locate their dens on promontories that provide them with a good view of the surrounding area. This particular den was located on a hillside above a small lake. I erected a blind across the lake, allowing a clear view of the den entrance. During the day when the adults were away hunting, the pups wandered out. Although I remained hidden 100 meters away, the pups clearly sensed my presence.

Canon F3, Canon EF 800mm lens, Canon Extender EF 2x, f/8 at 1/15 second, Fujichrome 100 film (pushed 1 stop)

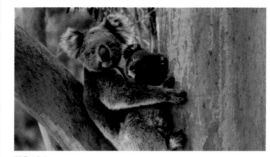

KOALA
(Phascolarctos cinereus)

The icon of Australian wildlife, the koala is a member of the order Diprotodontia, the largest of the marsupial orders. Found only in Australia's eucalyptus forests, these adorable antipodeans feed on the leaves and bark of about twelve different species of eucalyptus. The fibrous leaves are hard to digest, and koalas have a long 1.8- to 2.5-meter caecum to aid in the digestive process. Before widespread human settlement in Australia, koalas likely numbered in the millions, but habitat losses, forest fires, and hunting for pelts wiped out many regional populations in the first two decades of the twentieth century. In 1924 alone, more than two million pelts were exported. By the time protection came, only a few thousand animals remained. Today, koalas have lost 50 to 90 percent of their habitat to development. Population estimates range from a low of 40,000 to about ten times that number.

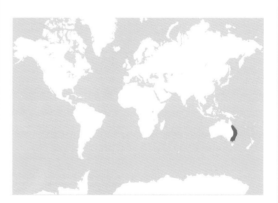

AW: On Australia's Kangaroo Island, 14 meters above the ground, a koala cradles its baby on a limb of a giant eucalyptus tree. To get this shot and its unusual perspective, I climbed the tree, keeping myself concealed behind the trunk. The koalas were sleeping so soundly on this chilly morning that I was able to approach to within 0.5 meter. I selected a 17–35mm wide-angle lens for two reasons. First, it is easy to handhold while balancing on a branch. Second, I wanted to capture a "sense of place" only a wide-angle lens can achieve.

Canon EOS-3, Canon EF 17–35mm lens, f/8 at 1/60 second, Fujichrome Astia film (pushed 1 stop)

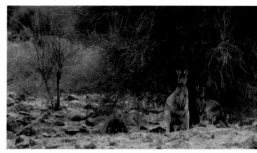

WESTERN GRAY KANGAROO
(Macropus fuliginosus)

Along with their eastern relatives (*M. giganteus*), western gray kangaroos are the largest surviving marsupials. About 1.5 meters tall, with tails up to a meter long, kangaroos are the "deer" of Australia, grazing on grass and other vegetation. Their heavy tails act as a balance when leaping, and as an "extra" leg when sitting. Females with young often gather in "mobs" of two to ten or more; males join such groups only if a female is in estrus. Population estimates for western grays exceed one million; however, populations of all three kangaroo species (western, eastern, and red [*M. rufus*]) have fluctuated greatly in response to droughts and hunting pressures. Considerable hunting of kangaroos for meat and skins occurs in Australia; in 1992, 10 percent of the entire kangaroo population (all three species) was harvested. Regional populations have declined, and some subspecies, including *M. f. fuliginosus* of Kangaroo Island, are considered threatened.

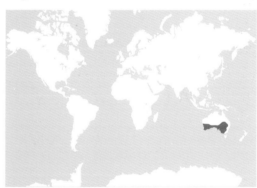

AW: A mother kangaroo and her joey watch as I cross a small clearing on Australia's aptly named Kangaroo Island. In situations such as this, I always try to keep the primary subject out of the center of the composition. Since the entire composition was primarily the same tone, I took an overall exposure reading rather than my usual spot reading.

Canon EOS-3, Canon EF 500mm IS lens, Canon Extender EF 1.4x, f/8 at 1/60 second, Fujichrome Provia film

NOTES FROM THE FIELD

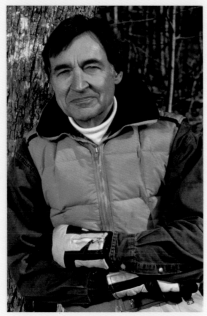

© JAMES KEGLEY

What is it about animals roaming freely in their native habitats that so captures the human imagination? Do they represent a kind of life force that enriches beyond measure the intricate landscapes of our planet? In his classic 1949 work, *A Sand County Almanac*, Aldo Leopold certainly thought so.

In writing about the time that he spent in the Mexican states of Chihuahua and Sonora, Leopold described the thick-billed parrot as "the numenon of the Sierra Madre," just as "the grouse is the numenon of the north woods, the blue jay of the hickory groves, the whisky-jack of the muskegs, the piñonero of the juniper foothills." A numenon, Leopold explained, is the "imponderable essence" or spiritual force of a place, embodied in its unique creatures. "Everybody knows, for example, that the autumn landscape in the north woods is the land, plus a red maple, plus a ruffed grouse," wrote Leopold. "In terms of conventional physics, the grouse represents only a millionth of either the mass or the energy of a hectare. Yet subtract the grouse and the whole thing is dead. An enormous amount of some kind of motive power has been lost."

As you leaf through these pages and admire Art Wolfe's exquisite work, imagine what each scene would look like without such numenons as California sea lions, arctic foxes, Przewalski's horses, giant pandas, Florida panthers, South American tapirs, and Andean condors gracing their native habitats. Like the north woods without the grouse, each of these landscapes would be barren without its full complement of native species.

Picturing these habitats devoid of their characteristic plants and animals soberly reminds us of what we are in danger of losing if the ranks of our planet's declining, vanishing, and expired species continue to grow. Unfortunately, the reports from the field are often bleak. We continue to imperil some of the planet's most noble creatures by failing to halt the unwise and excessive clearing and burning of forests; the overgrazing of pasturelands; the draining of wetlands; the polluting of rivers, streams, and lakes; and the cruel black-market slaughter of species such as rhinoceroses, and tigers.

Knowing what's at stake, what then do we do? Just give up and consign the world's dwindling diversity of wildlife—including many of the creatures photographed for this book—to at most a few isolated preserves and the care of the world's zoos? Or should the growing ranks of people who care deeply about our precious natural heritage take a stand and respond to the world's biodiversity crisis with intelligence, passion, and conviction?

The good news is that all over the world, ordinary people imbued with a conservation ethic are taking such a stand. In this essay, I celebrate the stories of special individuals who are taking extraordinary measures to help stem the tide of extinction in the twenty-first century. It may seem odd to have such a focus, given the degree to which the thoughtlessness or indifference of many of our fellow humans has contributed to the extinction of species. But in the long run, people who feel connected to nature, whether through their livelihoods, their recreational pursuits, or their appreciation of books like this, must and will be an essential part of the solution.

Author Barry Lopez takes this idea one step further, encouraging people to reclaim their ties with nature to help strengthen their bonds to the human community. After all, community, he reminds us, means everyone and everything. Eliminate any of the parts—people, species, landscapes—and we erode the sense of cohesion and common purpose that has tied people to the land and each other for millennia. Indeed, there is even a person tangible in Art Wolfe's photographs to help confirm Barry Lopez's notion that community incorporates people, species, and landscapes. It just so happens that the person in those exotic habitats is at the other end of the camera lens.

I believe our twenty-first-century challenge as nature lovers is to approach the outdoors as Art does, as people with strong connections to special places, motivated to walk respectfully and lightly on the land. Beyond this, our challenge is to convince friends and neighbors to act on our shared instincts toward nature, and to work on a daily basis to be more protective of and connected with our natural surroundings.

There are numerous examples of ordinary people whose commitment and dedication to conservation are worth celebrating. Looking back at how conservation issues were forced onto the national agenda, there is also one famous person who deserves his due— Theodore Roosevelt. Nearly a century ago, Roosevelt, appalled by the destruction of egrets and other wading birds—whose plumage was valued as mere hat decorations—didn't just accept the birds' demise as a given. He acted boldly and swiftly to create our first Federal Bird Reservation in 1903 on Pelican Island, Florida, and then worked to create a larger system of "national wildlife refuges," which today encompass over 38 million hectares. Roosevelt, known today as our greatest conservation president, also expanded the national forests from 17 million hectares to 70 million and preserved eighteen areas as national monuments, including the Grand Canyon and the Petrified Forest.

Roosevelt's solution of protecting the most biologically diverse lands still makes sense, and basic land protection is the foundation upon which other useful conservation strategies can be built. But we still have a long way to go. Currently, only about 4 to 6 percent of the Earth's surface is under some sort of protected status. The eminent Harvard biologist Edward O. Wilson, among others, believes that the nations of the world need to afford concrete protection to at least 10 percent of our planet's land areas in order to forestall a global extinction crisis.

Does that mean closing off one-tenth of the Earth's surface from human enterprise? Absolutely not. One of the more promising developments in the field of conservation biology is the realization that there are a number of economic activities that can be conducted harmoniously in protected land areas, such as ecotourism and the sustainable harvest of native plants. For example, in her essay for this book, Jane Goodall describes how her institute is helping peasant farmers near Tanzania's Gombe Stream Game Reserve achieve a better standard of living through activities that do not harm ongoing conservation activities in the park. Goodall rightly suggests that when you give people a better stake in the landscape, they become its greatest defenders.

You don't have to travel halfway across the globe, either, to find inspiring examples of people and communities figuring out how they can earn a decent living off the land, while also protecting the land's capacity to support a rich diversity of life. Here in the United States, in the course of my travels for The Nature Conservancy, I have met many memorable land stewards who are deeply committed to conservation.

In Colorado's scenic Yampa Valley, I have met ranchers such as Jay and Gail Fetcher, who are striving to reconcile the region's ranching heritage with the need to protect a globally imperiled cottonwood forest along the Yampa River. On their own, the Fetchers have installed fencing in sensitive streamside areas to better manage livestock grazing, encouraging restoration of the cottonwoods and reduction of streambank erosion.

Similarly, in the Peloncillo Mountains of southeastern Arizona, ranchers Matt and Anna Magoffin, and their sons Mike and Chris, spent much of a recent summer hauling tanker trucks full of water to a cattle watering hole to help sustain a group of drought-affected endangered Chiricahua leopard frogs. With the help of fellow conservation-minded ranchers, the Magoffins also drilled a well and built a windmill to provide a steady water supply for the frogs. The Magoffins and their compatriots have also entered into a voluntary association, the Malpais Borderlands Group, that is working to institute compatible grazing regimes and ward off subdivision of the rangelands.

Back east, on Block Island, Rhode Island, longtime residents like Keith Lewis have placed habitat protection for migratory waterfowl and a variety of terrestrial species above the millions in profits they could have made by selling their properties to developers. "There are more things in life besides money," said Lewis when he sold his 34 hectares of water-view land to The Nature Conservancy. Keith also spent an entire year—at his own expense—in a successful effort to lobby the Rhode Island General Assembly to allow Block Island to levy a local real-estate transfer tax to raise money to help buy more open space. Today, thanks to Lewis and like-minded Block Islanders, public or conservation ownership has risen to almost 20 percent of the island's total land area.

The passion that people such as Keith Lewis have for special places like Block Island motivated The Nature Conservancy to change its fundamental strategies toward land

conservation in the past decade. During the first forty years of our existence, The Nature Conservancy frankly did not pay much attention to people like the Fetchers and Keith Lewis, who have lived near the places we acquired. Our focus was on managing the land we had acquired or on acquiring more, and our structure was relatively centralized. But as we began to plan and work on larger scales, we have undergone a transformation. Not only have we aggressively expanded our operations at the local level, but we have come to recognize the critical importance of neighboring human communities in helping us achieve our goals. Engaging local communities in our work, we have found, offers us our best, highest-leverage, and often only opportunity for conserving large portions of the landscape, especially those managed by private landowners.

Consider our work on Virginia's Eastern Shore. Over the past quarter century, The Nature Conservancy has acquired 20,000 Eastern Shore hectares, including the last chain of migratory waterfowl– and sea turtle–friendly undeveloped barrier islands on the East Coast. To ensure the long-term protection of this resource, we reached out to the local community. We convened key local stakeholders to conduct a "visioning" exercise about the desired future for the community; worked with the local National Association for the Advancement of Colored People chapter on low-income housing and waste water issues; and helped support local environmentally sound businesses. When we heard back from the stakeholders that ensuring a stable job base was vital to the Eastern Shore's future, The Nature Conservancy took the initiative to create a for-profit venture capital subsidiary to bring compatible economic development activities to the area, ranging from agriculture to ecotourism. Not all our activities here have succeeded. But we have learned lessons from the initiative that can be applied in other communities seeking a balance between environmental protection and economic opportunity.

As we look to the future, the support of dedicated conservationists will be crucial to the success of another promising conservation activity—land restoration. In *The Diversity of Life*, Edward O. Wilson writes, "There can be no purpose more enspiriting than to begin the age of restoration, reweaving the wondrous diversity of life that still surrounds us." Wilson points out that conservation-minded landowners are already hard at work on their properties, restoring functioning freshwater and saltwater marsh wetlands, replanting forests, and regenerating ecosystems such as the tallgrass prairie of the Great Plains.

Deep in the Osage Hills of Oklahoma, one of the most beautiful grassland oases in the American heartland, I first met Mary Barnard Lawrence, the gracious lady who is making possible one of The Nature Conservancy's most important tallgrass prairie restoration projects. For decades, Mary's parents, Horace and Frankie Barnard, left their 12,000-hectare Barnard Ranch unplowed and managed cattle with due regard for the

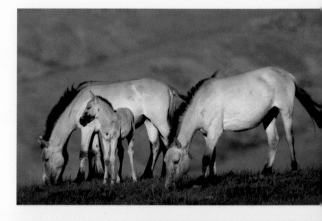

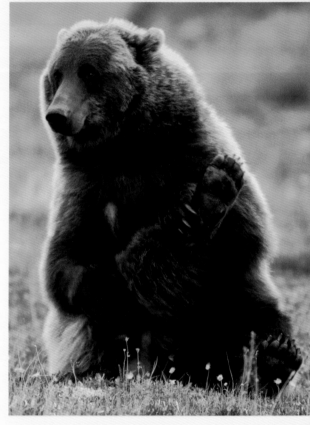

▲▲ PRZEWALSKI'S HORSE

(*Equus caballus przewalskii*), Hustain Nururu National Reserve, Mongolia

▲ BROWN BEAR

(*Ursus arctos*), Denali National Park, Alaska, USA

JOHN C. SAWHILL

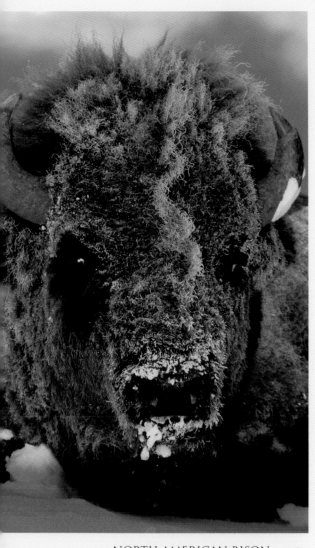

NORTH AMERICAN BISON
(*Bison bison*), YELLOWSTONE NATIONAL PARK,
WYOMING, USA

land's "carrying capacity." Ten years ago, Mary put the family property up for sale, and after considering many offers, agreed to convey the ranch to The Nature Conservancy. Mary was receptive to our plan to reintroduce bison and fire to the ranch, the missing natural elements crucial for regenerating the characteristic big bluestem, Indian grass, and switch grass of the prairie. When the sale of the ranch was completed, Mary remarked, "During the past couple of years, I have come to a deeper sense of the early Native American belief that one can never really own land. It is to be understood and protected."

And indeed, we took four years to better understand the landscape before we allowed the crackle of fire and the thunder of bison to return to the Osage Hills. When we commenced restoration activities, we began by burning portions of the prairie in the spring, late summer, and fall to mimic the seasonality of fires that occurred in presettlement times. Then, on a crisp October morning, for the first time in nearly a century, 300 bison were released to roam freely throughout 2,000 hectares of tallgrass.

Recently, we paused to celebrate the tenth anniversary of the preserve and to take stock of the progress of our restoration effort. Encouragingly, populations of prairie-nesting birds such as Henslow's sparrows, eastern meadowlarks, and grasshopper sparrows are rebounding. We are seeing more birds because of the increased diversity of cover, resulting from bison grazing and prescribed burning—just as we had hoped. We are so pleased with the initial results of this restoration project that we plan to increase both the herd size and the amount of bison range that is annually burned.

Just last year, over 30,000 people from throughout the United States and from forty-three foreign countries traveled to the Osage Hills in order to gaze in wonder at the bison and the other species that inhabit our Tallgrass Prairie Preserve. Perhaps the most special preserve visitor is a woman from the local Osage Tribe. Preserve Director Harvey Payne tells me that this woman visits the preserve daily and carefully records on videotape the comings and goings of the bison, while saying silent prayers of thanks for the return of these noble creatures to the tallgrass.

Mary Barnard Lawrence expressed similar sentiments when she spoke at the preserve's tenth-anniversary celebration: "As I drive across this vast land and feel the seasons come and go, I am constantly amazed—and thankful—for the continued growth and beauty of the Tallgrass Prairie Preserve. I thrill at the sight of the glorious wildflowers in the spring, the variety of grasses growing even taller through the summer—and the bison—always the majesty of the bison, increasing in healthy numbers as I had envisioned. . . . Thank God for the gift of being temporary caretakers of one of the most beautiful creations of His Earth. This is sacred land. We have been truly blessed."

Of course, it is a fairly straightforward matter to restore natural diversity when blessed with a landscape as intact and beautiful as the Tallgrass Prairie Preserve. What makes restoration ecology promising as a means for protecting biodiversity and as a focus for twenty-first-century human initiative is that it also can work in smaller landscapes. In the suburbs of Chicago, Illinois, community volunteers are working in Forest Preserve Districts to restore the scarce Midwest oak savannah landscape, by planting grasses and flowers scrounged from unmowed margins of cemeteries, golf courses, railroad rights-of-way, and horse trails, and by cutting brush and periodically burning understory. If successful, the savannah restoration will help species like swamp white oak, glade mallow, Kirtland's snake, Cooper's hawk, and the silvery blue butterfly recover.

In south Florida, a massive environmental engineering project involving the state and federal government, private landowners, and conservation groups is seeking to restore the natural water flows that are so crucial to the Everglades and the entire Florida Bay ecosystem. A vital element of the Everglades rescue project will be the attempt by the U.S. Army Corps of Engineers to undo the channelization that has straitjacketed the once-free-flowing Kissimmee River.

Meanwhile, in thousands of backyards around the country, homeowners are discovering that they can regenerate habitat for birds, bees, and butterflies by planting native grasses, flowers, shrubs, and trees. These actions go to the core of that bumper-sticker slogan, "Think globally, act locally," which expresses the notion that to save the Earth, we must begin with our own backyards.

But acting locally is just the beginning. We must also act collaboratively at regional, national, and international levels to ensure that future generations are able to enjoy great creatures in their natural habitats. Let me suggest a framework for fashioning a positive local, national, and international agenda for long-term wildlife protection.

1. USE NATURAL, NOT GEOPOLITICAL, BOUNDARIES AS THE BASIS FOR HABITAT AND WILDLIFE PROTECTION EFFORTS. Natural resources and wildlife protection require new ways of thinking about conservation planning. Traditionally, geopolitical boundaries like state, county, and national lines have dominated conservation actions by government agencies and nonprofit organizations alike. But if you think about it, plants and animals don't respect these artificial boundaries; neither do rivers, prairies, forests, deserts, mountains, or marshes. Grizzly bear habitat, for instance, stretches from the United States into Canada. Accordingly, governments, conservation groups, landowners, and other interested parties must organize their conservation planning and implementation actions around ecosystems and functional landscapes, not on man-made boundaries. California is leading the way among states, with state officials adopting the ecosystem

model as a template for action and as a means of improving decision-making and on-the-ground conservation outcomes. Others should follow.

2. PROVIDE AMERICANS BETTER INCENTIVES TO CONSERVE NATURE. Roughly two-thirds of the landscape in the United States is privately owned, with well over half of all imperiled species found on private land. I believe landowners have a positive responsibility to be environmental stewards. To really make a difference in how the American landscape is managed, we need to galvanize millions of people to take positive action to protect wildlife habitat. Regrettably, the controversy over laws like the Endangered Species Act has led in some cases to perverse outcomes, such as landowners deliberately destroying habitat lest a threatened or endangered species be found on their property and trigger regulatory restrictions on how they can use their land.

It would be preferable if public policies were changed to accomplish the following three goals: First, expand incentives for landowners to protect or enhance habitat on their properties. The U.S. Department of Agriculture has two incentive-based programs—the Conservation Reserve and Wetlands Reserve programs—that are highly popular with farmers. However, because they are underfunded, they have not been able to capture a high level of participation in the programs. Another underfunded incentive for conservation is the U.S. Fish and Wildlife Service's "Safe Harbor" policy that provides landowners assurances that if they take voluntary conservation actions on their properties to protect habitat for species listed as "threatened or endangered," they will not be subject to additional restrictions on how they can use the land.

Second, change local, state, and federal tax laws to encourage the sale, gift, or exchange of land for easements for conservation. States such as Delaware, Maryland, North Carolina, and Virginia have taken the lead in promoting progressive tax treatment of conservation, and thousands of hectares have been permanently protected as a result. Now other states and Congress are considering using the tax code as an effective carrot for saving our country's best places. One proposal being seriously considered by Congress would exempt from taxation one-half of the capital gains due if a landowner sells conservation land to a public or private conservation agency. If passed, this proposal could protect 80,000 hectares per year. Given our current period of fiscal solvency, there is no time like the present to enact laws like this that will provide some tax relief for conservation-minded Americans and that will benefit future generations.

And third, use tax and other laws to discourage the breakup and subdivision of farms and other large intact landholdings. In 1998 New Jersey voters passed a major bond initiative that will help keep intact much of the "Garden State's" large farmlands.

Other state and local entities are following suit by identifying pools of funds that can be used to acquire development rights for farmlands. I hear often from farmers and other landowners, who are positively inclined to manage or dispose of their landholdings with conservation stewardship in mind, provided the right incentive structure is put in place. Given our current turn-of-the-millennium focus on the long-term future, there is no time like the present to enact such positive public policy changes.

Government agencies also need to work to eliminate or reduce actions and policies that are destructive of wildlife habitat. By focusing on habitat restoration projects, government agencies and the private sector can direct their creative energies to as challenging and meaningful a goal as dam building and rocket launching offered in the past century.

3. SIGNIFICANTLY EXPAND INTERNATIONAL CONSERVATION ACTIVITIES. Finally, we must significantly expand our efforts to address the international dimensions of the wildlife and habitat crisis. In the twenty-seven countries where we support local conservation groups and projects in Latin America, the Caribbean, South America, and the Asia/Pacific region, The Nature Conservancy is providing funding to employ local residents in conservation-friendly pursuits. But we recognize the need to do more, and accordingly are working with our partners to upgrade and expand these programs.

The international community also needs to be more engaged in habitat and wildlife conservation. International financial institutions, which all too often in the past have subsidized ill-thought-out dam- and road-building projects that have resulted in the destruction of large landscapes, are taking a hard look at their practices and instituting much-needed reforms. Hopefully, these institutions will strongly support in the coming decades such innovative policies as debt-for-nature swaps and projects to support forest conservation as a means of containing carbon gas emissions.

One of Theodore Roosevelt's most significant actions as president was to convene a conference of all the nation's governors to address the country's conservation needs. It is about time that a summit of world leaders be held specifically to promote expanded cooperative international actions to protect wildlife and natural habitat.

We can make significant progress toward conservation of wildlife and wild places in the coming decades by focusing on the shared links between people, species, and landscapes that are so important to the human and natural communities that we aspire to pass on to future generations. On these pages, I know you will savor the images of species and landscapes that Art Wolfe has photographed around the world. His gift to us vividly portrays a treasured part of the world that should not, and need not, vanish.

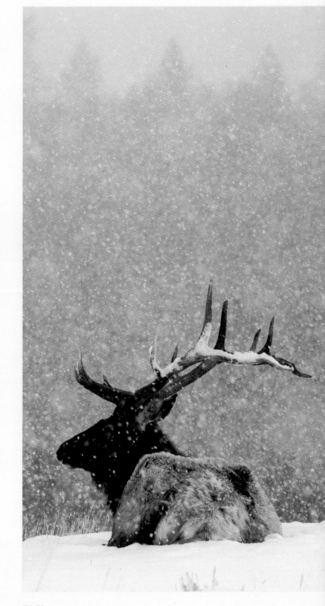

ELK

(*Cervus elaphus*), YELLOWSTONE NATIONAL PARK, WYOMING, USA

JOHN C. SAWHILL

185

SUBTROPICAL

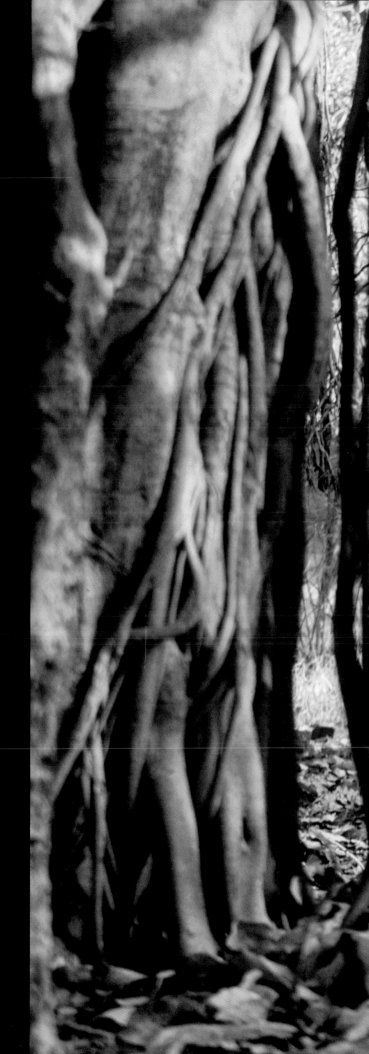

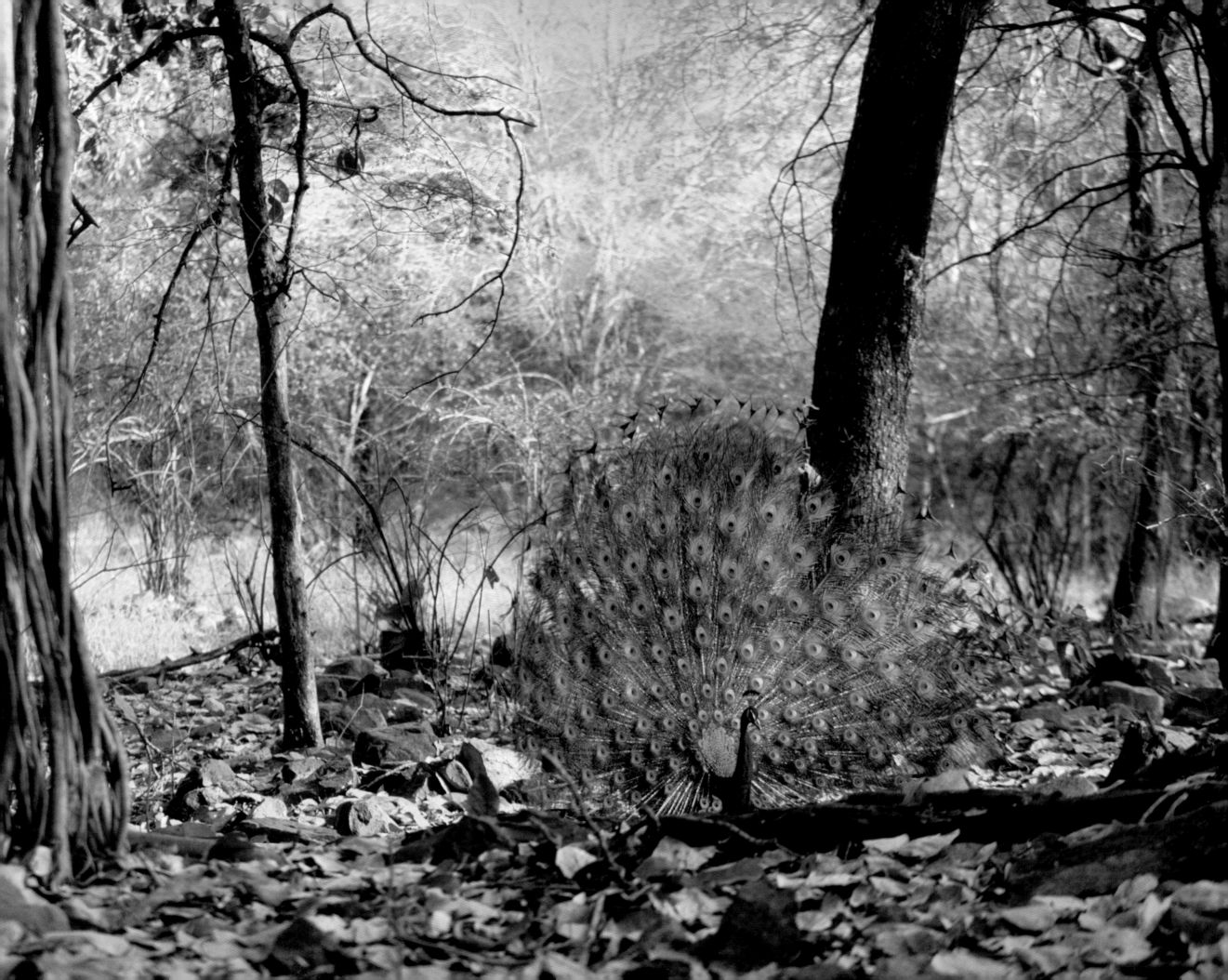

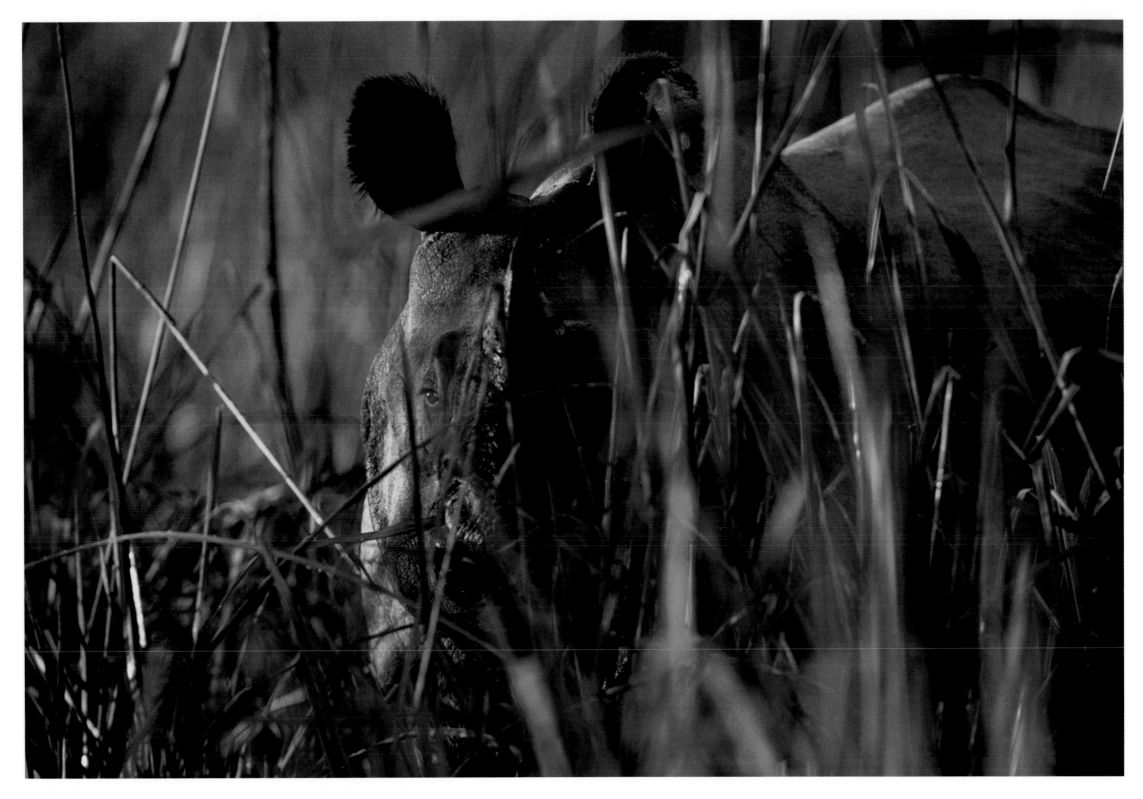

◂ INDIAN PEAFOWL

Ranthambore National Park, Rajasthan, India

GREATER INDIAN RHINOCEROS

Royal Chitwan National Park, Nepal

THE LIVING WILD

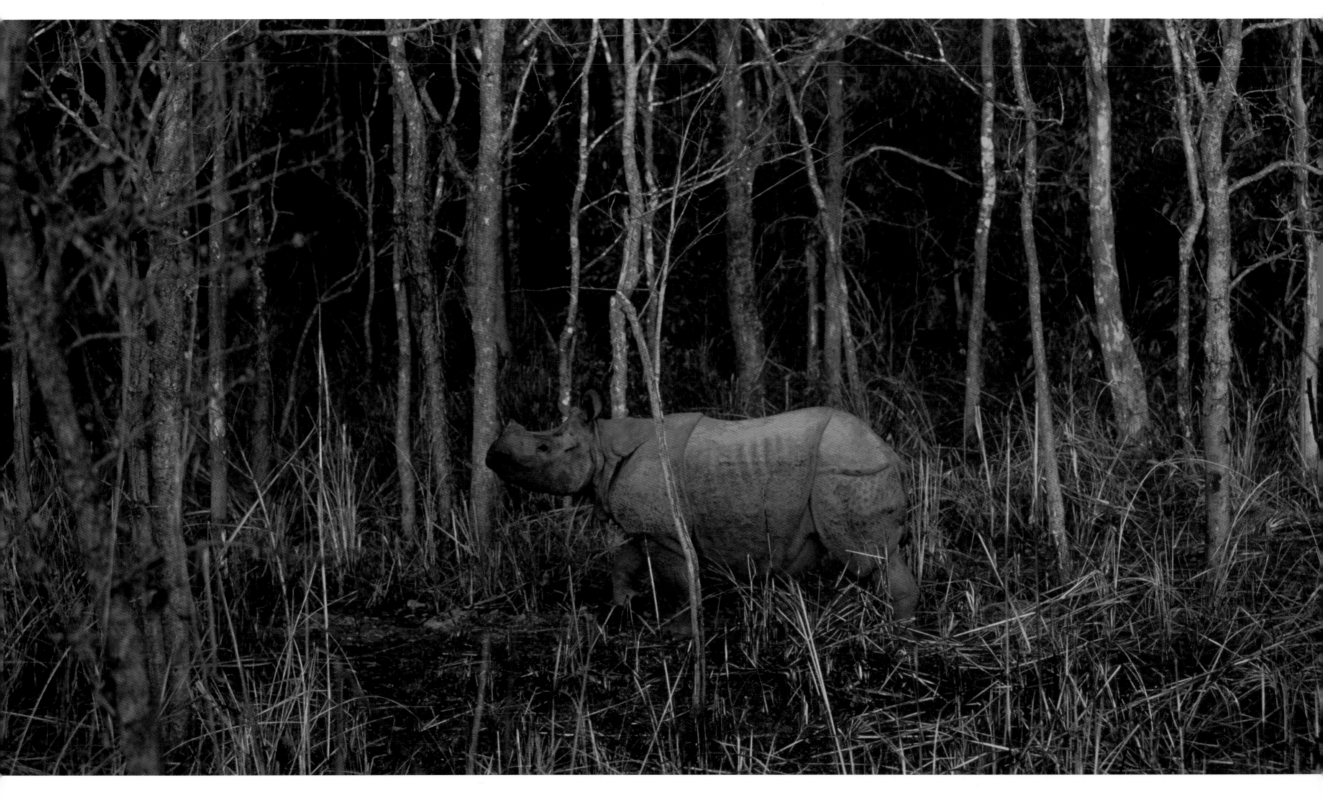

GREATER INDIAN RHINOCEROS

Royal Chitwan National Park, Nepal

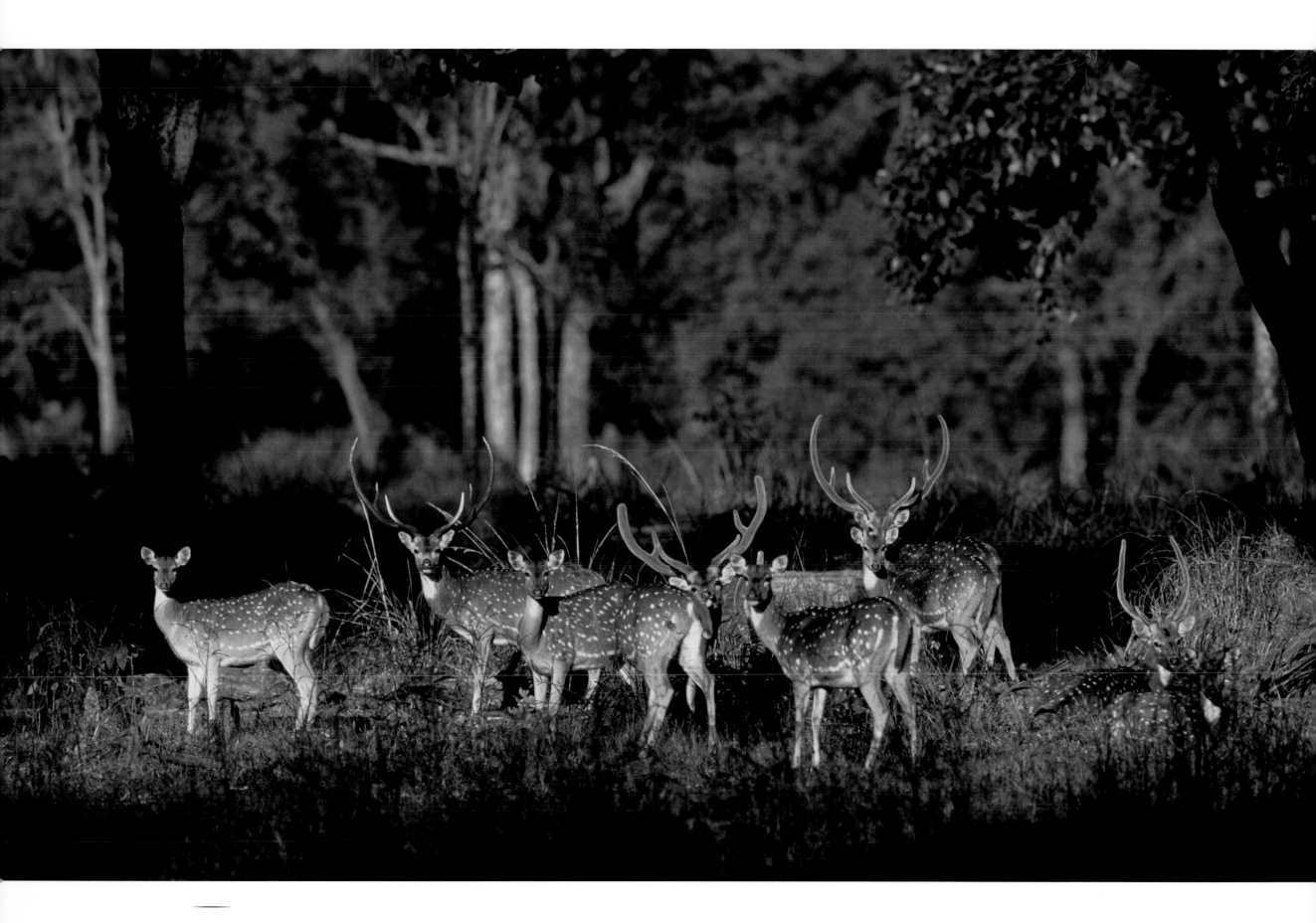

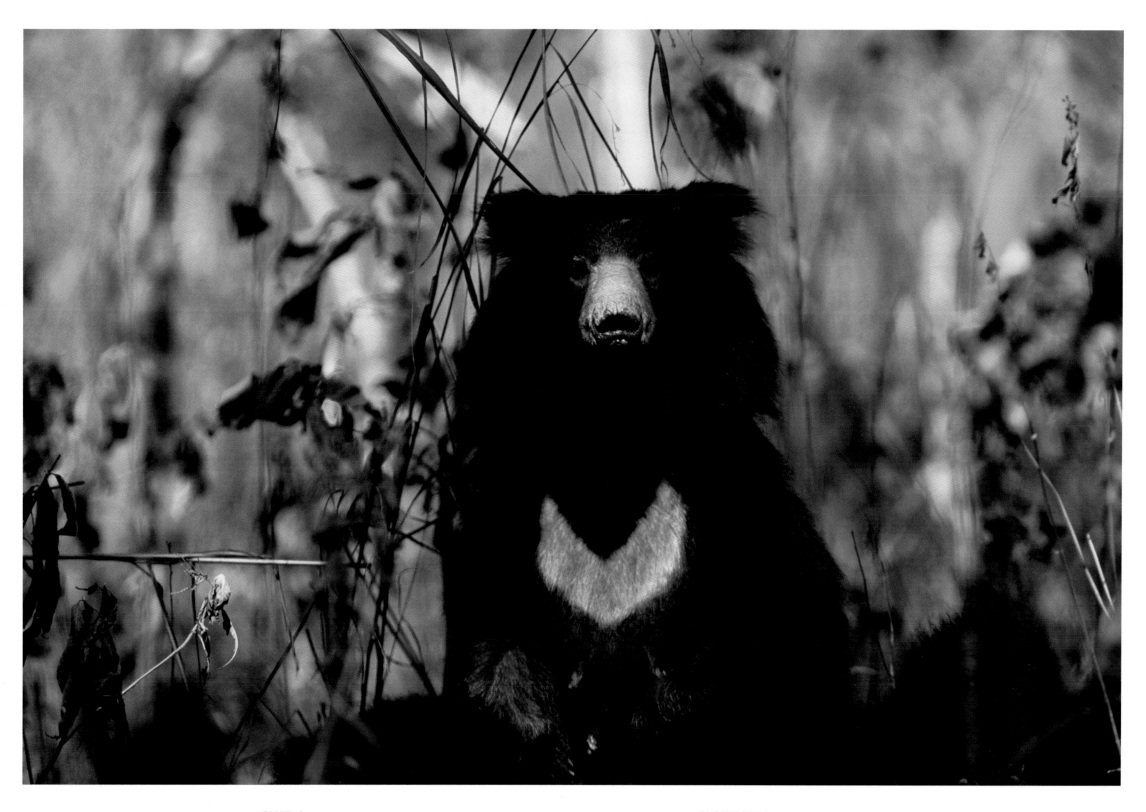

◄ CHITAL

Kanha National Park, Madhya Pradesh, India

SLOTH BEAR

Royal Chitwan National Park, Nepal

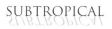

SUBTROPICAL

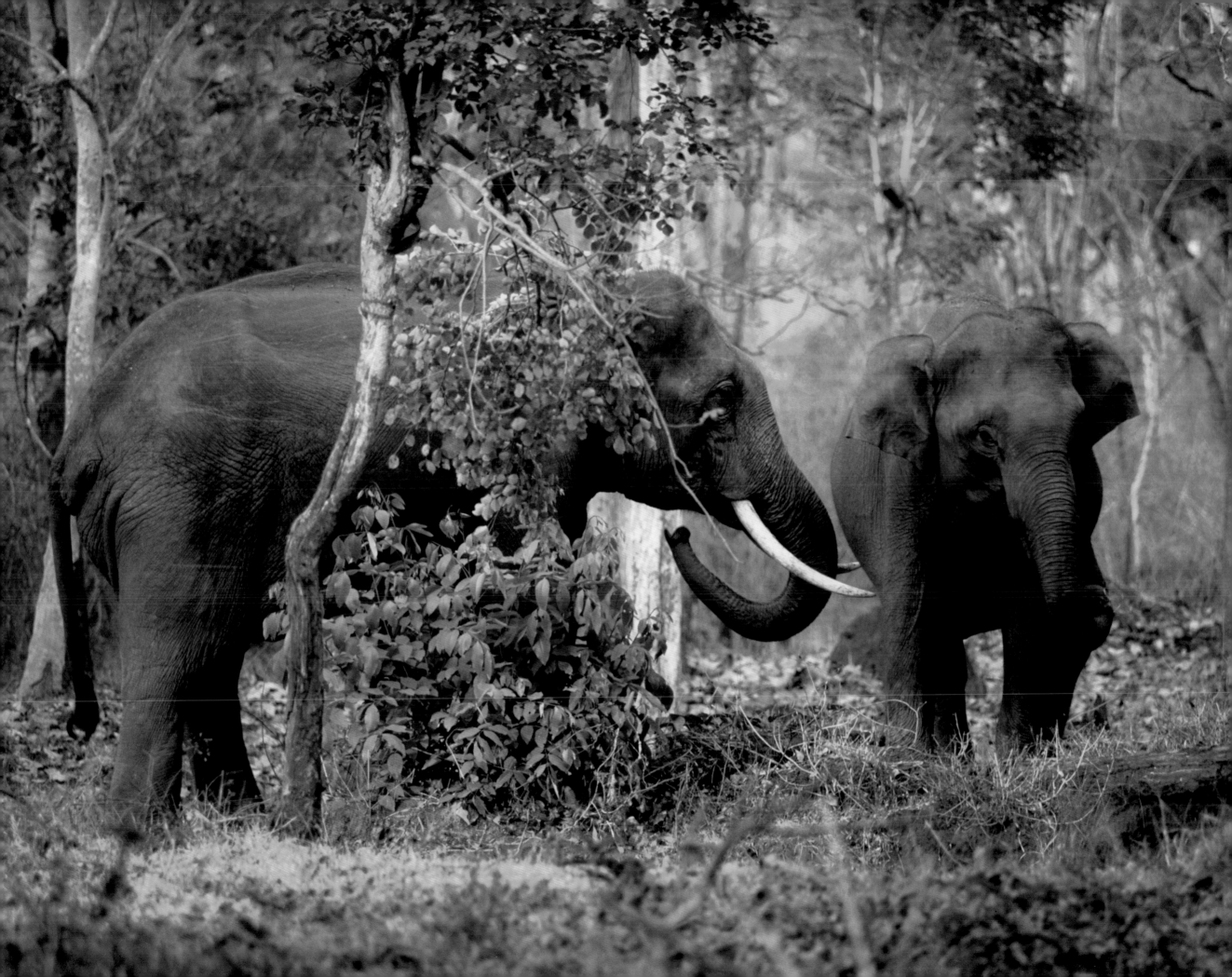

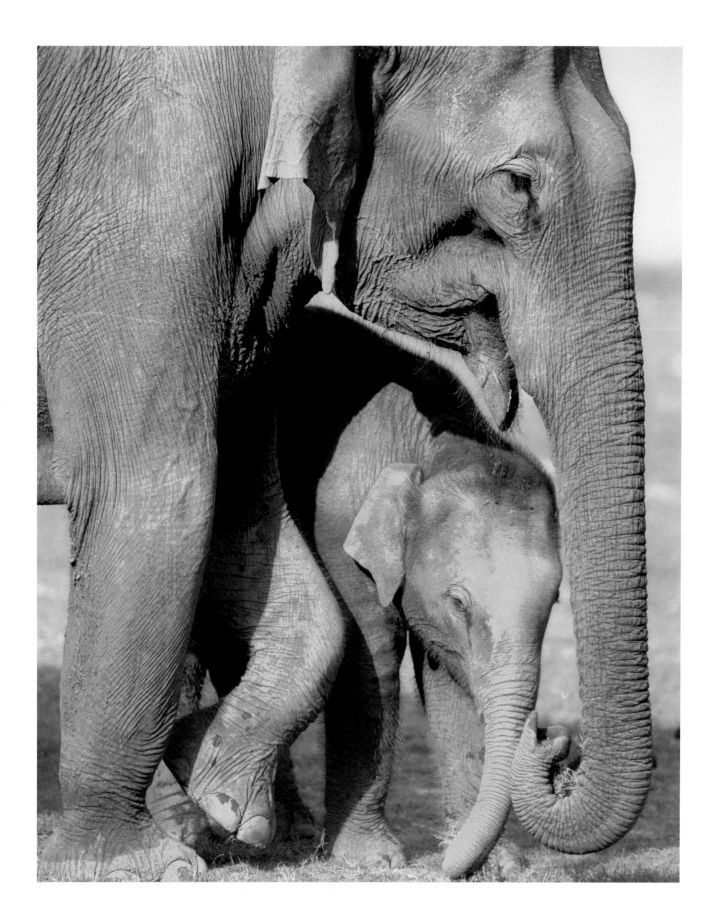

◄ AND ► ASIATIC ELEPHANT

NAGARAHOLE NATIONAL PARK, KARNATAKA,

INDIA

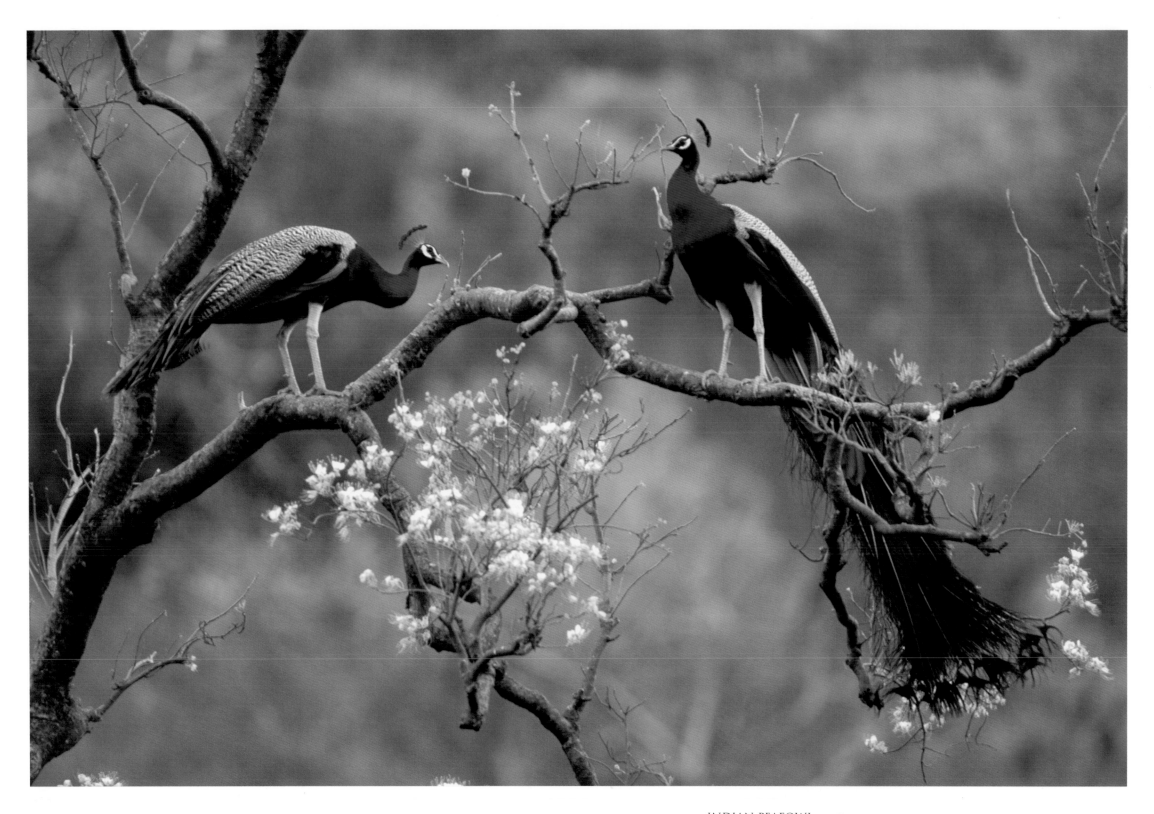

INDIAN PEAFOWL
Ranthambore National Park, Rajasthan, India

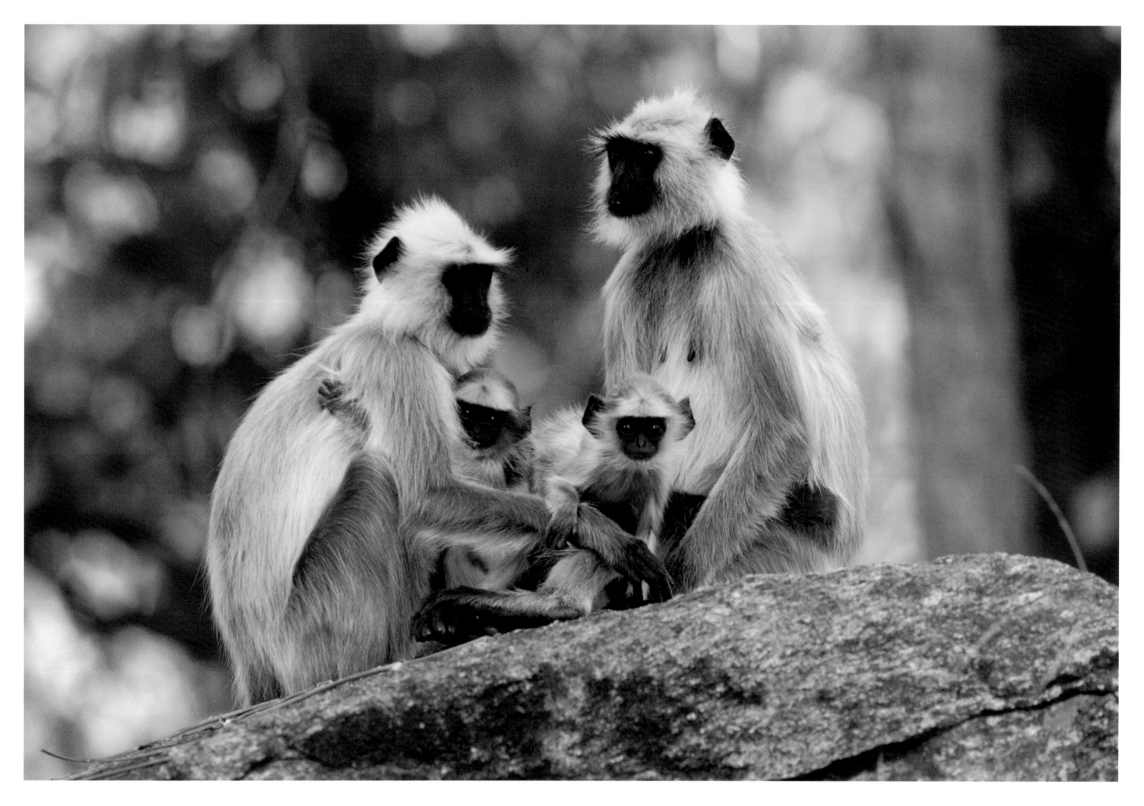

HANUMAN LANGUR

Kanha National Park, Madhya Pradesh, India

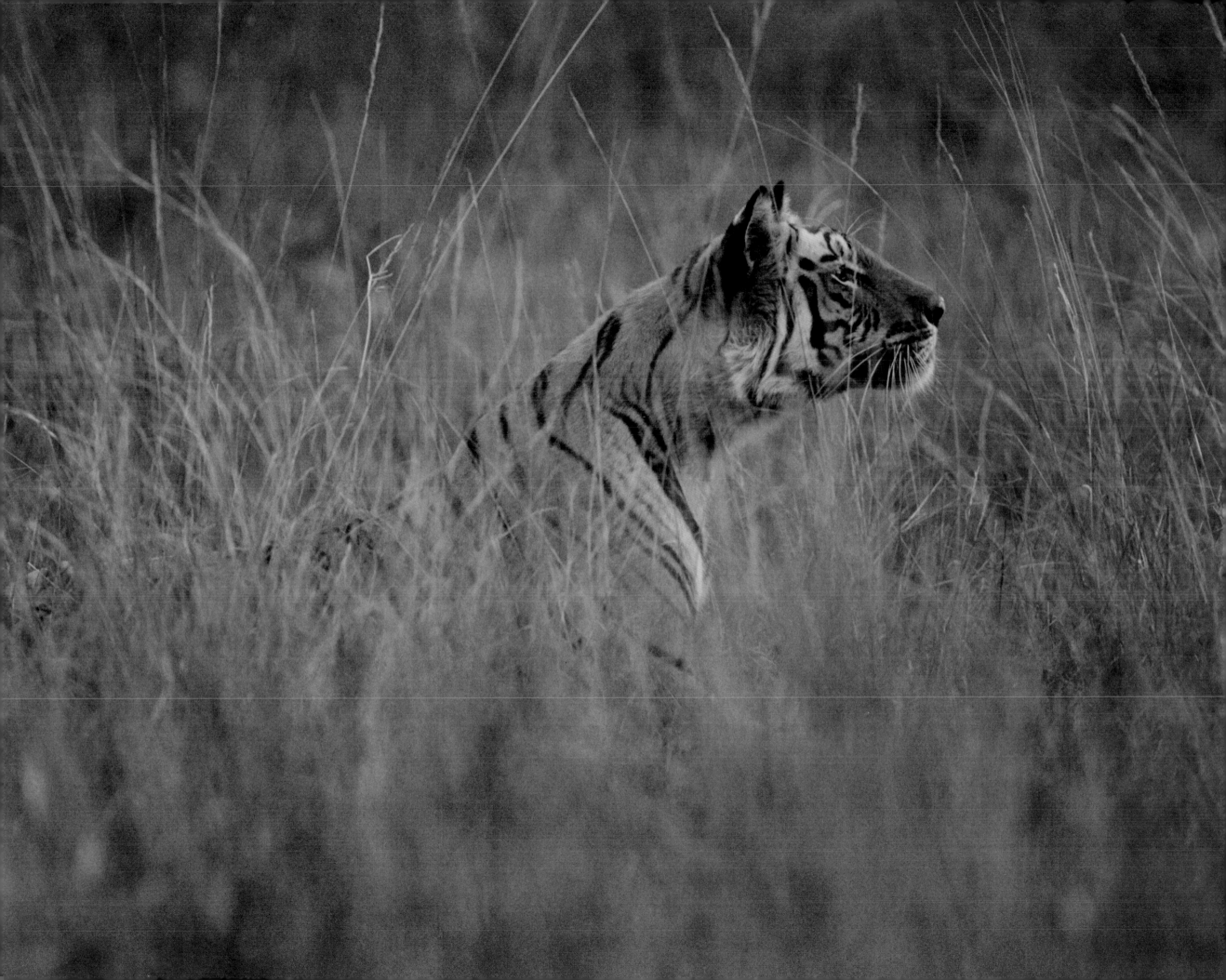

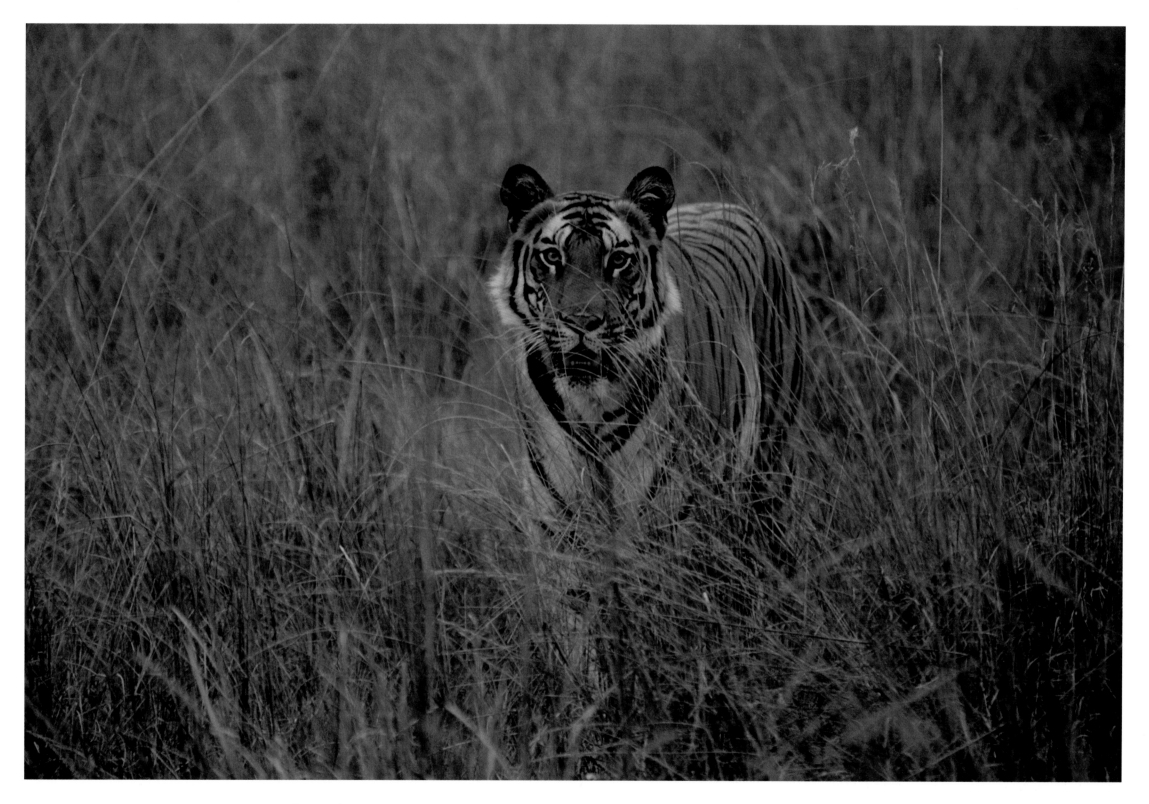

◄ AND ▲ TIGER

Bandhavgarh National Park, Madhya Pradesh, India

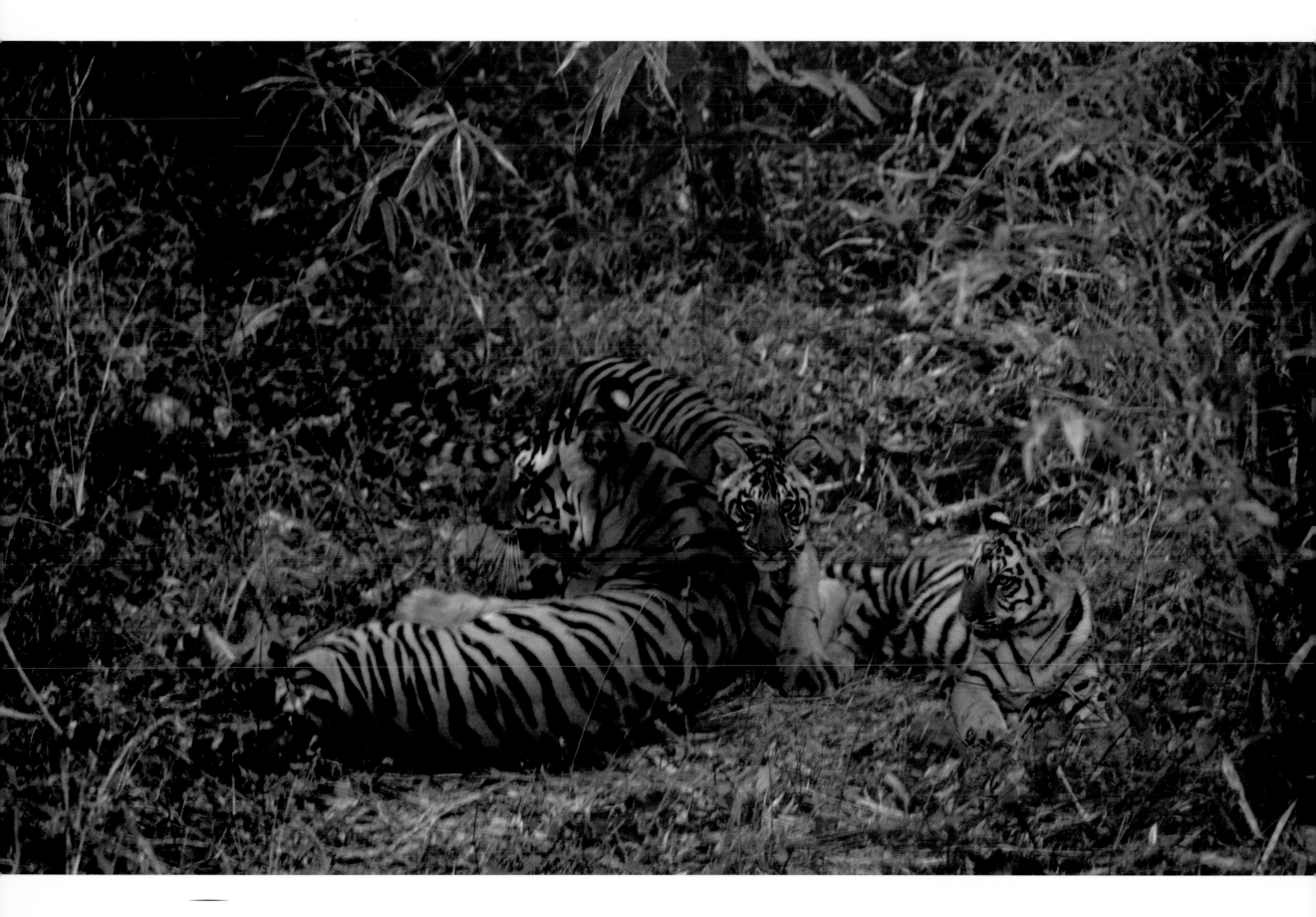

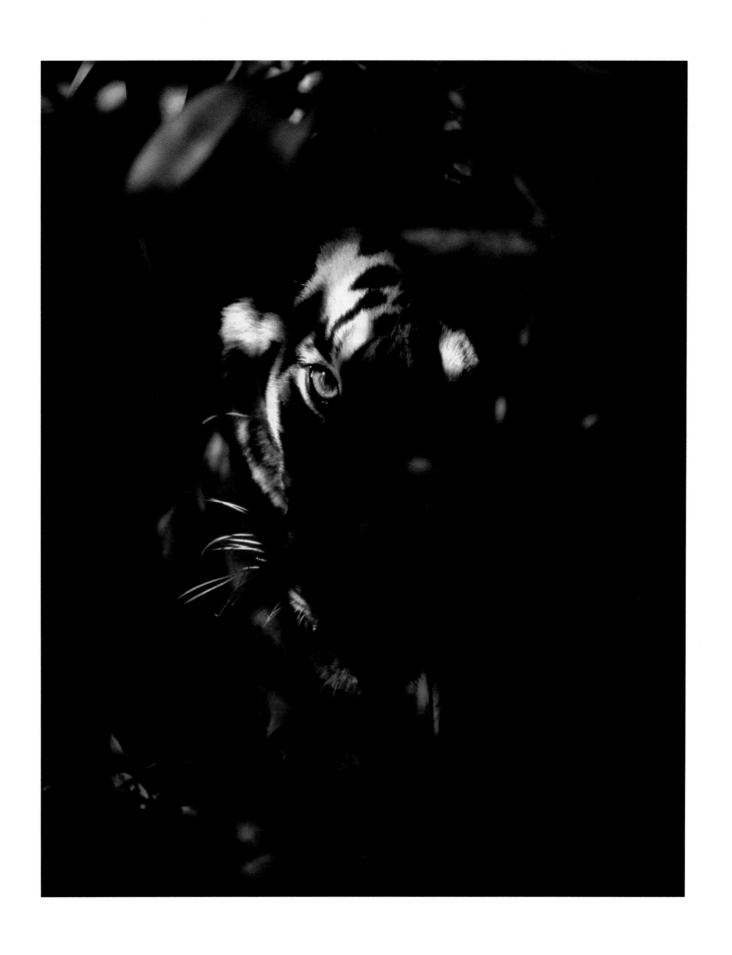

◄ AND ► TIGER

KANHA NATIONAL PARK, MADHYA

PRADESH, INDIA

SUBTROPICAL

199

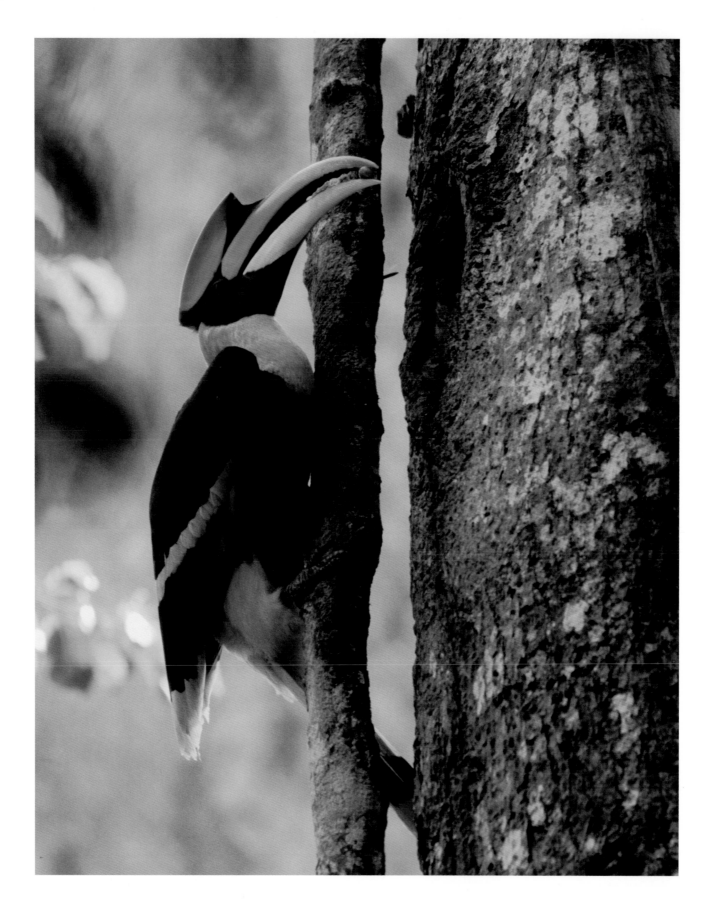

GREAT INDIAN HORNBILL

KHAO YAI NATIONAL PARK, THAILAND

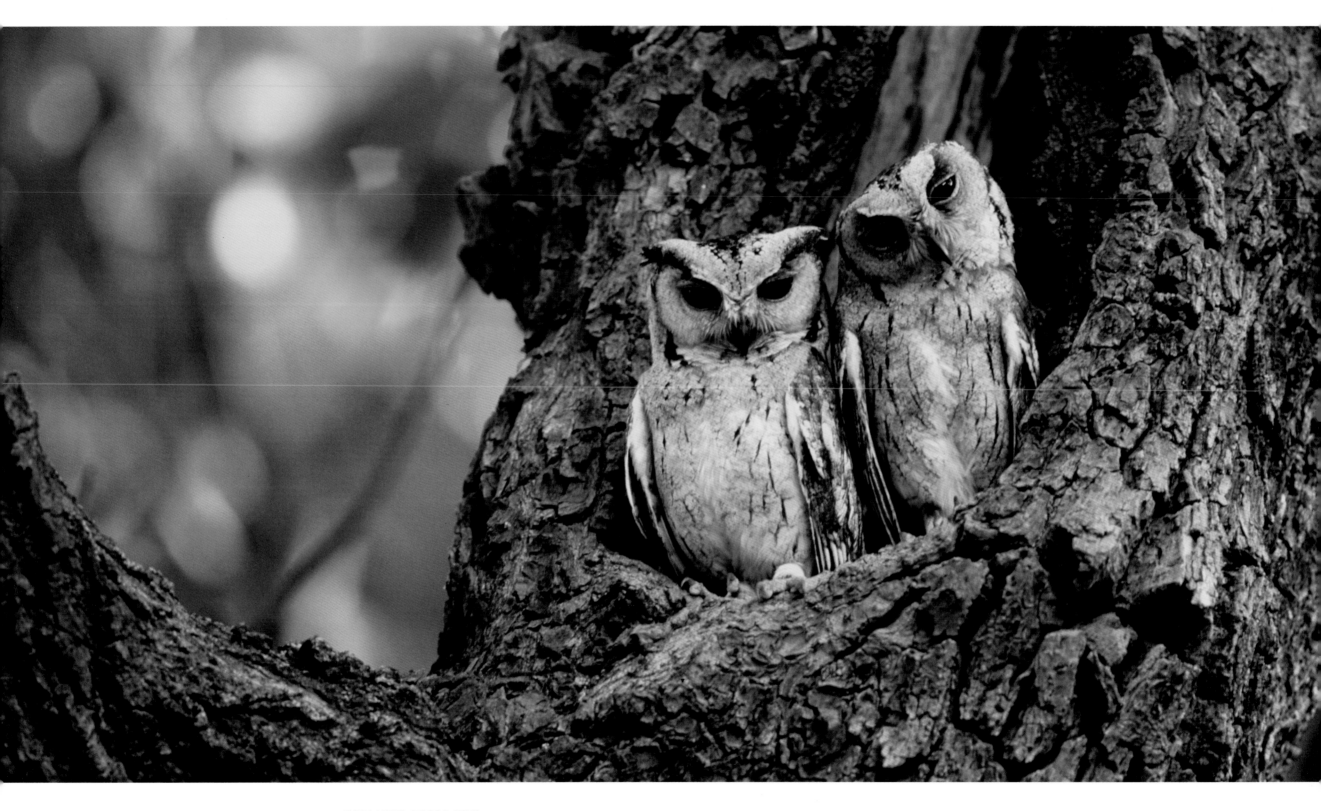

COLLARED SCOPS-OWL

Ranthambore National Park, Rajasthan, India

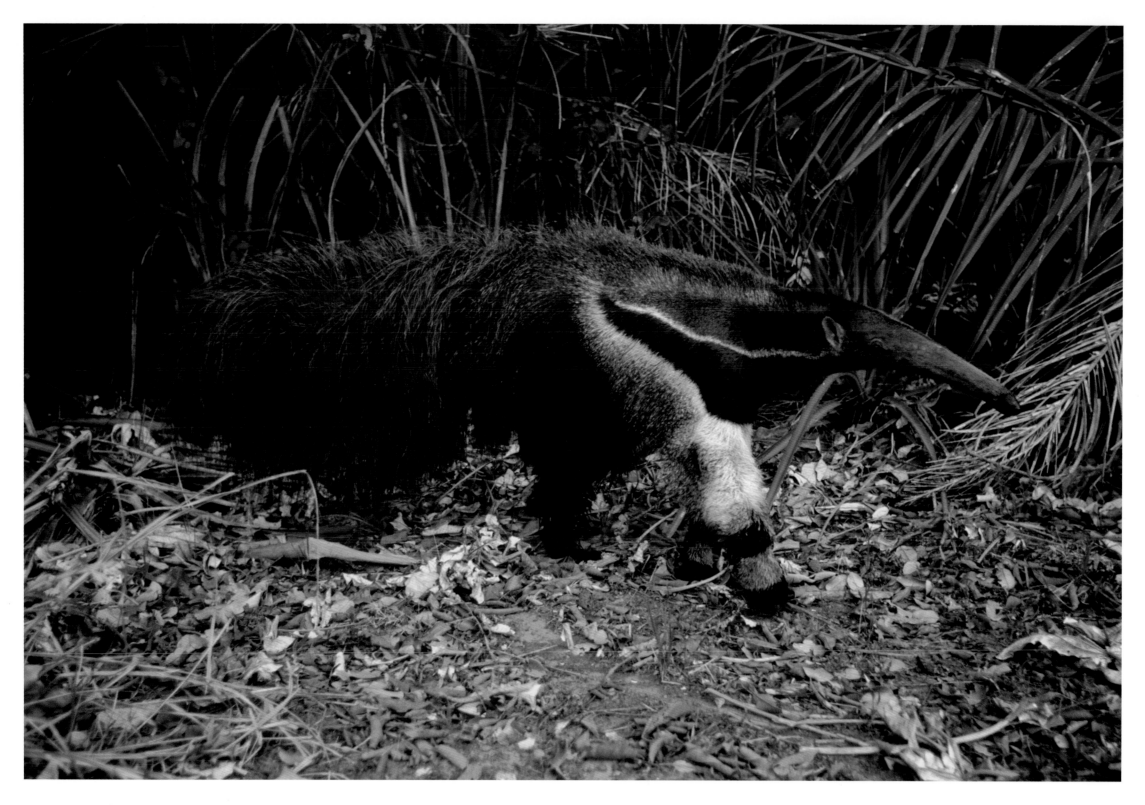

GIANT ANTEATER

Pantanal, Brazil

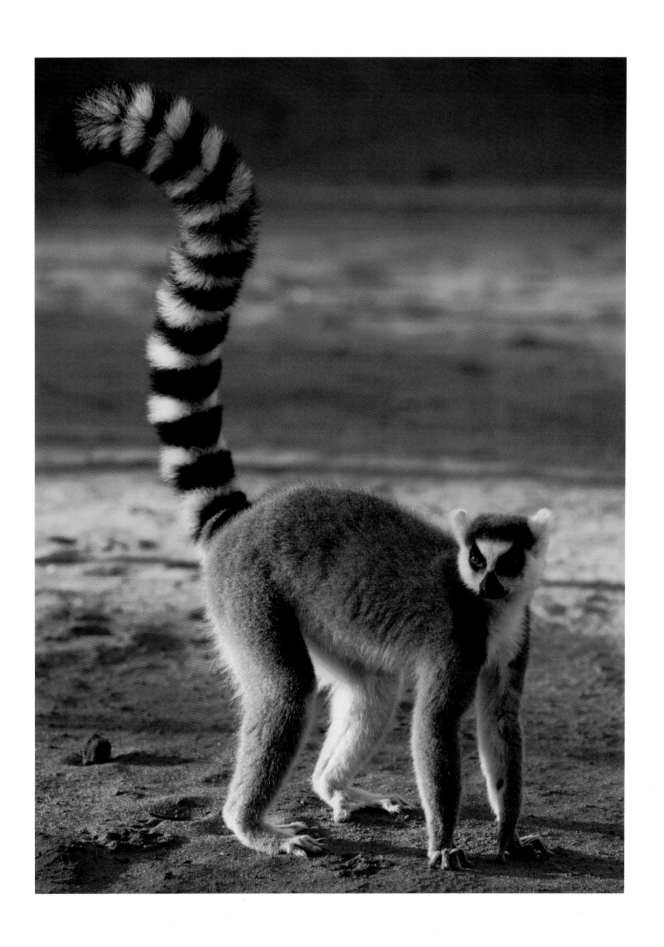

RING-TAILED LEMUR

SUBTROPICAL

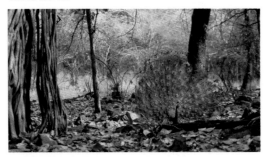

INDIAN PEAFOWL
(*Pavo cristatus*)

The Indian peafowl is one of the world's most distinctive birds. It is immediately recognizable. Found around the world in parks and ornate gardens, the peafowl is actually native only to the Indian subcontinent—it is the national bird of India and is considered sacred to both Hindus and Buddhists. In the wild, peafowl favor open habitats, particularly moist and dry deciduous forests near streams. The peacock's train may measure more than 1.5 meters in length, and he uses the "eye-filled" feathers to attract a harem of females to his side. When he is not displaying, his outrageous fan is folded neatly behind him. The peahen constructs a nest concealed in shrubs and lays an average of three to six eggs; she is solely responsible for incubation. Outside of the breeding season, the sexes segregate into parties of females with their young, and groups of bachelor males.

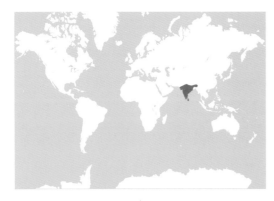

AW: Like many people, I had become a little blasé about peacocks, especially after seeing them roam freely in practically every zoological park I have ever visited. However, I gained a new appreciation for this giant fowl when I traveled to India and saw them in the wild. They are truly remarkable birds, particularly when the male does the courtship display. This photograph was taken from the back of a jeep. If I had approached on foot, the wild peacock would certainly have folded his feathers and fled into the forest.

Canon EOS-3, Canon EF 70–200mm lens, f/11 at 1/15 second, Fujichrome Velvia film

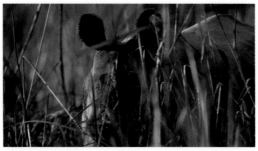

GREATER INDIAN RHINOCEROS
(*Rhinoceros unicornis*)

Long before poaching took its toll on rhinos, loss of habitat was marginalizing all five species. The greater Indian rhinoceros was fairly common in India and Pakistan before 1600, but rapid human population growth and agricultural expansion led to precipitous declines in its numbers. Sport hunters in the nineteenth and early twentieth centuries took thousands of animals, and more were killed under a bounty established to protect crops. By 1910, the species was near extinction, with a little over a dozen in India and 50 in Nepal. Through conservation, about 460 rhinos live in Nepal's Royal Chitwan National Park, under the watchful eye of nearly 1,000 armed guards, while another 1,200 inhabit India's Kaziranga National Park. Other areas have an additional 340 animals, giving a global wild population of about 2,000 individuals. Poaching is still a very real threat, and whether the rescue becomes permanent remains to be seen.

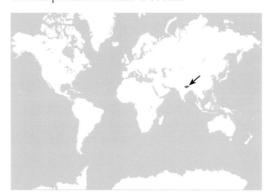

AW: I spotted this rhinoceros from an elevated viewing platform overlooking a large marsh. Accompanied by two guides, I cautiously approached to within 15 meters of where it stood in the tall elephant grass. When I released the shutter, the rhinoceros reacted immediately and we made a prudent retreat. These animals have been so heavily hunted in the past—and are still hunted today by poachers—that they remain wary of any approach by people on foot.

Canon EOS-3, Canon EF 600mm lens, f/8 at 1/60 second, Fujichrome Velvia film

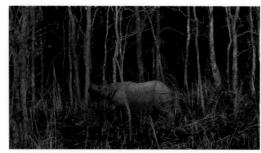

GREATER INDIAN RHINOCEROS
(*Rhinoceros unicornis*)

The greater Indian rhinoceros is one of just two species of Asian one-horned rhinos (the other being the critically endangered Javan rhinoceros [*R. sondaicus*]). One-horned rhinos differ from their African and Sumatran cousins in their single horn and their platelike "armor"—something that makes them seem all the more prehistoric. Indian rhinoceroses favor alluvial grasslands, where they can hide amid 8-meter-high plants. But their range is now so restricted that in some areas they are forced into more open habitats. As with Africa's rhinos, the greater Indian has suffered at the hands of poachers seeking the riches they see encapsulated in the 50-centimeter-long horns. At times, Asian rhino horn has garnered as much as US$50,000 per kilogram—four times the price of pure gold—so that a single horn could earn traders more than US$150,000.

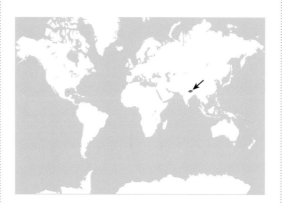

AW: From the back of an elephant, I photographed this rhinoceros at the edge of the dense forest of Royal Chitwan National Park in Nepal. The setting sun gives the entire scene a reddish cast. I selected my 70–200mm zoom lens for two reasons. First, its f/2.8 maximum aperture allows a fast enough shutter speed to freeze the motion caused by riding on an elephant. Second, the 80mm range of the lens allowed me to take in the surrounding environment after zooming to find the ideal focal length for the situation.

Canon EOS-3, Canon EF 70–200mm lens, f/2.8 at 1/25 second, Fujichrome Velvia film

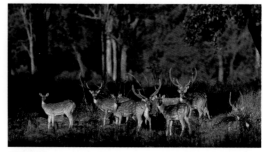

CHITAL
(*Axis axis*)

The chital or spotted deer is one of four species of *Axis* deer. The males carry splendid three-tined antlers, giving them a majestic bearing. As in many deer species, the male with the longest antlers is usually dominant and the most successful breeder. Found in grassland and open forest habitats, chital rarely penetrate dense forests. Both sexes have quite small ranges, and although gregarious—forming herds of fewer than ten to as many as several hundred animals—they spend much of their time in ranges of 180 to 500 hectares, with males generally covering more ground. Hunting and habitat destruction have had population-level impacts over many parts of the chital's former range. However, wild-living populations have been transplanted to several countries, including the United States, and parts of Europe and South America. If regularly disturbed, chital may become largely nocturnal, making them hard to approach and census.

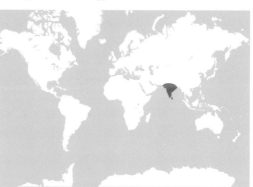

AW: Chital are one of the primary prey for the tigers in central India's Kanha National Park. Consequently, these deer are always on guard, always alert. To get this image, I had to resort to the equivalent of an 840mm lens—a 600mm lens with a 1.4 extender—and two tripods—one for the camera and one for the lens. Nonetheless, this herd stared at me anxiously.

Canon EOS-3, Canon EF 600mm lens, Canon Extender EF 1.4x, f/11 at 1/60 second, Fujichrome Astia film

THE LIVING WILD

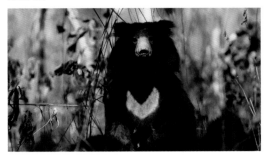

SLOTH BEAR
(Ursus ursinus)

This shaggy black bear with its distinctive crescent of white or yellow on its chest is native to the Indian subcontinent. Sloth bears have mobile, protruding lips and a naked snout; they can also close their nostrils at will. These adaptations help the bears when they are feeding on biting termites. The termites are dug from their nest and then noisily sucked up by the bear. Sloth bears also feed on carrion, eggs, grasses, and fruit. Comparable in size and weight with female black bears, they have poor eyesight and hearing, and will attack in self-defense if surprised by a person's close approach. As a result, they have earned a somewhat undeserved reputation for aggression. Partly because of fear over attacks—but also to provide gallbladders for alleged medicines—sloth bears have been heavily hunted. They have also lost significant amounts of their habitat to agriculture and logging. Only an estimated 7,500 to 10,000 remain.

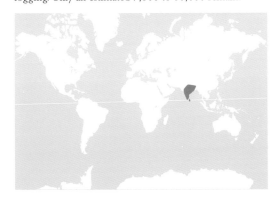

AW: A sloth bear stands to gain a better view as I move closer. Two nearly full-grown cubs stay close to their mother. It is unwise to venture too close to these long-furred black bears of India and Nepal. Many people are killed each year by sloth bears defending their territory—and their young. I photographed this bear with a long telephoto lens plus a 1.4 extender to enable me to maintain a safe and respectful distance between us.

Canon EOS-3, Canon EF 600mm lens, Canon Extender EF 1.4x, f/11 at 1/250 second, Fujichrome MS100/1000 film (exposed at 400 ISO)

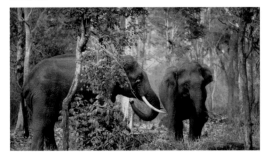

ASIATIC ELEPHANT
(Elephas maximus)

Just as their African cousins have suffered heavy losses from ivory poachers, so too have Asiatic elephants. An estimated 34,000 to 54,000 wild Asiatic elephants remain. Elephants require large areas to survive and as people move in to grow their crops, human-elephant conflicts increase. Crop raiding in India is a serious problem in many areas and 100 to 150 people are killed each year by elephants. Approximately 17,000 to 23,000 elephants survive in India, Nepal, Bangladesh, and Bhutan; 11,000 to 20,000 exist in mainland Southeast Asia; and 6,000 to 11,000 can be found in Sri Lanka, Sumatra, and Borneo. Since many populations are isolated, with limited or no gene flow between groups, their long-term viability is questionable. In addition to the wild elephants, there are about 16,000 domesticated elephants working as draft animals or attached to temples for ceremonial use in Asia.

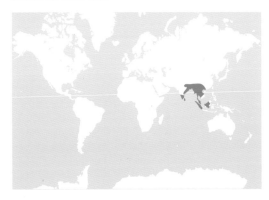

AW: I visited India for the first time for *The Living Wild*. I did not know what to expect of an Asiatic elephant after having photographed literally thousands of African elephants. Would they be comparatively meek? The answer came quickly as the large bull in this photograph charged our vehicle. I like this image for its soft quality of light as well as the "interior forest" that gives a sense of atmosphere.

Canon EOS-3, Canon EF 70–200mm lens, f/11 at 1/30 second, Fujichrome Velvia film (pushed 1 stop)

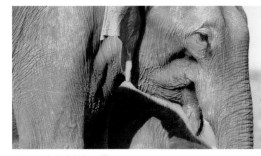

ASIATIC ELEPHANT
(Elephas maximus)

Elephants can give birth at any time of year, following a long gestation period of about 21 months. Newborns average 107 kilograms at birth and are able to stand within hours. Infants are much hairier than adults, which gives them a rather fuzzy appearance. Young elephants suckle regularly and may nurse for up to 18 months, although they begin to eat grass and other vegetation when just a few months old. Although they mainly suckle from their own mothers, infants will suckle from any lactating female in the group (in all likelihood an aunt or sibling). Females keep a close eye on their youngsters, and it is several years before a juvenile will stray far from its mother. Young males may form all-male subgroups when they are seven or eight years old, but females will stay in their natal herd, remaining close to their female relatives throughout their lives.

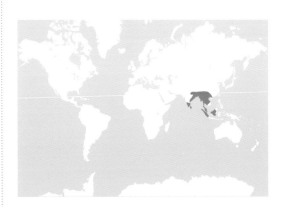

AW: A baby elephant casts a wary glance as my vehicle moves for a better view. As are African elephants, Asiatic elephant mothers are very protective of their offspring. They rarely allow their infants to venture more than a few "trunk lengths" away. During the hottest part of the day, the youngsters remain in the cooling shadow cast by their mothers' enormous bodies. I composed this image vertically to emphasize the vertical line of the female's trunk.

Canon EOS-3, Canon EF 600mm lens, f/11 at 1/125 second, Fujichrome Velvia film

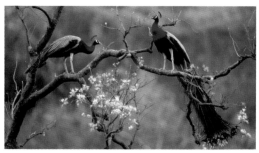

INDIAN PEAFOWL
(Pavo cristatus)

Peafowl have taken the concept of "sexual selection" to its extreme. Peacocks carry around their gaudy tails as badges of genetic fitness. Since the most stunning males tend to be the most successful breeders, other males are often left out. However, penhens are attracted to large groups of males, and males sometimes cooperate with each other by forming groups. These groups are not made up randomly, but consist of closely related males—usually brothers. Even when the birds have been raised separately, and thus have no previous association with each other, they still form groups based on kinship; they may recognize each other by feather patterns, smell, or call. By forming these "brother-bands," males increase the chance that at least some of them will breed, and by doing so, all of the brothers benefit since their genes are also being passed on to the next generation.

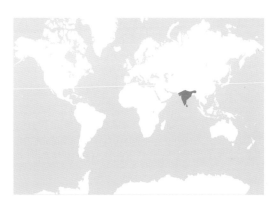

AW: During the day, peafowl scour the forest floor hunting for insects, lizards, and frogs. As nightfall approaches, the hunters could easily become the hunted, so these large, gregarious birds return to the safety of their roosts high in the forest canopy. I am particularly drawn to this image, because its simplicity evokes thoughts of Chinese silk embroidery. The flowering branches complement the graceful lines of the peafowl and bring the composition into balance.

Canon EOS-3, Canon EF 600mm lens, Canon Extender EF 1.4x, f/16 at 1/4 second, Fujichrome Velvia film (pushed 1 stop)

NOTES FROM THE FIELD

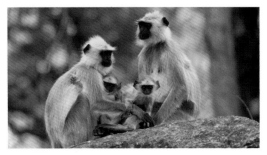

HANUMAN LANGUR
(Semnopithecus entellus)

The Hanuman langur is an adaptable primate, and seems equally at home in deserts or tropical rainforests, on the ground or in the trees. They are mainly vegetarian, favoring leaves, fruits, flowers, and crops—the latter often brings them into conflict with farmers. They form groups of 13 to 37 animals—although some groups may grow to over 100; there are typically two adult females for every adult male. Males may also band together to form single-sex groups. All groups are led by a dominant male, who fights other males to secure his position; a particularly adept animal may lead for a decade. When a new male takes over a group, he kills any dependent infants to bring the females back into breeding condition. Langurs are becoming increasingly rare as their habitats are cleared for agriculture, and their numbers are declining. The largest population, in India, is estimated at 233,800.

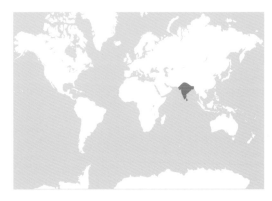

AW: For guides and trackers searching for tigers and leopards in India's national parks, langurs often become their eyes and ears. The ever-alert primates give a series of spirited, scolding calls whenever they see a large cat. For this reason, it is not uncommon to see herds of deer—primary prey for the big cats—staying close to troops of langurs. In a more quiet moment, two langur mothers cradle their young on a rocky promontory overlooking the forest. I chose a very long telephoto lens to avoid disturbing a classic scene.

Canon EOS-3, Canon EF 600mm lens, f/8 at 1/30 second, Fujichrome Velvia film (pushed 1 stop)

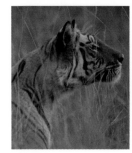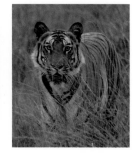

TIGER
(Panthera tigris)

In 1920, there were an estimated 100,000 tigers in Asia. Fear about attacks on humans, predation on livestock, habitat destruction, and hunting for skins and other body parts have dramatically cut those numbers. Of the eight recognized subspecies, three are believed to be extinct—the Caspian tiger (*P. t. virgata*), Javan tiger (*P. t. sondaica*), and Bali tiger (*P. t. balica*). Of the remaining five, the most abundant is the Bengal tiger (*P. t. tigris*), numbering 3,550 to 5,000 and surviving in India, Bangladesh, Myanmar/Burma, Nepal, and Bhutan. The Indochinese tiger (*P. t. corbetti*) numbers 1,050 to 1,750 animals and is found in Myanmar/Burma, Vietnam, Thailand, and the Malay Peninsula. There are fewer than 80 Chinese tigers (*P. t. amoyensis*) in the wild, 150 to 200 Siberian tigers (*P. t. altaica*), and about 400 Sumatran tigers (*P. t. sumatrae*).

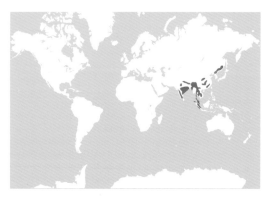

AW: Page 196 – For this early evening photograph, I used a high-speed film that I exposed at ISO 400, allowing me to avoid motion blur.

Canon EOS-3, Canon EF 600mm lens, f/4 at 1/15 second, Fujichrome MS100/1000 film (exposed at ISO 400)

AW: Page 197 – This tiger's curiosity makes him an easy photographic subject. But when tigers become too comfortable with people, they become easy targets for poachers. This male's mother, Sita, disappeared in 1998. In 2000 her skin was found in the house of a local poacher.

Canon EOS-3, Canon EF 70–200mm lens, f/4 at 1/8 second, Fujichrome Astia film (pushed 1 stop)

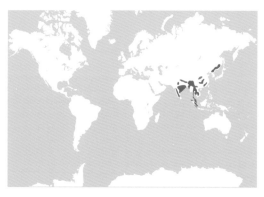

TIGER
(Panthera tigris)

Tigers are known to mate year-round, but most breeding takes place from November to April. Females reach sexual maturity at three or four years of age, while males do so at age four or five. Females are receptive for a maximum of just six days every three to nine weeks, and give birth to their cubs—up to six, but usually two or three—after a gestation period that averages 105 days. Males have nothing to do with the raising of their cubs, and depart after copulation, leaving the female alone. At birth, infant tigers weigh 780 to 1,600 grams; their eyes are tightly closed for up to two weeks. Females typically give birth in a cave or hidden in dense vegetation, and the cubs remain concealed until they are old enough to begin following their mother, at about five or six months of age.

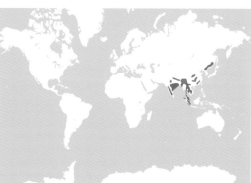

AW: A tiger and two four-month old cubs lounge in the dense forest of Kanha National Park. For 10 days I searched from atop an elephant for this trio. With good reason, tigers with cubs are extremely secretive. Males regularly kill cubs that are not their own offspring, making the female receptive to mating again. Photographing from an elephant is difficult at best. But when the light level is low, as it was in this case, it is truly challenging. For this image, I used fast film, an image stabilizer lens, and fill flash.

Canon EOS-3, Canon EF 75–300mm IS lens, f/5.6 at 1/30 second, fill flash, Fujichrome MS100/1000 film (exposed at ISO 400)

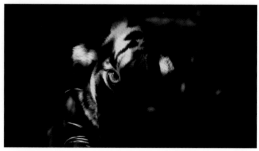

TIGER
(Panthera tigris)

During the 1960s and 1970s, a single tiger skin could bring in excess of US$4,000. International conventions and changing perceptions toward fur reduced the demand for skins. But today, the animals face other lethal pressures. Tiger bones have been used in eastern traditional medicines for thousands of years, but with rising human populations and international trade, their use is no longer sustainable. Tiger bones are ground up for use in concoctions to enhance the users' strength, and to relieve pain and cure diseases. Tiger penises are even used to make soup. Chinese tigers (*P. t. amoyensis*) initially bore the brunt of hunting for medicinal products. But with the virtual elimination of that subspecies, tigers are now targeted throughout their remaining range. Tiger-based products are still legal in Taiwan, South Korea, China, and Japan, and many researchers fear that the remaining 5,180 to 7,430 wild tigers will not endure much longer.

AW: A tiger sits silently in the dense undergrowth of India's Kanha National Park. I am personally drawn to photographs that require imagination to complete them. In this case, the fact that the cat is only partially seen lends a sense of mystery to the image. I spot read my exposure off the tiger's illuminated face.

Canon EOS-3, Canon EF 600mm lens, f/4 at 1/60 second, Fujichrome Velvia film

THE LIVING WILD

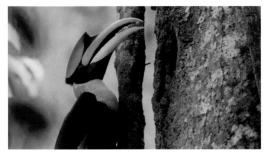

GREAT INDIAN HORNBILL
(*Buceros bicornis*)

The great Indian hornbill is a massive bird, growing to a length of 1.4 meters; the tail alone may be a meter long. Hornbills are found in southeast Asia, from sea level to about 1,500 meters. They are mainly frugivorous, picking fruits with their huge bills and swallowing them whole; pits and other indigestible matter are regurgitated. Because the seeds are usually regurgitated, hornbills are important seed dispersers. Hornbills generally mate for life, laying their two to four eggs in a protective tree cavity. The female remains with the clutch and is fed by her mate. Incubation lasts 28 to 40 days, and the chicks are completely dependent on their parents for up to eight weeks. As during incubation, the female stays with the chicks while the male forages for food. Hornbills face threats from hunting and habitat loss; regional populations have been depleted in many areas.

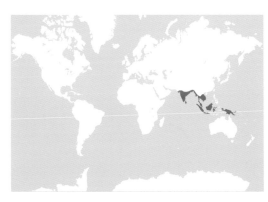

AW: This is a six-hour photograph. That is how long I waited for this hornbill to return to its nest cavity to feed its chick. This image required a 600mm lens plus a 1.4 extender and two tripods, one for the camera and one for the lens. I will never forget the sound this bird made as it swooped down onto the nest tree. I nearly forgot to take the photograph. Only a few exposures were sharp; the dark forest and the bird's movement combined to make conditions difficult. Even pushing my film left me with a painfully slow shutter speed.

Canon EOS-1N/RS, Canon EF 600mm, Canon Extender EF 1.4x, f/5.6 at 1/8 second, Fujichrome Astia film (pushed 1 stop)

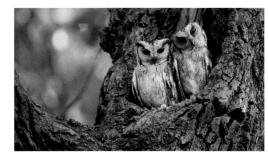

COLLARED SCOPS-OWL
(*Otus bakkamoena*)

The small (23 centimeters) collared scops-owl is a wide-ranging Asian owl consisting of more than twenty subspecies. It seems to prefer lightly forested habitats, but is also frequently seen near towns, where it hunts insects that are attracted to streetlights. Its curious "whut?" call can be heard after dusk. Insects form the bulk of its diet, but it will also take small mammals such as mice and voles, birds, and even geckos and bats. Human-induced habitat changes over parts of its range, where more dense forests are cleared, creating open habitats, have actually favored the collared scops-owl over some other owl species, including the rufous scops-owl (*O. rufescens*) and the spotted scops-owl (*O. spilocephalus*).

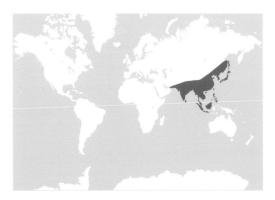

AW: Each day as I entered Ranthambore National Park, I passed this pair of owls sitting outside their nest cavity. At dusk as I left the park after my day of shooting, the tiny owls were already off hunting for the night. To get this photograph, I placed a tripod under my 600mm lens with a 2x extender attached, and then put a second tripod under my camera body. A tripod is always advisable to ensure the best composition and truly sharp images; two tripods are a necessity with such a long lens, especially with the attached extender.

Canon EOS-3, Canon EF 600mm lens, Canon Extender EF 2x, f/16 at 1 second, Fujichrome Velvia film

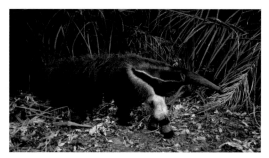

GIANT ANTEATER
(*Myrmecophaga tridactyla*)

Giant anteaters are members of the order Xenarthra that includes sloths and armadillos. They can be up to 1.2 meters long, and their bushy tail adds another 0.65 to 0.9 meter to their overall length. Their hair is coarse and stiff, and they weigh up to 60 kilograms. Anteaters possess powerful claws that are used to break into ant mounds; their long tongues can extend as much as 61 centimeters and they are capable of eating as many as 35,000 ants or termites a day. They are found in a variety of different habitats, including savannahs, grasslands, and humid forests. Anteaters are often active during the day, but become largely nocturnal when disturbed by people. Habitat loss has marginalized the species in many parts of its former range, and it has largely vanished from Central America. Trophy hunting is still a serious problem in many areas.

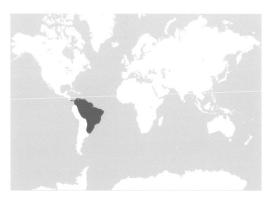

AW: The giant anteater is an extremely odd-looking creature. It inhabits much of the savannah and woodlands of South America. Equipped with a large, powerful tail and long, sharp claws, it is capable of inflicting serious injury to any predator. I kept this in mind as I approached to within 1 meter with a wide-angle lens. I found that if I positioned myself quietly in front of the nearsighted anteater, I could get very close without interfering with its foraging.

Canon EOS-3, Canon EF 17–35mm lens, f/11 at 1/60 second, Fujichrome Provia film

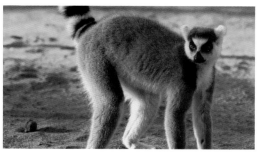

RING-TAILED LEMUR
(*Lemur catta*)

The ring-tailed lemur is one of eleven species of lemur in the family Lemuridae (twenty one other species of lemurs are classified in different families). It is the most terrestrial of the lemurs, and frequently spends more time on the ground than it does in the trees. They live in mixed groups of twelve to twenty-four animals, and feed on fruits, leaves, and other plant parts. Females are dominant over males and are also responsible for defending the groups' territory of 6 to 8.8 hectares. Although they can survive in partly wooded habitats, ring-tailed lemurs need primary, undisturbed vegetation. They also favor habitats along rivers, which are increasingly being cleared and developed by people. The size of the ring-tailed lemur population is unknown, with some estimating as few as 10,000 and others as many as 100,000 animals remaining.

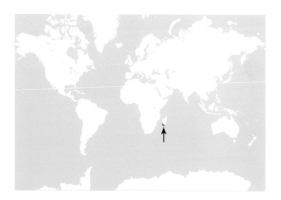

AW: In Madagascar's Berenty Preserve, the lemurs have become so habituated that they will literally climb onto your shoulder. With such willing subjects, it is hard not to come away with good images. For this photograph, I isolated a single lemur in the late-afternoon light. I selected a 70–200mm lens, since these hyperactive lemurs are in constant motion. Once they did stop— even momentarily—I could quickly zoom in or out, framing the lemur perfectly to fill all four corners of my composition.

Canon F1, Canon EF 70–200mm lens, f/8 at 1/125 second, Fujichrome 50 film

NOTES FROM THE FIELD

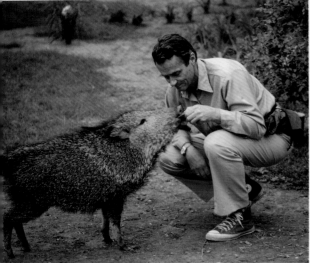

© GEORGE B. SCHALLER

George B. Schaller spent four years in the forests of the Wolong and Tangjiahe panda reserves in China during the early 1980s. His book The Last Panda (Chicago and London: University of Chicago Press, 1993) documents the successes, frustrations, and failures of the panda project conducted under the auspices of both the Chinese government and the World Wildlife Fund (WWF–World Wide Fund for Nature). The following are selected excerpts, with slight abridgments, from The Last Panda.

The ridge lunged upward like a dragon's spine bristling with fir and birch, and clouds were low and flying out from the mountains. Snow from a late-winter storm balanced on boughs and logs. When a riffle of wind stirred the branches, the snow drifted down in crystal veils that added a ghostlike radiance to the forest. Bamboo grew in the understory, the crowded ranks of stems claiming the hillside so completely that the light beneath the bamboo's canopy was a translucent undersea green. The sunless scent of moss and moldering wood choked the gloom. The bamboo was rigid with frost, and a dense silence hung over the ridge; there was no movement and seemingly no life.

In the stillness, leaves suddenly rustled and a stem cracked like breaking glass. Shrouded in bamboo was a giant panda, a female, slumped softly in the snow, her back propped against a shrub. Leaning to one side, she reached out and hooked a bamboo stem with the ivory claws of a forepaw, bent in the stem, and with a fluid movement bit it off near the base. Stem firmly grasped, she sniffed it to verify that it was indeed palatable, and then ate it end-first like a stalk of celery. While her powerful molars sectioned and crushed the stem, she glanced around for another, her movements placid and skillful, a perfect ecological integration between panda and bamboo. She ate within a circle of 1 meter, moved a few steps, and ate some more, consuming only coarse stems and discarding the leafy tops; she then sat hunched, forepaws in her lap, drowsy and content. Within a circle of 1,000 meters was her universe, all that she needed: bamboo, a mate, a snug tree-den in which to bear young.

Minutes later, she ambled in her rolling sailor's gait to a nearby spur where among gnarled rhododendrons she halted. No bamboo grew here. A shaft of sun escaped through a fissure of cloud and penetrated the twilight. Among bamboo the panda's form and color had seemed blurred and difficult to define; now in sun the panda shone with sparkling clarity. Near her was a massive fir. She knew that tree: It was a landmark, it defined the edge of her favored haunts, it served as a scent post. The tree's many dimensions helped give her an identity. The snow around the tree was unmarked by tracks, but when she sniffed the bark, she learned that a male had marked the site with his anal glands a few days before. Though she fixed the scent in her mind, she did not cover his odor with hers.

She angled down to the nearest bamboo patch and there once again foraged, the recycling of bamboo being the essence of her existence. She lived leisurely. Alone in these heights, the panda conveyed a sense of absolute solitude, an isolation that was almost mythic. A flock of tit babblers skittered like airborne mice through the bamboo above her head, yet her small dark eyes showed no awareness. Having eaten, she rolled over to sleep, her body at rest in the snow against a log, her dense coat making her impervious to the elements.

From below, near where the forest gave way to field, came the sounds of an ax. The bamboo around her like armor against intruders, she listened and then moved away, shunning any possible confrontation. She traveled on a private path along the slope, insinuating herself from thicket to thicket, moving like a cloud shadow, navigating with precision through the sea of stems, with only her tracks a record of her silent passing.

I have long been fascinated by pandas. As a high school student, I visited the St. Louis Zoo and watched a panda shuffling around its moated enclosure in the stifling heat. I had read Trailing the Giant Panda by the Roosevelt brothers, who on 13 April 1929 were the first Westerners to shoot a panda. Though I avidly read about their quest, I found myself even as a teenager reluctant to applaud their success.

I was also familiar with The Lady and the Panda, by Ruth Harkness, an account of the happy furor created by the infant Su-Lin, who in 1936 was the first panda to reach the West alive. I had searched for and located Chengdu on the map, for it had been the base of operations for all panda-collecting expeditions until the early 1940s.

Years later in 1963, after I had completed my biological studies at the University of Wisconsin, I remember reading news reports of the first panda birth in captivity at the Beijing Zoo. As a zoologist, I became intrigued by the animal's paradoxes and illogicalities. Science, with its penchant for creating neat categories, had been unable to force the panda into a definite taxonomic position, the animal showing resemblances to both bears and raccoons. Might a study of its behavior help solve the riddle? The panda further stimulated the elusive quality of scientific passion by its peculiar life-style. Here was a bearlike animal devoted wholly to recycling bamboo, a creature as improbable as a carnivorous cow. How had it adapted to such a specialized diet?

My interest, however, was based on more than the challenge of untying biological knots. There was the lure of the remote and rare and the opportunity to be the first Westerner to study the panda's marginal life. As a scientific wanderer imbued with a missionary urge, I also wanted to help the species survive. Research has little fascination and pleasure for me unless an animal also inspires more than intellectual involvement, unless

I enjoy its companionship. Like the mountain gorilla, tiger, lion, and other species I had previously studied, an animal must provide an emotional experience if I am to involve myself in its world for years, a perpetual emigrant isolated in an alien culture, afield night and day in whatever weather as, gradually and with care, I try not just to know the species but to understand it, slowly unfolding its life like an origami. The panda's real assets are understated and hidden behind its attractive exterior. In short, I thought the panda an animal worth knowing.

Political turmoil, civil war, and Japanese aggression preceded the success of the Communist revolution in 1949. Panda country was closed to outsiders and seemed likely to remain so. But then, in April 1971, the Chinese government sent one of its oblique hints that a policy change was imminent by inviting the U.S. table tennis team to China. I thought it an auspicious time to initiate a panda project. Starting in July 1971, William Conway, general director of the New York Zoological Society, wrote letters on my behalf to the Beijing Zoo, China's Academy of Sciences, and the Chinese embassy in Canada (for China and the United States did not have diplomatic relations then) proposing a collaborative study. He also contacted Sir Peter Scott to make WWF aware of our interests. I was in Pakistan when I received a letter from Conway: "Peter says that the World Wildlife Fund would be delighted to join in sponsorship of your efforts to study the giant pandas. Peter . . . tells me that neither the World Wildlife Fund nor IUCN now has a special project on the panda."

Not surprisingly the Chinese never replied to our letters, for they were in the midst of the Cultural Revolution. Pandas receded from my mind as I worked on wildlife in the Himalaya, Karakoram, and other ranges. Then, having completed that project, I settled into the swamps of the Mato Grosso in Brazil to study jaguars and their prey. I was in Brazil in the autumn of 1979 when Wayne King, then the director of the Florida State Museum and a person deeply involved in conservation matters, telephoned and left an urgent message for me to call him. A few days later I did.

"George, World Wildlife Fund and China have just agreed on a joint panda study. Are you interested in doing the field work?"

Most certainly I was interested. But being involved in another project, I first needed to decide how to do both. I wanted a few days to think about the matter.

In a letter dated 12 October 1979, to Lee Talbot, then director of conservation for WWF, I gave my answer: "I am tremendously eager and excited about taking part in this project."

Fourteen months later, I joined my Chinese colleagues at Wuyipeng to begin field work. Research aside, I was naturally keen just to meet a panda in its wilderness home,

something no foreigner had done for decades. After I had strived two months for that electric first sighting, the pandas had with uncanny ability still eluded me. At least my failure was not without precedent.

The botanist Ernest Wilson spent many months in panda country, including a visit to Wolong in 1908, but he never saw more than panda spoor. Most other travelers were no more successful than Wilson in encountering a panda, though some saw captive animals or dead ones. The first Westerners who definitely saw pandas alive in the forest were members of the expeditions that went to shoot them: the Roosevelts in 1929; the Dolan expedition in 1931; the Sage expedition in 1934; and a lone British hunter, Captain C. H. Brocklehurst, in 1935. Jack Young shot a panda in 1937, probably the last sighting of a panda in the wild by a foreigner. I hoped to be the next to see one.

The pandas, however, were extraordinarily elusive at Wuyipeng, and during weeks of tracking them in late 1980 and early 1981 I never encountered one in the snowbound forest. Late one day, unseen by any of us, a panda had even traveled past our tents, and that night passed the tents again, as if taunting us with its tracks.

2 March 1981. At dawn I leave for Bai Ai where Xiao Wang, on his way back to Wuyipeng after checking traps yesterday evening, met a panda ambling along the trail. A light snow has fallen during the night, and within minutes of camp I find fresh tracks going uphill. Slowly I follow the prints, placing my feet softly to avoid snapping branches beneath the snow, my senses straining to perceive any motion, any sound. Three droppings are still warm to my touch. Ahead a twig breaks, then silence. I move several steps. Bamboo rustles, and once more a tense hush. The panda is obviously trying to detect me too. Unseen we confront each other, the atmosphere almost tangible with emotional intensity. But having perceived potential danger, the panda withdraws, and, disappointed, I retrace my route.

Nearby is yet another fresh track, that of a smaller animal, probably a subadult, and it is traveling parallel to the one I have followed. Howard Quigley decides to find out where the small animal has come from, while I backtrack the other. Around dawn the larger panda had approached to within 30 meters of our tent, detected something worrisome, retreated a little, then arced around the camp on its way uphill. I continue downslope, following its tracks through dense umbrella bamboo, an impenetrable tangle of stems, their snow-laden tops bent into a solid canopy. Unable to bend the stout stems apart, I crawl through them, head facing downhill, smashing dead stems aside with stiff, raw hands. Near the base of the slope, I come upon the panda's bed at the base of a maple.

On my way back to camp, I meet Howard, his clothes as sodden as mine, dead bamboo

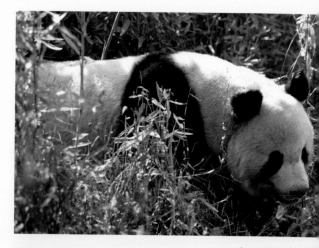

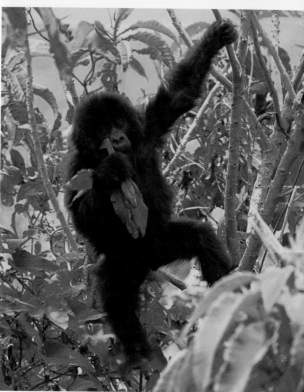

▲▲ GIANT PANDA

(*Ailuropoda melanoleuca*), QINLING MOUNTAINS, CHINA

▲ MOUNTAIN GORILLA

(*Gorilla gorilla beringei*), MGAHINGA NATIONAL PARK, UGANDA

GEORGE B. SCHALLER

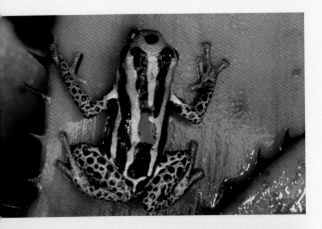

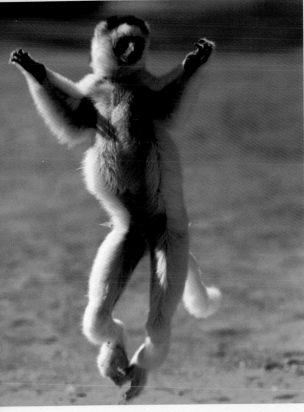

▲▲ AMAZONIAN POISON
FROG ◡

(*Dendrobates ventrimaculatus*), RIO NAPO, PERU

▲ VERREAUX'S SIFAKA ◡

(*Propithecus verreauxi*), MANDRARE RIVER,

MADAGASCAR

leaves clinging to his hair and beard. His panda had also gone down into the valley. Did the two travel near each other by accident? I want to follow the animals uphill, but fog has already erased the upper part of the Choushuigou and it might soon snow again, obliterating all tracks. As the pandas have angled uphill, they might cross a trail of ours above Bai Ai, so rather than following the animals, I will try to bisect their tracks there.

The trail above Bai Ai follows the rim of a valley. As I ascend, a moaning hoot fills the silence, soft yet resonant. Ahead I see the still figure of Hu Jinchu, and when he notices me he points to a tall, lone spruce downhill of us. There, crouched on a bough near the top, is a small panda. "Finally," I say to myself. At 5:15 P.M. it hoots again, sending its plaintive call across the hills. A few minutes later it calls once more, and as the sound fades we spot another panda, a bulky adult, among the dense lower branches of the same tree. It descends ponderously, hind legs first, sliding the last feet in a shower of bark, and disappears in the bamboo. We think it is a male who for reasons known only to himself is ill disposed toward the other. Relieved of its tormentor, the small panda gives up its insecure perch to huddle against the trunk of the spruce. In determined disregard of the cold and gathering darkness it quietly remains there, a lustrous fragment of life, idealized but real, as fog fills the valley, linking the slopes, arriving so quietly that we are aware of its coming only when the panda fades from view. Hu Jinchu and I smile at each other. It is a day of double happiness.

◡

We are fortunate that the panda is still with us, that our evolutionary paths have crossed. Values should not, I suppose, be assigned to creatures to whom values are unknown, and who all have equal claim to our fascination and respect. Still, the panda would seem more of a loss that a primrose or piranha, for it epitomizes the stoic defiance of fate and stirs our emotions with pity and admiration. If we lose the panda, we will never look on its black-and-white face again, its evolution will stop, its unique genetic code destroyed; its name will soon have little more significance than that of thousands of other species listed in the dusty catalogues of the world's museums, *Ailuropoda melanoleuca*, meaning the "black-and-white panda-foot." As the obscurity of centuries separates the animal from us, we will be left with only memories, a few massive bones, some faded hides. The pandas' lives will be forgotten, gone from our collective memories like the moa and mammoth. What a melancholy fate for so extraordinary an animal. All creatures, of course, are transitory, flourishing for a while, then fading away. However, pandas are survivors who were present several million years ago, before humankind became human, and they have outlived many other large mammals that vanished during the upheavals of the Ice Age. Their time as a species should not yet be over.

The many books on dead or dying species almost seem to lessen the intensity with which one views extinction. Repetition begins to trivialize a terrible event. No matter how much we may decry species extinction, nature still remains peripheral to the consciousness of most people. Are these books mostly bought as tokens of a belief that nature does count? Too often treatises on endangered species seem to be mere memorials, with all the finality that this implies, accounts of those animals whose drama has irrevocably ended: the dodo, passenger pigeon, great auk, and Steller's sea cow. My own emotions at least cannot respond to the ever-expanded list of dying animals; my capacity for concern is finite.

Yet there is justification for these volumes. Telling and retelling is a moral imperative; forgetting is a luxury we cannot afford. Neglect is a form of abuse. There are those who think that if only we can hold on to our biological diversity, all those millions of species of plants and animals, into the next century, destruction will end—yet there is no indication that it will. So we must at least record our experiences with the hope that our writings will encourage action to preserve species and stimulate a unity of compassion. Even in a truly moral world, destruction would not end, but at least we would view nature with finer sentiments, based on a revolution in the spirit of humankind. We would adjust our values and priorities and develop a land ethic that decries waste and needless destruction. Such changes cannot come through passion and strident rhetoric but only through a new concept of ourselves, a new design in the strategy of human survival.

Perhaps the panda in a small way can help change our concepts. Its seeming simplicity permits us to discern the qualities that make it so alluring. Having transcended its mountain home to become a citizen of the world, the panda is a symbolic creature that represents our efforts to protect the environment. Though dumpy and bearlike, it has been patterned with such creative flourish, such artistic perfection, that it almost seems to have evolved for this higher purpose. A round, rather flat face; large black eye patches; and a cuddly and clumsy appearance give the panda an innocent, childlike quality that evokes universal empathy, a desire to hug and protect. And it is rare. Survivors are somehow more poignant than casualties. Together, these and other traits have created a species in which legend and reality merge, a mythic creature in the act of life.

It is the difficult fate of this generation to finally grasp the magnitude of all the offenses against the panda and other forms of life; the extent of environmental destruction has been nothing less than a spiritual divestment, a renunciation of past and future. That the panda has been enshrined as an icon of our environment is not surprising. The animal has the power to touch and transform all those who gaze upon it; it has only to appear to brighten a scene. Yin and Yang are the two great Chinese forces of separation and unity: black and white, dark and light, sun and moon, summer and winter, life and death. Each force carries part of the other, each needs the other to retain a balanced whole with an emphasis on suppleness and endurance. The panda personifies this Yin and Yang. But humankind has upset the balance, and the panda's existence is now shadowed by fear of extinction.

I can only view with irony the fact that never has the panda's destruction been as rapid as during the years we studied it, during a period when it received more attention than at any time in its long history. Our years of intensive effort to protect the panda have certainly not yielded a victory and perhaps only a modest postponement of defeat. Indeed I am haunted by the realization that the project may have harmed rather than helped the panda. Many persons and several institutions have genuinely had the panda's interest at heart and their good intentions are unquestioned. But had the panda remained in the obscurity of its bamboo thickets, free from worldwide publicity and the greed this publicity helped to fuel, there might not now be so many captives, needlessly caught during and after the bamboo die-off, and not so many breeding stations. Pandas might not have huge prices on their heads and be sent alive overseas as rentals or sold dead as grisly trophies to Taiwan and Japan. However, even if pandas had been left undisturbed, their peace would soon have been shattered by loggers and an ever-growing population that turns mountain slopes into fields. The project provided for the first time basic information about the panda's obscure life, it defined conservation problems, and it proposed solutions to these problems. That is the project's important legacy. The continuing decline of the panda must not cripple our sense of purpose, our will to save the species. The panda survives, as does its habitat, and a realistic plan to save the animal exists. But unless we act *now* to implement the plan, our brief pang of love for the panda will end with an eternity of remorse.

For pandas there exists no freedom other than the peaceful security of bamboo shaded by forest. It cannot adjust its existence to ours, it cannot compromise its needs. To think otherwise, to continue gambling on its future, would be a costly blunder. All our fine sentiments and humanitarian concerns, all our attempts to immortalize the animal while it still exists, are of no consequence if the panda is allowed to vanish. To provide assurance that the panda will remain as a perennial witness to the wonder of evolution and as a talisman of ecological redemption, we must make a global commitment.

The ultimate responsibility for saving the panda in its natural home rests with China: It alone can implement the measures needed for the animal's protection. The rest of the world must, however, offer guidance, funds, and moral support. The gravity of the situation represents both hope and opportunity. But if we fail to make the correct choices now, the last pandas will disappear, leaving us with the nostalgia of a failed epic, an indictment of civilization as destroyer. We cannot recover a lost world.

The panda has no history, only a past. It has come to us in a fragile moment from another time, its obscure life illuminated through the years we tracked it in the forests. My years of involvement with the panda permeate my soul just as a panda defines and fills the bamboo forest with its luminous presence. Although they shuttle between heartache and happiness, my memories dwell mainly on Wei and Tang and the other free-living pandas who touched my life. The image of Zhen lingers most in my mind. I remember Zhen vividly on the day when I left Wuyipeng, when her brief appearance seemed like a parting gift.

I had found her not far from camp sitting hunched on a moss-covered boulder, muzzle tucked into her folded arms. Quietly I approached to within 15 meters and waited. She raised her head and with a disinterested gaze looked at me, then leaned forward, her back to me, and continued her rest. There was a startling self-assurance, a striking kind of freedom, in the way she ignored me. At intervals she changed position, resting on side or belly, and occasionally she sat up to scratch or paw flies off her face. Once she glanced in the direction of loud voices from camp. After two and a half hours, with the onset of a heavy rain, she raised her arms above her head, stretched, and yawned cavernously. She descended from the boulder and began to munch shoots. I left her there, her pelage gleaming softly in the bamboo twilight, until like falling snow she melted gently into the forest.

Years have passed since I last saw giant pandas in the wild, yet their powerful image continues to impinge on my life. Pandas are creatures so gentle and self-contained that they still affect me by the force of their uniqueness, by their aura of mystery. Our research on pandas gained only superficial insights into their alien existence, yet to see a panda again in a zoo or photograph releases a cascade of memories, of snowbound forests, of tracking animals over mountains lost in fog, of a female panda named Zhen-Zhen methodically crunching shoots in the bamboo's shadows.

George B. Schaller

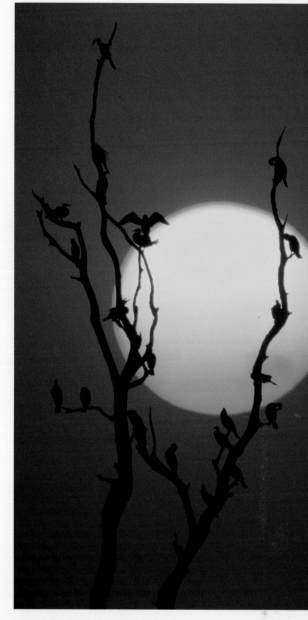

LITTLE CORMORANT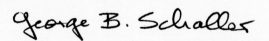
(*Phalacrocorax niger*), NAGARAHOLE NATIONAL PARK, KARNATAKA, INDIA

GEORGE B. SCHALLER

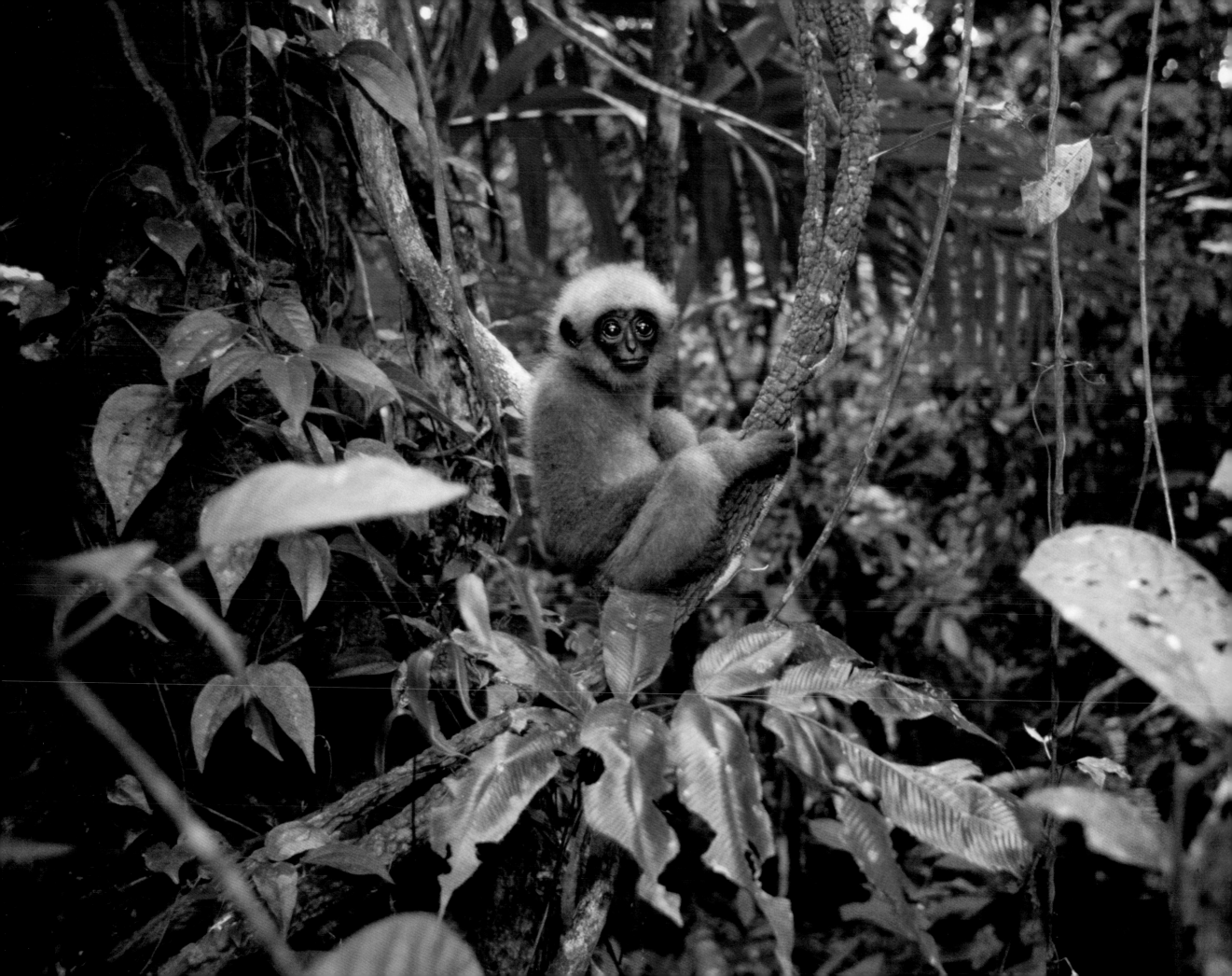

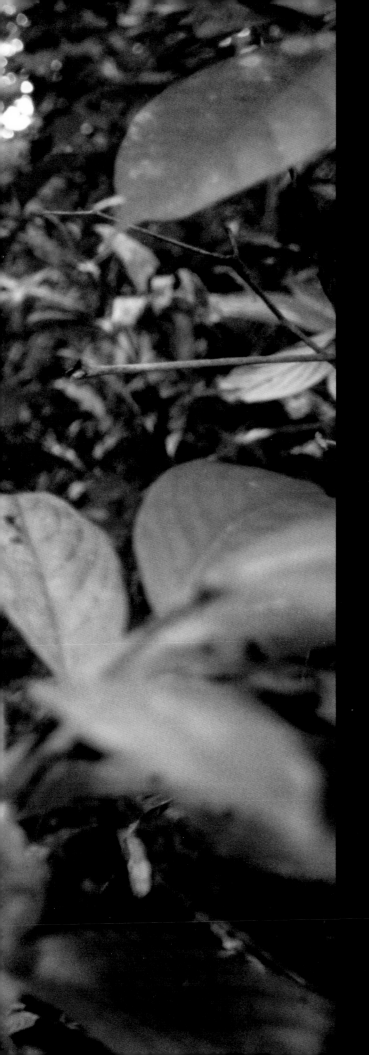

TROPICAL

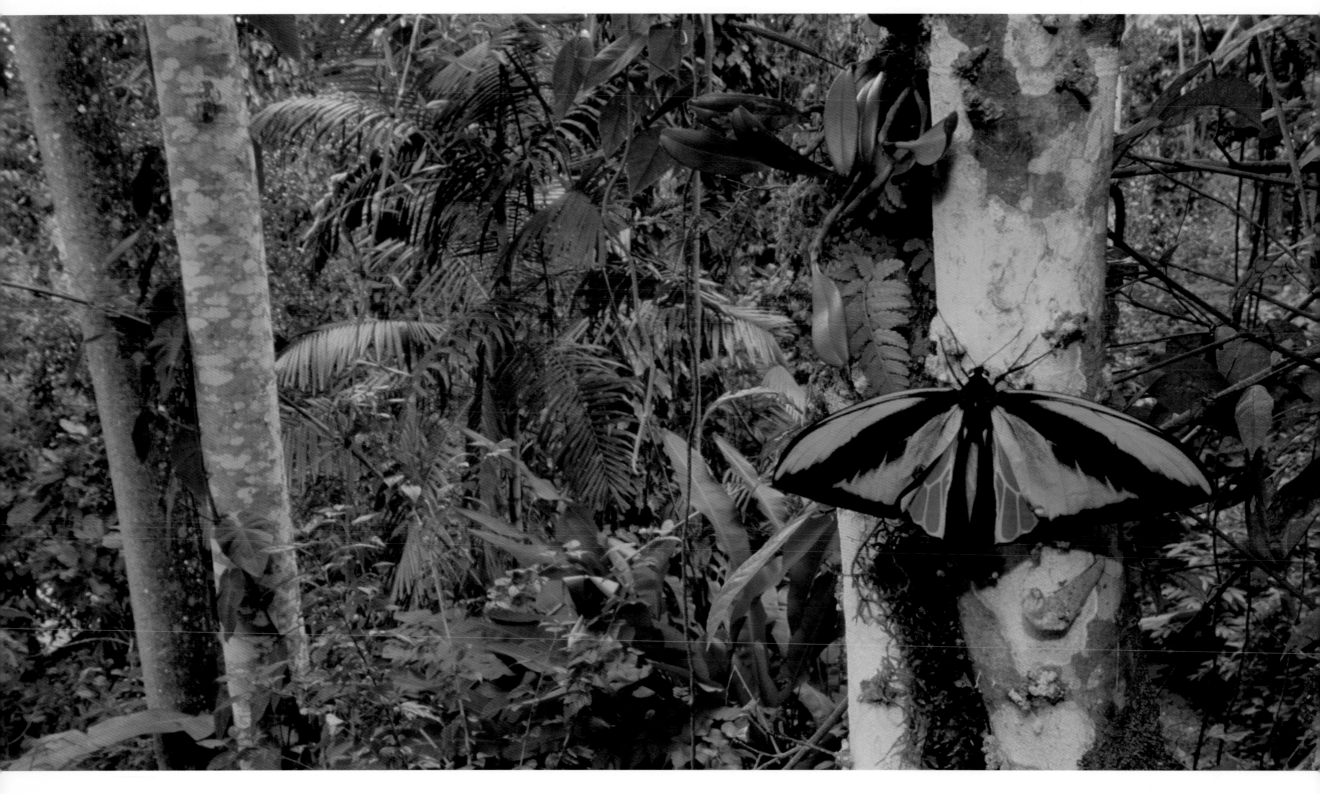

◄ GRAY GIBBON

Sarawak, Borneo, Malaysia

BIRDWING BUTTERFLY

Mount Amungwiwa, Papua New Guinea

THE LIVING WILD

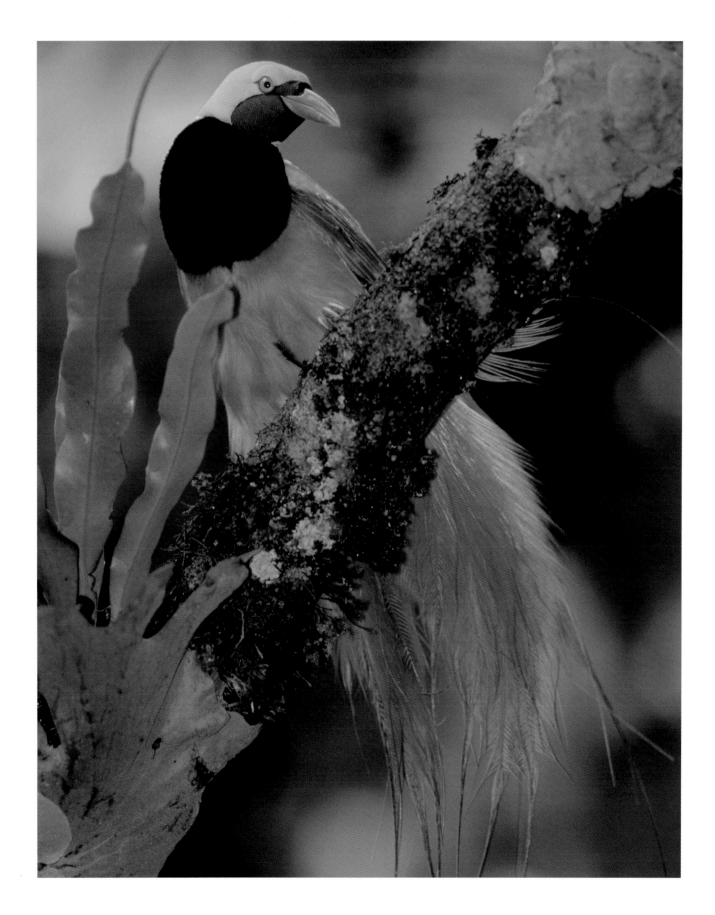

RAGGIANA
BIRD-OF-PARADISE
Mount Amungwiwa, Papua New Guinea

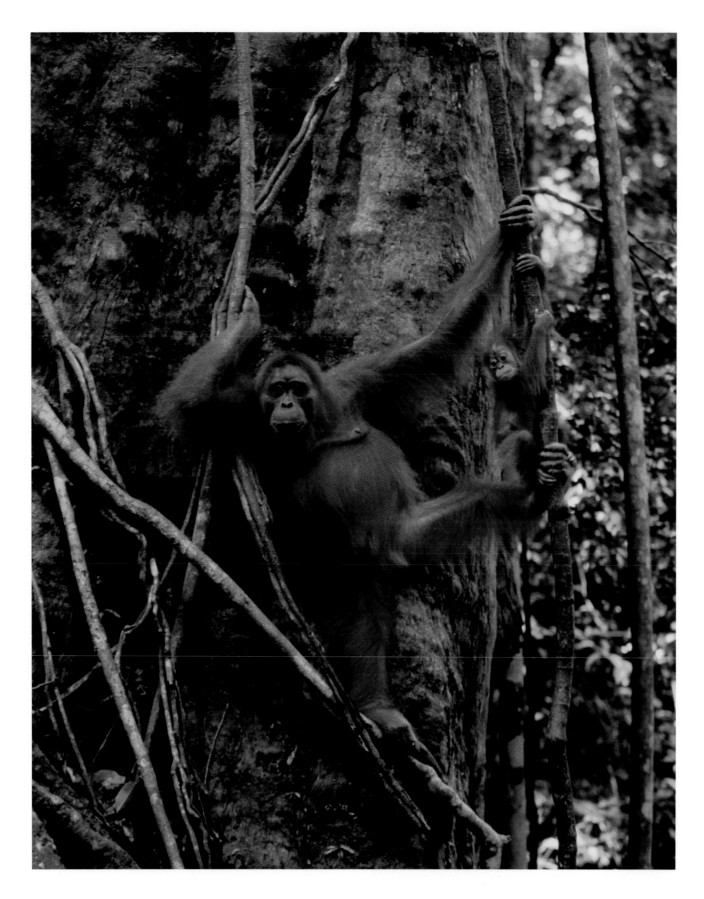

◄ AND ► ORANGUTAN

Gunung Leuser National Park, Sumatra,

Indonesia

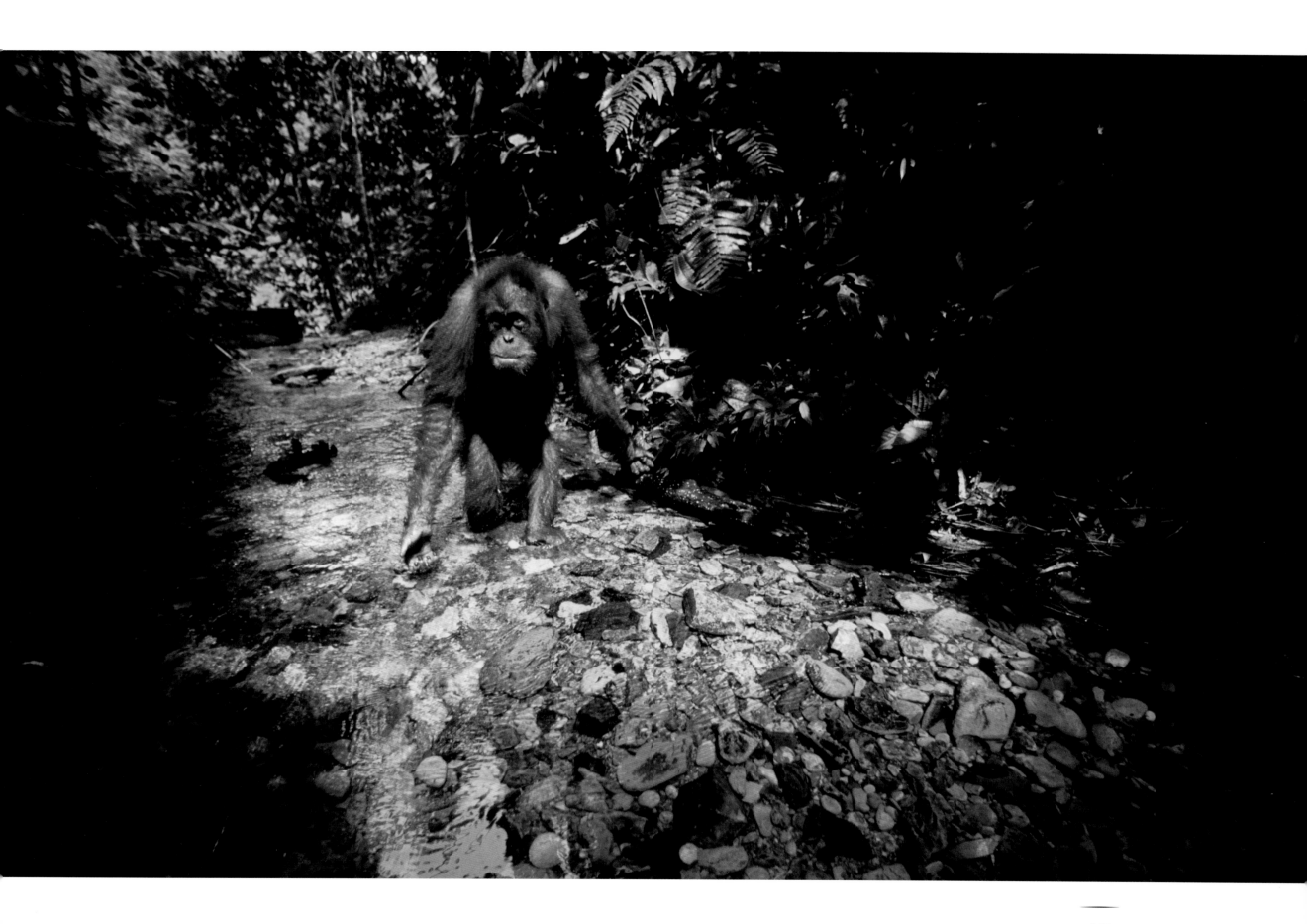

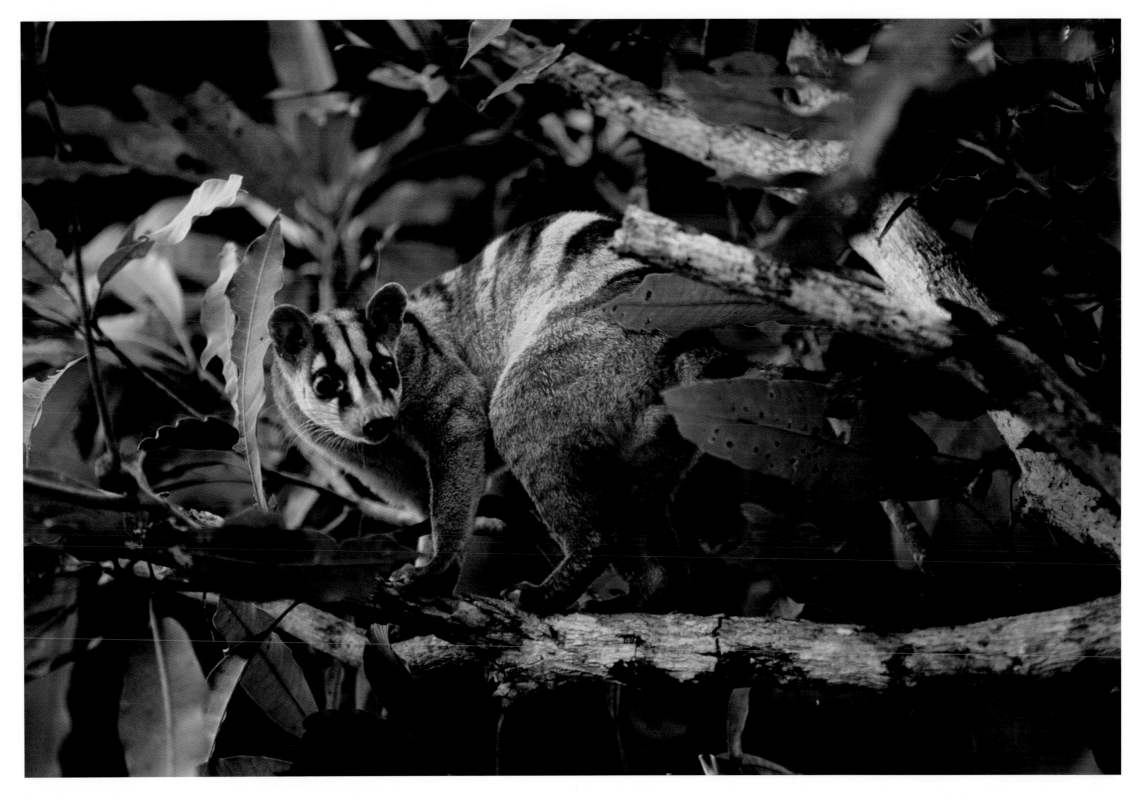

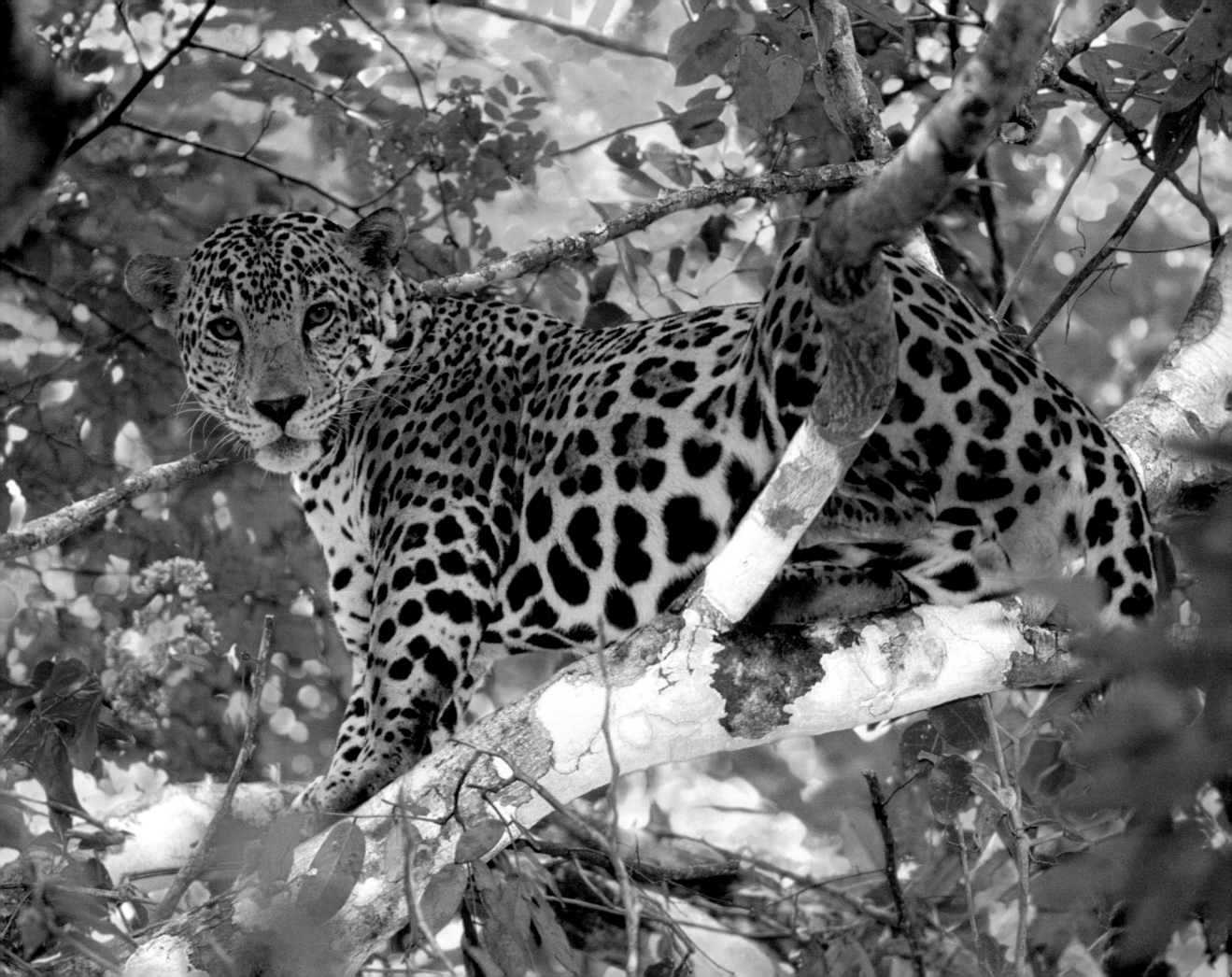

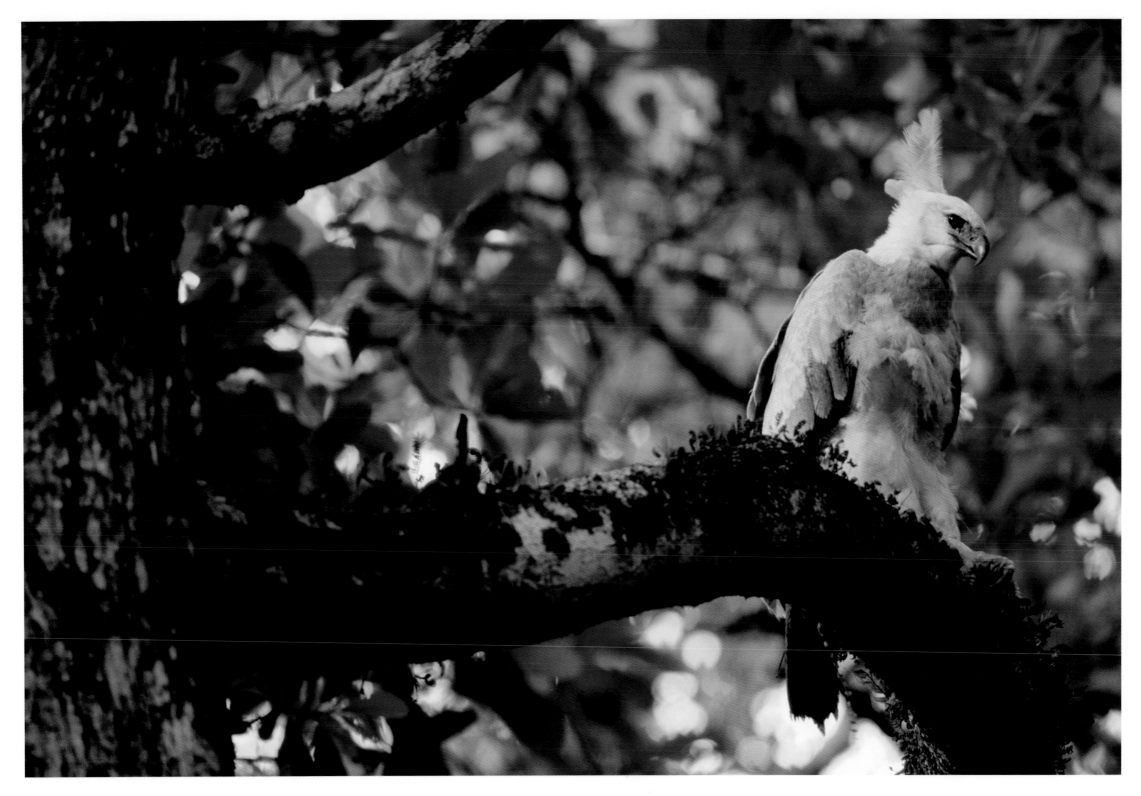

HARPY EAGLE

Panama

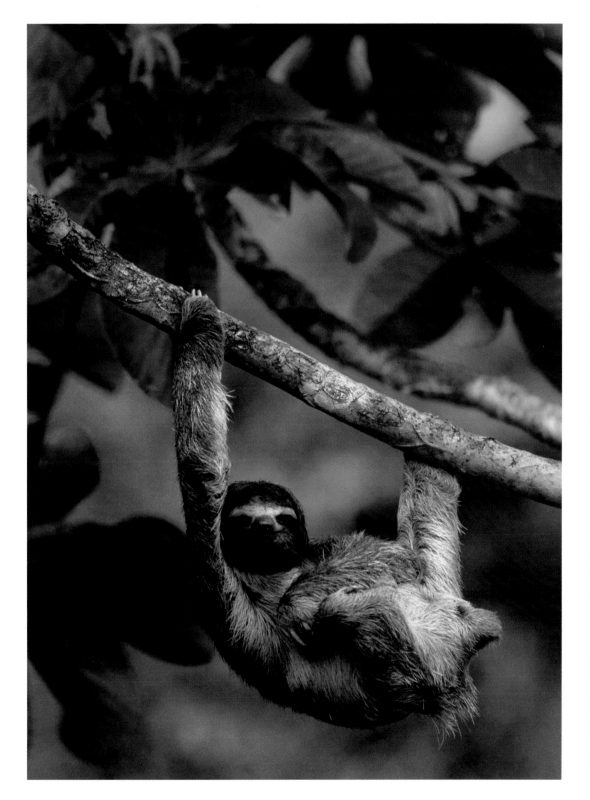

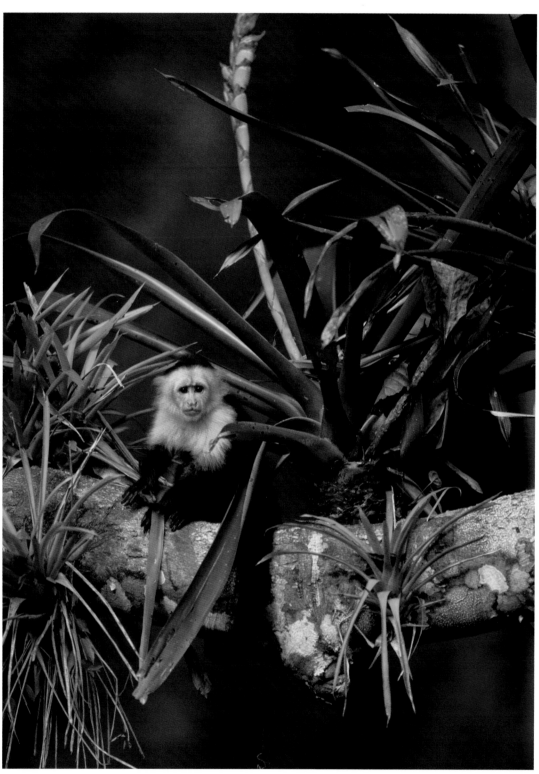

THREE-TOED TREE SLOTH ⌒

ISLAS BOCAS DEL TORO, PANAMA

WHITE-FACED SAPAJOU ⌒

ISLAS BOCAS DEL TORO, PANAMA

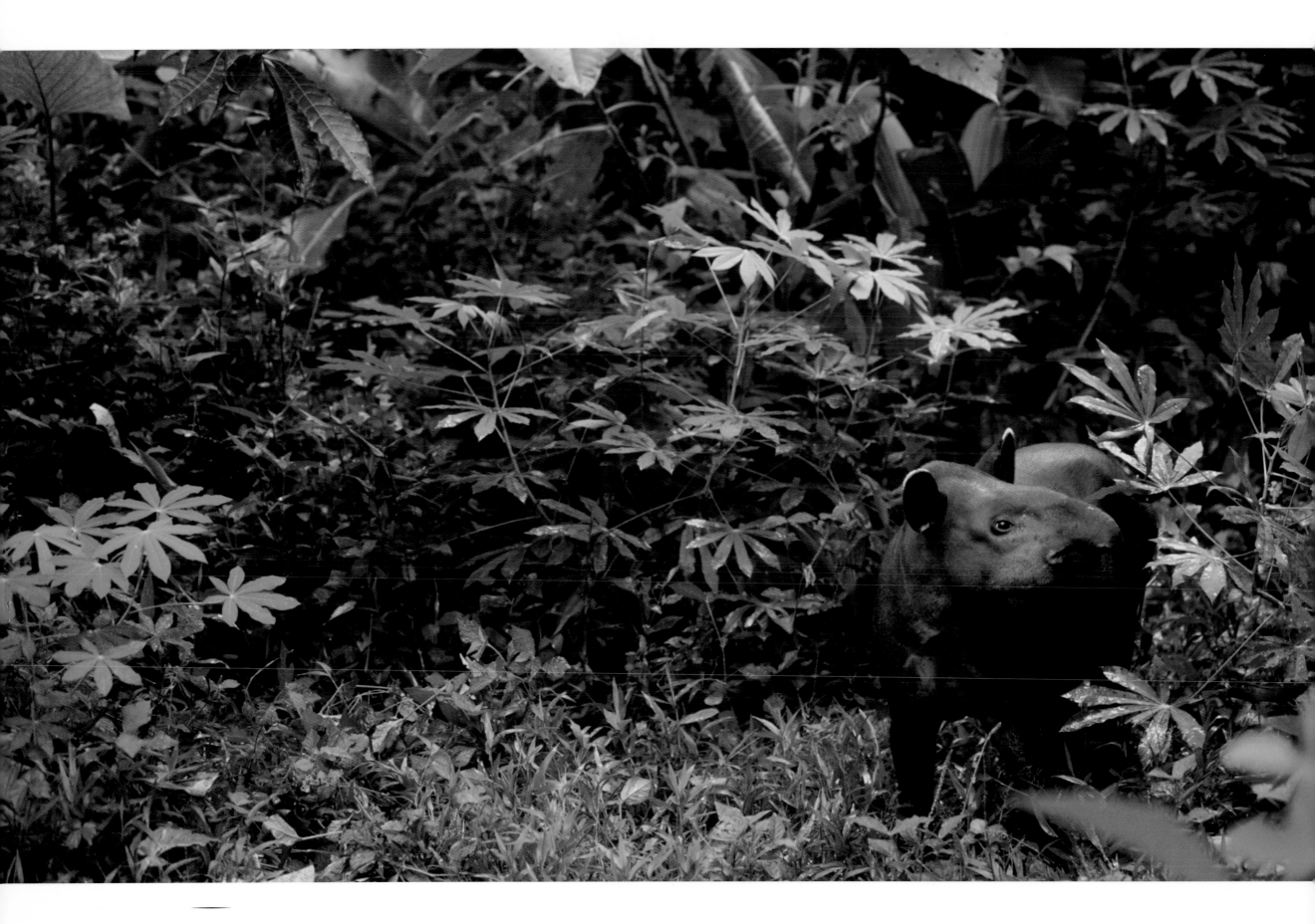

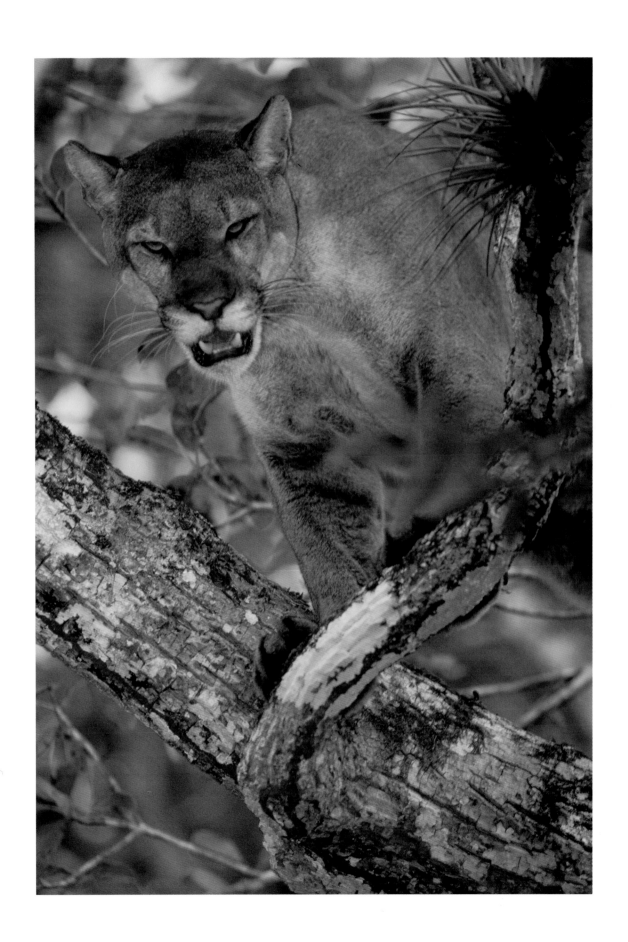

◄ SOUTH AMERICAN TAPIR
Lago Agrio, Ecuador

COUGAR
Calakmul Biosphere Reserve,
Campeche State, Mexico

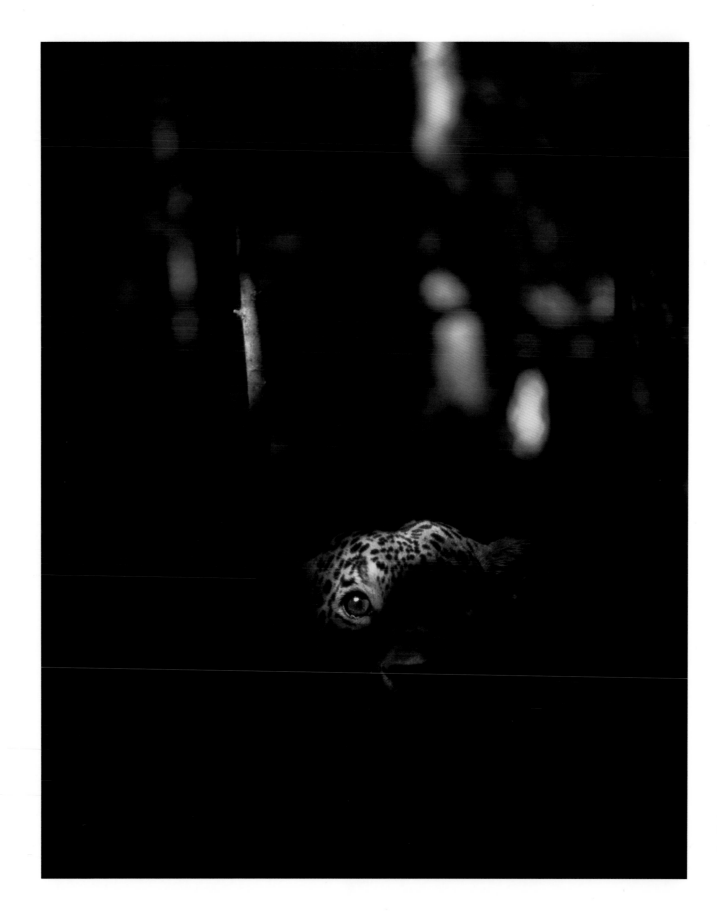

JAGUAR

Calakmul Biosphere Reserve,
Campeche State, Mexico

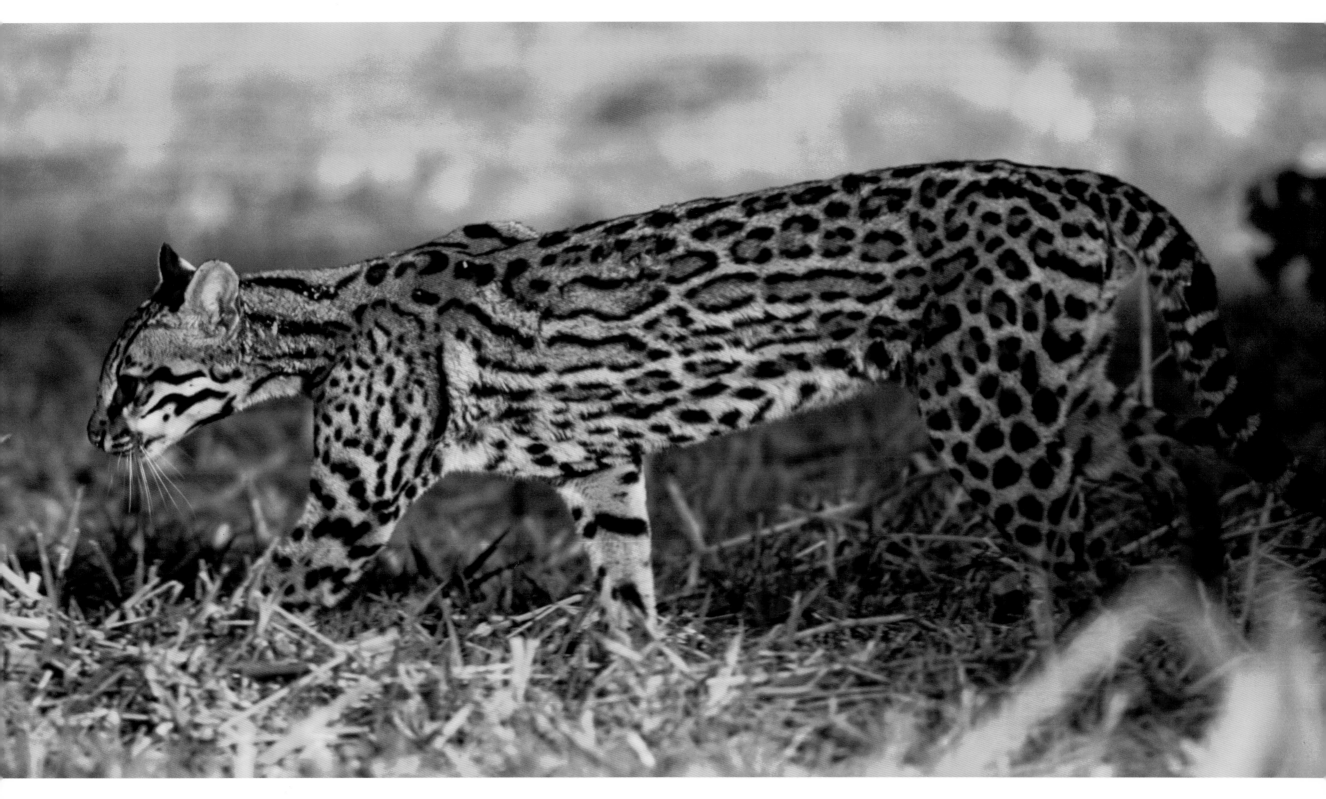

OCELOT

Llanos, Venezuela

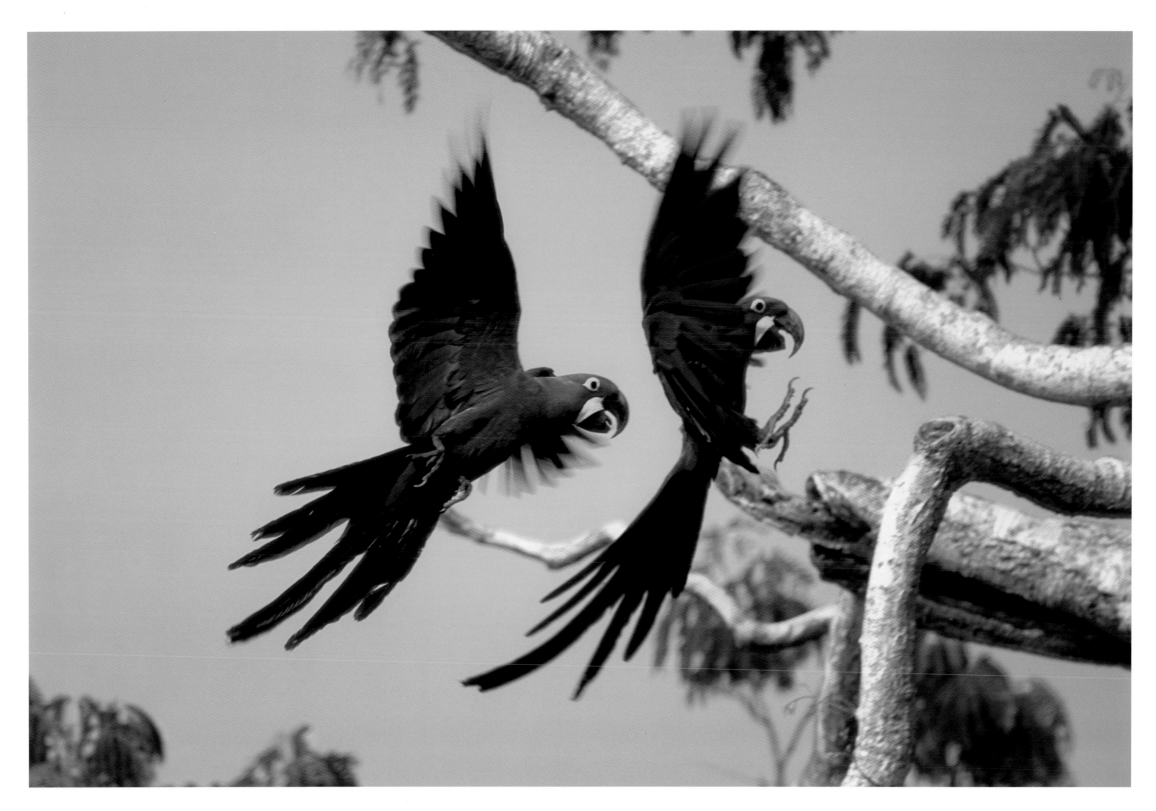

HYACINTH MACAW
Pantanal, Brazil

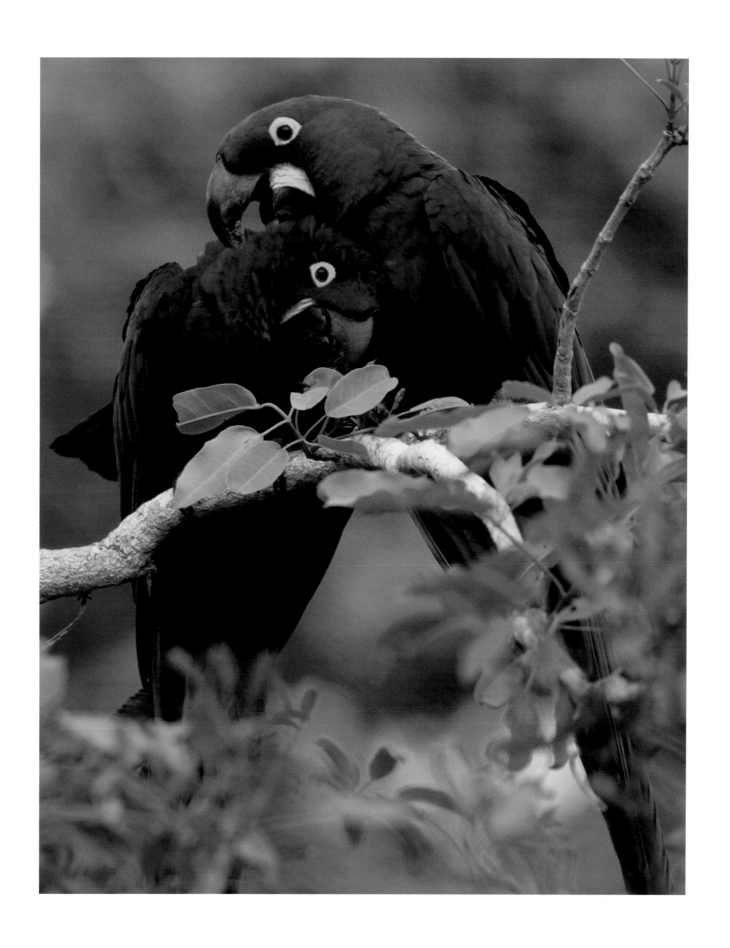

HYACINTH MACAW

TROPICAL

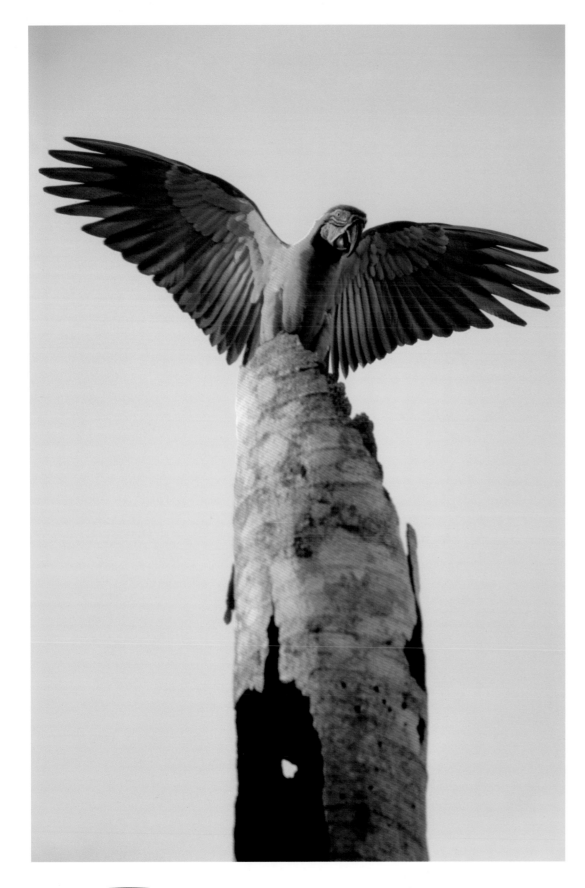
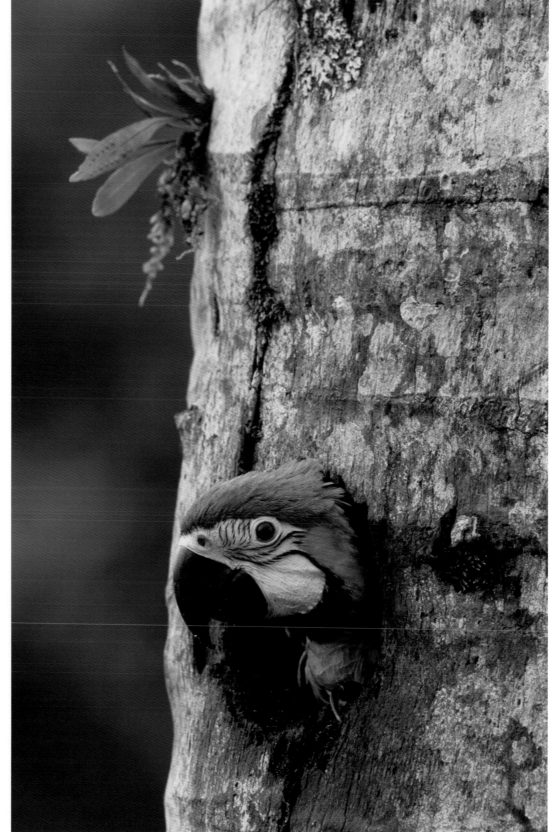

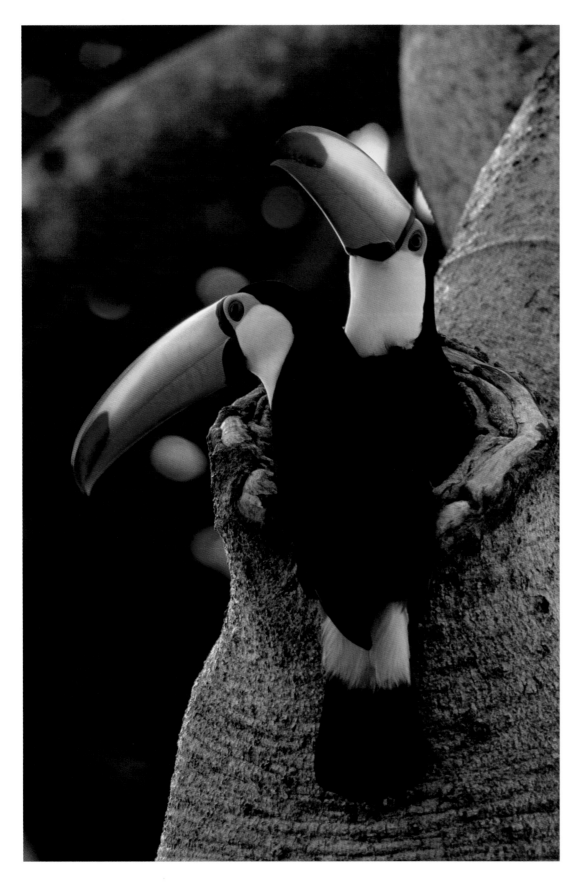

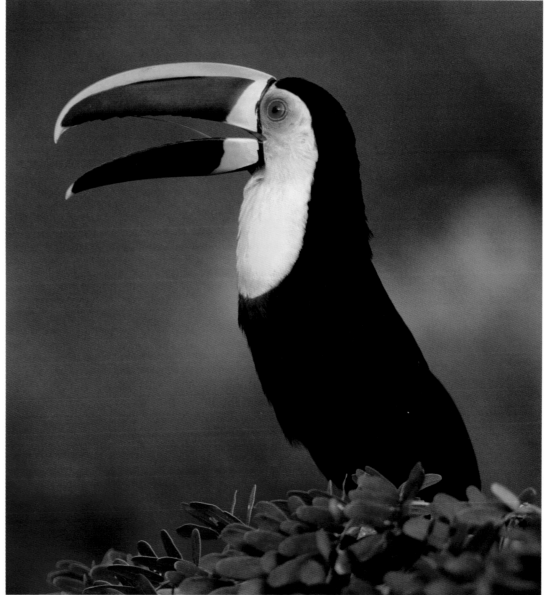

◄◄◄ BLUE-AND-YELLOW MACAW ∽

RESERVA DEL MANÙ, PERU

▲ CITRON-THROATED TOUCAN ∽

CARIBBEAN COAST, COLOMBIA

◄◄ BLUE-AND-YELLOW MACAW ∽

RIO AQUARICO, ECUADOR

◄ TOCO TOUCAN ∽

PANTANAL, BRAZIL

► GREEN-WINGED MACAW ∽

RESERVA DEL MANÙ, PERU

TROPICAL

229

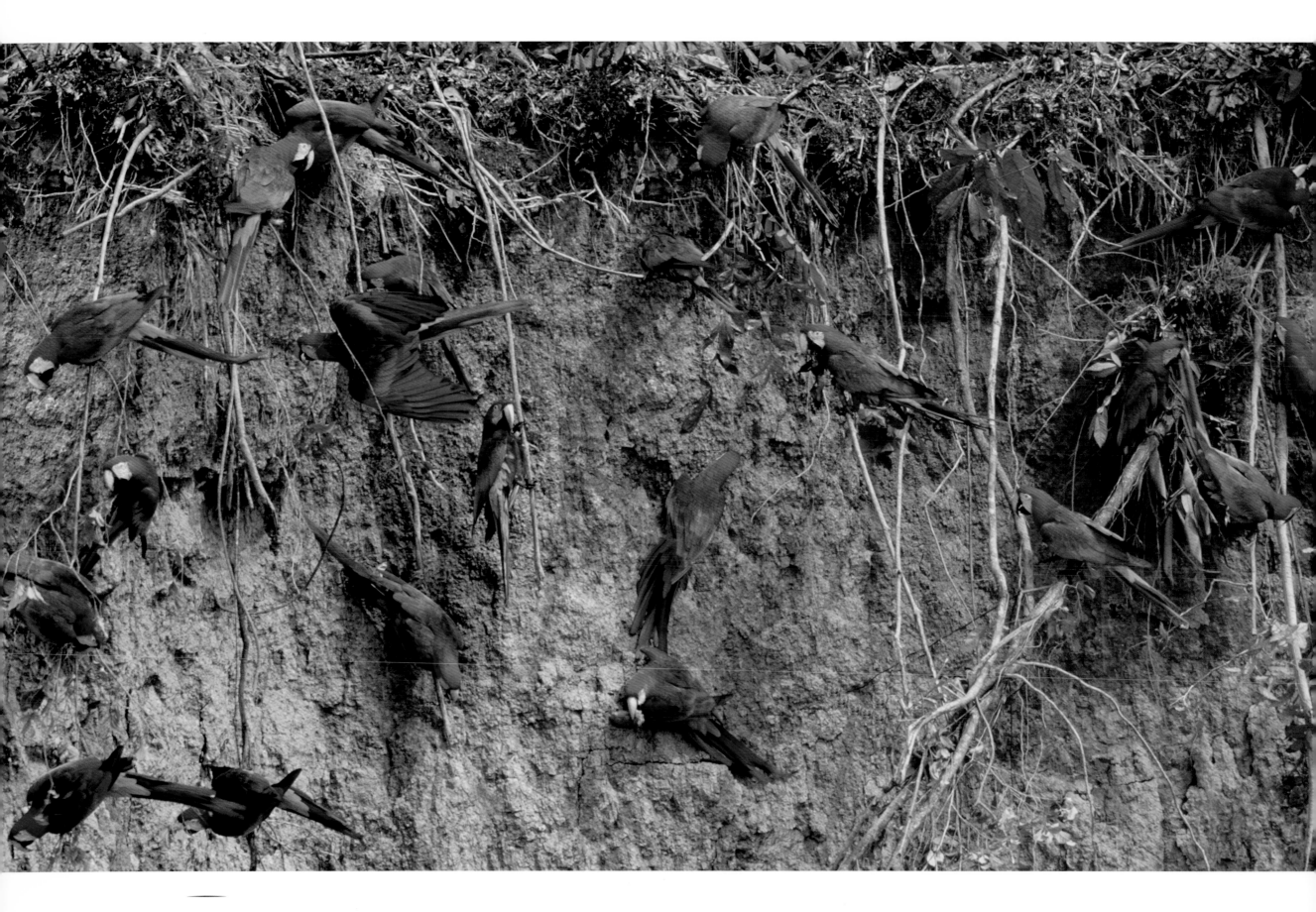

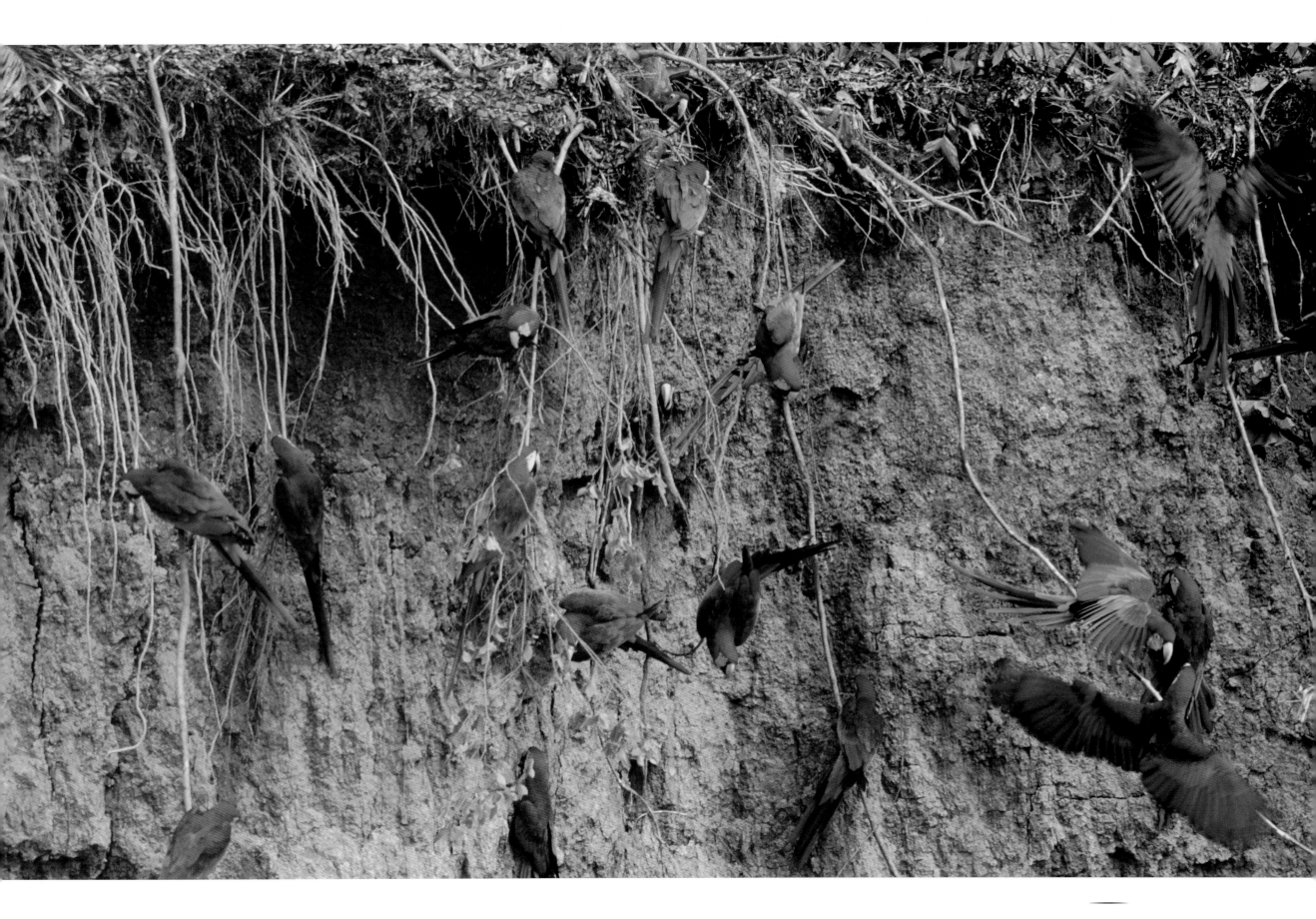

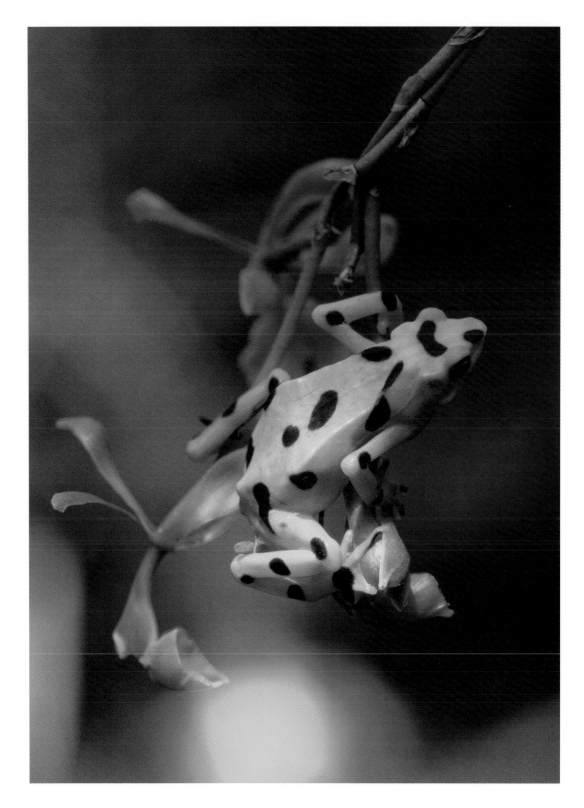

GOLDEN FROG

Pacific Lowlands, Panama

SOUTH AMERICAN MARBLED TREEFROG

Rio Tambopata, Peru

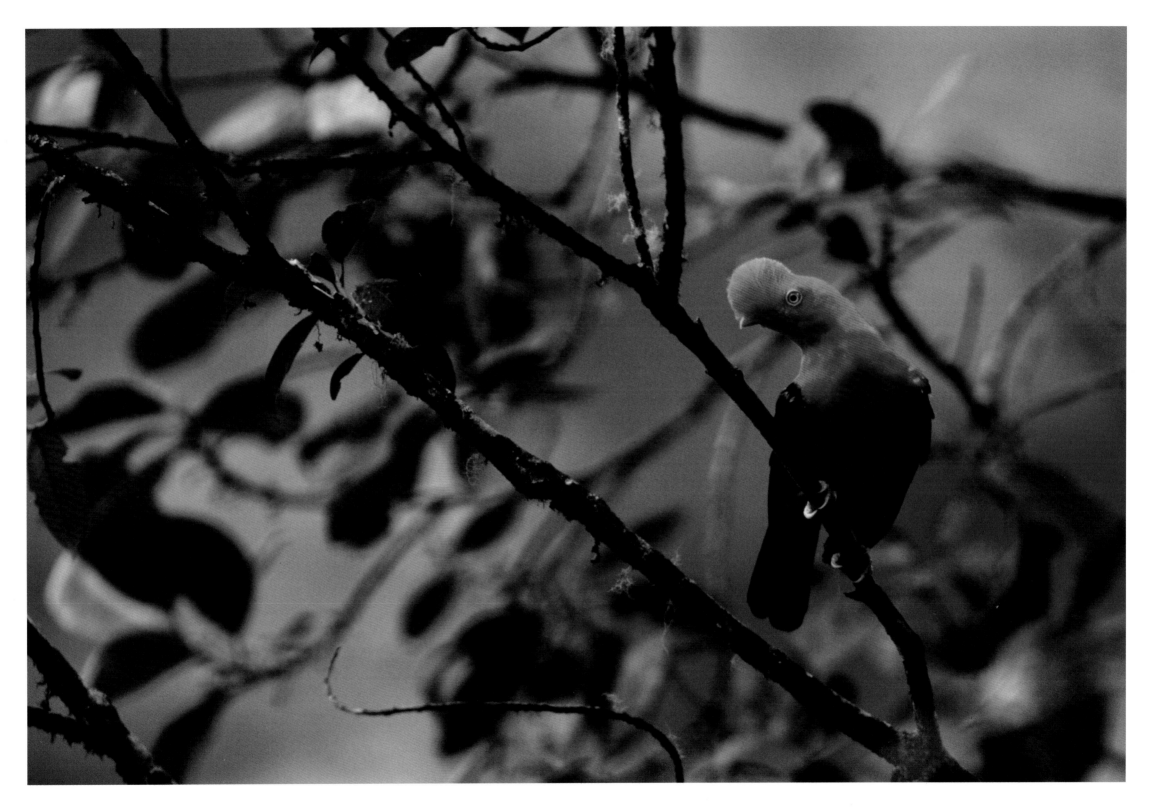

ANDEAN COCK-OF-THE-ROCK

ANDES MOUNTAINS, VENEZUELA

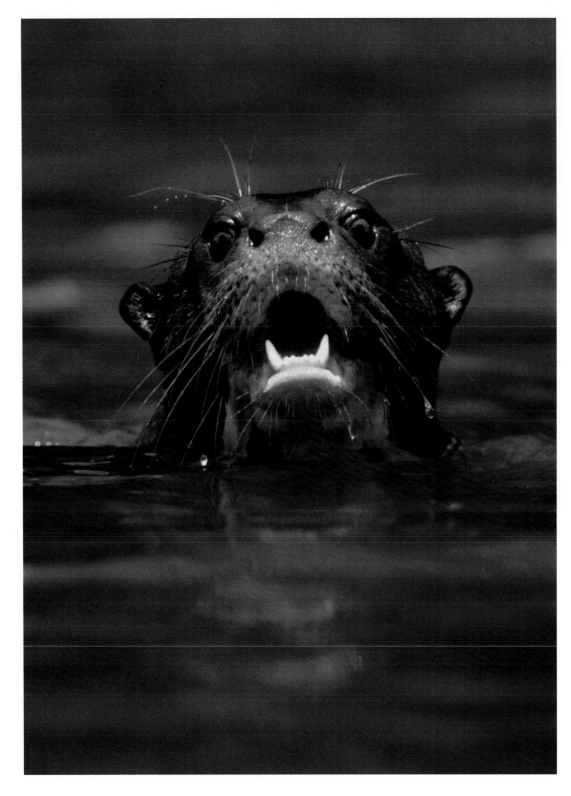

GIANT OTTER ⤳

Reserva del Manú, Peru

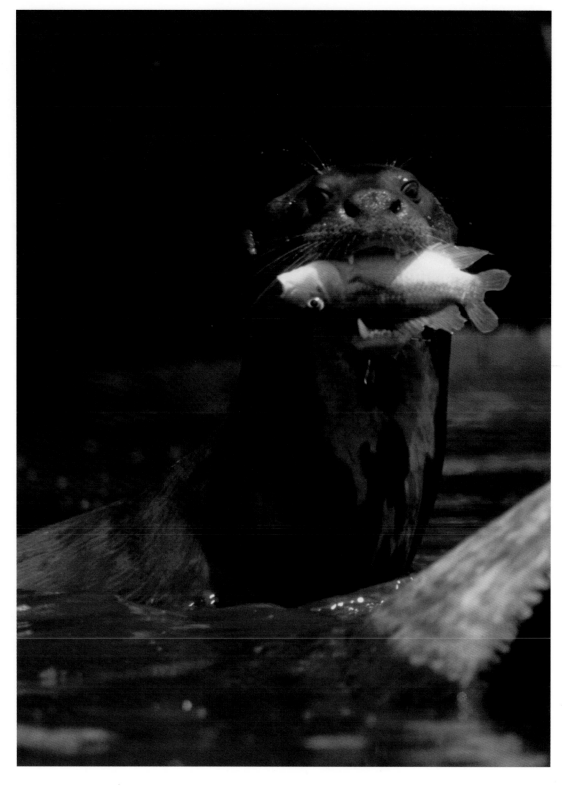

▲ AND ▶ GIANT OTTER ⤳

Reserva del Manú, Peru

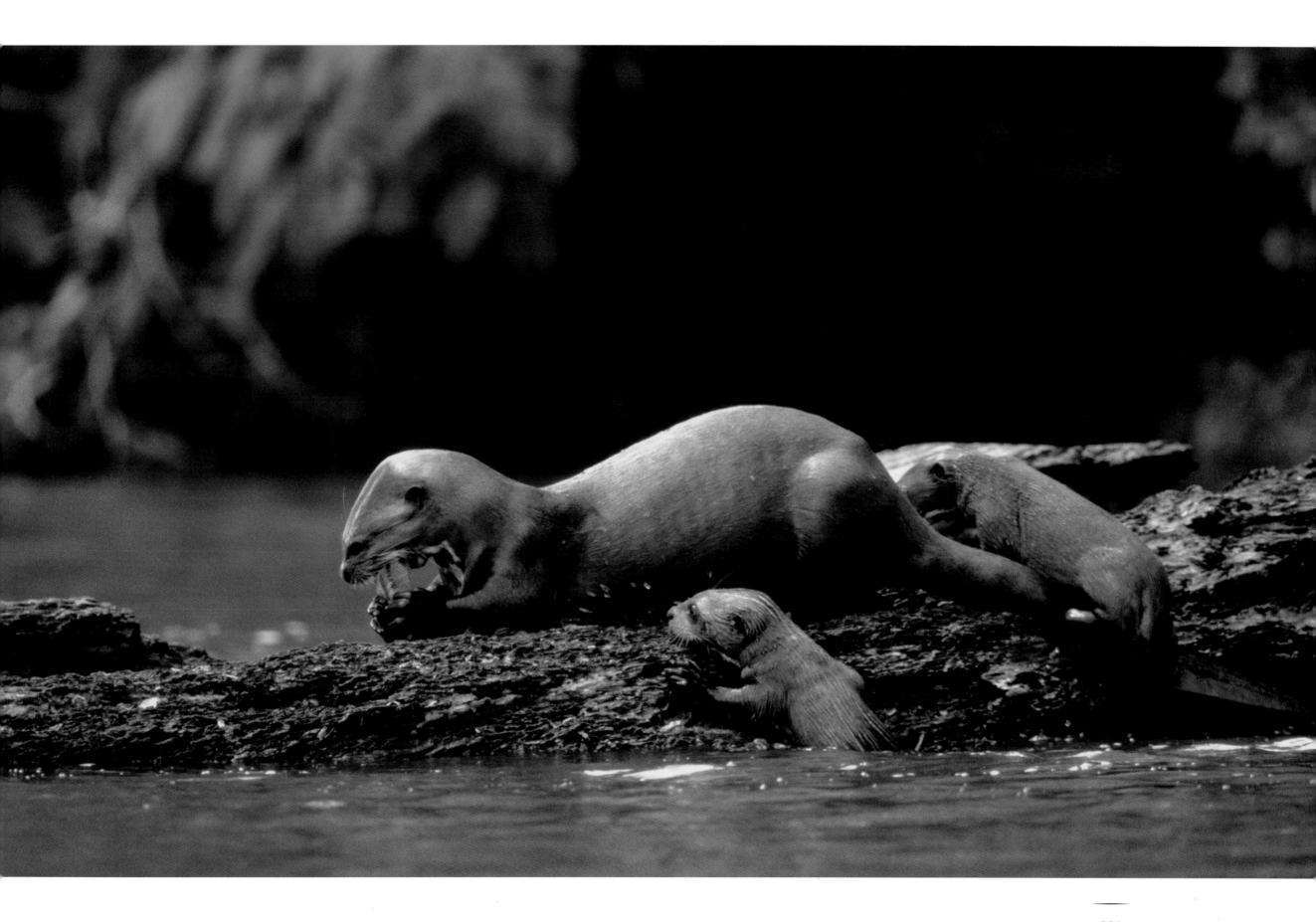

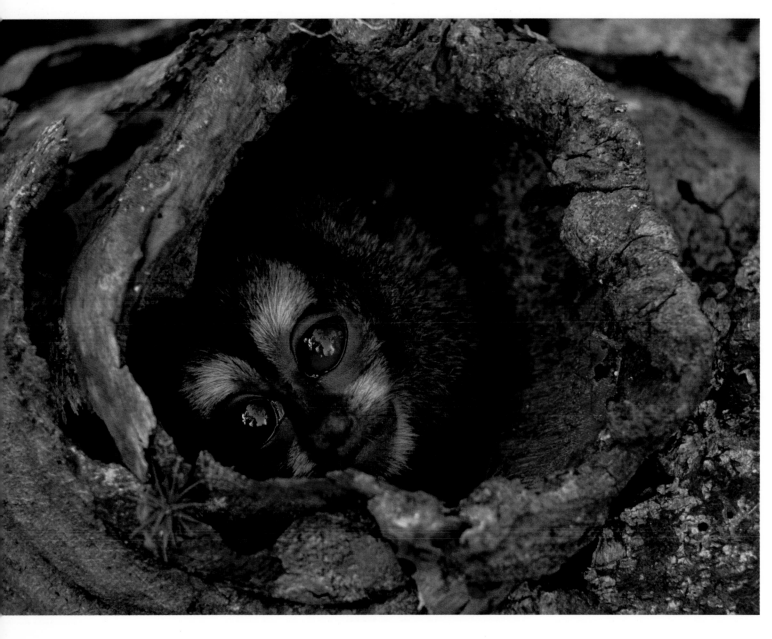

▲ NIGHT MONKEY

ISLAS BOCAS DEL TORO, PANAMA

► BLACK HOWLER MONKEY

ISLAS BOCAS DEL TORO, PANAMA

THE LIVING WILD

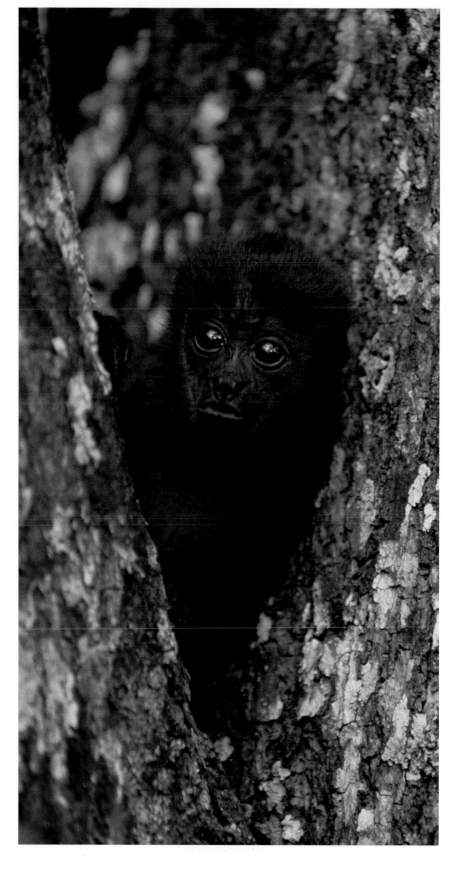

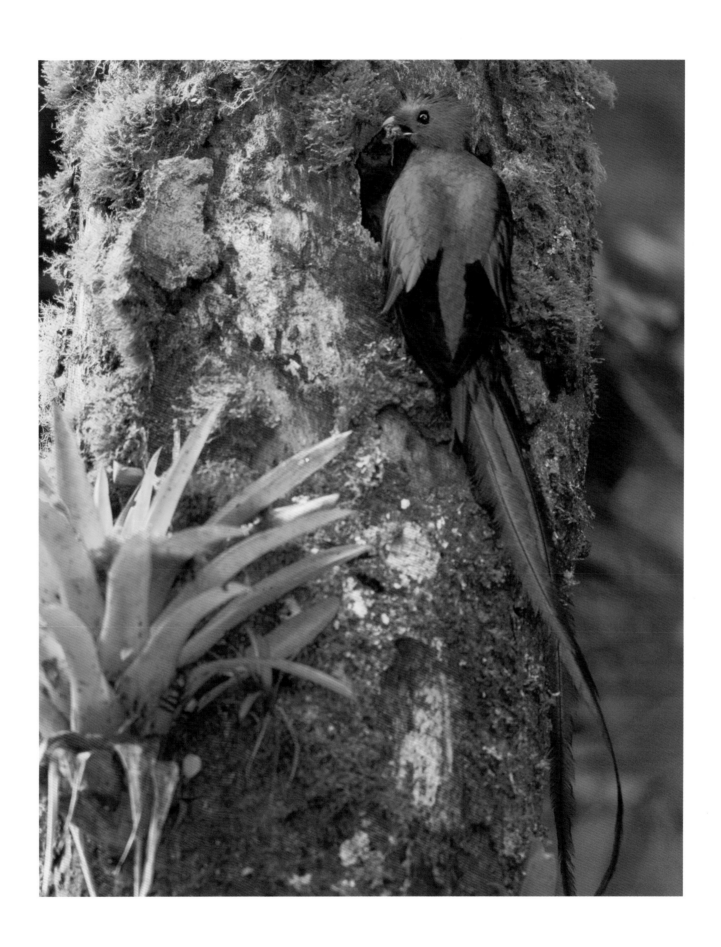

RESPLENDENT QUETZAL
La Amistad National Park, Panama

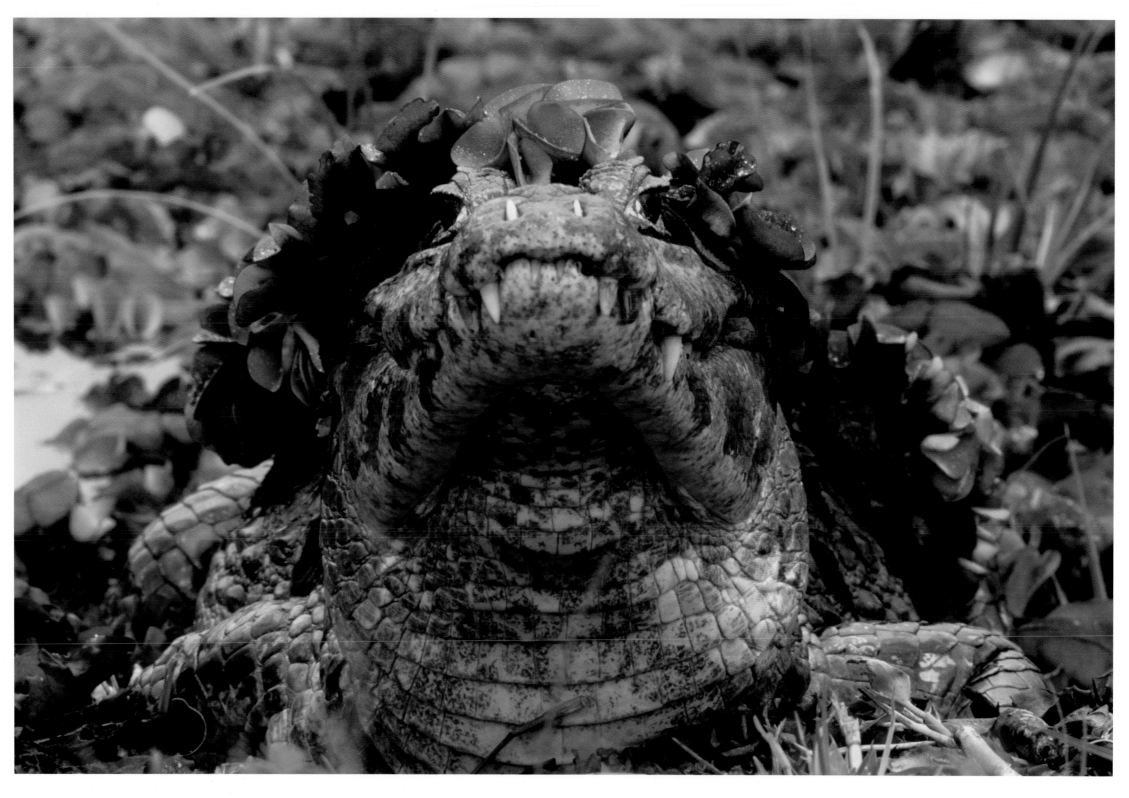

YACARE CAIMAN
Pantanal, Brazil

► SPECTACLED CAIMAN
Rio Orinoco, Venezuela

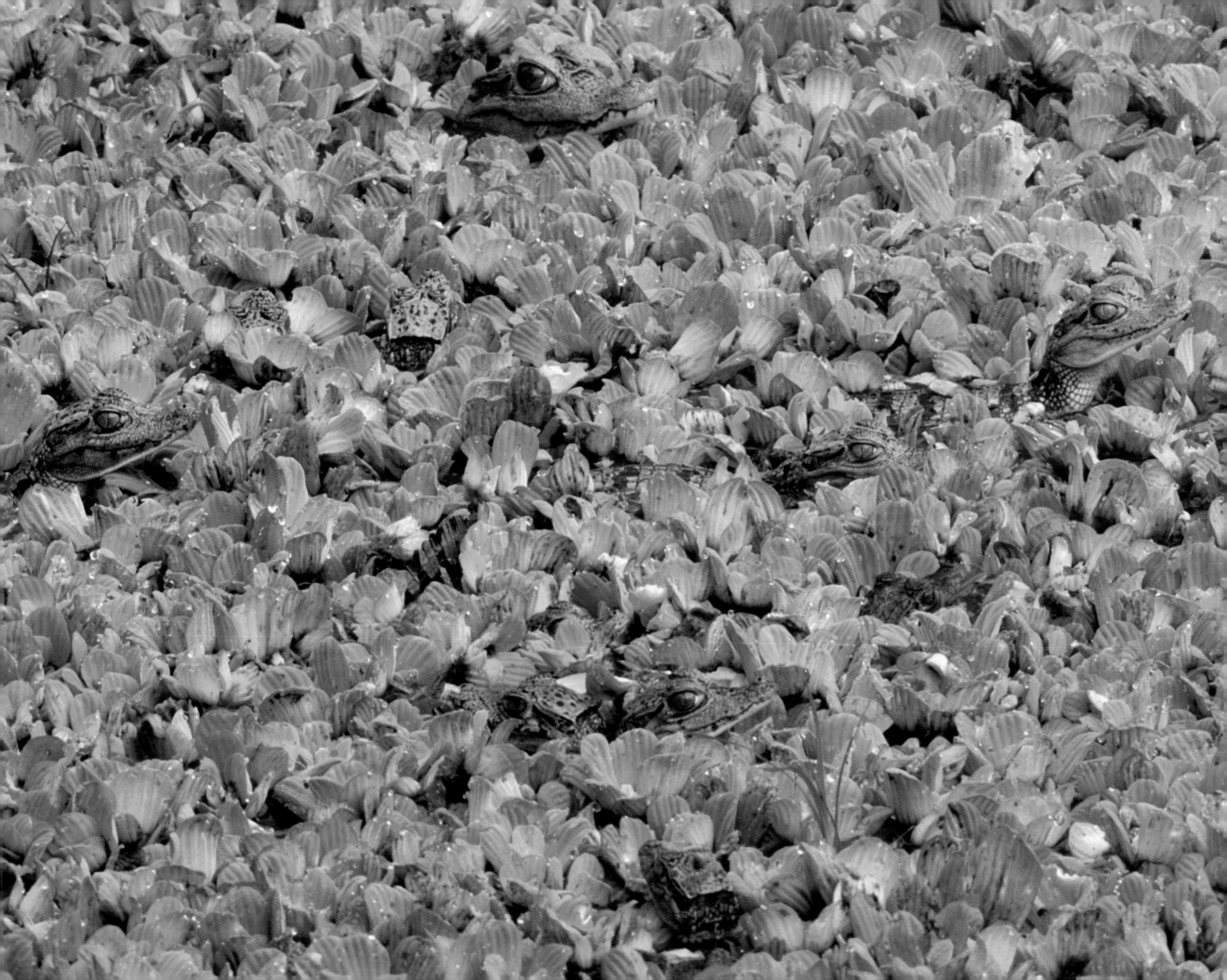

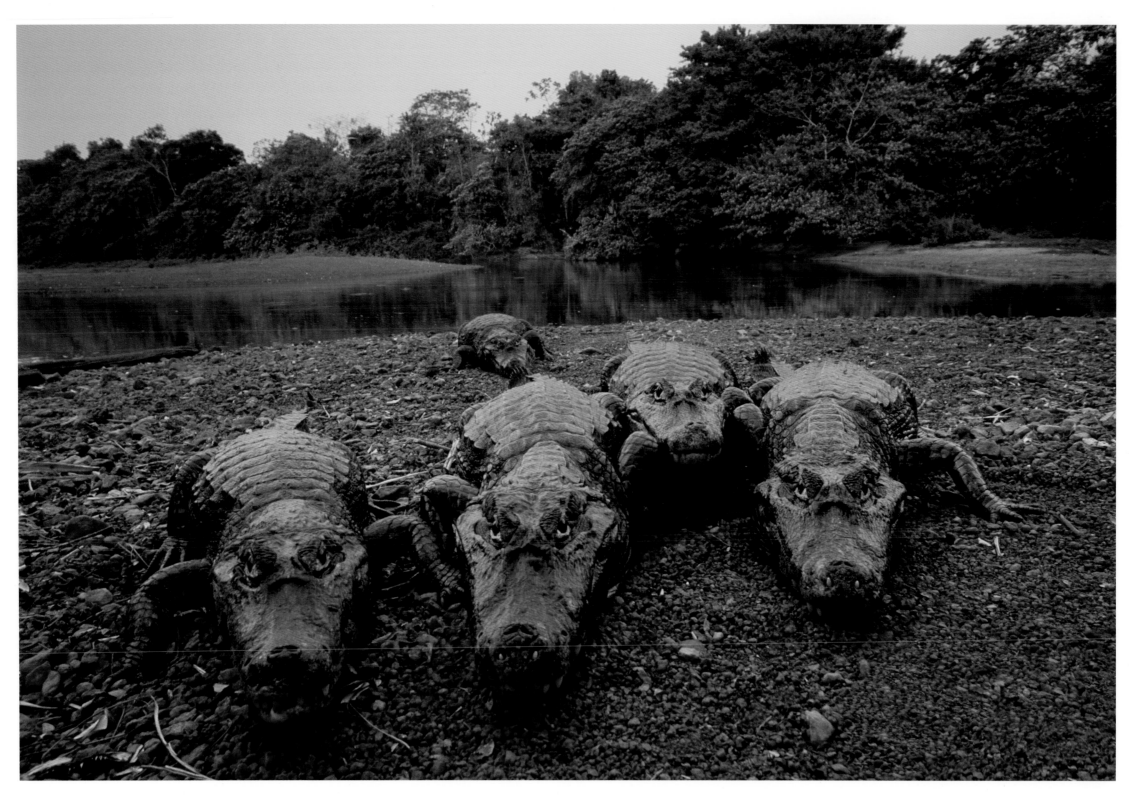

YACARE CAIMAN
Pantanal, Brazil

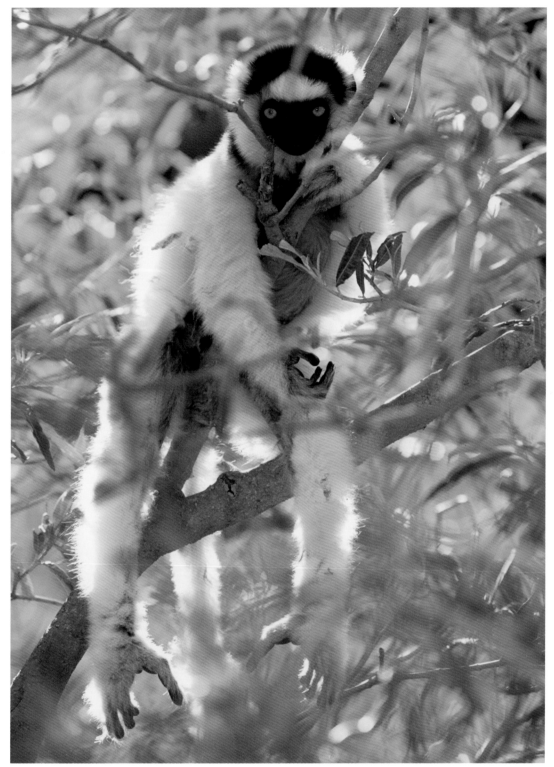

VERREAUX'S SIFAKA

MANDRARE RIVER, MADAGASCAR

INDRI

PERINET–ANALAMAZOATRA RESERVE, MADAGASCAR

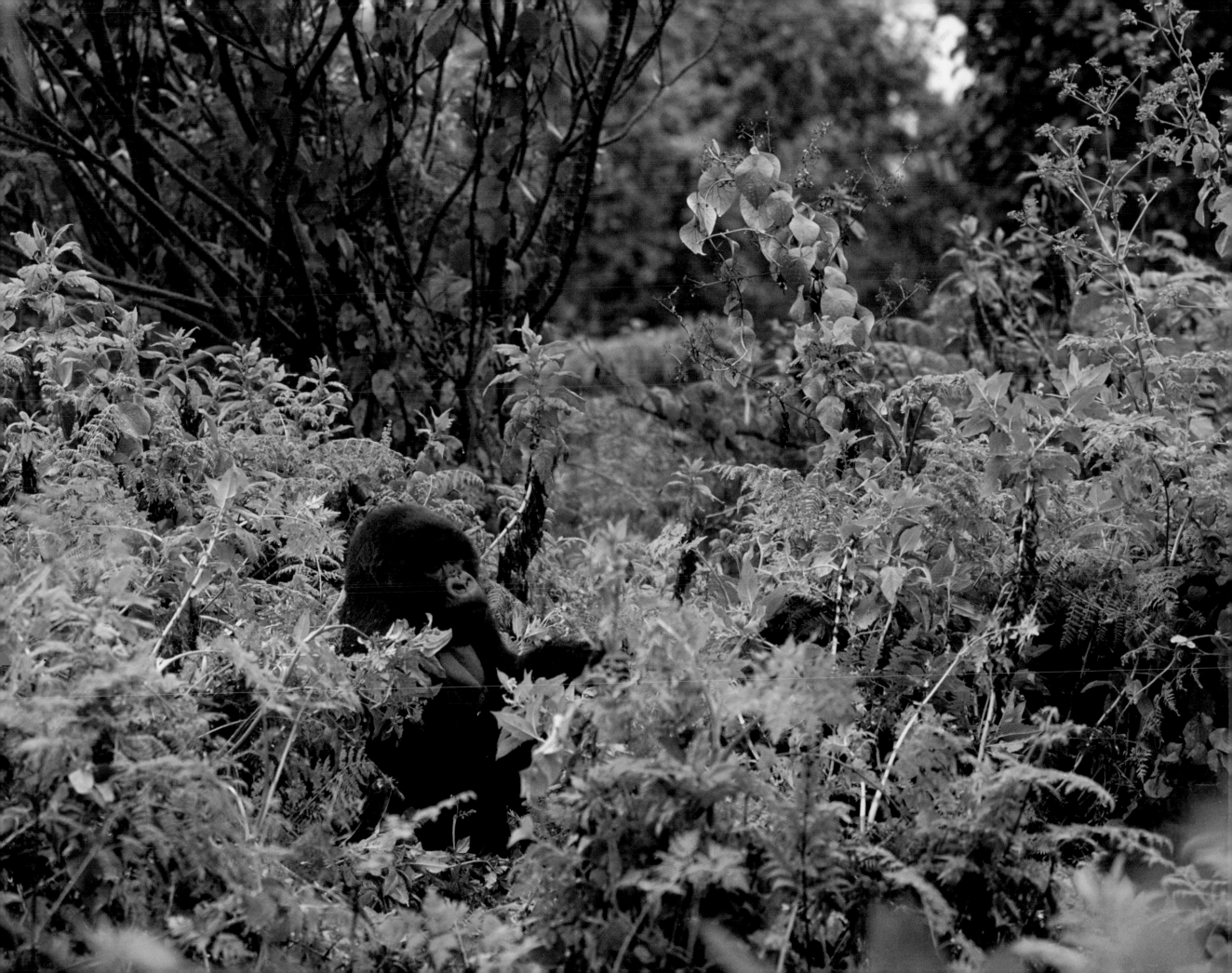

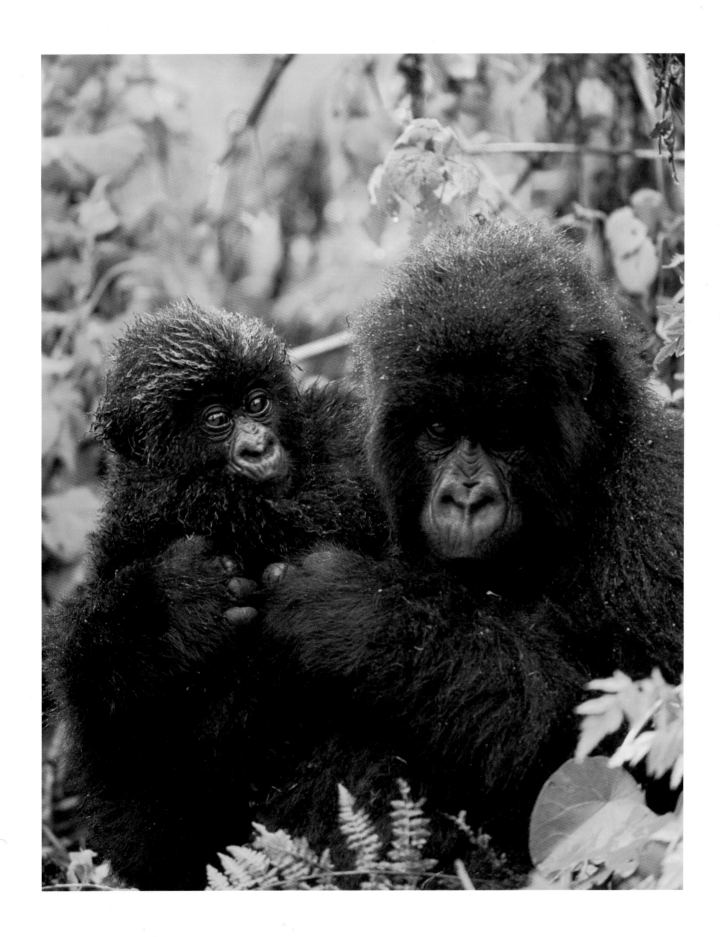

◀ AND ▶ MOUNTAIN GORILLA

Parcs national des Volcans, Rwanda

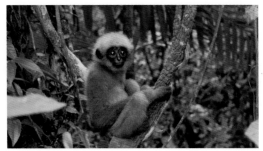

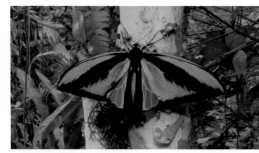

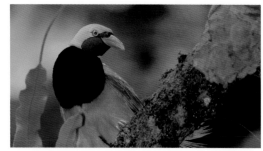

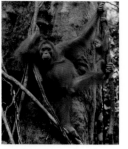 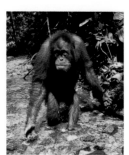

GRAY GIBBON
(Hylobates muelleri)

Gray or Mueller's gibbons are so-called "lesser apes." Gibbons are the closest primate relatives of the Hominidae (the great apes, including humans); they diverged from our common ancestors between 20 and 12 million years ago. Today gibbons are restricted to Southeast Asia; the gray gibbon is only found on Borneo. Well known for their death-defying leaps—more than 9 meters in a single bound—and melodious voices—their unique calls carry for several kilometers—these monogamous, tailless primates are built for life in the trees, with both sexes weighing between 4 and 8 kilograms. Deforestation, poaching, and trapping continue to take a toll on gibbon populations. Although legally protected, gray gibbons can still be found for sale in "bird markets" for less than US$100. In 1977, their population was estimated at almost two million, since then the vast majority of their habitat has been lost, and no reliable population data is available.

BIRDWING BUTTERFLY
(Ornithoptera priamus)

The male birdwing butterfly is a stunning, iridescent green insect with black and yellow markings on its wings. The larger female is somewhat drab by comparison, being mainly brown with white markings on her 20-centimeter-wide wings. Females are receptive to mating as soon as they have emerged from their cocoons, and male birdwings often conduct an early morning patrol through rainforest clearings, searching for "newly born" females. So keen are the males to mate that, at times, two or three may attempt to copulate with a single female at once. The birdwing butterflies' need for rainforest habitats makes them potentially vulnerable to habitat disturbances, particularly those resulting from logging, mining,. or land clearing for agriculture.

RAGGIANA BIRD-OF-PARADISE
(Paradisaea raggiana)

The highly vocal Raggiana or Count Raggi's bird-of-paradise can be found throughout much of eastern New Guinea; it is the national emblem of Papua New Guinea. The Spanish of the sixteenth century named "birds-of-paradise" after seeing the beautiful skins brought back to Europe by traders. Of the forty-three species, thirty-five are found only in New Guinea. The males that have the magnificent plumes, using their adornments to attract the relatively drab females. Their dances are striking, with the males contorting themselves to present the most stunning sight possible. Males are polygamous, and the females are left to raise the one to two chicks. It is the birds' plumage that has been the main threat to their existence. Hunting for feathers and skins, combined with habitat destruction, have decimated many populations. Although the international feather trade has been largely curtailed, indigenous peoples still use feathers in traditional costumes.

ORANGUTAN
(Pongo pygmaeus)

In the mid-1970s, there were an estimated 90,000 orangutans in Borneo (*P. p. pygmaeus*) and another 15,000 in Sumatra (*P. p. abelli*). Since then the population has crashed. Less than 2 percent of the orangutans' former range is protected, and those areas that are protected are increasingly compromised. Sumatra is losing its rainforests faster than any other Indonesian island. Logging and mining in Kalimantan—Indonesian Borneo—are decimating the forest, while the rainforest in Malaysian Borneo's Sabah region declined from 86 percent to 41 percent between 1953 and 1990. Across Indonesia, orangutans have lost over 80 percent of their forest in the last two decades. Current estimates number the Sumatran subspecies at about 9,200 animals, and the Bornean orangutan at fewer than 15,500. Compounding the effects of habitat loss, orangutans are still hunted for food and to provide infants for the "entertainment" industry.

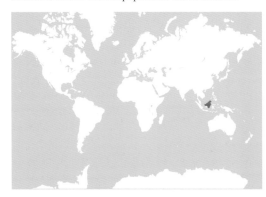

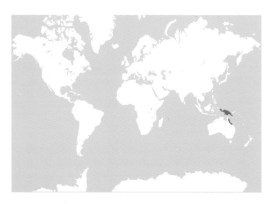

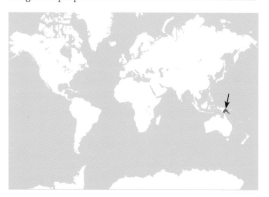

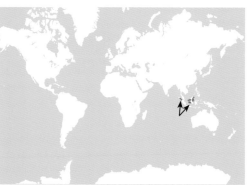

AW: Gibbon populations are increasingly threatened by the loss of their habitat. Yet some become habituated to human visitors, as demonstrated by this young animal. To get this photograph, I climbed a small tree next to the one in which the gibbon was perched. Surprisingly, it permitted me to approach within 4 meters, allowing me to use a wide-angle lens and create this environmental portrait that is as much about the habitat as it is about the gibbon.

Canon EOS-1N, Canon EF 24–85mm lens, f/11 at 1/15 second, Fujichrome Astia film

AW: A birdwing butterfly rests motionless in the dense highland rainforest. This is one of the world's largest butterflies. After emerging from its chrysalis, it takes hours for its huge wings to dry before it can take flight. I photographed this insect using a 17–35mm wide-angle lens, taking advantage of the butterfly's immobile state to get very close. I set my lens aperture at f/22 to maximize the depth of field. I used fill flash to bring out the color of the wings.

Canon EOS-3, Canon EF 17–35mm lens, f/22 at 1/2 second, fill flash, Fujichrome Velvia film

AW: This is a difficult bird to photograph in the wild, because it stays high in the forest canopy. To get this image, I visited a small research station that has several birds in enclosures. In the early morning and late afternoon, the captive females would call, attracting wild males from the surrounding forest. Low light levels in the dense forest required me to use a flash with an extender. I set the flash on fill mode, and spot read off the male's chest to arrive at the proper exposure. Even with the flash, I was able to get only a few sharp images.

Canon EOS-3, Canon EF 600mm lens, f/4 at 1/8 second, fill flash, Fujichrome Provia film (pushed 1 stop)

AW: Page 216 – I gained a clear view of this mother and baby by scrambling up a hillside across the ravine from their tree. They remained relaxed since they were over 30 meters above the ground.

Canon EOS-3, Canon EF 500mm IS lens, f/11 at 1/60 second, Fujichrome Provia film (pushed 1 stop)

AW: Page 217 – A chance encounter with an adolescent orangutan provides a unique photo opportunity. As this orangutan matures, he will lose his tolerance of humans, spending most of his time high in the forest canopy.

Canon EOS-3, Canon EF 17–35mm lens, f/8 at 1/125 second, Fujichrome Provia film

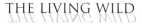

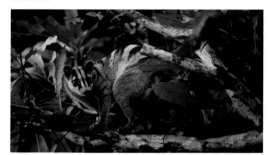

BANDED PALM CIVET
(*Hemigalus derbyanus*)

Banded palm civets are small (1.75- to 3-kilogram) carnivores found on the Southeast Asian mainland and various islands, including Sumatra and Borneo. They are rather doglike in appearance, but are actually members of a distinct family, the Viverridae. They have pointed faces marked by a dark medial strip and two lateral strips; their bodies are also striped with lighter and darker bands. Civets can climb, but banded palm civets are mainly terrestrial. They are most active at night, when they search the forest floor for earthworms and other invertebrates; they have strong, retractable, curved claws. Two subspecies—*H. d. minor* and *H. d. sipora*—are found only on the Mentawai Islands (located off the west coast of Sumatra) and are considered rare. Throughout their range, banded palm civets are losing habitat to commercial logging, and are persecuted by people who blame them for stealing chickens.

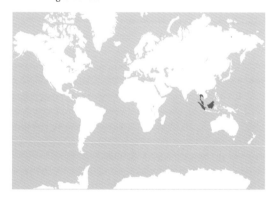

AW: While on an exploratory trip deep in the Bornean rainforest, I spotted this hyperactive little predator as it combed the forest for food. I pushed my film to increase my shutter speed. But without the "follow focus" capability of my camera and lens, I doubt that I would have been able to get a sharp image at all.

Canon EOS-1N, Canon EF 600mm lens, f/4 at 1/125 second, Fujichrome Astia film (pushed 1 stop)

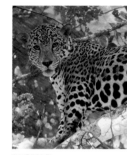 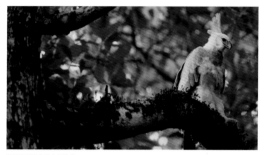

JAGUAR
(*Panthera onca*)

During the Pleistocene, jaguars roamed throughout the southern United States. However, as the climate changed and later as people expanded their range, the jaguars disappeared, although they may have bred in Arizona as late as 1950, and animals are still periodically seen in southern Arizona. Persecuted by farmers for killing livestock, killed for their skins, and facing a loss of habitat, jaguars have been virtually wiped out in Mexico and Central America. They have fared little better farther south. In the 1960s, 15,000 jaguars in the Brazilian Amazon were killed each year for their coats. With the skin trade no longer active, the Amazon basin is the jaguars' last stronghold; populations in grassland and pampas habitats were easier targets for hunters. With the elimination of many subpopulations, it is likely that the jaguar has lost much of its genetic diversity. Continued rainforest deforestation is likely to further fragment remaining populations.

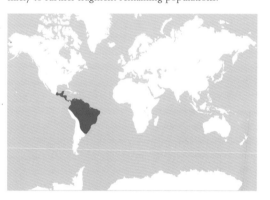

AW: Page 219 – Mexican researchers have discovered a population of jaguars along the Mexican–Guatemalan border. Here I accompanied a biologist conducting a census.

Canon EOS-3, Canon EF 600mm lens, Canon Extender EF 1.4x, f/8 at 1/30 second, fill flash, Fujichrome Velvia film (pushed 1 stop)

AW: Page 224 – Wild jaguars are difficult to photograph. Working with researchers using radio transmitters greatly increases one's odds. To get a proper exposure, I spot read off the patch of sun on the jaguar's head.

Canon EOS-1N, Canon EF 600mm lens, f/4 at 1/30 second, Fujichrome Astia film (pushed 1 stop)

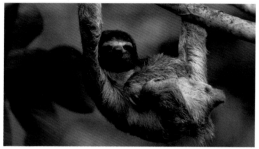

HARPY EAGLE
(*Harpia harpyja*)

This massive raptor—males weigh in at over 4 kilograms, while females range from 7.6 to 9 kilograms—has a wingspan of 2 meters. Found in undisturbed lowland tropical rainforests, harpy eagles prey on large animals such as sloths, howler and capuchin monkeys, porcupines, and large birds like macaws. Considered rare, harpy eagles are sparsely distributed in Central and South America; fewer than thirty nests have been confirmed since 1992. They have been severely impacted by habitat destruction and the loss of suitable nesting sites—they typically nest in the tallest emergent tree they can find. Although they lay two eggs, only one is generally raised to fledging. The juvenile remains within 100 meters of the nest for its first year, and as a result adults usually breed only every third year, giving them an exceedingly low recruitment rate. Reintroduction efforts are underway in Panama, but the numbers involved are small.

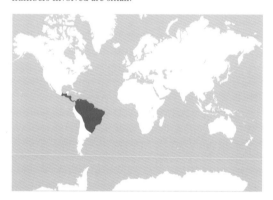

AW: An immature harpy eagle perches high in the rainforest canopy. From here the sharp-eyed eagle scans the surrounding forest looking for prey. This eagle was among a few released into the wild as American biologists teamed with their Panamanian colleagues to help restore the birds to their former range. For this shot, I walked in circles beneath the perch tree until I found a suitable opening in the dense limbs that allowed a clear view.

Canon EOS-3, Canon EF 600mm lens, f/11 at 1/60 second, Fujichrome Velvia film

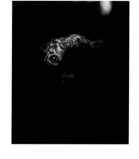

THREE-TOED TREE SLOTH
(*Bradypus variegatus*)

The three-toed tree sloth uses its strong claws as hooks to move, very slowly, through the trees. These unusual mammals have a low and variable body temperature, and are inactive during the colder part of the night. In the early mornings, they climb into the forest canopy to bask in the sun and raise their body temperature to something more typically mammalian. While their speed is limited, sloths are capable of rotating their heads an impressive 270 degrees, a useful adaptation as they search out the tasty young leaves of the *Cecropia* tree. Sloths are ill adapted to life on the ground; they descend to urinate and defecate only once or twice a week, and occasionally to change trees. As their forest habitats from Honduras to northern Argentina are cleared and fragmented, sloths can find themselves increasingly isolated from potential mates; attempts to cross open ground are frequently fatal.

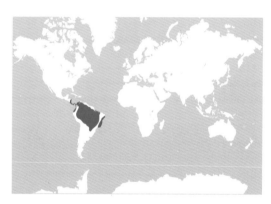

AW: Considering how slow the three-toed tree sloth moves, it is surprisingly difficult to photograph. Typically perched high in the trees eating leaves, it looks like a dark ball of fur silhouetted against the sky. I was lucky enough to find a sloth fairly low to the ground. By using an f/5.6 aperture setting for a shallow depth of field, I was able to incorporate the dark green backdrop of the trees in the distance for a "sense of place," while keeping the image simple and not distracting from the sloth.

Canon EOS-3, Canon EF 600mm lens, f/5.6 at 1/125 second, Fujichrome Velvia film

NOTES FROM THE FIELD

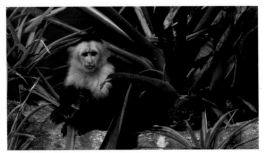

WHITE-FACED SAPAJOU
(Cebus capucinus)

White-faced sapajous are small capuchin monkeys found in Belize, from Honduras south to western Colombia, and in Ecuador. These endearing little primates are familiar to most as the "organ-grinder" monkey. When it was "chic" to have a monkey as a pet, this was the favored species. At 30 to 56 centimeters in length, with a comparably long tail, these black-and-white monkeys weigh 1.1 to 4.5 kilograms. Capuchins are also known as "ring-tail monkeys" because of the oft-coiled tip to their prehensile tails. Found mainly in humid forest habitats, capuchins can also be found in mangroves and secondary forests. They have a rich, varied diet that includes fruits, nuts, flowers, bark, insects, eggs, and—for those among the mangroves—even oysters and crabs. Although still fairly common in many areas, several subspecies of capuchin are critically endangered due to the loss of habitat, hunting, and trapping for the live-animal trade.

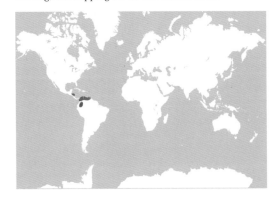

AW: The dense rainforests of Panama's Islas Bocas del Toro contain an abundant variety of animal life, including several species of primates. Here, a white-faced sapajou travels along a network of sprawling tree limbs that support epiphytes and bromeliads. I photographed this monkey with a 400mm lens with an extender so that I could stay far enough away so as not to frighten it.

Canon EOS-1N/RS, Canon EF 400mm lens, Canon Extender EF 2x, f/8 at 1/125 second, Fujichrome Provia film

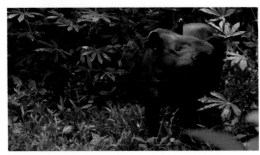

SOUTH AMERICAN TAPIR
(Tapirus terrestris)

The South American or lowland tapir is one of four species of tapirs (three of which are found in South America). They live in the dense tropical forests of Venezuela and Colombia, south to northern Argentina and southern Brazil, and can be found from sea level to 2,000 meters. Although considered to be at a lower risk of extinction than other tapir species, the lowland tapir's survival is dependent on active conservation efforts. Tapirs face intense pressure from poaching, hunting, and habitat loss through deforestation. They have a very low reproductive rate—a 13-month gestation period combined with (usually) a single offspring that remains with its mother for up to two years—which makes them highly susceptible to population declines. Tapirs feed on leaves, shrubs, and fruit, and the high percentage of fruit in their diet suggests that they are key seed dispersers.

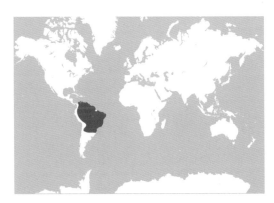

AW: While exploring the Rio Napo region of the Amazon basin, we stopped at one of the few Indian settlements along the river. The villagers informed us that a tapir came to a nearby tributary almost every morning, so we decided to set up camp. The next morning our decision to stay paid off. I took this photograph with a 600mm lens across a clearing near the stream. The tapir, although cautious, remained in the open for about 20 minutes.

Canon EOS-1N, Canon EF 600mm lens, f/8 at 1/30 second, Fujichrome Astia film

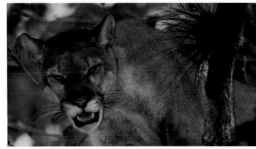

COUGAR
(Felis concolor)

The cougar has the greatest distribution of any mammal (except humans) in the Western Hemisphere (from Canada's Yukon and Nova Scotia to southern Chile and Patagonia). Cougars (also known as pumas, panthers, or mountain lions) are endangered in North America, but still occur in their former range in Central and South America. In Canada about 5,000 are found in British Columbia and Alberta; only small isolated populations survive farther east. In the eastern United States, the only confirmed population is in Florida, while in the West there are about 10,000. Although protected in some areas, they are still hunted for sport and killed to defend livestock in others. As the loss of habitat and gradual human encroachment bring people into closer proximity with cougars, the opportunities for harmful interactions increase; there are few areas in the world where humans and large predators are able to coexist.

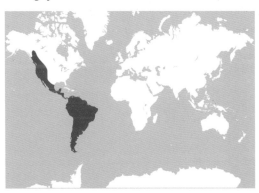

AW: While working with biologists conducting a census on jaguars in southern Mexico, I came across this cougar. Perched high in a tree, the cat seemed fairly relaxed. I photographed the cougar using a 600mm lens, aligning as much dark foliage behind it as possible to minimize the silhouetting effect of the bright sky. To bring out more color in this dark forest scene, I used fill flash.

Canon EOS-3, Canon EF 600mm lens, f/8 at 1/15 second, fill flash, Fujichrome Velvia film

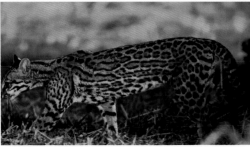

OCELOT
(Felis pardalis)

One of the most beautiful cats in the world, the ocelot has also been one of the most heavily exploited. The exquisite coat that camouflages the animal amid vegetation and shadows, from the rainforest to the grasslands, brought the small feline (they weigh 11.3 to 15.8 kilograms) to the attention of the fur industry. From the early 1960s until the mid-1970s, as many as 200,000 ocelots were trapped annually for their skins. As the demand for fur fell, the number taken dropped dramatically, and by the late 1980s the trade in ocelot pelts had been almost completely curtailed. The species has recovered from past hunting pressure and may now number more than 1.5 million. However, the subspecies *F. p. albescens*, found in southern Texas and northeastern Mexico, is considered critically endangered, with fewer than 250 adults remaining, out of which only 50 to 100 are in the United States.

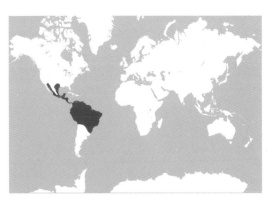

AW: As I photographed egrets along an oxbow lake in Venezuela's Llanos floodplain, I noticed a slight motion 75 meters ahead. At first I assumed it was a small heron jabbing at a fish. Then, as I scanned with binoculars, I discovered a twitching ear attached to a sleeping ocelot. With a 400mm lens and an extender mounted on a tripod, I quietly moved toward the sleeping cat. When I was about 40 meters away, the cat woke. As it got up and walked toward the surrounding forest, I was able to take this photograph.

Canon EOS-1N, Canon EF 400mm lens, Canon Extender EF 2x, f/5.6 at 1/125 second, Fujichrome Velvia film

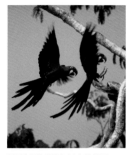
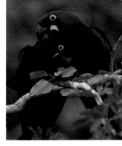

HYACINTH MACAW
(Anodorhynchus hyacinthinus)

Sometimes referred to as blue macaws, hyacinth macaws are large birds (90 to 100 centimeters in length), weighing more than 1.5 kilograms. Their coloring is a spectacular violet-blue with a bright yellow bare eye-ring and a yellow crescent-shaped lappet next to their lower mandible. Like all macaws, their heads and bills are large. Hyacinth macaws are often seen in pairs, and the sexes cannot be distinguished by sight. Flocks often gather at communal roosts in the evening, and they can be quite vocal at that time, producing sounds that range from croaks and screeches, to yapping, growling, and even purring. Their range is centered on Brazil, although they do extend into eastern Bolivia and northern Paraguay. Once considered "common," their distribution is now patchy. Birds are often captured, illegally, for the pet trade, while others are killed for their plumes, and for food. Fewer than 3,000 survive in the wild.

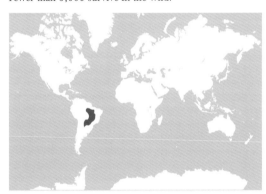

AW: Page 226 – Hyacinth macaws are one of the largest of the macaws. They fly with a relatively slow wingbeat, making them easier to film while in flight.

Canon EOS-3, Canon EF 500mm IS lens, f/11 at 1/500 second, Fujichrome Velvia film (pushed 1 stop)

AW: Page 227 – Biologists had studied these two rare birds for several seasons, so they were relatively easy to approach. Their plumage was best photographed under overcast light; in direct light, it turns a muddy grayish blue.

Canon EOS-3, Canon EF 600mm lens, f/8 at 1/30 second, Fujichrome Velvia film

---

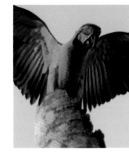
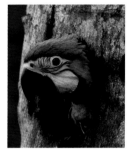

BLUE-AND-YELLOW MACAW
(Ara ararauna)

The blue-and-yellow macaw is one of the most familiar of the large parrots because of the large numbers in captivity. Principally found in South America's Amazon basin, these macaws are usually seen in pairs—although, as is the case with many parrots, the sexes are indistinguishable. They can often be seen flying along regularly used routes between their feeding and roosting areas, and making use of mineral-rich clay soils. Macaws forage high in the canopy, feeding on fruits, nuts, and leafbuds, and flocks of more than twenty individuals may congregate at a single feeding site. Trapping for the pet trade, although generally illegal, has resulted in significant population declines in many regions. The blue-and-yellow macaw became extinct in Trinidad in the early 1970s, and has vanished from much of southern and eastern Brazil; distribution in the northern part of the continent has also become patchy due to heavy trapping.

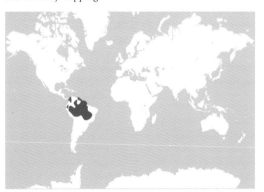

AW: Page 228 (left) – Macaws return to their nest only at sunset, allowing precious few minutes for photography. I worked from a survey tower 10 meters above the ground.

Canon EOS-3, Canon EF 600mm lens, Canon Extender EF 1.4x, f/5.6 at 1/15 second, Fujichrome MS100/1000 film (exposed at ISO 400)

AW: Page 228 (right) – Using a blind 9 meters off the ground, a 600mm lens, and a lot of patience, I was able to get several exposures of this chick as it looked out of a nest hole high in a palm tree.

Canon EOS-1N/RS, Canon EF 600mm lens, f/8 at 1/60 second, Fujichrome Velvia film

---

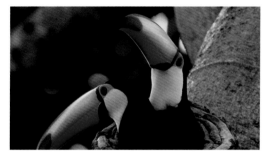

TOCO TOUCAN
(Ramphastos toco)

The toco toucan is the largest of the thirty-seven species of toucans. Found from Central America to northern Argentina, these vivid birds are instantly recognizable. The toco toucan sports a bill that makes up one-third of its total body length (about 20 centimeters out of a total body length of 66 centimeters). Despite its size, the toucan's bill is actually light. The outer sheath of the bill is made up of thin bone, while the bill itself is largely hollow. Toco toucans live in the rainforest canopy, using their large bills to pluck berries, fruits, seeds, insects, and even lizards from the branches. When a toucan successfully grasps some food, it tosses its head up to throw the morsel to the back of its throat. Although these delightful birds are still considered abundant, habitat destruction, particularly the loss of the rainforests, may soon threaten their survival.

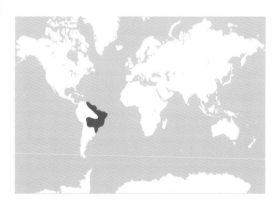

AW: A mated pair of toucans pause briefly as they exchange incubating duty at the entrance to their nest cavity. I used a 600mm lens with a 1.4 extender, placing tripods under both the lens and camera body to ensure the sharpest possible image. I composed the image to fill the background with as much dark foliage as possible. Then I waited patiently for the moment when both adults were perched at the nest opening. After several days I discovered that this happened only once a day, between eight and nine in the morning.

Canon EOS-3, Canon EF 600mm lens, Canon Extender EF 1.4x, f/11 at 1/60 second, Fujichrome Provia film

---

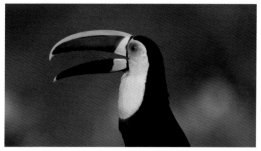

CITRON-THROATED TOUCAN
(Ramphastos citreolaemus)

At 53 centimeters in length, the citron-throated toucan is a large, charismatic bird. It closely resembles both the white-throated (*R. tucanus*) and the yellow-ridged (*R. culminatus*) toucans, but is found in the more northerly humid forests of Colombia up to about 900 meters; both of the other toucan species are present farther to the south. The bill of the citron-throated toucan measures 152 to 178 millimeters in length and is largely black with blue and yellow markings. Toucans are often seen in pairs or small groups. They favor the high canopy, and observers frequently comment that they appear top-heavy in flight. Their flight pattern usually involves several wing flaps, followed by a brief glide. When calling—citron-throated toucans deliver a froglike croak—the birds position themselves on an exposed perch and bob their heads from side to side as they "sing" each note.

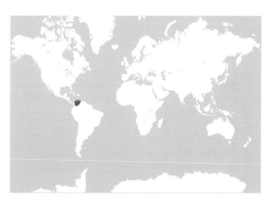

AW: Toucans are favorite subjects for photographers, because of their striking colors and huge, improbable bills. They are also very difficult to photograph, since they prefer to stay high in the forest canopy. Occasionally, they become habituated to bird feeders placed near lodges in the rainforest. Here, a toucan comes in close to a lodge, looking for slices of papaya.

Canon EOS-1N, Canon EF 600mm lens, f/11 at 1/125 second, Fujichrome Velvia film

NOTES FROM THE FIELD

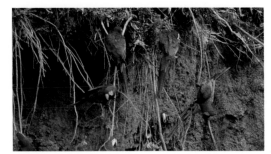

GREEN-WINGED MACAW
(*Ara chloroptera*)

Macaws are some of the bird world's most stunning members. The green-winged macaw is conspicuously red, with a long pointed tail, blue flight feathers, and green underwing-coverts. It closely resembles its sympatric relative, the scarlet macaw (*Ara macao*). These raucous birds are found from Panama to northern Argentina, including much of the Amazon basin. However, they have vanished from large parts of their former range, due to habitat loss, hunting, and collecting for the international pet trade. They are now considered uncommon and are declining throughout much of their peripheral range. Green-winged macaws favor the tropical rainforest in the northern part of their range, while to the south they venture into drier habitats, including savannah. They are most often seen in pairs—both sexes look identical—or in small flocks. They feed on fruits and seeds that they deal with easily with their large, powerful bills.

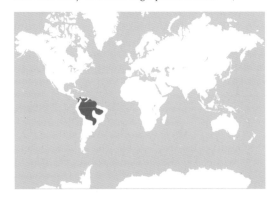

AW: By ten each morning, 100 green-winged macaws gather in the trees above the banks of the Rio Manú. Cautious at first, they soon descend to nibble on the mineral-rich clay. It is believed that these minerals neutralize the toxins contained in the nuts and fruits the birds eat. I spent four consecutive mornings in a floating blind. Unfortunately the weather was just too good. Bright sun kept the birds in harsh light. Finally a passing cloud provided enough shade to bring out the rich colors of the birds on my film.

Canon EOS-3, Canon EF 500mm IS lens, f/11 at 1/125 second, Fujichrome Provia film (pushed 1 stop)

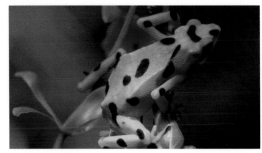

GOLDEN FROG
(*Atelopus varius zeteki*)

For most species in the rainforest, coloration is about camouflage or attracting a mate. That is not the case with the golden, or harlequin, frog (actually a true toad). Found only in the Pacific lowland forests of Panama, the golden frog has skin toxins that may cause hypertension, hallucinations, or paralysis. Predators quickly learn to associate the colors with an unpleasant experience and avoid contact with the diminutive creatures. While most of the sixty-six species in the genus *Atelopus* are diurnal, terrestrial, and often described as being somewhat bold, the golden frog is nocturnal, can be found up to 4 meters aboveground, and is considered very shy. Populations of golden frogs are declining, mainly due to loss of habitat to farming, logging, and cattle ranching. However, amphibians are also particularly susceptible to ultraviolet radiation, and high mutation rates in some populations have been linked to the thinning ozone layer.

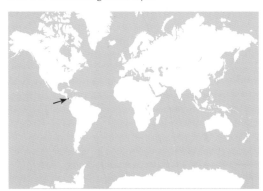

AW: Golden frogs, like poison arrow frogs, are relatively easy subjects to photograph. The difficulty lies with finding them in the first place. These tiny amphibians live secretly in the rotting debris of the rainforest floor. I photographed this frog with an extension tube placed between my 70–200mm lens and camera body. This permitted me to frame the frog tightly without having to get so close that I would have scared it away. This is a technique that I have often used while photographing amphibians, reptiles, and insects.

Canon EOS-1N, Canon EF 70–200mm lens, extension tube, f/11 at 1/30 second, Fujichrome Velvia film

---

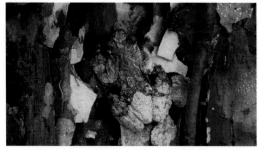

SOUTH AMERICAN MARBLED TREEFROG
(*Hyla marmorata*)

Hylid frogs—of which there are more than 700 species—are found in much of the world, including the Americas, Australia, and parts of Europe and Asia. The greatest diversity among the Hylidae is in the treefrog genus *Hyla*. In Central and South America, these frogs inhabit a variety of habitats, from lowland forests to montane rainforests. While most species are arboreal, others are aquatic or terrestrial. The South American marbled treefrog is widely distributed on the continent, and is identified by its highly cryptic coloration—the animal resembles the lichenous tree bark on which it climbs. Camouflage, however, protects the frog from only its natural enemies. Today, amphibians are threatened by habitat loss, pollution, competition with introduced species, mutations caused by increased ultraviolet radiation, and capture for the pet trade. Habitat protection and the careful regulation of live exports are essential to their survival.

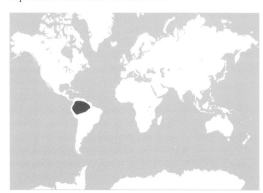

AW: Frogs come in an incredible variety of shapes, sizes, and colors. There are brightly colored poison arrow frogs and cryptic-colored treefrogs. They have provided nature photographers, including myself, with endless hours of delightful photography over the years. In the Peruvian Amazon, I came across this small treefrog, perfectly adapted to blend with the bark of this tree. When I shoot macrocompositions, I often use a 100mm macro lens. This lens enables me to focus closely without frightening my subject—or casting my shadow on it.

Canon EOS-1N/RS, Canon EF 100mm macro lens, f/16 at 1/4 second, Fujichrome Velvia film

---

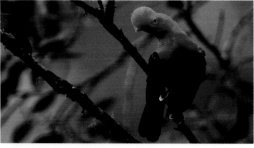

ANDEAN COCK-OF-THE-ROCK
(*Rupicola peruviana*)

The dramatic plumage of the male cock-of-the-rock ranges from scarlet (*R. p. sanguinolenta*) to orange-red (*R. p. aequatorialis*). While the male is vividly attired, with his erect crest, bright head, and breast starkly contrasting with his black wings and tail, the female is more subdued. She is a dark reddish brown color, and as such she blends in with the shadows of the forest. Cock-of-the-rocks are polygamous and the males gather communally at leks in the mid- to upper-story of their humid, wet forest habitats, where they display vocally for mates—their calls have been described as "piglike squeals." They nest on rocky outcrops, building mud nests for their two eggs. Although still locally common, they are frequently trapped for the cage bird trade and, as with most rainforest species, cock-of-the-rocks are increasingly threatened by habitat loss as their forests are cleared for agriculture and development.

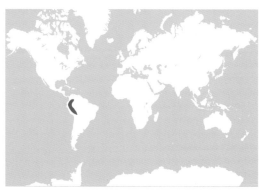

AW: Cock-of-the-rock is one of the most interesting birds in the Andes. But their dense forest habitat makes them difficult to photograph. To make matters worse, most of their elaborate breeding displays take place during the early morning and late afternoon, when light levels are the lowest. To get a sharp image, I used a 400mm f/2.8 lens, and fired my shutter every time a bird paused on a branch. I also remained in a blind, so as not to startle the wary birds.

Canon EOS-1N/RS, Canon EF 400mm lens, f/5.6 at 1/8 second, Fujichrome Velvia film (pushed 1 stop)

THE LIVING WILD

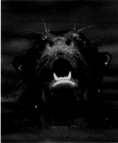 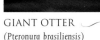

GIANT OTTER
(*Pteronura brasiliensis*)

Giant otters are in the same family, Mustelidae, as river otters, but they are the only member of the genus *Pteronura*. Once found across much of South America, from Colombia to northeastern Argentina, today giant otters have vanished from most of their former range. Weighing up to 34 kilograms and measuring 0.8 to 1.4 meters in length (plus a 0.3- to 1-meter tail), giant otters have thick, short, velvety fur that looks brown when dry and black when wet. Their lips, chin, throat, and chest are usually creamy white in color, forming a biblike marking. It is the otter's pelt that has led to its decline. In the 1980s a single pelt could bring a hunter $50 in the United States; the same pelt could then bring more than $250 in Europe. Although hunting is no longer legal, poaching continues. Giant otters have been virtually eradicated from Argentina, Uruguay, and southeastern Brazil.

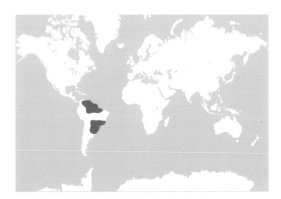

AW: Page 234 (left) – I worked from a floating platform made from two dugout canoes lashed together. I used a 500mm Image Stabilizer lens to minimize motion—the otter's and my own.

Canon EOS-3, Canon EF 500mm IS lens, f/8 at 1/250 second, Fujichrome Provia film

AW: Page 234 (right) – I followed a family of seven adults and four youngsters for four days from my platform. Eventually I was able to get portraits like this.

Canon EOS-3, Canon EF 500mm IS lens, f/5.6 at 1/125 second, Fujichrome Provia film

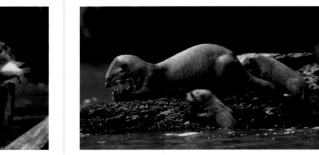

GIANT OTTER
(*Pteronura brasiliensis*)

Giant otters are well adapted to the water. They have large webbed feet and their tail is thick and muscular, as well as being slightly flattened. Giant otters favor slow-moving rivers and usually select areas with good cover for concealment. They are strong swimmers, and use their tail for thrust while their feet are used for steering. They catch fish with their mouths and though small fish are often eaten in the water, larger fish are carried to shore. Otters range over about 12 kilometers of river, actively defending their territories. At times they are quite sociable, and as many as twenty animals have been seen together. More usually, a group is made up of a mated pair, one or more subadults, and the young of the year. Giant otters are very vocal and that, combined with their diurnal nature, has made them easy targets for poachers.

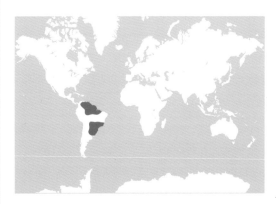

AW: Just a week prior to my arrival, the adult otters brought out their three-month-old babies for the first time. During my four-day stay, I photographed the adults teaching their young how to swim and fish. The family was highly social, often hunting communally. They used their whiskers to detect fish in the murky waters. In this photograph, an adult emerges with a fish and is quickly mobbed by the ever-hungry young.

Canon EOS-3, Canon EF 500mm IS lens, f/11 at 1/125 second, Fujichrome Provia film

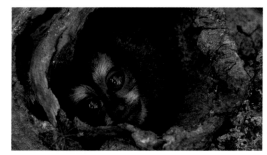

NIGHT MONKEY
(*Aotus lemurinus*)

There are ten species of night monkeys or douroucoulis. Although the taxonomy of the genus is uncertain, night monkeys may be the most primitive of the New World primates; they may also be the oldest member of the entire Anthropoidea (the suborder that includes all monkeys and apes). These petite primates weigh less than a kilogram and they have dense, woolly fur. Night monkeys live in the primary and secondary forests of Central America and northern South America. Unlike most other monkeys, they are nocturnal. At night they forage in the trees for fruits, nuts, flowers, insects, and small animals. Night monkeys have long been popular as pets and for use in biomedical research, and their collection has impacted local populations; in some areas they are also hunted for meat and fur. The destruction of forest habitat has completely eliminated some populations, and habitat loss is the greatest threat to their survival.

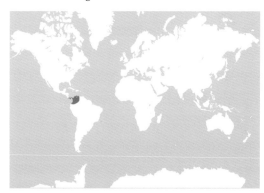

AW: Often when visiting remote villages, I ask whether there are any wild animals living nearby. On one occasion, a villager pointed out an old tree and said that a monkey lived in it. I erected a makeshift platform and then gently tapped on the tree. To my surprise, this small monkey sheepishly peered out of the cavity.

Canon EOS-1N, Canon EF 70–200mm lens, f/4 at 1/125 second, Fujichrome Astia film

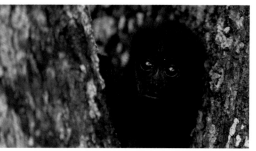

BLACK HOWLER MONKEY
(*Alouatta palliata*)

Howler monkeys are the largest of the New World monkeys. Only adult male black howler monkeys are actually black; females and juveniles are brownish in color. Males are also substantially larger than females, and may weigh more than twice as much (10 kilograms versus 4 kilograms). The species gets its name from its remarkable call that can be heard more than 3 kilometers away and sounds like a deep growl or a roaring lion. Groups of black howler monkeys may have as many as forty-five members, although most are in the ten to twenty range, with two to four adult males. Howler monkeys face habitat loss throughout Mexico and Central America, and group sizes are falling in areas where the forest is fragmented. In southern Mexico, 90 percent of the rainforests have been lost in the last 40 years and as a result monkey populations are now small and isolated, with little chance of long-term survival.

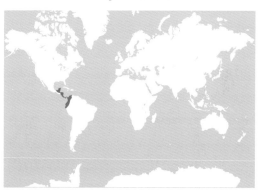

AW: When I first heard a howler monkey, I was on Islas Barro Colorado in the Panama Canal. So chilling was the sound they made in the predawn light that I was sure something was being killed. Later, when I discovered the source of the sound, I was greatly relieved. Howlers have a rather comical appearance—they have a pronounced hunchback profile, thanks to their large lower jaws, thick neck, and low facial angle. In this photograph, a young howler peers around the trunk of a tree, while adults nearby scold me.

Canon EOS-1N, Canon EF 600mm lens, f/5.6 at 1/60 second, Fujichrome Velvia film

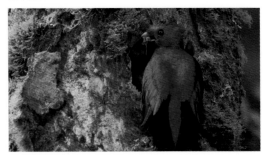

RESPLENDENT QUETZAL
(Pharomachrus mocinno)

The resplendent quetzal is found at high altitudes (between 1,300 and 3,200 meters) throughout Central America, and is considered endangered in almost every country within its range. The male sports a 0.6-meter-long tail and vibrant coloring, a combination that makes it one of the world's most beautiful birds. Unlike many species that migrate along north-south routes, quetzals migrate vertically between the cloud-forests (where they nest between March and June) and mid-slope altitudes. These birds are increasingly threatened as cultivation and logging reaches 2,000 meters and beyond. They also face continuing threats from illegal trading in live birds, skins, and feathers. Considered to be excellent dispersers of seeds since they feed on many different fruits, the quetzal's loss could have far-reaching implications for the long-term health of the cloud-forest.

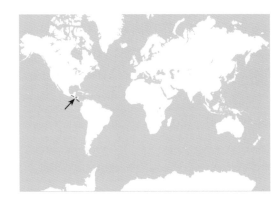

AW: I traveled high in the Panamanian mountains to photograph this quetzal. When I found a nest, I set up my camera with a 600mm lens 30 meters away. The nest tree was on a steep slope, so I was able to place my camera up the slope from the nest. Every 20 minutes, the adult birds returned to feed their chicks. They often paused for several seconds before entering the nest, and this is when I took my photographs. I was in the deep rainforest, so I used fill flash to add highlights to the iridescent feathers, as well as to add a catchlight to the eyes.

Canon EOS-1N, Canon EF 600mm lens, f/4 at 1/15 second, fill flash, Fujichrome Velvia film (pushed 1 stop)

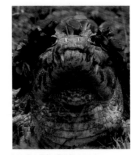 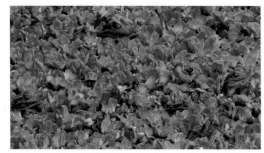

YACARE CAIMAN
(Caiman yacare)

Yacare caiman were severely affected by illegal hunting during the 1970s and 1980s. Poaching—for their skins—is still a major threat to the species, along with loss of their wetland habitats. Females are able to lay up to thirty-eight eggs during the breeding season, something that has helped alleviate some of the hunting pressure faced by the species, since the females' fecundity permits fairly rapid population recovery if hunting is relaxed. Females guard their mound nests during incubation, but may abandon their nests if disturbed. In areas with intensive hunting pressure or other disturbances, even prolific females may not successfully raise their offspring. To counter the impacts of poaching, sustainable-yield breeding programs have been introduced, and caiman are ranched (for their skins) in both Brazil and Argentina.

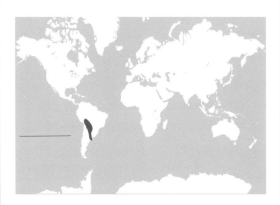

AW: Page 238 – To get this shot, I approached the reptile in a prone position, gaining a low enough angle to achieve this in-your-face perspective.

Canon EOS-3, Canon EF 600mm lens, Canon Extender EF 1.4x, f/16 at 1/15 second, Fujichrome Velvia film

AW: Page 240 – Accustomed to being fed by local ranch-hands, these caiman approach within 30 centimeters of where I knelt along the lakeshore. Not one to pass up an opportunity, I selected a wide-angle lens to record the scene.

Canon EOS-3, Canon EF 17–35mm lens, f/22 at 1/2 second, 2-stop graduated neutral density filter, fill flash, Fujichrome Velvia film

---

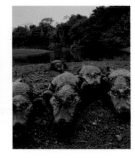

SPECTACLED CAIMAN
(Caiman crocodilus)

Spectacled caiman (sometimes referred to as the common caiman), so-named because of a bony ridge that joins the eyes like a pair of spectacles, is a highly adaptable species found in a variety of wetland habitats, although it prefers still water. Adults reach 2 to 2.5 meters, although exceptionally large males may be 3 meters long. Juveniles feed on aquatic invertebrates such as insects, crustaceans, and molluscs; as they grow, so does the size of their prey. Adults feed on fish, other reptiles, and even mammalian prey such as wild pigs. The skin of this caiman is not considered as valuable as that of other species, but since so many of the other species have been depleted, the spectacled caiman is now the hunters' mainstay; most of the hide market in America is served by this species. Numbers have been depleted in many areas (such as El Salvador), and the subspecies *C. c. apaporiensis* is considered severely threatened in Colombia.

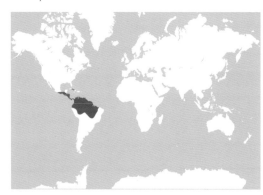

AW: Baby caiman hide amid floating vegetation filling this oxbow lake. The vegetation provides cover for the vulnerable babies since herons, egrets, and hawks frequently hunt the lake's shallow waters. As I approached these tiny reptiles, I found that the slightest movement would send them down into the water. It took several minutes before they surfaced again. To get this photograph, I chose a long lens and stopped down to f/22 to ensure that all of the caiman were in focus.

Canon EOS-1N, Canon EF 400mm lens, f/22 at 1/8 second, Fujichrome Velvia film

---

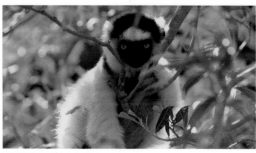

VERREAUX'S SIFAKA
(Propithecus verreauxi)

Verreaux's sifakas are one of three species of sifakas. Smaller than indris (*Indri indri*), they have a head and body length of about 0.5 meter and a tail about the same length. They weigh between 3 and 7 kilograms and are covered in soft, woolly fur. As with indris, their color can range from white to gray, brown, or black. They live in Madagascar's deciduous and evergreen forests and are capable of leaping 10 meters from tree to tree. Within home ranges of 6.75 to 8.5 hectares, groups of two to thirteen sifakas forage for leaves, fruit, flowers, and bark. Human population growth on the small island has led to the loss of much of the forest habitat as the land is cleared for agriculture and grazing. Verreaux's sifakas are still believed to number more than 100,000, but the steady loss of habitat and their highly restricted range suggest that either such estimates may be overly optimistic or they may be facing imminent decline.

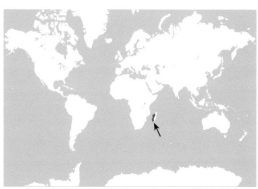

AW: A sifaka relaxes in a tall tree on a steep hillside. I was able to move to a spot upslope from the tree, gaining an almost unobstructed view of the lemur. The alert animal seemed to take all my motion in stride, watching me with what could only be described as nonchalance.

Canon EOS-1N, Canon EF 600mm lens, f/8 at 1/60 second, fill flash, Fujichrome Velvia film

---

THE LIVING WILD

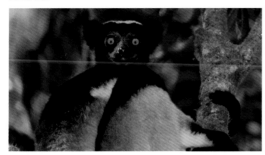

INDRI ～
(*Indri indri*)

The indri is the largest prosimian (a member of the suborder Prosimii that includes bushbabies and tarsiers)—with a head and body length of 0.6 to 0.9 meter. Along with sifakas, indris are known as leaping lemurs. They are endemic to Madagascar—as are thirty-two other types of lemurs. Restricted to northeastern Madagascar, indris occur in a variety of colors; some animals are largely white, others are black, gray, or brown. They live in coastal and montane rainforests up to 1,800 meters, and feed on leaves, flowers, and fruits. Indris are active during the day and live in family groups of between two and five animals. Over the last 1,500 years, sixteen species of lemurs have become extinct as a direct result of habitat destruction and hunting by humans. Today, the indri is considered highly endangered and fewer than 10,000 remain; some put the number as low as 1,000—none exist in captivity.

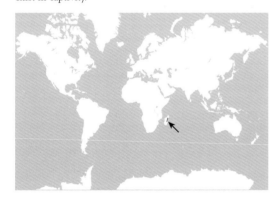

AW: Indris spend most of their lives high in the forest canopy. To photograph this lemur, I used a 600mm lens with a flash attached to my camera body. I set the flash on fill mode, so that I could bring highlights to the animal's eyes while making the lighting look as natural and as pleasing as possible.

Canon EOS-1N, Canon EF 600mm lens, f/4 at 1/125 second, fill flash, Fujichrome 50 film

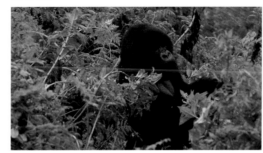

MOUNTAIN GORILLA ～
(*Gorilla gorilla beringei*)

The mountain gorilla is one of three currently recognized subspecies of gorillas. It is also the rarest, with fewer than 650 remaining in a small region that overlaps the high montane rainforests of Rwanda, Uganda, and Congo-Zaire, and possibly Uganda's Bwindi Impenetrable Forest. Every mountain gorilla family group is centered around a mature adult male, the silverback. In many cases, there may be more than one silverback in the group, and in those cases they are usually father and son(s). The silverback is the group's protector. He will guard his family against human attackers and outside males alike, performing blustering, noisy displays that can turn from bluff to real in an instant. More than 75 percent of silverbacks show signs of healed head wounds received in battles with other males. If the male loses his group to another male, the usurper will kill any dependent offspring in the group to bring the females back into breeding condition.

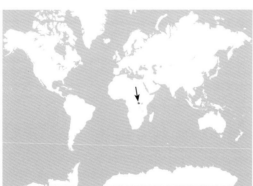

AW: As I photographed a group of gorillas, the silverback remained aloof, keeping his distance, while always keeping both me and his charges in sight. Rather than choosing to make a tight portrait of him with a longer lens, I opted to use a 70–200mm lens. Doing so enabled me to include more of the dense vegetation that typifies the mountain gorillas' habitat, consistent with the way I preferred to shoot for *The Living Wild*.

Canon F3, Canon EF 70–200mm lens, f/8 at 1/60 second, Fujichrome Velvia film

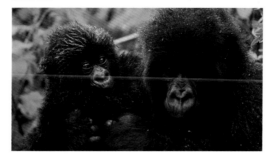

MOUNTAIN GORILLA ～
(*Gorilla gorilla beringei*)

Female mountain gorillas reach sexual maturity at about age 8, but they do not breed until at least age 10, when they emigrate from their natal group. Since the silverback in her natal group is also, in all likelihood, her father, a young female leaves the group she was born into to avoid incest. Females never range alone, but always transfer to another male—either one who already has a group, or a solitary male attempting to build his harem. When an outside male approaches a females' group, she sizes him up by observing how he interacts with the silverback in her own group. A male who is regularly defeated and driven away by other males is unlikely to attract many females to his side. In general, females prefer mature males who have been silverbacks for at least a few years, and will thus probably be good protectors for themselves and their offspring.

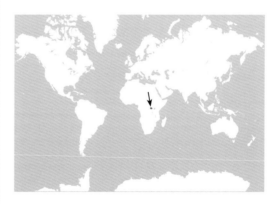

AW: Photographing mountain gorillas is one of the most enjoyable experiences of my 28 years spent photographing wildlife. I rose early this morning and trekked up one of Rwanda's Virunga Volcanoes, led by a seasoned tracker. We eventually found fresh tracks that led us to a troop of gorillas. The drizzle that I had cursed earlier actually proved beneficial; it softened the light, allowing for easier exposures. Had it been a bright, sunny day, the correct exposure for a black animal in dense vegetation would have been very difficult to achieve.

Canon F3, Canon EF 70–200mm lens, f/4 at 1/60 second, Fujichrome 100 film

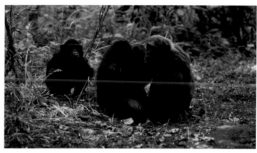

CHIMPANZEE ～
(*Pan troglodytes*)

Chimpanzees were once found across Africa, from the rainforests to the wooded savannahs. Several million may have lived at the beginning of the twentieth century. One hundred years later, some 105,000 survive: 12,000 are western chimpanzees (*P. t. verus*), most of them in Côte d'Ivoire; 80,000 are central chimpanzees (*P. t. troglodytes*), mainly found in Gabon and Congo-Zaire; and 13,000 are eastern chimpanzees (*P. t. schweinfurthii*) living east of the Congo River. We share 98.4 percent of our genes with them. They use tools and medicinal plants; they show the beginnings of culture. We have so much in common, and yet we have flirted with their extinction. Their habitats are being cleared. They are shot and trapped to provide bushmeat to rural settlements, and infants are torn from their mothers to serve as sad attractions in resort towns. They, along with "bonobos," are our nearest relatives. If we lose them, we lose part of ourselves.

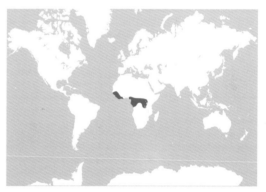

AW: Social grooming among chimpanzees occupies much of their time. For a photographer, it is a welcome activity, for it keeps the active chimpanzees relatively stationary. It also provides some interesting behavior to capture on film. Here two adults groom each other, while an adolescent watches. To record this, I chose a 70–200mm zoom lens with a maximum aperture of f/2.8. This allowed me to take a reasonably fast exposure in a dark setting, while the 200mm range of the lens permitted me to stay far enough away so as not to disrupt the scene.

Canon EOS-1N, Canon EF 70–200mm lens, f/4 at 1/30 second, Fujichrome 100 film

NOTES FROM THE FIELD

RESOURCES

African Wildlife Foundation
1400 16th Street, N.W., Suite 120
Washington, DC 20036, USA
Tel: 202-939-3333
Fax: 202-939-3332
africanwildlife@awf.org
www.awf.org

Agrupación Sierra Madre, S.C.
Prado Norte 324
Lomas de Chapultepec
11000 México City, México
Tel: 525-520-8820
Fax: 525-520-5717
asmupc@infosel.net.mx

Australian Mammal Society
Department of Environment and
    Natural Resources
Adelaide, South Australia, Australia
sgibbs@picknowl.com.au
http://ikarus.jcu.edu.au/mammal/

Canadian Parks and Wilderness Society
880 Wellington Street, Suite 506
Ottawa, ON K1R 6K7, Canada
Tel: 800-333-WILD
Fax: 613-569-7098
info@cpaws.org
www.cpaws.org

Canadian Wildlife Federation
2740 Queensview Drive
Ottawa, ON K2B 1A2, Canada
Tel: 800-563-WILD
Fax: 613-721-2902
info@cwf-fcf.org
www.cwf-fcf.org

Center for Marine Conservation
1725 DeSales Street, N.W., Suite 600
Washington, DC 20036, USA
Tel: 202-429-5609
Fax: 202-872-0619
cmc@dccmc.org
www.cmc-ocean.org

Cetacean Society International
P.O. Box 953
Georgetown, CT 06829, USA
Tel/Fax: 203-431-1606
William_Rossiter@compuserve.com
http://elfnet1a.elfi.com/csihome.html

Conservation International Foundation
2501 M Street, N.W., Suite 200
Washington, DC 20037, USA
Tel: 202-429-5660
Fax: 202-887-0193
www.conservation.org

CORAL: The Coral Reef Alliance
2014 Shattuck Avenue
Berkeley, CA 94704, USA
Tel: 510-848-0110
Fax: 510-848-3720
info@coral.org
www.coral.org

Defenders of Wildlife
1101 Fourteenth Street, N.W.,
    Suite 1400
Washington, DC 20005, USA
Tel: 202-682-9400
Fax: 202-682-1331
www.defenders.org

Dian Fossey Gorilla Fund International
800 Cherokee Avenue, S.E.
Atlanta, GA 30315, USA
Tel: 800-851-0203
Fax: 404-624-5999
2help@gorillafund.org
www.gorillafund.org

East African Wildlife Society
P.O. Box 20110, Nairobi, Kenya
Tel: 254-2-506671
Fax: 254-2-501752
www.cheetah.demon.nl/eawls.html

Fish & Wildlife Information Exchange
Conservation Management Institute
Virginia Tech, 203 W. Roanoke Street
Blacksburg, VA 24061, USA
Tel: 540-231-7348
Fax: 540-231-7019
fwiexchg@vt.edu
http://fwie.fw.vt.edu/index.htm

Friends of the Earth—U.S.
1025 Vermont Avenue, N.W.,
    Third Floor
Washington, DC 20005, USA
Tel: 877-843-8687
Fax: 202-783-0444
foe@foe.org
www.foe.org

International Society for
    Endangered Cats
3070 Riverside Drive, Suite 160
Columbus, OH 43221, USA
Tel: 614-487-8760
Fax: 614-487-8769
felineinfo@isec.org
www.isec.org

International Union for the
    Conservation of Nature and
    Natural Resources
IUCN—The World Conservation Union
Rue Mauverney 28
CH-1196 Gland, Switzerland
Tel: 41-22-999-00-01
Fax: 41-22-999-00-02
mail@hq.iucn.org
www.iucn.org

National Audubon Society
700 Broadway
New York, NY 10003, USA
Tel: 212-979-3000
Fax: 212-979-3188
www.audubon.org

National Parks Conservation
    Association
1300 Nineteenth Street, N.W., Suite 300
Washington, DC 20036, USA
Tel: 800-NAT-PARKS
npca@npca.org
www.npca.org/home/npca/

National Wildlife Federation
8925 Leesburg Pike
Vienna, VA 22184, USA
Tel: 703-790-4000
Fax: 703-790-4040
www.nwf.org

Natural Resources Defense Council
40 W. 20th Street
New York, NY 10011, USA
Tel: 212-727-2700
Fax: 212-727-1773
nrdcinfo@nrdc.org
www.nrdc.org

Orangutan Foundation International
822 S. Wellesley Avenue
Los Angeles, CA 90049, USA
Tel: 310-207-1655
Fax: 310-207-1556
redape@ns.net
www.orangutan.org

Rainforest Action Network
221 Pine Street, Suite 500
San Francisco, CA 94104, USA
Tel: 415-398-4404
Fax: 415-398-2732
rainforest@ran.org
www.ran.org

Rainforest Alliance
65 Bleecker Street, Sixth Floor
New York, NY 10012, USA
Tel: 212-677-1900
Fax: 212-677-2187
canopy@ra.org
www.rainforest-alliance.org

Royal Society for the Protection
    of Birds
The Lodge, Sandy
Bedfordshire, SG19 2DL,
    United Kingdom
Tel: 44-1767-680551
www.rspb.org.uk

Sierra Club
85 Second Street, Second Floor
San Francisco, CA 94105, USA
Tel: 415-977-5500
Fax: 415-977-5799
information@sierraclub.org
www.sierraclub.org

The Jane Goodall Institute
P.O. Box 14890
Silver Spring, MD 20911, USA
Tel: 301-565-0086
Fax: 301-565-3188
JGIinformation@janegoodall.org
www.janegoodall.org

The Nature Conservancy
4245 N. Fairfax Drive, Suite 100
Arlington, VA 22203, USA
Tel: 703-841-5300
Fax: 703-841-1283
www.tnc.org

Wildlife Conservation Society
2300 Southern Boulevard
Bronx, NY 10460, USA
Tel: 718-220-5100
Fax: 718-364-4275
feedback@wcs.org
www.wcs.org

World Conservation Monitoring Centre
219 Huntingdon Road
Cambridge, CB3 0DL, United Kingdom
Tel: 44-1223-277314
Fax: 44-1223-277136
info@wcmc.org.uk
www.wcmc.org.uk

World Wide Fund for Nature (WWF)
1126 Avenue du Mont Blanc
Gland, Switzerland
Tel: 41-22-364-9111
Fax: 41 22 364 4238
ddenhardt@wwfnet.org
www.panda.org

World Wildlife Fund—U.S.
1250 Twenty-Fourth Street, N.W.
P.O. Box 97180
Washington, DC 20037, USA
Tel: 202-293-4800
Fax: 202-293-9211
www.worldwildlife.org

Worldwatch Institute
1776 Massachusetts Avenue, N.W.
Washington, DC 20036, USA
Tel: 202-452-1999
Fax: 202-296-7365
worldwatch@worldwatch.org
www.worldwatch.org

Yellowstone Park Foundation
37 E. Main Street, Suite 4
Bozeman, MT 59715, USA
Tel: 406-586-6303
Fax: 406-586-6337
yellowstn@aol.com
www.ypf.org

Zero Population Growth
1400 Sixteenth Street, N.W., Suite 320
Washington, DC 20036, USA
Tel: 202-332-2200
or 800-POP-1956
Fax: 202-332-2302
info@zpg.org
www.zpg.org

For additional links to extensive
wildlife and environmental
Internet resources, visit
www.michellegilders.com

FURTHER READING

RECOMMENDED BY THE ESSAYISTS

Adams, Douglas, and Mark Carwardine. *Last Chance to See.* New York: Ballantine Books, 1990.

Attenborough, David. *The Living Planet.* London: William Collins Sons & Co., 1984.

Axelrod, Robert. *The Evolution of Cooperation.* Reprinted. New York: Basic Books, 1985.

Barbato, Joseph, and Lisa Weinerman, eds. *Heart of the Land: Essays on Last Great Places.* New York: Vintage Books, 1996.

Carson, Rachel. *Silent Spring.* Boston: Houghton Mifflin Co., 1994.

Cavalieri, Paola, and Peter Singer, eds. *The Great Ape Project: Equality Beyond Humanity.* New York: St. Martin's Press, 1993.

Cohen, Joel E. *How Many People Can the Earth Support?* New York: W. W. Norton & Co., 1995.

Croze, Harvey, and John Reader. *Pyramids of Life: Patterns of Life and Death in the Ecosystem.* London: The Harvill Press, 2000.

Diamond, Jared. *Guns, Germs, and Steel: The Fates of Human Societies.* New York: W. W. Norton & Co., 1997.

Dillard, Annie. *Pilgrim at Tinker Creek.* New York: Buccaneer Books, 1998.

Dobson, Andrew. *Conservation and Biodiversity.* New York: W. H. Freeman & Co., 1996.

Douglas-Hamilton, Ian, and Oria Douglas-Hamilton. *Battle for the Elephants.* New York: Doubleday, 1992.

Hardin, Garrett. *The Ostrich Factor: Our Population Myopia.* New York: Oxford University Press, 1999.

Leakey, Richard E., and Roger Lewin. *The Sixth Extinction: Patterns of Life and the Future of Humankind.* New York: Anchor Books, 1996.

Leopold, Aldo. *A Sand County Almanac.* New York: Oxford University Press, 1949.

Lopez, Barry. *Crossing Open Ground.* New York: Vintage Books, 1989.

Quammen, David. *The Song of the Dodo: Island Biogeography in an Age of Extinctions.* New York: Scribner, 1996.

Ridley, Matt. *The Origins of Virtue: Human Instincts and the Evolution of Cooperation.* New York: Penguin USA, 1998.

Roosevelt, Theodore. *Theodore Roosevelt: An Autobiography.* New York: Da Capo Press, 1988.

Terborgh, John. *Requiem for Nature.* Washington, D.C.: Shearwater Books, 1999.

Weiner, Jonathan. *The Beak of the Finch: A Story of Evolution in Our Time.* New York: Alfred A. Knopf, 1994.

Western, David. *In the Dust of Kilimanjaro.* Washington, D.C.: Island Press, 1997.

Wilcove, David S. *The Condor's Shadow: The Loss and Recovery of Wildlife in America.* New York: W. H. Freeman & Co., 1999.

Wilson, Edward O. *The Diversity of Life.* Cambridge, MA., and London: The Belknap Press of Harvard University Press, 1992.

RECOMMENDED BY THE EDITOR

Bonner, Raymond. *At the Hand of Man.* New York: Alfred A. Knopf, 1993.

Brown, Lester R., et al. *State of the World: A Worldwatch Institute Report on Progress Toward a Sustainable Society.* New York & London: W. W. Norton & Co., annual.

Chadwick, Douglas H. *The Fate of the Elephant.* Toronto, Ont., Canada: Key Porter Books, 1992.

Darwin, Charles. *On the Origin of Species by Means of Natural Selection, or Preservation of Favoured Races in the Struggle for Life.* Reprinted. London: Penguin, 1859.

——. *The Voyage of the Beagle.* Reprinted. London: J. M. Dent & Sons, 1839.

Dawkins, Richard. *The Blind Watchmaker.* London: Longman Books, 1986.

Fossey, Dian. *Gorillas in the Mist.* Boston: Houghton Mifflin Co., 1983.

Goodall, Jane. *Through a Window: My Thirty Years with the Chimpanzees of Gombe.* London: George Weidenfeldt & Nicolson, 1990.

Gould, Stephen Jay. *Full House: The Spread of Excellence from Plato to Darwin.* New York: Harmony Books, 1996.

McKibben, Bill. *The End of Nature.* New York: Random House, 1989.

Muir, John. *Travels in Alaska.* Boston: Houghton Mifflin, 1915.

Schaller, George B. *The Last Panda.* Chicago: The University of Chicago Press, 1994.

——. *The Year of the Gorilla.* Chicago: The University of Chicago Press, 1988.

Sessions, George, ed. *Deep Ecology for the 21st Century.* Boston: Shambhala Publications, 1995.

Suzuki, David. *The Sacred Balance: Rediscovering Our Place in Nature.* Vancouver, B.C. David Suzuki Foundation, Greystone Books, 1997; Seattle: The Mountaineers Books, 1997.

Van der Post, Laurens. *A Far-Off Place.* New York: William Morrow and Co., 1974.

Wilson, Edward O., ed. *Biodiversity.* Washington, D.C.: National Academy Press, 1988.

World Resources Institute, The United Nations Environment Programme, The United Nations Development Programme, and The World Bank. *World Resources: A Guide to the Global Environment.* New York & Oxford: Oxford University Press, biannual.

First edition published 2000 by Wildlands Press, an imprint of Art Wolfe, Inc.

Distributed in the U.S. and Canada by Publishers Group West

Printed and bound in China by C & C Offset Printing Co.,Ltd.

09 08 07 06 05 04 03 02 01   10 9 8 7 6 5 4

Wildlands Press gratefully acknowledges The University of Chicago Press for permission to reprint excerpts from *The Last Panda* (1994 paperback edition by George B. Schaller): Prologue (pp. 1–2); pp. 44–46 (in part); pp. 49, ¶7–51; Preface (pp. xvi, ¶2–xvii, ¶2); Epilogue (pp. 250, ¶3, 6–251, ¶1 l. 2); Epilogue (pp. 251, ¶2–252); Preface (p. xi, ¶1).

Design and Typography: Elizabeth Watson

Executive Editor: Ray Pfortner, Wildlands Press

Image Management and Digital Prepress: Gilbert Neri, Art Wolfe, Inc.

Digital Production Management: Richelle Barnes and Matthew Flor, Getty Images/Seattle

Color Profiling: Peter Constable, Getty Images/Seattle

Image Scanning: Stacey Lester, Jason Wiley, Lou Kings, Johnny Hubbard, Curt Waller, Getty Images/Seattle

Digital Coordination: Jay Sakamoto and Tim Perciful, Getty Images/Seattle

Maps: Marge Mueller, Gray Mouse Graphics

Photo Editor: Deirdre Skillman

Project Planner: Christine Eckhoff

Copyediting and Proofreading: Marlene Blessing and Kris Fulsaas

Production Editing: Louise Helmick

Production Manager, Printing and Binding: Nancy Duncan-Cashman

Science Advisor: Gary M. Stolz, Ph.D., US Fish & Wildlife Service

Corporate Sales: Annie Woodward

Product Development: Kate Campbell and Craig Scheak

Publicist: Alice B. Acheson

Front cover - southern elephant seal (*Mirounga leonina*), South Georgia Island, UK; pp. 1, 3 and 256, emperor penguin (*Aptenodytes forsteri*), Weddell Sea, Antarctica; flaps - polar bear (*Ursus maritinus*), Churchill, Manitoba, Canada; back cover - scarlet macaw (*Ara macao*), Rio Tambopata, Peru.

Technical notes: This book was produced using an ICC/ColorSync color managed workflow. Images were drum scanned at GettyImages/Seattle on a Heidelberg Chromagraph S3400. Scanned images were tagged with the GettyRGB ICC profile and transferred to Art Wolfe, Inc. for design production. Final design layouts were made in Quark 4.0 and hard proofed on a Fuji PictroProof digital proofer. An ICC profile was created for the specific printing conditions at C & C Offset Printing Company. All separations were made using this profile. Images were scanned at 400 dpi and screened at 200 lines per inch.

All of the images in this book were taken in the wild (with the exception of the Bornean bay cat on page 7 and the bactrian camel on page 8) and created in the camera. To allow for inclusion in this book and for print production purposes, the images on the cover and pages 44, 140, 166, 172, and 239 were digitally retouched. Such retouching ranged from removing fill-flash catchlights in the eyes of the jaguar on page 239 to removing an out-of-focus branch in front of the eye of the panda on page 172 and man-made elements behind the snow macaques on page 140.

Maps: All distribution maps have been compiled using a variety of sources. Often a species (or subspecies) is not continuous throughout the area shown Individuals or small groups may occur outside of that area. A number of species are so poorly known in the wild, that their distribution is only estimated by researchers.

Library of Congress Cataloging-in-Publication Data

Wolfe, Art.

    The living wild / Art Wolfe ; William Conway…[et al.] ; edited by Michelle A. Gilders.

        p. cm.

        Includes bibliographical references.

        ISBN 0-9675918-0-5 (hc)

        1. Animals. 2. Animals—Pictorial works. 3. Wildlife conservation. I. Gilders, Michelle A., 1966- II. Title.

    QL45.2.W66 2000

    59—dc21 00-026050

    CIP

For more information about Art Wolfe and his photography, visit www.ArtWolfe.com

Wildlands Press

1944 First Avenue S

Seattle, WA 98134, USA

Phone: 888-973-0011

info@WildlandsPress.com

www.WildlandsPress.com

INDEX

ART WOLFE ON LOCATION

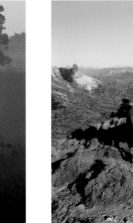
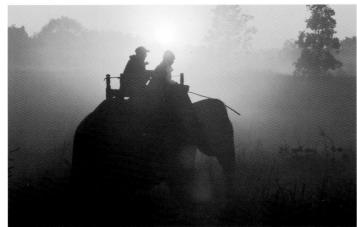

Kanha National Park, Madhya Predesh, India

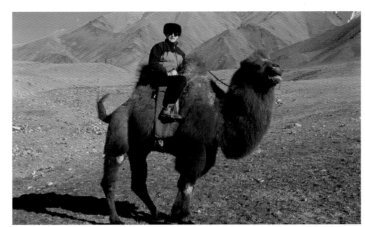

Andes Mountains, Argentina

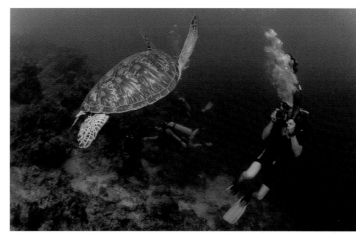

Pulau Sipidan, Malaysia

Western Mongolia

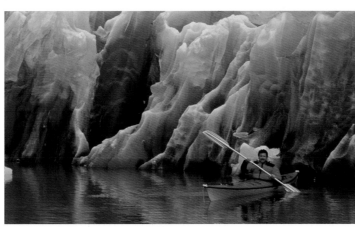

Tracy Arm, Southeast Alaska, USA

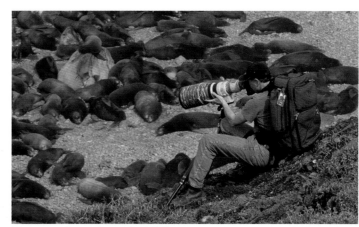

Northern Coast, California, USA

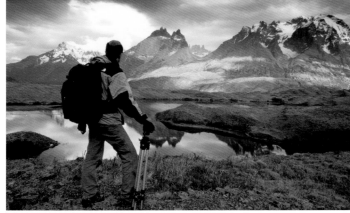

Torres del Paine National Park, Chile

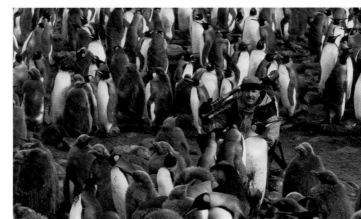

South Georgia Island, United Kingdom

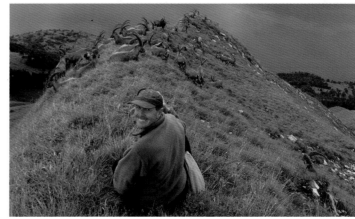

Interlaken, Alps, Switzerland

All photographs this page © Gavriel Jecan, except Art Wolfe kayaking © Charles Sleicher.

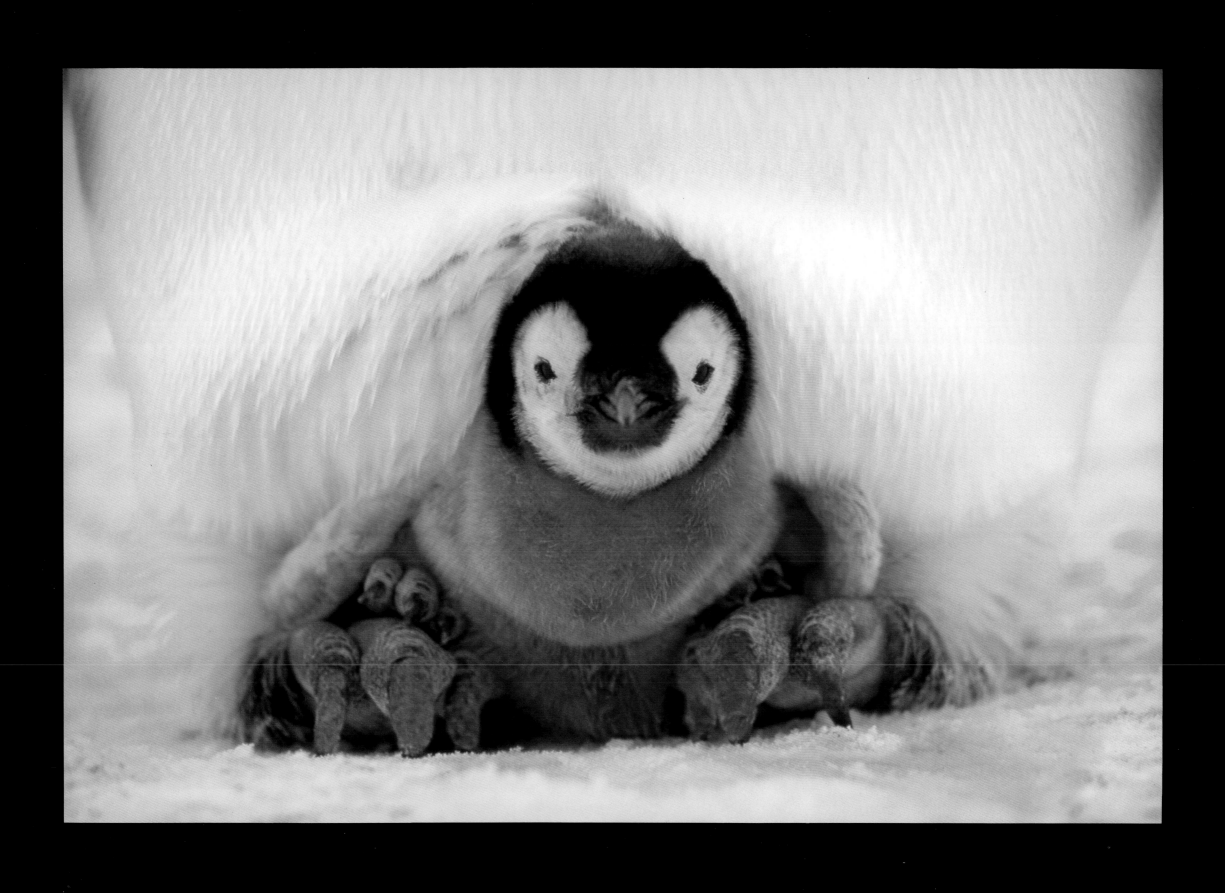